# THE POLITICS OF HEROIN

# THE POLITICS OF HEROIN

## CIA COMPLICITY IN

## THE GLOBAL DRUG TRADE

Alfred W. McCoy

A completely revised and expanded edition of
*The Politics of Heroin in Southeast Asia*

LAWRENCE HILL BOOKS

**Library of Congress Cataloging-in-Publication Data**

McCoy, Alfred W.
  The politics of heroin : CIA complicity in the global drug trade /
Alfred W. McCoy. — 1st ed.
    p.   cm.
  Rev. and expanded ed. of : The politics of heroin in Southeast
Asia. 1972.
  Includes bibliographical references and index.
  ISBN 1-55652-126-X : $29.00. — ISBN 1-55652-125-1 (pbk) : $16.95
    1. Heroin.   2. Drug traffic—History—20th century.   3. Drug
traffic—Asia, Southeastern—History—20th century.   4. Narcotics,
Control of—History—20th century.   I. McCoy, Alfred W.   Politics of
heroin in Southeast Asia.   II. Title.
HV5822.H4M33 1991
363.4'5'0959—dc20                                                    90-47398
                                                                        CIP

This book is a completely revised and expanded edition of *The Politics of
Heroin in Southeast Asia.* Copyright © 1972 by Alfred W. McCoy and
Cathleen B. Read, Harper & Row, Publishers, Inc.

Reprinted by arrangement with Harper & Row, Publishers, Inc. All rights
reserved. For information address Harper & Row, Publishers, Inc., 10 East
53rd St., New York, NY 10022.

We would like to thank the University of Wisconsin-Madison Cartographic
Laboratory for providing the maps for this edition.

Front cover photo: "Man Incising Opium Poppy." © Michael Freeman. First
published in *Peoples of the Golden Triangle.* Reprinted with permission.

Printed in the United States of America
First edition
First Printing
Published by Lawrence Hill Books, Brooklyn, New York
An imprint of Chicago Review Press, Inc.
814 North Franklin Street
Chicago, Illinois 60610

*For my teachers*
*Lee Ahlborn*
*Harry J. Benda*
*Robert Cluett*
*T. Dixon Walker*

# Contents

# Maps

# Charts

# Preface

WRITING THIS BOOK HAS BEEN A LONG JOURNEY, FROM AMERICA to Asia and from youth to middle age. In 1971, then twenty-five and in my second year at Yale Graduate School, I set out on a trip around the world to study the politics of the global heroin trade. Somehow I survived the unanticipated adventures that followed and two years later I published *The Politics of Heroin in Southeast Asia*, a book that was more exposé than explanation. Over the next fifteen years, I returned to Southeast Asia several times to research revisions to that first book and to gather materials for a second, entitled *Drug Traffic*, a study of heroin's impact on crime and corruption in Australia. Finally, in the summer of 1990, I combined my own data on Southeast Asia with the research of others on Central America and South Asia to produce the present volume.

My work on the heroin trade began in the fall of 1970 as an outgrowth of a book I had edited on Laotian politics. Elisabeth Jakab, my editor at Harper & Row, suggested that I use my knowledge of Southeast Asian politics to write a book providing a historical perspective on the sudden spread of heroin addiction among American troops in South Vietnam. What began as a small project based on library research soon mushroomed into a much larger one after three more or less chance encounters.

During spring break, I took time off from research in Yale's Sterling Memorial Library to conduct interviews in Paris with former French officers about the opium trade during their Indochina War of the early 1950s. My meeting with General Maurice Belleux, the former chief of

French intelligence for Indochina, inadvertently revealed that the CIA was involved in the opium trade as their French counterparts had been before them. Receiving me in the offices of a helicopter company he now headed, Belleux responded to a broad question about opium by explaining in detail how his agency had controlled Indochina's illicit drug trade and used it to finance clandestine operations against Communist guerrillas. The general added that "your CIA" had inherited his network of covert action allies when the French quit Vietnam in 1954. He suggested that a trip to Saigon would reveal that American intelligence was, like its earlier French counterpart, involved in the opium traffic. Other French veterans, notably the paratroop commander Colonel Roger Trinquier, confirmed both the general's information and his suggestion.

It was not only General Belleux who convinced me that the Vietnam drug problem needed investigation. At a street demonstration in New Haven for Black Panther leader Bobby Seale, I met the beat poet Allen Ginsberg, who insisted that the CIA was deeply involved in the Southeast Asian opium trade. To back his claims and aid my research, he mailed me a carton containing years' worth of unpublished dispatches from Time-Life correspondents that documented the involvement of America's Asian allies in the opium traffic.

The third chance encounter was the most unlikely of all. At a society wedding in New York City for the sister of a former Columbia fraternity brother, I was astonished to hear a group of marine officers, guests of the groom, tell stories of North Vietnamese soldiers found dead with syringes in their arms on the slopes of Khe Sanh and Communist truck convoys rolling down the Ho Chi Minh trail in South Vietnam loaded with heroin for American troops.

After submitting overdue term papers to my tolerant Yale professors, Karl Pelzer and John Whitmore, I started for Southeast Asia in the summer of 1971. On the way, I stopped in Washington, D.C. to interview the legendary CIA operative Edward Lansdale, General Belleux's successor in Saigon. Both Lansdale and his former CIA aide Lucien Conein received me in their modest suburban homes not far from the CIA's Langley headquarters and told stories about drug trafficking in Saigon by the French, the Corsicans, and the intimates of President Ngo Dinh Diem. A former Saigon coup leader, General Nguyen Chanh Thi, now exiled to an apartment near Dupont Circle, confirmed the CIA stories and, more important, gave me introductions to some of his friends in South Vietnam. The Washington bureau of Dispatch News Service, a fledgling agency best known for its exposé of the My Lai massacre, told me that one of its stringers, an Australian named John Everingham, was writing about CIA helicopters carrying opium in Laos.

How could I find him? Easy. Everingham was the only white man in Saigon who wore a blond ponytail and "Viet Cong–style black pajamas."

During one of my last interviews in the States, I received the first of the death threats that accompanied this research. Moving west, I stopped at a restored nineteenth-century flour mill on the banks of a stream in Readyville, Tennessee. Its owner, a young man named Joe Flipse, had recently returned from volunteer service with tribal refugees in Laos. Over coffee at his kitchen table, he finished the interview by threatening to kill me if I sourced any information to him.

By the time I landed at Saigon's Tan Son Nhut airport in July, I was armed with some introductions and an idea for a new way to ask controversial questions. Instead of working like a journalist tracking the visible signs of the current heroin trail, I would start my interviews with questions about opium use in the past—when it was legal and not at all controversial. Working forward to the present, I would compile information about the illicit traffic and individual involvement that would lead, slowly perhaps, to those who controlled the current trade. Instead of confronting the protectors and drug dealers with direct accusations, an unproductive and dangerous method, I would try oblique and apparently unrelated questions, seeking to confirm the profile I had built up from documents and other interviews. In short, I would use historical methods to probe the present.

During my first days in Saigon, General Thi's introduction opened the door to the home of Colonel Pham Van Lieu, an influential leader of South Vietnam's "third force" who had once commanded the country's marines and national police. Over the next month, Lieu arranged meetings in his living room with senior Saigon officers who presented details and documentation about the role of senior government officials in the sale of heroin to U.S. troops.

A number of young Americans working in Saigon as stringers and researchers for the famous by-line reporters helped me check this information. Mark Lynch, now a Washington lawyer, gave me access to the files in *Newsweek*'s offices, where he worked as a researcher. A Cornell graduate student, D. Gareth Porter, was in Saigon working on current politics and shared information. A friend from Yale Graduate School, Tom Fox, now editor of the *National Catholic Reporter*, was then in Saigon stringing for *The New York Times*. One night he took me on a six-hour odyssey from the flashy neon bars at Saigon's center to the tin-shed brothels at the fringe of Cholon's sprawling shantytowns, rebuffing the advances of prostitutes and calling for heroin at every stop. For an outlay of twenty dollars, I returned to my hotel room with pockets bulging from vials of high-grade heroin worth maybe five thousand dollars on the street in New York. As I flushed the powder down the drain that night, I thought about trying it just once. I can recall raising a vial to my nose before hesitating and tipping it into the toilet.

During my last week in Saigon, I was walking up and down Tu Do Street at Saigon's center looking for the Dispatch stringer when I spotted a tall white man in black pajamas striding down the other side of the street. I screamed out "Everingham, Everingham" above the roar of the rock music spilling from the bars and the revs of the Saigon-cowboy motorcycles. He paused. Over coffee, we agreed to meet at 5:00 P.M. two weeks later at the bar of the Constellation Hotel in Vientiane, Laos. Yes, he had been in tribal villages where CIA helicopters had flown out the opium. He could take me to those villages to see for myself. He was trying to get a start as a photographer and asked that I use his pictures in my book.

Two weeks later, I was sitting at the bar of the Constellation Hotel nursing a Coca-Cola when John Everingham walked in with Phin Manivong, our young Lao interpreter. Next day at dawn, we took a taxi out of Vientiane, hitched a ride on a USAID highway truck north for most of the day, and then started hiking up a steep path that climbed from road's edge into the hills. By nightfall we were sleeping in a Yao hill tribe village near the peak of a mile-high mountain. After a few days spent watching the women plant opium in the valleys around the village, we traveled north through mist-shrouded mountains with the look of ancient Chinese scroll paintings to Long Pot village, a Hmong settlement at the edge of the battle lines. Approaching just before dark, we were escorted to the house of Ger Su Yang, the local Hmong leader who held the post of district officer.

Over a dinner of pig fat and sticky rice, Ger Su Yang asked Everingham, through our interpreter, what we were doing in his village. Knowing the Hmong leader from earlier visits, Everingham was frank and told him that I was writing a book on opium. For a man who did not read a daily newspaper, Ger Su Yang proposed a bargain that showed a keen sense of media management. He would provide armed men to escort us anywhere in his district and would allow us to ask anything we wanted about the opium. If he did that, could I get an article in a Washington newspaper reporting that the CIA had broken its promise? For ten years, he explained, the men of his village had died fighting in the CIA's army until only the fourteen-year-old boys were left. When he refused to send these boys to die, the CIA had stopped the rice airdrops that fed his village of women and children. After six months the children were visibly weak from hunger. Once the Americans in Washington knew about his situation, surely, said Ger Su Yang, they would send the rice. I promised.

Over the next five days, we conducted our opium survey, door-to-door, at every house in the village. Do you grow opium? Yes. After the harvest, how do you market the opium? We take it over to that hill, and the American helicopters come with Hmong soldiers who buy the opium and take it away in the helicopters.

We also learned that we were being watched. A Hmong captain in the CIA's Secret Army was radioing reports to the agency's secret base at Long Tieng. On our fourth day in Long Pot, a helicopter marked "Air America," the CIA's airline, spotted us on a nearby hill as it took off from the village. It hovered just above our heads, pilot and copilot staring for a long minute before flying off. On the fifth day, we were hiking to the next village with an escort of five Hmong armed with carbines when a shot rang out. The escort went ahead to the next ridge and waited momentarily before motioning for us to proceed. As we slipped down the face of that slope wet from the monsoon rains, several automatic weapons opened up from the next ridge, spraying the hillside with bullets. We fell back into a small hollow. While our escorts gave us a covering fire, we slithered on our bellies through the elephant grass to get away. Overweight and out of shape from months in Sterling Memorial Library, I rose to my knees. Everingham slammed my face into the mud. Somehow we all made it to safety behind the ridge and assembled, laughing at our luck to escape from the "Communist guerrillas" who we assumed were the authors of our ambush.

The next day, as we were interviewing in a nearby village, a tribesman whispered to our interpreter that it had not been the Communists. We had been ambushed by the Hmong soldiers of General Vang Pao, commander of the CIA's Secret Army. The next morning, we cut short our research and fled down the path toward the highway, later hitching a ride on a truck heading north, not south for Vientiane, fearful of another ambush. An hour later, we came to a junction where a U.S. army major was supervising a helicopter ferrying Royal Lao troop detachments into the Communist zone. Worried about what might be waiting for us on the road south to Vientiane, I decided to lie. I told the major that I was an adviser to the U.S. embassy on tribal matters and needed to borrow his helicopter for an urgent trip to Vientiane. He was going back to the capital anyway and would give us a lift. When we landed at the outskirts of the city later that afternoon, two unshaven Americans approached us with light machine guns slung over their shoulders. They demanded that we go with them, claiming that they were U.S. embassy security officers. We refused and took a taxi instead.

Several days later, I told Don Ronk, *The Washington Post*'s Vientiane stringer, about the rice situation in Long Pot. Ger Su Yang was right.

When the story appeared in the paper's back pages a few days later, the U.S. embassy bombarded the village with sacks of rice.

Resting at the Constellation Hotel a few days after our return, I got a telephone call from a legend, Edgar "Pop" Buell, the Indiana farmer who had played a key role in building the CIA's Secret Army of 30,000 Hmong guerrillas. He wanted to show me what was really happening in Laos. I agreed and the next morning took a helicopter to an upland valley that was the hub of his Hmong refugee operations. After we toured hospital and schools, Pop Buell and his assistant, George Cosgrove, took me on a flight to a mountaintop village for the funeral of a Hmong commander killed in an air crash. As the rice wine flowed and Hmong crossbows shot the soul of the deceased toward heaven, Cosgrove, a supposed social worker with the body of a linebacker, leaned over and told me the correct name and address of my interpreter Phin. "If you keep going the way you are," George warned, "he will be dead before long."

The next day, I called at the office of Ambassador Charles Mann, director of USAID for Laos, who promised that Phin would live. Ambassador Mann kept his word and Phin survived to flee Laos after 1975 when the Communists took power.

By now I was reasonably certain that the CIA was involved in transporting the opium of its Hmong hill tribe allies. I knew too that somebody in the CIA's Vientiane station had enough knowledge of Air America's involvement to try to stop my research. After all, if the agency had nothing to hide, why the ambush and the death threats? But that was low-level complicity at best, far removed from the upper echelons of the Laotian government. I had one source, an American adviser in the USAID public safety program, who insisted that the chief of staff of the Royal Lao army, General Ouane Rattikone, owned the largest heroin refinery in Laos and was producing the Double U-O Globe brand then flooding U.S. army camps in South Vietnam. I needed confirmation and it had to come from the only reliable source, General Ouane himself.

One afternoon, I hailed a taxi in downtown Vientiane and asked the driver to take me to General Ouane's house. I did not know the address and I did not have an appointment. After the driver dropped me at a suburban bungalow, I knocked at the door and a young woman, who turned out to be the general's daughter, let me in and told me to wait. About a half hour later, a beige Mercedes pulled into the drive and General Ouane's inimitably large figure entered. Sweating heavily as he sank into a couch, the general whispered with his daughter before motioning me to his side. He asked what I wanted and I evaded the truth. Presenting my card as a correspondent for *Harper's* magazine, which I was, I said that I was in Indochina to profile America's allies and their crusade against communism, which I was not. For an hour, he chatted about his family and the career path he had followed in his rise to command. General, I said, that was fine but what about the allegations by your enemies that you stole money when managing the opium syndicate just a few years ago. *"Merde!* That bastard Phoumi is gossiping again. I am going to stop these rumors for good," muttered General Ouane, referring to his old rival General Phoumi Nosavan, then exiled in Bangkok. Suddenly, that elephantine figure leapt up the stairs with a catlike grace and returned a few minutes later with a heavy, leather-bound ledger. On the cover was the title "Opium Régie du Laos" (Laotian Opium Monopoly). The general took me through every page, showing what he had paid the tribes for opium in the 1960s, how many kilograms he exported to Vietnam, and the profits he had deposited in the syndicate's bank accounts. I was impressed, particularly since all the transactions took place after 1961 when Laos had abolished its official opium monopoly and made drug dealing illegal. With the general's encouragement, I copied down sample transactions, which appear in the footnotes of this book.

Just to test the U.S. position on drugs, I called on the press attaché at the American embassy in Vientiane, saying that "a reliable source" had alleged that General Ouane, commander of an army funded entirely by U.S. military aid, had once run an opium smuggling syndicate. Next day, the embassy's press officer informed me that my source was not reliable. America's ally General Ouane was not now nor had he ever been in any way involved in drugs. Could I quote him? Yes, he was speaking on the record.

My method seemed to be working. The past was proving a reliable guide to the present. By going back to the past where documents were available and facts firm, I was able to move forward to the present, knowing where to look and what sort of questions to ask.

But my success was also making me wildly overconfident. After surviving my encounters with the CIA, I jettisoned the caution that had served me well and became aggressive in my search for the heroin trail that led from the hills to Vientiane and then to Saigon. Learning that General Ouane's partner in the Double U-O Globe heroin factory was a Chinese merchant named Huu Tim-heng, I decided to force my way behind the paper facade of his front corporations, which included local franchises for Esso and Pepsi-Cola. I called at his home in downtown Vientiane, demanding to see Huu Tim-heng. Fortunately, he was out. I took a taxi to the Pepsi-Cola bottling plant near the Mekong River that served as Huu's front for the import of acetic anhydride, the chemical used in making heroin. I broke into the abandoned factory and prowled the premises for some evidence of illegal activity, which of course, was not there.

In northwestern Laos, I sped up the Mekong River in a sleek power boat to meet the CIA's Yao tribal leader, Chao La, reputedly a major heroin manufacturer. A polite man, Chao La entertained me at his armed camp in a kindly fashion and handled my questions about opium without a flicker of irritation, evading some and answering others. Opium was the only profitable business in these hills. Tribal leaders in the Golden Triangle seemed nonplussed when I asked about the progress of the poppy crop.

From Laos, I faced a month-long journey for home through northern Thailand, where former CIA agent William Young spent days recounting his experiences as hill tribe guerrilla leader; along the Burma-Thailand border, where rebel commanders received me in their camps; and on to Singapore, where I drank for days in the bar at the Shangri-La Hotel with an aging Australian blonde named Norma "Silky" Sullivan, an intimate of Saigon's leading Corsican gangsters. She gave me the name and Paris phone number for one Lars Bugatti, whom she described as an ex-Gestapo officer and major drug dealer.

Landing at Paris only 22 hours after my last meeting with Norma, I made a stupid mistake. From my hotel, I rang Mr. Bugatti, gave Norma's name, and took a taxi to his apartment in a fashionable area. The door opened to a lavish foyer where five well-muscled young men lounged about, chatting and smoking. In the privacy of Bugatti's manicured study, I said that Norma had told me that he "knew something" about drugs. *"Elle est mythomane,"* he said in a threatening tone. That instant, I realized where I was. I was no longer in the Golden Triangle where people talked openly about an opium business that fed everyone from tribal farmers to Laotian generals. I was back in the First World where even powerful men went to jail for drugs. "What does *mythomane* mean?" I asked, suddenly unsure of my French. He rose from his desk and pulled me forward to a giant Larousse dictionary with a motion of his fat finger. *"Mythomane,"* it read, "a compulsive or habitual liar." Yes, of course, so she was. I excused myself, exited past the five young men, and changed taxis before returning to my hotel.

Although the threats stopped once I finished the final draft of the book in the spring of 1972, I began to face other kinds of problems. President Richard Nixon had just declared "war on drugs," making the global drug traffic a major domestic political issue for the first time in U.S. history. Evidently, the Nixon administration was not about to be embarrassed by a political issue of its own making. On June 12, I testified about CIA complicity in the Indochina drug traffic before Senator William Proxmire's Committee on Appropriations. A few days later, Elisabeth Jakab rang from New York, summoning me from Washington for a meeting with the president and vice-president of Harper & Row.

Receiving us in Harper & Row's executive suite looking out on the groves of Gothic spires on the roof of St. Patrick's Cathedral, the company's president, Winthrop Knowlton, announced that Cord Meyer, Jr., a senior CIA official, had recently visited Harper's owner and president emeritus, Cass Canfield, Sr., apparently an old friend from New York social circles. Claiming that my book represented a threat to national security, the CIA had asked Harper's owner to suppress it. To his credit, Canfield had refused. But he had agreed to allow the CIA to review the manuscript prior to publication. Although Knowlton argued forcefully in favor of the CIA review, I resisted the idea and withheld my approval.

A month later Knowlton gave me an ultimatum: If I did not agree to a CIA review of the manuscript, Harper & Row, contract notwithstanding, would refuse to publish my book. I spent almost twenty-four hours struggling with the dilemma. My friend David Obst, a freelance literary agent in Washington, put me in touch with Hal Dutton of the publishing house E. P. Dutton, who was, David said, very upset by Harper's decision to grant the CIA prior review of any manuscript. Dutton was willing to publish the book but warned that editorial work and legal battles with Harper & Row could mean a delay of six months.

Rather than slow the publication of timely material, I worked out a compromise with Harper & Row. We created a procedure for submitting the manuscript to the CIA for prior review in a way that would preserve some semblance of editorial integrity.

Tipped off to a potential story by our mutual friend David Obst, Seymour Hersh, recently hired as an investigative reporter for *The New York Times*, interviewed Harper's staff and published his exposé of the CIA's attempt to suppress the book on page 1 of the *The New York Times*. Over the next week, *The Washington Post* ran an editorial attacking the CIA's infringement of freedom of the press and NBC's *Chronolog* program televised an hour-long report by Garrick Utley on the agency's complicity in the Laotian drug trade.

Faced with a barrage of negative media exposure, the CIA studied my manuscript for a week before delivering a review full of undocumented and unconvincing denials. It was a dishonest document, indicating that Harper & Row's trust in the agency's integrity had been ill advised. For example, to counter my thesis that the CIA's alliance with Nationalist Chinese irregulars in Burma had expanded local opium production, the CIA simply denied that the Chinese irregulars had been involved in drug dealing. But only five months before, the CIA had spent nearly $2 million to buy and burn the "last" 26 tons of opium that its Chinese clients had hauled out of northern Burma.

In August 1972, Harper & Row ran quarter-page advertisements in *The New York Times* announcing publication of my book—without any changes.

Humiliated in the public arena, the CIA turned to covert harassment. Over the coming months, my federal education grant was investigated, my phone was tapped, my income tax was audited, and my sources were intimidated. After the agency's inspector general ordered an internal investigation, an Air America helicopter landed in Ger Su Yang's village and a CIA man ordered him aboard for a flight to a covert combat base in northern Laos. Interrogated for an hour by an irate CIA agent, the Hmong leader, fearing arrest or execution, lied and denied everything. Soon after Ger Su Yang landed back in his village, John Everingham arrived on one of his periodic mountain treks. Ger Su Yang apologized for lying and asked the photographer: "Do you think they will send a helicopter to arrest me, or send Vang Pao soldiers to shoot me?"

Shortly after my book was published, New York Congressman Ogden Reid, a ranking member of the House Foreign Relations Committee, telephoned me to say that he was sending investigators to Laos to look into the opium situation. By the time they arrived, the CIA had silenced my sources, and the investigators returned to Congress with the agency's sanitized story.

Although I had scored in the first engagement with a media blitz, the CIA won the longer bureaucratic battle. By silencing my sources and publicly protesting its abhorrence of drugs, the agency convinced Congress that it had been innocent of any complicity in the Southeast Asian opium trade. In its hearings on CIA assassinations and covert operations in 1975, Senator Frank Church's committee accepted the results of the agency's own internal investigation, which had found, not surprisingly, that none of its operatives had ever been in any way involved in the drug trade. Although the CIA's report had expressed some concern about opium dealing by its Southeast Asian allies, Congress did not question the agency about its alliances with leading drug lords—the key aspect, in my view, of CIA complicity in narcotics trafficking. As the flow of drugs into America slowed and the number of addicts declined during the mid-1970s, the heroin problem receded into the inner cities for much of the decade. The media moved on to new sensations, and the issue was largely forgotten.

If the CIA had not interfered in the congressional investigations, legislative restraints on future covert operations might have prevented the agency's complicity in the disastrous heroin and cocaine epidemics of the 1980s. Denied CIA logistic support and political protection, the drug lords of Asia and the Americas might not have been able to deliver such limitless supplies of heroin and cocaine, perhaps slowing the spread of the U.S.'s drug problem. As it was, the CIA convinced Congress of its integrity on the drug issue, thus preventing an honest appraisal and blocking any chance of reform.

The DEA's enforcement shield that had allowed America's brief respite from drugs during the 1970s simply deflected the Golden Triangle's heroin exports to new markets in Europe and Australia. For the first time in over a half century, both continents suffered widespread narcotics abuse. Indeed, heroin's spread created a worldwide narcotics market with unprecedented enforcement problems. I followed this heroin trail during a twelve-year residence in Australia, an experience that gave me a sharper sense of the global nature of the narcotics trade.

In the summer of 1989, I returned to America to take up a post at the University of Wisconsin, arriving a few months before President George Bush declared his "war on drugs." Listening to my thoughts on the latest drug war, Dr. Ruby Paredes felt that I had something to add to the public debate and urged me to publish a revised edition of my first book. Soon after I arrived in Madison, the news director at the city's community radio station, Jeffrey W. Hansen, stoked my enthusiasm for the project with several hours of interviews about America's drug wars. Simultaneously, an independent New York publisher, Shirley Cloyes of Lawrence Hill Books, proposed publishing a revised edition that would allow major changes to old material and the inclusion of new chapters on the current drug war.

I did not have to risk my life to update this book in 1990. As the narcotics trade expanded beyond the Golden Triangle to much of Asia and Latin America, the localized, dangerous field interviews of the early 1970s in places such as Saigon and Vientiane were no longer the most appropriate method for researching a vast global narcotics industry. Once an obscure subject, the documentation on the international narcotics traffic, particularly of criminal organizations and government complicity, has grown tremendously over the past twenty years. Consequently, this book required a massive research effort instead of the on-site investigations of the early 1970s.

Because the global drug trade has now expanded far beyond Europe and Southeast Asia, I had to call on the expertise of many scholars for this new book. At the University of Wisconsin, John Roosa assisted with research into southern Asian history. David Streckfuss contributed his considerable insights on current Thai politics and worked with dedication as the main researcher for the whole project. Steve Galster and Craig Nelson at the National Security Archives in Washington, D.C. demonstrated the enormous value of their collections by locating recently declassified documents on current U.S. drug policy. Marian Wilkinson of the *Sydney Morning Herald* provided documents on the CIA involvement in the Nugan Hand Bank scandal and helped me understand its complexities.

The new section on southern Asian heroin could not have been written without the help of Lawrence Lifschultz, a specialist on Indian and Pakistani politics. As a Yale undergraduate twenty years ago, Larry had helped me research my first book. With the same generosity, he now opened files from his years as a distinguished South Asian correspondent to provide me with press clippings, documents, and his own seminal articles on Pakistan's heroin industry. Larry also put me in touch with another former Yale student, Barnett Rubin, now resident South Asian specialist at the U.S. Institute for Peace, who sent me his materials on the Afghan guerrilla situation.

To update the section on organized crime in Europe and America, I benefited from the encyclopedic expertise and archives of Professor Alan A. Block at Pennsylvania State University. I told him my interests and he sent me a carton of declassified documents that he has collected over the past fifteen years. During the period of revisions and corrections, the book's copy editor, Barbara Flanagan, managed the formidable task of integrating the old text with the new, solving many complex editorial problems.

With all this help, I was able to discard obsolete data from my first book and write new material, comprising more than half the present volume. Moving beyond exposé to explanation, I have included new analytic sections on the political dynamics of the global narcotics trade, two chapters that cover the past twenty years of drug trafficking, and material that places the current drug war in historical perspective. Although I am grateful for all this assistance, I remain, as always, solely responsible for any errors of fact or interpretation.

Alfred W. McCoy
Madison, Wisconsin
December 1990

# Introduction: A History of Heroin

ON MARCH 15, 1990, U.S. ATTORNEY GENERAL RICHARD THORN-burgh called a press conference to announce a major initiative in America's war on drugs. Speaking to reporters at the Justice Department on Pennsylvania Avenue in Washington, the attorney general revealed that federal prosecutors in Brooklyn had filed a sealed indictment the previous December against one Khun Sa, an opium warlord then living half a world away in the jungles of northern Burma. The indictment accused Khun Sa of importing 3,500 pounds of heroin into New York City over an eighteen-month period. Specifically, it charged that he was the owner of a 2,400-pound shipment intercepted en route to New York at Bangkok in 1988—the largest single heroin seizure ever made. Justice Department officials claimed that the Burmese warlord was New York City's leading heroin supplier. The head of the Drug Enforcement Administration, John Lawn, called Khun Sa "the self-proclaimed king of opium," and federal prosecutors labeled him "the most powerful drug trafficker in the Golden Triangle."[1]

Filed only months after President Bush had declared war on drugs, the charges against Khun Sa seemed to promise a second front in the global battle. In December 1989, some 24,000 U.S. combat forces had invaded Panama in pursuit of the Caribbean "drug lord" General Manuel Noriega. The troops fought their way through Panama City and brought the dictator back to Miami to face charges of conspiring to smuggle cocaine into the United States. With the filing of similar charges against the Asian opium king, would the United States now pursue equally radical measures against Khun Sa? "We do have an extradition treaty with Burma," answered the attorney general. "It has never been utilized, but we will follow whatever avenues are open to secure the cooperation of the Burmese government.[2]

After the dramatic claims about Khun Sa's paramount importance in the global heroin traffic, the attorney general's appeal for assistance from a corrupt Rangoon regime was, to say the least, an anticlimax. For nearly thirty years, Rangoon had played politics with its opium trade, protecting favored drug lords like Khun Sa and allowing them use of government roads to transport their opium. Indeed, Kung Sa's rise to preeminence among rival opium warlords was a direct result of Rangoon's protection. If Burma's cooperation were not forthcoming, would U.S. combat forces now fly halfway around the world to storm Khun Sa's opium empire scattered across 100,000 square miles of the most rugged Southeast Asian mountains?

Even if Khun Sa were brought before a Brooklyn judge, his successful prosecution would not slow the march of opium caravans out of the Golden Triangle. At the very moment the U.S. attorney general was pleading for Burma's cooperation, the Rangoon military regime was grooming a new warlord to succeed Khun Sa in the event that diplomatic pressures should force them to deliver the reigning opium king.

The gap between the attorney general's harsh accusations and impotent actions demonstrates the limitations of a global drug war still fighting its first battles. The invasion of Panama, with all of its difficulties, was only a strike against a downstream drug finance center and never approached the narcotics heartland of the Andes. For all of its drama, General Noriega's arrest had no impact on the Caribbean cocaine trade. Unlike conventional combat in which the capture of a great general or leader is tantamount to victory, the war on drugs is being fought against a global commodity—controlled not by humans but by invisible market forces.

The capture of Noriega and the indictment of Khun Sa were the culmination of a U.S. drug policy that has, for the past seventy years, refused to recognize the failure of repression. Driven by a myopic moralism, U.S. policy ignores the fundamental dynamics of the drug trade. Over the past two centuries, narcotics have become major global commodities that operate on fluid laws of supply and demand not susceptible to simple repression. Over the past half century, every attempt at interdiction not only has failed to eradicate this global trade but has contributed, quite directly, to an expansion of both production and consumption of narcotics.

Although opium is very much a commodity, its prohibition gives its trade some peculiar properties. The very illegality of opium allows its trade far greater profits than any other commodity yields, producing a vast cash flow that has ramified into global networks linking tribal opium lords in the highlands of the Third World with criminal syndicates in the cities of the First World. This illicit traffic allows opium and heroin traders at all levels enormous incomes that they can use to purchase enough protection to survive any attempt at suppression. To understand the dynamics of the global heroin trade we must probe the history of this peculiar commodity in a way that America's policymakers have not. Narcotics are not simply illegal and immoral. Opium and coca products are global commodities with a unique politics and economics that cannot be ignored.

## A Social History of Heroin

Most societies in most times, regardless of locale or level of development, have used drugs for both medication and recreation. Alcohol is used in many societies across Europe and Asia, kava root is common in the Pacific, and the pre-Columbian societies of the Americas chewed peyote and coca leaf. Discovered and domesticated during prehistoric times in the eastern Mediterranean, opium first appears in formal Greek pharmacopeia during the fifth century B.C. and in Chinese texts during the eighth century A.D. Homer's *Odyssey* describes it as a drug that will "lull all pain and anger, and bring forgetfulness of every sorrow." Opium's healing properties were first detailed in the works of the Greek physician Hippocrates (466–377 B.C.) and were later explored by the Roman-era physician Galen (130–200 A.D.).[3]

From the eastern Mediterranean, the opium poppy, a temperate-climate plant that will grow only in the cool highlands of tropical Asia, spread into the mountains of India and China following in the path of Arab traders who also appreciated its medicinal properties. In the *Herbalist's Treasury* of 973 A.D., a commission of nine Chinese scholars wrote that the poppy's "seeds have healing power" and recommended a cure made by "mixing these seeds with bamboo juice boiled into gruel." The first reference to the modern method of harvesting the poppy's morphine content comes in the work of Wang Hi in the fifteenth century: "Opium is produced in Arabia from poppies with red flowers. . . . [A]fter the flower has faded, the capsule while still fresh is pricked for the juice."[4] Today the great bulk of the world's opium is still grown in a band of mountains that extends along the southern rim of the Asian landmass—from Turkey's Anatolian plateau through Iran, Afghanistan and Pakistan to India, and from there to the Golden Triangle where Burma (now called Myanmar), Thailand, and Laos converge.

Opium, morphine, and heroin are all drugs made from the opium poppy, or *Papaver somniferum*. Ancient peoples learned first to boil its seeds and later to incis its head to extract the sap. By the sixteenth century, residents of Persia and India began eating and drinking opium mixtures as a purely recreational euphoric, a practice that soon made opium an important item in intra-Asian trade. But it was European merchants who discovered opium's commercial potential. During the era of their dominion over Asian trade in the sixteenth century, Portuguese merchant captains carried ever increasing cargoes of Indian opium to China. The Dutch who succeeded them in the seventeenth century exported shipments of Indian opium to China and the islands of Southeast Asia, totaling more than 50 tons per year after 1650. More important, the Dutch introduced the practice of smoking opium in a tobacco pipe, thus popularizing the drug among the Chinese. Reacting to the rapid spread of opium smoking, the emperor ordered the prohibition of opium use in 1729, the first of many failed attempts by the Chinese at suppression.

The opium trade's modern era began in 1773 when the British East India Company took control of the export of Indian opium to China. Using its power as the colonial overlord of Bengal in eastern India, the company established a monopoly over the production and sale of opium. As the British colonial regime expanded its exports of Bengal opium to China over the next seventy-five years, opium became a major global commodity, giving this modern commerce a scale and organizational sophistication that distinguish it from its earlier forms—opium as folk pharmacopeia or luxury item in Asia's long-distance trade. Using opium to barter for China's tea, silk, and porcelains, British merchants controlled a profitable triangular trade between India, China, and Europe that smuggled growing quantities of opium to China. Although China's emperor banned opium completely in the 1790s, making the trade illegal, the law failed to slow the expansion of opium smuggling by British and American merchants.

The British East India Company's centralized controls accelerated the export of Indian opium to China—from only 15 tons in the 1720s to 75 tons in the 1770s when the company began its monopoly, to 3,200 tons in 1850. In 1839 and 1856, Britain fought two successful opium wars to force the Chinese Empire to rescind its opium ban. During the late nineteenth century, addiction grew and commercial opium cultivation spread across China. By 1900, China's population of 400 million included an estimated 13.5 million opium addicts who consumed 39,000 tons of smoking opium annually. Not only was China the world's largest consumer, but it harvested more than 35,000 tons of opium, over 85 percent of the world's total.

During the first century of the modern drug trade, British commerce had transformed opium from a luxury good into a bulk commodity of the same proportions as commercial stimulants—coffee, tea, and cacao. Although China's opium tonnage was less than its national tea harvest of 90,000 tons, opium's value was far higher. By any standard, opium had become a major commodity in legitimate international trade.

By the late nineteenth century, mass opium use spread beyond China to Southeast Asia and Europe. All the European colonial governments in Southeast Asia generated tax revenues by selling imported Indian opium to both Chinese immigrants and indigenous populations through state-licensed opium dens. At their peak in the early twentieth century, Southeast Asia's state opium monopolies accounted for close to 20 percent of total tax revenues in Siam and nearly 60 percent in British Malaya.[5]

In the West, opium addiction spread through bottled medical remedies. In 1821, the British writer Thomas De Quincey first drew attention to the problem of medical addiction when he published an essay entitled *Confessions of an English Opium-Eater*. Addicted during his student days at Oxford, De Quincey remained an opium user for the rest of his life. Such domestic drug use within the confines of middle-class homes became a characteristic of nineteenth-century life in England, America, and Australia.

Although Europeans and Americans consumed growing quantities of bottled opium, it was the chemical production of its derivatives, morphine and heroin, that popularized narcotics use in the West during the 1800s. If opium is a drug of venerable antecedents, morphine and heroin are products of the modern pharmaceutical industry. Medical science first learned to extract morphine, the poppy sap's active chemical ingredient, in 1805. E. Merck & Company of Darmstadt, Germany, began commercial manufacture of morphine in 1827, but it was not until the 1860s, in combination with the hypodermic syringe, that it gained popularity as an anesthetic. In 1874, the English researcher C. R. Wright synthesized heroin, or diacetylmorphine, for the first time when he boiled morphine and a common chemical, acetic anhydride, over a stove for several hours. After biological testing on dogs showed that diacetylmorphine induced "great prostration, fear, sleepiness speedily following the administration . . . and a slight tendency to vomiting," the English researcher decided to discontinue his experiments.[6]

In 1898, however, the Bayer Company of Elberfeld, Germany, began mass production of diacetylmorphine and coined the trade name heroin to market the new remedy. A year later, Bayer discovered a milder pain reliever, which it named aspirin, and used the same commercial acumen to popularize both products. In its international advertising campaign,

Bayer described heroin as a nonaddictive panacea for adult ailments and infant respiratory diseases. The drug's popularity encouraged imitators, and scores of patent medicine manufacturers appeared in Europe, America, and Australia in the late nineteenth century. Concealing the high narcotic content of their nostrums from consumers by steadfast refusal to publish their "secret remedies," the patent medicine companies promoted their products through saturation advertising in mass-circulation newspapers—claiming near-miraculous properties that would restore vitality to the aged, heal children, and cure dozens of unrelated ailments. In 1906, the American Medical Association approved heroin for general use "in place of morphine in various painful injections," as did its counterparts in Europe and Australia. In short, physicians believed that heroin was an effective, nonaddictive substitute for morphine whose dependency-inducing properties were, at last, well understood.[7]

During the late nineteenth century, the same manufacturers also promoted another narcotic, cocaine. Unlike opium, cocaine is a relatively recent arrival in the canons of Western pharmacopeia. During the 1830s, the Swiss naturalist J. J. von Tschudi published an account of coca leaf chewing among the Andean Indians in his book *Travels in Peru*, claiming that his porters could travel for five nights on no food and little sleep while chewing this leaf. European medical experiments with the coca leaf began in the 1850s, and Merck became the first to manufacture cocaine, the leaf's active ingredient, in concentrated crystal form. Between 1884 and 1887, Sigmund Freud, inspired by his American colleagues, conducted a series of experiments with cocaine and published three enthusiastic articles ascribing beneficial, if not miraculous, effects to the new drug. In particular, Freud praised cocaine for its ability to cure morphine and alcohol addiction in the course of a ten-day treatment program. Although Freud wrote that the user experienced "absolutely no craving for the further use of cocaine," other medical researchers of the 1880s found that prolonged use had a negative effect on the nervous system and produced a strong desire for the drug. More substantive medical research discovered that cocaine was an important medication for both teeth extractions and ophthalmic surgery.[8]

While medical science gave cocaine its qualified approval, the drug manufacturers sold massive quantities in the form of popular remedies and daily tonics. Until 1903, for example, the popular soft drink Coca-Cola contained a dose of cocaine. The Parke-Davis pharmaceutical company of Detroit became one of the world's leading cocaine manufacturers, producing coca cordials, cocaine cigarettes, hypodermic capsules, ointments, and sprays.[9] Such successful marketing made mass addiction to cocaine and heroin a significant feature of late-nineteenth-century life.

Although aggressive advertising no doubt played a part in the popularity of the new narcotic remedies, they would not have been consumed for so long and in such large quantities if they had not met some basic consumer need. In retrospect, the growth of mass narcotics abuse seems part of the transformation of daily living in the 1800s. Indeed, one of the most important manifestations of modernity in the West was the creation of a new diet based on a global trade in protein and stimulants. In the eighteenth century, American and European workers had been employed on farms or in small firms where they could control the pace of their work according to their own biorhythms, perhaps lazing through the morning and speeding up in the afternoon. In such societies, a low-energy, grain-based diet was no doubt adequate nutrition. As the population shifted from country to city and from farm to factory, both the means and the need to transform the character of the working person's diet developed. Bound to an industrial regimen that required a constant level of performance throughout the twelve-hour day, the modern factory worker felt pressed to use stimulants that could accelerate the body's rhythms artificially to match the pace of industry. Factories set their machines at a high pitch, and the price of inattention to their hazardous mechanisms was often injury or death.

During the nineteenth century, the Western diet replaced low-energy grains with proteins and stimulants. After a century of unchanging dietary habits, the average Englishman's annual consumption of sugar, a quick energy source, jumped fourfold from 20 pounds per person in 1850 to 80 pounds in 1900. During the same period, England's per capita consumption of tea increased threefold from 2 to 6 pounds. By century's turn, the ordinary English worker stoked his or her body in the morning with a breakfast comprising an Argentine beef sausage, an egg or two from China, and a cup of Chinese or Indian tea energized with two or three spoons of Caribbean sugar.[10] In the United States the change in diet was just as dramatic. Between 1865 and 1903, annual coffee consumption increased nearly threefold from 4.7 to 13.3 pounds per person, while sugar jumped fourfold from 18.2 to 78.8 pounds.[11] The simple eighteenth-century diet of milled grains had given way to one spiced with large quantities of protein (eggs and beef), glucose (sugar), and stimulants (coffee and tea).

If an energized diet of proteins, glucose, and caffeine could be used to stimulate the body and maintain a constant level of performance through a long working day, then narcotic-based medicines could be used to soothe and relax it artificially during the short hours of rest. In the mid- to late-1800s, patent medicine manufacturers produced legal drugs to assist every bodily function and induce any desired state of mind. There were cocaine-based drugs to overcome fatigue, morphine remedies to soothe worn nerves, and heroin medications to calm the agitated mind or respiratory system. Paralleling the increase in sugar and coffee use, Americans' annual consumption of opium rose fourfold from 12 grains per person in the 1840s to 52 grains in the 1890s.[12] Narcotics addiction followed this rising curve, peaking at about 313,000 addicts in 1896.[13] In the United Kingdom, sales of patent medicines, most of them opium-based, increased sevenfold between 1850 and 1905.[14]

In an era when Western medical practice was still rudimentary, mass self-medication was a practice that also encouraged opium abuse. During the nineteenth century, English and American medicine was locked into a long transition from the eighteenth century's heroic remedies of bleeding and blistering to the genuine therapeutic remedies that first appeared in the early twentieth century. In this protracted crisis their practice was undergoing, medical doctors were the most enthusiastic advocates of opium treatment, injecting morphine to cure adult ailments and prescribing opium tonics for childhood diseases. In an era of poor sanitation in crowded cities, dehydrating diseases such as cholera were epidemic and opium was a genuinely effective remedy. "Opium," explains historian Terry Parssinen, "was the Victorian's aspirin, Lomotil, Valium and Nyquil, which could be bought at the local chemist for as little as a penny."[15]

There were significant gender differences in drug abuse during the 1800s. Although everyone used opium when ill, women abused the drug more frequently than men. In the custom of the day, women were informally banned from the American barroom or English pub, where men met to maintain their alcohol addiction. At home, women were introduced to opium through the patent medicines they used to treat themselves and their families. The advertising at century's turn confirms this contrast. Drinking alcohol was a manly activity portrayed in press advertisements with themes of male sports and barrooms. Narcotic remedies showed women nurturing their children in home settings. Both the anecdotal and statistical evidence indicates that most American, Australian, and English addicts—like Mary Tyrone, the mother in Eugene O'Neill's drama *Long Day's Journey into Night*— were middle-class women.[16]

After 1900, growing medical awareness of narcotics addiction and an international temperance movement combined to produce new laws that restricted and then prohibited the use of narcotics. Led by the clergy and laity of the Protestant churches, the temperance movement attacked alcohol addiction first before turning its attention to narcotics.

Although medical science began to analyze the problem of opiate addiction in the eighteenth century, it was not until the 1890s that the profession became generally aware of the dependency-inducing properties of the new miracle drugs cocaine, heroin, and morphine. It took several decades, however, to translate medical knowledge into legislative reforms. Patent medicine dealers were the largest newspaper advertisers in the United States, Britain, and Australia, and the press consequently had an interest in not publicizing information detrimental to sales. In a famous series of muckraking articles on the patent medicine trade published by *Collier's* magazine in 1905, Samuel Hopkins Adams reported that many leading American newspapers had long-term advertising contracts with patent medicine advertisers containing a single escape clause—the drug companies could break the contract if state or local legislation restricted the sale of their products. Protected from criticism, the patent medicine trade grew into a $250 million a year industry by 1900.[17]

Despite strong resistance, U.S. reform movements succeeded in exposing the narcotic content of patent medicines and securing regulatory legislation. In 1897 Illinois banned cocaine sales without prescription and in 1906 the U.S. Pure Food and Drug Act required labeling of patent medicines showing their precise contents. Within two years sales of the once secret remedies had dropped by one-third. Pressed by further state and federal legislation restricting patent medicine sales, manufacturers reduced and then removed the alcoholic and narcotic contents. The manufacturers of one popular nostrum, Mrs. Winslow's Soothing Syrup, a child's sedative, reduced its morphine content by three-quarters within a three-year period.[18]

Although many states passed laws banning narcotics, the manufacturers frustrated these efforts with mail-order sales, finally provoking a response from the U.S. Congress. With strong support from religious movements, Congress passed the Harrison Narcotics Act in 1914 requiring a doctor's prescription for the purchase of heroin or cocaine. After decades of promoting narcotics use, however, medical doctors often ignored the act's intentions and simply sold prescriptions. In one month, for example, a single New York City "dope doctor" wrote prescriptions for 68,282 grains of heroin, 54,097 grains of morphine, and 30,280 grains of cocaine.[19] But over the next decade, a combination of Supreme Court decisions and additional legislation turned this loose law into an effective prohibition of all legal narcotics sales. By 1923, the Treasury Department's new Narcotics Division, the first federal drug agency, was actively banning all legal narcotics sales and pursuing the criminal drug pushers who had replaced pharmacists.[20]

The U.S. prohibition of narcotics was part of a global movement that extended from America to Europe and Asia. Responding to pressure from English Protestants and Chinese nationalists, the Shanghai Opium Commission of 1909 launched an antinarcotics diplomacy that slowly reduced global opium production. Drafted under the auspices of the League of Nations, the Geneva Convention of 1925 imposed strict regulations on the export of heroin. These controls were reinforced by the League's Limitation Convention of 1931, which stipulated that drug manufacturers could produce enough heroin only to meet legitimate "medical and scientific needs." Through these treaties, the world's legal heroin production plummeted from nearly 20,000 pounds in 1926 to only 2,200 five years later.[21] Likewise, through a broad range of regulations and restrictions, drug diplomacy reduced global opium production from its peak of 41,600 tons in 1906 to just 7,600 in 1934.[22] Following the collapse of the League of Nations during World War II, its narcotics committee transferred to the newly established United Nations and continued its drug diplomacy, finally achieving a total ban on legal narcotics sales in 1961.

The sharp decline in legal pharmaceutical production did not end widespread heroin addiction. No longer able to procure a regular dosage of drugs from pharmacy or doctor, American addicts were forced to turn to illegal street dealers. Although the profile of a typical addict shifted from a middle-class white woman to a lower-class white man, America still had some 200,000 addicts in the mid-1920s.[23] After the United States prohibited the legal sale of narcotics in the 1920s, criminal syndicates emerged in many cities to meet the illicit demand for heroin and cocaine. Exploiting the prohibition of both alcohol and narcotics in the 1920s, American organized crime grew from localized gangs into nationwide syndicates with substantial economic and political influence in the cities of the industrial Midwest and Northeast. Although the prohibition of alcohol lasted just thirteen years until its repeal in 1933, the ban on narcotics sales was permanent, making the illicit heroin traffic the most constant source of income for organized crime in America.

Thus, the events of the 1920s mark a major transition in the history of the global drug trade. For 150 years opium had operated as a normal commodity, expanding into a global trade that linked the highland poppy growers of Asia with urban consumers in Europe and America. In the seventy years that followed Prohibition in the 1920s, narcotics have moved from legal commerce to illicit traffic, acquiring thereby a peculiar politics while still retaining many attributes as ordinary commodities. Despite prohibition, the illicit heroin industry still unites urban addicts with highland opium growers through an informal alliance of international smugglers and domestic distributors. Instead of moving through the normal arteries of commerce, the global drug trade has shifted to illicit networks that link the opium and coca highlands of the Third World with the cities of the First World.

The global prohibition of opium and coca sales did not change the economic dependence of highland farmers on the global drug trade. Over the past century, peasants along the Andes and the southern rim of Asia have relied on these drugs as their major cash crops. In such remote, rugged regions with costly transport and poor roads, narcotics—with their light weight and sure market—remain the only appropriate cash crops. These mountain regions, moreover, provide refuge to rebels who find narcotics, with both production and marketing outside government control, an ideal economic base for revolution. The Asian and South American highland zones lie at the intersection of trade, terrain, national boundaries, and ethnic frontiers that make them natural outlaw zones beyond the reach of any modern state. In these zones, the merchants who control the opium crop are often legitimate tribal leaders who can mobilize arms and armies to defend their trade. Whether at peace or in rebellion, many highland regions of Asia and Latin America are dominated by narcotics, which create potent political support for their survival.

As the raw drugs come down from the highlands, they usually move to centers of secondary services essential to the global traffic—processing, finance, and smuggling. In Southeast Asia's Golden Triangle, Burma's Shan Plateau produces bumper opium crops under the protection of tribal warlords. But the finance, processing, and export are done through Bangkok, a sophisticated city with the economic base to provide such services. While all Latin America's cocaine is grown in the highlands of the Andes, the Caribbean basin provides the support services—export and finance through Medellín and Cali, Colombia; money laundering through Panama City; and smuggling through the Bahamas and other island states.

Since the highland drug farmers require credit and markets to finance each new crop, a major expansion of drug production has three requirements—finance, logistics, and politics. Thus, the sudden growth of Burma's opium production in the 1950s required CIA air logistics, Thai military protection, and Taiwanese capital. Similarly, the upsurge of opium production in Afghanistan during the 1980s relied on the logistical support of Pakistan's Inter Service Intelligence, the cover of a CIA covert operation, and the services of Pakistani banks, just as the simultaneous expansion of the Colombian cocaine trade required capital from illicit financiers, the loose protection of the covert Contra war, and the illegal services of banks based in Caribbean free ports such as Panama City.

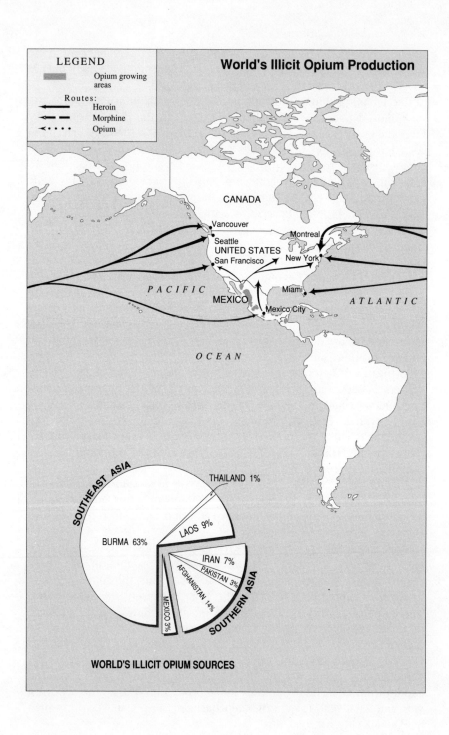

LEGEND

Opium growing areas

Routes:
→ Heroin
⇠ Morphine
◁···· Opium

**World's Illicit Opium Production**

CANADA

Vancouver
Seattle
Montreal
UNITED STATES
San Francisco
New York
MEXICO
Miami
Mexico City

PACIFIC

ATLANTIC

OCEAN

SOUTHEAST ASIA

THAILAND 1%

LAOS 9%

BURMA 63%

IRAN 7%
PAKISTAN 3%
AFGHANISTAN 14%

MEXICO 3%

SOUTHERN ASIA

**WORLD'S ILLICIT OPIUM SOURCES**

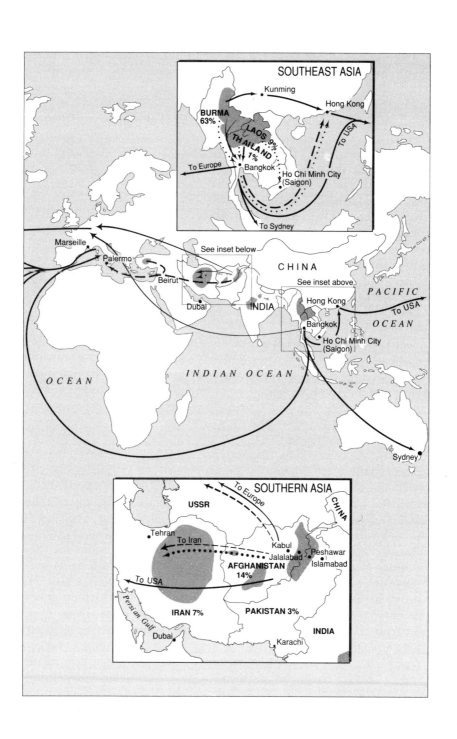

SOUTHEAST ASIA

Kunming

Hong Kong

BURMA
63%

LAOS
9%

THAILAND
1%

To Europe

Bangkok

Ho Chi Minh City
(Saigon)

To USA

To Sydney

Marseille

Palermo

Beirut

CHINA

See inset below

Dubai

INDIA

See inset above

Hong Kong

PACIFIC

To USA

OCEAN

Bangkok

Ho Chi Minh City
(Saigon)

OCEAN

INDIAN OCEAN

Sydney

SOUTHERN ASIA

USSR

To Europe

CHINA

Tehran

To Iran

Kabul

Peshawar

Jalalabad

Islamabad

AFGHANISTAN
14%

To USA

Persian Gulf

IRAN 7%

PAKISTAN 3%

INDIA

Dubai

Karachi

Once grown, processed, and smuggled, drugs often enter national distribution systems through major port cities. Indeed, the rise of criminal syndicates after the prohibition of drugs in the 1920s is closely identified with the world's great port and transport cities—New York, Chicago, Marseille, Shanghai, Hong Kong, Bangkok, Saigon, and Sydney. During the 1920s, Marseille's French-Corsican syndicates began smuggling narcotics across the Atlantic; in Shanghai the Green Gang took control of the Yangtze Valley and opened heroin laboratories to control the region's opium trade; and in New York Jewish crime syndicates distributed prohibited drugs—alcohol, cocaine, and heroin. Port cities such as Marseille and New York have been built around transport and cargo handling, a commerce of movement that allows organized theft, smuggling, and black market trading. With entrepôt economies dependent on the up-and-down cycles of world trade, these cities spawn vice sectors—prostitution, gambling, protection, and organized theft—that offer alternative employment for the underclass. Often by default, vice operators in these rough cities can translate their economic influence into political power.

The prohibition of narcotics has contributed to the growth of modern organized crime. While the governments of the laissez-faire nineteenth century tolerated or taxed most forms of personal vice, the moralistic regimes of the twentieth century have tried to use state power to control personal behavior. The prohibition of personal vice, narcotics included, simply transferred these trades from legitimate merchants to entrepreneurs in vice and violence.

As with all commodities, there is a politics of heroin. Since opium and coca are large, capital-intensive industries, investors at all levels try to minimize risk by seeking political protection. As drug syndicates have expanded from local into international operations, the quality of their protection has kept pace. In the mountains, the opium warlords protect the poppy harvest by forming their own armies and cultivating external allies, such as national politicians or intelligence agencies like the CIA. As drugs move out of the mountains into global markets, dealers seek support from national police and intelligence organizations. Finally, in the cities of the First World drug dealers cultivate links with local police to protect their illicit distribution networks. In some cities, drug distribution has achieved a de facto symbiosis with law enforcement. In Hong Kong during the 1970s, for example, corrupt senior police worked closely with the syndicates to regulate the colony's heroin traffic, taking a major share of the profits and using the law to crush any competition. In New York during the 1960s, the regional office of the Bureau of Narcotics and Dangerous Drugs achieved a similar symbiosis with a Mafia drug syndicate, accepting regular bribes to arrest only those dealers nominated by the syndicate. The system gave federal agents an impressive record of arrests and allowed them rapid promotions while simultaneously eliminating any competition for the Mafia.

Since prohibition of narcotics in the 1920s, alliances between drug brokers and intelligence agencies have protected the global narcotics traffic. In Nationalist China during World War II, the regime's most powerful intelligence agency was allied with the Green Gang, a syndicate that controlled the opium trade along the vast Yangtze Valley. Similarly, in postwar France successive Gaullist governments worked with Marseille's Corsican milieu to fight an underground war against military terrorists. Most important, during the cold war the U.S. Central Intelligence Agency formed alliances with drug syndicates that have had a significant impact on the global heroin traffic.

Given the frequency of such alliances, there seems a natural attraction between intelligence agencies and criminal syndicates. To gain a covert capacity for operations outside normal channels, intelligence agencies have cultivated alliances with criminals in waterfronts and mountain borderlands. In return for their cooperation, port city criminals get protection that allows them to conduct their illegal business in full view of the state and its police. Similarly, highland drug lords benefit from improved logistics in rough terrain, access to capital for larger opium crops, and improved arms to seize and hold territory.

Beyond these practicalities, there seems a natural affinity between covert operatives and criminal syndicates. Both are practitioners of what one retired CIA operative has called the "clandestine arts"—the basic skill of operating outside the normal channels of civil society.[24] Among all the institutions of modern society, intelligence agencies and criminal syndicates alone maintain large organizations capable of carrying out covert operations without fear of detection. For example, when the CIA needed a legion of thugs to break the 1950 Communist dock strike in Marseille, it turned to that city's Corsican milieu. When the agency attempted to assassinate Cuban leader Fidel Castro in the 1960s, it retained American Mafia syndicates who could not only kill on contract but ensure confidentiality—something no official U.S. agency, except the CIA itself, could do. Operating in the mountains of Asia, the CIA has allied itself with heroin merchants in Laos, Chinese opium dealers in Burma, and rebel opium armies in Afghanistan.

Over the past forty years, CIA covert operations have often overwhelmed the interdiction efforts of the weaker U.S. drug enforcement agencies. In Southeast Asia, for example, the U.S. Bureau of Narcotics opened its first office in Bangkok with just three agents in the late 1960s, more than a decade after a major CIA covert operation—

backed by several hundred agents and a fleet of aircraft—had installed a 12,000-man opium army in the mountains of northern Burma. While a handful of drug agents worked out of lowland offices trying to intercept drug shipments or discover the names of the smugglers, the CIA's massive covert apparatus had been operating in the opium highlands, allied with the very drug lords that U.S. narcotics agents were trying to arrest.

Moreover, America's attempts at narcotics control, both domestic and international, have been crippled by major problems inside U.S. enforcement agencies. After a decade of poor performance, the first federal drug agency, the Treasury's Narcotics Division, collapsed in 1929 when a New York City grand jury discovered systematic corruption. Field agents were protecting the City's drug dealers and the division chief's son was working as a tax agent for the country's most notorious racketeer, Arnold Rothstein. Reacting to the scandal, Congress created the Federal Bureau of Narcotics (FBN) in 1930, and President Herbert Hoover named a young Prohibition officer, Harry Anslinger, as its director. Although alcohol prohibition ended in 1933, the FBN's antinarcotics campaign continued for another thirty years under Anslinger, a tough bureaucratic infighter whose survival skills rivaled those of J. Edgar Hoover at the FBI. Regarding all drugs as absolutely evil, Anslinger dedicated the FBN's resources to domestic enforcement, pursuing addicts and dealers with equal enthusiasm. Absorbed in domestic drug control, Anslinger did not assign FBN agents abroad before the war, and instead relied on the League of Nations or liaisions with foreign police.[25]

After World War II, the United States abandoned its multilateral approach to international control and extended the FBN's operations into Europe and the Middle East, achieving only limited success. In retrospect, it seems that Anslinger's intelligence connections compromised his bureau's antinarcotics mission. As a strong anti-Communist and a specialist in counterintelligence, Anslinger maintained close ties to the U.S. intelligence community. During World War II, he had lent his bureau's key personnel to form the Office of Strategic Services (OSS), forerunner of the CIA, thereby setting a postwar pattern of cross-fertilization between the two agencies.[26] Aware of France's strategic importance on the European front of the cold war, Anslinger avoided pressuring Paris over its promotion of the Indochina opium trade during the early 1950s and covered his oversight by falsely accusing Vietnam's Communists of complicity.[27] Insisting that Communist China controlled the Asian heroin trade, Anslinger refused to assign any agents to Southeast Asia, which had become, by his retirement in 1962, the world's major opium producer.[28] Did Anslinger knowingly keep his FBN agents out of Southeast Asia during the 1950s to avoid exposing the CIA's complicity in the Golden Triangle opium trade? Were his false allegations of Communist Chinese control over the Asian heroin trade, now repudiated by his own agency, a knowing attempt to protect Nationalist China's control over Burma's opium exports? Whatever his motivation, Anslinger's politics denied his bureau any Asian expertise. As an indication of its total ignorance of Asia, in 1965 the Bureau of Narcotics compiled a dossier of the world's 246 leading drug traffickers. Although the information on some 200 European and American dealers was detailed and largely accurate, the list showed only two opium traffickers for all of Southeast Asia. Both were minor European traffickers—Rolf Schmoll, who was married to a Hmong princess, arranged for small shipments of opium out of Laos and Michel Libert, a French Corsican smuggler, operated out of Saigon and Bangkok in the mid-1960s. There was not a single reference to the Burmese drug lords or Hong Kong heroin syndicates, which had already emerged as the world's major illicit drug traffickers.[29]

Crippled by corruption and strategic myopia, the FBN and its successor, the Bureau of Narcotics and Dangerous Drugs (BNDD), failed to stem an expanded international narcotics traffic that was increasingly concentrated in Southeast Asia by the late 1960s. After superseding the BNDD in the early 1970s, the Drug Enforcement Administration (DEA) has emerged in the last two decades as a much more professional antinarcotics agency with a global network of agents and offices. Reflecting its origins, however, the DEA remains unwilling to challenge the CIA when any of the CIA's covert operations become involved in the drug trade.

In this internecine bureaucratic struggle for the opium hills of Asia, the FBN's and DEA's weak, distant attempts at interdiction of the heroin flow have often been overwhelmed by the CIA's logistic and political support for the drug lords. Indeed, a brief survey of the international traffic over the past forty years shows that the CIA's covert alliances have played a significant, albeit inadvertent, role in opening new opium zones for the global drug traffic. At two critical junctures after World War II, the late 1940s and the late 1970s, when America's heroin supply and addict population seemed to ebb, the CIA's covert action alliances generated a sudden surge of heroin that soon revived the U.S. drug trade.

The CIA's complicity in the drug trade was a product of the cold war. In the late 1940s when Soviet troops occupied Eastern Europe and China's Communist revolutionaries seized power, America's postwar leaders were faced with an immediate threat of global Communist expansion. Needing new weapons to fight a new kind of global war, the

Truman administration created the Central Intelligence Agency (CIA) in 1947 with two main missions—espionage and covert action. In effect, the CIA became the vanguard of America's global anti-Communist campaign. Practicing a radical pragmatism, its agents made alliances with any local group, drug merchants included, capable of countering Communist influence. Although these covert action alliances represent only a fraction of CIA operations, they still have had a profound impact on the postwar heroin trade.

The CIA's alliance with the drug lords in the late 1940s came at a time when the global opium trade was at its lowest ebb in nearly two centuries. World War II had disrupted international shipping and imposed tight waterfront security that blocked the smuggling of heroin into the United States. As America's narcotics use fell to its lowest level in half a century, the purity of illicit heroin packets dropped from 28 percent in 1938 to only 3 percent three years later. America's addict population plummeted from 200,000 in 1924 to a tenth of that figure in 1944–1945.[30] At the end of World War II, the possibility existcd that heroin addiction might decline and eventually disappear as a major social problem in the United States. Heroin supplies were small, international criminal syndicates were in disarray, and the American addict population had declined to a level where treatment was finally possible. Within a decade, however, the illicit heroin industry had revived. By the early 1950s, the global drug syndicates were again operating, Southeast Asia's poppy fields were expanding, and heroin refineries were multiplying in both Marseille and Hong Kong. Many of the reasons for the revival of the illicit narcotics trade lie with the conduct of U.S. foreign policy and its covert action arm.

The cold war was a global confrontation, but Europe was the most important battleground in the late 1940s. Determined to restrict Soviet influence in Western Europe, American CIA operatives intervened in the internal politics of Italy and France. From 1948 to 1950, the CIA allied itself with the Corsican underworld in its struggle against the French Communist party for control over the strategic Mediterranean port of Marseille. With CIA support, the Corsicans overcame their rival and for the next quarter century used their control over the Marseille waterfront to dominate the export of heroin to the U.S. market.

Simultaneously in Southeast Asia, the CIA ran a series of covert warfare operations along the China border that were instrumental in the creation of the Golden Triangle heroin complex. In 1951, the agency supported the formation of a Nationalist Chinese army for a covert invasion of southwestern China. When the invasion attempts failed in 1951–1952, the CIA installed Nationalist troops along the Burma-China border as a tripwire for an anticipated Communist Chinese invasion of

Southeast Asia. Over the next decade, the Nationalist Army transformed Burma's Shan states into the world's largest opium producer.

Applying the same tactics in Laos from 1960 to 1975, the CIA created a secret army of 30,000 Hmong tribesmen to battle Laotian Communists near the border with North Vietnam. Since the Hmong's main cash crop was opium, the CIA adopted a complicitous posture toward the traffic, allowing the Hmong commander, General Vang Pao, to use the CIA's Air America to collect opium from his scattered highland villages. In late 1969, the CIA's various covert action clients opened a network of heroin laboratories in the Golden Triangle. In their first years of operation, these laboratories exported high-grade no. 4 heroin to U.S. troops fighting in Vietnam. After their withdrawal, the Golden Triangle laboratories exported directly to the United States, capturing one-third of the American heroin market.

During the mid-1970s, the temporary success of some DEA operations in Turkey, Thailand, and Mexico cut the heroin flow to the United States, reducing the number of American addicts by more than half, from an estimated 500,000 to 200,000. In 1979, however, the CIA covert warfare operation in Afghanistan provided the support for a major expansion of the southern Asian* drug trade. To support the Afghan resistance against the Soviet occupation, the CIA, working through Pakistan's intelligence, allied with Afghan guerrillas, notably Gulbuddin Hekmatyar, who used the agency's arms, logistics, and support to become the region's largest drug lord. Within a year, a surge of southern Asian heroin had captured more than 60 percent of the American market, breaking the long drug drought and raising the addict population to its previous peak.

From 1934 to 1970, the slow pressure of League drug diplomacy had forced a gradual reduction in global opium production from 7,600 tons to only 1,000. In the following twenty years, however, the failure of the DEA's suppression efforts combined with CIA complicity in global traffic allowed world opium production to multiply fourfold to 4,200 tons by 1989. Significantly, some 3,000 tons, or 73 percent of the 1989 total, came from Southeast Asia, where the CIA had worked with the region's drug lords for twenty-four years. Most of the balance comes from southern Asian opium hills and heroin laboratories controlled by the CIA's Afghan guerrilla clients.

Unlike some national intelligence agencies, the CIA did not involve itself directly in the drug traffic to finance its covert operations. Nor was its culpability the work of a few corrupt agents eager to share in the

---

*The term "southern Asia" refers to the geographical area encompassing Iran, Afghanistan, Pakistan, and northern India.

enormous profits. The CIA's role in the heroin traffic was an inadvertent but almost inevitable consequence of its cold war tactics.

## The Logistics of Heroin

America's heroin addicts are victims of the most profitable of criminal enterprises—one that involves millions of peasant farmers in the mountains of Asia, thousands of corrupt government officials, disciplined criminal syndicates, and agencies of the U.S. government. America's heroin addicts are the final link in a chain of secret criminal transactions that begin in the opium fields of Asia, pass through clandestine heroin laboratories in Europe and Asia, and enter the United States through a maze of international smuggling routes.

Almost all of the world's illicit opium is grown in the narrow 4,500-mile stretch of mountains that extends across southern Asia from Turkey through Pakistan to Laos. Peasants and tribesmen of eight different nations harvest some 4,000 tons a year of raw opium, which eventually reaches the world's heroin and opium addicts.[31] A small percentage of these 4,000 tons is diverted from legitimate pharmaceutical production in Turkey, Iran, and India, but most of it is grown expressly for the international narcotics traffic in southern and Southeast Asia. Although Turkey was the major source of American narcotics through the 1960s, the hundred tons of raw opium its licensed peasant farmers diverted from legitimate production never accounted for more than 7 percent of the world's illicit supply.[32] About 24 percent is harvested by poppy farmers in southern Asia (Afghanistan, Pakistan, and India). However, much of this is consumed by local opium addicts, and only a small share finds its way to Europe or the United States.[33] It is Southeast Asia that has become the world's most important source of illicit opium. Every year the hill tribe farmers of Southeast Asia's Golden Triangle harvest approximately 3,000 tons of raw opium, or about 70 percent of the world's illicit supply.[34]

Despite countless minor variations, all of Asia's poppy farmers use the same basic techniques when they cultivate the opium poppy. The annual crop cycle begins in late summer or early fall as the farmers scatter handfuls of tiny poppy seeds across the surface of their hoed fields. At maturity the greenish poppy plant has one main tubular stem, which stands about three or four feet high, and perhaps half a dozen to a dozen smaller stems. About three months after planting, each stem produces a brightly colored flower; gradually the petals drop to the ground, exposing a green seed pod about the size and shape of a bird's egg. For reasons still unexplained by botanists, the seed pod synthesizes a milky white sap soon after the petals have fallen away. This sap is opium, and the farmers harvest it by cutting a series of shallow parallel incisions across the bulb's surface with a special curved knife. As the white sap seeps out of the incisions and congeals on the bulb's surface, it changes to a brownish-black color. The farmer collects the opium by scraping off the bulb with a flat, dull knife.

Even in this age of jumbo jets and supersonic transports, raw opium still moves from the poppy fields to the morphine refineries on horseback. There are few roads in these underdeveloped mountain regions, and even where they exist, smugglers generally prefer to stick to the mountain trails where there are fewer police. Most traffickers do their morphine refining close to the poppy fields, since compact morphine bricks are much easier to smuggle than bundles of pungent, jellylike opium. Although they are separated by more than four thousand miles, criminal "chemists" of the Middle East and Southeast Asia use roughly the same technique to extract pure morphine from opium. The chemist begins the process by heating water in an oil drum over a wood fire until his experienced index finger tells him that the temperature is just right. Next, raw opium is dumped into the drum and stirred with a heavy stick until it dissolves. At the propitious moment the chemist adds ordinary lime fertilizer to the steaming solution, precipitating out organic waste and leaving the morphine suspended in the chalky white water near the surface. While filtering the water through an ordinary piece of flannel cloth to remove any residual waste matter, the chemist pours the solution into another oil drum. As the solution is heated and stirred a second time, concentrated ammonia is added, causing the morphine to solidify and drop to the bottom. Once more the solution is filtered through flannel, leaving chunky white kernels of morphine on the cloth. Once dried and packaged for shipment, the morphine usually weighs about 10 percent of the weight of the raw opium from which it was extracted.[35]

The heroin manufacturing process is a good deal more complicated and requires the supervision of an expert chemist. At the end of World War II, Marseille and Hong Kong established themselves as the major centers for heroin laboratories. However, their dominance was challenged by newer clusters of heroin laboratories in the wilds of the Golden Triangle and the arid valleys of Pakistan. Most laboratories are staffed by a three-person team consisting of an experienced "master chemist" and two apprentices. In most cases the master chemist is really a master chef who has simply memorized the complicated four-part recipe after several years as an assistant. The goal of the four-stage process is to chemically bind morphine molecules with acetic acid and then process the compound to produce a fluffy white powder that can be dissolved and injected from a syringe.

STAGE ONE.  To produce ten kilos of pure heroin (the normal daily output of many labs), the chemist heats ten kilos of morphine and ten kilos of acetic anhydride in an enamel bin or glass flask. After being heated six hours at exactly 185°F, the morphine and acid become chemically bonded, creating an impure form of diacetylmorphine (heroin).

STAGE TWO.  The solution is treated with water and chloroform until the impurities precipitate out, leaving a somewhat higher grade of diacetylmorphine. The solution is drained off into another container, and sodium carbonate is added until the crude heroin particles begin to solidify and drop to the bottom.

STAGE THREE.  After the heroin particles are filtered out of the sodium carbonate solution under pressure by a small suction pump, they are purified in a solution of alcohol and activated charcoal. The new mixture is heated until the alcohol begins to evaporate, leaving relatively pure granules of heroin at the bottom of the flask. This is known as no. 3 heroin.

STAGE FOUR.  This final stage produces the fine white powder prized by American addicts and requires considerable skill on the part of an underworld chemist. The heroin is placed in a large flask and dissolved in alcohol. As ether and hydrochloric acid are added to the solution, tiny white flakes begin to form. After the flakes are filtered out under pressure and dried through a special process, the result is a white powder, 80 to 99 percent pure, known as no. 4 heroin. In the hands of a careless chemist the volatile ether gas may ignite and produce a violent explosion that can level the clandestine laboratory.[36]

Once it is packaged in plastic envelopes, heroin is ready for its trip to the United States via an infinite variety of couriers—stewardesses, diplomats, businesspeople, Marseille gangsters, Chinese merchants. But regardless of the means used to smuggle, almost all of these shipments are financed and organized by one of the major American distribution syndicates. Although the top bosses of organized crime never even see, much less touch, the heroin, their financial resources and their connections with Chinese syndicates and Corsican gangs play a key role in the importation of America's heroin supply. The top brokers usually deal in bulk shipments of 20 to 100 kilos of no. 4 heroin. After a shipment arrives, the brokers divide it into wholesale lots of 1 to 10 kilos for sale to their underlings. From there the process of dilution and profit making continues downward through another three levels in the distribution network until it finally reaches the street.[37] By this time the heroin's value has increased tenfold and it is so heavily diluted that the average street packet sold to an addict is less than 5 percent pure.

To an average American who witnesses the dismal spectacle of the narcotics traffic at the street level, it must seem inconceivable that the government could be implicated in the international narcotics trade. Unfortunately, American diplomats and CIA agents have been involved in the narcotics traffic at three levels: (1) coincidental complicity by allying with groups actively engaged in the drug traffic; (2) support of the traffic by covering up for known heroin traffickers and condoning their involvement; and (3) active engagement in the transport of opium and heroin. It is ironic, to say the least, that America's heroin plague is of its own making.

# 1

# Sicily: Home of the Mafia

AT THE END OF WORLD WAR II, THERE WAS A STRONG CHANCE that heroin addiction could be eliminated in the United States. The wartime security measures designed to prevent infiltration of foreign spies and sabotage to naval installations made smuggling into the United States virtually impossible. Most American addicts were forced to break their habits during the war, and consumer demand just about disappeared. Moreover, the international narcotics syndicates were weakened by the war and could have been decimated with a minimum of police effort.

During the 1930s much of America's heroin had come from China's refineries centered in Shanghai and Tientsin. This supply was supplemented by the smaller amounts produced in Marseille by the Corsican syndicates and in the Middle East by the notorious Eliopoulos brothers. Mediterranean shipping routes were disrupted by submarine warfare during the war, and the Japanese invasion of China interrupted the drug flow to the United States from the Shanghai and Tientsin laboratories. The last major wartime seizure took place in 1940, when 42 kilograms of Shanghai heroin were discovered in San Francisco. During the war only tiny quantities of heroin were confiscated, and laboratory analysis by federal officials showed that its quality was constantly declining; by the end of the war most heroin was a crude Mexican product, less than 3 percent pure. And a surprisingly high percentage of the samples were fake.[1] Most addicts were forced to undergo an involuntary withdrawal

24

from heroin, and at the end of the war the Federal Bureau of Narcotics reported that there were only 20,000 addicts in all of America.[2]

After the war, Chinese traffickers had barely reestablished their heroin labs when Mao Tse-tung's peasant armies captured Shanghai and drove the traffickers out of China.[3] The Eliopoulos brothers had retired from the trade with the advent of the war, and a postwar narcotics indictment in New York discouraged any thoughts they may have had of returning to it.[4] The hold of the Corsican syndicates in Marseille was weakened, since their most powerful leaders had made the tactical error of collaborating with the Nazi Gestapo and so were either dead or exiled. Most significantly, Sicily's Mafia had been smashed almost beyond repair by two decades of Mussolini's police repression. It was barely holding on to its control of local protection money from farmers and shepherds.[5]

With American consumer demand reduced to its lowest point in fifty years and the international syndicates in disarray, the U.S. government had a unique opportunity to eliminate heroin addiction as a major American social problem. Instead, the government—through the CIA and its wartime predecessor, the OSS—created a situation that made it possible for the Sicilian-American Mafia and the Corsican underworld to revive the international narcotics traffic.[6] These operations were the first signs of the CIA's willingness to form tactical, anti-Communist alliances with major narcotics dealers, whether in the cities of Europe or the jungles of the Third World. During the forty years of the cold war, several of the CIA's covert action allies were to play a significant role in sustaining a global narcotics industry that supplied the United States.

In Sicily the OSS, through the Office of Naval Intelligence, initially allied with the Mafia to assist the Allied forces in their 1943 invasion. Later, the alliance was maintained to check the growing strength of the Italian Communist party on the island. In Marseille the CIA joined forces with the Corsican underworld to break the hold of the Communist party over city government and to end two dock strikes—one in 1947, the other in 1950—that threatened the efficient operation of the Marshall Plan and the First Indochina War. After the CIA withdrew in the early 1950s, Marseille's Corsicans won political protection from France's intelligence service, the SDECE, which allowed their heroin laboratories to operate undisturbed for nearly 20 years. In partnership with Italy's Mafia syndicates, the Corsicans smuggled raw opium from Turkey and refined it into no. 4 heroin for export.

Their biggest customer was the United States, the richest nation in the world, the only one of the great powers that had come through World War II relatively untouched, and the country that had the biggest potential for narcotics distribution. For, in spite of their forced withdrawal during the war years, America's addicts could easily be won back to their heroin persuasion.

## The Mafia in America

At first the American Mafia had ignored the new business opportunity afforded by the prohibition of drugs in the early 1920s. Steeped in the traditions of the Sicilian "honored society," which absolutely forbade involvement in either narcotics or prostitution, the Mafia had left the heroin business to the powerful Jewish gangsters who dominated organized crime in the 1920s.

Prohibition transformed the character of both narcotics use and organized crime in America. During the 1890s, the typical drug abuser was a white, middle-class housewife who purchased bottled opiates from her pharmacist or physician. After prohibition, the typical addict was a "hustling, mainlining [white] male junkie" who sought his heroin on the streets from the new criminal syndicates that now serviced this illicit demand.[7] Although middle-class medical addiction declined after 1920, drug prohibition failed to reduce the number of recreational addicts and simply transferred a large, lucrative clientele to criminal syndicates. By the late 1920s, these new vice trades would transform inner-city criminals from parochial gangs preying on ethnic neighborhoods into national syndicates controlling vast, profitable enterprises.

The career of the Jewish criminal Irving "Waxey Gordon" Wexler illustrates the relationship between drug and alcohol prohibition and the growth of organized crime. Born in 1888, Gordon first appeared in the Jewish underworld of New York's Lower East Side as a member of the Benjamin Fine gang. Between 1910 and 1914, Gordon accumulated $100,000 from gambling and took control of Fine's gang, by then active in the city's garment district as a "power broker" among the unions. Only two years after passage of the 1914 Harrison Narcotics Act, Gordon had become a "major partner in at least five different cocaine mobs" operating in Manhattan and Philadelphia. Over the next fifteen years, he remained one of New York's largest cocaine distributors and was eventually indicted, but not convicted, for transporting narcotics to Minnesota.[8] In both drug dealing and, later, bootlegging, Gordon and younger gangsters drew on the capital and contacts of New York's most powerful racketeer, Arnold Rothstein, a Jewish gambling broker best known for fixing the 1919 World Series.[9]

As a Jewish gangster emerging from the Lower East Side, Waxey Gordon was typical of the new drug dealers created by passage of the Harrison Act. In 1917, the New York Kehillah, a Jewish community agency, tried to counter sensational press allegations about Jewish criminality with a serious study of the problem. Of the 263 drug dealers discovered in New York City, there were, among those of identifiable ethnicity, 83 Jews, 23 Italians, 8 Irish, 5 blacks, and 3 Greeks. When the Kahillah investigators examined the 22 "combinations" or syndicates that dominated the cocaine traffic, they found that 85 percent of their members were Jewish and the remaining 15 percent Italian. While cocaine wholesalers covered territory that reached from Philadelphia to Boston, about 44 percent of the city's 129 retailers with known addresses were found on the Lower East Side.[10]

During the 1920s, Jewish syndicates also controlled much of New York's heroin distribution and supplied their dealers by smuggling narcotics from Europe and Asia. Indeed, the New York drug dealer Jacob "Yasha" Katzenberg "knew more about procuring heroin in Asia and smuggling it into the United States than anyone else in the world."[11] Since international narcotics controls were lax during the interwar period, New York's dealers could procure limitless supplies through their overseas criminal contacts who simply bought narcotics legally in Paris in the 1920s and Shanghai in the 1930s.[12]

The Katzenberg-Lvovsky-Buchalter case is the most spectacular instance of such heroin smuggling. This venture had its origins in February 1935 when a New York City apartment exploded and investigators discovered raw morphine, processed heroin, and processing paraphernalia. Although the heroin chemist was convicted, evidence against the principals, Yasha Katzenberg and Jacob Lvovsky, was weak. Seeking new sources after the loss of the laboratory, Lvovsky, financed by Katzenberg and Louis Buchalter, sent "emissaries" to China. In Shanghai, the New Yorkers made contact with Yanis Tsouanis, described in a U.S. consular report as "the most notorious Greek smuggler at present," and through him purchased heroin from a Greek syndicate that controlled illicit exports from the legal Japanese laboratories at Tientsin. Between October 1935 and February 1937, this New York combine of thirty men organized six trips to Shanghai and sent back tourist steamer trunks packed with 649 kilograms of heroin for a profit of $519,220.[13] The power behind this lucrative operation was Louis "Lepke" Buchalter, the leading Jewish gangster in New York during the 1930s. Lepke coordinated an organization of some 250 men and since the late 1920s had been the preeminent racketeer in the city's clothing industry. Indicted for heroin smuggling in November 1937, Lepke went into hiding around New York and made headlines two years later with his sensational surrender to radio celebrity Walter Winchell and FBI Director J. Edgar Hoover. With testimony from his partner Yasha Katzenberg, Lepke was sentenced to twelve years for drug dealing.[14]

When alcohol prohibition started in 1920, Waxey Gordon and other

Jewish criminals—Benjamin "Bugs" Siegel, Arthur "Dutch" Schultz, and Meyer Lansky—soon dominated much of New York's bootleg liquor trade. Among the seventeen major bootleggers active in New York during the mid-1920s, seven were Jewish, five Italian, and three Irish. In 1928–1929, the so-called Jewish syndicate, comprising Gordon and eight associates, operated thirteen breweries in the New York area and was perhaps the largest beer distributor in the United States.[15]

Although Arnold Rothstein was shot at the Park Central Hotel in 1928, Waxey Gordon was jailed for tax evasion in 1933, and Lepke was electrocuted for murder in 1944, other Jewish gangsters, notably Lansky, survived the tumult of these decades to play a leading role in syndicate crime for the next thirty years. But the passing of these Jewish crime leaders and their generation did indeed bring change. Rothstein could ignore the Mafia in the 1920s and Lepke still dealt largely with Jewish criminals in the 1930s, but Lansky would achieve his power through an alliance with Italians such as Lucky Luciano.

While Jewish gangs thus controlled much of New York alcohol, narcotics, and gambling during the 1920s, the Mafia contented itself with a smaller share of the bootleg liquor industry.[16] However, in 1930–1931, only seven years after heroin was legally banned, a war erupted in the Mafia ranks. Out of the violence that left more than sixty gangsters dead came a new generation of leaders with little respect for the traditional code of honor prohibiting involvement in narcotics.[17]

The leader of this mafioso youth movement was the legendary Salvatore C. Lucania, known to the world as Charles "Lucky" Luciano. Charming and handsome, Luciano must rank as one of the leading criminal executives of the modern age. For, at a series of meetings after the killings that eliminated the old guard, Luciano outlined his plans for a modern, nationwide crime cartel. His modernization scheme quickly won support from the leaders of America's twenty-four Mafia "families," and within a few months the National Commission was functioning smoothly. This was an event of some significance: Almost single-handedly, Luciano built the Mafia into the most powerful criminal syndicate in the United States and pioneered organizational techniques that are still the basis of organized crime today. Luciano also forged an alliance between the Mafia and Meyer Lansky's Jewish gangs that survived for almost 40 years and became a key characteristic of organized crime in the United States.

With the end of Prohibition in sight, Luciano decided to take the Mafia into the lucrative prostitution and heroin rackets, a move determined largely by financial considerations. The Mafia's success had been based on illegal distilling and rumrunning. Its continued prosperity, which

Luciano hoped to maintain through superior organization, could be sustained only by developing new sources of income.

Heroin was an attractive substitute for liquor because its relatively recent prohibition had left a large market that could be exploited and expanded. Although heroin addicts in no way compared with drinkers in numbers, heroin profits could be just as substantial: heroin's light weight made it less expensive to smuggle, and its relatively limited number of sources made it easier to monopolize.

Heroin, moveover, complemented Luciano's other new business venture—the organization of prostitution on an unprecedented scale. Luciano forced many small-time pimps out of business as he found that addicting his prostitute labor force to heroin kept them quiescent, steady workers, with a habit to support and only one way to gain enough money to support it. This combination of organized prostitution and drug addiction, which later became so commonplace, was Luciano's trademark in the 1930s. By 1935 he controlled two hundred New York City brothels with twelve hundred prostitutes, providing him with an estimated income of more than $10 million a year.[18] Supplemented by growing profits from gambling and the labor movement as well, organized crime was once again on a secure financial footing.

As Mafia drug distributors supplanted the Jewish networks during the 1930s, the effect was soon felt on the streets of New York. By threatening rival dealers and undercutting their prices, the Mafia soon won a near monopoly over the street trade.[19] Once in control, the Italians adulterated the heroin far more than their Jewish predecessors had. As purity dropped to 27.5 percent by 1938, heroin "sniffing" was no longer effective, and addicts were forced to use hypodermic injection. "When the Chinese and Jews had it, it was beautiful," recalled one Times Square drug dealer. "But when the Italians got it—bah! They messed it all up. . . . They started thinking people were just a herd of animals—just give them anything."[20] An Italian-American heroin dealer who worked with Jewish distributors in the early 1930s was also critical of the Mafia: "See, the Jews were businessmen; they gave it to you the way they got it. . . . Then the wops started to get in it, and they started to knock off the Jews, they started to clip them. . . . The Italians were selling shit, chemical, acid. . . . These sons of bitches were so hungry for money that they cut it half a dozen times."[21]

But in the late 1930s the American Mafia fell on hard times. Federal and state investigators launched a major crackdown on organized crime that produced one spectacular narcotics conviction and forced a number of powerful mafiosi to flee the country. In 1936 Thomas Dewey's organized crime investigators indicted Luciano himself on sixty-two counts of forced prostitution. Although the Federal Bureau of Narcotics had gathered enough evidence about Luciano's involvement in the drug traffic to indict him for narcotics, both the bureau and Dewey's investigators felt that the forced prostitution charge would be more likely to offend public sensibilities and secure a conviction. Moreover, Luciano's centralization of the city's brothels had not increased their income or efficiency, and he had had to use simple terror to extract his share of house profits. His grandiose scheme for a quasi-industrial brothel trade strained the economics of the "$2 house" beyond endurance. Despite regular beatings by his "vicious" enforcer Jimmie Fredericks, the madams cheated the syndicate in every possible way to protect their profits.[22] In the end, Luciano lost control of his clients, and three of his prostitutes testified against him. With this evidence, Dewey, already famous for his prosecution of Waxey Gordon, scored a sensational conviction against Luciano and his nine codefendants, a mix of Jews and Italians. The New York court sentenced Luciano to a thirty-to-fifty-year jail term.[23]

Luciano's arrest and conviction were a major setback for organized crime: they removed the underworld's most influential mediator from active leadership and probably registered as a shock among lower-ranking gangsters. Some months later, Mafia leader Vito Genovese fled New York for Italy since "he knew the police were trying to arrest him as an accomplice of Luciano."[24]

However, the Mafia suffered even more severe reverses on the mother island of Sicily. Although Dewey's reputation as a racket-busting district attorney was rewarded by a governorship and later by a presidential nomination, his efforts seem faint compared with Mussolini's personal vendetta against the Sicilian Mafia. During a state visit to a small town in western Sicily in 1924, the Italian dictator offended a local Mafia boss by treating him with the same condescension he usually reserved for minor municipal officials. The mafioso made the foolish mistake of retaliating by emptying the piazza of everyone but twenty beggars during Mussolini's speech to the "assembled populace."[25] Upon his return to Rome, the outraged Mussolini appeared before the Fascist parliament and declared total war on the Mafia. Cesare Mori was appointed prefect of Palermo and for two years conducted a reign of terror in western Sicily that surpassed even the Inquisition. Combining traditional torture with modern innovations, Mori secured confessions from and long prison sentences for thousands of mafiosi, thereby reducing the venerable society to its weakest state in a hundred years.[26] Although the campaign ended officially in 1927 as Mori accepted the accolades of the Fascist parliament, local Fascist officials continued to harass the mafiosi. By the beginning of World War

II, the Mafia had been driven out of the cities and was surviving only in the mountain areas of western Sicily.[27]

## The Mafia Restored

World War II gave the Mafia a new lease on life. In the United States, the Office of Naval Intelligence (ONI) became increasingly concerned over a series of sabotage incidents on the New York waterfront, which culminated in the burning of the French liner *Normandie* on the eve of its christening as an Allied troop ship. In the words of William B. Herlands, New York's commissioner of investigation, who examined the operation in detail after the war: "We were faced with a grave national emergency. . . . A blackout was imposed over the . . . waterfront area within the Third Naval District, which included New York and New Jersey. Many of our ships were being sunk by enemy submarines off the Atlantic Coast . . . and the outcome of the war hung in the balance."[28]

Powerless to infiltrate the waterfront itself, ONI decided to recruit local gangsters and contacted New York District Attorney Frank Hogan, who suggested Joseph "Joe Socks" Lanza, then under indictment for extortion. Officially Joseph Lanza was a "business agent for the United Seafood Workers' Union," but in reality Joe Socks was "the rackets boss of the Fulton Fish Market . . . in downtown New York City."[29] In March 1942 when the navy first approached Lanza, ONI was preoccupied with coastal security. Captain Roscoe C. McFall, the district intelligence officer, later told investigators that he was concerned about "subversive activities by enemy agents in and along the harbor" and "the suspected danger that enemy submarines might be refuelled through fishing boats . . . operated by criminal elements."[30] Since Lanza had "a great number of contacts in the fish market and among fishing boat . . . captains . . . along the Atlantic Coast," he was an ideal contact for this phase of ONI's operation.[31] Accordingly, Commander Charles R. Haffenden, McFall's subordinate, met with Lanza every week for the next nine months to plan a range of operations—information on the refueling of enemy submarines, acquisition of false union cards to place ONI agents on the fishing boats, and organization of the city's Italian fishermen "as part of the submarine look-out system."[32]

After only three weeks, however, ONI realized that Lanza was a middle-ranking racketeer of limited influence. Unable to deliver information that ONI had requested on matters outside the fishing industry, Lanza told his navy contacts that people feared he was "going to use the information as an informer . . . to get consideration on his then pending indictment."[33] In April, Lanza told Haffenden that "Luciano could be of great assistance" and could "send some word out to Joe Adonis or Frank (Costello), his friend."[34]

Luciano at that time was confined in Clinton State Prison, near the Canadian border in upstate New York, and the navy contacted his attorney, Moses Polakoff. Asked to serve as the intermediary, Polakoff demurred, suggesting instead a person "whose patriotism, or affection for our country, irrespective of his reputation, was of the highest."[35] The next morning, Polakoff introduced the U.S. navy to the patriot Meyer Lansky, Luciano's partner in narcotics and bootlegging, at Longchamps Restaurant in Manhattan. Citing an intimate relationship with Luciano dating from the early 1920s, Lansky assured the navy representatives that Luciano was trustworthy. At Polakoff's suggestion, in May 1942 Commander Haffenden agreed to expedite a meeting with Luciano by arranging his transfer from remote Clinton Prison to Great Meadow Prison near Albany.[36]

Several weeks later, Polakoff and Lansky met Luciano in a prison interview room and "explained the Naval Intelligence situation to him." Luciano agreed to cooperate and suggested that Lansky should "act as a liaison between Luciano and the people . . . whose aid was to be enlisted. Those people know that if Lansky said he was acting for Luciano, that statement would not be questioned." Over the next three years, Luciano met with Lansky eleven times and with Polakoff another twenty. Although Haffenden never saw Luciano, he met frequently with Lansky, who became, as Luciano had suggested, the intermediary between the navy and the underworld. Haffenden, Lansky later recalled, "would tell me . . . just what he wanted; . . . I would seek the man I . . . thought could do best to fulfill his needs; . . . anyone that could be of assistance in the war effort; . . . I would introduce them."[37]

Although ONI was still interested in sabotage and security on the New York docks, it also sought Luciano's help in gathering intelligence for the Allied invasion of Sicily, then planned for sometime in 1943. Through Luciano, Lansky brought a number of Sicilain immigrants to ONI's offices in Manhattan for intense interrogation by Italian-American agents in Commander Haffenden's unit, now known as the Ferret Squad. At Luciano's suggestion, for example, Lansky contacted racketeer Joe Adonis, who brought six Sicilians to provide "strategic intelligence" about the island's coast. "Prior to our attack on Sicily," Lansky recalled of these meetings with Haffenden, "the conversations ran of their knowledge of the coastline and the contour of the land off the coast." Commander Haffenden, Lansky said, "pulled out big maps—and he showed them the maps for them to recognize their villages and to compare the maps with their knowledge of their villages." Working with ONI cartographers, Haffenden prepared numerous maps and charts of the Sicilian coast, including one large map with overlays based on "several thousand" of these reports.[38]

Most important, the commissioner of investigation reported that, through Luciano and his associates, "the names of friendly Sicilian natives and even Sicilian underworld and Mafia personalities who could be trusted were obtained and actually used in the Sicilian campaign."[39] In mid-1942, Commander Haffenden delivered these "names of individuals in Sicily" to a Captain Wharton at ONI headquarters in Washington, who later reported that the names "turned out to be 40% correct . . . on the basis of actual experience."[40]

As the Allied forces assembled along the North Africa coast for the invasion of Sicily in May 1943, Vice Admiral Henry K. Hewitt, U.S. navy area commander, found a flaw in the plans. Since Sicily, once liberated, was to become a base for U.S. navy operations in the Italian campaign, the invasion forces would need to establish close relations with the island's population to facilitate a long-term occupation. His headquarters intelligence staff did not have any Italian speakers, and the admiral sent an urgent request to Naval Intelligence headquarters for six Italian-speaking agents. By May 15, four of Commander Haffenden's New York agents involved in gathering the strategic intelligence on Sicily were en route to North Africa by plane.[41]

On the night of July 9–10, 1943, Allied forces numbering 160,000 landed on the beaches of western Sicily, the British in the north and the Americans farther south. At 2:30 A.M., the U.S. Seventh Army under General George Patton came ashore in two separate waves at the towns of Gela and Licata on the southern coast. "It was incomprehensible to me that the OSS should have been given such meager information about both the planning and execution of the invasion of Sicily," wrote Max Corvo, recalling his frustration when his OSS team arrived to board the landing craft and found that they were supposed to sit out the first four days of the invasion in Africa.[42] In his history of the OSS, former CIA official R. Harris Smith explained that "OSS responsibilities for Italian espionage were preempted by the Office of Naval Intelligence through a mysterious arrangement with the American Mafia."[43]

While Corvo's OSS team waited in Africa, ONI's New York operatives landed in Sicily with the first wave, two agents at Gela and two at Licata. "One of the most important plans," recalled Commander Paul A. Alfieri, one of the ONI agents, "was to contact persons who had been deported for any crime from the United States . . . and one of my first successes after landing at Licata was in connection with this." Alfieri later told the commissioner that he "made it my business to make that [Mafia contact] my first stop" and found that these "criminal and underworld characters in Sicily who . . . were members of the Mafia . . . were 'extremely cooperative to me and also to various other intelligence officers.' "[44]

With mafiosi guides, Alfieri set out through the scattered fighting for the "secret headquarters of the Italian naval command," identified in the New York interrogations, and found it in a villa set back from the beach. Unopposed, Alfieri walked past the surprised Italian officers into an admiral's office, blew open the safe with a short fuse, and returned to the beachhead with an armful of documents. According to Alfieri's team leader, Commander Anthony J. Marsloe, these "documents embodying the entire disposition of the Italian and German naval forces in the Mediterranean—together with the minefields . . . —were taken on board Admiral Connolly's flagship . . . and were successfully used to accelerate the Italian surrender." For these exploits, Alfieri won the Legion of Merit with a presidential citation commending him for "contribution in large measure to the success of our invasion forces."[45]

In his report in 1954, Commissioner Herlands noted that "Alfieri pursued the same technique of contacting former underworld characters in the subsequent invasions and operations on the Italian mainland with the same success."[46] Calling the subject classified, however, the U.S. navy refused, a full ten years after the invasion of Italy, to divulge details about this aspect of its alliance with the Mafia. Thus, the history of ONI and OSS relations with the Mafia during the Sicily campaign must be extracted from unofficial sources.[47]

After crushing mild resistance by the Italian army and securing the beachheads at Gela and Licata, Patton's Seventh Army launched an offensive into Sicily's western hills, Italy's Mafialand, and headed for Palermo.[48] Although there were more than 60,000 Italian troops and a hundred miles of booby-trapped roads between Patton and Palermo, his troops covered the distance in a remarkable four days.[49]

The dean of Italy's Mafia experts, Michele Pantaleone, argues that it was the mafiosi who were responsible for the surprising speed of General Patton's advance to Palermo. Five days after the Allies landed in Sicily, an American fighter plane flew over the village of Villalba, about forty-five miles north of General Patton's beachhead on the road to Palermo, and jettisoned a canvas sack addressed to "Zu Calo." Zu Calo, better known as Don Calogero Vizzini, was the unchallenged leader of the Sicilian Mafia and lord of the mountain region through which the American army would be passing. The sack contained a yellow silk scarf emblazoned with a large black L. The L, of course, stood for Lucky Luciano, and silk scarves were a common form of identification used by mafiosi traveling from Sicily to America.[50]

The story of the scarf may be apocryphal, but ONI's ongoing operations with the Mafia lend credibility to reports of contact, direct or indirect, between Luciano and Don Calogero. In fact, Luciano was born less than fifteen miles from Villalba in Lercara Fridi, where his mafiosi relatives still worked for Don Calogero.[51] Two days later, three

American tanks rolled into Villalba after driving thirty miles through enemy territory. Don Calogero climbed aboard and spent the next six days traveling through western Sicily organizing support for the advancing American troops.[52] As General Patton's Third Division moved onward into Don Calogero's mountain domain, the signs of its dependence on Mafia support were obvious to the local population. The Mafia protected the roads from snipers, arranged enthusiastic welcomes for the advancing troops, and provided guides through the confusing mountain terrain.[53]

While the role of the Mafia is little more than a historical footnote to the Allied conquest of Sicily, the Mafia's cooperation with the American military occupation was important. Although there is room for speculation about Luciano's precise role in the invasion, there can be little doubt about the relationship between the Mafia and the American military occupation.

This alliance developed in the summer of 1943, when the Allied occupation's primary concern was to release as many of its troops as possible from garrison duties on the island so they could be used in the offensive through southern Italy. Practicality was the order of the day, and in October the Pentagon advised occupation officers "that the *carabinieri* and Italian Army will be found satisfactory for local security purposes."[54] But the Fascist army had long since deserted, and Don Calogero's Mafia seemed far more reliable at guaranteeing public order than Mussolini's powerless *carabinieri*. So in July the Civil Affairs Control Office of the U.S. army appointed Don Calogero mayor of Villalba and his later successor as Sicily's Mafia boss, Genco Russo, mayor of Mussumeli. Under the command of Colonel Charles Poletti, the former lieutenant governor of New York, the Allied Military Government (AMGOT) selected mafiosi as mayors in many towns across western Sicily.[55] Whether Poletti was simply supporting the military's alliance with the Mafia or had personal ties to the underworld through his career in New York politics is difficult to determine. Several months later, the colonel would appoint fugitive New York gangster Vito Genovese as his interpreter, and after the war Luciano was quoted as calling Poletti "one of our good friends."[56]

During the weeks following the landing, Sicily's mafiosi maneuvered to infiltrate the new Allied government. In August 1943, Lord Rennell, commander of British occupation forces, reported that "in their exuberance to remove Fascist Podestas and municipal officials in rural towns, my officers have . . . appointed a number of Mafia 'bosses' or allowed such 'bosses' to propose suitable malleable substitutes." Using the Sicilian *omertà*, or code of silence, to conceal their Mafia affiliations, local mafiosi were "naturally not slow in levelling accusations of Fascist sympathies against their own pet enemies." Elimination of fascism and the *carabinieri*, the "two great enemies of the Mafia," had allowed a sudden increase of homicides that were "of the Mafia type or bear indications of Mafia antecedents."[57]

As Allied forces crawled north through the Italian mainland, American intelligence officers became increasingly upset about the leftward drift of Italian politics. Between late 1943 and mid-1944, the Italian Communist party's membership had doubled, and in the German-occupied northern half of the country a radical resistance movement was gathering strength; in the winter of 1944, more than 500,000 Turin workers shut the factories for eight days despite brutal Gestapo repression, and the Italian underground grew to almost 150,000 armed fighters. Rather than being heartened by the underground's growing strength, the U.S. army became increasingly concerned about its radical politics and began to cut back its arms drops to the resistance in mid-1944.[58] "More than twenty years ago," Allied military commanders reported in 1944, "a similar situation provoked the March on Rome and gave birth to Fascism. We must make up our minds—and that quickly—whether we want this second march developing into another 'ism.' "[59]

In Sicily the decision had already been made. To combat expected Communist gains, occupation authorities used Mafia officials in the AMGOT administration. Since any changes in the island's feudal social structure would cost the Mafia money and power, the "honored society" was a natural anti-Communist ally. So confident was Don Calogero of his importance to AMGOT that he killed Villalba's overinquisitive police chief to free himself of all restraints.[60]

When the U.S. army liberated Naples in October 1943, Colonel Poletti's military government hired the notorious New York racketeer Vito Genovese as "interpreter for the Allied Military Government in Italy."[61] A Luciano lieutenant who fled New York in 1937 to avoid indictment, Genovese had returned home to Naples. There, according to a U.S. army intelligence report, "Genovese was enrolled in a Fascist organization . . . and while living in Naples led a life of luxury and entertained a mistress."[62]

After joining the Allied government, Genovese dominated the black market in stolen military goods across southern Italy. In mid-1944, a U.S. army investigator, Sergeant Orange C. Dickey, learned that "Genovese used to meet all the big contraband dealers secretly in his apartment in Nola." Through his network, Genovese was using U.S. army trucks to traffic in "contraband wheat," olive oil, and military cargoes hijacked from the Naples docks.[63] In its review of the evidence, the military intelligence service described Genovese as "a civilian translator for the

Allied Military Government" and concluded that he was "a big black-market operator" who had "led a gang which bribed truck drivers to drive trucks carrying American supplies into groves . . . where his men stole the supplies"[64] In August, Dickey arrested Genovese and, acting almost on his own, brought him back to Brooklyn to face trial for murder. The sergeant then filed a complete report with his army superiors about the black market in Italy, implicating "a great many people who are quite prominent . . . in the Allied Military Government."[65] When the report reached the War Department, Brigadier General Carter W. Clarke called it "a very *hot* paper" and suggested that "it be filed and no action taken."[66]

Although Genovese's deportation eliminated his influence in Italy, his Mafia friends would remain, their power and prestige restored by their alliance with the Allied government. During his nine months with AMGOT, Genovese's black market operations had reached Sicily and brought him into a commercial alliance with the island's Mafia boss, Don Calogero Vizzini. The two had used their official positions to establish one of the largest black market operations in all of southern Italy. Don Calogero sent enormous truck caravans loaded with all the basic commodities for the Italian diet rolling northward to hungry Naples, where their cargoes were distributed by Genovese's organization.[67] These trucks were issued passes and export papers by AMGOT in Naples and Sicily, and some corrupt American army officers even made contributions of gasoline and trucks to the operation.

In exchange for these favors, Don Calogero became one of the major supporters of the Sicilian independence movement, which was enjoying the covert support of the OSS. As Italy veered to the left in 1943–1944, the American military became alarmed about its future position in Italy, and OSS felt that the island's naval bases and strategic location in the Mediterranean might provide a future counterbalance to a Communist mainland.[68] Don Calogero supported this separatist movement by recruiting most of western Sicily's mountain bandits for its volunteer army, but he quietly abandoned it shortly after the OSS dropped it in 1945.

Don Calogero rendered other services to the anti-Communist effort by breaking up leftist political rallies. On September 16, 1944, for example, the Communist leader Girolama Li Causi held a rally in Villalba that ended abruptly in a hail of gunfire as Don Calogero's men fired into the crowd and wounded nineteen spectators.[69] Michele Pantaleone, who observed the Mafia's revival in his native village of Villalba, described the consequences of AMGOT's occupation policies:

> By the beginning of the Second World War, the Mafia was restricted to a few isolated and scattered groups and could

have been completely wiped out if the social problems of the island had been dealt with . . . . The Allied occupation and the subsequent slow restoration of democracy reinstated the Mafia with its full powers, put it once more on the way to becoming a political force, and returned to the Onorata Societa the weapons which Fascism had snatched from it.[70]

## Lucky Luciano in Europe

In 1946 American military intelligence made one final gift to the Mafia—they released Lucky Luciano from prison and deported him to Italy, thereby freeing one of the criminal talents of his generation to rebuild the heroin trade. Appealing to the New York State Parole Board in 1945 for his immediate release, Luciano's lawyers based their case on his wartime services to the navy. Although naval intelligence officers called to give evidence at the hearings were extremely vague about what they had promised Luciano in exchange for his services, one naval officer, Commander Haffenden, wrote a number of confidential letters on Luciano's behalf that were instrumental in securing his release.[71] In January 1946, New York Governor Thomas E. Dewey, the prosecutor who had sent Luciano to prison ten years earlier, announced that his thirty-to-fifty-year sentence would be commuted to allow deportation on grounds that he had aided the war effort by "inducing others to provide information concerning possible enemy attack."[72]

Within two years after Luciano's return to Italy, the U.S. government deported more than one hundred more mafiosi as well. And with the cooperation of his old friend Don Calogero and the help of many of his former followers from New York, Luciano was able to build an international narcotics syndicate soon after his arrival in Italy.[73]

The narcotics syndicate Luciano organized after World War II remains one of the more remarkable in the history of the traffic. For more than a decade it moved morphine base from the Middle East to Europe, transformed it into heroin, and then exported it in substantial quantities to the United States—all without suffering a major arrest or seizure. The organization's comprehensive distribution network within the United States helped raise the number of addicts from an estimated 20,000 at the close of the war to 60,000 in 1952 and to 150,000 by 1965.

After resurrecting the narcotics traffic, Luciano's first problem was securing a reliable supply of heroin. Initially he diverted legally produced heroin from one of Italy's most respected pharmaceutical companies, Schiaparelli. However, investigations by the U.S. Federal Bureau of Narcotics in 1950—which disclosed that at least 700 kilos of heroin had been diverted to Luciano over a four-year period—led to a tightening of Italian pharmaceutical regulations.[74] But by this time

Luciano had built up a network of clandestine laboratories in Sicily and Marseille and no longer needed to divert the Schiaparelli product.

Morphine base was now the necessary commodity. Thanks to his contacts in the Middle East, Luciano established a long-term business relationship with a Lebanese who was quickly becoming knowing as the Middle East's major exporter of morphine base—Sami El Khoury. Through judicious use of bribes and his high social standing in Beirut society,[75] El Khoury established an organization of unparalleled political strength. The directors of Beirut Airport, Lebanese customs, the Lebanese narcotics police, and, perhaps most important, the chief of the antisubversive section of the Lebanese police[76] protected the import of raw opium from Turkey's Anatolian plateau into Lebanon, its processing into morphine base, and its final export to the laboratories in Sicily and Marseille.[77]

After the morphine left Lebanon, its first stop was the bays and inlets of Sicily's western coast. There Palermo's fishing trawlers would meet oceangoing freighters from the Middle East in international waters, pick up the drug cargo, and smuggle it into fishing villages scattered along the rugged coastline.[78]

Once the morphine base was safely ashore, it was transformed into heroin in one of Luciano's clandestine laboratories. Typical of these was the candy factory opened in Palermo in 1949: it was leased to one of Luciano's cousins and managed by Don Calogero himself.[79] The laboratory operated without incident until April 11, 1954, when the Roman daily *Avanti!* published a photograph of the factory under the headline "Textiles and Sweets on the Drug Route." That evening the factory was closed, and the laboratory's chemists were reportedly smuggled out of the country.[80] After Marseille's laboratories began operating in the early 1950s with superior chemists and more secure political protection, Luciano apparently abandoned production and concentrated on smuggling.

Once heroin had been manufactured and packaged for export, Luciano used his Mafia and Corsican connections to send it through a maze of international routes to the United States. Not all of the mafiosi deported from the United States stayed in Sicily. To reduce the chance of seizure, Luciano had placed many of them in such European cities as Milan, Hamburg, Paris, and Marseille so they could forward the heroin to the United States after it arrived from Sicily concealed in fruits, vegetables, or candy. From Europe heroin was shipped directly to New York or smuggled through Canada and Cuba.[81]

While Luciano's prestige and organizational ability were an invaluable asset, a large part of his success was due to his ability to pick reliable allies. After he was deported from the United States in 1946, he charged his longtime associate Meyer Lansky with the responsibility of managing his financial empire. Lansky also played a key role in organizing Luciano's heroin syndicate: he supervised smuggling operations, negotiated with Corsican heroin manufacturers, and managed the collection and concealment of the enormous profits. Lansky's control over the Caribbean and his relationship with the Florida-based Trafficante family were of particular importance, since many of the heroin shipments passed through Cuba or Florida on their way to America's urban markets. For almost twenty years the Luciano-Lansky-Trafficante partnership remained a major feature of the international heroin traffic.[82]

Organized crime was welcome in prerevolutionary Cuba, and Havana was probably the most important transit point for Luciano's European heroin shipments. The leaders of Luciano's heroin syndicate were at home in the Cuban capital and regarded it as a "safe" city: Lansky owned most of the city's casinos, and the Trafficante family served as Lansky's resident managers in Havana.[83]

Luciano's 1947 visit to Cuba laid the groundwork for Havana's subsequent role in international narcotics smuggling traffic. Arriving in January, Luciano summoned the leaders of American organized crime, including Meyer Lansky, to Havana for a meeting and began paying extravagant bribes to prominent Cuban officials as well. The director of the Federal Bureau of Narcotics at the time felt that Luciano's presence in Cuba was an ominous sign.

> I had received a preliminary report through a Spanish-speaking agent I had sent to Havana, and I read this to the Cuban Ambassador. The report stated that Luciano had already become friendly with a number of high Cuban officials through the lavish use of expensive gifts. Luciano had developed a full-fledged plan which envisioned the Caribbean as his center of operations. . . . *Cuba was to be made the center of all international narcotic operations.* [Emphasis added.][84]

Pressure from the United States finally resulted in the revocation of Luciano's residence visa and his return to Italy, but not before he had received commitments from organized crime leaders in the United States to distribute the regular heroin shipments he promised them from Europe.[85]

The Caribbean, on the whole, was a profitable place for American racketeers—most governments were friendly and did not interfere with the "business ventures" that brought some badly needed capital into their generally poor countries. Organized crime had been well established in Havana long before Luciano's landmark voyage. During the 1930s Meyer Lansky "discovered" the Caribbean for northeastern syndicate bosses and invested their illegal profits in an assortment of lucrative gambling ventures. In 1933 Lansky moved into the Miami Beach area and took over most of the illegal off-track betting and a variety of hotels and casinos.[86] He was also reportedly responsible for organized crime's decision to declare Miami a "free city" (that is, not subject to the usual rules of territorial monopoly).[87] Following his success in Miami, Lansky moved to Havana for three years, and by the beginning of World War II he owned the Hotel Nacional's casino and was leasing the municipal racetrack from a reputable New York bank.

Burdened by the enormous scope and diversity of his holdings, Lanksy had to delegate much of the responsibility for daily management to local gangsters.[88] One of Lansky's earliest associates in Florida was Santo Trafficante, Sr., a Sicilian-born Tampa gangster. Trafficante had earned his reputation as an effective organizer in the Tampa gambling rackets and was already a figure of some stature when Lansky first arrived in Florida. By the time Lansky returned to New York in 1940, Trafficante had assumed responsibility for Lansky's interest in Havana and Miami.

By the early 1950s Trafficante had himself become such an important figure that he delegated his Havana concessions to Santo Trafficante, Jr., the most talented of his six sons. The younger Santo's official position in Havana was that of manager of the Sans Souci Casino, but he was far more important than his title indicates. As his father's financial representative, and ultimately Meyer Lansky's, Santo controlled much of Havana's tourist industry and became quite close to the pre-Castro dictator Fulgencio Batista.[89] Moreover, it was reportedly his responsibility to receive the bulk shipments of heroin from Europe and forward them through Florida to New York and other major urban centers, where their distribution was assisted by local Mafia bosses.[90]

## Harold Meltzer in Mexico

The significance of Lucky Luciano's success in Europe is perhaps best explained by its contrast with the sordid saga of Harold Meltzer in Mexico. During the late 1940s while Luciano and Lansky were knitting their crime connections into the Mediterranean heroin trade, Meltzer failed dismally in his bid to make Mexico a major supplier of opiates for American addicts. Each of Meltzer's many failings highlights another aspect of Luciano's success.

An obscure but diligent Jewish drug dealer, Meltzer had been sentenced to two years for selling narcotics by a New York court in 1928 and remained an active distributor throughout the 1930s in areas as diverse as Boston and Oklahoma. During the war, in the words of a Federal Bureau of Narcotics report, "heroin prices skyrocketed to fantastic heights, with a complete scarcity of heroin." When prices reached $1,200 per pound for crude opium and $600 per ounce for heroin in 1945, Meltzer decided to open up Mexico as a new source of raw opium for the American market. Through his contacts, Meltzer befriended Salvatore Duhart, the Mexican consul in Washington, playing on the diplomat's "degenerate fondness for women." With Duhart's promise to fix the Mexican border police as his main asset, Meltzer, according to the FBN, "borrowed . . . up to $50,000.00 from Nig Rosen, Willie Weisberg, Frank Livorsi, and other leading New York and Philadelphia racketeers, primarily Jewish, to finance the narcotic deal." Through three widely separated sources, the bureau heard that Meltzer was managing a "million dollar narcotics venture for Meyer Lansky."

Armed with his Jewish capital and Mexican contact, Meltzer closed his apartment at 30 Central Park South in June 1945 and moved his family to Mexico City for the next four years. Driven by an insatiable U.S. demand for opiates, Meltzer's Mexican enterprise prospered in its first months. While Salvatore Duhart located Mexican suppliers and bribed the border guards, Meltzer moved about America arranging delivery of opium to Jewish dealers for smoking and to Italian laboratories for conversion into heroin.

Then things started going wrong. Meltzer himself was smoking opium and carrying on an affair with a black prostitute. When the operation started working well, Meltzer, in a typical move, decided to dispense with Duhart's costly services and give the Mexican end to an American gangster named Max Cossman. Without Duhart to supervise quality, the Mexican dealers began filling opium containers with coins, nails, and bullets for weight. In utter innocence, Meltzer delivered the short-weight containers to his American distributors on consignment and they ultimately refused to pay for the inferior goods. Even an appeal to "Trigger Mike" Coppola to enforce payment failed, and Mexican suppliers kidnapped partner Cossman when Meltzer failed to send the promised payment.

Visiting New York in early 1947, Meltzer won a partial reprieve when his friend Fred Reiner, a dealer who had once worked with Waxey Gordon, introduced him to Charlie "The Jew" Yacknowsky, a New Jersey waterfront boss, who interceded with the Jewish creditors. Desperate to raise the money for Cossman's ransom, Meltzer then worked through Reiner, first to arrange for a European chemist to staff his Mexican laboratory and then to place an order for delivery of three kilograms of Italian heroin. When the heroin approached Havana harbor several months later, Meltzer drove south out of New York, crashed Reiner's car in an accident near Jacksonville, and made it to Cuba by air. After removing the heroin from the doors of an imported auto, Meltzer flew to

Miami and then disappeared with the drugs. Back in New York, Meltzer became the last man seen with Yacknowsky before he was shot. Fleeing to Los Angeles where he joined forces with racketeer Mickey Cohen, Meltzer left behind a trail of angry creditors, notably Fred Reiner.

Determined to get even, Reiner turned informant for the FBN in 1949 and identified many of Meltzer's buyers. When several were charged, they too were happy to turn against Meltzer. A Miami dealer named Charles Drucker who had lent him $10,000 "testified as to his association with Harold Meltzer in the narcotic traffic." Based on this evidence, Mexican police charged Max Cossman with drug dealing, and U.S. officials indicted Meltzer for giving false information to customs. Moreover, there were reports that Max "Chink" Rothman, muscle for the Nig Rosen–Meyer Lansky–Willie Weisberg organization in Philadelphia, was looking for Meltzer to collect the original mob money invested in his Mexican scheme.

The contrast with Luciano and Lansky is instructive. Like Luciano, Meltzer had the business sense to see that America's postwar heroin market could no longer rely on diversion of legal drugs from Europe or Asia. Both Luciano and Meltzer realized that postwar syndicates would have to integrate all phases of the trade: opium processing, smuggling, and street distribution. Meltzer may have had the vision, but his group lacked Luciano's contacts, Trafficante's strategic territory, and Lansky's finances—all essentials for the creation of a stable connection between foreign suppliers and U.S. dealers. Moreover, Lansky and Luciano had leadership qualities beyond Meltzer's slender abilities. While Luciano could rely on his Marseille contacts for skilled Corsican chemists, Meltzer failed in his attempts to recruit a European manager for his Mexican laboratory. In Florida, criminals feared Trafficante but testified against Meltzer. If Meyer Lansky's word was his bond, Howard Meltzer's was an overture to a bad debt.

Finally, and perhaps most important, Meltzer's failure shows the paramount importance of politics in the international drug trade. Despite its natural geographical advantages, Meltzer's Mexican venture did not enjoy the political protection of Luciano's more remote European operation. Meltzer's project prospered briefly with the support of a minor Mexican patron, the "degenerate" Consul Duhart, and then failed without him. By contrast, Luciano's partners had strong political connections. By 1950, the Mafia controlled politics in Sicily, and Marseille's Corsican syndicates enjoyed the patronage of both the city government and the CIA. While Meltzer tried to launch Mexican opium exports solely on their commercial merits, Marseille's Corsicans had the added advantage of a political alliance with the CIA when they began processing heroin for the U.S. market.

By 1951, Lansky and Luciano were millionaires many times over and Howard Meltzer was under arrest.[91] In the drug business, as in any business, it took leadership, capital, contacts, and, above all, politics to turn demand into profits.

## The Marseille Connection

The basic Turkey-Italy-America heroin route continued to dominate the international heroin traffic for more than twenty years with only one important alteration—during the 1950s the Sicilian Mafia began to divest itself of the heroin manufacturing business and started relying on Marseille's Corsican syndicates for their drug supplies. There were two reasons for this change. As the diverted supplies of legally produced Schiaparelli heroin began to dry up in 1950 and 1951, Luciano was faced with the alternative of expanding his own clandestine laboratories or seeking another source of supply. While the Sicilian mafiosi were capable international smugglers, they seemed to lack the ability to manage the laboratories. Almost from the beginning, illicit heroin production in Italy had been plagued by a series of arrests—owing more to mafiosi incompetence than anything else—of couriers moving supplies in and out of laboratories. The implications were serious: if the seizures continued, Luciano himself might eventually be arrested.[92]

Preferring to minimize the risks of direct involvement, Luciano apparently decided to shift his major source of supply to Marseille. There, Corsican syndicates had gained political power and control of the waterfront as a result of their involvement in CIA strikebreaking activities. Thus, Italy gradually declined in importance as a center for illicit drug manufacturing, and Marseille became the heroin capital of Europe.[93]

Although it is difficult to probe the inner workings of such a clandestine business under the best of circumstances, there is reason to believe that Meyer Lansky's 1949–1950 European tour was instrumental in promoting Marseille's heroin industry.

After crossing the Atlantic in a luxury liner, Lansky visited Luciano in Rome, where they discussed the narcotics trade. He then traveled to Zurich and contacted prominent Swiss bankers through John Pullman, an old friend from the rumrunning days. These negotiations established the financial labyrinth that organized crime used for decades to smuggle its enormous gambling and heroin profits out of the country into numbered Swiss bank accounts without attracting the notice of the U.S. Internal Revenue Service.

Pullman was responsible for the European end of Lansky's financial operation: depositing, transferring, and investing the money when it arrived in Switzerland. He used regular Swiss banks for a number of years until the Lansky group purchased the Exchange and Investment Bank of Geneva. Across the Atlantic, Lansky and other gangsters used two methods to transfer their money to Switzerland: "friendly banks" (those willing to protect their customers' identity) were used to make ordinary international bank transfers to Switzerland; and in cases when the money was too hot for even a friendly bank, it was stockpiled until a Swiss bank officer came to the United States on business and could "transfer" it simply by carrying it back to Switzerland in his luggage.[94]

After making the financial arrangements with Pullman in Switzerland, Lansky traveled through France, where he met with high-ranking Corsican syndicate leaders on the Riviera and in Paris. After lengthy discussions, Lansky and the Corsicans are reported to have arrived at some sort of agreement concerning the international heroin traffic.[95] Soon after Lansky returned to the United States, heroin laboratories began appearing in Marseille. On May 23, 1951, Marseille police broke into a clandestine heroin laboratory—the first to be uncovered in France since the end of the war. After discovering another on March 18, 1952, French authorities reported that "it seems that the installation of clandestine laboratories in France dated from 1951 and is a consequence of the cessation of diversions in *Italy* during the previous years [emphasis added]."[96] During the next five months French police uncovered two more clandestine laboratories. In future years, U.S. narcotics experts were to estimate that the majority of America's heroin supply was being manufactured in Marseille.

# 2

# Marseille: America's Heroin Laboratory

FOR MOST AMERICANS DURING THE 1960s, MARSEILLE MEANT only heroin, but for the French this bustling Mediterranean port represented the best and the worst of their national traditions. Marseille has been the crossroads of France's empire, a stronghold of its labor movement, and the capital of its underworld. Through its port have passed citizens on their way to colonial outposts, notably in North Africa and Indochina, and "natives" permanently or temporarily immigrating to the mother country. Marseille has long had a tradition of working-class militancy. The city became a stronghold of the French Communist party and was the hard core of the violent general strikes that racked France in the late 1940s. Since the turn of the century Marseille has been depicted in French novels, pulp magazines, and newspapers as a city crowded with gunmen and desperadoes of every description—a veritable Chicago of France.

Traditionally, these underworld characters are not properly French by language or culture—they are Corsican. Unlike the gangsters in most other French cities, who are individualistic and operate in small, ad hoc bands, Marseille's criminals belong to tightly structured clans, which recognize a common hierarchy of power and prestige. This cohesiveness on the part of the Corsican syndicates has made them an ideal counterweight to the city's powerful Communist labor unions. Almost inevitably, many of the foreign powers and local politicians who have ruled Marseille allied themselves with the Corsican syndicates: French Fascists used them to battle Communist demonstrators in the 1930s; the

Nazi Gestapo used them to spy on the Communist underground during World War II; and the CIA paid them to break Communist strikes in 1947 and 1950. The last of these alliances proved the most significant, since it put the Corsicans in a powerful enough position to establish Marseille as the postwar heroin capital of the Western world and to cement a long-term partnership with Mafia drug distributors.

The Corsicans have usually worked well with the Sicilians, for there are similarities of culture and tradition between the two groups. Separated by only three hundred miles of blue Mediterranean water, both Sicily and Corsica are arid, mountainous islands lying off the west coast of the Italian peninsula. Although Corsica has been a French province since the late 1700s, its people have been strongly influenced by Italian Catholic culture. Corsicans and Sicilians share a pride in family and village that has given both islands a history of armed resistance to foreign invaders and a heritage of family vendettas. Their common poverty has resulted in the emigration of their most ambitious sons. Just as Sicily has sent its young to America and the industrial cities of northern Italy, so Corsica has sent its youth to French Indochina and the port city of Marseille. After generations of migration, Corsicans account for more than 10 percent of Marseille's population.

Despite all the similarities between Corsican and Sicilian society, Marseille's Corsican gangsters do not belong to any monolithic "Corsican Mafia." In their pursuit of crime and profit, the Mafia and the Corsican syndicates have adopted different styles, different techniques. The Mafia, in both Sicily and the United States, has operated like a plundering army. While "the grand council" or "the commission" maps strategy on the national level, each regional "family" has a clear hierarchy with a "boss," "underboss," "lieutenants," and "soldiers." Rivals are eliminated through force, "territory" is assigned to each boss, and legions of mafiosi use a range of rackets—prostitution, gambling, narcotics, protection—to milk the population. Over the last century the Mafia has devoted most of its energies to occupying and exploiting western Sicily and urban America.

In contrast, Corsican racketeers have formed smaller, more sophisticated criminal syndicates. The Corsican underworld lacks the Mafia's formal organization, although it does have a strong sense of corporate identity and almost invariably imposes a death sentence on those who divulge information to outsiders. A man who is accepted as an ordinary gangster by the Corsicans "is in the milieu," while a respected syndicate boss is known as *un vrai Monsieur*. The most powerful are known as *paceri*, or "peacemakers," since they can impose discipline on the members of all syndicates and mediate vendettas. While mafiosi usually lack refined criminal skills, the Corsicans are specialists in heroin manufacturing, sophisticated international smuggling, art thefts, and counterfeiting. Rather than restricting themselves to Corsica or Marseille, Corsican gangsters have migrated to Indochina, North Africa, the Middle East, Latin America, Canada, and the South Pacific. In spite of the distances that separate them, Corsican racketeers keep in touch, co-operating efficiently in complex intercontinental smuggling operations, which stymied the efforts of law enforcement authorities for a quarter century.[1]

Cooperation between Corsican smugglers and Mafia drug distributors inside the United States was the major reason the Mafia was able to circumvent every effort U.S. officials made at reducing the flow of heroin into the United States in the decades after World War II. When Italy responded to U.S. pressure by reducing its legal pharmaceutical heroin production in 1950–1951, the Corsicans opened clandestine laboratories in Marseille. When U.S. customs tightened baggage checks along the eastern seaboard, the Corsicans originated new routes through Latin America. When Turkey began to phase out opium production in 1968, Corsican syndicates in Indochina developed new supplies of morphine and heroin.

For a full quarter century, from 1948 to 1972, the Corsicans thus dominated the U.S. heroin market and dispatched, through their alliance with the Mafia, a steady flow of high-grade heroin across the Atlantic. Compared with the volatile global drug trade that followed, the Corsican era seems a period of unique stability when Turkish opium moved without disruption through Marseille's heroin laboratories and into America through Canada or the Caribbean.

Under the terms of their informal alliance with France's Gaullist governments, the Marseille syndicates manufactured their heroin exclusively for export. Marseille may have become the world's largest heroin producer, but France remained drug-free—an essential element in the political equation that allowed this illicit industry to operate. Protected and connected, the Corsicans, according to the Federal Bureau of Narcotics, produced an estimated 80 percent of America's heroin supply.[2] Although the FBN may have inflated the estimate to justify its own emphasis on European enforcement, the Corsicans seem, from available data, to have sustained the American heroin market during this critical quarter century.

Marseille is the hub of the Corsicans' international network. During the First Indochina War (1946–1954), Corsican syndicates made a fortune in illegal currency manipulations by smuggling gold bullion and paper currency between Saigon and Marseille. In the 1950s Corsican gangsters supplied a booming black market in "tax-free" cigarettes by smuggling American brands into Marseille from North Africa. During their twenty years of peak activity, Corsican heroin laboratories were located in Marseille's downtown tenements or in luxurious villas scattered through the surrounding countryside. Most of the laboratories' morphine base supplies were smuggled into the port of Marseille from Turkey or Indochina. Marseille is the key to the Corsican underworld's success, and the growth of its international smuggling operations has been linked to its political fortunes in Marseille. From the time of their emergence in the 1920s, Marseille's Corsican syndicates were shaped by the dynamics of French politics.

## Genesis

The first link between the Corsicans and the political world came about with the emergence in the 1920s of Marseille's first "modern" gangsters, François Spirito and Paul Bonnaventure Carbone. Until their rise to prominence, the milieu was populated by colorful pimps and gunmen whose ideal was a steady income that ensured them a life of leisure. The most stable form of investment was usually two or three prostitutes, and few gangsters of the premodern age demonstrated any higher aspirations.[3]

Carbone and Spirito changed all that. They were close friends, and their twenty-year partnership transformed the character of the Marseille milieu. Of the two, Spirito was the more innovative, and his influence spans the entire history of the modern Marseille milieu. Born in Marseille in January 1900 as Charles Henri Faccia, a name he would later write with a shaky, semiliterate hand, Spirito became an active transatlantic drug smuggler and was twice convicted in Boston before the war—in 1929 for trespassing and in 1939 for smuggling 55 pounds of opium aboard the SS *Exeter*. Carbone was killed by the resistance in 1943, but Spirito lived into his late sixties; retiring to his restaurant at Sausset-les-Pins on the Riviera and respected in the milieu as "le Grand." Indicative of his influence, a 1965 survey by the Bureau of Narcotics still credited him with active criminal associates ranging from Marseille heroin merchants through transatlantic smugglers to New York drug distributors.[4]

This partnership's first major venture was the establishment of a French-staffed brothel in Cairo in the late 1920s. They repeated and expanded their success on their return to Marseille, where they proceeded to organize prostitution on a scale previously unknown. But more significantly, they recognized the importance of political power in protecting large-scale criminal ventures and its potential for providing a source of income through municipal graft.

In 1931 Carbone and Spirito reached an "understanding" with Simon Sabiani, Marseille's Fascist deputy mayor, who appointed Carbone's brother director of the municipal stadium and opened city employment to associates of the two underworld leaders.[5] In return for these favors, Carbone and Spirito organized an elite corps of gangsters that spearheaded violent Fascist street demonstrations during the depression years of the 1930s. All across Europe fascism was gaining strength: Mussolini ruled Italy, Hitler was coming to power in Germany, and emerging French Fascist groups were trying to topple the republic through mass violence. Communist and Socialist demonstrators repeatedly rushed to the defense of the republic, producing a series of bloody confrontations throughout France.[6] In Marseille, Carbone and Spirito were the vanguard of the right wing. In February 1934, for example, several days after an inflammatory speech by a Fascist army general, massive street demonstrations erupted on the Canebière, Marseille's main boulevard. The thousands of leftist dock workers and union members who took to the streets dominated this political confrontation until Carbone and Spirito's political shock force fired on the crowd with pistols. The national police intervened, the workers were driven from the streets, and the wounded were carted off to the hospital.[7]

After four years of battling Sabiani's underworld allies in the streets, the left settled its political differences long enough to mount a unified electoral effort that defeated Sabiani and placed a Socialist mayor in office.[8] Although the leftist electoral victory temporarily eclipsed the Fascist-Corsican alliance, the rise of fascism had politicized the Marseille underworld and marked its emergence as major force in city politics.

To those schooled in the Anglo-American political tradition, it might seem strange that the underworld should play such a critical role in Marseille politics. However, in France the street demonstration has often been as important as the ballot box in influencing the course of politics. From the downfall of King Louis Phillippe in 1848, to the Dreyfus scandal of the 1890s, through the May revolution of 1968, the ability to mass muscle on the boulevards has been a necessary political asset.

Although they had lost control of the municipal government, Carbone and Spirito's economic strength hardly declined. The emergence of organized narcotics trafficking in the United States provided Carbone with the opportunity to open a heroin laboratory in the early 1930s, while the outbreak of the Spanish civil war enabled him to engage in the arms traffic.[9]

Carbone and Spirito found their political influence restored in 1940, when German troops occupied Marseille after France's precipitous military collapse. Faced with one of the more active resistance movements in France, the Nazi Gestapo unit assigned to Marseille became desperate for informants and turned to the leading figures in the underworld, who were willing to collaborate.

On July 14, 1942, the Resistance showed its strength for the first time by machine-gunning the headquarters of a pro-German political organization in downtown Marseille (the PPF, whose regional director was the Fascist ex-mayor Simon Sabiani). The following afternoon Carbone and Spirito handed the Gestapo a complete list of all those involved. For these and other services, they were well rewarded. This prosperity was short-lived, however, for in 1943 Carbone was killed en route to Marseille when his train was blown up by the Resistance,[10] and following the Normandy landing in 1944 Spirito fled to Spain with Sabiani.

In 1947 Spirito came to the United States, where he enjoyed an active role in the New York–Marseille heroin traffic. Three years later he was arrested in New York on a heroin smuggling charge and sentenced to two years in Atlanta federal prison.[11] On his release he returned to France, where he was arrested and tried for wartime collaboration with the Nazis; however, after only eight months in prison he retired to manage a restaurant on the French Riviera. While he remained active in the heroin business, Spirito no longer wielded any visible power in Marseille. Occasionally, the city's warring gangs asked him to use his prestige to mediate their bloody vendettas. But mostly he played bocce on the sand, arranged drug deals and enjoyed his position as a respectable citizen of Toulon until his death in 1967.[12]

## From Underworld to Underground

A significant element of the Corsican underworld sided secretly with the Resistance, thus ensuring the consolidation of some sort of power base for the milieu at the end of World War II. Their patriotic activities set the scene for the emergence of a new generation of criminal leaders, embodied in the Guerini brothers.

While Carbone and Spirito were happy enough to help themselves by helping the Germans, most Corsicans, both in Marseille and on the island itself, were bitterly opposed to the German occupation. It was increasingly apparent that the island would be annexed by the Third Reich's ally Italy—something abhorrent to most Corsicans, who felt that their unique language as well as their sense of cultural identity would be jeopardized.

In 1940 a group of Corsican Resistance fighters issued a statement concerning the possibility of Italian annexation:

> Corsica will never accept being handed over to Italy. Since 1789, she has embraced France. She has given France

Napoleon. In the course of the Great War, 40,000 Corsicans died on the field of battle in northeastern France. . . .

An Italian Corsica? What a monstrosity! If this crime were ever committed, history would have to reserve some bloody pages for the fight to the death a small people of 300,000 would wage against a powerful nation of 45 million inhabitants.[13]

In Corsica, this strong anti-Italian chauvinism mobilized the most effective resistance movement in France, and the island's mass uprising in 1943 is unparalleled in the annals of the Resistance.[14]

The Resistance in France was divided between the Communists and non-Communists. Although wartime American propaganda films and postwar French cinema have projected an image of France as a nation in chains, with every other citizen a nighttime warrior, most French collaborated with the Germans and were indifferent, if not hostile, toward the Resistance.

In contrast, the Communist party, with its anti-Fascist ideology and disciplined cell structure, began resistance activities almost immediately and remained one of the most effective armed organizations in France until the 1944 Allied landings in Normandy. Despite their alliance with the Soviet Union, America and Britain refused to work directly with French Communist guerrillas and throughout most of the war never knowingly parachuted them arms or supplies.[15] The French Resistance remained deeply factionalized for most of the war and never amounted to anything more than a nuisance for the German occupation army.

The situation in Marseille was typical. Generally, the movement was divided between the Communist party's FTP (Franc-Tireurs et Partisans), with 1,700 to 2,000 members, and a non-Communist coalition group, MUR (Mouvements Unis de Résistance), with fewer than 800. Among the MUR's most important components was Marseille's Socialist party (whose leader was Gaston Defferre, also head of an Allied intelligence network).[16] Both MUR and FTP recognized the need for unity. But the persistence of rather unheroic squablings, mainly over MUR's adherence to the Allied command's policy of denying arms to the Communist FTP, prevented any meaningful cooperation.[17] The Communists and non-Communists finally managed to form a unified resistance army (Forces Françaises de l'Intérieur) in February 1944, but for most of the war they had remained at odds.[18]

As a result of their prewar anti-Communist activities in Marseille's politics, few of the resistance-minded Corsicans were accepted into the Communist underground. However, several of Marseille's Corsican syndicates became the backbone of the non-Communist underground, which lacked the necessary covert experience to carry out effective resistance work. For instance, within a month after its formation in March 1943, MUR was virtually decimated when one of its officers, captured by the Gestapo, informed on many of its members.[19] But with their law of silence and their experience in secret criminal operations, the Corsicans easily adapted to the world of espionage and urban guerrilla warfare.

The most famous of the Corsican Resistance heroes were the Guerini brothers. Antoine Guerini, a former triggerman for Carbone and Spirito, worked as an agent for Anglo-American intelligence. When English intelligence officers were parachuted into the Marseille area to make contact with MUR, they were hidden in the cellars of Antoine's nightclubs. Antoine was also responsible for smuggling arms into the city for MUR after they had been parachuted from British aircraft. During the twelve-day battle for the liberation of Marseille in August 1944, Antoine's younger brother Barthélemy supplied intelligence, arms, and men to Gaston Defferre's socialist militia, and was later awarded the Legion of Honor for his wartime exploits.[20]

When the U.S. army occupied Marseille in August, the city's milieu infiltrated the ranks of the Resistance, creating a problem for both the U.S. army and the local Communist party. Soon after the city's liberation, the Resistance swelled from 1,600 to 4,500 troops, "as all the hoodlums and grudgeholders flocked to the colors after the fighting was over." Within a month, reputable citizens had returned to peacetime pursuits, leaving "criminals and undisciplined young hoodlums" in control of the Resistance units.[21] After two Resistance militia with criminal records murdered several American soldiers without provocation, the U.S. army began disbanding the Resistance forces. Unaware that the Resistance had changed character from Communist to criminal in the weeks since liberation, the U.S. army was surprised when the Communist party offered no opposition to the dissolution.[22]

## The Socialists, the Guerinis, and the CIA

Although the Corsican underworld's wartime alliances had laid the foundation for Marseille's future criminal dynasty, the end of the German occupation generally meant hard times for the Marseille milieu. For more than twenty years Carbone and Spirito had dominated the underworld, pioneering new forms of criminal activity and providing leadership, discipline, and, most important, political alliances. Now they were gone, and none of the surviving syndicate bosses had as yet acquired the power to assume their mantle.

To add to its problems, the milieu's traditional enemies, the Communist and Socialist parties, remained firmly allied until mid-1946, thus denying a conservative-underworld alliance any chance of acquiring political power.

In the first municipal elections of April 1945, a left-wing coalition swept Socialist party leader Gaston Defferre into the mayor's office. Splitting with the Socialists in 1946, the Communist party mounted a successful independent effort and elected its candidate mayor in November.[23]

Moreover, a new police unit, the CRS (Compagnies Républicaines de Sécurité) had become the bane of the Marseille underworld. Formed during the liberation struggles of August 1944, when most of the municipal police force (who had cooperated with the Germans) disappeared,[24] the CRS was assigned the task of restoring public order, tracking down collaborators, restricting smuggling, and curbing black market activities. A high percentage of its officers was recruited from the Communist Resistance movement, and they performed their duties too effectively for the comfort of the milieu.[25]

But the milieu's rise to power was not long in coming. In the fall of 1947 bloody street fighting, electoral reverses, and the clandestine intervention of the CIA toppled the Communist party from power and brought about a permanent realignment of Marseille's politics. When the strikes and rioting finally came to an end, the Socialists had severed their contacts with the Communists, a Socialist-underworld alliance was in control of the city's politics, and the Guerini brothers had emerged as the unchallenged "peacemakers" of the Marseille milieu. For the next twenty years their word would be law in the Marseille underworld.

The confrontation began innocently enough with the municipal elections of October 19 and 26, 1947. On the national level, General Charles de Gaulle's new anti-Communist party (Reassemblement du Peuple Français, RPF) scored substantial electoral successes throughout France. In Marseille, the revitalized conservatives won enough seats on the municipal council to unseat the Communist mayor and elect a conservative, Michel Carlini. One of Carlini's first offical acts was to raise the municipal tram fares, a seemingly uncontroversial move justified by growing fiscal deficits. However, this edict had unforeseen consequences.

More than two years after the end of the war, Marseille was still digging itself out from the rubble left by the Allied bombing. Unemployment was high, wages were low; the black market was king, and a severe shortage of the most basic commodities lent an air of desperation to morning shoppers.[26] The tramways were the city's lifeline, and the increased fare pinched pocketbooks and provoked bitter outrage. The Communist-Socialist labor coalition (Confédération Génerale du Travail, CGT) responded with a militant boycott of the tramways. Any motorman daring to take a tram into the streets was met with barricades and a shower of rocks from the angry populace.[27]

Marseille's working class was not alone in its misery. Across France, blue-collar workers were suffering through the hard times of a painful postwar economic recovery. Workers were putting in long hours, boosting production and being paid little for their efforts. Prodded by their American advisers, successive French cabinets held down wages to speed economic recovery. By 1947 industrial production was practically restored to its prewar level, but the average Parisian wage for skilled labor was only 65 percent of what it had been during the depths of the depression.[28] Workers were literally hungry as well: food prices had skyrocketed, and the average worker was eating 18 percent less than in 1938. Even though their wages could barely cover their food expenditures, workers were forced to shoulder the bulk of the national tax burden. The tax system was so inequitable that the prestigious Parisian daily *Le Monde* labeled it "more iniquitous than that which provoked the French Revolution."[29]

In Marseille, throughout early November, ugly incidents heated political tensions in the wake of the tramways boycott, culminating in the escalating violence of November 12. That day began with a demonstration of angry workers in the morning, saw a beating of Communist councilors at the city council meeting in the afternoon, and ended with a murder in the early evening.[30] Early that morning, several thousand workers had gathered in front of the courthouse to demand the release of four young sheet metal workers who had been arrested for attacking a tram. As the police led two of them toward the hall for their trial, the crowd rushed the officers and the men escaped. Emboldened by their initial success, the crowd continued to try to break through police cordons for several hours, demanding that the charges against the workers be dropped. Responding to the determined mood of the crowd, the court was hastily convened, and at about four in the afternoon the charges were reduced to the equivalent of a misdemeanor. The demonstrators were just preparing to disband when an unknown worker arrived to announce, "Everybody to City Hall. They are beating our comrades."[31]

The assault had occurred in the course of a regular meeting of the municipal council, when Communist councilors raised the issue of the tramway fares. The discussions became overheated, and some of the mayor's well-muscled supporters, most members of the Guerini gang, rushed forward and administered a severe beating to the Communist councilors.[32] Word of the beatings spread quickly through Marseille, and within an hour 40,000 demonstrators had gathered in front of City Hall.[33] The handful of police present were able to bring the situation under control only when Communist ex-mayor Jean Cristofol calmed the crowd. Within thirty minutes it had dispersed, and by 6:30 P.M. all was quiet.

While most of the demonstrators went home, a contingent of young workers rushed back across the waterfront and charged into the narrow streets around the opera house. Crowded with nightclubs and brothels, the area was commonly identified as the headquarters of the underworld. It was generally believed that the black market was controlled from these clubs, and they were deemed a just target for working-class anger. As the crowd roamed the streets breaking windows, Antoine and Barthélemy Guerini fired guns into the crowd, wounding several of the demonstrators. Later that evening a young sheet metal worker died of his wounds.[34]

The next morning banner headlines in the Communist newspaper, *La Marseillaise*, read, CARLINI AND DE VERNEJOUL REINSTATE SABIANI'S METHODS IN THE MAYOR'S OFFICE OF MARSEILLE. The paper reported that an investigation had disclosed it was Guerini men who had attacked the municipal councilors.[35] This charge was not seriously rebutted in the Socialist paper, *Le Provençal*, or the Gaullist *Méridional*. In a court hearing on November 16, two police officers testified seeing the Guerinis shooting into the crowd. At the same hearing one of the younger Guerini brothers admitted that Antoine and Barthélemy had been in the area at the time of the shooting. But four days later the police mysteriously retracted their testimony, and on December 10 all charges against the Guerinis were dropped.[36] The morning after the shooting, November 13, the local labor confederation called a general strike, and the city came to a standstill.

Marseille workers had reached the breaking point at about the same time as their comrades in the rest of France. Spontaneous wildcat strikes erupted in factories, mines, and railway yards throughout the country.[37] As militant workers took to the streets, demonstrating for fair wages and lower prices, the Communist party leadership was reluctantly forced to take action. On November 14, the day after Marseille's unions went on strike, the leftist-labor confederation, CGT, called for a nationwide general strike.

Contrary to what one might expect, French Communist leaders of this era were not radical revolutionaries. For the most part they were conservative middle-aged people who had served their nation during the wartime resistance and now wanted, above all else, to take part in the governance of their country. Their leadership of the wartime resistance had earned them the loyalty of the working class, and thanks to their efforts French unionists had accepted low postwar wages and abstained from strikes in 1945 and 1946. However, their repeated support for draconian government austerity measures began to cost them votes in union elections, and in mid-1946 one U.S. State Department analyst reported that Communist leaders "could no longer hold back the discontent of the rank and file."[38] When wildcat strikes and demonstrations erupted in mid-November 1947, the Communist party was forced to support them or forfeit its leadership of the working class. At best its support was halfhearted. But by late November, 3 million workers were out on strike and the French economy was almost paralyzed.

Ignoring their own analysts, U.S. foreign policy planners interpreted the 1947 strike as a political ploy on the part of the Communist party and "feared" that it was a prelude to a "takeover of the government." The reason for this myopia was simple: by mid-1947 the cold war had started and Washington viewed political events in terms of "the world-wide ideological clash between Eastern Communism and Western Democracy."[39] Apprehensive over Soviet gains in the eastern Mediterranean and the growth of Communist parties in Western Europe, the Truman administration drew up in May the multibillion-dollar European Recovery Plan (known popularly as the Marshall Plan) and established the CIA in September.[40] Determined to save France from an imminent Communist coup, the CIA moved in to help break up the strike, choosing the Socialist party as its nightstick.

After decades of research, the weapons and warriors are emerging from the veil of official secrecy that has long obscured these covert operations. When Congress voted $400 million for the fight against communism in early 1947, President Harry Truman "used it overtly in Greece and Turkey and covertly in France and Italy, through the CIA, to support . . . democratic political parties."[41] In the bureaucratic chaos that followed the agency's creation that summer, intelligence functions were scattered among the Defense and State departments and the executive branch, with only loose coordination by the CIA's new head, the director of central intelligence. In the rush to construct an intelligence capacity, the National Security Council created the Office of Policy Coordination (OPC) in June 1948 to develop "a covert political action capability," a broad mission that made it responsible for active clandestine operations such as union infiltration. Paid through the CIA but housed in the State and Defense departments, OPC flourished in this anomalous situation—freed from normal bureaucratic controls and funded far more liberally than even the CIA itself.[42] OPC's founding director was Frank Wisner, a former OSS operative who had spent the postwar years in Europe recruiting ex-Nazis, many of them major war criminals, to operate behind Soviet lines. Under his brilliant and unconventional leadership, the OPC soon attracted talented OSS veterans, such as Thomas Braden and William Colby, who shared his pragmatic viewpoint that any enemy of communism, whether Gestapo officer or Corsican gangster, could become America's ally.[43] As Colby, a future CIA director, explained, Wisner's OPC was "operating in the atmosphere of an order of Knights Templar, to save Western freedom from Communist darkness."[44]

In the early days of the cold war, the CIA and OPC identified unions as the key to the struggle for Western Europe. Working through the American Federation of Labor (AFL), which was already operating its own secret networks in Europe, the agency began sending some $2 million a year to anti-Communist labor leaders.[45] "I think the AFL/CIO interest in protecting the docks in Marseille and things like that antedated the establishment of the agency," recalled Braden, the OPC official who managed these operations. "I suspect it was done by the OSS or the Army or the State Department."[46] Indeed, in early 1947, the U.S. ambassador to Paris, Jefferson Caffery, was already warning Washington that "the long hand of the Kremlin is increasingly exercising power . . . through . . . the French Communist Party and its fortress the CGT."[47] In an indirect call for the covert funding, the ambassador complained that "the labor leaders who are resisting the Communist grip on the C.G.T. have not been able (mostly from lack of funds) to organize effective opposition groups."[48]

When French Communists attacked the Marshall Plan with strikes in 1947, the CIA, in one of its earliest operations, launched a covert counterattack. Through the AFL, the agency engineered the first split in postwar European labor by channeling clandestine funds to Léon Jouhaux, the Socialist leader, who then led his Force Ouvrière union out of the Communist-dominated CGT.[49] Without admitting his source of funds, AFL President George Meany would later boast that his union had "financed the split in the Communist-controlled union in France—we paid for it, we sent them American trade union money, we set up their offices, we sent them supplies."[50]

On the surface it may have seemed a bit out of character for the CIA to be backing anything so far left as a Socialist party. However, there were only three major political parties in France—Socialist, Communist, and Gaullist—and by a simple process of elimination the CIA wound up allying itself with the Socialists. While General de Gaulle was too independent for American tastes, Socialist leaders were rapidly losing political ground to the Communists and thus were willing to collaborate with the CIA.

Writing in the *Saturday Evening Post* in 1967, Thomas Braden, former director of the CIA's international organizations division, explained the agency's strategy of using the left to fight leftists:

> It was personified by Jay Lovestone, assistant to David
> Dubinsky in the International Ladies' Garment Workers' Union.
> Once Chief of the Communist Party in the United States,

Lovestone had an enormous grasp of foreign-intelligence operations. In 1947 the Communist *Confédération Générale du Travail* led a strike in Paris which came very close to paralyzing the French economy. A takeover of the government was feared.

Into this crisis stepped Lovestone and his assistant, Irving Brown. With funds from Dubinsky's union, they organized *Force Ouvrière*, a non-Communist union. When they ran out of money they appealed to the CIA. Thus began the secret subsidy of free trade unions which soon spread to Italy. Without that subsidy, postwar history might have gone very differently.[51]

CIA payments on the order of $1 million a year guaranteed the Socialist party a strong electoral base in the labor movement[52] and gave its leaders the political strength to lead the attack on striking workers. While Marseille Socialist leader Gaston Defferre called for an anti-Communist crusade from the floor of the National Assembly and in the columns of *Le Provençal*,[53] Socialist Minister of the Interior Jules Moch directed massive police actions against striking workers.[54] With the advice and cooperation of the U.S. military attaché in Paris, Moch requested the call-up of 80,000 reserves and mobilized 200,000 troops to battle the strikers. Faced with this overwhelming force, the CGT called off the strike on December 9, after less than a month on the picket lines.[55]

The bloodiest battleground of the general strike was not Paris, as Braden indicated, but Marseille. Victory in Marseille was essential for U.S. foreign policy. As one of the most important international ports in France, Marseille was a vital beachhead for Marshall Plan exports to Europe. Continued Communist control of its docks would threaten the efficiency of the Marshall Plan and any future aid programs. Because Marseille was the second largest city in France, continued Communist domination of its electorate would increase the chance that the Communist party might win enough votes to form a national government. (The Communist party already controlled 28 percent of the vote and was the largest party in France.)

The growing split between Marseille's Communist and Socialist parties and Defferre's willingness to serve American interests had already been revealed in National Assembly debates over the bloody November 12 incidents in Marseille. Instead of criticizing the Guerinis for beating the municipal councilors and murdering the sheet metal worker, Socialist leader Defferre chose to attack the Communists:

> The American and English flags which were hanging from city hall were slashed by Communist hordes. . . . We have proof

of what the Communists are capable: I trust that the
government will take note of the consequences.

The Socialist Party deplores these incidents, but it will not
tolerate that those who try to pass here as representatives will
be able to defy the law.[56]

Several days later, Communist deputy Jean Cristofol rebutted
Defferre's accusations, charging that the Guerinis' gangsters were in the
employ of both Gaullist and Socialist parties in Marseille. When Defferre
rose to deny even knowing Guerini, another Communist deputy
reminded him that a Guerini cousin was the editor of Defferre's
newspaper, Le Provençal. Then Cristofol took over to reveal some
disturbing signs of the Marseille milieu's revival: underworld collaborators were being paroled from prison and government officials
were allowing milieu nightclubs to reopen, among them the Guerinis'
Parakeet Club. Only six months earlier, Cristofol himself, then
Marseille's mayor, had ordered the clubs closed.[57]

The Socialists' first step in breaking Marseille's strike was to purge
suspected Communist supporters from the CRS police units. Once this
was accomplished these units could be ordered to use violent tactics
against the striking workers. Although official reports had nothing but
praise for the professionalism of these officers,[58] Socialist mayor
Gaston Defferre unjustly accused them of having sided with the
demonstrators during the rioting of November 12.[59] After Socialist
cadres drew up a list of suspected CRS Communists, Defferre passed it
along to Socialist minister Jules Moch, who ordered the blacklisted
officers fired.[60] This action by the Socialists was certainly appreciated
by the hard-pressed Corsican syndicates as well. In contrast to the
regular police, CRS units had been cracking down on the milieu's
smuggling and black market activities.[61] Once these Communist officers
had been purged, CRS units started attacking picket lines with
unrestrained violence.[62]

But it would take more than ordinary police repression to break the
determination of Marseille's 80,000 striking workers. If the United States
was to have its victory in Marseille it would have to fight for it. Through
the CIA, the United States proceeded to do just that.

The CIA, through its contacts with the Socialist party, had sent agents
and a psychological warfare team to Marseille, where they dealt directly
with Corsican syndicate leaders through the Guerini brothers. The CIA's
operatives supplied arms and money to Corsican gangs for assaults on
Communist picket lines and harassment of important union officials.
During the month-long strike the CIA's gangsters and the purged CRS
police units murdered a number of striking workers and mauled the
picket lines. Finally, the CIA psychological warfare team prepared

pamphlets, radio broadcasts, and posters aimed at discouraging workers from continuing the strike.[63] Some of the psy-war team's maneuvers were inspired: at one point the American government threatened to ship 65,000 sacks of flour meant for the hungry city back to the United States unless the dockers unloaded them immediately.[64] The pressure of violence and hunger was too great, and on December 9 Marseille's workers abandoned the strike, along with their fellow workers in the rest of France. There were some ironic finishing touches. On Christmas Eve 1947, eighty-seven boxcars arrived at the Marseille train station carrying flour, milk, sugar, and fruit as "gifts from the American people" amidst the cheers of hundreds of schoolchildren waving tiny American flags.[65]

The Guerinis gained enough power and status from their role in smashing the 1947 strike to emerge as the new leaders of the Corsican underworld. While the CIA was instrumental in restoring the Corsican underworld's political influence, it was not until the 1950 dock strike that the Guerinis gained enough power to take control of the Marseille waterfront. This combination of political influence and control of the docks created the ideal environment for the growth of Marseille's heroin laboratories—fortuitously at the same time that Mafia boss Lucky Luciano was seeking an alternative source of heroin supply.

The same austere economic conditions that had sparked the 1947 strike also produced the 1950 shutdown. Conditions for the workers had not improved in the intervening three years; if anything, they had grown worse. Marseille, with its tradition of working-class militancy, had even more reason for striking than the rest of France. Marseille was France's "Gateway to the Orient," through which material (particularly American munitions and supplies) was transported to the French Expeditionary Corps fighting in Indochina. Among the city's left-wing unions, France's Indochina War was generally unpopular. Moreover, Ho Chi Minh had helped to found the French Communist party and was a popular hero in France among the leftist working class, especially in Marseille with its many resident Indochinese.[66] In January, Marseille dock workers began a selective boycott of those freighters carrying supplies to the war zone. Then on February 3 the CGT convened a meeting of Marseille dock workers, which issued a declaration demanding "the return of the Expeditionary Corps from Indochina to put an end to the war in Vietnam" and urging "all unions to launch the most effective actions possible against the war in Vietnam." The movement of arms shipments to Indochina was "paralyzed."[67] Although the Atlantic ports joined the embargo in early February, that action was not as effective or as important as the Marseille strike.[68] By mid-February, the shutdown had spread to the metal industries, the mines, and the railways.[69] But most of the strikes were halfhearted. On February 18 the Paris newspaper *Combat* reported that Marseille was once again the hard core; 70 percent of Marseille's workers supported the strike, compared with only 2 percent in Bordeaux, 20 percent in Toulouse, and 20 percent in Nice.[70]

Once more Marseille's working-class militancy called for special methods, and the CIA's Thomas Braden later recalled how he dealt with the problem:

> On the desk in front of me as I write these lines is a creased and faded yellow paper. It bears the following inscription in pencil:
>
> "Received from Warren G. Haskins, $15,000 (signed) Norris A. Grambo."
>
> I went in search of this paper on the day the newspapers disclosed the "scandal" of the Central Intelligence Agency's connections with American students and labor leaders. It was a wistful search, and when it ended, I found myself feeling sad.
>
> For I was Warren G. Haskins, Norris A. Grambo was Irving Brown, of the American Federation of Labor. The $15,000 was from the vaults of the CIA, and the yellow paper is the last memento I possess of a vast and secret operation. . . .
>
> It was my idea to give $15,000 to Irving Brown. He needed it to pay off *his strong-arm squads in the Mediterranean ports*, so that American supplies could be unloaded against the opposition of Communist dock workers. [Emphasis added.][71]

With some $2 million in CIA funds channeled through OPC, the AFL's Irving Brown delivered scab laborers from Italy to his Marseille ally, Pierre Ferri-Pisani.[72] Described by *Time* magazine as a "rugged, fiery Corsican," Ferri-Pisani used the Italian scabs and a crew of local Corsican criminals to work the docks, unloading shipments of U.S. weapons and ultimately breaking the strike. Surrounded by his gangster hirelings, Ferri-Pisani stormed into local Communist headquarters and threatened to make the party's leadership "pay personally" for the continuing boycott. As *Time* noted with satisfaction, "The first Communist who tried to fire Ferri-Pisani's men was chucked into the harbor."[73]

In addition, the Guerini's gangsters were assigned the job of pummeling Communist picketers to allow troops and scabs onto the docks, where they could begin loading munitions and supplies. By March 13 government officials were able to announce that, despite a continuing boycott by Communist workers, 900 dockers and supplementary troops had restored normal operations on the Marseille waterfront.[74] Although sporadic boycotts continued until mid-April, Marseille was now subdued and the strike was essentially over.[75]

But there were unforeseen consequences of these cold war victories. In supplying the Corsican syndicates with money and support, the CIA broke the last barrier to unrestricted Corsican smuggling operations in Marseille. When control over the docks was compounded with the political influence the milieu had gained with CIA assistance in 1947, conditions were ideal for Marseille's growth as America's heroin laboratory. The French police later reported that Marseille's first heroin laboratories were opened in 1951, only months after the milieu took over the waterfront.

Gaston Defferre and the Socialist party also emerged victorious when the 1947 and 1950 strikes weakened the local Communist party. After 1953, Defferre and the Socialists enjoyed an unbroken political reign over the Marseille municipal government that lasted a quarter century. Throughout this period, the Guerinis maintained a close relationship with Marseille's Socialists, acting as bodyguards and campaign workers for local Socialist candidates until the family's downfall in 1967.

## The Corsican Milieu

While it is impossible to quantify their precise percentage of the invisible transatlantic heroin trade, Marseille's Corsicans, according to a 1965 survey by the Federal Bureau of Narcotics, had become America's main suppliers. In its "international list" of 246 major traffickers, the bureau demonstrated that the Corsicans, through their heroin laboratories and smuggling networks, had linked Turkey's opium fields with New York's heroin market for the previous fifteen years. Protected by their national and local political patrons, the major Corsican heroin brokers worked through criminal subcontractors to import morphine from Lebanon, process it into heroin in Marseille's laboratories, and then export high-grade powder to American Mafia distributors through criminal associates in Canada and the Caribbean.

Marseille's role as the Mediterranean's heroin free port relied on a small cadre of skilled Corsican chemists who produced high-grade, no. 4 heroin. At peak in 1965, Marseille syndicates operated some twenty to twenty-five clandestine laboratories with outputs ranging from 50 to 150 kilograms per month. Although operations were intermittent and loosely structured, this illicit industry still demonstrated a certain efficiency. Responding to rising U.S. demand, Marseille's laboratories doubled their output in just five years, exporting an estimated 4.8 tons of pure heroin to the United States in 1965.[76]

These Corsican syndicates were not large, quasi-military hierarchies with all aspects of the trade under their direct control. Often consisting of brothers or close friends, Marseille's Corsican cells had two essential elements that sustained their clandestine commerce—local political protection and a global criminal network. A trace of the linkages noted in the FBN's "international list" shows how major Marseille brokers supplied the U.S. heroin market through loose networks of "associates" that extended from Turkey to New York.

François Spirito was still associated with a Corsican smuggling network that reached New York and included Jean-Baptiste Giacobetti, a Marseille Corsican who "financed large quantities of heroin, usually in 50 kilogram lots, for shipment to the United States"; Antoine D'Agostino, a Corsican who was "engaged in the smuggling of large quantities of narcotics into the United States from France"; and Giacomo Reina, a "member of the Gaetano Lucchese organization in New York City which is engaged in narcotics."

Younger and more powerful, Corsica-born Marcel Francisci managed a network from his Parisian casino that integrated every phase of the heroin trade. In Marseille, his brothers Jeannot and Zeze organized "the importation of morphine base from the Middle East"; and their Corsican contact Gabriel Carcassonne "operated a clandestine laboratory in Marseille." After the morphine was processed, local associate Dominique Venturi organized "the smuggling of heroin from French clandestine laboratories to Canada, utilizing the services of his brother." Finally, from his home in Montreal, brother Jean Venturi, described as "one of the major distributors of heroin to the United States," worked closely with Quebec's Guiseppe Cotroni, "head of Canada's largest narcotics syndicate having . . . furnished huge amounts of heroin to . . . distributors in New York City headed by Carmine Galante" and his successor Joseph "Bayonne Joe" Zicarelli, "a dominant figure in Northern New Jersey . . . narcotic activities."

Reflecting his preeminent position within the milieu, Barthélemy Guerini was Marseille's leading heroin merchant. The bureau reported that he "finance[d] various criminal activities in the Marseille area, particularly the illicit narcotics traffic" and described him as "an arbiter and overlord in the Marseille underworld" with associates among the "top echelon of French narcotic traffickers." From his Bar de la Méditerranée in Marseille and his Bar Ascot at Cannes, Guerini associated with Achille Cecchini, who "organize[d] the importation of morphine base from the Middle East," and Antoine Cordoliani, who "supplie[d] heroin to various important traffickers in Marseille" from his "clandestine heroin laboratory installed near Marseille." As testimony to the strength of his political connections, Guerini had "never been convicted" despite his prominence in the Marseille milieu.[77]

The control of the Guerini brothers over Marseille's heroin industry was so complete that for nearly twenty years they were able to impose an absolute ban on drug peddling inside France at the same time they were exporting vast quantities of heroin to the United States. After their decline through a long, losing vendetta against Marcel Francisci in the mid-1960s, their embargo on domestic drug trafficking became unenforceable, and France developed a heroin problem of its own.[78]

## The Guerini-Francisci Vendetta

From its very beginning, postwar heroin production in Marseille had been so dominated by the Guerinis and their operations were so extensive that some of their subordinates, such as Dominique and Jean Venturi, earned independent reputations as major traffickers. Their only serious rival was Marcel Francisci, the owner of an international gambling syndicate. In the 1960s, the Federal Bureau of Narcotics described Francisci as a longtime "understudy" to Spirito and "an equally important figure in the French underworld,"[79] while its intelligence files noted that Francisci "participated with his brothers in organizing the smuggling into France of morphine base produced in the Middle East."[80] Born at Giamammacce, Corsica, in 1919, Francisci was a veteran of the wartime resistance and was awarded four medals for his heroics.[81] While Marcel lived in Paris and frequented fine restaurants such as Fouquets on the Champs Elysées, his two younger brothers, Jeannot and Zeze, lived in Marseille where they managed the family's interests in the city's heroin trade.[82] Although they coexisted happily enough throughout the 1950s, when the Guerinis clearly had the upper hand, Francisci's growing influence in the 1960s produced serious tensions. Competition over control of some casino interests provided the spark, and a silent war began in 1965 that continued for three years with little more than extended obituary notices in the French press.

In late 1967, two gangsters tried to demolish Francisci's Corsican villa with 220 pounds of explosives, and six months later two snipers tried to assassinate him in a public square. After the two suspected snipers were found murdered in Paris, a police investigation uncovered their associations with Jean-Baptiste Andreani, a Paris casino owner associated with the Guerinis.[83] Following these attempts on Francisci's life, three more Guerini associates were found murdered. In the end the Guerinis were decisively defeated. On June 23, 1967, two assassins pumped eleven bullets into Antoine Guerini in a Marseille gas station.[84] Antoine's murder marked the beginning of the end for the Guerini dynasty, and Barthélemy's downfall was not long in coming.

During Antoine's funeral at Calenzana, Corsica, on July 4, two Marseille burglars took advantage of the absence of the family retainers to break into Antoine's villa and steal family jewelry worth thousands of dollars.[85] Unless Barthélemy acted quickly to avenge his brother's death and catch the burglars, the blow to his prestige would destroy his authority over the milieu. Barthélemy's rage did not go unnoticed, and on July 10 one of the burglars, Jean Paul Mandroyan, returned the jewels, while the other thief fled to Spain. On July 22 the police found Mandroyan shot dead—and a witness reported that he had seen Barthélemy forcing Mandroyan into his Mercedes just before the young burglar's murder. On August 4 police entered the Guerinis' Club Méditerranée and arrested Barthélemy and his five bodyguards. All six were armed.[86]

Barthélemy's trial began on schedule on January 5, 1970, but from the beginning the prosecution suffered reverses. In his distinguished black suit, carefully trimmed hair, and a red lapel pin indicating his wartime decoration, Barthélemy hardly looked the part of a desperate gangster. On the second day of the trial, the key prosecution witness retracted his testimony.[87] A road test proved that it was impossible for Barthélemy's Mercedes to have been the murderer's car. With each day of testimony the prosecution's case grew weaker, as the defense attorney demonstrated that most of the state's evidence was circumstantial. In his summation, the prosecutor could not help admitting his failure and demanded that the Guerini gang must be sentenced, not so much because of their possible guilt, but because they were criminal types who were a menace to Marseille.[88]

On January 15 the court returned a verdict of guilty: Barthélemy received twenty years; his younger brother Pascal and two others, fifteen years apiece. Spectators screamed "scandal." Cries of "This is justice?" were heard. And the defendants themselves shouted, "Innocent, innocent, innocent."[89]

Why were the Guerinis convicted? There had been serious accusations against them in the past that could have become solid cases had the Ministry of Justice been interested. But the Guerinis were guaranteed immunity to local investigations by their relationship with Marseille's Socialists. However, by 1967 Socialist party influence had declined substantially after a decade of Gaullist rule. Francisci, according to informed French observers, had earned considerable political influence through his services to the Gaullist government. During the early 1960s, he had helped organize a group of Corsican gangsters known popularly as the *barbouzes* to combat a right-wing terrorist campaign following General de Gaulle's announcement of Algerian independence. As the owner of Paris's most exclusive casino, Cercle Haussmann, Francisci was in daily contact with high-ranking government officials.[90] He was a close personal friend of a former Gaullist cabinet minister and was himself a Gaullist provincial counselor in Corsica.

In the aftermath of Barthélemy Guerini's conviction, the balance of power in the Marseille heroin trade shifted somewhat. The Guerini family's reduced fortunes were represented by Pierre, a younger brother, and Barthélemy's wife, a former nightclub dancer. The Guerini decline was matched by the growing influence of the Venturi brothers, longtime Guerini associates, as well as by Francisci himself. In 1972 the U.S. Bureau of Narcotics labeled Jean Venturi the "major distributor of French heroin into the United States" and described his younger brother Dominique as "his major source of supply."[91] The Venturis also seem to have inherited the Guerinis' influence with Marseille's Socialist party; during the city elections it was their men who served as Mayor Defferre's bodyguards. Interestingly, in February 1972 *The New York Times* reported that Dominique Venturi's contracting firm was "redoing the Marseille town hall for the city's Socialist Mayor Gaston Defferre."[92] Although Marcel Francisci publicly denied any involvement in the drug traffic, the FBN had long identified him as a principal in the smuggling of morphine from the Middle East to Marseille.[93]

Francisci was not the only gangster associated with the ruling Gaullist party. The FBN believed that the Gaullists replaced corrupt Marseille politicians as the milieu's most important protectors, and some U.S. narcotics agents were quite concerned about the complicity of high-level French intelligence officials in the narcotics traffic.

During the May revolution of 1968, when thousands of students and workers surged through the streets of Paris, barricades were thrown up, and government buildings were occupied, General de Gaulle's government came close to crumbling. To aid the restoration of public order, Jacques Foccart, the general's top intelligence adviser, organized five thousand men, many of them Corsican and French gangsters, into the Service d'Action Civique (SAC). While there were known criminals in SAC's rank and file, police officers and top intelligence officials took on positions of responsibility within the organization. SAC was assigned such tasks as silencing hecklers at pro-Gaullist rallies, breaking up opposition demonstrations, and providing bodyguards for cabinet ministers and high government officials.[94] When President Georges Pompidou inspected the Concorde supersonic aircraft at Toulouse in August 1971, five hundred SAC men turned out to protect him. The same month another five hundred were mobilized to maintain harmony at the Gaullist party's national convention.[95] In addition, both the national police and SDECE (a French equivalent of the CIA) used SAC to execute "dirty" missions that would have compromised their regular agents.[96]

In exchange for their services, SAC men were protected from police investigation and given safe-conduct passes—necessary for their more sensitive assignments—which granted them immunity to stop-and-search by police.[97] In spite of SAC's protection, there were occasional slipups, and, according to the U.S. Bureau of Narcotics, at least ten SAC gangsters were arrested in France carrying major shipments of heroin during 1970–1971. In the fall of 1970, when the police arrested Serge Constant, a member of SAC in Nice, and charged him with having smuggled two heroin shipments into the United States, he threatened them, saying, "We have protection, so watch your step." A Grenoble bar proprietor named Mrs. Bonnet was arrested with 105 pounds of heroin destined for the United States in her car. She was the widow of SAC leader Matthieu Bonnet, who had chauffeured President Pompidou during the 1967 election. In September 1971 a notorious heroin courier, Ange Simonpiéri, was finally arrested after a Swiss lawyer accused the Gaullists of protecting him on a prime-time radio show. Predictably, Simonpiéri was a retired *barbouze* and a close friend of the Gaullist deputy who organized a "parallel police" group in 1961.[98]

Moreover, informed observers were convinced that some of SDECE's top intelligence officers had been organizing narcotics shipments to the United States to finance SAC operations, using SDECE's counterintelligence net to protect their shipments. Although U.S. narcotics agents working undercover against French heroin traffickers had little fear of being unmasked by the milieu, they became increasingly concerned about being discovered by SDECE. In early 1971, for example, a U.S. undercover narcotics agent met with representatives of Marseille's biggest heroin syndicate in a New York City hotel room. Posing as an American mafioso, the undercover agent offered to purchase a hundred kilos of heroin and agreed to pay a top price. Convinced that they were dealing with a real American gangster, the Corsican smugglers flew back to Marseille, elated at their success, and began to put together the shipment. However, just as they were about to depart for New York and walk into a carefully laid trap, another Corsican gangster phoned to warn them that the American mafioso was really a U.S. narcotics agent. Incredulous, the smugglers asked the informant over the phone, "How do you know?" And the caller responded, "Colonel —— passed this information on to me." According to informed observers, that colonel was a high-ranking SDECE intelligence officer. As these observers admitted, some corrupt elements of SDECE seem to have done a good job of penetrating their undercover network.

The extent of SDECE's involvement in the heroin trade was finally exposed in November 1971, when a New Jersey prosecutor indicted Colonel Paul Fournier, one of SDECE's top supervisory agents, for conspiring to smuggle 45 kilos of heroin into the United States. On April 5 a U.S. customs inspector assigned to the Elizabeth, New Jersey, waterfront had discovered the heroin concealed in a Volkswagen camper and arrested its owner, a retired SDECE agent named Roger de

Louette. After confessing his role in the affair, de Louette claimed that he was only working as a courier for Colonel Fournier.[99] Fournier's indictment rated banner headlines in the French press and prompted former high-ranking SDECE officials to come forward with some startling allegations about SDECE's involvement in the heroin traffic.[100]

Even with SDECE's clandestine support, however, Marseille's days as the heroin capital of Europe were numbered. The Guerinis' collapse threw open the field to younger gangsters with little respect for their ban on drug peddling inside France. As one of France's top police officials put it, "These new guys are guys who don't follow the rules. With tougher U.S. suppression effort, the cost of smuggling got too much for some of them, so they took the easy way out and began to sell here." Within two years after Antoine Guerini's death and Barthélemy's incarceration, France itself was in the grip of an escalating heroin plague. By early 1972 fifteen out of every thousand French army draftees were being rejected because of drug addiction, and Marseille itself had an addict population estimated at anywhere from 5,000 to 20,000. As France developed a drug crisis of its own, the French government dropped its rather blasé attitude and declared narcotics "France's number one police problem." Marseille's police narcotics unit was expanded from eight officers in 1969 to seventy-seven only two years later. The stepped-up police effort scored several spectacular heroin seizures and prompted speculation in the French press that Marseille's heroin manufacturers might eventually be forced out of business.[101]

These French police operations, supported by President Richard Nixon's "war on drugs," produced a major assault on Marseille's heroin industry. As U.S. diplomatic pressure on the Turkish front forced the abolition of opium production and slowed the supply of Middle Eastern morphine, French police enjoyed unprecedented success against Marseille's syndicates.

The campaign began in October 1971 when a joint DEA-French operation arrested Corsican trafficker André Labay in Paris with 106 kilograms of no. 4 heroin. Following leads from this seizure, French police filed charges that produced heavy sentences for sixteen syndicate members. Four months later, French officers found 415 kilograms of heroin on a fishing boat, *Caprice des Temps*, at sea near Marseille—establishing a new world record for heroin seizures.[102] Most significantly, the French then raided a Marseille laboratory, apprehending 119 kilograms of heroin and arresting veteran Corsican drug broker Joseph Cesari.[103] Similar French-American operations produced a wave of prosecutions against a Corsican milieu that had operated with impunity for decades.

In 1973, the DEA's Paris agent reported that police actions in Marseille had reduced French drug exports and had "contributed considerably to the present heroin shortage on the eastern seaboard of the United States."[104] Citing the arrest of many of the milieu's *gros bonnets*, the head of Marseille's narcotics police noted that "it appears impossible to obtain pure heroin in Marseille" because "the suppliers have almost disappeared."[105]

## Decline of the European Heroin Trade

By the early 1970s, police pressure in Marseille, combined with Turkey's ban on opium cultivation, brought to an end the European heroin trade as it had operated since the late 1940s. A mix of police operations, heroin seizures, poppy eradication, and Mafia violence disrupted the smooth flow of heroin out of the Mediterranean basin. After the Turkey-Marseille corridor collapsed, leading U.S. heroin brokers were forced into a major reorganization of the trade. By the time Corsican and Sicilian syndicates revived the Mediterranean trade in the late 1970s, American drug syndicates had found new sources of heroin in Asia and Latin America. In an expanded global heroin traffic, European dealers could no longer dominate the U.S. market.

Denied political refuge in Marseille, the Corsican laboratories closed for several years before reappearing, scattered across southern France and down the length of Italy. After five years without any signs of illicit manufacturing, French police seized several laboratories in 1978 and 1979. More significantly, Italian police found their first heroin laboratory in November 1979 and, over the next ten months, raided five more in locations ranging from a medieval castle near Milan in the north to a modern villa in Palermo in the south.

Each raid produced evidence of a close alliance between Corsican syndicates and the Sicilian Mafia. When French police raided the first of these new laboratories at La Ciotat near Marseille in February 1978, the DEA reported that the 40 kilograms of morphine base seized "had been delivered to the laboratory by Italian traffickers." Similarly, in August 1979, Italian police intercepted 2.5 kilograms in Sicily, part of a 6-kilogram shipment en route from a Corsican laboratory near Nice to American mafiosi waiting for delivery in Palermo.[106] In June 1980, the Italian police assault on laboratories concealed in the Milan castle found four Corsican chemists and evidence that led to the arrest of the legendary Marseille broker Jean Jehan, inspiration for the nemesis in the two *French Connection* films.[107]

In retrospect, the French police campaign against the Marseille milieu seems to have forced the Corsicans into a closer alliance with the

Sicilian Mafia. As the Corsicans began moving their operations across the border into Italy, the Mafia's role in the Mediterranean traffic suddenly expanded in the early 1970s, producing a new round of mafiosi murders in Sicily. Losing none of their capacity for violence and vendetta, Sicilian families, particularly Palermo's "new mafia," had been battling over the heroin trade since the mid-1950s.

In Sicily a costly eight-year battle (1955–1963) between the "old" and the "new" Mafia factions had reduced the "honored society" to its weakest state since the end of World War II. The "old" Mafia was made up of traditional rural gangsters, the semi-literate tyrants who ruled by fear and exploited the impoverished peasants. In contrast, the "new" Mafia was attracted by the modern business methods and the international heroin smuggling that Lucky Luciano and his American deportee cohorts had introduced in the late 1940s. Moreover, Sicily was changing and so was its Mafia. As the landed estates began a "gradual disintegration" in the late 1940s and the poorest peasants migrated to the cities of Italy's industrial north, the unjust rural order that had required Mafia violence for its protection was disappearing.[108] During the 1950s, rural mafiosi migrated to the booming capital Palermo on Sicily's northern coast, with each Mafia family controlling city districts and killing to expand its territory. In 1955 Palermo's violence began with a battle over the city's food market that left sixty mafiosi dead by the end of the year.[109] In the first three years of the ensuing war eighteen major mafiosi and countless minor gunmen were eliminated.[110]

Weakened by the enormous cost in leadership, the feud subsided, but it broke out again in 1963 when part of a heroin shipment was stolen by a courier en route to the United States. It was a singularly inopportune moment for headline murders, as the Mafia itself was well aware, for a parliamentary investigating commission was finally looking into the Mafia. Even though the honored society's grand council ordered a moratorium for the duration of the inquiry, passions could not be restrained, and the murders began again. The fast Alfa Romeo sedans favored by mafiosi were being blown up in Palermo with such frequency that the mere sight of one parked was enough for the police to clear the street.

The violence finally produced a reaction from Rome after seven police were killed when a Mafia car bomb exploded in Palermo's Ciaculli district. Called to investigate a theft of an Alfa Romeo, the police officers were vaporized when they opened the trunk and 200 pounds of dynamite exploded, destroying a nearby villa and leaving a large crater in the street. On orders from Rome, the Italian army's regional commander for Sicily, General Aldo de Marco, swept Palermo with 10,000 troops and made 1,903 arrests of suspected mafiosi.

The Parliamentary Commission of Inquiry into the Activities of the Mafia began in the midst of the explosions, and its reports contained the first serious legislative suggestions for combating the venerable society.[111] In 1964, 800 mafiosi were arrested in a major sweep and locked up in Palermo prison. The arrests continued: in 1968, 113 more were arrested (though many subsequently released), and in May 1971, 33 of the top leadership were exiled to Filicudi and Linosa islands.[112] Faced with a repression that exceeded even that of Mussolini's Fascist government in the 1920s, many Mafiosi sought refuge in rural Sicily or fled to the Americas.[113]

After these last arrests, however, the repression slowed and the "new" Mafia began to emerge in Sicily, fueled by its expanded role in the heroin trade. According to later testimony by mafioso Tomasso Buscetta before a Palermo court, the original Mafia commission had "scattered" during the fighting of 1963 and did not revive until the early 1970s.[114] Using their contacts with migrant mafiosi in America, the Sicilians began working as brokers by purchasing heroin from Mediterranean suppliers and arranging their own smuggling operations.

U.S. narcotics agents first learned of this new operation on September 24, 1971, when they stopped a twenty-nine-year-old Sicilian migrant named Francisco Rappa, an employee of Piancone Pizzeria in Perth Amboy, New Jersey, and arrested him for possession of 86 kilograms of heroin.[115] Investigators later learned that the heroin had been shipped from Sicily by Gaetano Badalamenti, the new boss of the Mafia commission, and its intended recipients were his nephews, owners of the Perth Amboy pizzeria and leading heroin distributors.[116] In the late 1970s, the Sicilians, by allying more closely with the Corsicans and extending their sources to Asia, would become global heroin brokers. But as the Rappa arrest shows, the first Sicilian smuggling efforts of the early 1970s were often inept and would require several years to achieve the sophistication of the early Corsican operations.

The most important blow the the Mediterranean heroin complex came in 1967, when the Turkish government announced plans to reduce, and eventually abolish, opium production. The U.S. government contributed $3 million to build up a special 750-man police narcotics unit, finance research for substitute crops, and improve the managerial efficiency of the government regulatory agency, the Turkish Marketing Organization.[117] By early 1972, Turkey had reduced its opium-growing provinces from twenty-one to four. In those areas where poppy production had been prohibited, "U.S. agents have reported little evidence of illicit production, . . . and such crops when found have been immediately destroyed."[118] After the Nixon Administration used a mixture of diplomatic pressure and promises of $35 million in aid, the Turkish government imposed a total opium ban after the 1972 harvest.

There were immediate signs that Turkey's ban had severely disrupted global drug traffic. In March 1972, French police made their last seizure of Middle East morphine when they arrested Turkish Senator Kudret Bayhan for smuggling 321 pounds of morphine base. As Turkey's poppy fields went out of production, its usual illicit markets, Iran and America, experienced a sharp drop in drug smuggling. Iran's seizures of illicit Turkish opium fell from 8,000 kilograms in 1969 to only 200 in 1973. Reflecting the same trend, total U.S. heroin seizures declined from 1,036 pounds in 1971 to only 481 pounds in 1973.[119] Since Turkey's poppy fields were the major source of raw materials for Marseille's heroin laboratories, the impact of the Turkish government's declaration was obvious. According to analysts at the Federal Bureau of Narcotics, the Corsican syndicates "saw the handwriting on the wall" and quickly realized that they would have to find an alternative source of opium if their lucrative drug racket were to survive.[120]

Thus, the international heroin trade was at a crossroads in the late 1960s. If it were to continue, a major effort would be required to reorganize the traffic. This could hardly be done by letter or telephone but would necessitate the personal intervention of a high-ranking underworld figure. As in any other business enterprise, the leaders of organized crime have little to do with daily operations but are the only ones who can initiate major corporate changes or new enterprises. While ordinary businesspeople transact much of their basic negotiations by telephone, correspondence, and intermediaries, police surveillance and telephone taps make these methods impractical for the tycoons of organized crime. Moreover, mafiosi do not sign binding contracts with other gangsters and can hardly take a partner to court if he fails to honor an agreement. Therefore, it is one of the basic characteristics of organized crime that all important deals require a meeting of the bosses involved so that they can exchange their personal "word of honor." This need for face-to-face discussions also explains why Mafia leaders have repeatedly exposed themselves to conspiracy indictments and banner headlines by arranging large underworld conferences, such as the ill-fated 1957 Apalachin meeting.

After Luciano's death in 1962, the logical successors to his leadership in the narcotics trade were his two subordinates Meyer Lansky and Vito Genovese. However, in 1958 Genovese had been indicted for heroin trafficking by a New York court and was later sentenced to fifteen years imprisonment. Although he continued to direct many of his enterprises from the Atlanta federal penitentiary, where he was treated with great respect by prisoners and guards alike, he was in no position to conduct the reorganization of the narcotics trade.[121] Lansky at sixty-six was now too old and too carefully watched to repeat his 1949 business trip. By November 1970, when he retired to Israel, he had already turned over much of the major decision making to his subordinates.[122] Thus, by death and default, the responsibility logically fell to Santo Trafficante, Jr.

At fifty-seven Trafficante was one of the most effective organized crime leaders then operating in the United States. Avoiding the ostentatious lifestyle of Cadillacs and diamonds that was so attractive to many mafiosi, Trafficante cultivated the austerity of the old Sicilian dons. But unlike the old Sicilians, he managed the organization with reason rather than force and was one of the few major Mafia leaders whose "family" was not torn apart by internal power struggles or vendettas with other families.[123] Despite his prestige within the organization, Trafficante's good sense prevented him from campaigning for a leading position on the Mafia's national commission. This self-effacing attitude no doubt accounted for his personal safety and considerable influence. Through his studious avoidance of publicity, he was one of the least known and most underestimated leaders of organized crime.

Trafficante himself was reportedly involved in the narcotics traffic only at the level of financing and crisis management; he never saw, much less handled, any heroin. His organization was so airtight, and he was so discreet, that federal narcotics agents considered him virtually untouchable.[124] In its 1965 "international list" of narcotics traffickers, the Federal Bureau of Narcotics described Trafficante as a "powerful Mafia figure in Tampa, Florida" who "knows most of the major sources of supply of narcotics in Central and South America. Suspected of smuggling narcotics into the United States."[125]

Trafficante's territory was Florida and the Caribbean, where he served as one of Meyer Lanksy's chief retainers. During the late 1940s and 1950s Trafficante was heavily involved in Luciano's and Lansky's heroin smuggling operations, and after his father's death in 1954 he succeeded him as Mafia boss of Florida and fell heir to his relationship with Lansky. Trafficante always did his best to look after Lansky's interests. When Anastasia, the head of Murder, Inc., tried to open a competing casino in Meyer Lansky's Havana in 1957, Trafficante arranged a friendly meeting with him in New York. An hour after Trafficante checked out of the Park-Sheraton Hotel, three gunmen murdered Anastasia in the hotel barbershop.[126]

The Cuban revolution in 1959 forced Trafficante to write off his valuable Havana casino operations as a total loss, but he was partially compensated by the subsequent flood of Cuban refugees to Miami. His association with leading Cuban gangsters and corrupt politicians when he was living in Havana enabled him to expand his control over the Florida *bolita* lottery, a Cuban numbers game, which became enormously lucrative when the refugees started pouring into Florida in 1960.[127] By recruiting Cubans into Trafficante's organization to expand the *bolita* lottery, organized crime may have acquired a new group of narcotics couriers and distributors who were unknown to American police or Interpol. With Latin couriers, new routes could be opened up, bringing European heroin into Miami through Latin America.

The Mafia's transfer of narcotics importation and distribution to its new Cuban associates caused some confusion in the press; many analysts misinterpreted the appearance of Cuban and South American couriers and distributors to mean that organized crime had given up the heroin trade. The Justice Department's "Operation Eagle" revealed something of this new organization in June 1970 when 350 federal narcotics agents made 139 arrests "in the largest federal law enforcement operation ever conducted against a single narcotics distribution ring." Although the arrests were carried out in ten cities, the Bureau of Narcotics stated that all five of the ringleaders were Spanish-speaking and three were Cubans residing in Miami.[128] In addition, federal authorities reported that bulk heroin seizures in the Miami area increased 100 percent during 1971, indicating that the beachfront city had remained a major distribution hub.[129]

While the recruitment of Cuban gangsters may have solved the problems with couriers and distributors, the Mafia still had to find an alternative source of morphine base and, if possible, a reserve source of heroin in case of problems in Marseille and Europe. There were a number of alternatives, among which Southeast Asia was the most promising. While Mexico had been refining small amounts of low-grade, brown heroin for a number of years, its syndicates had never been able to produce the fine white powder demanded by American addicts. Though India and Afghanistan had some lively local opium smuggling, they had no connections with the international criminal syndicates. But Southeast Asia was already growing more than 70 percent of the world's illicit opium, and the Chinese laboratories in Hong Kong were producing some of the finest heroin in the world. Moreover, entrenched Corsican syndicates based in Vietnam and Laos had been supplying the international markets, including Marseille and Hong Kong, with opium and morphine base for almost a decade. Obviously this was an area ripe for expansion.

In 1947, when Lucky Luciano wanted to use Havana as a narcotics transfer point, he went there personally. And just before Marseille embarked on large-scale heroin production for the American market in 1951–1952, Meyer Lansky went to Europe and met with Corsican leaders in Paris and on the Riviera.

So in 1968, in the tradition of the Mafia, Santo Trafficante, Jr., went to Saigon, Hong Kong, and Singapore.[130]

# 3

## Opium for the Natives

WHEN SANTO TRAFFICANTE, JR., BOARDED A COMMERCIAL JET for the flight to Southeast Asia, he was probably unaware that Western adventurers had been coming to Asia for hundreds of years to make their fortunes in the narcotics trade. Earlier adventurers had flown the flags of the Portuguese Empire, the British East India Company, and the French Republic; Trafficante was a representative of the American Mafia. He was traveling on a jet aircraft, but they had come in tiny, wooden-hulled Portuguese caravels, British men-of-war, and steel-ribbed steamships. With their superior military technology, these agents of empire used their warships to open up China and Southeast Asia for their opium merchants and conquered the Asian landmass, dividing it into spheres and colonies. Empire builders subjected millions of natives to opium addiction, generating revenues for colonial development and providing profits for European stockholders. Thus, the Mafia was following a long tradition of Western drug trafficking in Asia—but with one important difference. It was not interested in selling Asian opium to the Asians; it was trying to buy Asian heroin for Americans.

The rise of large-scale heroin production in Southeast Asia is the culmination of four hundred years of Western intervention. In the 1500s European merchants introduced opium smoking; in the 1700s the British East India Company became Asia's first large-scale opium smuggler, forcibly supplying an unwilling China; and in the 1800s every European colony had its official opium dens. At almost every stage of its development, Asia's narcotics traffic has been influenced by the rise and fall of Western empires.

Before the first Portuguese ships arrived in the 1500s, opium smoking and the long-distance drug trade were not well developed in Asia. Like most cultures in most times, early Asian societies used a variety of drugs—rice wine, coconut wine, betel nut—for both recreation and medication. Discovered and domesticated in Neolithic times, opium first appeared in Greek medical documents during the fifth century B.C. and in those of the Chinese during the eighth century A.D. In his poem "The Cultivation of the Medicinal Plant Poppy," written around 970 A.D., Su Che rhapsodized that the poppy's "seeds are like autumn millet; when ground they yield a sap like cow's milk; when boiled they become a drink fit for Buddha." The pharmacopeia of Su Sung, compiled in 1057 A.D., noted that the "poppy is found everywhere" and advised that "in cases of nausea, it will be found serviceable to administer a decoction of poppy seeds."[1] From such slender evidence, we can infer that opium was first cultivated in the eastern Mediterranean and spread gradually along Asia's trade routes to India, reaching China by the eighth century A.D.

Although the poppy spread along the southern rim of Asia in medieval times, opium was used mainly for medication and its cultivation was still limited. It was not until the fifteenth century that opium became a regular item in intra-Asian trade to supply Persians and Indians who used it as a recreational euphoric. Indeed, under the reign of Akbar (1556–1605), the great Mogul state of northern India relied on opium land as a significant source of revenue. Although cultivation covered the whole Mogul empire, it was concentrated in two main areas—upriver from Calcutta in the east along the Ganges Valley for "Bengal opium" and upcountry from Bombay in the west for "Malwa opium."[2]

Europe's Age of Discovery coincided with the start of Asia's modern opium trade. Only six years after Columbus crossed the Atlantic, Portuguese explorer Vasco da Gama rounded the tip of Africa and became the first European sea captain to reach India. Later Portuguese captains ventured farther east, encountering some resistance from the Muslim captains who controlled the lively, long-distance trade that reached from Arabia to China. Realizing that he needed strategic ports to control the sea lanes, the Portuguese captain Affonso de Albuquerque occupied Goa on India's west coast in 1510 and the next year conquered the great port of Malacca on the Malay Peninsula. Over the next half century, Portugal's constellation of coastal enclaves extended north up the China coast to Macao and east to the Spice Islands of Indonesia.

Like the Dutch and British who followed, the Portuguese found that the spices, textiles, and porcelains of Asia commanded a high price in

Europe, but few European goods found a market in Asia. To sustain commerce without exhausting their supply of gold and silver coin, Portuguese captains had to finance their business by becoming brokers in the intra-Asian trade. Fortifying their small coastal enclaves against attack, the Portuguese sortied out into the sea lanes from the Red Sea to the South China Sea, confiscating native cargoes, plundering rival ports, and expropriating the local trade.

As the Portuguese fought Chinese, Japanese, Indians, and Arabs for control of Asia's seaborne trade, they soon realized the potential of opium. "If your Highness would believe me," the conqueror Albuquerque wrote his monarch from India in 1513, "I would order poppies . . . to be sown in all the fields of Portugal and command *afyam* [opium] to be made . . . and the laborers would gain much also, and people of India are lost without it, if they do not eat it."[3] From their ports in western India, the Portuguese began exporting Malwa opium to China, competing aggressively with Indian and Arab merchants who had once controlled this trade.[4] Eager for another commodity to barter for Chinese silks, the Portuguese also began importing tobacco from their Brazilian colony half a world away.

Although the Chinese frustrated Portuguese hopes by growing their own tobacco, the tobacco pipe itself, which had been introduced by the Spanish, turned out to be the key to China's riches. Indian opium mixed with tobacco and smoked through a pipe was pleasing to the Chinese palate. This fad first became popular among the overseas Chinese of Southeast Asia, and Dutch merchants witnessed Chinese smoking an opium-tobacco mixture in Indonesia as early as 1617.[5] By the early eighteenth century, opium smoking was growing so rapidly in China that the Emperor Yung Chen banned the practice in 1729, an edict that did little to stem its spread.

Arriving in Asia a century after the Portuguese, the Dutch proved aggressive competitors for control of the region's opium trade. Sailing directly across the Indian Ocean from Africa to the Indies in 1599, a Dutch fleet of twenty-two ships established a temporary enclave on Java and returned to Europe with a fabulous cargo of spices. Instead of extending themselves across the whole of Asia as the Portuguese had done, the Dutch concentrated their fleets in the Indonesian archipelago, establishing a permanent port at Jakarta in 1619 and battling desperately for decades to secure their hold over the sprawling Indies. In 1640, the Dutch East India Company began purchasing the Malwa opium of western India for export to the Indies, where there was already a small market. After the price of the Malwa variety became prohibitive, the Dutch began buying larger shipments of Bengal opium from eastern India. As Dutch colonials negotiated monopoly rights for Java's populous districts, their company's opium imports from India rose dramatically, from 617 kilograms in 1660 to 72,280 kilograms only twenty-five years later. Dutch profits from the opium trade were spectacular. Buying opium cheaply in India and selling it high in Java allowed the company a 400 percent profit on its 1679 shipments. The Asian merchants who landed at Jakarta with cargoes of silk, porcelains, tin, and sugar for the Dutch began accepting Indian opium as payment. By 1681, opium represented 34 percent of the cargo on Asian ships sailing out of Jakarta.[6] No longer a lightweight luxury or medical item, opium was becoming a basic trade commodity. In 1699, the Dutch imported 87 tons of Indian opium for distribution to Java and the Indies.[7]

Although the last Europeans to enter the trade, it was the British who finally transformed opium from luxury good to bulk commodity. The British East India Company had acquired coastal enclaves at Calcutta in 1656 and at Bombay in 1661 but did not enter the opium trade for another fifty years. In the interim, a syndicate of Indian merchants up the Ganges River at Patna held a monopoly over the Bengal opium trade, making cash advances to peasant farmers and selling the processed opium to Dutch, British, and French merchants. Marching inland from their port at Calcutta, the British conquered Bengal in 1764 and soon discovered the financial potential of India's richest opium zone.

## Opium for the Pipes of China

In 1773, the modern era in the Asian opium trade began when Warren Hastings, the new governor-general of Bengal, established a colonial monopoly on the sale of opium. As the East India Company expanded production, opium became India's main export, traded with a volume and commercial sophistication unknown during its earlier phase as an item in the intra-Asian trade. Over the next 130 years, Britain actively promoted the export of Indian opium to China, defying Chinese drug laws and fighting two wars to open China's opium market for its merchants. Using its military and mercantile power, Britain played a central role in making China a vast drug market and in accelerating opium cultivation throughout China. By 1900 China had 13.5 million addicts consuming 39,000 tons of opium. When Britain formally abandoned its advocacy of the drug trade in August 1907, opium was a global commodity comparable in every respect to coffee, cacao, tea, or tobacco. China itself harvested 35,000 tons of opium, making its own crop comparable in bulk to Japan's tea harvest (31,000 tons), Brazil's cacao yield (39,000 tons), and Colombia's coffee production (55,000 tons).[8]

With a unanimous vote of approval from Bengal's colonial council on

November 23, 1773, Governor Hastings abolished the Indian opium syndicate at Patna and established a state monopoly on sound principles that were to operate for the next half century. Under the new regulations, the East India Company or its agents had the exclusive right to purchase opium from Bengal's farmers and auction it for export. Realizing that opium was a harmful drug, Hastings tried to limit production to a level sufficient to stabilize the colony's chaotic finances. Most important, he barred the company from handling the drug beyond its auction halls in the port of Calcutta. The company's ships that called at China's ports to load tea were not allowed to carry opium, leaving actual sale of the addictive drug in China and the Indies to the private European merchants who bid at the Calcutta auctions.[9]

From the outset, the trade's corrupting character defeated the company's bid for propriety in such a sordid business. Instead of collecting opium directly from the farmers, Hastings had reserved the right to sell this service to a private contractor. In 1781 he awarded the contract, without bidding, to an intimate friend, Stephen Sullivan, son of the company's chairman who had come to India to recoup his family's finances. In April 1786 Edmund Burke rose in the House of Commons in London to charge Hastings with "high crimes and misdemeanors" and to condemn "the prodigal and corrupt system which Mr. Hastings had introduced into the finances of India." Although the House of Lords exonerated Hastings nine years later, his humiliation and growing problems with contractors finally forced the monopoly to assume full control of the opium trade.[10]

In 1797 the company eliminated the contractors and set up a system that was to last for more than a century. Under the new procedures, the East India Company and the colonial state that succeeded it controlled the opium from cultivation through processing to export. Bengal's opium country stretched for 500 miles across the Ganges Valley, with more than a million registered farmers growing poppy plants exclusively for the company on 500,000 acres of prime land.[11] From their factories at Patna and Benares in the heart of opium country, senior British officers directed some 2,000 Indian agents who circulated through the poppy districts, extending credit and collecting opium. After an eighty-day growing season, the farmers collected the opium sap in January by lancing and scraping each egg-shaped poppy bulb up to eight times and then delivered the liquid sap to the Indian agents. Processed under strict supervision at the two factories, the opium was dried into balls, checked to ensure a purity of 70 percent for Patna and 77 percent for Benares, and then packed into wooden chests, each containing forty balls and weighing 140 pounds. Bearing the Patna and Benares trademarks that were synonymous with quality, the chests were sent down to Calcutta under guard and sold at auction to private British merchants.[12] Since China had damned opium as a "destructive and ensnaring vice" and banned all imports in 1799, British sea captains bribed Canton's mandarins and smuggled the chests into southern China where the Bengal brands commanded twice the price of the inferior local products.[13]

For its first quarter century, this system ensured prosperity for British India and a stable opium supply for China. Not only did opium solve the fiscal crisis that accompanied the conquest of Bengal, it remained a staple of colonial finances, providing from 6 to 15 percent of British India's tax revenues during the nineteenth century.[14] Far more important, these opium exports were an essential component of an India-China-Britain trade that was the envy of the world. Trade figures for the 1820s, for example, show that the triangular exchange was remarkably large and well balanced: £22 million of Indian opium and cotton to China; £20 million in Chinese tea to Britain; and £24 million in British textiles and machinery back to India. In managing this trade, the East India Company prized stability above profit and for more than twenty years held India's opium exports at 4,000 chests—just enough to finance its purchase of China's tea crop.[15]

The system's success was the cause of its downfall. The vast profits of Britain's opium trade attracted competitors. Moreover, the company's steadfast refusal to raise Bengal's opium exports beyond the quota of 4,000 chests per year left a vast unmet demand for drugs among China's swelling population of opium smokers. As demand drove the price per chest upward from 115 rupees in 1799 to 2,428 rupees just fifteen years later, the East India Company's monopoly on Bengal opium faced strong competition from Turkey and western India.

Britain's most daring rivals were the Americans. Barred from bidding at the Calcutta auctions, Yankee traders loaded their first cargoes of Turkish opium at Smyrna on Turkey's Mediterranean coast in 1805 and sailed them around the tip of Africa to China. Within a decade, the Turkish trade had attracted major American merchants such as John Jacob Astor and constituted 30 percent of all U.S. cargoes reaching China.[16] Just as the British controlled Benal opium, so these American merchants won a de facto monopoly over the Turkish drug trade to China. Although the Americans increased their shipments from 102 chests in 1805 to 1,428 twenty-five years later, their largest cargoes were still just a quarter of the 5,672 chests the British brought from Bengal.[17] Nonetheless, through the efforts of these adventurous Americans, Turkish opium would remain a low-cost alternative to the Bengal brands until 1834 when the Yankee captains were finally allowed to bid at Calcutta.[18]

The real challenge to the East India Company's monopoly came from Malwa opium grown in the princely states of western India. Collected by Indian merchants and shipped from Portuguese ports on the west coast, often by Parsee merchants, Malwa opium had captured 40 percent of the China market by 1811, challenging the British company's monopoly. By 1818, however, the British completed their conquest of western India, giving them indirect control over the opium districts there. At first, the British tried to buy up the rival Malwa crop and auction it in Bombay, replicating the procedure they used to sell Bengal opium in Calcutta. This attempt at a preemptive buy was a dismal failure. The British purchase stimulated poppy production in the west, and the amount of Malwa opium reaching the China coast doubled in just one year.[19]

Determined to defend their monopoly, the company's directors decided to promote unlimited production in Bengal, thereby producing opium "at a price which would make competition unprofitable." In a move indicative of opium's importance, in 1831 the governor-general of India, Lord William Bentinck, toured the upper Ganges with revenue officers to explore new areas for poppy farming. Within the decade, fifteen new opium districts opened in Bengal, doubling the area of poppy cultivation.[20]

To export this expanded production, the governor-general also sponsored a challenged to the tyranny of the northwest monsoon. In years past when the company sold just 4,000 chests, private opium traders made only one trip to China each year on Indian country craft, sailing north through the China Sea before the winds of the southwest monsoon and returning to India with the northwest monsoon at their stern. Built of heavy Malabar teak at local yards, the broad-beamed Indian craft lacked the maneuverability to tack toward China in the face of monsoon winds that blew with steady strength down the China Sea for months after the opium harvest. In 1829 Captain William Clifton, a retired Royal Navy officer who had married into a Calcutta dockyard family, wrote to the governor offering to build a new kind of ship that could beat into the monsoon and carry three opium cargoes to China every year. With funds from the governor and the plans of a sleek American privateer captured in the War of 1812, Clifton launched the *Red Rover*, the first of the "opium clippers," and set sail for China in December 1829 with 800 chests of opium. With a long, low hull for speed and maneuver, the *Red Rover* tacked its way northward into the monsoon winds, reaching Macao and returning to Calcutta in just eighty-six days. At a banquet in Calcutta, the governor toasted Clifton's triumph and presented him with a reward of £10,000.[21] Realizing that the new ship meant competition for his conventional fleet, the most powerful of Calcutta's Parsee opium merchants, Rustomjee Cowasjee, commissioned Britain's leading naval architect to build him a faster ship. A year later, his company launched the *Sylph*, a 300-ton barque of shapely hull that later raced the *Red Rover* to China. Over the next decade, the Cowasjee family would launch five more of these fast ships to maintain its share of the opium trade against British and American competition.[22]

After the East India Company lost its charter in 1834, its informal regulation of the China opium trade collapsed, allowing profit-minded American and British captains to take control. Indeed, the company's demise launched a fleet of new opium clippers. During the next five years, twenty-five sleek ships joined the opium fleet, including three fast slave ships seized by the Royal Navy between Africa and America.[23] Speed was now an essential element in the new free-market opium trade. A fast ship could capture the best prices at the start of each season and maximize its owner's profit by making three return voyages on the Calcutta-to-Canton opium run. Along with their naval artillery, the clippers relied on speed to outrun the Malay and Chinese pirates who preyed on their valuable cargoes between Singapore and Shanghai.

India's export boom flooded the China coast with illicit opium, rending the fragile political fabric that had veiled the smuggling trade for decades. Rising slowly from 15 tons in 1720 to 75 tons with the start of the Bengal monopoly in 1773, China's imports of Indian opium had stabilized at about 250 tons after 1800. When the East India Company lifted its restrictions, China's imports increased tenfold—from 270 tons in 1820 to 2,555 tons twenty years later. Instead of the discreet smuggling of previous decades, British and American clippers crowded China's anchorages with their illicit cargoes, fending off Chinese customs with bribes and artillery barrages.[24] Opium addiction spread rapidly, reaching some three million Chinese addicts by the 1830s and provoking some angst among the British clergy.[25] "I call upon all British Christians," wrote Rev. Algernon Thelwall of Cambridge University in 1839, "to come forward as one man, in opposition to this nefarious traffic, which brings such deep disgrace upon the Christian name."[26]

Unlike Bengal's opium, moral indignation was not a British monopoly. Long concerned by the situation in Canton, the Chinese imperial court at Beijing was appalled by the developments of the 1830s. As addiction and corruption spread, two mandarins appeared before the emperor to debate the drug problem, a realist urging legalization of opium and an idealist insisting on the enforcement of prohibition.

In June 1836 the mandarin Hsu Nai-tsi, vice president of the Sacrificial Court, knelt before his emperor to earnestly entreat his Sacred Majesty to issue orders for an investigation of the opium problem. "I would humbly represent that opium was originally ranked among the medicines," Hsu began. "When one is long habituated to inhaling it, the habit of using it is destructive of time, injurious to property, and yet dear to one even as life." Although opium had been banned in 1799, "the smokers of the drug have increased in number and the practice has spread throughout the whole empire." Before the opium trade grew to its present size, "the barbarian merchants brought foreign money to China which was a source of pecuniary advantage to the people of the seaboard provinces. But latterly, the barbarian merchants have clandestinely sold opium for money."

The smuggling trade, Hsu reported, was well organized. At Canton "are constantly anchored seven or eight large ships, in which the opium is kept and which are therefore called the receiving ships. There are carrying boats plying up and down the river, and these are vulgarly called 'fast crabs' and 'scrambling dragons.' They are well armed with guns and are manned with some scores of desperadoes, who ply their oars as if they were wings to fly with. All the custom houses and military posts which they pass are largely bribed." Such smuggling, said Hsu, was spreading opium addiction within the ranks of the officials. "It becomes my duty, then to request that any officer, scholar or soldier found guilty of secretly smoking opium, shall be immediately dismissed from public employ." As a solution to the problem, Hsu recommended that the prohibition on opium use for the common people be lifted and opium imports be legalized to provide taxes. Since "vulgar or common people who have no official duties to perform" are not important, then it would make little difference if they were to become opium addicts.[27]

Six months later, the mandarin Chu Tsun, member of the board of rites, also knelt before his emperor and entreated "his Sacred Majesty to remove a great evil from among the people." Referring to those like Hsu who favored legalizing opium imports "as means of preventing money from secretly oozing out of the country," Chu argued that "this would be, indeed, a derogation of the true dignity of government." As for those who favor encouraging local opium growing to reduce imports, Chu replied: "Shall the fine fields of Kwangtung, that produce their three crops every year, be given up for the cultivation of this noxious weed?"

Chu found the idea of allowing the ordinary people to smoke opium repugnant. "The wide spreading and baneful influence of opium, when regarded as injurious to property, is of inferior importance; but when regarded as hurtful to the people, it demands most anxious considera-tion; for in the people lies the very foundation of the Empire." Through their moral force, laws could discourage the people from opium. "While the Empire preserves and maintains its laws, the plain and honest rustic will see what he has to fear and will be deterred from evil. Though the laws be declared by some to be but waste paper, yet these their unseen effects will be of no trifling nature. If the prohibitions be suddenly repealed, and the action which was a crime be no longer counted such by the Government, how shall the dull clown know that the action is still in itself wrong? In open day, and with unblushing front, they will continue to use opium till they find it as indispensable as their daily meat and drink."

Reminding the emperor of his dynasty's maxim that "horsemanship and archery are the foundations of its existence," Chu pointed out that the army sent to crush a rebellion of the Yao minority in 1832 found "that great numbers of the soldiers were opium smokers; so that, although their numerical force was large there was hardly any force found among them."

To protect the strength of the army and the virtue of the people, Chu argued that the prohibition on both the import and the smoking of opium must be enforced. The English at Canton must be reminded of China's regulations about opium "in order to eradicate from their minds all their covetous and ambitious schemes." If the English still refuse to obey, "forbearance must then cease, and thundering fire from our cannon must be opened upon them, to make them quake before the terror of our arms."[28]

In the end, it was China that quaked before the terror of British arms in the First Opium War (1839–1842).[29] In 1838 the emperor adopted the moralistic position on the opium problem and appointed the mandarin Lin Tse-hsu as special commissioner to Canton with extraordinary powers to "go, examine, and act." After eight days of investigation, Lin, a formidable official well informed about Canton's corruption, ordered the British merchants to surrender their opium cargoes and to sign bonds promising to honor China's prohibition on imports. After much delay, the foreign merchants surrendered 15,000 chests containing 95 tons of opium, including 10 tons from the American firm Russell & Co. For days, 500 workers broke up the opium balls and dissolved the fragments in a trench filled with salt and lime. Lin's campaign threatened the British China trade, and London dispatched a fleet of six warships and 7,000 troops that captured Canton in May 1839. For the next two years, the British expedition moved north, sacking China's major coastal cities. Forced to sue for peace at Nanking in 1842, China ceded Hong Kong, opened five new ports to foreign trade, and agreed to an indemnity of $21 million for the destruction of the opium.[30] But China still refused to legalize opium.

The fifteen years following the First Opium War were the high tide of the China trade. Illicit imports of Indian opium nearly doubled, rising to 4,810 tons in 1858.[31] At the Calcutta auctions, frenzied bidding drove opium prices and colonial profits to new heights, making a fast run to the China coast essential to ensure a quick return on the investments. In the five years following the start of the Opium War, forty-eight new clippers joined the opium fleet. Four of the fastest were built in American yards for Russell & Co., the Yankee trading house that would use their speed to challenge the great British opium merchants Jardine Matheson & Co. Under a commission from Russell & Co., in 1844 a Boston yard launched the *Coquette*, a 450-ton opium clipper with shallow hull and narrow beam that set new speed records on the Calcutta-to-Canton route. Reflecting the intense competition, British shipyards countered with the *Torrington*, a ship of similar design built in 1846 for Jardine Matheson.[32] Rival clipper captains bet heavily on opium races up the China coast, and conservative maritime journals celebrated new speed records. As the largest of the opium traders, Jardine had eight heavily armed receiving ships anchored off Chinese ports, five clippers cruising the coast, and five more ships carrying opium from India. The fastest clippers may have sailed for the American house Russell & Co., but even its largest cargoes could not challenge the dominion of Jardine's flotilla over the opium trade. Among the ninety-five clippers in the opium fleet, Calcutta's Cowasjee family owned six, the Americans of Russell & Co. had eight, and the British giants of the trade, Dent and Jardine, operated a total of twenty-seven.[33]

Although skilled seafarers and folk heroes in their day, the clipper captains shared a certain cynicism about their trade. "How should you like to be a smuggler?" Captain James Prescott wrote to his brother Henry in New York from the China coast in 1845. "What do the folks think I am up to here? What a pity you had not come with me, you might now be a smuggler, have a fine command and ere this making your fortune."[34] Nonetheless, this cynical commerce did bring "the dawn of a new era of naval architecture" in New York in 1845 with the launch of the *Rainbow*, the first of the true transoceanic clippers. The design concept of narrow beam and shallow draft that American dockyards had first developed for the peculiar requirements of the opium cutters was perfected in these larger "California clippers." With twice the tonnage of the largest opium ships, the *Rainbow* showed its speed on its maiden voyage when it sailed from New York to China in just ninety-two days.[35] Driven by their clouds of sails and slender hulls, American clippers such as the *Sea Witch* and *Flying Cloud* set new speed records on the sea lanes to China and even captured the London tea route from British shipping, lending an aura of romance to what remained, at its economic core, a tawdry trade.

The era of the opium clipper ended when China finally legalized the drug trade after its defeat in the Arrow War, or Second Opium War (1856–1858). The Treaty of Nanking that settled the First Opium War had left many ambiguities over the terms of Western access to China, producing numerous diplomatic incidents as foreign merchants became more active and aggressive along China's coast. When Chinese maritime officers arrested the British captain of the ship *Arrow* on minor charges in 1856, these accumulated tensions erupted into war. After combined Anglo-French forces occupied both Canton and Tientsin, the Chinese government agreed to open the country to free foreign trade.[36] In negotiations over the tariff provisions of this new treaty, the British emissary Lord Elgin urged the legalization of opium imports.[37] Desperate for new tax revenues to rebuild after years of war and rebellion, the Chinese government agreed but reserved both the customs duties and the domestic opium trade for itself. In the aftermath of China's legalization of opium, smugglers became registered importers, plodding steamships displaced the fast clippers, and state monopolies replaced private traders.

In the wake of opium's legalization, China achieved a level of mass addiction never equaled by any nation before or since: in 1906 the imperial government reported that 27 percent of all adult Chinese males were opium smokers.[38] But by the turn of the century, China was relying less and less on imported Indian opium. As addiction spread, so did poppy cultivation within China. Indian imports rose from 4,800 tons in 1859 to 6,700 tons twenty years later and then declined slowly for the rest of the century as cheaper, China-grown opium began to supplant the high-grade Bengal brands.[39]

Beginning in the early nineteenth century, as China's addict population had begun to swell, the opium poppy had spread out from its original home in mountainous Yunnan and Szechwan to most of the other provinces in southern and central China. Despite the proliferation of the poppy seed, opium was still an illegal crop, and sporadic enforcement of the ban limited cultivation even among remote hill tribes. Once opium imports were legalized in 1858, however, many officials no longer bothered to discourage local cultivation. Writing in the October 15, 1858 edition of the *New York Daily Tribune*, Karl Marx commented that "the Chinese Government will try a method recommended by political financial considerations—viz: legalize the cultivation of poppy in China."[40]

Indeed, Chinese provincial officials began encouraging production, and by the 1880s China was in the midst of a major opium boom, particularly in the rugged southwestern provinces of Szechwan and Yunnan, where cultivation had begun. Observers claimed that China's leading opium-producing province, Szechwan, was harvesting 10,000 tons of raw opium annually.[41] Trekking through Yunnan during the early 1880s, the British consul Alexander Hosie once walked for five miles "without seeing a crop other than the poppy." Two Western missionaries who explored Yunnan, China's second opium province, claimed that "three-quarters of all the land seen" was planted to opium. In 1881, the British consul at Yichang estimated the total opium production in the southwest at 13,525 tons, a figure so high that at first it seemed incredible.[42] But when official figures finally became available at century's turn, Szechwan and Yunnan were in fact producing 19,100 tons, equivalent to 54 percent of China's total harvest.[43] Although estimates varied widely, by 1885 China was probably growing twice as much opium as it was importing.[44]

The harvest in the opium-rich southern provinces was so bountiful that Yunnan had begun exporting opium to Southeast Asia. In 1901 the governor-general of French Indochina reported that half of the opium retailed by the colony's opium monopoly was from neighboring Yunnan, and a French business periodical noted with interest that Yunnan was harvesting 3,000 tons of raw opium annually.[45] In addition, cheap Yunnanese opium became the staple of Southeast Asia's growing illicit traffic. Unable to pay the inflated prices demanded by the profit-hungry government monopolies, addicts in Burma, Siam, and Indochina turned to the black market for supplies of smuggled Yunnanese opium. Every year long mule caravans protected by hundreds of armed guards left Yunnan, crossed the ill-defined border into Burma, Siam, and French Indochina carrying tons of illicit opium.[46]

## The Opium Dens of Southeast Asia

The Southeast Asian opium trade was the creation of European colonialism. Just as the age of empire brought China mass addiction and India extensive poppy cultivation, so it gave Southeast Asia the omnipresent opium den. Some early records indicate that Indian and Chinese opium appeared as trade goods in the islands of Southeast Asia as early as the fifteenth century, but quantities were small and their use was usually medicinal. Lying astride the main sea lanes between India and China, Southeast Asia was drawn into the expanding Asian drug trade during the sixteenth century as Arab and Portuguese ships laden with Indian opium passed through its islands en route to Canton. But lacking China's vast population and appetite for opium, these islands remained only a minor market for Indian exports.[47] Southeast Asia's opium trade began with the arrival of the Europeans. When they occupied Jakarta in the seventeenth century, the Dutch found some addiction among the people of Java and began marketing imported Indian opium through licensed dealers. The Dutch developed a substantial opium trade on Java in the seventeenth and eighteenth centuries, but drug use remained uncommon elsewhere in the region.

During the nineteenth century, state-licensed opium dens became a unique Southeast Asian institution, spreading and sustaining addiction throughout the region. In 1930, Southeast Asia had 6,441 government opium dens where any adult could, for a nominal fee, smoke an unlimited number of "pipes." In just one year, those dens served 272 tons of opium to 542,100 registered smokers. Opium use, legal and illicit, was found throughout the region, but its spread was uneven. There were no legal dens in the Philippines after United States banned opium use in 1906. By contrast, French Indochina in 1930 had 3,500 licensed "opium divans," or one for every 1,500 adult males, and was home to 125,200 opium smokers, or twenty-three percent of all the addicts in Southeast Asia. Southeast Asia's only independent state, the Kingdom of Siam, earned 14 percent of its tax revenues by selling 84 tons of opium through 972 licensed dens to 164,300 opium smokers, the largest addict population in Southeast Asia.[48] In no other region of the world did so many governments promote mass drug abuse with such unanimity of means and moral certitude.

With the exception of Java, the great majority of Southeast Asia's opium smokers were Chinese immigrants. As the population of southern China reached the saturation point in the early decades of the century,[49] a severe economic crisis forced a massive migration, creating large communities of Chinese in Southeast Asia by 1900: 60,000 Chinese in Rangoon, 120,000 in Saigon, and 200,000 in Bangkok.[50] Leaving a country in which one in every four males was an opium smoker by 1900, many of the Chinese migrants were landing at cities such as Saigon and Singapore with an opium habit. To their profit, colonial governments discovered that they could release a rich flow of tax revenues by tapping an existing vice. In 1925, for example, 91 percent of the registered opium smokers in Burma were Chinese, leaving only 1,300 Burmese among the colony's 18,200 addicts.[51] Not surprisingly, the rate of opium addiction among these immigrants was high, reaching seven percent of all overseas Chinese in Malaya during the 1920s.[52]

At first, the colonial governments restricted their role in importing the opium from India. Instead of managing the dens directly, the colonial overlords auctioned "opium farms," or franchises, to the highest bidder, usually a consortium of Chinese influentials who managed this complex business among their people without troubling the state. In 1881, however, the French administration in Saigon established the Opium Régie, a direct state marketing monopoly that showed far greater efficiency and profitability. Over the next forty years, the new model spread to the Dutch Indies, British Burma, and Siam. Aware of the rising criticism of their opium trading, many colonial governments announced the new monopoly as a drug control measure. Although the Dutch, like many colonial governments, introduced the reform with the stated aim of reducing native opium use, on Java the Régie expanded sales and forcibly spread opium to areas such as the Priangan that had previously resisted opium use.[53] Similarly, after the British established a new monopoly for the Federated Malay States in 1911, per capita opium sales to the Chinese doubled.[54] By century's turn, every Southeast Asian state, from Burma to the Philippines, had an opium monopoly.[55]

Although state opium sales began by cultivating a Chinese vice, the habit spread gradually to Southeast Asia's local populations. Through Chinese opium contractors and illicit dealers, some of the indigenous peoples developed the habit, thus fostering a moderate demand for opium among the Burmese, Malays, Thai, and Vietnamese. "The Chinese," wrote a U.S. commission that visited Rangoon in 1904, "have been known to distribute opium gratis among the Burmese in order to cause them to acquire the opium habit. After this has been done, the Chinese sell, and generally at any figure they please." Among Rangoon's estimated 5,500 Burmese opium addicts, only 90 visited the licensed government opium dens and the great majority dealt with the illicit Chinese traffickers.[56]

No mere vice, opium became a major factor in Southeast Asian economic growth, in both public and private sectors, reflecting and reinforcing the region's ongoing modernization. In many parts of nineteenth-century Southeast Asia, the opium franchises were integral to the rise of overseas Chinese capital. From the time Sir Stamford Raffles established a British colony on Singapore in 1819, the island government earned more than half its revenue by leasing an opium franchise to influential Chinese. By the mid-nineteenth century, Singapore's Chinese merchants and their partners in the hinterland controlled a two-way trade, exporting opium to coolies working on their plantations in the jungles of nearby Johor and importing the tropical products of those plantations. When a scarcity of labor drove wages to uneconomic levels, the Chinese planters balanced their books by extracting some 30 to 70 percent of coolie wages by selling opium to the coolies through the franchise. The synergy of this trade between opium and plantation products financed both the clearing of Johor's jungles and the growth of the Chinese capital in Singapore.[57] Indicative of opium's central role in Singapore's economy, a struggle between rival Chinese ethnic syndicates, Chiu chau and Hokkien, over the opium franchise in the early 1860s produced two years of riots, arson, and opium smuggling.[58] Similarly, opium was central to the Chinese tin mines operating along the west coast of the Malay Peninsula during the nineteenth century. With profits earned from selling opium to their own workers, tin mine operators cushioned themselves against periodic drops in the world tin price.[59]

During the same period, Chinese opium contractors on Java controlled both the legal opium sales and a vast illicit commerce. During their three centuries on Java, the Dutch created the largest and most lucrative of the colonial opium monopolies. Unlike the Portuguese, Parsees, and British who competed to export opium to China, the Dutch concentrated on opium distribution within their domains on Java.[60] From 1640 to 1799, the Dutch East India Company imported an average of 56 tons of opium annually, large quantities for the day, and the amount rose steadily throughout the nineteenth century to 208 tons by 1904.[61] By starting their retail monopoly two centuries before the other European powers, the Dutch developed a large clientele of native Javanese opium smokers. Although almost all opium contractors were Chinese, most users were Javanese. Thus the Dutch opium trade, unlike the French, was not limited to a small Chinese community. With their wages from Java's thriving plantation economy, ordinary villagers earned the cash, scarce elsewhere in Southeast Asia, to sustain a habituation to low-grade opium.[62] Indeed, at the Shanghai Opium Commission in 1909, the Dutch delegation reported that "the greater portion of the total quantity of opium sold is consumed by natives."[63] Although the Dutch monopoly began reducing sales in the early twentieth century, in 1929 it was still operating 1,065 opium dens that retailed 59 tons of opium to 101,000 registered smokers.[64]

If opium smoking elsewhere in Southeast Asia was a relatively minor problem, on Java it was central to the island's social and economic history. Across Java, the official Chinese contractors purchased small amounts of high-priced Indian opium through the Dutch company while simultaneously using their licenses to mask the distribution of far larger illicit quantities. Purchasing the same Indian opium at a far lower price in Singapore's free port, smugglers supplied the Chinese contractors with large quantities of illicit opium that the Chinese sold at less than half the official price. Dutch investigations along the northern Java coast in 1883 discovered that just one group of smugglers had brought in 41 tons of illicit opium that year.[65] As such large-scale smuggling indicates, the opium trade created a nexus of corruption that spanned the whole of Indies colonial society. At the apex, wealthy Chinese contractors bribed Dutch officials with lavish gifts to win the opium contracts. At the nadir, the opium dens were the centerpiece in Java's floating world of vice where gamblers, prostitutes, outlaws, and opium police congregated. In between, the Chinese opium contractors raised a retinue of spies, or "little eyes," to track down smugglers whose illicit opium eroded their profits or to collect information to use against their rivals in the contract bidding.[66]

Despite Dutch claims that their Opium Régie would control and eventually eradicate the problem, the monopoly remained central to colonial finances until World War II. When Indonesian nationalists launched their revolution against the Dutch in 1945, they captured control of the opium stocks and engaged in an illicit traffic with Singapore to fund their armed forces.[67]

While the addiction weakened the local populations, it strengthened the finances of colonial governments. In 1905–1906, for example, opium sales provided 16 percent of taxes for French Indochina, 16 percent for Netherlands Indies, 20 percent for Siam, and 53 percent for British Malaya.[68] These revenues, sometimes reaching as high as 59 percent of total taxes, financed construction of the cities, canals, roads, and rails that remain as the hallmarks of the colonial era.[69]

Despite heavy opium consumption, Southeast Asia remained a minor producer until the 1950s. At the 1909 Shanghai Opium Commission, the Thai delegates could report with some honesty that "Siam does not produce opium because it does not cultivate the poppy."[70] After World War II, Southeast Asia's Golden Triangle would become the world's leading opium grower, with an annual harvest of 1,000 to 3,300 tons of raw opium. But in the late 1930s, the highlands of Burma, Thailand, and Laos—the future Golden Triangle—still produced an insignificant harvest of only 15 tons of raw opium. The reason for this slow growth of poppy cultivation in Southeast Asia lies in the economics of the opium monopolies. For as long as the colonial monopolies survived, they did everything possible to discourage local opium production.

## Opium Production in Southeast Asia

In the nineteenth century, poppy cultivation in the highlands of Southeast Asia began as an indirect response to the political and economic turmoil sweeping Yunnan province just across the border in southern China. For several centuries, Muslim merchants had linked the markets of the Yunnan Plateau with highland kingdoms that stretched from Bengal to Vietnam. With strings of some fifty mules, caravans went west along the old Burma Road to India and then south across the Shan Plateau toward Siam or southeast into the highland valleys of Laos. By the mid-nineteenth century, the Yunnan Muslims, known as Panthays or Haw, were carrying shipments of opium and tea to undercut the high price of both commodities in Siam. Crossing the Shan states, these merchants added to their opium supply by bartering for the local production, thus stimulating Burma's opium crop.[71] "The Panthays are a virile, sturdy and aggressive race," wrote a Christian missionary who observed them firsthand. "The men who guide the long trains of mules . . . through the wild mountain passes of Yunnan and the Burmese frontier must be rugged in constitution and spirit. The . . . exposure to all kinds of weather—drenching rains, scorching heat, or . . . the bitter frost and raw damps of the mountains slopes—would indeed daunt any but men of iron mould."[72]

As the Chinese empire extended its reach into the country's southern borderlands during the late nineteenth century, imperial armies faced rebellions from the autonomous ethnic states that had existed for centuries without interference. Brutal in every respect, these campaigns were similar to the slaughters of aboriginal populations by states across the globe in the modern era—whether the Plains Indians of the American West, the Australian aboriginals, or the tribes of the Argentine Pampas.

In China, highland ethnic rebels often won the early battles, but the slow, grinding force of imperial armies eventually broke the organized resistance. In 1856 the Muslims of Yunnan province rebelled and established an independent kingdom at the city of Tali in the western mountains, one hundred miles from Burma, under a leader who crowned himself Sultan Suleiman. Sending his caravans west for arms, the sultan contacted British officials in Burma and dispatched his son to London to plead for diplomatic support. The Muslims found local allies among the Hmong mountain tribes of Yunnan, who had launched their own rebellion against the Chinese in 1853.[73] After fifteen years of intermittent fighting, imperial forces used modern artillery directed by Western advisers to breach the walls of the Muslim fortress at Tali and overwhelm its 30,000 defenders. The Chinese commander, in the words of one British explorer, ordered a "general massacre of the disarmed . . . garrison, and an indiscriminate slaughter of thousands of men, women and children completed the conquest."[74] In the aftermath, surviving Muslims fled west to the mountain towns of Burma and northern Siam where they survived by trading with the opium-growing tribesmen of Southeast Asia.[75]

During this period, imperial armies were also fighting a massive revolt of Hmong hill tribes across China's southern borderlands. Again, imperial forces broke the revolt with slaughters during the 1870s, forcing a mass migration of Hmong opium farmers into Vietnam and Laos.[76] Throughout much of the nineteenth century, these imperial campaigns sent waves of Hmong and Yao southward into the mountains of Indochina, bringing with them the knowledge of poppy cultivation.

China's conquests forced two streams of migration into Southeast Asia, the Muslims moving southwest toward Siam and the hill tribes arcing to the southeast through Vietnam and Laos. After settling in Southeast Asia, the Muslim merchants integrated the Hmong and Yao tribes into an overland opium trade that stretched from Yunnan to Bangkok. With their strings of mules and horses, the Muslims became the logistic link between the opium supplies of southern China and the demand for illicit drugs in the cities of Southeast Asia. Unaware of the boom in poppy cultivation that was sweeping Yunnan and Szechwan in the 1880s, state opium monopolies had raised official prices in the smoking dens of Bangkok and Saigon to levels beyond the reach of most addicts.

Starting their journeys in the markets of Yunnan, the Muslims bartered textiles for opium and then led their mule caravans through the hill villages of Burma and Laos, trading for opium at each stage until they reached Siam and northern Vietnam. Through this overland smuggling, the Muslims gradually stimulated opium production in the highlands of Southeast Asia.[77]

During the late nineteenth century, travelers passing through the highlands of Southeast Asia noticed widespread opium production. In a scientific essay of 1888, a British observer in Laos reported that recently arrived Hmong were cultivating opium as a cash crop.[78] Similarly, a British explorer who crossed northeastern Burma in the 1890s saw "miles of slopes covered with poppy" and noted that the "fields climb up steep ravines and follow the sheltered sides of ridges." French colonials inspecting the highlands of Laos and Vietnam also observed Hmong and Yao tribesmen cultivating the opium poppy.[79]

After 1900, Siam and French Indochina found that this overland smuggling trade was taking a major share of their legal opium markets. In 1928, for example, French officials formed "a special surveillance corps covering a wide area" along the China-Vietnam border and attacked seventeen armed caravans with 15.5 tons of opium, equivalent to 22 percent of government sales.[80] In 1935 Bangkok described this overland smuggling as "one of the most serious problems of the Siamese administration" and reported seizures of 14 tons, equivalent to 18 percent of legal opium sales. After its investigators found that the official opium price was 300 percent higher than the illicit, Bangkok cut its prices, producing a 121 percent rise in legal opium sales.[81]

Despite the spread of poppy cultivation in the highlands of Southeast Asia, the region still remained a minor producer in the decades before World War II. In 1909 French Indochina claimed that rigid regulation of Hmong villages had reduced cultivation to "an absolutely insignificant area" and held production to only 3.5 tons of opium.[82] After allowing production to reach 29 tons in 1923, the French found the diversion to smugglers troublesome and forced Hmong opium production back to "small quantities" in the 1930s.[83] Faced with the inevitability of smuggling from neighboring Yunnan, British officials in Burma licensed opium growing in the Shan state borderlands and used those controls to reduce production from 31 tons in 1932 to 8 tons just four year later.[84]

Even at its peak in the 1920s, Southeast Asia's 60 tons of opium were dwarfed by the 6,380 tons produced across the border in China.[85] The demand for illicit opium remained strong in the region's cities, but Southeast Asia did not develop widespread poppy cultivation until the late 1940s, more than fifty years after China.

The explanation for this half-century delay in the growth of the Golden Triangle's opium production is simple: British Burma, French Indochina, and the Kingdom of Siam did everything in their power to discourage their hill tribes from growing opium. While British India and imperial China generated revenues by producing and exporting opium, Southeast Asian governments gained their revenues from the sales of refined opium to addicts, not from the production and export of raw opium. Through their own official monopolies or licensed franchise dealers, Southeast Asian governments imported raw opium from abroad (usually from India, China, or Persia), refined it into smoking opium, and then made an enormous profit by selling it to addicts at inflated prices. Official monopolies and franchises were continually raising prices to maximize their profits, frequently forcing addicts onto the black market, where smuggled Yunnanese opium was available at a more reasonable cost. Smuggling became the bane of official dealers, forcing their government sponsors to mount costly border patrols to keep cheaper opium out and to lower prices to win back customers. It was their concern over the smuggling problem that led colonial governments to reduce and restrict hill tribe opium production. Knowledgeable colonial officials felt that poppy cultivation by local hill tribes would magnify the smuggling because customs officers patrolling the hills would find it impossible to distinguish between legitimate hill tribe opium and smuggled Yunnanese opium. Moreover, the hill tribes would divert opium to the black market, adding to the flow of illicit supplies and further reducing government revenues.[86]

These concerns influenced colonial opium policy in the Golden Triangle from the very beginning of European rule in the northern borderlands of Burma and Indochina. After the British pacified northeastern Burma in the late 1880s, they made sporadic attempts at reducing tribal opium production along the Chinese border until 1923, when they launched a systematic campaign in these areas.[87] Following their annexation of Tonkin in 1884 and Laos in 1893, French colonials experimented with large-scale commercial poppy plantations but consistently avoided promoting hill tribe production for almost fifty years.[88] Thus, while provincial officials in southern and western China promoted poppy cultivation, colonial officials across the border in the Golden Triangle were either restraining or actively reducing hill tribe opium production.

## International Drug Diplomacy

In the late nineteenth century, the scandal of Far Eastern opium trade inspired a global anti-opium movement, led by Protestant clergy and laity, that forced Western nations to adopt a drug diplomacy aimed at suppressing the international trade in narcotics. The Hague Opium Conference of 1911–12 and subsequent negotiations led to a series of opium control treaties under the League of Nations in 1925 and the United Nations after 1945. What today remains a routine, sometimes dreary diplomacy began more than a century ago as an impassioned religious crusade.

The early anti-opium movement was a loose alliance between British Protestants, Western missionaries in China, and Chinese imperial officials. With a generous endowment from a British Quaker, the Anglo-Oriental Society for the Suppression of the Opium Trade formed in 1874 and soon attracted the patronage of a Catholic cardinal and the archbishop of Canterbury.[89] At mass meetings, the society proclaimed its intention to "urge the British government entirely to disconnect itself from . . . the opium traffic" and to restore China's "perfect independence of action to deal with opium," which it had lost in the two Opium Wars. "This Opium Trade is a Christian's monopoly," proclaimed the Rev. A. E. Moule before the Shanghai Missionary Conference of 1877. "Its history is a Christian sin, a Christian shame. Take away this abnormal, this unnatural ally of heathenism, and we can meet the enemy without doubt of the final outcome."[90] Declaring his support for the anti-opium movement, China's leading mandarin, Li Hung-chang, informed the society that "China views the question from a moral standpoint; England from a fiscal." While proclaiming his moral opposition to opium, Li, like many of his class, grew a substantial poppy crop on ancestral lands, a contradiction that sparked British colonial suspicions that China merely wished to eliminate competition from Indian imports.[91]

For thirty years Britain's missionaries and moralists fought a relentless campaign through meetings and petitions that culminated in 1906 when Parliament passed a motion to end India's opium trade. Triumphant at last, British crusaders linked arms and marched out of Parliament House singing hymns. Long humiliated by every aspect of the traffic, China's nationalists were strongly opposed to the pandemic of opium addiction that seemed to spread without restraint. With strong mandates for suppression, British and Chinese diplomats agreed on a ten-year, step-by-step reduction in both Indian imports and Chinese cultivation. As the Indian opium shipments diminished, China pursued a rigorous anti-opium campaign that eliminated smoking in Beijing and reduced cultivation in provinces such as Szechwan.

After the revolution of 1911 against the Manchu emperor, however, the new republican government proved corrupt and its opium suppression campaign faltered. China's poppy cultivation revived, morphine and heroin pills appeared as substitutes for smoking opium, and the new republic's cabinet was found taking a bribe from the opium syndicate. Nonetheless, in January 1919, the republic burned the last chest of Indian opium at a public ritual before invited guests at Shanghai. After three hundred years, the India-China opium trade had ended.[92] It was, however, an event of less than historic importance. India now exported opium elsewhere and China grew enough to supply its own addicts.

While Britain engaged in bilateral negotiations with China, the United States sought a solution through global drug diplomacy. After occupying the Philippines in 1898, the United States discovered that it had inherited a state opium monopoly similar to those elsewhere in Southeast Asia. In 1903, for example, Manila had 190 dens retailing a total of 130 tons of opium.[93] Aware that opium provided nearly 4 percent of colonial revenues, the U.S. governor, William Howard Taft, was inclined to continue the traffic, until an outpouring of protest in the United States forced Washington to intervene. In 1903 the colonial regime appointed the Episcopal missionary Bishop Charles Brent, formerly an assistant minister in a poor Boston parish, to head a committee investigating the opium problem. After touring Asia to study the matter, Bishop Brent recommended an ultimate prohibition.[94] In 1906 the U.S. regime responded by restricting sales to adult Chinese males and registering 12,700 smokers. Two years later, Manila slashed imports to just 38 pounds, raising the illicit price to a level that made smuggling profitable. Although opium smuggled from China met the illicit demand, drug abuse in the Philippine Islands declined, through a mix of prohibition and high illicit price, to levels far below that in other Southeast Asian colonies.[95]

Whatever its actual impact might have been, the Philippine ban won fame for Bishop Brent and launched America's attempt at drug diplomacy. Aware that illicit Chinese opium was sabotaging the Philippine prohibition, the bishop wrote to President Theodore Roosevelt suggesting an international conference to assist China in its struggle against the opium trade. As an enthusiastic amateur diplomat who had won the Nobel Peace Prize for his role in settling the Russo-Japanese War, Roosevelt embraced the bishop's idea and committed American resources to convening the first International Opium Commission. With Bishop Brent in the chair, delegations from thirteen countries— including Britain, France, Persia, Siam, and China—met at Shanghai for a month early in 1909.[96] With stunning self-confidence, the European colonial powers portrayed their profit-oriented opium monopolies as drug control measures, thus pushing the conference toward a consensus that government regulation was the solution. "Being proud of the Java Régie system and also deeply convinced of its useful effect," the Dutch delegate A. A. de Jongh suggested that the opium trade be removed from "the hands of private wholesale dealers" and be "limited to the Governments of opium-producing and opium-consuming countries"— just what the colonial regimes were already doing. In unanimous, nonbinding resolutions, the commission defended the colonial interest by advising "the *gradual* suppression . . . of *opium*," the drug its members did sell, and urging "*drastic* measures" against the "grave danger" of *morphine*, the drug its members did not sell.[97] Thus, the commission left a mingled legacy, defending Asia's colonial opium trade while simultaneously launching a global antinarcotics diplomacy.

Two years later, the United States used its influence to convene a second round of drug diplomacy, the International Conference on Opium at the Hague. With the support of William Taft, the former Philippine governor who was now the U.S. president, Bishop Brent again chaired the conference and maintained its moral momentum against the colonial interest. Moving beyond the mere recommendations of the Shanghai commission, these sessions drafted the Hague Opium Convention, which required each signatory nation to pass its own domestic drug legislation. As a party to these proceedings, the United States was thus required to pass its first federal drug laws, a diplomatic pressure that translated into enactment of the Harrison Narcotics Act by the U.S. Congress in 1914.[98] Before the Hague convention could take effect, World War I intervened, delaying further drug diplomacy until the League of Nations convened the Geneva Conference of 1925 and began a rigorous round of negotiations. Under the Geneva narcotics convention and its later protocols, drug controls moved away from voluntary national laws to mandatory international controls over the production and sale of drugs.[99]

Restrained by the influence of the European colonial lobby, this cautious diplomacy could never achieve the total eradication advocated by the anti-opium movement. Although the diplomacy moved with a slowness that moral reformers found abhorrent, it nonetheless produced international treaties that gradually restricted the right of governments to traffic in narcotics. Faced with the threat of diplomatic censure, the major trafficking nations were forced to restrict their trade, and the result was an 82 percent decline in world opium supply—from 42,000 tons in 1906 to 8,000 tons in 1934.[100] Although none of Southeast Asia's states actually abolished its opium monopoly, all made gestures, genuine and cosmetic, that reduced the region's opium sales by 65 percent in the fifteen years after World War I. The Netherlands Indies, for example, which had been selling opium since the seventeenth century, cut the colony's consumption by 88 percent, from 127 to 15 tons.[101]

Although these reforms reduced the region's legal opium sales, they could not eradicate a mass demand for the drug cultivated by three centuries of colonial rule. Colonial regimes could break their fiscal dependence opium taxes by fiat, but colonized societies could not cut the cultural and economic roots of mass opium addiction so quickly. As soon as governments slashed imports or closed opium dens, smugglers and dealers emerged to service the unmet demand.

In the islands of Southeast Asia, a colonial customs service could, with some difficulty, patrol the sea lanes and enforce the prohibition on opium imports from India and Persia. But on the mainland, Thailand and French Indochina found it impossible to close their mountain borders to the overland caravan trade from Yunnan and Burma. With 50 percent of its smokers and 70 percent of its dens,[102] Bangkok and Saigon were Southeast Asia's premier opium markets, offering high profits to draw the caravans southward from the opium hills. There were, moreover, politics to the opium economy. When the excise departments of Thailand and French Indochina stopped taxing the legal trade, their military factions imposed an informal tax on the illicit traffic. Creation of the colonial opium trade had proved far easier than its abolition.

## Royal Thai Opium Monopoly

Although opium was clearly a colonial vice, the independent Kingdom of Siam was an apt imitator. After legalizing opium in 1851, Siam (today Thailand), developed one of the most successful monopolies in Southeast Asia. The large Chinese population in Bangkok provided a ready market, and opium became a mainstay of royal finances.[103] By 1905 the royal government was earning 20 percent of its taxes by selling 95 tons of opium through Bangkok's 900 opium dens.[104] As opium became integrated in the country's economy, the government found it increasingly difficult to disengage from the traffic.

"It is unquestionable that the drug has evil effects upon its consumers; and casts degradation upon every country where the inhabitants are largely addicted to the habit of opium smoking," said Siam's King Chulalongkorn in 1908. "But unfortunately there are many obstacles in the way of attainment of this object [eradication of the vice]. Briefly speaking, there is the considerable shrinkage in the State revenues to be faced. It is nevertheless Our bounden duty not to neglect Our people and allow them to become more and more demoralized by indulgence in this noxious drug. We have accordingly decided the spread of the opium habit among Our people shall become gradually lessened until it shall be entirely suppressed."[105]

Not even a god-king could reverse the inexorable tide of modern economics. Over the next ten years, the number of opium dens increased by 360 percent to 3,245 and opium's share of royal revenues climbed to 25 percent.[106] Twenty years after the king had promised an end to the drug trade, the opium monopoly's imports doubled to 180 tons, sustaining the largest addict population in Southeast Asia.[107]

At its start in the early nineteenth century, Siam's thriving opium trade simply reflected the size of the Chinese population. As the Bangkok dynasty imported legions of Chinese laborers for construction of canals across its central plains, its Chinese population became the largest in Southeast Asia, reaching 440,000 in 1821 and constituting half of Bangkok by 1880.[108]

And with the Chinese came the opium problem. In 1811 King Rama II promulgated Siam's first formal ban on the sale and consumption of opium. In 1839 another Thai king reiterated the prohibition and ordered the death penalty for major traffickers. Despite the good intentions of royal courts, legislative efforts failed. Although Chinese distributors could be arrested and punished, the British merchant captains who smuggled the illicit narcotic were virtually immune to prosecution. Whenever a British captain was arrested, ominous rumblings issued from the British embassy, and the captain was soon freed to smuggle in another cargo. Finally, in 1852, King Mongkut bowed to British pressure and established a royal opium franchise that was leased to a wealthy Chinese merchant.[109]

In 1855 King Mongkut yielded to further British pressure and signed a commercial treaty with the British Empire which lowered import duties to 3 percent and abolished the royal trading monopolies, the fiscal basis of the royal administration. To replace these lost revenues, the king expanded the four Chinese-managed vice franchises—opium, lottery, gambling, and alcohol—which provided between 12 and 22 percent of all government revenues in the latter half of the nineteenth century.[110] After only a decade of operation, the court found that an "influx of contraband opium" was undercutting "the Opium Monopoly which has yielded much profit to the Metropolis of the Kingdom" and passed the first comprehensive regulations to bar smuggling.[111]

In 1907, after a half century of legal drug sales, Siam's king announced his program for the suppression of "this noxious drug." Following the example of the Dutch and French, his government eliminated the Chinese contractors and assumed direct distribution of opium to the dens. Almost mocking the king's intentions, the new monopoly, like those in French Indochina and the Netherlands Indies, produced a sustained increase in opium sales. The number of dens and retail shops jumped from 1,200 in 1900 to more than 3,000 in 1917;[112] the number of opium addicts reached

200,000 by 1921;[113] and the opium profits continued to provide between 15 and 20 percent of all government tax revenues.[114]

Responding to mounting international opposition to legalized opium trafficking, the Thai government finally began reducing the volume of the opium monopoly's business in the 1920s. By 1930 almost 2,000 shops and dens were closed, but the remaining 837 were still handling 89,000 customers a day.[115] To demonstrate the royal commitment to ending the drug trade, Siam hosted the Bangkok Opium Conference in 1931, another meeting in the ongoing anti-opium diplomacy.[116]

In 1932, however, an elite revolution of middle-ranking military and civil servants seized power and imposed a constitution on the monarch. Led by an ultranationalist, Colonel Phibun Songkhram, the military gradually took control of the new regime and used its growing influence to reverse the opium eradication policy. Determined to reclaim the Tai-speaking Shan states from British Burma, younger officers around Phibun apparently began using the opium trade as a vehicle for extending their influence into northern Siam and Burma. Whatever the cause, official involvement in the opium trade along the northern borderlands increased markedly after 1932. These trends became particularly evident in 1938 when Colonel Phibun became prime minister and focused greater attention on the northern borderlands a matter of state policy. To reinforce the regime's expansionist aims, Phibun changed the country's name from Siam to Thailand—an implicit claim to the Tai-speaking region of northern Burma.[117]

During the 1930s, Bangkok's opium market developed direct links with the opium hills that stretched north from Siam across Burma to China. When the revolutionary government came to power in 1932, the rapid reduction in legal opium dens—to only 860 from a peak of 3,250 in 1917—had already encouraged a sharp rise in caravan smuggling from Burma.[118] Continuing the royal suppression effort, the new government did not import any opium in 1932–1933. But reflecting its own support for the trade, the revolutionary regime raised the number of opium dens to 1,400 in 1938. By increasing opium outlets while cutting supplies, the regime produced an upsurge of smuggling from Burma and Yunnan.[119] In 1935 alone, Siam's government seized 5 tons of illegal opium.[120] Over the next five years, seized opium totaled 27 tons and amounted to 23 percent of the opium sold by the monopoly.[121] The contradictions in a policy that cut opium imports while continuing to sell the drug in licensed dens produced Siam's first major instance of opium corruption.

The incident began in May 1934 when the director of Siam's excise department, the unit responsible for opium sales, was visiting Kengtung in Burma's Shan states and, without proper authorization, contracted with some local dealers who would supply 15 tons of opium for the monopoly. Under loose British controls, the Shan states were harvesting 20 to 30 tons for licensed dens and unknown quantities for the illicit caravan trade.[122] After his finance minister rejected the offer as improper and illegal, the excise director nonetheless notified his Kengtung contact that he would pay a "reward" for the seizure of the opium once it arrived across the border. Thus, on January 9, 1935, Siam's excise officers seized nine trucks loaded with 9 tons of opium just inside the border, and the director doubled his department's reward budget to pay the "informers." The case became an open scandal when the British adviser to Siam's finance ministry, James Baxter, wrote an open letter to the Singapore *Straits Times* exposing the details of the transaction. In the end, the finance minister denied everything and the national assembly refused, by a vote of 48 to 17, to discuss the matter. As planned, the excise department marketed the opium officially through its licensed dens.[123]

After Phibun became prime minister in 1938, the government abandoned any pretense of opium suppression and revived the monopoly. Since it was, officials claimed, "impossible to prevent the transporting of this contraband opium across a border strip of mountains and jungle," the prohibition effort encouraged "clandestine smoking by addicts deprived of a convenient licensed establishment."[124] To supply its expanded network of opium dens, the regime announced that it would promote poppy cultivation among the hill tribes of northern Siam to cut the costs of imports and control smuggling.[125] Twenty years earlier, Siam had demonstrated its potential for local production when it made a trial purchase of 5 tons of tribal opium.[126] In December 1938, the government agreed to purchase the opium harvest from two mountain villages and two years later, in March 1940, announced that the local experiment had been successful. Henceforth, the Phibun government proclaimed, Thailand would be able to grow its own opium.[127]

The government's active promotion of poppy cultivation, combined with increasing migration of hill tribes into Thailand, stimulated a gradual increase in the country's opium production during the 1940s. Although large numbers of Hmong and Yao had started moving into Indochina from southern China during the mid-1800s, it was not until the early twentieth century that substantial numbers of the highland opium farmers had started crossing into Thailand from Laos.[128] Other opium-growing tribes—such as the Akha, Lisu, and Lahu—took a more direct route, moving slowly southward through northern Burma before crossing into Siam. Since the tribal population was small and production sporadic, their meager harvests rarely got much farther than the local trading towns at the base of the mountain ranges. For example, in Ban

Wat, a small trading town south of Chiangmai, hill traders recalled that the opium business was so small in the prewar period that all of their opium was sold directly to Thai and Chinese addicts in the immediate area. Although they were close to Chiangmai, which was a major point for forwarding illicit Chinese opium to Bangkok, the local production rarely got beyond neighboring towns and villages.[129] Nor was it possible for the lowland Thai peasants to cultivate the opium poppy. The Yunnan variety of the opium poppy that was grown in southern China and Southeast Asia prospered only in a cool, temperate climate. And in these tropical latitudes, it had to be grown in mountains above three thousand feet in elevation, where the air was cool enough for the sensitive poppy. Since the Thai peasants clung resolutely to the steamy lowland valleys where they cultivated paddy rice, opium production in Thailand, as in the rest of Southeast Asia, became the work of mountain tribesmen.

Although Thailand was cut off from its major opium suppliers, Iran and India, during World War II, it had no difficulty securing an adequate supply of raw opium for the royal monopoly. Through its military alliance with the Japanese Empire, Thailand occupied the Shan states in northeastern Burma and gained access to its opium-growing regions along the Chinese border.

After allying with Japan in 1940, Prime Minister Phibun proclaimed a quasi-Fascist program for Thailand, involving mass mobilization at home and expansion abroad.[130] In a secret agreement signed in early 1940, Phibun agreed to support Japan's war effort in exchange for recognition of Thai claims to the Shan states.[131] Jumping off from bases in Thailand, the Japanese 15th Army invaded lower Burma at the outbreak of the war and occupied Rangoon in March 1942. Determined to cut the famed Burma Road that was supplying Chinese forces in Yunnan with munitions from India, the Japanese pushed north in three columns, shattering Allied defenses. Driving the demoralized Nationalist Chinese before them, Japan's eastern column entered the Shan states, with the main force reaching the Burma Road junction on April 30 and a smaller group advancing toward Kengtung in the south.[132]

As the battle lines moved away toward India in the west, the Japanese commanders invited their Thai allies to occupy the southern Shan states, now safely distant from combat. In May 1942 the Thai Northern Army marched into the Shan states and occupied the main market town at Kengtung. There Major General Phin Choonhawan, governor of what Bangkok now called the United Thai State, established a military administration that would control the area for the next two years. After the end of the monsoon rains in September, the Northern Army continued its march toward China, overcoming weak resistance from scattered Nationalist Chinese (Kuomintang, KMT) garrisons and reaching the China border in January 1943.[133] A few months after the military occupation of Kengtung, the Thai opium monopoly imported 36 tons from the Shan states, raising opium revenues to a record level.[134] At war's end, when Japanese forces began to suffer reverses on the Indian front, Thailand's Northern Army began its withdrawal from the Shan states. Four months after a new civilian cabinet ousted Prime Minister Phibun in July 1944, Bangkok ordered Governor Phin home from Kengtung and demobilized his Northern Army.[135]

In the annals of World War II, the Thai advance into the Shan states appears as a minor military operation, a footnote to the big battles fought elsewhere. Viewed from a different perspective, the occupation gains significance as an important phase in the development of the modern Southeast Asian drug trade. Many of the political links that would bind these disparate highlands into the Golden Triangle opium zone were forged during the Thai occupation. By the early 1950s, just a few years after the war, General Phibun's faction, including many veterans of the Northern Army, would use its contacts with the Nationalist Chinese military to import substantial quantities of Shan state opium. This alliance shaped a Burma-to-Bangkok opium corridor that remains, even forty years later, central to Southeast Asia's drug trade.

By allowing the Thai army direct contact with the Shan states for the first time, the wartime occupation fostered alliances between local elites and influential Thai military factions. Recalling his departure from Kengtung in 1944, Phin, later Thailand's chief of staff, recalled that "over 1,000 government officials and other well-wishers came to send me off. Many of them cried."[136] Of equal importance, the occupation also allowed contact with the Nationalist Chinese military in nearby Yunnan. Although the Chinese were enemies at the start of the war, Japan's slow decline led the Thai military, on orders from Prime Minister Phibun, to meet the commander of the KMT's 93rd Division, General Lu Wi-eng, at the border in April 1944.[137] When American OSS agents operating in Yunnan sought clandestine contacts among the Thai military in neighboring Kengtung, they learned that General Lu already had detailed lists of the Northern Army's officers.[138] After the war when Chinese Communist forces captured Yunnan, remnants of this same unit, the 93rd Division, retreated into Burma where they later developed the Shan opium trade in alliance with General Phin's faction.

The 36 tons of Shan opium exported to Thailand during the Northern Army's occupation of Kengtung hints at the politics that would underlie the postwar drug trade. The logistics for this particular shipment remain obscure, but the political connections that emerged from the Shan campaign are more obvious. Significantly, many of the Thai military who dominated the opium traffic with Burma after World War II were veterans of Shan state occupation. As architect of the 1947 coup and later chief of staff, General Phin—with the support of factional allies from his old northern command—emerged as Thailand's leading soldier-politician during the postwar decade. With a retinue of loyal subalterns, four daughters married to rising young officers, and a prominent soldier son in Colonel Chatchai Choonhawan, Phin played a preeminent role in structuring the military factions that dominated postwar Thai politics. The list of his Northern Army veterans thus reads like a lineage of Thai military strongmen—General Phao Siyanan (1947–1957), Field Marshal Sarit Thanarat (1957–1963), General Krit Siwara (1957–1976), and General Kriangsak Chamanan (1976–1980).[139]

Although not every leader of every faction was involved in the Shan opium trade, drug revenues would remain a major source of Thai military power in the decades following World War II. Moreover, the war in no way reduced Yunnan's exports to Southeast Asia. Both the Japanese army and the Nationalist Chinese government actively encouraged the opium traffic during the war. Even though they were at war with each other, the Nationalist Chinese government (which controlled the opium-growing provinces of southern China) sold substantial quantities of raw opium to the Japanese army (which occupied Burma and the coastal regions of China).[140] In addition, smugglers' caravans continued to filter across the border from Yunnan, providing substantial quantities of inexpensive opium for Thai addicts. Thus Thailand emerged from World War II with its large addict population intact and its dependence on imported opium undiminished.[141]

## Burma: Opium on the Shan Plateau

The British opium monopoly in Burma was one of the smallest and least profitable in all of Southeast Asia. Perhaps because Burma was administered as an appendage to their wealthy Indian empire, British colonial officials in Burma were rarely plagued by acute fiscal deficits and never pursued the opium business with the same vigor as their counterparts in the rest of Southeast Asia.

Soon after their arrival in Lower Burma in 1852, the British had begun importing large quantities of opium from India and marketing it through a government-controlled opium monopoly. However, in 1878 the British parliament passed the Opium Act and began to take steps to reduce opium consumption. Now opium could be sold only to registered Chinese opium smokers and Indian opium eaters, and it was absolutely illegal for any Burmese to smoke opium. However, a large number of Burmese had become introduced to the habit in the quarter century of unrestricted sale before prohibition.[142] While the regulations succeeded in reducing opium profits to less than 1 percent of total colonial revenues in 1939[143]—the lowest in Southeast Asia—they had limited success in controlling addiction. In 1930 a special League of Nations Commission of Inquiry reported that there were 55,000 registered addicts buying from the government shops and an additional 45,000 using illicit opium smuggled from China or the Shan states.[144]

In 1886 the British acquired an altogether different sort of opium problem when they completed their piecemeal conquest of the Kingdom of Burma by annexing the northern half of the country. Among their new possessions were the Shan states located in Burma's extreme northeast—the only area of Southeast Asia with any significant hill tribe opium production. Flanking the western border of China's Yunnan province, the Shan states are a rough mountainous region somewhat larger than England itself. While it did not take the British long to subdue the lowland areas of Upper Burma, many of the mountain tribes inhabiting the Shan states' vast, rugged terrain were never brought under their control. Until the very end of their colonial rule, opium from these hill tribe areas would continue to be smuggled into Lower Burma, mocking British efforts at reducing the addict population and cutting into the profits from their opium monopoly. Although the British made a number of efforts at abolishing opium cultivation in the Shan states, geography, ethnography, and politics ultimately defeated them.

The mountain ridges and wide rivers that crisscross the Shan states have their beginnings far to the north in the mountains of Tibet. The jagged, east-west crescent of the Himalayan mountain range is twisted sharply to the south at the point where Tibet and China meet, thereby channeling its waters into the southward plunge of Asia's great rivers—the Yangtze, Mekong, Salween, and Irrawaddy. As the Irrawaddy's tributaries cross the extreme northern tip of Burma—the Kachin state—they flow through long north-south alluvial plains and relatively narrow upland valleys that lie between 7,000-to-10,000 foot mountain ridges. Soon after the Irrawaddy turns west near the Kachin state's southern border and spills out onto the broad plains of central Burma, the sharp mountains of the Kachin state give way to the wide plateaus of the western Shan states and the large upland valleys of the eastern Shan states.

It is this striking interplay of sharp mountain ranges and upland valleys—not any formal political boundary—that has determined the ethnic geography of the Shan and Kachin states. The Shans are lowland rice cultivators who keep to the flat, wide valleys where their buffalo-drawn plows can till the soil and ample water is available for irrigation. Throughout the Kachin and Shan states the Shans dominate the flatlands of the upland valleys and plateaus.[145] Most practice some form of the Buddhist religion, and all speak a dialect of the Thai language similar to that spoken by their neighbors across the border in northern Thailand. Their irrigated paddy fields have always produced a substantial surplus, providing for the formation of relatively large towns and strong governments. Generally, the larger valleys have become tiny autonomous principalities ruled by feudal autocrats known as *sawbwas* and clans of supporting nobility.

Ringing the upland valleys are mountain ridges inhabited by a wide variety of hill tribes. The hills of the Kachin state itself are populated mainly by Kachins. Farther south the Kachns thin out and the hills are populated with Wa, Pa-o, Lahu, and Palaung. All these mountain dwellers till the soil by cutting down the trees and burning the forest to clear land for dry rice, tea, and opium. Needless to say, this kind of agriculture is hard on the soil, and erosion and soil depletion force the hill tribes to seek new villages periodically. As a result, the political organization of the hill tribes is much less tightly structured than that of the Shans. Many of the tribes practice a form of village democracy, while others, particularly some of the Kachins, have an aristocracy and a rigid social structure.[146] Whatever their own political structure might be, few of these tribes are larger or concentrated enough to be truly autonomous, and most owe some allegiance to the feudal Shan *sawbwas*, who control local commerce and have more powerful armies.

As British colonial officials traveled through the Shan states in the late 1880s and the early 1890s seeking native allies, they quickly discovered that the region's population of 1,200,000 Shans and tribesmen was ruled by thirty-four independent *sawbwas*. Their kingdoms ranged from Kengtung (a little larger than Massachusetts and Connecticut combined) all the way down to several tiny fiefs with an area of less than twenty square miles. The British position was very insecure: the Shan territories east of the Salween River were tied economically to China, and many of the other *sawbwas* were considering changing their political allegiance to the king of Siam. The British secured the *sawbwas'* wavering loyalties by "showing the flag" throughout the Shan states. In November 1887 two columns of about 250 men each set off to "conquer" the Shan states.[147] Bluffing their way from state to state, the British convinced the *sawbwas* that the British Empire was far stronger than their meager forces might indicate and thus was deserving of their allegiance.

But the British were hardly eager to spend vast sums of money administering these enormous territories; and so, in exchange for the right to build railways and control foreign policy, they recognized the *sawbwas'* traditional powers and prerogatives.[148] In granting the *sawbwas* control over their internal affairs, the British doomed their future efforts at eradicating opium cultivation in northeastern Burma. The *sawbwas* received a considerable portion of the tribal opium harvest as tribute, and opium exports to Siam and Lower Burma represented an important part of their personal income. However, after years of determined refusal, the *sawbwas* finally acceded to British demands for opium controls and in 1923 the Shan States Opium Act was passed into law. Growers were registered, attempts were made to buy up all the opium,[149] and the total harvest was gradually reduced from 37 tons in 1926 to 8 tons in 1936. While the British were the police, army, and government in the rest of Burma, in the Shan states they were merely advisers, and there were limits to their power. Opium production was never fully eradicated, and the British soon abandoned their unpopular campaign.[150]

After World War II, weakened by a costly war on the European continent, the British yielded to the rising demand and gave Burma its independence. But they had left a troublesome legacy. Although the new government was able to ban opium consumption completely with the Opium Den Suppression Act of 1950,[151] it found no solution to the problem of poppy cultivation in the trans-Salween Shan states.[152] The British had saddled the Burmese with autonomous *sawbwas* who would tolerate no interference in their internal affairs and steadfastly resisted any attempts at opium suppression. Although there was only limited opium production when the British left in 1947, the seeds had been planted from which greater things would grow.

## Opium Finance in French Indochina

Vietnam was one of the first stops for Chinese emigrating from overpopulated Kwangtung and Fukien provinces in the late eighteenth and early nineteenth centuries. While the Vietnamese emperors welcomed the Chinese because of their valuable contributions to the nation's commercial development, they soon found the Chinese opium habit a serious economic liability. Almost all of Vietnam's foreign trade in the first half of the nineteenth century was with the ports of southern China. Vietnam's Chinese merchants managed the trade efficiently, exporting Vietnamese commodities such as rice, lacquerware, and ivory to Canton to pay for the import of Chinese luxury and manufactured goods. In the 1830s, however, British opium began flooding into southern China in unprecedented quantities, seriously damaging the entire fabric of Sino-Vietnamese trade. The addicts of southern China and Vietnam paid for their opium in silver, and the resulting drain of specie from both countries caused inflation and skyrocketing silver prices.[153]

The Vietnamese court was adamantly opposed to opium smoking on moral as well as economic grounds. Opium was outlawed almost as soon as it appeared, and in 1820 the emperor ordered that even sons and younger brothers of addicts were required to turn the offenders over to the authorities.[154]

The imperial court continued its efforts, which were largely unsuccessful, to restrict opium smuggling from China, until military defeat at the hands of the French forced it to establish an imperial opium franchise. In 1858 a French invasion fleet arrived off the coast of Vietnam, and after an abortive attack on the port of Dangang, not far from the royal capital of Hué, sailed south to Saigon, where they established a garrison and occupied much of the nearby Mekong Delta. Unable to oust the French from their Saigon beachhead, the Vietnamese emperor finally agreed to cede the three provinces surrounding Saigon and to pay an onerous, long-term indemnity worth 4 million silver francs. But the opium trade with southern China had disrupted the Vietnamese economy so badly that the court found it impossible to meet this onerous obligation without finding a new source of revenue. Yielding to the inevitable, the emperor established an opium franchise in the northern half of the country and leased it to Chinese merchants at a rate that would enable him to pay off the indemnity in twelve years.[155]

More significant in the long run was the French establishment of an opium franchise to put the new colony on a paying basis only six months after they annexed Saigon in 1862. Opium was imported from India, taxed at 10 percent of value, and sold by licensed Chinese merchants to all comers.[156] Opium became a lucrative source of income, and this successful experiment was repeated as the French acquired other areas in Indochina. As the French annexed Cambodia (1863), Annam (1883), Tonkin (1884) and Laos (1893), they founded autonomous opium monopolies to finance the heavy initial expenses of colonial rule. While the opium franchise had succeeded in putting southern Vietnam on a paying basis within several years, the rapid expansion of French holdings in the 1880s and 1890s created a huge fiscal deficit for Indochina as a whole. Moreover, a hodgepodge administration of five separate colonies was a model of inefficiency, and legions of French functionaries were wasting what little profits these colonies generated. While a series of administrative reforms repaired much of the damage in the early 1890s, continuing fiscal deficits still threatened the future of French Indochina.[157]

The man of the hour was a former Parisian budget analyst named Paul Doumer, and one of his solutions was opium. Soon after he stepped off the boat from France in 1897, Governor-General Doumer began a series of major fiscal reforms: a job freeze was imposed on the colonial bureaucracy, unnecessary expenses were cut, and the five autonomous colonial budgets were consolidated under a centralized treasury.[158] But most important, Doumer reorganized the opium business in 1899, expanding sales and sharply reducing expenses. After consolidating the five autonomous opium agencies into the single opium monopoly, Doumer constructed a modern, efficient opium refinery in Saigon to process raw Indian resin into prepared smoker's opium. The new factory devised a special mixture of prepared opium that burned quickly, thus encouraging the smoker to consume more opium than he might ordinarily.[159] Under Doumer's direction, the opium monopoly made its first purchases of cheap opium from China's Yunnan province so that government dens and retail shops could expand their clientele to include the poorer workers who could not afford the high-priced Indian brands.[160] More dens and shops were opened to meet expanded consumer demand. By 1918 French Indochina was home to 1,512 dens and 3,098 retail shops. Business boomed.

As Governor-General Doumer himself has proudly reported, these reforms increased opium revenues by 50 percent during his four years in office, accounting for over one-third of all colonial revenues.[161] For the first time in more than ten years there was a surplus in the treasury. Moreover, Doumer's reforms gave French investors new confidence in the Indochina venture, and he was able to raise a 200-million-franc loan, which financed a major public works program, part of Indochina's railway network, and many of the colony's hospitals and schools.[162]

Nor did the French colonists have any illusions about how they were financing Indochina's development. When the government announced plans to build a railway up the Red River valley into China's Yunnan province, a spokesman for the business community explained one of its primary goals:

> It is particularly interesting, at the moment one is about to vote funds for the construction of a railway to Yunnan, to search for ways to augment the commerce between the province and our territory. . . . The regulation of commerce in *opium* and salt in Yunnan might be adjusted in such a way as to facilitate commerce and increase the tonnage carried on our railway. [Emphasis added.][163]

While a vigorous international crusade against the "evils of opium" during the 1920s and 1930s forced other colonial administrations in Southeast Asia to reduce the scope of their opium monopolies, French officials remained immune to such moralizing. When the Great Depression of 1929 pinched tax revenues, they managed to raise opium monopoly profits (which had been declining) to balance the books.

Opium revenues climbed steadily and by 1938 accounted for 15 percent of all colonial tax revenues—the highest in Southeast Asia.[164]

In the long run, however, the opium monopoly weakened the French position in Indochina. Vietnamese nationalists pointed to the opium monopoly as the ultimate example of French exploitation.[165] Some of Ho Chi Minh's most bitter propaganda attacks were reserved for those French officials who managed the monopoly. In 1945 Vietnamese nationalists reprinted this French author's description of a smoking den and used it as revolutionary propaganda:

> Let's enter several opium dens frequented by the coolies, the longshoremen for the port.
>
> The door opens on a long corridor; to the left of the entrance, is a window where one buys the drug. For 50 centimes one gets a small five gram box, but for several hundred, one gets enough to stay high for several days.
>
> Just past the entrance, a horrible odor of corruption strikes your throat. The corridor turns, turns again, and opens on several small dark rooms, which become veritable labyrinths lighted by lamps which give off a troubled yellow light. The walls, caked with dirt, and indented with long niches. In each niche a man is spread out like a stone. Nobody moves when we pass. Not even a glance. They are glued to a small pipe whose watery gurgle alone breaks the silence. The others are terribly immobile, with slow gestures, legs strung out, arms in the air, as if they had been struck dead. . . . The faces are characterized by overly white teeth; the pupils with a black glaze, enlarged, fixed on god knows what; the eyelids do not move; and on the pasty cheeks, this vague, mysterious smile of the dead. It was an awful sight to see walking among these cadavers.[166]

This kind of propaganda struck a responsive chord among the Vietnamese, for the social costs of opium addiction were heavy indeed. Large numbers of plantation workers, miners, and urban laborers spent their entire salaries in the opium dens. The strenuous work, combined with the debilitating effect of the drug and lack of food, produced some extremely emaciated laborers, who could only be described as walking skeletons. Workers often died of starvation, or more likely their families did. While only 2 percent of the population were addicts, the toll among the Vietnamese elite was considerably greater. With an addiction rate of almost 20 percent, the native elite, most of whom were responsible for local administration and tax collection, were rendered less competent and more liable to corruption by their expensive opium habits.[167] In fact, the village official who was heavily addicted to opium became something of a symbol for official corruption in Vietnamese literature of the 1930s. The Vietnamese novelist Nguyen Cong Hoan has written an unforgettable portrait of such a man:

> Still the truth is that Representative Lai is descended from the tribe of people which form the world's sixth race. For if he were white, he would have been a European; if yellow, he would have been an Asian; if red, an American; if brown, an Australian; and if black, an African. But he was a kind of green, which is indisputably the complexion of the race of drug addicts.
>
> By the time the Customs officer came in, Representative Lai was already decently dressed. He pretended to be in a hurry. Nevertheless, his eyelids were still half closed, and the smell of opium was still intense, so that everyone could guess that he had just been through a "dream session." Perhaps the reason he had felt he needed to pump himself full of at least ten pipes of opium was that he imagined it might somehow reduce his bulk, enabling him to move about more nimbly.
>
> He cackled, and strode effusively over to the Customs officer as if he were about to grab an old friend to kiss. He bowed low and, with both of his hands, grasped the Frenchman's hand and stuttered.
>
> "Greetings to your honor, why has your honor not come here in such a long time?"[168]

## World War II Opium Crisis

At the beginning of World War II Indochina's 2,500 opium dens and retail shops were still maintaining more than 100,000 addicts and providing 15 percent of all tax revenues. The French imported almost 60 tons of opium annually from Iran and Turkey to supply this vast enterprise. However, as World War II erupted across the face of the globe, trade routes were blocked by the battle lines and Indochina was cut off from the poppy fields of India and Persia. Following the German conquest of France in the spring of 1940 and the Japanese occupation of Indochina several months later, the British navy imposed an embargo on shipping to Indochina. Although the Japanese military occupation was pleasant enough for most French officials who were allowed to go on administering Indochina, it created enormous problems for those who had to manage the opium monopoly. Unless an alternative source of opium could be found, the colony would face a major fiscal crisis.

While smuggled Yunnanese opium might solve the addicts' problem, the opium monopoly needed a more controllable source of supply. The only possible solution was to induce the Hmong of Laos and northwest Tonkin to expand their opium production, and in 1940 the opium monopoly did just that.

However, as French officials embarked on this massive poppy production campaign, some of the more experienced of them must have had their doubts about the chances of success. Past efforts at either expanding Hmong opium production or reducing the amount of opium they diverted to smugglers had sparked at least two major revolts and countless bloody incidents. Only three years after the French arrived in Laos, ill-advised demands for increased opium deliveries from Hmong farmers in the Plain of Jars region had prompted these independent tribesmen to attack the local French garrison.[169] Later French mismanagement of their opium dealings with the Hmong had been a contributing factor in the massive Hmong uprising that swept across Laos and Tonkin from 1919 until 1922.[170] Their attempts at dealing with the smuggling problem were even more disastrous. In 1914 a French crackdown on Yunnanese opium smugglers provoked one of the most violent anti-French uprisings in Laotian history. After French colonial officials started harassing their caravans trading in the Plain of Jars region, Yunnanese opium traders led thousands of hill tribesmen into revolt and occupied an entire Laotian province for almost a year, until two French regiments finally drove them back into China.[171]

Despite this long history of armed insurgency in response to French attempts at dealing with smugglers and Hmong opium farmers, the opium monopoly had no choice but to expand the Hmong production and repress smuggling so that the increased harvests would not become contraband. The fiscal consequences of doing nothing were too serious, and the French had to accept the risk of provoking an uprising in the hills.

As the opium monopoly set out to transform the tribal opium economy in 1939–1940, instructions similar to these were telegrammed to colonial officials throughout the highlands advising them on how to expand poppy cultivation:

> Your role may be summed up as follows:
> —encourage cultivation;
> —survey the cultivations and know as exactly as possible the surface cultivated;
> —repress clandestine traffic.[172]

The French devised new tactics to increase the chances of their success and minimize the risk of violence. No longer were customs officers sent out with heavily armed horsemen to patrol the highland ridges and market towns for smugglers; instead, they were given pack horses loaded with cloth, silver, and trade goods and ordered to eliminate the smugglers by outbidding them. Rather than sending out French officers to persuade the tribesmen to increase their opium crops and creating possible occasions for ugly incidents, the opium monopoly instead selected prestigious tribal leaders as its opium brokers. These leaders relayed the new demand for opium to the tribesmen, imposed whatever particular tax or law was most likely to include compliance, and delivered the opium to French officials after paying the farmer a negotiated price.

Purely from the viewpoint of increasing opium production, this policy was a substantial success. Indochina's opium production jumped from 7.4 tons in 1940 to 60.6 tons in 1944—an 800 percent increase in four years. These crops were enough to maintain an adequate supply for Indochina's 100,000-plus addicts and produce a steady rise in government opium revenues—from 15 million piasters in 1939 to 24 million in 1943.[173]

In exchange for their cooperation, the French supported the political aspirations of tribal leaders. The most important opium-growing regions in Indochina were Xieng Khouang province in northeastern Laos and the Tai country of northeastern Tonkin. Both regions had a high concentration of opium-growing Hmong tribesmen and lay astride major communication routes. By choosing Touby Lyfoung as their opium broker in Xieng Khouang and Deo Van Long in the Tai country, the French made political commitments that were to have unforeseen consequences for the future of their colonial rule.

## Highland Poppy Farmers

In the 1970s the Hmong of Laos could still recall that there had once been "great Hmong kingdoms" in the highland plateaus of southern China several hundred years ago. In fact, Chinese imperial archives show that large numbers of Hmong lived in southwestern China (Szechwan, Yunnan, Hunan, and Kweichow provinces) for more than two thousand years. In 1971 there were still more than 2.5 million Hmong living in the mountains of these four provinces. Until the seventeenth century, these rugged provinces were of little importance to the imperial court in Peking, and the emperors were generally content as long as the Hmong nobles sent regular tribute. In exchange, the emperor decorated the Hmong leaders with titles and recognized the legitimacy of their autonomous kingdoms.[174] When the emperors of the Ming dynasty (1368–1644), for example, were confronted with Hmong dissidence, they rarely sent in exterminating armies. Instead they weakened the powerful Hmong kingdoms by appointing more kings and nobles, thereby creating a host of squabbling tribal principalities.[175]

This policy of indirect rule produced a rather curious political hybrid. In the midst of an imperial China divided into systematic provinces and governed by a meritocracy respected for its erudition, there sprang up a random mosaic of Hmong fiefs. These kingdoms were ruled by hereditary "little kings," known as *kaitong*, who commanded a quasi-religious reverence from their subjects. Each kingdom was dominated by a different clan, the *kaitong* and the ruling aristocracy usually sharing the same family name.[176] But trouble descended on the Hmong tribes after the Manchu dynasty was established in 1644. Among their many bureaucratic innovations, the Manchus decided to abolish the autonomy of the Hmong kingdoms and integrate them into the regular bureaucracy. When this policy met with resistance, the Manchus began to exterminate these troublesome tribes and to repopulate their lands with the more pliable ethnic Chinese.[177] After a two-hundred-year extermination campaign culminated in a series of bloody massacres in the mid-nineteenth century, thousands of Hmong tribesmen fled southward toward Indochina.[178]

Most of the retreating Hmong moved southeastward and burst on northern Vietnam's Tonkin Delta like an invading army. But the Vietnamese army drove the Hmong back into the mountains without great difficulty since the invaders were weakened by the humid delta climate and frightened by the Vietnamese elephant battalions.[179] The defeated Hmong scattered into the Vietnamese highlands, finally settling in semipermanent mountain villages.

Three Hmong *kaitong*, however, avoided the headlong rush for the Tonkin Delta and turned to the west, leading their clans past Dien Bien Phu and into northeastern Laos. One of these clans was the Ly, from southern Szechwan province. Their *kaitong* had been the leader of the Hmong resistance in Szechwan, and when the Chinese massacres began in 1856 he ordered his four sons to lead the survivors south while he remained to hold back the Chinese armies. His third son, Ly Nhiavu, invested with the title of *kaitong*, led the survivors on a year-long march that ended in Nong Het district in Laos, near the present Laos-Vietnam border.[180] The hills surrounding Nong Het were uninhabited and the rich soil was ideal for their slash-and-burn agriculture. The location had already attracted two other refugee clans—the Mua and Lo. Since the Lo *kaitong* was the first to arrive, he became the nominal leader of the region. As the word spread back to China and Vietnam that the Laotian hills were fertile and unoccupied, thousands of Hmong began to migrate southward. Since no other *kaitong* arrived to challenge the original triumvirate, Nong Het remained the most important Hmong political center in Laos.

Soon after the French arrived in 1893, their colonial officers began purchasing opium for the Laotian opium monopoly and ordered the Hmong to increase their production. Angered that the French had failed to consult him before making the demand, the Lo *kaitong* ordered an attack on the provincial headquarters in Xieng Khouang City. But

Hmong flintlocks were no match for modern French rifles, and the uprising was quickly suppressed. Humiliated by his defeat, the Lo *kaitong* conceded his position in the triumvirate to the Mau *kaitong*. The French, however, were considerably chastened by their first attempt at dealing directly with the Hmong and thereafter dealt with them only through their own leaders or through Lao administrators.

Until the opium crisis of 1940 forced them to intervene in Hmong politics once more, the French exercised a more subtle influence over tribal affairs. But they still had ultimate political authority, and those Hmong leaders ambitious and clever enough to ingratiate themselves with the French could not fail to gain an important advantage. Ly Foung and his son Touby Lyfoung were such men.

Although Ly Foung was a member of the Ly clan, he was no relation to *kaitong* Ly Nhiavu or his aristocratic family. Ly Foung's father had arrived in Nong Het as a porter for a Chinese merchant in 1865, eight years after *kaitong* Ly Nhiavu. Although Ly Foung's father asked Ly Nhiavu and his three brothers to accept him as a fellow clansman, they refused. He was from Yunnan, not Szechwan, and his willingness to work as a porter—a virtual slave—for a hated Chinese made him unacceptable in the eyes of the Ly aristocrats.[181]

Rejected by the aristocracy, Ly Foung's father founded his own small village in the Nong Het area and married a local tribeswoman, who bore him a large family. Unfortunately, some of his children were born with serious congenital defects, and he had to center all of his ambitions on his third son, Ly Foung, who grew up to become a remarkable linguist, speaking Chinse and Lao fluently and having an adequate command of Vietnamese and French. Ly Foung, aware that kinship and marriage ties were the basis of power among the Hmong, set out to marry into *kaitong* Lo Bliayao's family. Reportedly a rather strong, hard man, Bliayao possessed undeniable talents as a leader that had enabled him to establish himself as the premier *kaitong* of Nong Het.

The traditional Hmong wedding is unusual. When a young man has decided he wants to marry a particular woman, he forcibly abducts her with the help of his friends and bundles her off to a makeshift forest cabin until the marriage is consummated. The custom has declined in popularity and even in its heyday the kidnapping was usually not performed unless the parents gave their tacit consent. In 1918 Ly Foung decided to marry Lo Bliayao's favorite daughter, May, but instead of consulting with the father himself, Ly Foung reportedly paid the bride's uncle to arrange the abduction. Whatever Bliayao may have thought before the marriage (there are reports that he disliked Ly Foung), he made no protest and hired Ly Foung as his personal assistant and secretary.[182] Although May gave birth to Touby, the postwar Hmong political leader, in August 1919 and to a healthy daughter as well, the marriage was not a happy one. During a particularly bitter quarrel in their fourth year of marriage, Ly Foung beat May severely. She became despondent and committed suicide by eating a fatal dosage of opium. In his rage and grief, Lo Bliayao fired Ly Foung as his secretary and severed all ties with the Ly clan.[183]

To avoid a seemingly inevitable confrontation between the Lo and Ly clans, the French accepted the Hmong suggestion of separating the feuding clans by dividing Nong Het district into two administrative districts. Lo Bliayao's eldest son was appointed chief of Keng Khoai district, and several years later Ly Foung's elder son was appointed chief of Phac Boun district.[184]

The division of Nong Het district was accepted without protest, and the quarreling ceased. In December 1935, however, *kaitong* Lo Bliayao died, severing the last link with the "great Hmong kingdoms" of southern China and creating serious political problems for the Lo clan. Lo Bliayao's eldest son and successor, Song Tou, was in no way his equal Devoting his time to gambling and hunting, Song Tou avoided his political responsibilities and soon dealt a serious blow to his family's prestige by mismanaging local tax collections and losing his position as chief of Keng Khoai district.[185] When Ly Foung agreed almost immediately to make up the taxes Song Tou lost, the French colonial government appointed him district chief.

It was a great victory for the Ly Foung family. Seventy years after his father had been rejected by the Ly aristocrats, Ly Foung had made himself leader of the Ly clan and the most powerful Hmong in Nong Het. With Nong Het's two districts governed by him and his son, Ly Foung had excluded the Lo from all the high political offices open to the Hmong and secured a monopoly on political power.

The Lo clan's decline deeply disturbed Song Tou's younger brother, Faydang, who had inherited his father's strong character. Shortly after Ly Foung assumed office, Lo Faydang set off on a 120-mile journey to the Lao royal capital, Luang Prabang, where he petitioned the popular Prince Phetsarath, known as one of the few Lao aristocrats with any sympathy for the hill tribes. The prince interceded on his behalf and got everyone involved—the French, Ly Foung, and Laotian aristocrats—to agree that Faydang would become district chief of Keng Khoai when death or illness removed Ly Foung from office.[186]

But when Ly Foung died in September 1939, the French broke their promise to Faydang and gave the post to Ly Foung's son, Touby. They had regarded Faydang's petition to the royal court two years before as an act of insubordination and were unwilling to entrust Faydang with any authority in the region. Chastened by their earlier experiences with the tribes, the French were interested in dealing only with tribal leaders of proven loyalty who would act as brokers to purchase the opium harvest and reduce the amount diverted to smugglers.

While Faydang was a possible troublemaker, Touby's loyalty and competence were proven. His father had understood how much the French valued a good colonial education, and Touby was the first Hmong ever to attend high school, graduating from the Vinh Lycée in the spring of 1939 with a good academic record. When Ly Foung died that September, both Touby and Faydang clearly intended to present themselves before the assembly of Keng Khoai village for election to the now vacant office of district chief. Without any explanation, the French commissioner announced that Faydang was disbarred from the election. Touby ran virtually unopposed and won an overwhelming victory.[187]

With the outbreak of World War II, the French launched a massive effort to boost tribal opium production and Touby's political future was guaranteed. Several months after his election Touby began an eight-year tenure as the only Hmong member of the opium purchasing board, providing valuable technical information on how best to expand Hmong production.[188] In Nong Het region itself, Touby raised the annual head tax from three silver piasters to an exorbitant eight piasters but gave the tribesmen the alternative of paying 3 kilograms of raw opium instead.[189] Most Hmong were too poor to save eight silver piasters a year and took the alternative of paying in opium. Since an average Hmong farmer probably harvested less than 1 kilogram of raw opium a year before Touby's election, the tax increase precipitated an opium boom in Nong Het. With its fertile hills, excellent communications (Laos's major road to the sea passed through the district), and concentrated Hmong population, Nong Het became one of Indochina's most productive opium-growing areas.

Moreover, these measures were applied to Hmong districts across northern Laos, changing the hill tribe economy from subsistence agriculture to cash-crop opium farming. Touby himself felt that Laos's opium harvest more than doubled during this period, rising to as much as 30 or 40 tons a year. As one French colonial official put it, "Opium used to be one of the nobles of the land; today it is king."[190]

Although Faydang pleaded continually throughout World War II with French authorities to install him as district officer as they had promised, the opium imperative tied the French firmly to Touby. Faced with a situation where two clans in a village or district were incompatible, the Hmong usually separated them by splitting the village or district, as they had done earlier in Nong Het. But the French were firmly behind Touby, who could guarantee them an increasing supply of opium, and rejected

Faydang's requests. As a result of their opium policy, Touby became a loyal official, while his uncle Faydang became increasingly embittered toward colonial rule. The French betrayal of Faydang was probably a significant factor in his evolution as one of Laos's more important revolutionary leaders. Moreover, the French policy created intolerable tensions between the Lo and Ly clans—tensions that exploded at the first opportunity.

After the Japanese surrender in August 1945 the Laotian and Vietnamese (Viet Minh) nationalist movements took advantage of the weakened French posture to occupy the major cities and towns. Throughout Indochina the French began to gather intelligence, seize strategic points, and generally maximize their minimal resources to prepare for reoccupation. Realizing the strategic importance of the Plain of Jars, the Free French had parachuted commandos and arms into secret bases set up for them by Touby Lyfoung and his followers in 1944 and 1945.[191] Then, on September 3, French officers and Touby's Hmong commandos reoccupied Xieng Khouang City, near the Plain of Jars, without firing a shot. Touby was sent back to Nong Het to secure the region and guard the mountain pass leading into Vietnam against a possible Viet Minh assault. Doubting Faydang's loyalty to the French, Touby sent a messenger to his village demanding that he declare his loyalty.[192] Although Faydang had not yet made contact with the Viet Minh or the Lao nationalist movement, he refused. Now that Touby had some modern arms and surplus ammunition, he decided to settle the matter once and for all. He sent sixty men to encircle the village and massacre the Lo clansmen. But Faydang had been expecting the move and had ordered the villagers to sleep in the fields. When the attack began, Faydang and some two hundred of his followers fled across the border to Muong Sen and made contact, for the first time, with the Viet Minh.[193] Guiding a Viet Minh column into Laos several months later, Faydang urged his fellow Lo clansmen to rise in revolt, and several hundred of them followed him back into North Vietnam.

When Faydang began to organize the guerrilla movement later known as the Hmong Resistance League, the oppressive French opium tax administered by Touby was evidently a major factor in his ability to recruit followers. During World War II, many Hmong had been driven into debt by the onerous tax, and some of the poorer farmers had been forced to sell their children to deliver a sufficient amount of opium.[194] According to Faydang's own account, the Hmong began joining his movement "with great enthusiasm" after he abolished the opium tax and introduced some other major reforms in 1946.[195]

More than thirty years after the French began boosting Hmong opium production, almost 30,000 of Touby's followers were fighting as mercenaries for the CIA. And on the other side of the battle lines, thousands of Faydang's Hmong guerrillas joined the Pathet Lao revolutionary movement. This simple clan conflict, which was pushed to the breaking point by the French opium imperative, became a permanent fissure and helped to fuel twenty-five years of Laotian civil war.

## Opium in the Tai Country

With the exception of Laos, the largest opium-producing region in Indochina was the adjacent area of northwestern Vietnam known as the Tai country. Its ethnic geography was quite similar to that of the Shan states of Burma; the upland valleys were inhabited by wet-rice farmers at altitudes too low for poppy cultivation. But Hmong tribes lived on the cool mountain ridges where slash-and-burn agriculture was ideal for poppy cultivation. Since the Hmong of northwestern Tonkin had no large population centers or powerful political leaders like Lo Bliayao and Ly Foung, French efforts to organize local militia or regular civil administration in the 1930s had consistently failed.[196] In contrast, the French found it easy to work with the valley populations, the White Tai and Black Tai.

Consequently, as French administrators mapped their strategy for expanding opium production in northwestern Tonkin in 1940, they decided not to work directly with the Hmong as they were doing in Laos. Instead, they allied themselves with powerful Tai feudal leaders who controlled the lowland market centers and most of the region's commerce. To make the Tai leaders more effective opium brokers, the French suspended their forty-year policy of culturally Vietnamizing the Tai by administering the country with Vietnamese bureaucrats.

Although the French had confirmed the authority of Deo Van Tri, White Tai ruler of Lai Chau, when they first pacified the Tai country in the 1890s, they had gradually reduced the authority of his successors until they were little more than minor district chiefs.[197] Potentially powerful leaders like Deo Van Tri's second son, Deo Van Long, had been sent to school in Hanoi and posted to minor positions in the Tonkin Delta. However, in 1940 the French reversed this policy and began using the Tai leaders as opium brokers. Deo Van Long returned to Lai Chau as a territorial administrator.[198] In exchange for French political support, Deo Van Long and the other Tai leaders negotiated with their Hmong mountain neighbors for the purchase of opium and sent the increased harvest to the opium monopoly in Saigon for refining and sale. After 1940 these feudal chiefs forced Hmong farmers to expand their opium harvest;[199] by the war's end there were 4.5 to 5 tons of Hmong opium available for shipment to Saigon.[200]

This use of Tai leaders as opium brokers may have been one of the most significant administrative decisions the French made during their entire colonial rule. In 1954 the French decided to risk the outcome of the First Indochina War on a single decisive battle in a remote mountain valley of northwestern Tonkin named Dien Bien Phu. The French commanders, hoping to protect their ongoing operations in the Tai country and block a Viet Minh offensive into Laos, felt it would be impossible for the Viet Minh to set up artillery on the ridges overlooking the new fortress. They planned a trap for the Viet Minh, who would be destroyed in the open valley by French aircraft and artillery fire. But on the commanding mountain ridges lived the Hmong who had been cheated and underpaid for their opium for almost fifteen years by the Tai feudal leaders, who were closely identified with the French. Thousands of these Hmong served as porters for the Viet Minh and eagerly scouted the ridges they knew so well for ideal gun emplacements. The well-placed Viet Minh artillery batteries shattered the French fortifications at Dien Bien Phu and France's colonial empire along with them.

## Postwar Opium Boom

During the postwar decade, Southeast Asia began producing its own supplies of raw opium. After major changes in the world market cut off the Indian and Chinese imports that had sustained its smokers for over three centuries, Southeast Asia's highland tribes began harvesting enough opium to supply local urban markets, making the region self-sufficient in opium for the first time in its history.

The Southeast Asian opium economy had emerged from World War II essentially unchanged. The amount of opium harvested in what would later become the world's largest opium-producing area, Burma and northern Thailand, had increased very little, if at all. True, Indochina's total production had grown to 60 tons—a 600 percent increase—but Laos's total, only 30 tons, was still a long way from its estimated 1968 production of 100 to 150 tons. On balance, the Golden Triangle was still producing less than 80 tons annually—insignificant when compared with its 1970 production of 1,000 tons.

While Southeast Asia had not produced enough opium to make itself self-sufficient, the moderate increases in local production, combined with smuggled Yunnanese opium, were enough to maintain the seriously addicted and the affluent. Although Southeast Asian consumers faced rising prices—the Indochina monopoly's charge for a kilogram of opium increased 500 percent from 1939 to 1943—they experienced nothing comparable to the collective withdrawal American addicts suffered during World War II.[201] Thus, the core of Southeast Asia's opium consumers emerged from the war intact.

Immediately after the war, foreign opium supplies reappeared; Iranian opium was imported legally by the Thai and French opium monopolies, while overland smuggling from China's Yunnan province flourished. Not only was prewar consumer demand restored, but the addict population grew steadily. Thailand's addicts, for example, rose from an estimated 110,000 in 1940 to 250,000 in 1970.[202] While there were promising exceptions in the region—Singapore's and Malaysia's addict population dropped from an estimated 186,000 before the war to 40,000 in 1970[203]—the number of addicts in Southeast Asia as a whole increased substantially in the postwar period.

Yet within ten years after the end of World War II, Southeast Asia was totally cut off from all the foreign opium on which its addicts had depended for over three centuries. By 1955 three governmental decisions created a serious crisis in international opium trade and denied Southeast Asia all its foreign opium. In 1953 the major opium-producing countries in Europe, the Middle East, and South Asia signed the U.N. protocol and agreed not to sell opium on the international market for legalized smoking or eating. Although this international accord ended large shipments of Iranian opium to the Thai and French opium monopolies, international smugglers simply took over the Iranian government's role.

A far more serious blow to the Southeast Asian opium economy had come in 1949, when the Chinese People's Liberation Army won the civil war and drove the last remnants of Chiang Kai-shek's Nationalist Army out of Yunnan province. Yunnan was China's second largest opium grower and much of its vast poppy harvest had been smuggled into Southeast Asia. When the People's Liberation Army began patrolling the border in the early 1950s to prevent an expected counterattack by CIA-supported Nationalist Chinese troops, most opium caravans were halted. By the mid-1950s People's Republic agriculturalists and party workers had introduced substitute crops, and any possible opium seepage into Southeast Asia ceased.[204]

The key to China's suppression campaign was a massive detoxification program that eliminated demand among the world's largest addict population, estimated at 40 million in the 1930s. As a part of the revolutionary mobilization of the new regime, Communist cadres identified addicts and sent them to local drug clinics where opium use was denounced as an "imperialist and capitalist activity." Those who persisted in their addiction were branded criminals and dispatched to labor camps.[205] Through the process of land reform, extensive poppy fields were reclaimed for food production and further opium cultivation was banned under regulations approved at the State Administrative Council in February 1950.[206]

Despite the importance of China's policy for global drug trade, the U.S. Bureau of Narcotics simply refused to recognize the realities. Under the leadership of its militantly anti-Communist director, Harry Anslinger, the bureau conjured up images of a vast Communist state heroin complex pumping heroin into Asia and the West. "One primary outlet for the Red Chinese traffic has been Hong Kong," Anslinger wrote in 1961. "A prime target area in the United States was California. The Los Angeles area alone has probably received forty percent of the smuggled contraband from China's heroin and morphine plants."[207] After Anslinger's retirement and mass firings of corrupt bureau agents in the 1960s, a reformed federal agency, the Bureau of Narcotics and Dangerous Drugs, repudiated his position on China. "On the basis of information available to the U.S. Government," the new bureau reported, "there is no evidence that the People's Republic of China sanctions the illicit export of opium . . . or is involved in the illicit trafficking of narcotic drugs."[208]

Once the bureau removed Anslinger's ideological blinders, its analysts produced some perceptive commentary on the impact of China's successful prohibition. In a 1970 report titled "The World Opium Situation," the bureau described China's involvement in two major events that had changed the structure of world's narcotics traffic in recent decades:

> The world market for opium has experienced dynamic change—including two major upheavals—from the beginning of the postwar period down to the present. In order of importance the landmark events were (1) the shutdown of China's vast illicit market with the change of governments there in 1949 and (2) the abolition of cultivation in Iran after 1955 coupled with the rapid suppression of China's illicit production at about the same time.[209]

With the end of China's illicit contribution to Southeast Asia's opium supplies, Iran had become the region's major supplier in the early 1950s. In 1953, for example, Iranian opium accounted for 47 percent of all opium seized by Singapore police and customs and a higher percentage in other Southeast Asian nations.[210] Most of Iran's illegally diverted opium was smuggled eastward to Southeast Asia, but a substantial portion was also sent to Lebanon, the Arab states, and Europe.

In addition to its substantial exports, Iran had an addict population second only to China's. In 1949 Garland Williams, district supervisor for the U.S. Federal Bureau of Narcotics in Tehran, estimated that 11 percent of Iranian adults were drug users—1.3 million opium addicts in an adult population of 11.6 million. Although only 40 percent of Tehran's adults smoked, in provinces such as Kerman and Khorasson addiction reached 80 percent, and opium pipes were found in almost every house. Tehran itself had 500 opium dens with twenty to fifty people smoking in each at any given hour of the night.[211] "I have seen infants at their mother's breasts while the mothers are smoking opium in the dens,"[212] Williams reported in February 1949. "In another of these dens I saw child prostitutes, some of whom were less than ten years of age, and these little girls were playing with the men and . . . took their turns when some man would pay the price." Another den was a social club for local housewives who smoked while "there were many small children playing around in the rooms and breathing the opium smoke from the busy pipes." Outside the dens, Williams found opium pipes in the ubiquitous teahouses and in the homes of the elite where they "were very expensive and elaborate and [were] greatly treasured." If the residents did not smoke, then the pipe was necessary for guests. The country's fifty great families who owned "farmland in tremendous quantities" were convinced that "no crop will take the place of opium" since it was uniquely adapted for the harsh winter planting season. Since these great families controlled the Parliament (Majlis), the opium laws were weak, the office charged with the enforcement of restrictions on cultivation was "highly inefficient and corrupt," and "opium [was] growing all over Iran."[213]

Despite Williams's pessimistic appraisal, Iran began to reduce production sharply in 1950 with exports declining from 246 tons to only 41 tons by 1954.[214] Under the Shah's authoritarian rule, the final blow came in 1955 when the government announced the complete abolition of opium growing. According to a later CIA analysis, the Shah was motivated by "the poor health of military recruits and by increased international pressure." The Shah's prohibition, which was rigorously enforced, had a double impact on Asia's opium trade, first cutting its substantial exports to Southeast Asia and then creating a sudden demand for imports to sustain its vast addict population. Although the addict population declined slowly to some 350,000 opium users in 1969, the last year of the ban, Iran still consumed an average of 240 tons of opium, a considerable drain on the world's illicit supplies.[215] Since Iran played such a large role in Asia's opium trade as both producer and consumer, its decision disrupted the global traffic. Iran's sudden surge in illicit demand stimulated opium production in its neighbors to the east and west, Afghanistan and Turkey. Of equal importance, the shortage of illicit opium in southern Asia created a crisis for Southeast Asia's drug trade, long dependent on imports to sustain its large addict population.[216]

These dramatic events, which had changed the pattern of the international narcotics traffic, were the result of government action; and it would take equally bold initiatives on the part of Southeast Asia's governments if mass opium addiction were to survive. Decisions of this magnitude were not within the realm of the petty smugglers and traffickers who had supplied the region's poor addicts with Yunnanese and Shan state opium. Almost without exception it had been governmental bodies—not criminals—whose decisions made the major changes in the international narcotics trade. It was the French colonial government that expanded Indochina's production during World War II, the Chinese government that sealed the border and phased out Yunnan's opium production, and the Iranian government that decreed that Iran would no longer be Asia's major supplier of illicit opium.

In the 1950s the Thai, Lao, Vietnamese, and American governments made critical decisions that would expand Southeast Asia's opium production and transform the Golden Triangle into the largest single opium-producing area in the world.

# 4

## *Cold War Opium Boom*

IT IS MARCH OR APRIL, THE END OF THE DRY SEASON, IN SOUTH-east Asia's Golden Triangle. From the Kachin hills and Shan Plateau of Burma to the mountains of northern Thailand and northern Laos, the ground is parched and the rains are only weeks away. In every hill tribe village—whether it be Hmong, Yao, Lahu, Lisu, Wa, or Kachin—it is time to clear the fields for planting. On one of these hot, dusty mornings men, women, and children gather at the bottom of a wide hillside near the village, where for weeks the men have been chopping and slashing at the forest growth with single-bit axes. The felled trees are tinder-box dry.

Suddenly, the young men of the village race down the hill, igniting the timber with torches. Behind them, whirlwinds of flame shoot four hundred feet into the sky. Within an hour a billowing cloud of smoke rises two miles above the field. When the fires die down, the fields are covered with a nourishing layer of wood ash and the soil's moisture is sealed beneath the ground's fire-hardened surface. But before the planting can begin, these farmers must decide what crop they are going to plant—rice or poppies?

Although their agricultural techniques are traditional, these mountain farmers are very much a part of the modern world. And like farmers everywhere, their basic economic decisions are controlled by larger forces—by the international market for commodities and the prices of manufactured goods. In their case the high cost of transportation to and from their remote mountain villages rules out most cash crops and leaves only two choices—opium or rice. The safe decision has always been to plant rice, since it can be eaten if the market fails. Farmers can cultivate a small patch of poppy on the side, but they will not commit full time to opium production unless they are sure that there is a market for this crop.

A reliable market for their opium had developed in the early 1950s, when several major changes in the international opium trade slowed, and then halted, the imports of Chinese and Iranian opium that had supplied Southeast Asia's addicts for almost a hundred years. During World War II the United States had "extracted the agreement from its European allies" that they would abolish the opium monopolies when their colonies were recaptured and had maintained the pressure for prohibition after 1945.[1] As the official opium trade collapsed in the decade following the war, the region's military and intelligence agencies expanded the illicit traffic and expropriated a share of its profits to fund their operations. During the 1950s, Thai police, the Nationalist Chinese army, the French military, and the CIA adopted policies that allowed Southeast Asia's mass opium addiction to survive and even thrive.

As a result of these military and intelligence activities, Southeast Asia was approaching its present level of production by the end of the decade. Research by the U.S. Bureau of Narcotics showed that by the late 1950s Southeast Asia's Golden Triangle region was harvesting approximately 700 tons of raw opium, or about 50 percent of the world's total illicit production.[2] This rapid growth in opium production changed Southeast Asia's role in the global narcotics market. Starting as a drug-deficient region reliant on imports in the 1930s, Southeast Asia became self-sufficient in opium during the 1950s and would by the 1980s emerge as the world's main heroin supplier.

The transformation of the disparate highland ridges that sprawl for 100,000 square miles across the northern edges of Southeast Asia into an integrated opium zone was not simply the product of global market forces. Without the supply, the large addict populations of Bangkok and Saigon might have disappeared gradually like those in Manila and Jakarta. Without demand, the poppy fields of Burma and Laos might have faded over time like those of Yunnan just to the north. Searching for the catalytic forces that brought supply and demand together with such dramatic effect leads to the covert warfare, French and American, fought in these mountains during the early decades of the cold war.

In the struggle to contain Asian communism, the United States fought hot wars in Korea and Vietnam using its full array of conventional combat forces. Along China's southern border, however, the West waged the cold war with unconventional tactics. Instead of artillery and infantry, covert combat in the mountains of Southeast Asia became a war by proxy in which local allies were more important than firepower.

Operating beyond the controls of bureaucracy in Paris and Washington, a small cadre of clandestine warriors struck ad hoc alliances with the tribes and warlords who inhabited the mountains of the Golden Triangle. With their support, the CIA and its French counterparts were able to penetrate China on intelligence missions, monitor its long border for signs of an impending Chinese attack, and mobilize tribal armies to battle Communist guerrillas in this harsh terrain. Although the sheer size of these operations was unprecedented, America had already discovered the craft of covert action during World War II when OSS operatives parachuted behind enemy lines to work with French, Thai, and Burmese guerrillas.

For different reasons, both French and American operatives integrated their covert warfare with the Golden Triangle opium trade. The French motivation seems, on its face, simple. Denied funds by a National Assembly tired of an inconclusive Indochina War that dragged on for a decade, French intelligence did not have adequate covert funds. Faced with tight fiscal constraints, French officers merged the opium supply of Laos with the drug demand of Saigon to fund covert operations against Communists in both combat zones.

The CIA's motivation was more complex. Although the agency's funding was generous, it was not limitless, and all of its operations, no matter how important, faced fiscal constraints. By drawing on the resources of a powerful tribal leader or local warlord, a CIA agent could achieve a covert operational capacity far beyond his budgetary limits. Thus, an effective covert warrior had to find a strong local leader willing to merge his people's resources with the agency's operations. In a region of weak microstates and fragmented tribes, such strongmen usually combined traditional authority with control over the local economy. In the Golden Triangle, the only commodity was opium, and the most powerful local leaders were the opium warlords. "To fight you must have an army," explained General Tuan Shi-wen, a veteran of the CIA's covert war in Burma, "and an army must have guns, and to buy guns you must have money. In these mountains the only money is opium."[3]

This interplay among opium, money, and political power drew the CIA into a complicitous relationship with the Golden Triangle drug trade. In its covert warfare, the CIA's strength was no more or less than that of its local clients. To maintain the power that mobilized tribal armies and marched them into battle, these warlords used the CIA's resources—arms, ammunition, and, above all, air transport—to increase their control over the opium crop. Instead of opposing the expansion of their ally's autonomous economic base, most CIA operatives embraced it, knowing it increased their client's combat effectiveness and thereby gave the entire operation a certain independence from Washington's directives. As the warlord's power from opium profits increased, so did the agent's combat capacity and personal power. Thus, the CIA's complicity was not, like that of the French, a matter of mere financial pressure. It represented, at a superficial level, a bid for an increase in combat efficiency. At a more primal level, the embrace of the warlord and his opium trade was a perverse personal triumph, the act of a machismo warrior casting off the bureaucratic controls of his commanders half a world away. Whether a corrupt Thai police general, ruthless Hmong tribal commander, or a cynical Chinese opium warlord, CIA agents embraced them all, reveling in their defiance of civil standards for politics and warfare. Since the CIA headquarters in Washington saw the field operatives as front-line troops in the cold war, agency officials did not ask questions about methods as long as they produced results. There was, then, a certain congruence of interest between the warlords, the field operatives, and CIA headquarters that led to the agency's multi-faceted complicity in the Golden Triangle opium trade.

In Indochina during the 1950s, it was the French military's direct involvement in the drug trade that linked the Hmong opium supply with the demand of Saigon's opium dens. Across the Mekong in Burma and Thailand, the CIA fought a purer kind of covert warfare, operating entirely through its local clients. Thus, it was the CIA's informal alliances that tied the Kuomintang's opium supply in Burma to the demand for drugs in Bangkok. Despite tactical differences, both operations provided the logistics that merged supply and demand: the French military, through its own air force, opened a Laos-to-Saigon air corridor; the CIA, through the mule caravans of its clients, presided over the formation of a Burma-to-Bangkok overland corridor.

When the cold war came to Asia, the Hmong of Indochina were among the first of the Golden Triangle hill tribes drawn into the conflict as mercenary warriors. Since the Hmong's only cash crop was opium, their counter-guerrilla operations were soon intertwined with the region's rising drug trade. And the region was singularly poised to take on a central role in the global traffic: it had a local market of close to a million addicts; it had the organization, provided by military- and intelligence-backed syndicates, to move the opium from the mountains to urban markets; and it had skilled highland farmers devoting most of their labor to cultivating the poppy. Although Southeast Asia still exported only limited amounts of morphine and heroin to Europe and the United States, the region's trafficking capabilities were well enough developed by the late 1950s to meet any demands from the global market.

# French Indochina: Operation X

The French colonial government's campaign to eliminate opium addiction, which began in 1946 with the abolition of the opium monopoly, never had a chance of success. Desperately short of funds, French intelligence and paramilitary agencies expropriated the opium traffic to finance their covert operations during the First Indochina War. As soon as the civil administration would abolish some aspect of the trade, French intelligence services proceeded to take it over. By 1951 intelligence controlled most of the opium trade—from mountain poppy fields to urban smoking dens. Dubbed Operation X by insiders, this clandestine opium traffic produced a cast of Corsican narcotics syndicates and corrupt French intelligence officers who became key figures in the international drug trade.

The First Indochina War was a bitter nine year struggle (1946–1954) between a dying French colonial empire and an emerging Vietnamese nation. It was a war of contrasts. On one side was the French Expeditionary Corps, one of the proudest, most professional armies in the world, with a modern military tradition of more than three centuries. Arrayed against it was the Viet Minh, a communist-led coalition of weak guerrilla bands, the oldest of which had only two years of sporadic military experience when the war broke out. The French commanders struck poses of almost heroic proportions: General de Lattre, the gentleman warrior; General Raoul Salan, the hardened Indochina hand; Major Roger Trinquier, the cold-blooded, scientific tactician; and Captain Antoine Savani, the Corscian Machiavelli. The Viet Minh commanders were shadowy figures, rarely emerging into public view and, when they did, attributing their successes to the correctness of the party line or the courage of the rank and file. French military publicists wrote about the brilliance of a general's tactics or maneuvers, while the Viet Minh press projected Socialist caricatures of struggling workers and peasants, heroic front-line fighters, and party wisdom.

These superficialities were indicative of the profound differences in the two armies. At the beginning of the war the French high command viewed the conflict as a tactical exercise whose outcome would be determined, according to traditional military doctrine, by controlling territory and winning battles. The Viet Minh understood the war in radically different terms; to them, the war was not a military problem but a political one. As the Viet Minh commander, General Vo Nguyen Giap, has noted:

> political activities were more important than military activi-
> ties, and fighting less important than propaganda; armed

activity was used to safeguard, consolidate, and develop political bases.[4]

The Viet Minh's goal was to develop a political program that would
draw the entire population—regardless of race, religion, sex, or class
background—into the struggle for national liberation. Theirs was a
romantic vision of the mass uprising: resistance becoming so widespread and so intense that the French would be harassed everywhere.
Once the front-line troops and the masses in the rear were determined
to win, the tactical questions of how to apply this force were elementary.

The French suffered through several years of frustrating stalemate
before realizing that their application of classical textbook precepts was
losing the war. But they slowly developed a new strategy of counterguerrilla, or counterinsurgency, warfare. By 1950–1951 younger, innovative French officers had abandoned the conventional war tactics that
essentially visualized Indochina as a depopulated staging ground for
fortified lines, massive sweeps, and flanking maneuvers. Instead Indochina became a vast chessboard where hill tribes, bandits, and religious
minorities could be used as pawns to hold strategic territories and prevent
Viet Minh infiltration. The French concluded formal alliances with a
number of these ethnic or religious factions and supplied them with arms
and money to keep the Viet Minh out of their area. The French hope was
to atomize the Viet Minh's mobilized, unified mass into a mosaic of
autonomous fiefs hostile to the revolutionary movement.

Major Roger Trinquier and Captain Antoine Savani were the most
important apostles of this new military doctrine. Savani secured
portions of Cochin China (comprising Saigon and the Mekong Delta) by
rallying river pirates, Catholics, and messianic religious cults to the
French side. Along the spine of the Annamite Mountains from the
Central Highlands to the China border, Major Trinquier recruited a wide
variety of hill tribes; by 1954 more than 40,000 tribal mercenaries were
busy ambushing Viet Minh supply lines, safeguarding territory, and
providing intelligence. Other French officers organized Catholic militia
from parishes in the Tonkin Delta, Nung pirates on the Tonkin Gulf, and
a Catholic militia in Hué.

Although the French euphemistically referred to these local troops as
"supplementary forces" and attempted to legitimize their leaders with
ranks, commissions, and military decorations, they were little more than
mercenaries—and very expensive mercenaries at that. To ensure the
loyalty of the Binh Xuyen river pirates who guarded Saigon, the French
allowed them to organize a variety of lucrative criminal enterprises and
paid them an annual stipend of $85,000 as well.[5] Trinquier may have had
40,000 hill tribe guerrillas under his command by 1954, but he also had

to pay dearly for their services; he needed an initial outlay of $15,000 for basic training, arms, and bonuses to set up each mercenary unit of 150 men.[6] It is no exaggeration to say that the success of Savani's and Trinquier's work depended almost entirely on adequate financing; if they were well funded they could expand their programs almost indefinitely, but without capital they could not even begin.

The counterinsurgency efforts were continually plagued by a lack of money. The war was tremendously unpopular in France, and the French National Assembly reduced its outlay to the minimum for regular military units, leaving almost nothing for extras such as paramilitary or intelligence work. Moreover, the high command itself never really approved of the younger generation's unconventional approach and was unwilling to divert scarce funds from the regular units. Trinquier still complained years later that the high command never understood what he was trying to do, and said that they consistently refused to provide sufficient funds for his operations.[7]

The solution was Operation X, a clandestine narcotics traffic so secret that only high-ranking French and Vietnamese officials even knew of its existence. The anti-opium drive that began in 1946 had received scant support from the "Indochina hands"; customs officials continued to purchase raw opium from the Hmong, and the opium smoking dens, cosmetically renamed "detoxification clinics," continued to sell unlimited quantities of opium.[8] However, on September 3, 1948, the French high commissioner announced that each smoker had to register with the government, submit to a medical examination to ascertain the degree of his addiction, and then be weaned of the habit by having his dosage gradually reduced.[9] Statistically the program was a success. The customs service had bought 60 tons of raw opium from the Hmong and Yao in 1943, but in 1951 they purchased almost nothing.[10] The detoxification clinics were closed and the sealed opium packets each addict purchased from the customs service contained a constantly dwindling amount of opium.[11]

But the opium trade remained essentially unchanged. The only real differences were that the government, having abandoned opium as a source of revenue, now faced serious budgetary problems; and the French intelligence community, having secretly taken over the opium trade, had solved theirs. The opium monopoly had gone underground to become Operation X.

Unlike the American CIA, which has its own independent administration and chain of command, French intelligence agencies have always been closely tied to the regular military hierarchy. The most important French intelligence agency, and the closest equivalent to the CIA, is the SDECE (Service de Documentation Extérieure et du Contre-

Espionage). During the First Indochina War, its Southeast Asian representative, Colonel Maurice Belleux, supervised four separate SDECE "services" operating inside the war zone: intelligence, decoding, counterspionage, and action (paramilitary operations). While SDECE was allowed a great deal of autonomy in its pure intelligence work—spying, decoding, and counterespionage—the French high command assumed much of the responsibility for SDECE's paramilitary Action Service. Thus, although Major Trinquier's hill tribe guerrilla organization, the Mixed Airborne Commando Group (MACG), was nominally subordinate to SDECE's Action Service, in reality it reported to the Expeditionary Corps' high command. All of the other paramilitary units, including Captain Savani's Binh Xuyen river pirates, Catholics, and armed religious groups, reported to the 2$^{eme}$ Bureau, the military intelligence bureau of the French Expeditionary Corps.

During its peak years from 1951 to 1954, Operation X was sanctioned on the highest levels by Colonel Belleux for SDECE and General Raoul Salan for the Expeditionary Corps.[12] Below them, Major Trinquier of MACG assured Operation X a steady supply of Hmong opium by ordering his liaison officers serving with Hmong commander Touby Lyfoung and Tai Federation leader Deo Van Long to buy opium at a competitive price. Among the various French paramilitary agencies, the work of MACG was the most inextricably interwoven with the opium trade, even beyond the problem of financing covert operations. For its field officers in Laos and Tonkin had soon realized that unless they provided a regular outlet for the local opium production, the prosperity and loyalty of their hill tribe allies would be undermined.

Once the opium was collected after the annual spring harvest, Trinquier had his paratroopers fly it to Cap Saint Jacques (Vungtau) near Saigon, where the Action Service school trained hill tribe mercenaries at a military base. There were no customs or police controls to interfere with the illicit shipments here. From Cap Saint Jacques the opium was trucked the sixty miles into Saigon and turned over to the Binh Xuyen bandits, who were there serving as the city's local militia and managing its opium traffic, under the supervision of Captain Savani of the 2$^{eme}$ Bureau.[13]

The Binh Xuyen operated two major opium-boiling plants in Saigon (one near their headquarters at Cholon's Y-Bridge and the other near the National Assembly) to transform the raw poppy sap into a smokable form. The bandits distributed the prepared opium to dens and retail shops throughout Saigon and Cholon, some of which were owned by the Binh Xuyen (the others paid the gangsters a substantial share of their profits for protection). The Binh Xuyen divided its receipts with Trinquier's MACG and Savani's 2$^{eme}$ Bureau.[14] Any surplus opium the

Binh Xuyen were unable to market was sold to local Chinese merchants for export to Hong Kong or to the Corsican criminal syndicates in Saigon for shipment to Marseille. MACG deposited its profits in a secret account managed by the Action Service office in Saigon. When Touby Lyfoung or any other Hmong tribal leader needed money, he flew to Saigon and personally drew money out of the *caisse noire*, or "black box."[15]

MACG had had its beginnings in 1950 following a visit to Indochina by the SDECE deputy directory, who decided to experiment with using hill tribe warriors as mountain mercenaries. Colonel Grall was appointed commander of the fledgling unit, twenty officers were assigned to work with hill tribes in Central Highlands, and a special paramilitary training camp for hill tribes, the Action School, was established at Cap Saint Jacques.[16] However, the program remained experimental until December 1950, when Marshal Jean de Lattre de Tassigny was appointed commander in chief of the Expeditionary Corps. Realizing that the program had promise, General de Lattre transferred 140 to 150 officers to MACG and appointed Major Trinquier to command its operation in Laos and Tonkin.[17] Although Grall remained the nominal commander until 1953, it was Trinquier who developed most of MACG's innovative counterinsurgency tactics, forged most of the important tribal alliances, and organized much of the opium trade during his three years of service.

His program for organizing country guerrilla units in Tonkin and Laos established him as a leading international specialist in counter-insurgency warfare. He evolved a precise four-point method for transforming any hill tribe area in Indochina from a scattering of mountain hamlets into a tightly disciplined, counterguerrilla infrastructure—a *maquis*. Since his theories also fascinated the CIA and later inspired American programs in Vietnam and Laos, they bear some examination.

**Preliminary Stage.** A small group of carefully selected officers flew over hill tribe villages in a light aircraft to test the response of the inhabitants. If somebody shot at the aircraft, the area was probably hostile, but if tribe members waved, then the area might have potential. In 1951, for example, Major Trinquier organized the first *maquis* in Tonkin by repeatedly flying over Hmong villages northwest of Lai Chau until he drew a response. When some of the Hmong waved the French tricolor, he realized that the area qualified for stage 1.[18]

**Stage 1.** Four or five MACG commandos were parachuted into the target area to recruit about fifty local tribesmen for counterguerrilla training at the Action School in Cap Saint Jacques, where up to three hundred guerrillas could be trained at a time. Trinquier later explained his criteria for selecting these first tribal cadres:

## 1. French Intelligence and Paramilitary Organizations
## During the First Indochina War, 1950–1954

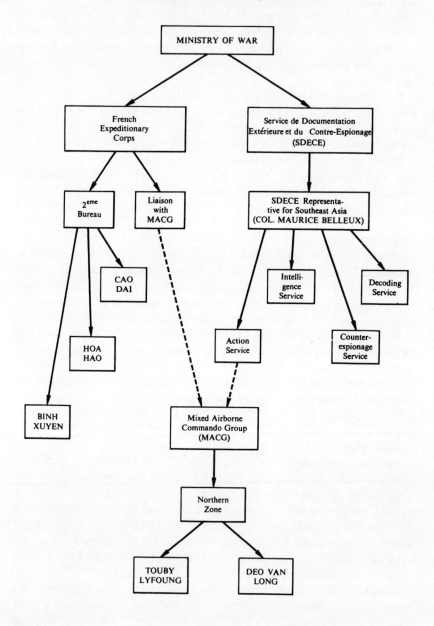

They are doubtless more attracted by the benefits they can expect than by our country itself, but this attachment can be unflagging if we are resolved to accept it and are firm in our intentions and objectives. We know also that, in troubled periods, self-interest and ambition have always been powerful incentives for dynamic individuals who want to move out of their rut and get somewhere.[19]

These ambitious mercenaries were given a forty-day commando course comprising airborne training, radio operation, demolition, small arms use, and counterintelligence. Afterward the group was broken up into four-man teams made up of a combat commander, radio operator, and two intelligence officers. The teams were trained to operate independently of one another so that the *maquis* could survive if any of the teams were captured. Stage 1 took two and a half months and was budgeted at $3,000.

**Stage 2.** The original recruits returned to their home area with arms, radios, and money to set up the *maquis.* Through their friends and relatives, they began propagandizing the local population and gathering basic intelligence about Viet Minh activities in the area. Stage 2 was considered completed when the initial teams had managed to recruit a hundred more of their fellow tribesmen for training at Cap Saint Jacques. This stage usually took about two months and $6,000, with most of the increased expenses consisting of the relatively high salaries of the mercenary troops.

**Stage 3.** This was by far the most complex and critical part of the process. The target area was transformed from an innocent scattering of mountain villages into a tightly controlled *maquis.* After the return of the final hundred cadres, any Viet Minh organizers in the area were assassinated, a tribal leader "representative of the ethnic and geographic group predominant in the zone" was selected, and arms were parachuted to the hill tribesmen. If the planning and organization had been properly carried out, the *maquis* would have up to three thousand armed tribesmen collecting intelligence, ferreting out Viet Minh cadres, and launching guerrilla assaults on nearby Viet Minh camps and supply lines. Moreover, the *maquis* was capable of running itself, with the selected tribal leader communicating regularly by radio with French liaison officers in Hanoi or Saigon to ensure a steady supply of arms, ammunition, and money.

While the overall success of this program proved its military value, the impact on the French officer corps revealed the dangers inherent in clandestine military operations that allow its leaders the discretion to violate military regulations and moral norms. The Algerian war, with its methodical torture of civilians, continued the inexorable brutalization of France's elite professional units. Afterward, while his comrades in arms were bombing buildings and assassinating government leaders in Paris in defiance of President de Gaulle's decision to withdraw from Algeria, Trinquier, who had directed the torture campaign during the battle for Algiers, flouted international law by organizing Katanga's white mercenary army to fight a U.N. peacekeeping force during the 1961 Congo crisis.[20] Retiring to France to reflect, Trinquier advocated the adoption of "calculated acts of sabotage and terrorism"[21] and systematic duplicity in international dealings as an integral part of national defense policy.[22] While at first glance it may seem remarkable that the French military could have become involved in the Indochina narcotics traffic, in retrospect it can be understood as another consequence of allowing officers to do whatever seems expedient.

Trinquier had developed three important counterguerrilla *maquis* for MACG in northeastern Laos and Tonkin from 1950 to 1953: the Hmong *maquis* in Laos under the command of Touby Lyfoung; the Tai *maquis* under Deo Van Long in northwestern Tonkin; and the Hmong *maquis* east of the Red River in north central Tonkin. Since opium was the only significant economic resource in each of these regions, MACG's opium purchasing policy was just as important as its military tactics in determining the effectiveness of highland counterinsurgency programs. When MACG purchased the opium directly from the Hmong and paid them a good price, they remained loyal to the French. But when the French used non-Hmong highland minorities as brokers and did nothing to prevent the Hmong from being cheated, these tribesmen joined the Viet Minh—with disastrous consequences for the French.

Unquestionably, the most successful MACG operation was the Hmong *maquis* in Xieng Khouang province, Laos, led by the French-educated Hmong Touby Lyfoung. When the Expeditionary Corps assumed responsibility for the opium traffic on the Plain of Jars in 1949–1950, they appointed Touby their opium broker, as had the opium monopoly before them.[23] Major Trinquier did not need to use his four-stage plan when dealing with the Xieng Khoung province Hmong; soon after he took command in 1951, Touby came to Hanoi to offer to help initiate MACG commando operations among his followers. Because there had been little Viet Minh activity near the Plain of Jars since 1946, both agreed to start slowly by sending a handful of recruits to the Action School for radio instruction.[24] Until the Geneva truce in 1954 the French military continued to pay Touby an excellent price for the Xieng Khouang opium harvest, thus ensuring his followers' loyalty and providing him with sufficient funds to influence the course of Hmong politics. This arrangement also made Touby extremely wealthy by

Hmong standards. In exchange for these favors, Touby remained the most loyal and active of the hill tribe commanders in Indochina.

Touby proved his worth during the 1953–1954 Viet Minh offensive. In December 1952 the Viet Minh launched an offensive into the Tai country of Vietnam and were moving quickly toward the Laos-Vietnam border when they ran short of supplies and withdrew before crossing into Laos.[25] Since rumors persisted that the Viet Minh were going to drive for the Mekong the following spring, an emergency training camp was set up on the Plain of Jars and the first of some five hundred young Hmong were flown to Cap Saint Jacques for a crash training program. Just as the program was getting under way, the Viet Minh and their local guerrilla allies, the Pathet Lao, launched a combined offensive across the border into Laos, capturing Sam Neua City on April 12, 1953. The Vietnam 316th People's Army Division, Pathet Lao irregulars, and local Hmong partisans organized by Lo Faydang drove westward, capturing Xieng Khouang City two weeks later. But with Touby's Hmong irregulars providing intelligence and covering their mountain flanks, French and Lao colonial troops used their tanks and artillery to good advantage on the flat Plain of Jars and held off the Pathet Lao–Viet Minh units.[26]

In May the French Expeditionary Corps built a steel mat airfield on the plain and began airlifting in 12,000 troops, some small tanks, and heavy engineering equipment. Under the supervision of General Albert Sore, who arrived in June, the plain was soon transformed into a virtual fortress guarded by forty to fifty reinforced bunkers and blockhouses. Having used mountain minorities to crush rebellions in Morocco, Sore appreciated their importance and met with Touby soon after his arrival. After an aerial tour of the region with Touby and his MACG adviser, Sore sent out four columns escorted by Touby's partisans to sweep Xieng Khouang province clean of any remaining enemy units. After this operation, Sore arranged with Touby and MACG that the Hmong would provide intelligence and guard the mountain approaches while his regular units garrisoned the plain itself. The arrangement worked well, and Sore remembered meeting amicably on a regular basis with Touby and Lieutenant Vang Pao, then company commander of a Hmong irregular unit and later the commander of CIA mercenaries in Laos, to exchange intelligence and discuss paramilitary operations. He also recalled that Touby delivered substantial quantities of raw opium to MACG advisers for the regular DC-3 flights to Cap Saint Jacques and felt that the French support of the Hmong opium trade was a major factor in their military aggressiveness. As Sore put it, "The Hmong were defending their own region, and of course by defending their region they were defending their opium."[27]

Another outsider also witnessed the machinations of the covert Operation X. During a six-week investigative tour of Indochina during June and July 1953, Colonel Edward G. Lansdale of the American CIA discovered the existence of Operation X. Trying to put together a firsthand report of the Viet Minh invasion of Laos, Lansdale flew up to the Plain of Jars, where he learned that French officers had bought up the 1953 opium harvest, acting on orders from General Salan, commander in chief of the Expeditionary Corps. When Lansdale later found out that the opium had been flown to Saigon for sale and export, he complained to Washington that the French military was involved in the narcotics traffic and suggested that an investigation was in order. General Lansdale recalled that the response ran something like this:

> Don't you have anything else to do? We don't want you to open
> up this keg of worms since it will be a major embarrassment to
> a friendly government. So drop your investigation.[28]

By mid-1953, repeated Viet Minh offensives into northern Laos, like the spring assault on the Plain of Jars, had convinced the French high command that they were in imminent danger of losing Laos. To block future Viet Minh offensives, they proceeded to establish a fortified base, or "hedgehog," in a wide upland valley called Dien Bien Phu near the Laos–North Vietnam border.[29] In November the French air force and CAT (Civil Air Transport, later Air America) began airlifting 16,000 men into the valley, and French generals confidently predicted they would soon be able to seal the border.

By March 1954, however, the Viet Minh had ringed Dien Bien Phu with well-entrenched heavy artillery; within a month they had silenced the French counterbatteries. Large-scale air evacuation was impossible, and the garrison was living on borrowed time. Realizing that an overland escape was their only solution, the French high command launched a number of relief columns from northern Laos to crack through the lines of entrapment and enable the defenders to break out.[30] Delayed by confusion in high command headquarters, the main relief column of 3,000 men did not set out until April 14.[31] As the relief column got under way, Colonel Trinquier, by now MACG commander, proposed a supplementary plan for setting up a large *maquis*, manned by Touby's irregulars, halfway between Dien Bien Phu and the Plain of Jars to aid any of the garrison who might break out. After overcoming the high command's doubts, Trinquier flew to the Plain of Jars with a large supply of silver bars. Half of Touby's 6,000 irregulars were given eight days of intensive training and dispatched for Muong Song, sixty miles to the north, on May 1. Although Trinquier managed to recruit yet another 1,500 Hmong mercenaries elsewhere, his efforts proved futile.[32] Dien

Bien Phu fell on May 8, and only a small number of the seventy-eight colonial troops who escaped were netted by Touby's *maquis.*[33]

Unlike the Hmong in Laos, those in northwestern Tonkin, where Dien Bien Phu was located, had good cause to hate the French and were instrumental in their defeat. Although in Laos Operation X had purchased raw opium directly from the Hmong leaders, in northwestern Tonkin political considerations forced MACG officials to continue the earlier opium monopoly policy of using Tai leaders, particularly Deo Van Long, as their intermediaries with the Hmong opium growers. By allowing the Tai feudal lords to force the Hmong to sell their opium at extremely low prices, they embittered the Hmong toward the French and made them enthusiastic supporters of the Viet Minh.

After the Vietnamese revolution began in 1945 and the French position weakened throughout Indochina, the French command decided to work through Deo Van Long, one of the few local leaders who had remained loyal, to restore their control over the strategically important Tai highlands in northwestern Vietnam.[34] In 1946 three highland provinces were separated from the rest of Tonkin and designated an autonomous Tai Federation, with Deo Van Long, who had only been the White Tai leader of Lai Chau province, as president. Ruling by fiat, he proceeded to appoint his friends and relatives to every possible position of authority.[35] Since there were only 25,000 White Tai in the federation as opposed to 100,000 Black Tai and 50,000 Hmong,[36] his actions aroused bitter opposition.

When his political manipulations failed, Deo Van Long tried to put down the dissidence by military force, using two 850-man Tai battalions that had been armed and trained by the French. Although he drove many of the dissidents to take refuge in the forests, this was hardly a solution, since they made contact with the Viet Minh and thus became an even greater problem.[37]

Moreover, French support for Deo Van Long's fiscal politics was a disaster for France's entire Indochina empire. The French set up the Tai Federation's first autonomous budget in 1947, based on its only marketable commodity—Hmong opium. As one French colonel put it:

> The Tai budgetary receipts are furnished exclusively by the Hmong who pay half with their raw opium, and the other half, indirectly, through the Chinese who lose their opium smuggling profits in the [state] gaming halls.[38]

Opium remained an important part of the Tai Federation budget until 1951, when a young adviser to the federation, Jean Jerusalemy, ordered it eliminated. Since official regulations prohibited opium smoking,

Jerusalemy, a strict bureaucrat, did not understand how the Tai Federation could be selling opium to the government.

So in 1951 opium disappeared from the official budget. Instead of selling it to the customs service, Deo Van Long sold it to MACG officers for Operation X. In the same year French military aircraft began making regular flights to Lai Chau to purchase raw opium from Deo Van Long and local Chinese merchants for shipment to Hanoi and Saigon.[39]

With the exception of insignificant quantities produced by a few Tai villages, almost all of the Opium purchased was grown by the 50,000 Hmong in the federation. During World War II and the immediate postwar years, they had sold about 4.5 to 5 tons of raw opium annually to Deo Van Long's agents for the opium monopoly. Since the monopoly paid only one-tenth of the Hanoi black market price, the Hmong preferred to sell the greater part of their harvest to the higher-paying local Chinese smugglers.[40] During this time, Deo Van Long had no way to force the Hmong to sell to his agents at the low official price. By 1949, however, backed by three Tai guerrilla battalions and retainers in government posts at all of the lowland trading centers, he was in a position to force the Hmong to sell most of their crop to him, at gun point, if necessary.[41] Many of the Hmong who had refused to sell at his low price became more cooperative when confronted with a squad of well-armed Tai guerrillas. Moreover, when Deo Van Long stopped dealing with the opium monopoly after 1950, there was no longer any official price guideline, and he was free to increase his own profit by reducing the already miserable price paid the Hmong.

While these methods may have made Deo Van Long a rich man by the end of the Indochina War (after the Geneva cease-fire he retired to a comfortable villa in France), they seriously damaged his relations with the Hmong. When they observed his rise in 1945–1946 as the autocrat of the Tai Federation, many joined the Viet Minh.[42] As Deo Van Long acquired more arms and power in the late 1940s and early 1950s, his rule became even more oppressive, and the Hmong became even more willing to aid the Viet Minh.

This account of the Tai Federation opium trade would be little more than an interesting footnote to the history of the Indochina opium monopoly were it not for the battle of Dien Bien Phu. Although it was an ideal base from a strategic viewpoint, the French command could not have chosen a more unfavorable battlefield. It was the first Black Tai area Deo Van Long had taken control of after World War II. His interest in it was understandable: Dien Bien Phu was the largest valley in the Tai Federation and in 1953 produced 4,000 tons of rice, about 30 percent of the federation's production.[43] Moreover, the Hmong opium cultivators in the surrounding hills produced three-fifths of a ton of raw opium for the monopoly, or about 13 percent of the federation's legitimate sale.[44] But soon after the first units were parachuted into Dien Bien Phu, experienced French officials in the Tai country began urging the high command to withdraw from the area. Jerusalemy, the young French adviser, sent a long report to the high command warning that if they remained at Dien Bien Phu defeat was only a matter of time. The Hmong in the surrounding mountains were extremely bitter toward Deo Van Long and the French for their handling of the opium crop, explained Jerusalemy, and the Black Tai living on the valley floor still resented the imposition of White Tai administrators.[45]

Confident that the Viet Minh could not possibly transport sufficient heavy artillery through the rough mountain terrain, the French generals ignored these warnings. French and American artillery specialists filed reassuring firsthand reports that the "hedgehog" was impenetrable. When the artillery duel began in March 1954, French generals were shocked to find themselves outgunned; the Viet Minh had two hundred heavy artillery pieces with abundant ammunition, against the French garrison's twenty-eight heavy guns and insufficient ammunition.[46] An estimated 80,000 Viet Minh porters had hauled this incredible firepower across the mountains, guided and assisted by enthusiastic Black Tai and Hmong. General Vo Nguyen Giap, the Viet Minh commander, recalled that "convoys of pack horses from the Meo [Hmong] highlands" were among the most determined of the porters who assisted this effort.[47]

Hmong hostility prevented French intelligence and counterintelligence operations. It is doubtful that the Viet Minh would have chosen to attack Dien Bien Phu had they been convinced that the local population was firmly against them, since trained Hmong commandos could easily have disrupted their supply lines, sabotaged their artillery, and perhaps given the French garrison accurate intelligence on their activities. As it was, Colonel Trinquier tried to infiltrate five MACG commando teams from Laos into the Dien Bien Phu area, but the effort was almost a complete failure.[48] Unfamiliar with the terrain and lacking contacts with the local population, the Laotian Hmong were easily brushed aside by Viet Minh troops with local Hmong guides. The anti-colonial Hmong guerrillas enveloped a wide area surrounding the fortress, and all of Trinquier's teams were discovered before they could approach the encircled garrison. The Viet Minh divisions overwhelmed the fortress on May 7–8, 1954.

Less than twenty-four hours later, on May 8, 1954, Vietnamese, French, Russian, Chinese, British, and American delegates sat down together for the first time at Geneva, Switzerland, to discuss a peace settlement. The news from Dien Bien Phu had arrived that morning, and it was reflected in the grim demeanor of the Western delegates and the confidence of the Vietnamese.[49] The diplomats finally compromised on a peace agreement almost three months later: on July 20 an armistice was declared and the war was over.

But to Colonel Roger Trinquier a multilateral agreement signed by a host of great and small powers meant nothing—his war went on. Trinquier had 40,000 hill tribe mercenaries operating under the command of 400 French officers by the end of July and was planning to take the war to the enemy by organizing a huge new *maquis* of up to 10,000 tribesmen in the Viet Minh heartland east of the Red River.[50] Now he was faced with a delicate problem: his mercenaries had no official status and were not covered by the cease-fire. The Geneva agreement prohibited overflights by the light aircraft Trinquier used to supply his mercenary units behind Viet Minh lines and thus created insurmountable logistics and liaison problems.[51] Although he was able to use some of the Red Cross flights to the prisoner-of-war camps in the Viet Minh–controlled highlands as a cover for arms and ammunition drops, this was only a stopgap measure.[52] In August, when Trinquier radioed his remaining MACG units in the Tai Federation to fight their way out into Laos, several thousand Tai retreated into Sam Neua and Xieng Khouang provinces, where they were picked up by Touby Lyfoung's Hmong irregulars. But the vast majority stayed behind. Although some kept broadcasting appeals for arms, money and food, by late August their radio batteries went dead, and they were never heard from again.

There was an ironic footnote to this last MACG operation. Soon after several thousand of the Tai Federation commandos arrived in Laos, Touby realized that it would take a substantial amount of money to resettle them permanently. Since the MACG secret account had netted almost $150,000 from the previous winter's opium harvest, Touby went to the Saigon paramilitary office to make a personal appeal for resettlement funds. But the French officer on duty was embarrassed to report that an unknown MACG or SDECE officer had stolen the money, and MACG's portion of Operation X was broke. "Trinquier told us to put the five million piasters in the account where it would be safe," Touby recalled with great amusement, "and then one of his officers stole it. What irony! What irony!"[53]

When the French Expeditionary Corps began its withdrawal from Indochina in 1955, MACG officers approached American military personnel and offered to turn over their entire paramilitary apparatus. CIA agent Lucien Conein was one of those contacted, and he passed the word along to Washington, But "DOD [Department of Defense] responded that they wanted nothing to do with any French program" and the offer was refused.[54] Many in the agency regretted the decision when the CIA sent Green Berets into Laos and Vietnam to organize hill tribe guerrillas several years later. In 1962 American representatives visited Trinquier in Paris and offered him a high position as an adviser on mountain warfare in Indochina. But fearing that the Americans would never give a French officer sufficient authority to accomplish anything, Trinquier refused.[55]

Looking back on the machinations of Operation X from the vantage point of almost four decades, it seems remarkable that its secret was so well kept. Almost every news dispatch from Saigon that discussed the Binh Xuyen alluded to their involvement in the opium trade, but there was no mention of the French support for hill tribe opium dealings and certainly no comprehension of the full scope of Operation X. Spared headlines, or even rumors, about their involvement in the narcotics traffic, neither SDECE nor the French military were pressured into repudiating the drug trade as a source of funding for covert operations. Apparently there was one internal investigation of this secret opium trade, which produced a few reprimands, more for indiscretion than anything else, and Operation X continued until the French withdrew from Indochina.

The investigation began in 1952, when Vietnamese police seized almost a ton of raw opium from a MACG warehouse in Cap Saint Jacques. Colonel Belleux had initiated the seizure when three MACG officers filed an official report claiming that opium was being stored in the MACG warehouses for eventual sale. After the seizure confirmed their story, Belleux turned the matter over to Jean Letourneau, high commissioner for Indochina, who started a formal inquiry through the comptroller-general for Overseas France. Although the inquiry uncovered a good deal of Operation X's organization, nothing was done. The inquiry did damage the reputation of MACG's commander, Colonel Grall, and Commander in Chief Salan. Grall was ousted from MACG and Trinquier was appointed as his successor in March 1953.[56]

Following the investigation, Colonel Belleux suggested to his Paris headquarters that SDECE and MACG should reduce the scope of their narcotics trafficking. If they continued to control the trade at all levels, the secret might get out, damaging France's international relations and providing the Viet Minh with propaganda. Since the French had to continue buying opium from the Hmong to retain their loyalty, Belleux suggested that it be diverted to Bangkok instead of being flown directly to Saigon and Hanoi. In Bangkok the opium would become indistinguishable from much larger quantities being shipped out of Burma by the Nationalist Chinese army, and thus the French involvement would be concealed. SDECE Paris, however, told Belleux that he was a "troublemaker" and urged him to give up such ideas. The matter was dropped.[57]

Apparently SDECE and the French military emerged from the Indochina War with narcotics trafficking as an accepted gambit in the espionage game. In November 1971 the U.S. attorney for New Jersey caused an enormous controversy in both France and the United States when he indicted a high-ranking SDECE officer, Colonel Paul Fournier, for conspiracy to smuggle narcotics into the United States. Given the long history of SDECE's official and unofficial involvement in the narcotics trade, surprise seems to have been unwarranted. Fournier had served with SDECE in Vietnam during the First Indochina War at a time when the clandestine service was managing the narcotics traffic as a matter of policy. The involvement of some SDECE agents in later Corsican heroin smuggling indicated that SDECE's acquaintance with the narcotics traffic had not ended.

## The Binh Xuyen in Saigon

Just as the history of SDECE's role in the tribal opium trade was repeated by the CIA in Laos and Afghanistan, so the involvement of Saigon's Binh Xuyen river pirates was the product of a political relationship that has recurred many times over the last half century— the alliance between governments and gangsters. While the CIA-Corsican alliance in the early years of the cold war contributed to the resurrection of the European heroin trade, the French 2$^{eme}$ Bureau's alliance with the Binh Xuyen allowed Saigon's opium commerce to survive during the First Indochina War. The 2$^{eme}$Bureau was not integral to the mechanics of the opium traffic in the way that MACG had been in the mountains; it remained in the background providing overall political support, allowing the Binh Xuyen to take over the opium dens and establish their own opium refineries. By 1954 the Binh Xuyen controlled virtually all of Saigon's opium dens and dominated the distribution of prepared opium throughout Cochin China (the southern part of Vietnam). Since Cochin China had usually consumed over half of the monopoly's opium, and Saigon—with its Chinese twin city, Cholon— had the highest density of smokers in the entire colony[58] the 2$^{eme}$ Bureau's decision to turn the traffic over to the Binh Xuyen guaranteed the failure of the government's anti-opium campaign and ensured the survival of mass addiction in Vietnam.

The 2$^{eme}$ Bureau's pact with the Binh Xuyen was part of a larger French policy of using ethnic, religious, and political factions to deny territory to the Viet Minh. By supplying these splinter groups with arms and money, the French hoped to strengthen them enough to make their localities into private fiefs, thereby neutralizing the region and freeing regular combat troops from garrison duty. But Saigon was not just another province, it was France's "Pearl of the Orient," the richest, most

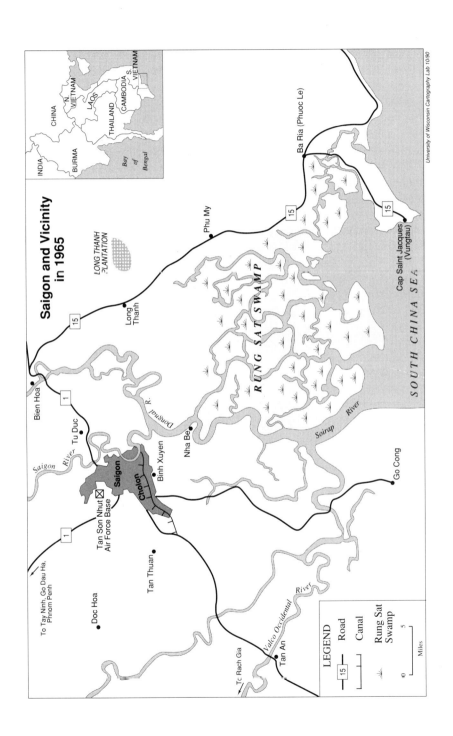

# Saigon and Vicinity in 1965

INDIA

CHINA

BURMA

N. VIETNAM

LAOS

THAILAND

CAMBODIA

S. VIETNAM

Bay of Bengal

Ba Ria (Phuoc Le)

15

15

Cap Saint Jacques (Vungtau)

Phu My

LONG THANH PLANTATION

Long Thanh

15

RUNG SAT SWAMP

SOUTH CHINA SEA

Bien Hoa

1

Tu Duc

Saigon River

Dongnai R.

Binh Xuyen

Nha Be

Soirap River

Go Cong

Saigon

Cholon

Tan Son Nhut Air Force Base

1

To Tay Ninh, Go Dau Ha, Phnom Penh

Doc Hoa

Tan Thuan

Vaico Occidental River

To Rach Gia

Tan An

LEGEND

15 — Road

Canal

Rung Sat Swamp

0   5
Miles

University of Wisconsin Cartography Lab 10/90

important city in Indochina. In giving Saigon to the Binh Xuyen, block by block, over a six-year period, the French were not just building up another fiefdom, they were making these bandits the key to their control of Cochin China. Hunted through the swamps as river pirates in the 1940s, by 1954 their military commander was director-general of the national police and their chief, the illiterate Bay Vien, was nominated as prime minister of Vietnam. The gangsters had become the government.

The Binh Xuyen river pirates first emerged during the early 1920s in the marshes and canals along the southern fringes of Saigon-Cholon as a loose coalition of pirate gangs, about two hundred to three hundred strong. Armed with old rifles, clubs, and knives and schooled in Sino-Vietnamese boxing, they extorted protection money from the sampans and junks that traveled the canals to the Cholon docks. Occasionally they sortied into Cholon to kidnap or rob a wealthy Chinese merchant. If too sorely pressed by the police or the colonial militia, they could retreat through the streams and canals south of Saigon deep into the impenetrable Rung Sat Swamp at the mouth of the Saigon River, where their reputations as popular heroes and the maze of mangroves protected them from capture. If the Binh Xuyen pirates were the Robin Hoods of Vietnam, then the Rung Sat (Forest of the Assassins) was their Sherwood Forest.[59]

Their popular image was not entirely undeserved, for there is evidence that many of the early outlaws were ordinary contract laborers who had fled from the rubber plantations that sprang up on the northern edge of the Rung Sat during the rubber boom of the 1920s. Insufficient food, harsh work schedules, and beatings made most of the plantations slave labor camps with annual death rates higher than 20 percent.[60]

But the majority of those who joined the Binh Xuyen were just ordinary Cholon street toughs, and the career of Le Van Vien, known as "Bay" Vien, was rather more typical. Born in 1904 on the outskirts of Cholon, Bay Vien found himself alone, uneducated, and in need of a job after an inheritance dispute cost him his birthright at age seventeen. He soon fell under the influence of a small-time gangster who found him employment as a chauffeur and introduced him to the leaders of the Cholon underworld.[61] As he established his underworld reputation, Bay Vien was invited to meetings at the house of the underworld leader Duong Van Duong ("Ba" Duong), in the hamlet of Binh Xuyen just south of Cholon.

The early history of the Binh Xuyen was an interminable cycle of kidnapping, piracy, pursuit, and occasional imprisonment until late in World War II, when Japanese military intelligence, the Kempeitai, began dabbling in Vietnamese politics. During 1943–1944 many individual gang leaders managed to ingratiate themselves with the Japanese army, then administering Saigon jointly with the Vichy French. Thanks to Japanese protection, many gangsters were able to come out of hiding and find legitimate employment; Ba Duong, for example, became a labor broker for the Japanese and under their protection carried out some of Saigon's most spectacular wartime robberies. Other leaders joined Japanese-sponsored political groups, where they became involved in politics for the first time.[62] Many of the Binh Xuyen bandits had already had an intense exposure to Vietnamese nationalist politics while imprisoned on Con Son (Puolo Condore) island. Finding themselves sharing cells with political prisoners, they participated in their heated political debates. Bay Vien himself escaped from Con Son in early 1945 and returned to Saigon politicized and embittered toward French colonialism.[63]

On March 9, 1945, the fortunes of the Binh Xuyen improved further when the Japanese army became wary of growing anti-Fascist sentiments among their French military and civilian collaborators and launched a preemptive coup. Within a few hours all French police, soldiers, and civil servants were behind bars, leaving those Vietnamese political groups favored by the Japanese free to organize openly for the first time. Some Binh Xuyen gangsters were given amnesty; others, like Bay Vien, were hired by the newly established Vietnamese government as police agents. Eager for the intelligence, money, and men the Binh Xuyen could provide, almost every political faction courted the criminal organization. Rejecting overtures by conservatives and Trotskyites, the Binh Xuyen made a decision of considerable importance—they chose the Communist-led Viet Minh as their allies.

While this decision would have been of little consequence in Tonkin or central Vietnam, where the Communist-dominated Viet Minh was strong enough to stand alone, in Cochin China the Binh Xuyen support was crucial. After launching an abortive revolt in 1940, the Cochin division of the Indochina Communist party had been weakened by mass arrests and executions.[64] When the party began rebuilding at the end of World War II, it was already outstripped by more conservative nationalist groups, particularly politicoreligious groups such as the Hoa Hao and Cao Dai. In August 1945 the head of the Viet Minh in Cochin China, Tran Van Giau, convinced Bay Vien to persuade Ba Duong and the other chiefs to align with the Viet Minh.[65] When the Viet Minh called a mass demonstration on August 25 to celebrate their installation as the new nationalist government, fifteen well-armed, bare-chested bandits carrying a large banner declaring "Binh Xuyen Assassination Committee" joined the tens of thousands of demonstrators who marched through downtown Saigon for more than nine hours.[66] For almost a month the Viet Minh ran the city, managing its public utilities and patrolling the streets, until late September, when arriving British and French troops took charge.

World War II had come to an abrupt end on August 15, when the Japanese surrendered to the Allies in the wake of the atom bomb attacks on Hiroshima and Nagasaki. Allied commanders had been preparing for a long, bloody invasion of the Japanese home islands and were suddenly faced with the enormous problems of disarming thousands of Japanese troops scattered across eastern and Southeast Asia. On September 12 some 1,400 Indian Gurkhas and a company of French infantry under the command of British General Douglas D. Gracey were airlifted to Saigon from Burma. Although he was under strict orders to stay out of politics, General Gracey, an archcolonialist, intervened decisively on the side of the French. When a Viet Minh welcoming committee paid a courtesy call he made no effort to conceal his prejudices. "They came to see me and said 'welcome' and all that sort of thing," he later reported. "It was an unpleasant situation and I promptly kicked them out."[67] Ten days later the British secretly rearmed some fifteen hundred French troops, who promptly executed a coup, reoccupying the city's main public buildings. Backed by Japanese and Indian troops, the French cleared the Viet Minh out of downtown Saigon and began a house-to-house search for nationalist leaders. With the arrival of French troop ships from Marseille several weeks later, France's reconquest of Indochina began in earnest.[68]

Fearing further reprisals, the Viet Minh withdrew to the west of Saigon, leaving Bay Vien as military commander of Saigon-Cholon.[69] Since the Binh Xuyen then had less than a hundred men, the Viet Minh suggested that they merge forces with the citywide nationalist youth movement, the Avant-Garde Youth.[70] After meeting with Bay Vien, one of the Avant-Garde's Saigon leaders, the future police chief Lai Van Sang agreed that the merger made sense: his two thousand men lacked arms and money, while the wealthy Binh Xuyen lacked rank and file.[71] It was a peculiar alliance; Saigon's toughest criminals were now commanding idealistic young students and intelligentsia. As British and French troops reoccupied downtown Saigon, the Binh Xuyen took up defensive positions along the southern and western edges of the city. Beginning on October 25, French thrusts into the suburbs smashed through their lines and began driving them back into the Rung Sat swamp.[72] Ba Duong led the amphibious retreat of thousands of Binh Xuyen troops, Avant-Garde Youth, and Japanese deserters deep into the Rung Sat's watery maze. However, they left behind a network of clandestine cells known as action committees, or assassination committees, totaling some 250 men.

While Binh Xuyen waterborne guerrillas harassed the canals, its Saigon action committees provided intelligence, extorted money, and unleashed political terror. Merchants paid the action committees regular fees for a guarantee of their personal safety, while the famous casino the Grand Monde paid $2,600 a day as insurance that Binh Xuyen terrorists would not toss a grenade into its gaming halls.[73] These contributions, along with arms supplies, enabled the Binh Xuyen to expand their forces to seven full regiments totaling ten thousand men, the largest Viet Minh force in Cochin China.[74] In 1947, when the Viet Minh decided to launch a wave of terror against French colonists, the Binh Xuyen action committees played a major role in the bombings, knifings, and assaults, that punctuated the daily life of Saigon-Cholon.[75]

Despite their important contributions to the revolutionary movement, the Binh Xuyen marriage to the Viet Minh was doomed from the start. It was not sophisticated ideological disputes that divided them, but rather more mundane squabblings over behavior, discipline, and territory. Relations between Binh Xuyen gangs had always been managed on the principle of mutual respect for each chief's autonomous territory. In contrast, the Viet Minh were attempting to build a mass revolution based on popular participation. Confidence in the movement was an imperative, and the excesses of any unit commander had to be punished before they could alienate the people and destroy the revolution. On the one hand the brash, impulsive bandit, on the other the disciplined party cadre—a clash was unavoidable.

A confrontation came in early 1946 when accusations of murder, extortion, and wanton violence against a minor Binh Xuyen chieftain forced the Viet Minh commander, Nguyen Binh, to convene a military tribunal. In the midst of the heated argument between the Binh Xuyen leader Ba Duong and Nguyen Binh, the accused grabbed the Viet Minh commander's pistol and shot himself in the head. Blaming the Viet Minh for his friend's suicide, Ba Duong began building a movement to oust Nguyen Binh but was strafed and killed by a French aircraft a few weeks later, well before his plans had matured.[76]

Shortly after Ba Duong's death in February 1946, the Binh Xuyen held a mass rally in the heart of the Rung Sat to mourn their fallen leader and elect Bay Vien as his successor. Although Bay Vien had worked closely with the Viet Minh, he was now more ambitious than patriotic. Bored with being king of the mangrove swamps, Bay Vien devised three stratagems for catapulting himself to greater heights: he ordered assassination committees to fix their sights on Nguyen Binh;[77] he began working with the Hoa Hao religious group to forge an anti-French, anti–Viet Minh coalition;[78] and he initiated negotiations with the French 2[eme] Bureau for some territory in Saigon.

The Viet Minh remained relatively tolerant of Bay Vien's machinations until March 1948, when he sent his top advisers to Saigon to negotiate a secret alliance with Captain Savani of the 2[eme] Bureau.[79] Concealing their knowledge of Bay Vien's betrayal, the Viet Minh invited him to attend a special convocation at their camp in the Plain of Reeds on May 19, Ho Chi Minh's birthday. Realizing that this was a trap, Bay Vien strutted into the meeting surrounded by two hundred of his toughest gangsters. While he allowed himself the luxury of denouncing Nguyen Binh to his face, the Viet Minh were stealing the Rung Sat. Viet Minh cadres who had infiltrated the Binh Xuyen months before called a mass meeting and exposed Bay Vien's negotiations with the French. The angry nationalistic students and youths launched a coup on May 28; Bay Vien's supporters were arrested, unreliable units were disarmed, and the Rung Sat refuge was turned over to the Viet Minh. Back on the Plain of Reeds, Bay Vien sensed an ugly change of temper in the convocations, massed his bodyguards, and fled toward the Rung Sat pursued by Viet Minh troops.[80] En route he learned that his refuge was lost and changed direction, arriving on the outskirts of Saigon on June 10. Hounded by pursuing Viet Minh columns and aware that return to the Rung Sat was impossible, Bay Vien found himself on the road to Saigon.

Unwilling to join the French openly and be labeled a collaborator, Bay Vien hid in the marshes south of Saigon for several days until 2eme Bureau agents finally located him. Bay Vien may have lost the Rung Sat, but his covert action committees remained a potent force in Saigon-Cholon and made him invaluable to the French. Captain Savani, known as "the Corsican bandit" among his fellow officers, visited the Binh Xuyen leader in his hideout and argued, "Bay Vien, there's no other way out. You have only a few hours of life left if you don't sign with us."[81] The captain's logic was irrefutable; on June 16 a French staff car drove Bay Vien to Saigon, where he signed a prepared declaration denouncing the Communists as traitors and avowing his loyalty to the Vietnamese emperor, Bao Dai.[82] Shortly afterward, the French government announced that it "had decided to confide the police and maintenance of order to the Binh Xuyen troops in a zone where they are used to operating" and assigned them a small piece of territory along the southern edge of Cholon.[83]

In exchange for this concession, eight hundred gangsters who had rallied to Bay Vien from the Rung Sat, together with the covert action committees, assisted the French in a massive, successful sweep through the twin cities in search of Viet Minh cadres, cells, and agents. As Bay Vien's chief political adviser, Lai Huu Tai, explained, "Since we had spent time in the *maquis* and fought there, we also knew how to organize the counter *maquis*."[84]

But once the operation was finished, Bay Vien, afraid of being damned as a collaborator, retired to his slender zone and refused to move. The Binh Xuyen refused to set foot on any territory not ceded to them and labeled an independent "nationalist zone." To avail themselves of the Binh Xuyen's unique abilities as an urban counterintelligence and security force, the French were obliged to turn over Saigon-Cholon block by block. By April 1954 the Binh Xuyen military commander, Lai Van Sang, was director-general of police, and the Binh Xuyen controlled the capital region and the sixty-mile strip between Saigon and Cap Saint Jacques. Since the Binh Xuyen's pacification technique required vast amounts of money to bribe thousands of informers, the French allowed them carte blanche to plunder the city. In giving the Binh Xuyen this economic and political control over Saigon, the French were both eradicating the Viet Minh and creating a political counterweight to Vietnamese nationalist parties gaining power as a result of American pressure for political and military Vietnamization.[85] By 1954 the illiterate, bullnecked Bay Vien had become the richest man in Saigon and the key to the French presence in Cochin China. Through the Binh Xuyen, the French 2$^{eme}$ Bureau countered the growing power of the nationalist parties, kept Viet Minh terrorists off the streets, and battled the American CIA for control of South Vietnam. Since the key to the Binh Xuyen's power was money, and quite a lot of it, their economic evolution bears examination.

The Binh Xuyen's financial hold over Saigon was similar in many respects to that of American organized crime in New York City. The Saigon gangsters used their power over the streets to collect protection, money and to control the transportation industry, gambling, prostitution, and narcotics. But while American criminals prefer to maintain a low profile, the Binh Xuyen flaunted their power: their green-bereted soldiers strutted down the streets, opium dens and gambling casinos operated openly, and a government minister actually presided at the dedication of the Hall of Mirrors, the largest brothel in Asia.

Probably the most important Binh Xuyen economic asset was the gambling and lottery concession controlled through two sprawling casinos—the Grand Monde in Cholon and the Cloche d'Or in Saigon—which were operated by the highest bidder for the annually awarded franchise. The Grand Monde had been opened in 1946 at the insistence of the governor-general of Indochina, Admiral Thierry d'Argenlieu, to finance the colonial government of Cochin China.[86] The franchise was initially leased to a Macao Chinese gambling syndicate, which made payoffs to all of Saigon's competing political forces—the Binh Xuyen, Emperor Bao Dai, prominent cabinet ministers, and even the Viet Minh. In early 1950 Bay Vien suggested to Captain Savani that payments to the Viet Minh could be ended if he were awarded the franchise.[87] The French agreed, and Bay Vien's adviser Lai Huu Tai (Lai Van Sang's brother) met with Emperor Bao Dai and promised him strong support if he agreed to back the measure.

But when Bao Dai made the proposal to President Huu and the governor of Cochin, they refused their consent, since both of them received stipends from the Macao Chinese. The Binh Xuyen broke the deadlock in their own inimitable fashion: they advised the Chinese franchise holders that the Binh Xuyen police would no longer protect the casinos from Viet Minh terrorists,[88] kidnapped the head of the Macao syndicate,[89] and, finally, pledged to continue everybody's stipends. After agreeing to pay the government a $200,000 deposit and $20,000 a day, the Binh Xuyen were awarded the franchise on December 31, 1950.[90] Despite these heavy expenses, the franchise was an enormous economic coup; shortly before the Grand Monde was shut down by a new regime in 1955, knowledgeable French observers estimated that it was the most profitable casino in Asia, and perhaps in the world.[91]

Sometime after 1950 the French military awarded the Binh Xuyen another lucrative colonial asset, Saigon's opium commerce. The Binh Xuyen started processing MACG's raw Hmong opium and distributing prepared smoking opium to hundreds of dens scattered throughout the twin cities.[92] They paid a fixed percentage of their profits to Emperor Bao Dai, the French 2[eme] Bureau, and the MACG commandos. The CIA's Colonel Lansdale later reported:

> The Binh Xuyen were participating in one of the world's major arteries of the dope traffic, helping move the prize opium crops out of Laos and South China. The profits were so huge that Bao Dai's tiny cut was ample to keep him in yachts, villas, and other comforts in France.[93]

The final Binh Xuyen asset was prostitution. They owned and operated a variety of brothels, from small, intimate villas staffed with young women for generals and diplomats to the Hall of Mirrors, whose twelve hundred inmates and industrial techniques made it one of the largest and most profitable in Asia.[94] The brothels not only provided income but also yielded a steady flow of political and military intelligence.

In reviewing Bay Vien's economic activities in 1954,[95] the French 2[eme] Bureau concluded:

> In summary, the total of the economic potential built up by General Le Van (Bay) Vien has succeeded in following exactly the rules of horizontal and vertical monopolization so dear to American consortiums.[96]

Bay Vien's control over Saigon-Cholon had enabled him to build "a multi-faceted business enterprise whose economic potential constitutes one of the most solid economic forces in South Vietnam."[97]

After allowing the Binh Xuyen to develop this financial empire, the

2<sup>eme</sup> Bureau witnessed its liquidation during the desperate struggle it waged with the CIA for control of Saigon and South Vietnam. Between April 28 and May 3, 1955, the Binh Xuyen and the Vietnamese army (ARVN) fought a savage house-to-house battle for control of Saigon-Cholon. More troops were involved in this battle than in the Tet offensive of 1968, and the fighting was almost as destructive.[98] In the six days of combat, 500 persons were killed, 2,000 wounded, and 20,000 left homeless.[99] Soldiers disregarded civilians and leveled whole neighborhoods with artillery, mortars, and heavy machine guns. When it was all over the Binh Xuyen had been driven back into the Rung Sat and Prime Minister Ngo Dinh Diem was master of Saigon.

This battle was a war by proxy; the Binh Xuyen and Diem's army were stand-ins, mere pawns, in a power struggle between the French 2<sup>eme</sup> Bureau and the American CIA. Although there were longstanding tactical disagreements between the French and the Americans, at the ambassadorial and governmental levels the atmosphere was one of friendliness and flexibility not to be found between their respective intelligence agencies.

Prior to the French debacle at Dien Bien Phu in May 1954, the two governments had cooperated with a minimum of visible friction in Indochina. During the early 1950s the United States paid 78 percent of the cost of maintaining the French Expeditionary Corps, and hundreds of American advisers served with French units. After Dien Bien Phu and Geneva, however, the partnership began to crumble.

France resigned itself to granting full independence to its former colony and agreed at Geneva to withdraw from the northern half of the country and to hold an all-Vietnam referendum in 1956—an election the Viet Minh were sure to win—to determine who would rule the unified nation. Under the guidance of French Premier Pierre Mendès-France, Paris planned "a precedent-setting experiment in coexistence"; France would grant the Viet Minh full control over Vietnam by adhering strictly to the Geneva accords and then work closely with Ho Chi Minh "to preserve French cultural influence and salvage French capital."[100] Needless to say, the French premier's plans did not sit well in a U.S. State Department operating on Secretary John Foster Dulles's anti-Communist first principles. Fundamental policy disagreements began to develop between Washington and Paris, though there was no open conflict.

The Pentagon Papers have summarized the points of disagreement between Washington and Paris rather neatly:

> All the foregoing tension resolved to two central issues between the United States and France. The first was the question

of how and by whom Vietnam's armed forces were to be trained. The second, and more far reaching, was whether Ngo Dinh Diem was to remain at the head of Vietnam's government or whether he was to be replaced by another nationalist leader more sympathetic to Bao Dai and France.[101]

The first question was resolved soon after Special Ambassador General J. Lawton Collins arrived in Vietnam on November 8, 1954. The Americans were already supplying most of ARVN's aid, and French High Commissioner General Paul Ely readily agreed to turn the training over to the Americans.

The second question—whether Diem should continue as prime minister—provoked the CIA-2eme Bureau war of April 1955. Diem was a political unknown who had acceded to the premiership largely because Washington was convinced that his strong anti-Communist, anti-French beliefs best suited American interests. But the immediate problem for Diem and the Americans was control of Saigon. If Diem were to be of any use to the Americans in blocking the unification of Vietnam, he would have to wrest control of the streets from the Binh Xuyen. For whoever controlled the streets controlled Saigon, and whoever controlled Saigon held the key to Vietnam's rice-rich Mekong Delta.

While the French and American governments disavowed any self-interest and tried to make even their most partisan suggestions seem a pragmatic response to the changing situation in Saigon, both gave their intelligence agencies a free hand to see if Saigon's reality could be molded in their favor. Behind the diplomatic amity, the CIA, led by Colonel Lansdale, and the French 2eme Bureau, under Captain Savani, engaged in a savage clandestine battle for Saigon.

In the movie version of Graham Green's novel about this period, *The Quiet American*, Colonel Lansdale was played by the World War II combat hero Audie Murphy, whose previous roles as the white-hat hero in dozens of westerns allowed him to project the evangelistic anti-communism so characteristic of Lansdale. What Murphy did not portray was Lansdale's mastery of the CIA's repertoire of covert action techniques, including sabotage, psychological warfare, and counter-terrorism. When Lansdale arrived in Saigon in May 1954 he was fresh from engineering President Ramón Magaysay's successful counterinsurgency campaign against the Philippine Communist party. As the prophet of a new counterinsurgency doctrine and representative of a wealthy government, Lansdale was a formidable opponent.

In seeking to depose Bay Vien, Lansdale was not just challenging the 2eme Bureau, he was taking on Saigon's Corsican community—Corsican businessmen, Corsican colonists, and the Corsican underworld. From the late nineteenth century onward, Corsicans had dominated the

Indochina civil service.[102] At the end of World War II, Corsican resistance fighters, some of them gangsters, had joined the regular army and come to Indochina with the Expeditionary Corps. Many remained in Saigon after their enlistment to go into legitimate business or to reap profits from the black market that flourished in wartime. Those with strong underworld connections in Marseille were able to engage in currency smuggling between the two ports. The Marseille gangster Barthélemy Guerini worked closely with contacts in Indochina to smuggle Swiss gold to Asia immediately after World War II.[103] Moreover, Corsican gangsters close to Corsican officers in Saigon's 2[eme] Bureau purchased surplus opium and shipped it to Marseille, where it made a small contribution to the city's growing heroin industry.[104]

The unchallenged leader of Saigon's Corsican underworld was the respectable merchant Mathieu Franchini. Owner of the exclusive Continental Palace Hotel, Franchini made a fortune playing the piaster gold circuit between Saigon and Marseille during the First Indochina War.[105] He became the Binh Xuyen's investment counselor and managed a good deal of their opium and gambling profits. When Bay Vien's fortune reached monumental proportions, Franchini sent him to Paris where "new found Corsican friends gave him good advice about investing his surplus millions."[106] According to reliable Vietnamese sources, it was Franchini who controlled most of Saigon's opium exports to Marseille. Neither he nor his associates could view with equanimity the prospect of an American takeover.

Many people within the 2[eme] Bureau had worked as much as eight years building up sect armies like the Binh Xuyen; many Corsicans outside the military had businesses, positions, rackets, and power that would be threatened by a decline in French influence. While they certainly did not share Premier Mendès-France's ideas of cooperation with the Viet Minh, they were even more hostile to the idea of turning things over to the Americans.

When Lansdale arrived in Saigon he faced the task of building an alternative to the mosaic of religious armies and criminal gangs that had ruled South Vietnam in the latter years of the war. Ngo Dinh Diem's appointment as premier in July 1954 gave Lansdale the lever he needed. Although he was handpicked by the Americans, Diem had spent most of the previous decade in exile and had few political supporters and almost no armed forces. Prime minister in name only, Diem controlled merely the few blocks of downtown Saigon surrounding the presidential palace. The French and their clients—ARVN, the Binh Xuyen, and the armed religious sects, Cao Dai and Hoa Hao—could easily mount an anti-Diem coup if he threatened their interests. Lansdale proceeded to fragment his opposition's solid front and to build Diem an effective military apparatus. French control over the army was broken and Colonel Duong Van Minh ("Big Minh"), an American sympathizer, was recruited to lead the attacks on the Binh Xuyen. By manipulating payments to the armed religious sects, Lansdale was able to neutralize most of them, leaving the Binh Xuyen as the only French pawn. The Binh Xuyen financed themselves largely from their vice rackets, and their loyalty could not be manipulated through financial pressures. But, deserted by ARVN and the religious sects, the Binh Xuyen were soon crushed.

Lansdale's victory did not come easily. Soon after he arrived he began sizing up his opponent's financial and military strength. Knowing something of the opium trade's importance as a source of income for French clandestine services, he now began to look more closely at Operation X with the help of a respected Cholon Chinese banker. But the banker was abruptly murdered and Lansdale dropped the inquiry. There was reason to believe that the banker had gotten too close to the Corsicans involved, and they killed him to prevent the information from getting any further.[107]

An attempted anti-Diem coup in late 1954 led to Lansdale's replacing the palace guard. After the embassy approved secret funding (later estimated at $2 million), Lansdale convinced a Cao Dai dissident named Trinh Minh Thé to offer his *maquis* near the Cambodian border as a refuge in case Diem was ever forced to flee Saigon.[108] When the impending crisis between the French and the Americans threatened Diem's security in the capital, Thé moved his forces into the city as a permanent security force in February 1955 and paraded 2,500 of his barefoot soldiers through downtown Saigon to demonstrate his loyalty to the prime minister.[109] The 2eme Bureau was outraged at Lansdale's support for Thé. Practicing what Lansdale jocularly referred to as the "unorthodox doctrine of zapping a commander,"[110] Thé had murdered French General Chanson in 1951 and had further incensed the French when he blew up a car in 1953 in downtown Saigon, killing a number of passersby. Officers from the 2eme Bureau personally visited Lansdale to warn him that they would kill Thé, and they "usually added the pious hope that I would be standing next to him when he was gunned down."[111]

On February 11, 1955, the French army abdicated its financial controls and training responsibilities for ARVN to the United States, losing not only ARVN but control of the Hoa Hao and Cao Dai religious sects as well. Approximately 20,000 of them had served as supplementary forces to the French and Vietnamese armies[112] and had been paid directly by the 2eme Bureau. Now, with their stipends cut and their numbers reduced, they were to be integrated into ARVN, where they would be controlled by Diem and his American advisers.

Lansdale was given $8.6 million to pay back salaries and "bonuses" to sect commanders who cooperated by "integrating" into ARVN.[113] Needless to say, this move aroused enormous hostility from the French. When Lansdale met with General Gambiez of the French army to discuss the sect problem, the tensions were obvious:

> We sat at a small table in his office. . . . A huge Alsatian dog crouched under it. Gambiez informed me that at one word from him, the dog would attack me, being a trained killer. I asked Gambiez to please note that my hands were in my pockets as I sat at the table; I had a small .25 automatic pointing at his stomach which would tickle him fatally. Gambiez called off his dog and I put my hands on the table. We found we could work together.[114]

By February the 2<sup>eme</sup> Bureau realized that they were gradually losing to Lansdale's team, so they tried to discredit him as an irresponsible adventurer in the eyes of his own government by convening an unprecedented secret agents' tribunal. But the session was unsuccessful, and the 2<sup>eme</sup> Bureau officers were humiliated; their animosity toward Lansdale was, no doubt, intensified.[115]

But the French were not yet defeated, and late in February they mounted a successful counteroffensive. When Diem refused to meet the sects' demands for financial support and integration into ARVN, the French seized the opportunity and brought all the sect leaders together in Tay Ninh on February 22, where they formed the United Front and agreed to work for Diem's overthrow. Money was to be provided by the Binh Xuyen. When a month of fruitless negotiations failed to wring any concessions from Diem, the United Front sent a five-day ultimatum to Diem demanding economic and political reforms.[116] Suddenly the lethargic quadrille of political intrigue was over and the time for confrontation was at hand.

Lansdale was now working feverishly to break up the United Front and was meeting with Diem regularly.[117] With the help of the CIA station chief, Lansdale put together a special team to tackle the Binh Xuyen, the financial linchpin of the United Front. Lansdale recruited a former Saigon police chief named Mai Huu Xuan, who had formed the Military Security Service (MSS) with two hundred to three hundred of his best detectives when the Binh Xuyen took over the police force in 1954. Embittered by four years of losing to the Binh Xuyen, the MSS began a year-long battle with the Binh Xuyen's action committees. Many of these covert cells had been eliminated by April 1955, a factor that Xuan felt was critical in the Binh Xuyen's defeat.[118] Another of Lansdale's recruits was Colonel Duong Van Minh, the ARVN commander for Saigon-Cholon.

Lansdale made ample discretionary funds available to Minh, whom he incorporated in his plans to assault the Binh Xuyen.[119]

The fighting began on March 28 when a pro-Diem paratroop company attacked the Binh Xuyen–occupied police headquarters. The Binh Xuyen counterattacked the following night, beginning with a mortar attack on the presidential palace at midnight. When French tanks rolled into the city several hours later to impose a cease-fire agreed to by the United States, Lansdale protested bitterly to Ambassador Collins, "explaining that only the Binh Xuyen would gain by a cease-fire."[120]

For almost a month French tanks and troops kept the Binh Xuyen and ARVN apart. Then on April 27 Ambassador Collins met with Secretary of State Dulles in Washington and told him that Diem's obstinacy was the reason for the violent confrontation in Saigon. Dismayed, Dulles cabled Saigon that the United States was no longer supporting Diem.[121] A few hours after this telegram arrived, Diem's troops attacked Binh Xuyen units and drove them out of downtown Saigon into neighboring Cholon. Elated by Diem's easy victory, Dulles cabled Saigon his full support for Diem. The embassy burned his earlier telegram.[122]

During the fighting of April 28 Lansdale remained in constant communication with the presidential palace, while his rival Captain Savani moved into the Binh Xuyen headquarters at the Y Bridge in Cholon, where he took command of the bandit battalions and assigned his officers to accompany Binh Xuyen troops in the house-to-house fighting.[123] The Binh Xuyen radio offered a reward to anyone who could bring Lansdale to their headquarters where, Bay Vien promised, his stomach would be cut open and his entrails stuffed with mud.[124]

On May 2 the fighting resumed as ARVN units penetrated Cholon leveling whole city blocks and pushing the Binh Xuyen steadily backward. Softened by years of corruption, the Binh Xuyen bandits were no longer the tough guerrillas of a decade before. Within a week most of them had retreated into the depths of the Rung Sat swamp.

Although the war between Diem and Bay Vien was over, the struggle between Lansdale and the Corsicans was not quite finished. True to the Corsican tradition, the defeated French launched a vendetta against the entire American community. As Lansdale describes it:

> A group of soreheads among the French in Saigon undertook a spiteful terror campaign against American residents. Grenades were tossed at night into the yards of houses where Americans lived. American owned automobiles were blown up or booby-trapped. French security officials blandly informed nervous American officials that the terrorist activity was the work of the Viet Minh.[125]

A sniper put a bullet through Lansdale's car window as he was driving through Saigon, and a Frenchman who resembled him was machine-gunned to death in front of Lansdale's house by a passing car. When Lansdale was finally able to determine that the ringleaders were French intelligence officers, grenades started going off in front of their houses in the evenings.[126]

During his May 8–11, 1955, meeting with French Premier Edgar Faure in Paris, Dulles announced his continuing support for Diem, and both agreed that France and the United States would pursue independent policies in Indochina. The partnership was over; France would leave, and the United States would remain in Vietnam to back Diem.[127]

Diem's victory brought about a three-year respite in large-scale opium trafficking in Vietnam. Without the Binh Xuyen and Operation X managing the trade, bulk smuggling operations from Laos came to an end and distribution in Saigon of whatever opium was available became the province of petty criminals. Observers also noticed a steady decline in the number of opium dens operating in the capital region. Although American press correspondents described the Binh Xuyen–Diem conflict as a morality play—a clash between the honest, moral Prime Minister Diem and corrupt, dope-dealing "super bandits"—the Binh Xuyen were only a superficial manifestation of a deeper problem, and their eviction from Saigon produced little substantive change.[128]

For more than eighty years French colonialism had interwoven the vice trades with the basic fabric of the Vietnamese economy by using them as legitimate sources of government tax revenue. During the late 1940s the French simply transferred them from the legitimate economy to the underworld, where they have remained a tempting source of revenue for political organizations. By exploiting the rackets for the French, the Binh Xuyen had developed the only effective method ever devised for countering urban guerrilla warfare in Saigon. Their formula was a combination of crime and counterinsurgency: control over the municipal police allowed systematic exploitation of the vice trade; the rackets generated large sums of ready cash; and money bought an effective network of spies, informants, and assassins.

The system worked so well for the Binh Xuyen that in 1952 Viet Minh cadres reported that their activities in Saigon had come to a virtual standstill because the bandits had either bought off or killed most of their effective organizers.[129] When the Diem administration was faced with large-scale insurgency in 1958, it reverted to the Binh Xuyen formula, and government clandestine services revived the opium trade with Laos to finance counterinsurgency operations. Faced with similar problems in 1965, Premier Ky's adviser General Loan would use the same methods.[130]

## Secret War in Burma: KMT and CIA

While the work of French clandestine services in Indochina enabled the opium trade to survive government supression efforts, CIA activities in Burma helped transform the Shan states from a relatively minor poppy-cultivating area into the largest opium-growing region in the world. The precipitous collapse of the Nationalist Chinese (Kuomintang, or KMT) government in 1949 convinced the Truman administration that it had to stem "the southward flow of communism" into Southeast Asia. In 1950 the Defense Department extended military aid to the French in Indochina. In that same year, the CIA began regrouping remnants of the defeated Kuomintang army in the Burmese Shan states for an invasion of southern China. Although the KMT army was to fail in its military operations, it succeeded in monopolizing and expanding the Shan states' opium trade.

The KMT shipped the opium harvests to northern Thailand, where they were sold to General Phao Siyanan of the Thai police, a CIA client. The CIA had promoted the Phao-KMT partnership to provide a secure rear area for the KMT, but this alliance soon became a critical factor in the growth of Southeast Asia's narcotics traffic.

With CIA support, the KMT remained in Burma until 1961, when a Burmese army offensive drove them into Laos and Thailand. By this time, however, the Kuomintang had already used their control over the tribal populations to expand Shan state opium production by almost 500 percent—from less than 80 tons after World War II to an estimated 300–400 tons by 1962.[131] From bases in northern Thailand the KMT continued to send mule caravans into the Shan states to bring out the opium harvest. In 1973, twenty years after the CIA first began supporting KMT troops in the Golden Triangle, these KMT caravans controlled almost one-third of the world's total illicit opium supply and enjoyed a growing share of Southeast Asia's thriving heroin business.[132]

Opium had long been a prerogative of power for the KMT warlords who controlled southern China before 1949. During his seventeen-year rule over Yunnan province in the remote southwest bordering Burma, General Lung Yun relied primarily on opium and banditry to sustain his independent army. A member of the Lolo minority of northern Yunnan, Lung Yun was heir to the mix of highland raiding, caravan trading, and opium farming characteristic of this remote region. When World War II made Yunnan the KMT's last bastion and landing point for U.S. military aid, this "one-eyed warlord governor" prospered. By 1945 he "maintained a private army to protect his extensive poppy fields along the . . . northwest border of Yunnan . . . and directed his son's systematic highjacking operations of American lend-lease arms . . . and rations traveling over the Burma Road to Kunming."[133] Working with his cousin General Lu Han, the warlord ran a "lucrative contraband traffic" that smuggled opium and U.S. supplies into the Japanese occupied areas of central China, Burma, and Thailand. As his demands for U.S. goods and his defiance of the KMT regime mounted in 1945, President Chiang Kai-shek ousted General Lung in a minor coup and replaced him with the equally notorious General Lu Han, a partner in the old warlord's most blatant black market dealing.[134]

As Mao's revolutionary army pushed into southern China in late 1949, Generalissimo Chiang Kai-shek and his Kuomintang regime planned to make craggy Yunnan province their last bastion. By now, however, the local warlord Lu Han harbored his own grievances against Chiang. At the end of World War II Lu Han had been ordered to occupy northern Indochina for the Allies while British forces moved into the southern sector. Eager for plunder, Lu Han sent his ragged divisions into Tonkin, where they settled on the countryside like locusts. To satiate Lu Han and win his tolerance for the nationalist movement, Premier Ho Chi Minh organized a "Gold Week" from September 16 to 23, 1945. Viet Minh cadres scoured every village, collecting rings, earrings, and coins from patriotic peasants. When Lu Han stepped off the plane at Hanoi airport on September 18, Ho Chi Minh presented him with a solid gold opium pipe.[135]

Absorbed in this systematic plunder, one of the KMT units, the Ninety-third Division, extended its occupation of Laos beyond the deadline for withdrawal so it could finish collecting the Hmong opium harvest.[136] During Lu Han's absence in Hanoi, Chiang sent two of his divisions to occupy Yunnan. When the Chinese withdrew from Indochina in early June 1946, Chiang ordered Lu Han's best troops to their death on the northern front against the Chinese Communists, reducing the warlord to the status of guarded puppet inside his own fiefdom.[137]

When the People's Liberation Army entered Yunnan in December 1949, Lu Han armed the population, who drove Chiang's troops out of the cities and threw the province open to the advancing revolutionary armies.[138] Nationalist Chinese stragglers began crossing into Burma, and in January 1950 remnants of the Ninety-third Division, Twenty-sixth Army, and General Li Mi's Eighth Army arrived in Burma. Five thousand of Li Mi's troops who crossed into Indochina instead of Burma were quickly disarmed by the French and interned on Phu Quoc Island in the Gulf of Thailand until they were repatriated to Taiwan in June 1953.[139]

However, the Burmese army was less successful than the French in dealing with the Chinese. By March 1950 some 1,500 KMT troops had crossed the border into Burma and were occupying territory between Kengtung and Tachilek. In June the Burmese army commander for

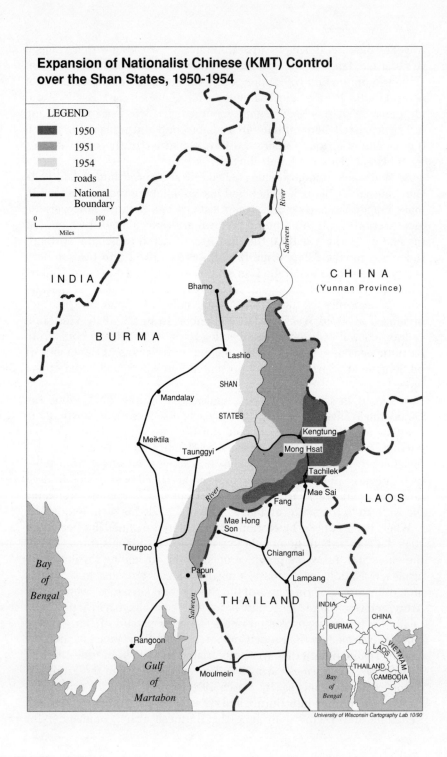

# Expansion of Nationalist Chinese (KMT) Control over the Shan States, 1950-1954

### LEGEND

- 1950
- 1951
- 1954
- —— roads
- – – National Boundary

0   100
Miles

CHINA
(Yunnan Province)

INDIA

BURMA

Salween River

Bhamo

Lashio

SHAN

Mandalay

STATES

Meiktila

Kengtung

Taunggyi

Mong Hsat

Tachilek

River

Mae Sai

Fang

LAOS

Mae Hong Son

Tourgoo

Chiangmai

Bay of Bengal

Papun

Lampang

Salween

THAILAND

INDIA

CHINA

BURMA

LAOS

VIETNAM

Rangoon

THAILAND

CAMBODIA

Gulf of Martabon

Moulmein

Bay of Bengal

University of Wisconsin Cartography Lab 10/90

Kengtung state demanded that the KMT either surrender or leave Burma immediately. When General Li Mi refused, the Burmese army launched a drive from Kengtung and captured Tachilek in a matter of weeks. Two hundred of Li Mi's troops fled to Laos and were interned, but the remainder retreated to Mong Hsat, about forty miles west of Tachilek and fifteen miles from the Thai border.[140] Since the Burmese army had been tied down for three years in central Burma battling four major rebellions, its Kengtung contingent was too weak to pursue the KMT through the mountains to Mong Hsat. But it seemed only a matter of months until the Burmese troops would become available for the final assault on the weakened KMT forces.

Isolated between hostile Burmese and Communist Chinese troops, General Li Mi's forces were desperate for outside support. In August the U.S. chargé in Taipei reported that Li Mi's officers "have made much trouble with [Nationalist] Chinese Embassy Bangkok, demanding money and supplies and diplomatic support." Since Taiwan's foreign ministry was "adamant against ordering troops to lay down arms in Burma," Li Mi was trapped and thus forced to pursue every option—asking the Thai government for ammunition to fight his way back into Yunnan, negotiating with Burmese rebels for ammunition to fight Rangoon, and demanding supplies from Taipei to hold his position in Burma.[141]

At this point the CIA entered the lists on the side of the KMT, drastically altering the balance of power. The Truman administration, ambivalent toward the conflict in Southeast Asia since it took office in 1945, was moved to action by the sudden collapse of Chiang Kai-shek's Kuomintang regime. All U.S. government agencies scrambled to devise policies "to block further Communist expansion in Asia,"[142] and in April 1950 the Joint Chiefs of Staff advised the secretary of defense that:

> resolution of the situation facing Southeast Asia would . . . be facilitated if prompt and continuing measures were undertaken to reduce the pressure from Communist China. In this connection, the Joint Chiefs of Staff have noted the evidences of renewed vitality and apparent increased effectiveness of the Chinese Nationalist forces.[143]

The Joint Chiefs went on to suggest the implementation of a "program of special covert operations designed to interfere with Communist activities in Southeast Asia."[144]

Six months after the fall of China, these plans gained a new priority when North Korean forces crossed the 38th Parallel into the South. As the Korean War intensified when China's massive army crossed the Yalu River in November 1950, President Truman authorized an expansion of covert action capabilities and approved a plan put forward by the Office of Policy Coordination (OPC) and the CIA for the invasion of southern China using the KMT remnants in Burma. The operation was controversial from the outset. At a White House meeting sometime in early 1951, the CIA's director, General Walter Bedell Smith, reportedly opposed the plan, arguing that it could not draw Chinese forces from the Korean front. But Truman overruled him and ordered the CIA to proceed on the basis of a strict confidentiality that denied knowledge to senior agency officials and U.S. diplomats, including the U.S. ambassador to Burma.[145]

After Truman approved the plan, the executive's covert action arm, the OPC, assumed control of the operation as part of an ongoing expansion on its global mission. In the months after the outbreak of the Korean War, the OPC had grown from a small unit of just 302 personnel with a budget of $4.7 million into a worldwide covert action apparatus of 5,954 employees funded at $82 million per year. Moreover, in October 1951, Truman had authorized an "intensification of covert action" in executive order NSC 10/5, in effect "condoning and fostering activity without providing scrutiny and control." Under the force of this rapid expansion, the OPC was achieving, in the words of one congressional analyst, an "institutional independence that was unimaginable at the time of its inception."[146] Although CIA Director Bedell Smith, a powerful figure, demanded and won nominal control over OPC within a week of his appointment in October 1950, its autonomous bureaucracy would remain intact for another two years. Armed with a budget that con sumed more than half the CIA's funds, the OPC enjoyed an extraordinary power within a U.S. intelligence community that was still little more than a "vague coalition of independent baronies."[147] Under the leadership of its founder, the messianic cold warrior Frank Wisner, the OPC recruited promising agents with lavish salaries and fought bureaucratic wars with its rivals, the CIA included. Wisner dismissed the CIA's analysts as "a bunch of old washerwomen exchanging gossip while they rinse through the dirty linen," and CIA agents regarded OPC as "a bunch of amateurs who didn't exercise good tradecraft."[148] As a covert action agency, instead of a passive data-collecting bureau like most CIA units, the OPC recruited a number of OSS war veterans like William Colby who had reveled in the thrill of parachuting into occupied France or Burma for missions of demolition, espionage, and guerrilla action.[149] Just as they had operated behind German and Japanese lines in World War II, OPC's agents now concocted derring-do schemes in the old OSS spirit to penetrate the iron curtain. While OPC's European operatives were hardened by their work with ex-Nazis and assorted Fascists, its Far East agents maintained a more exotic aura. Future CIA director William Colby, who joined the OPC's Far East division at this time, described it as "a rich stable of immensely colorful characters from . . . swashbucklers accustomed to danger to quiet students steeped in the culture of the Orient." The division's director, Colonel Richard Stilwell, was a future four-star general, and its deputy, Desmond Fitzgerald, was a New York socialite and China war veteran whose "romantic activism produced great dinner talk."[150] OPC colleagues delighted in recounting tales of Asian adventure, such as the stories of Paul Helliwell, on assignment with the OSS in wartime China, paying his Chinese informants with "three sticky brown bars" of opium.[151] But both divisions, Europe and Far East, were driven by the same radical pragmatism that allied the OPC with Gestapo officers or Corsican gangsters in Western Europe and opium warlords in Southeast Asia.

Not only did the OPC execute Truman's orders for an invasion of southern China, but it had probably originated the idea two years before. As Communist forces were sweeping south in May 1949 and their victory seemed certain, General Claire Chennault, commander of the famed Flying Tigers in China during World War II, came to Washington to lobby for an infusion of funds for the dying Nationalist regime. With "a small force of stout men who know the terrain" and ample air support, Americans could help the Nationalists and their tough provincial warlords dig in along China's western borderlands from the deserts of the north to the mountains of Yunnan in the south.[152] Although the State Department dismissed Chennault's plan as "impractical," he found a persuasive advocate in Helliwell. With Helliwell's endorsement, General Chennault met OPC director Frank Wisner at the Hotel Washington and convinced him to support the scheme by subsidizing Civil Air Transport (CAT), the general's own China airline that was then lurching toward bankruptcy. With Helliwell's strong endorsement, the OPC agreed to an annual subsidy of some $1 million for CAT's China operations and dispatched its guerrilla expert, OSS veteran Alfred T. Cox, to fly throughout China on CAT giving money and munitions to surviving warlords. Despite the OPC's last-hour support, the Nationalist regime continued its collapse. Within four months the Communists swept to the western border and CAT flew out of China carrying the last warlord with his treasury of $1.5 million in gold bars.[153]

Although quixotic in the extreme, this attempt at reversing the course of Chinese history with a fleet of aging aircraft nonetheless created both the inspiration and infrastructure for the later OPC/CIA invasions. Faced with certain bankruptcy after the loss of his China routes, Chennault, through his friends at OPC, sold CAT to the CIA in August 1950 for $950,000. With the purchase of Civil Air Transport, later renamed Air America, the CIA had acquired the air power that would sustain its covert operations, China invasions included, for the next quarter century.[154] Moreover, the abortive attempt seems to have excited OPC's field operative Alfred Cox about the possibilities for cross-border operations against Communist China. A tireless agent who had been football captain and Phi Beta Kappa at Lehigh University, Cox had joined OSS in 1942 and led aggressive commando teams in southern France and Yunnan, later claiming that his operations were "the first real use by the American Army of Organized Guerrillas . . . who operated in small hard hitting . . . bands behind enemy lines." Drinking heavily in his job at the Atlantic Coal Company in Providence after the war, Cox fled from "personal demons" into the OPC when Frank Wisner recruited him in 1949. Assigned to OPC's Far East division along with many OSS veterans, Cox was back in China by October to witness firsthand the collapse of the Nationalists.

Despite the debacle, Cox was still convinced that guerrilla operations inside Communist China were possible and played a central, perhaps seminal, role in developing the covert invasion plans.[155] Although the details have never been revealed, it seems that the essentials of the OPC/CIA plans involved an arms airlift to Burma via Bangkok, logistical support for KMT forces based in Burma under the command of General Li Mi, and, most important, ongoing air operations to supply the KMT forces once they had penetrated China. From external evidence it appears that the CIA hoped that Li Mi's invasion forces would link with the estimated 600,00 to 1 million Nationalist guerrillas believed to be waiting inside China.

Once Truman approved the plan, the OPC moved quickly to fashion a framework of "plausible denial" for a covert operation of unprecedented size and diplomatic delicacy.[156] In Washington, OPC official Paul Helliwell, a lawyer, formed the Sea Supply Corporation to mask the arms shipments.[157] Simultaneously, OPC negotiated with General Li Mi in Burma and Bangkok through a special military emissary to mainland Southeast Asia, Marine General Graves B. Erskine. At these meetings, Li Mi reported that he had escaped from Yunnan into northern Burma with 2,000 troops but had been forced, by lack of food and supplies, to withdraw south to Tachilek near the Thai border.[158]

In early 1951 the OPC's Far East division assigned operational control to Alfred Cox in Hong Kong and dispatched a team of operatives to Sea Supply's Bangkok offices under agent Sherman B. Joost, a Princeton man who had led Kachin tribal guerrillas in Burma during the war as a commander of OSS Detachment 101.[159] Once in Thailand, Joost made contact with fellow OSS veteran Willis Bird, a private Bangkok-based aviation contractor who had married the sister of Sitthi Sawetsila, a Thai air force officer close to the powerful police general Phao.[160] As the clandestine network grew, Willis Bird's relative William Bird became

CAT's representative in Bangkok.[161] Through such contacts, the CIA approached Thailand's Prime Minister Phibun Songkhram, a resolute anti-Communist, who "readily agreed . . . to provide certain facilities to support Li Mi." When the British ambassador later expressed dismay at his support for the CIA, Phibun reportedly replied, "Why are you surprised? Aren't you just as interested in killing Communists as I am, or as the Americans are?"[162]

After months of such intense preparations, Operation PAPER finally began on February 7, 1951, when four CAT air transports landed in Bangkok with a shipment of weapons for Sea Supply Corporation from CIA stores in Okinawa.[163] According to General Li Mi's account, there was a March meeting in Bangkok with two Americans, the OPC's Joost and businessman Willis Bird, before this initial shipment was flown north to Chiangmai—200 rifles, 150 carbines, 12 mortars, and 4 radio sets. "The Chief of Police of Thailand," Li Mi said, referring to General Phao, "delivered the arms personally to the Burma border accompanied by two U.S. Officers, one a Captain and the other a radio operator."[164]

The first signs of direct CIA aid to the KMT appeared in early 1951, when Burmese intelligence officers reported that unmarked C-46 and C-47 transport aircraft were making at least five parachute drops a week to KMT forces in Mong Hsat.[165] With its new supplies the KMT underwent a period of vigorous expansion and reorganization. Training bases staffed with instructors flown in from Taiwan were constructed near Mong Hsat, KMT agents scoured the Kokang and Wa states along the Burma-China border for scattered KMT survivors, and Li Mi's force burgeoned to 4,000 men.[166] In April Li Mi led the bulk of his force up the Salween River to Mong Mao in the Wa states, where they established a base camp near the China border. As more stragglers were rounded up, a new base camp was opened at Mong Yang; soon unmarked C-47s were seen making air drops in the area. When Li Mi recruited 300 troops from Kokang state under the command of the *sawbwa*'s younger sister, Olive Yang, more arms were again dropped to the KMT camp.[167]

In June 1951 the attempted reconquest of Yunnan began when the 2,000 KMT soldiers of the Yunnan Province Anti-Communist National Salvation Army based at Mong Mao crossed the border into China. Accompanied by CIA advisers and supplied by regular airdrops from unmarked C-47s, KMT troops moved northward in two columns, capturing Kengma and its airfield some sixty miles inside China without resistance. However, as they advanced north of Kengma, the People's Liberation Army (PLA) counterattacked. The KMT suffered huge casualties, and several of their CIA advisers were killed. Li Mi and his Salvation Army fled back to Burma, after less than a month in China. Undeterred by this crushing defeat, however, the General dispatched his

2,000-man contingent at Mong Yang into southern Yunnan; they too were quickly overwhelmed and driven back into Burma two months later.[168] Retreating from Yunnan with heavy losses of troops and equipment, the KMT forces began to live off the land. Among the remaining KMT troops, 7,300 were in the Wa states along the border and 4,400 were farther south in Kengtung state.[169] In August the U.S. ambassador to Rangoon, David M. Key, reported that the *sawbwa* of Kengtung was "greatly agitated over the extremely serious situation developing in his state." As the KMT collapsed in the wake of the defeat, the remnants were "becoming very unruly and indulging in outright looting."[170]

Rather than abandoning this doomed adventure, the CIA redoubled its efforts. Late in 1951 the KMT, assisted by American engineers, opened a landing strip at Mong Hsat so that it could handle the large two- and four-engine aircraft flying directly from Taiwan or Bangkok.[171] In November Li Mi flew to Taiwan for an extended vacation and returned three months later at the head of a CAT airlift, which flew 700 regular KMT soldiers from Taiwan to Mong Hsat.[172] Burmese intelligence reported that the unmarked C-47s began a regular shuttle service, with two flights a week direct from Taiwan. Sea Supply Corporation began forwarding enormous quantities of U.S. arms to Mong Hsat:[173] Burmese intelligence observed that the KMT began sporting brand-new American M1s, .50 caliber machine guns, bazookas, mortars, and anti-aircraft artillery.[174] With these lavish supplies the KMT press-ganged 8,000 soldiers from the hardy local hill tribes and soon had a force of 12,000 men.[175]

While preparing for the Yunnan invasion, the KMT had concentrated their forces in a long, narrow strip of territory parallel to the China border. Since Yunnan's illicit opium production continued until about 1955, the KMT were in a position to monopolize almost all of the province's smuggled exports. The Burmese government reported that "off and on these KMT guerrillas attacked petty traders plying across the border routes."[176]

After a year-long buildup, General Li Mi launched his final bid to reconquer Yunnan province. In August 1952, 2,100 KMT troops from Mong Yang invaded China and penetrated about sixty miles before the Chinese army drove them back into Burma.[177] This was the last of the large-scale invasions. While Li Mi and his American advisers had not really expected to overrun the vast stretches of Yunnan province with an army of 12,000, they had been confident that once the KMT secured a foothold in China, the remaining Nationalist partisans would rally to their redoubts. Although General Chennault had estimated the guerrillas at 1 million and the U.S. Joint Chiefs of Staff reported some 600,000, only a few scattered bands actually joined Li Mi once he had crossed into China.[178] Moreover, Li Mi's forces had demonstrated poor discipline and had demanded, soon after arriving in Burma, that their dependents be flown in from Taiwan, thereby reducing their mobility and combat effectiveness.[179] After three failed invasions had absorbed heavy casualties, Li Mi's forces settled along the border to gather intelligence and monitor signs of a possible Communist Chinese advance into Southeast Asia.

In a 1953 interview in Taipei with U.S. Ambassador Karl L. Rankin and U.S. military attaché Colonel John H. Lattin, General Li Mi gave a pessimistic account of his operations and showed, inadvertently, the pressures that were leading his troops into the opium trade. During his first invasion, which he dated June 24 to July 15, 1951, Li Mi had received five CAT airlifts inside Yunnan totaling 875 rifles with 40 rounds each and 2,000 carbines with 50 rounds. After the last airdrop on July 15, some 6,000 Communist troops attacked his positions at Kengtung. During the five days of continuous fighting, "I lost 800 men and inflicted 3,000 casualties on the Communists." Under "constant pressure" in August, Li Mi withdrew from Yunnan, accompanied by some "30–40,000 able-bodied men from the districts we had occupied." At the suggestion of two American officers with his forces in Burma, Li Mi then traveled to Bangkok for a conference. "One American officer stated that I should not have withdrawn from Yunnan," Li Mi recalled. "I stated that we fight to exist and not be wiped out." Despite the apparent dissatisfaction, the Americans had agreed to supply the KMT forces with $75,000 and delivered the funds in October with the orders to "lie low and train." General Li Mi's unwillingness to undertake a suicide mission for the CIA was straining relations with his American patrons.

Continuing his story, Li Mi gave an account of four contacts with Major-General Frank D. Merrill (ret.), a wartime commando leader in Burma on unspecified leave from his post as New Hampshire highway commissioner, that showed that the covert American alliance with the KMT was cracking under the strain of mounting diplomatic pressure. In early 1952 the contacts began at Clark Air Force Base in the Philippines where Merrill expressed concern that "at the next meeting of the General Assembly (United Nations) the Russians and the Burmese would surely bring up the questions of troops in Burma and that I was to lie low and personally keep out of Burma." After Li Mi reassured Merrill on this point, the KMT general then warned that the Karen ethnic guerrillas of northern Burma were contacting the "Chicoms." Evidently concerned, Merrill, whose wartime experience had been in Burma's Kachin state, replied that the Karen were "the best tribesmen in Burma" and advised Li Mi to "do everything you can to keep them from going Communist." Acting on these instructions, Li Mi made contact with the

Karen and created a permanent liaison office with their representatives in his headquarters. At a second meeting with Merrill in Tokyo in March, the American instructed the KMT general to continue his work with the Karen "to bring them closer to the Burmese government." Although Merrill refused several of Li Mi's requests for support, he "did promise to get me some sorely needed medical supplies for my troops." Clearly, the alliance was winding down. The third contact came in May when "I received a TRX from General Merrill in which he indicated displeasure because I was not living up to my promises. He stated that my supply planes (Taiwan to Mong Hsat) were flying over Thailand and causing embarrassment to the U.S. He stated that if this continued he could not continue to support me." Showing some independence, Li Mi replied that "my men had little food or ammunition and . . . I must use any means at hand to supply them." Finally, in July, Merrill wrote pleading "matrimonial difficulties" and stated that he would "be unable to support me further." With that letter, this channel for U.S. aid, which had dwindled to just $25,000 for 1952, apparently stopped.[180]

If General Li Mi's account is correct, U.S. financial support for his forces would have been declining just before two major KMT offensives—their last invasion of Yunnan in August and their later eruption out of the Burma-China borderlands across the whole of the Shan states in late 1952. Under the circumstances, it seems probable that both attacks, into Yunnan and across the Shan states, represented an attempt by the KMT to gain a local mass base for food and taxes once the United States had cut its aid.

Whatever the cause, the KMT stopped concentrating their forces near the China border in late 1952 and began spreading out across the Shan states in an effort to occupy as much territory as possible. With the Burmese army still preoccupied with insurgency in other parts of Burma, the KMT soon became the only effective government in all the Shan states' territories between the Salween River and the China border (Kokang, Wa, and Kengtung states). These territories were also Burma's major opium-producing region, and the shift in KMT tactics allowed them to increase their control over the region's opium traffic. The Burmese government reported:

> The KMTs took over the control and administration of circles (districts) and village tracts. They started opening up revenue collection centers, and local people were being subjected to pay gate-fees and ferry fees, in entering their occupied area. Customs duties were also levied on all commodities brought into their territories for trade. The taxes were collected in kind as well as money. . . . By means of threat and coercion, these

KMT aggressors forced the local inhabitants to comply with their demands.[181]

The KMT occupation centralized the marketing of opium, using hundreds of petty traders who combed the Shan highlands. The KMT also required that every hill tribe farmer pay an annual opium tax. One American missionary to the Lahu tribesmen of Kengtung State, Rev. Paul Lewis, recalled that the KMT tax produced a dramatic rise in the amount of opium grown in the highland villages he visited. Tribes had very little choice in the matter and he could remember, only too vividly, the agony of the Lahu who were tortured by the KMT for failing to comply with their regulations.[182] Moreover, many Chinese soldiers married Lahu tribeswomen; these marriages reinforced KMT control over the highlands and made it easier for them to secure opium and recruits. Through their personal contacts in mountain villages, powerful army, and control over the opium-growing regions, the KMT were in an ideal position to force an expansion of the Shan states' opium production when Yunnan's illicit production began to disappear in the early 1950s.

Almost all the KMT opium was sent south to Thailand, either by mule train or aircraft. Soon after their arrival in Burma, the KMT formed a mountain transport unit, recruiting local mule drivers and their animals.[183] Since most of their munitions and supplies were carried overland from Thailand, the KMT mule caravans found it convenient to haul opium on the outgoing trip from Mong Hsat and soon developed a regular caravan trade with Thailand. Burmese military sources claimed that much of the KMT opium was flown from Mong Hsat in "unmarked" C-47s flying to Thailand and Taiwan.[184] In any case, once the KMT opium left Mong Hsat it was usually shipped to Chiangmai, where a KMT colonel maintained in liaison office with the Nationalist Chinese consulate and with local Thai authorities. Posing as ordinary Chinese merchants, the colonel and his staff used raw opium to pay for the munitions, food, and clothing that arrived from Bangkok at the Chiangmai railhead. Once the matériel was paid for, it was this colonel's responsibility to forward it to Mong Hsat.[185] Usually the KMT dealt with the commander of the Thai police, General Phao, who shipped the opium from Chiangmai to Bangkok for both local consumption and export.[186]

While the three CIA-sponsored invasions of Yunnan at least represented a feebly conceived anti-Communist policy, the KMT expansion across the Shan states defied all logic. With what appeared to be CIA support, the KMT offensive soon became a full-scale invasion of eastern Burma. In late 1952 thousands of KMT mercenaries forded the Salween

River and began a well-orchestrated advance. The Burmese government claimed that this was the beginning of an attempt to conquer the entire country. In March 1953 the Burmese fielded three crack brigades and quickly drove the KMT back across the Salween. Significantly, after a skirmish with the KMT at the Wan Hsa La ferry, Burmese soldiers discovered the bodies of three white men who bore no identification other than some personal letters with Washington and New York addresses.[187]

As a result of the invasion, Burma went before the United Nations in March 1953 and charged the Nationalist Chinese government with un- unprovoked aggression. While the KMT troops had previously been only a bother—a minor distraction in the distant hills—they now posed a serious threat to the survival of the Union of Burma. Despite the United States' best efforts to sidetrack the issue and Taiwan's denial of any responsibility for General Li Mi, the Burmese produced reams of photos, captured documents, and testimony convincing enough to win a vote of censure for Taiwan. By now the issue had become such a source of international embarrassment for the United States that Washington used its influence to convene a Four-Nation Military Commission (Burma, the United States, Taiwan, and Thailand) in Bangkok on May 22. Although all four powers agreed to a complete KMT withdrawal from Burma after only a month of negotiations, the KMT guerrillas refused to cooperate and talks dragged on through the summer. Only after Burma again took the issue to the United Nations in September did the Taiwan negotiators in Bangkok stop quibbling and agree to the withdrawal of 2,000 KMT troops: the evacuees would march to the Burma-Thailand border, be trucked to Chiangmai, Thailand, and flown to Taiwan by the CIA's Civil Air Transport.

However, the Burmese were suspicious of the arrangements from the beginning, and when representatives of the Four-Nation Military Commission arrived in northern Thailand to observe the withdrawal, Thai police commander Phao refused to allow the Burmese delegation to accompany the others to the staging areas.[188] The next problem arose when the first batch of fifty soldiers emerged from the jungle carrying a nine-by-fifteen-foot portrait of Chiang Kai-shek instead of their guns, thus discrediting the withdrawal. The U.S. ambassador to Thailand, General William Donovan, cabled the U.S. embassy in Taiwan, demanding that the KMT be ordered to bring out their weapons. On November 9 the U.S. ambassador to Taiwan, Karl L. Rankin, replied that if the United States did not ease its pressure Chiang threatened to expose CIA support of the KMT in Burma. Donovan cabled back that the "Chicoms" and Soviets already knew about the CIA operations and kept up his pressure.

As the founder of OSS and an adviser to the current CIA director, Donovan brought an enormous authority to his demands for a full evacuation of all KMT arms and personnel. Indeed, acting on authority from the president, CIA Director Walter Bedell Smith had been personally responsible for Donovan's appointment to Bangkok.[189] But the CIA was to learn that installing the KMT in Burma was much easier than withdrawing them. Now that the KMT were entrenched in the Shan states with the full support of the Thai military, Taiwan, and CIA elements in Bangkok, not even an ambassador who spoke on behalf of the CIA director could remove them.

When the KMT withdrawal was later resumed, the soldiers carried rusting museum pieces as their arms.[190] The Burmese observers, now allowed into the staging areas, frequently protested that many of the supposed Chinese looked more like Lahus or Shans. Although other observers ridiculed these accusations, the Burmese were correct. Among the 1,925 "soldiers" evacuated in November-December 1953, there were large numbers of boys, Shans, and Lahus.[191] Even by 1971 there were an estimated 300 Lahu tribesmen still living on Taiwan who had been evacuated during this period. Although some were recruited by the promise of jobs as generals or jet pilots, most were simply press-ganged from their villages on a quota basis, given Chinese names, dressed in KMT uniforms, and shipped off to Taiwan. Many husbands and wives were separated for years, and some of the families moved to Thailand to await the return of their sons or husbands. Twenty years later only two men had come back.[192]

In the six months between November 1953 and March 1954, CAT completed a major airlift from Thailand to Taiwan, carrying 5,583 KMT soldiers, 1,040 dependents, 1,000 rifles, 69 machine guns, and 22 mortars. Paid at the rate of $128 for each passenger, the evacuations earned CAT $850,000, bolstering the precarious finances of the CIA's new airline.[193] Despite the impressive scale of the evacuation, much of the KMT's clandestine army remained in Burma.

Frustrated with its attempts to remove the KMT through international negotiations, in March 1954 Burma launched its largest military operation against the KMT. After the Burmese air force bombarded Mong Hsat for two days,[194] the army captured the KMT headquarters and drove its 2,000 defenders south toward the Thai border.[195] Negotiations were reopened in Bangkok, and during the next two months CAT flew another 4,500 KMT troops to Taiwan. On May 20, 1954, Li Mi announced the dissolution of the Yunnan Province Anti Communist National Salvation Army.[196] However, there were still 6,000 KMT troops left in Burma. Fighting began again a month later and continued sporadically for the next seven years.

While the continuing struggle faded from American headlines, in June 1955 the Rangoon *Nation* reported that 600 KMT troops had been smuggled into the Shan states from Taiwan.[197] A new commander was appointed, and a headquarters complex was opened at Mong Pa Liao near the Mekong River.[198] The KMT continued to rule the hill tribes with an iron hand. In 1957 an American missionary reported:

> For many years there have been large numbers of Chinese Nationalist troops in the area demanding food and money from the people. The areas in which these troops operate are getting poorer and poorer and some villages are finding it necessary to flee.[199]

Not only did the KMT continue to demand opium from the tribes, but they upgraded their role in the narcotics trade as well. When the Burmese army captured the KMT camp at Wanton in May 1959, they discovered three morphine base refineries operating near a usable airstrip.[200]

Although forgotten by the international press, the KMT guerrilla operations continued to create problems for both the Burmese and Chinese governments. When delegations from the Union of Burma and the People's Republic of China met to resolve a border dispute in the summer of 1960, they also concluded a secret agreement for combined operations against the KMT base at Mong Pa Liao.[201] This base, with a runway capable of handling the largest transport aircraft, was defended by some 10,000 KMT troops entrenched in an elaborate fortifications complex. After weeks of heavy fighting, 5,000 Burmese troops and three full People's Liberation Army divisions, totaling 20,000 men,[202] finally overwhelmed the fortress on January 26, 1961.[203] While many of their hill tribe recruits fled into the mountains, the crack KMT units retreated across the Mekong River into northwestern Laos. Burmese officers were outraged to discover American arms of recent manufacture and five tons of ammunition bearing distinctive red, white, and blue labels.[204] In Rangoon 10,000 angry demonstrators marched in front of the U.S. embassy, and Burma sent a note of protest to the United Nations saying that "large quantities of modern military equipment, mainly of American origin, have been captured by Burmese forces.[205]

State Department officials in Washington disclaimed any responsibility for the arms and promised appropriate action against Taiwan if investigation showed that its military aid shipments had been diverted to Burma.[206] Under pressure from the Kennedy Administration, Taiwan agreed to withdraw more of its irregulars from Thailand, and another round of airlifts began.[207] On April 5 Taiwan announced the end of the flights, declaring that 4,200 soldiers had been repatriated.[208] Six days later Taiwan joined the State Department in disavowing any responsibility for the 6,000 remaining troops.[209] However, within months the CIA began hiring these disowned KMT remnants as mercenaries for its secret operations in northwestern Laos.[210]

In retrospect, the entire Burma operation of the 1950s appears as one of the most dismal episodes in the history of the CIA. At the most basic level, the KMT's ragtag invasion was easily repulsed by Yunnanese militia after an advance of only sixty miles, thus failing in its main mission of drawing regular Chinese forces away from the Korean front. Moreover, at a time of delicate global diplomacy, an operation involving 15,000 troops and a fleet of aircraft became so obvious that its "plausible denial" was transparent. As soon as CAT's flights began in early 1951, *New York Times* correspondent Seymour Topping noticed CATs "clandestine air movements" at Saigon airport and pieced together the details of the entire operation in a matter of weeks, publishing much of it on page one.[211]

When Burma lodged protests and raised the issue at the United Nations, the Truman Administration's repeated denials by the highest officials, including CIA Director Walter Bedell Smith, became a diplomatic embarrassment. When the counselor of the British embassy in Washington asked for confirmation of "rumors that American arms were being smuggled" to the KMT, the CIA director was "very firm in his assurance that there was no official connection whatsoever with Li Mi." In an apparent attempt at disinformation, the director added that "any Americans who might be connected with this operation were freelance and he suspected might be connected with General Chennault."[212]

As the evidence of American involvement mounted, U.S. diplomats found repetition of the official denials demoralizing. In a confidential cable to the State Department from Rangoon, U.S. Ambassador David M. Key denounced the "American participation in the KMT operations which have brought chaos to [the] eastern Shan states and have been conducted in flagrant disregard [for] Burmese sovereignty." When his call for a "halt to any further American participation in these operations" was ignored, Ambassador Key returned to Washington and resigned in protest.[213]

Even the CIA was embarrassed by the failure of the operation. Outside the agency, CIA Director Bedell Smith flatly denied any American involvement in Burma, but inside the Langley headquarters he was outraged. After reading about covert U.S. support for the KMT in *The New York Times*, Bedell Smith, a retired army general, summoned the OPC's Far East director, Richard Stilwell, and, in the words of an agency eyewitness, gave him such a "violent tongue lashing" that "the colonel went down the hall in tears." Whatever the cause of the director's dissatisfaction, the Burma debacle was the worst in a string of OPC affronts that confirmed his decision to abolish the office. In 1952 he merged the OPC with the CIA's Office of Special Operations, a clandestine data collecting unit.[214] To smooth the transition and please a good friend, Bedell Smith appointed the OPC's founder, Frank Wisner, to head the new covert operations division, the directorate of plans.[215] Instead of eliminating OPC's style of covert action, the merger, in the words of a U.S. congressional review, "resulted in the maximum development of covert action over clandestine collection."[216]

The director's decision to preserve the OPC's influence within the plans directorate may well have undercut the CIA's later attempt to evacuate the KMT from Burma. Drawing on an interview with OPC veteran Tom Braden, one historian explained that the CIA would not admit that the KMT campaign had become "a drug-producing operation" and later "hatched elaborate plans for the army, knowing full well they were engaged in nonsense but not prepared to jeopardize careers . . . by admitting to so monumental a mistake."[217] Moreover, the CIA found its alliance with an opium army potentially embarrassing. After delivering the arms to the KMT in Burma, an unknown number of CAT's American pilots were loading the KMT's opium for the return flight to Bangkok. One of these, a U.S. China veteran named Jack Killam, was murdered in 1951 after an opium deal went wrong and was buried in an unmarked grave by CIA agent Sherman Joost.[218] With the OPC's tradition of radical pragmatism now housed in the CIA's plans directorate, the agency's alliance with the KMT opium armies in the Burma-Thai borderlands would last for a decade after the nominal 1954 withdrawals. More important, by refusing to repudiate the KMT and its involvement in the opium trade, the CIA had, in effect, created a precedent that would allow later covert operations to become similarly compromised.

At first glance the history of the KMT's involvement in the Burmese opium trade seems to be another case of a CIA client taking advantage of the agency's political protection to enrich itself from the narcotics trade. But on closer examination, the CIA appears to be much more seriously compromised in this affair. The CIA fostered the growth of the Yunnan Province Anti-Communist National Salvation Army in the borderlands of northeastern Burma—a potentially rich opium-growing region. There is no question of CIA ignorance or naiveté, for as early as 1952 *The New York Times* and other major American newspapers published detailed accounts of the KMT's role in the narcotics trade.[219] But most disturbing is the coincidence that the KMT's Bangkok connection, the commander of the Thai police, General Phao, was the CIA's man in Thailand.

# Thailand's Opium Trade

Under the military regimes that ruled Thailand for a quarter century after World War II, corruption became central to the seizing and holding of power. For a military faction plotting a coup, cash was essential to purchase intelligence, win loyalty, and ensure last-minute defections. "Once money was acquired, power and followers would come to heel like shadows," recalled Captain Anon, the leader of the 1951 coup attempt. "Money was the first weapon used in the overthrowing of the Government. No bullet was necessary."[220] Once in power, the ruling military clique required funds to block a possible coup by rival factions. The judicious manipulation of extralegal funding could purchase strategic intelligence about rivals, pacify insurgent subordinates, and, above all, maintain the loyalty of key garrison commanders.

Backed by the power of the state, successful military regimes combined official corruption with control over the more dynamic sectors of the Thai economy. By placing allies in key cabinet posts, the military regimes of the postwar era used the state's regulatory power to win corporate directorships and lucrative commercial licenses. One detailed study of the Thai factions during the 1950s showed leading military officers serving as directors of all the country's major corporations.[221] In addition to their control over the modern corporate sector, military factions also dominated the large informal sector of the Thai economy, most important a large smuggling trade in opium, rice, rubies, jade, wolfram, and teak. Since normal business was concentrated in the sprawling Bangkok metropolis, the military had a natural advantage in its bid to control illegal cross-border commerce.

After 1947 ruling Thai factions integrated control over the cross-border trade with a formal military mission, the defense of the nation's frontiers. Viewed from supreme command headquarters in Bangkok, Thailand's northern and eastern borders represented a grave strategic threat. To the east lay Vietnam, which posed an immediate challenge with its Communist revolution and its later potential for military invasion. To the north and west stood Burma, a traditional enemy that held contested territories, and further north was China, whose support for both Thai and Burmese Communists after 1949 was a cause of concern.

In postwar decades, the Thai military countered these dual threats through a subtle and little understood military strategy. Conventional military units were positioned along the eastern frontiers to meet a possible Vietnamese thrust through Laos and across the Mekong River into the rolling terrain of Thailand's northeast. But a radically different strategy was used to secure the rugged northern frontier facing Burma.

The strategy, a departure from the conventional Western tactics that deployed military forces along an armed frontier, was a more traditional form of Southeast Asian statecraft suited to this difficult terrain. Rather than assigning its conventional forces to patrol the northern mountains, where they usually performed poorly, the Thai supreme command cultivated alliances with highland clients—KMT remnants in the 1950s and numerous Shan opium armies in the 1960s. Through a dexterous manipulation of rivalries among Burma's ethnic insurgents, the Thai military fostered a situation of controlled chaos inside Burma along the mountains straddling the common frontier. Instead of the modern and Western concept of the *border* as an almost metaphysical line (thick on the map but thin on the ground) that divides the earth between two sovereign states, the Thai military saw their frontiers in traditional terms as a *borderland*, a broad, ill-defined highland zone where great lowland city-states battle for control through client armies.[222]

The Thai opium trade prospered because it served the strategic and financial interests of the nation's military rulers. For forty years the Thai military has provided sanctuaries, arms, and an opium market for the many mini-armies it has supported. Usually located in the mountains north of Chiangmai, the guerrilla camps were tightly controlled by the Thai military and housed the essential logistics of the Golden Triangle heroin trade—thousands of armed troops, vast mule caravans, and, after 1968, heroin refineries. Although numbers and size varied over time, Thailand's client mini-armies can be divided into three types: Nationalist Chinese (KMT) intelligence units, who have operated in northern Burma since 1950 and remained for decades the largest opium merchants; various ethnic rebel armies, especially those from the northeastern Shan states trying, after 1960, to secede from the Union of Burma; and the Yunnanese opium warlords. Significantly, the core of Bangkok's postwar military leadership were veterans of Thailand's wartime occupation of the Shan states and had formed political and logistical networks that allowed them to operate in the remote northern borderlands. Many of these Thai ultranationalists harbored the hope that Thailand would be able to annex the Shan states as it had during World War II. However, the Thai military maintained its closest alliances with the more mercenary armies—the Yunnanese opium warlords and the Nationalist Chinese units.

This frontier strategy freed troops for the military's dominion over Bangkok. While modern European armies deployed their main combat forces along their frontiers, the postwar Thai military arrayed its strategic units in the capital. Although U.S. military aid gave Thailand modern equipment during the 1950s, its army concentrated the new tanks and aircraft in the capital to control access to the throne—a tactic rooted in traditional Siamese statecraft. Since Field Marshal Phin's reorganization of the army in 1952, its heavy strategic unit, the First Division, has been based in downtown Bangkok.[223] Watching its tanks and crack infantry move into position along the boulevards during later crises, foreign military observers were impressed by the First Division's extraordinary efficiency as an integrated coup force.

From 1947 to 1957, Thai politics was dominated by an intense rivalry between two powerful military factions: one led by General Phao Siyanan, the country's notoriously corrupt police commander, and the other by Marshal Sarit Thanarat, a populist authoritarian who was the army's commander in chief. Both they and their patrons won power in the November 1947 coup, which toppled a liberal civilian government and restored Thailand's wartime dictator, Marshal Phibun Songkhram, to power. Tainted by his alliance with Japan, Phibun relied on a coalition of more junior military officers, many of whom had served in the Northern Army's occupation of the Shan states during the war. The driving force behind the coup was Major General Phin Choonhawan, the former commander of the Shan state occupation, who drew on two factions for support: one sparked by his own son-in-law, Colonel Phao, and the other led by Colonel Sarit, who then commanded the key coup force, the First Infantry Regiment.[224]

More than any other event, the 1947 coup shaped the dynamics of postwar Thai politics, installing the military in power and postponing democracy for a quarter century. Most of the military factions that would rule Thailand from the 1950s to the 1990s came to power in this coup. Determined to avoid Allied retribution for its wartime alliance with Japan, Thailand's postwar civilian government had demobilized the Northern Army in 1945, charged Phibun with collaboration, and returned the Shan states to Burma. In particular, the civilian government's harsh tactics in deactivating the Northern Army seems to have provided its commander with the justification for his later coup. Instead of providing transport home, Bangkok demobilized the forces in the northern borderlands, reducing the soldiers "to a rabble" that straggled southward feeding themselves through banditry and begging. Once back in Bangkok, the Northern Army's officers were faced with the threat of permanent deactivation, in effect the loss of commissions and careers.[225] "Many military officers . . . who fought with me in the war," said the cashiered Northern Army commander Phin, "came to express their concern practically every day about the worsening situation of the country. I therefore started to . . . listen to the ideas of military officers who commanded troops in the city. . . . I discovered that almost all of them wanted to see this government overthrown." Calling active troop commanders in Bangkok to his home, General Phin won support from all except two, whom he warned "had better keep quiet, otherwise they would be killed."[226] The motivation of many for joining Phin was clear. Phin's loyal subaltern and son-in-law Phao had been cashiered for serving as aide to the wartime dictator Phibun, and Sarit, a veteran of the Northern Army, was living in constant fear that he "would be put on inactive reserve status."[227] Moreover, active-duty officers were concerned about the new civilian constitution that made the Thai senate elective, thus depriving the military of its appointive seats.[228]

In November 1947 General Phin's coup forces occupied government radio stations, the telephone exchange, and the ministry of defense— capturing the capital and forcing the civilian government into exile. Over the next four years, Phin's core group, only nominally led by Prime Minister Phibun, attacked its military rivals through a succession of minor coups. As the ruling faction strengthened its control, it began to partition the kingdom's wealth and power. Appointed commander in chief of the army in 1948, Phin made his ally Sarit the army commander for Bangkok and his subaltern Phao the deputy director of national police. From his new position, Phao recruited a coterie of loyalists known as the Police Knights and used them to arrest and assassinate political opponents, including Thailand's chief of detectives and four former cabinet ministers. With his Knights, identifiable by their heavy diamond rings, Phao took control of "the smuggling rice and opium," arousing opposition in Parliament, which gave the navy "authority for smuggling suppression." In an apparent effort to protect his opium trading, Phao tried and failed to bring the navy's antismuggling Coastal Patrol Unit under police control.[229]

In 1951 the remaining opposition struck back when the navy command, formerly allied with the liberal civilian cabinet, kidnapped the prime minister at a shipboard ceremony and held him hostage aboard the battleship *HMS Si Ayutthaya*. Using its air force allies, Phin's army faction bombed the naval dockyards and sank the battleship, forcing its captain and the prime minister to swim for shore. After hundreds were killed in fighting that raged through the heart of Bangkok, Phao arrested more than a thousand navy personnel and later cut the Navy's forces by more than 75 percent.[230]

In the aftermath of victory, the Phin faction consolidated its hold on power and completed its division of the spoils. Still army commander, General Phin promoted his four sons-in-law to cabinet rank as deputy ministers for interior, communications, commerce, and agriculture. Promoted to director-general of police, General Phao expanded the force and used it to take control of the opium trade. Eventually, Phao and Sarit balanced their commands at 40,000 police and 45,000 army troops, respectively.[231] Phao took control of rice smuggling and Sarit received a lavish salary as head of the national lottery.[232] Although the two factions divided other areas amicably, a bitter struggle soon developed over control of the opium trade.

The illicit opium trade had only recently emerged as one of the country's most important economic assets. Its sudden significance may have served to upset the delicate balance of power between the Phao and Sarit cliques. Although the opium monopoly had thrived for almost a hundred years, by the time of the 1947 coup the high cost of imported opium and reasonably strict government controls made it an unexceptional source of graft. However, the rapid decline in foreign opium imports and the growth of local production in the early 1950s suddenly made the opium trade worth fighting over.

At the first United Nations narcotics conference in 1946, Thailand was criticized for being the only country in Southeast Asia still operating a legal government monopoly.[233] Far more threatening than the criticism, however, was the general agreement that all nonmedical opium exports should be ended as soon as possible. Iran had already passed a temporary ban on opium production in April 1946,[234] and although the Thai royal monopoly was able to import 22 tons from Iran for its customers in 1947, the future of foreign imports was uncertain.[235] Moreover, smuggled supplies from China began trickling to an end after 1950 as the People's Republic proceeded with its successful opium eradication campaign. To meet its projected needs for raw opium, the Thai government authorized poppy cultivation in the northern hills in 1947. The edict attracted a growing number of Hmong into Thailand's opium-growing regions and promoted a dramatic increase in Thai opium production.[236] But these gains in local production were soon dwarfed by the much more substantial increases in the Burmese Shan states. As Iranian and Chinese opium gradually disappeared in the early 1950s, the KMT filled the void by forcing an expansion of production in the Shan states they occupied. Since the KMT were at war with the Burmese and received their U.S. supplies from Thailand, Bangkok became a natural entrepôt for their opium. By 1949 most of the Thai monopoly's opium was from Southeast Asia,[237] and in 1954 British customs in Singapore stated that Bangkok had become the major center for international opium trafficking in Southeast Asia.[238] The traffic became so lucrative that Thailand quietly abandoned the anti-opium campaign announced in 1948 that had promised to end all opium smoking within five years.[239]

The "opium war" between Phao and Sarit was a hidden one, with almost all the battles concealed by a cloak of official secrecy. The most comical exception occurred in 1950 as one of Sarit's army convoys approached the railhead at Lampang in northern Thailand with a load of opium. Phao's police surrounded the convoy and demanded that the army surrender the opium since antinarcotics work was the exclusive responsibility of the police. When the army refused and threatened to shoot its way through to the railway, the police brought up heavy machine guns and dug in for a firefight. A nervous standoff continued for two days until Phao and Sarit themselves arrived in Lampang, took possession of the opium, and escorted it jointly to Bangkok, where it quietly disappeared.[240]

In the underground struggle for the opium trade, Phao slowly gained the upper hand. While the clandestine nature of this "opium war" makes it difficult to reconstruct the precise ingredients in Phao's victory, the critical importance of CIA support cannot be underestimated. In 1951 the CIA front organization, Sea Supply Corporation, began delivering lavish quantities of naval vessels, arms, armored vehicles, and aircraft to Phao's police force.[241] With these supplies Phao was able to establish a police air force, a maritime police, a police armored division, and a police paratroop unit. By 1953 the CIA had at least 275 overt and covert agents working with Phao's police and had delivered, through Sea Supply, $35 million worth of assistance. Aside from supplying the police with arms, communications equipment, and transport, the CIA created two new paramilitary police units destined for duty in the northern opium zone, the Police Aerial Reconnaissance Unit (PARU) and the Border Patrol Police (BPP).[242]

General Sarit's American military advisers repeatedly refused to grant his army the large amounts of modern equipment that Sea Supply Corporation gave Phao's police.[243] Since Sea Supply shipments to KMT troops in Burma were protected by the Thai police, Phao's alliance with the CIA also gave him extensive KMT contacts, through which he was able to build a virtual monopoly on Burmese opium exports. Phao's new economic and military strength quickly tipped the balance of political power in his favor; in a December 1951 cabinet shuffle, his clique captured five cabinet slots, while Sarit's faction got only one.[244] Within a year Sarit's rival had taken control of the government and Phao was recognized as the most powerful man in Thailand.

Phao used his new political power to further strengthen his financial base. He took over the vice rackets, expropriated the profitable Bangkok slaughterhouse, rigged the gold exchange, collected protection money from Bangkok's wealthiest Chinese businessmen, and forced them to appoint him to the boards of more than twenty corporations. Using his expanded police force, Phao mounted a massive repression of all dissidence, actual and potential. He created a network of civilian informants, organized the powerful Political Affairs Bureau with CIA support, and conducted a mass arrest of 104 leading intellectuals in

1952.[245] The man whom C. L. Sulzberger of *The New York Times* called "a superlative crook"[246] and whom a respected Thai diplomat hailed as the "worst man in the whole history of modern Thailand"[247] became the CIA's most important Thai client.

In an indication of the CIA's support for Phao, U.S. Ambassador William Donovan, founder of the OSS and senior adviser to the CIA, declared that "Thailand is not a police state" and hailed Phao's police as "a tough and well trained national police force." The ambassador's view that Thailand was "the free world's strongest bastion in Southeast Asia" may have encouraged his affection for General Phao's police.[248] Reflecting the ambassador's high esteem, in 1954 the U.S. secretary of the army awarded General Phao the Legion of Merit for "exceptionally meritorious service."[249] Phao became Thailand's most ardent anti-Communist, and it appears that his major task was to support KMT political aims in Thailand and its guerrilla units in Burma. Phao protected KMT supply shipments, marketed their opium, and provided such miscellaneous services as preventing Burmese observers from going to the staging areas during the November–December 1953 airlifts of supposed KMT soldiers to Taiwan.

In political terms, however, Phao's attempts to generate support for the Kuomintang among Thailand's overseas Chinese community, the richest in Asia, was probably more important. Until 1948 the KMT had been more popular than Mao's Communists among Thailand's Chinese and had received liberal financial contributions. As Mao's revolution moved toward victory during 1948–1949, Chinese sentiment shifted decisively in favor of the Communists.[250] The Thai government was indifferent to the change; in 1949 Prime Minister Phibun even announced that the sudden growth in pro-Mao sentiment among the Thai Chinese presented no particular threat to Thailand's security.[251]

But after the Phibun government allied itself with the United States in 1950, it took a harder line, generally urging the Chinese to remain neutral about politics in their mother country. In contrast, Phao began a campaign to steer the Chinese community back to an active pro-KMT position. Phao's efforts were part of a larger CIA effort to combat the growing popularity of the People's Republic among the wealthy, influential overseas Chinese community throughout Southeast Asia. The details of this program were spelled out in a 1954 U.S. National Security Council position paper, which suggested:

> Continue activities and operations designed to encourage the overseas Chinese communities in Southeast Asia: (a) to organize and activate anti-communist groups and activities within their own communities; (b) to resist the effects of

parallel pro-communist groups and activities; (c) generally, to
increase their orientation toward the free world; and, (d)
consistent with their obligations and primary allegiance to
their local governments, to extend sympathy and support to
the Chinese Nationalist Government as the symbol of Chinese
political resistance and as a link in the defense against
communist expansion in Asia.[252]

These pressures resulted in a superficial shift to the right among
Thailand's Chinese. However, since their support for the KMT was
largely dependent on police intimidation, when Phao was weakened by
political difficulties in 1955 pro-KMT activity began to collapse.[253]

By 1955 Phao's national police force had become the largest
opium-trafficking syndicate in Thailand and was intimately involved in
every phase of the narcotics traffic, producing a level of corruption that
was remarkable even by Thai standards. If the smuggled opium was
destined for export, police border guards escorted the KMT caravans
from the Thailand-Burma border to police warehouses in Chiangmai.
From there police guards brought it to Bangkok by train or police
aircraft. Then it was loaded onto civilian coastal vessels and escorted by
the maritime police to a mid-ocean rendezvous with freighters bound
for Singapore or Hong Kong.[254] However, if the opium was needed for
the government opium monopoly, theatrical considerations came to the
fore, with police border patrols staging elaborate shootouts with the
KMT smugglers near the Burma-Thailand frontier. Invariably the KMT
guerrillas dropped the opium and fled, while the police heroes brought
the opium to Bangkok and collected a reward worth one-eighth the
retail value.[255] The opium subsequently disappeared. Phao himself
delighted in posing as the leader in the crusade against opium
smuggling[256] and often made hurried, dramatic departures to the
northern frontier, where he personally led his men in these gun battles
with the smugglers of slow death.[257]

Opium profits may have helped build General Phao's political empire,
but an opium scandal contributed to its downfall. It began as another of
Phao's carefully staged opium seizures. During the night of July 9, 1955,
a squad of border police crouched in the underbrush at the Mesai River,
watching KMT soldiers ferrying 20 tons of opium from Burma into
Thailand.[258] When the last bundles were unloaded early the next
morning the Thai police burst from the jungle and rushed the smugglers.
Miraculously, the KMT soldiers again escaped unharmed. The police
escorted the opium to Bangkok, where General Phao congratulated
them. But for some reason, perhaps the huge size of the haul, Phao
became overanxious. He immediately signed a request for a reward of

$1,200,000 and forwarded it to the ministry of finance. Then he rushed across town to the finance ministry and, as deputy minister of finance, signed the check. Next, or so he claimed, Phao visited the mysterious "informer" and delivered the money personally.[259] On July 14 Phao told the press that the unnamed informant had fled the country with his money in fear of his life and therefore was not available for comment. He also said that most of the 20 tons would be thrown into the sea, though some would be sold to pharmaceutical companies to pay for the reward.[260] Even to the corruption-hardened Thai journalists the story seemed too specious to withstand any scrutiny.

Prime Minister Phibun was the first to attack Phao, commenting to the press that the high opium rewards seemed to be encouraging the smuggling traffic. More pointedly, he asked why the final reward was so much higher than the one first announced.[261] The police explained that since they had not had a chance to weigh the opium, they just estimated the reward, and their estimate was too low. Since it was common knowledge that the law prescribed no payments until after weighing, the press jumped on this hapless explanation and used it to attack Phao.[262] In August Phao was relieved of his position in the finance ministry after he left on a tour of Japan and the United States.[263] During his absence, Prime Minister Phibun released the press from police censorship, assumed veto power over all police paramilitary activities, and ordered the police to give up their business positions or quit the force.[264] After months of frustration, the finance ministry, now freed of Phao's influence, announced on August 31 that opium smoking would finally be outlawed. During early deliberations, the cabinet had proposed a complete ban by the end of the year, but the finance ministry, with General Phao as its deputy minister, had pointed out that "if opium use were ended according to the stipulated schedule . . . state revenues . . . could not be made up by alternate sources of taxation."[265] Since opium's share of revenues had already fallen to only 2.7 percent, the argument was not convincing.[266]

Phao returned in late September and delivered a public apology before the National Assembly, swearing that the police were in no way implicated in the 20-ton opium scandal.[267] But public opinion was decidedly skeptical, and the unleashed press began a long series of exposés on police corruption. General Sarit was particularly bitter toward Phao, and newspapers friendly to Sarit's clique began attacking Phao's relationship with the CIA, accusing him of being an American puppet. In November 1956 Phibun made Thailand's break with Phao's pro-KMT policy official when he said at a press conference, "The Kuomintang causes too much trouble; they trade in opium and cause

Thailand to be blamed in the United Nations."[268] Some of the press were even bold enough to accuse the CIA's Sea Supply Corporation of being involved in Phao's opium trafficking.[269]

As Sarit's fortunes rose, Phao's influence deteriorated so quickly that he felt compelled to try to use the February 1957 elections for a popular comeback. With his profits from the opium trade and other rackets, he took control of the ruling political party and began a public speaking campaign. His police issued immunity cards to Bangkok gangsters and paid them to break up opposition rallies and to beat up unfriendly candidates. In the 1957 balloting Phao's thugs perpetrated an enormous amount of electoral fraud, producing a series of Bangkok press attacks on the police for "hooliganism," opium smuggling, and extortion.[270] Phao did well enough in the elections to be appointed minister of the interior in the succeeding cabinet. But this position did him little good, for Sarit was preparing a coup.

On September 16, 1957, tanks and infantry from Sarit's old First Division moved into Bangkok's traditional coup positions. Phao flew off to Switzerland and Prime Minister Phibun fled to Japan. Sarit moved cautiously to reinforce his position. He allowed a divisive cabinet composed of competing military factions and anti-American liberals to take office, maintaining his control over the military by appointing a loyal follower, General Thanom Kittikhachon, as minister of defense. Next, Sarit broke the power of the police force. Police armored and paratroop units were disbanded and their equipment turned over to the army,[271] and all of the CIA agents attached to Phao's police force were thrown out of the country.[272] Sarit's longtime follower, General Praphat Charusathien, was made minister of the interior. Loyal army officers were assigned to key police positions, where they used an investigation of the opium trade to purge Phao's clique. For example, when police and military units seized 6 tons of raw opium on the northern frontier in November, they captured five Thai policemen as well. In Bangkok, the new director-general of police, General S. Swai Saenyakorn, explained that five or six gangs that controlled smuggling in the north operated "with police influence behind their backs" and that these arrests were part of a larger campaign to fire or transfer all those involved.[273] General Swai's words took on added meaning when police Brigadier General Thom Chitvimol was removed from the force and indicted for his involvement in the 6-ton opium case.[274]

New elections in December legitimized the anti-Phao coup, and on January 1, 1958, Thanom became prime minister. However, liberals in the cabinet were chafing under Sarit's tight rein, and they began organizing several hundred dissatisfied younger military officers for another coup. But Sarit reorganized his clique into an association known as the Revolutionary Group, and on October 20, 1958 seized power with a bloodless coup group that allowed his Group to rule openly.[275] Now that the police had been rendered ineffectual as a power base, Sarit's only major worry was the possibility of a countercoup by the younger colonels and lieutenant colonels whose loyalty to the regime was in doubt. These fears dominated the endless postcoup sessions of the Revolutionary Group, and discussion continued for hours as Sarit and his fellow generals grappled for a solution. They agreed that a coup could be prevented if they recruited the majority of the colonels into their faction by paying them large initial bonuses and regular supplemental salaries. But the Revolutionary Group faced the immediate problem of rapidly assembling millions of *baht* for the large initial bonuses. Obviously, the fastest way to amass this amount of money was to reorganize General Phao's opium trade.

The Revolutionary Group dispatched army and air force officers to Hong Kong and Singapore to arrange large opium deals; police and military officers were sent into northern Thailand to alert mountain traders that there would be a market for all they could buy. As the 1959 spring opium harvest came to an end, the army staged its annual dry-season war games in the north to maximize opium collection. Every available aircraft, truck, and automobile was pressed into service, and the hills of northern Thailand and Burma were picked clean. Soon after the opium had been shipped from Bangkok to previously arranged foreign buyers and the flickering flames of the countercoup doused with the opium money, the Revolutionary Group met to discuss whether they should continue to finance their political work with opium profits. Sarit was in favor of the idea and was not particularly concerned about international opinion. General Praphat, who helped manage the trade for Sarit, agreed with his leader. While most of the group was indifferent, Generals Thanom and Swai were concerned about possible international repercussions. General Swai was particularly persuasive, since he was respected by Sarit, who addressed him with the Thai honorific "elder brother." Finally Sarit decreed that the police and military would no longer function as a link between Burma's poppy fields and the oceangoing smugglers on Thailand's southern coast. However, no attempt would be made to stop the enormous transit traffic or punish those who discreetly accepted bribes from Chinese syndicates who would inherit the traffic.[276]

Aware that General Phao had been discredited by his open involvement in the opium trade, Sarit's faction moved quickly to distance itself from the traffic. Only months after his operatives had taken control of illicit opium trading in the northern mountains, Sarit launched a highly publicized opium suppression campaign in downtown Bangkok.

In December 1958 Sarit's Revolutionary Group issued decree number 37 denouncing opium smoking as "a serious danger to health and sanitation" and ordering that, as of June 30, 1959, "opium smoking and distribution is hereby prohibited throughout the Kingdom."[277]

With the same ruthless precision he demonstrated in his coups and countercoups, Field Marshal Sarit unleashed a full military assault on the opium trade. At one minute after midnight on July 1, 1959, Sarit's forces swept the country, raiding opium dens, seizing their stocks, and confiscating opium pipes. At Sanam Luang field, the ritual center of Bangkok, excise officers lit a bonfire of 43,445 opium pipes before the cameras of the country's press. During the next day, Sarit patrolled the city, personally inspecting the raided dens and captured paraphernalia. Speaking to his people, Sarit declared that "1 July 1959 can be considered a date of historical significance because it began the first chapter of a new age in the history of the Thai nation. We can say that it was on this date that we became a civilized nation. The honor of the nation has now risen above the contempt of the foreign newspapers that have printed pictures of our people smoking opium."[278]

Although Sarit's ban did indeed end the official opium monopoly after a full century of operation, it did not eliminate other key elements of the drug trade. Under the opium monopoly, Thailand had sustained the largest number of opium smokers in Southeast Asia. In the decades that followed, Bangkok's smokers shifted to heroin and Thailand still had the region's largest addict population. After the finance ministry abolished legal opium sales and banned drug revenues from its official ledgers, Thai military factions expropriated the now illicit opium profits for their covert operational funds. Avoiding the tawdry, open corruption of General Phao, later military leaders distanced themselves from the traffic, extracting an informal tribute from the opium warlords based in Thailand's north and accepting retainers from Bangkok's Chinese syndicates that continue to manage the heroin trade.

With the decline of military influence following Thailand's "Democratic Revolution" of October 1973, some remarkable revelations were forthcoming about the involvement of leading generals in the heroin industry. After Sarit's death in 1963, political power had been divided among the prime minister, General Thanom Kittikhachon; his minister of interior and master of political intrigue, General Praphat Charusathien; and Colonel Narong Kittikhachon, Thanom's son and Praphat's son-in-law. Following the triumvirate's forced resignation and flight into exile in October 1973, the Thai press published charges by police Colonel Pramual Vangibandhu, a high official in the Central Narcotics Bureau recently arrested for drug dealing, that "Narong has a nationwide network of trafficking. Most of the drug shipments by boats to Hong

Kong and South Vietnam all belonged to him."[279] Privately, Thai police and military officials confided that General Praphat received a share of the profits from the narcotics trade, as he did from almost every other legitimate and illegitimate business in the country.[280]

Although General Phao had been driven into exile in 1957, his Burma-to-Bangkok opium corridor remained. During his decade of extraordinary power, Phao had used his political networks to build the basic logistics of the Golden Triangle heroin trade. In retrospect, it appears that CIA support was of paramount importance to General Phao's role in the opium traffic. The agency supplied the aircraft, motor vehicles, and naval vessels that gave Phao the logistic capability to move opium from the poppy fields to the sea lanes. Moreover, his role in protecting Sea Supply's shipments to the KMT gave Phao a considerable advantage in establishing himself as the exclusive exporter of KMT opium.

Given its even greater involvement in the KMT's Shan states opium commerce, how do we evaluate the CIA's role in the evolution of large-scale opium trafficking in the Burma-Thailand region? Under the Kennedy administration presidential adviser Walt W. Rostow popularized a doctrine of economic development that preached that a stagnant, underdeveloped economy could be jarred into a period of rapid growth, an economic "takeoff," by a massive injection of foreign aid and capital, which could then be withdrawn as the economy coasted into a period of self-sustained growth.[281] CIA support for Phao and the KMT seems to have sparked such a "takeoff" in the Burma-Thailand opium trade during the 1950s: modern aircraft replaced mules, naval vessels displaced sampans, and well-trained military organizations expropriated the traffic from bands of mountain traders.

Never before had the Shan states encountered smugglers with the discipline, technology, and ruthlessness of the KMT. Under General Phao's leadership, Thailand had changed from an opium-consuming nation to the world's most important opium distribution center. The Golden Triangle's opium harvest began climbing to its 1989 peak of 3,300 tons; Burma's total harvest had increased from less than 40 tons[282] just before World War II to 300–400 tons in 1962,[283] while Thailand's expanded at an even greater rate, from 7 tons[284] to more than 100 tons.[285] In a 1970 report the U.S. Bureau of Narcotics concluded:

> By the end of the 1950s, Burma, Laos, and Thailand together had become a massive producer, and the source of more than half the world's present illicit supply of 1,250 to 1,400 tons annually. Moreover, with this increase in output the region of the Far East and Southeast Asia quickly became self-sufficient in opium.[286]

But was this increase in opium production the result of a conscious decision by the CIA to support its allies, Phao and the KMT, through the narcotics traffic? Was this the CIA's Operation X? There can be no doubt that the CIA knew that its allies were heavily involved in the traffic; headlines made it known to the whole world, and Phao was responsible for Thailand's censure by the U.N.'s Commission on Narcotic Drugs. Certainly the CIA did nothing to halt the trade or to prevent its aid from being abused. But whether the CIA actively organized the traffic is something only the agency itself can answer. In any case, by the early 1960s the Golden Triangle had become the largest single opium-growing region in the world—a vast reservoir able to supply America's lucrative markets should any difficulties arise in the Mediterranean heroin complex. The Golden Triangle had surplus opium and it had well-protected, disciplined syndicates. With the right set of circumstances it could easily become America's major heroin supplier.

# 5

## South Vietnam's Heroin Trade

THE BLOODY SAIGON STREET FIGHTING OF APRIL–MAY 1955 marked the end of French colonial rule and the beginning of direct American intervention in Vietnam. When the First Indochina War came to an end, the French government had planned to withdraw its forces gradually over a two- or three-year period to protect its substantial political and economic interests in southern Vietnam. The armistice concluded at Geneva, Switzerland, in July 1954 called for the French Expeditionary Corps to withdraw into the southern half of Vietnam for two years, until an all-Vietnam referendum determined the nation's political future. Convinced that Ho Chi Minh and the Communist Viet Minh were going to score an overwhelming electoral victory, the French began negotiating a diplomatic understanding with the government in Hanoi.[1]

But America's cold warriors were not quite so flexible. Speaking before the American Legion convention several weeks after the signing of the Geneva accords, New York's influential Catholic prelate Cardinal Spellman warned:

> If Geneva and what was agreed upon there means anything at all, it means . . . taps for the buried hopes of freedom in Southeast Asia! Taps for the newly betrayed millions of Indochinese who must now learn the awful facts of slavery from their eager Communist masters![2]

Rather than surrendering southern Vietnam to the "Red rulers' godless goons," the Eisenhower administration decided to create a new nation where none had existed before. Looking back on America's post-Geneva policies from the vantage point of the mid-1960s, the *Pentagon Papers* concluded that South Vietnam "was essentially the creation of the United States":

> Without U.S. support Diem almost certainly could not have consolidated his hold on the South during 1955 and 1956.
> Without the threat of U.S. intervention, South Vietnam could not have refused to even discuss the elections called for in 1956 under the Geneva settlement without being immediately overrun by Viet Minh armies.
> Without U.S. aid in the years following, the Diem regime certainly, and independent South Vietnam almost as certainly, could not have survived.[3]

The French had little enthusiasm for this emerging nation and its prime minister, and so the French had to go. Pressured by American military aid cutbacks and prodded by the Diem regime, the French stepped up their troop withdrawals. By April 1956 the once mighty French Expeditionary Corps had been reduced to less than 5,000 troops, and American officers had taken over their jobs as advisers to the Vietnamese army.[4] The Americans criticized the French as hopelessly "colonialist" in their attitudes, and French officials retorted that the Americans were naive. During this difficult transition period one French official denounced "the meddling Americans who, in their incorrigible guilelessness, believed that once the French army leaves, Vietnamese independence will burst forth for all to see."[5]

Although this French official was doubtlessly biased, he was also correct. There was a certain naiveté, a certain innocent freshness, surrounding many of the American officials who poured into Saigon in the mid-1950s. The patron saint of America's anti-Communist crusade in South Vietnam was a young navy doctor named Thomas A. Dooley. After spending a year in Vietnam helping refugees in 1954–1955, Dooley returned to the United States for a whirlwind tour to build support for Prime Minister Ngo Dinh Diem and his new nation. Dooley declared that France "had a political and economic stake in keeping the native masses backward, submissive and ignorant" and praised Diem as "a man who never bowed to the French."[6] But Dr. Dooley was not just delivering South Vietnam from the "organized godlessness" of the "new Red imperialism," he was offering them the American way. Every time he dispensed medicine to a refugee, he told the Vietnamese, "This is American aid."[7] And when the Cosmevo Ambulator Company of Paterson, New Jersey, sent an artificial limb for a young refugee girl, he told her it was "an American leg."[8]

Although Dooley's national chauvinism seems somewhat naive today, it was generally shared by Americans serving in South Vietnam. Even the CIA's tactician General Edward Lansdale seems to have been a strong ideologue. Writing of his experiences in Saigon during this period, Lansdale later said:

> I went far beyond the usual bounds given a military man after I discovered just what the people on these battlegrounds needed to guard against and what to keep strong. . . . I took my American beliefs with me into these Asian struggles, as Tom Paine would have done."[9]

The attitude of these crusaders was so strong that it pervaded the press at the time. Diem's repressive dictatorship became a "one man democracy." *Life* magazine hailed him as "the Tough Miracle Man of Vietnam," and a 1956 *Saturday Evening Post* article began: "Two years ago at Geneva, South Vietnam was virtually sold down the river to the Communists. Today the spunky little Asian country is back on its own feet, thanks to a mandarin in a sharkskin suit who's upsetting the Red timetable!"[10]

But American's fall from innocence was not long in coming. Only seven years after these journalistic accolades were published, the U.S. embassy and the CIA—in fact, some of the same CIA agents who had fought for him in 1955—engineered a coup that toppled Diem and left him murdered in the back of an armored personnel carrier.[11] By 1965 the United States found itself fighting a war that was strikingly similar to France's colonial war. The U.S. embassy was trying to manipulate the same clique of corrupt Saigon politicos that had confounded the French in their day. The U.S. army looked just like the French Expeditionary Corps to most Vietnamese. Instead of Senegalese and Moroccan colonial levies, the U.S. army was assisted by Thai and South Korean troops. The U.S. special forces were assigned to train the same hill tribe mercenaries that the French paratroopers had recruited ten years earlier.

Given the similarities between the French and American war machines, it is hardly surprising that the broad outlines of Operation X reemerged after U.S. intervention. As the CIA became involved in Laos in the early 1960s it became aware of the truth of Colonel Trinquier's axiom "To have the Meo,* one must buy their opium."[12] At a time when there was no ground or air transport to and from the mountains of Laos except CIA aircraft, opium continued to flow out of the villages of Laos to transit points such as Long Tieng. There, government air forces, this

---

*Meo is a derogatory name for the Hmong that Westerners adopted from the lowland peoples of China, Thailand, and Vietnam during the colonial period.

time Vietnamese and Lao instead of French, transported narcotics to Saigon, where close allies of Vietnam's political leaders were involved in both domestic distribution and international trafficking. And just as the French high commissioner had found it politically expedient to overlook the Binh Xuyen's involvement in Saigon's opium trade, the U.S. embassy, as part of its unqualified support of the Thieu-Ky regime, looked the other way when presented with evidence that Saigon's leaders were involved in the GI heroin traffic. While American complicity was certainly much less conscious and overt than that of the French a decade earlier, this time it was not just opium but morphine and heroin as well, and the consequences were far more serious. After a decade of American military intervention, Southeast Asia became the source of 70 percent of the world's illicit opium and the major supplier of raw materials for America's booming heroin market.

## Heroin in South Vietnam

Geography and politics dictated the fundamental "laws" that governed South Vietnam's narcotics traffic until 1975. Since opium was not grown inside South Vietnam, all of the country's drugs had to be imported— from the Golden Triangle region to the north, the source of all the country's opium and heroin. Although it has become the world's most important source of illicit opium, the Golden Triangle is landlocked, cut off from local and international markets by long distances and rugged terrain. In the early 1970s, the Golden Triangle's narcotics followed one of two "corridors" to reach the world's markets—an air route from Vientiane, Laos, to Vietnam, which closed after the fall of Saigon in 1975, and an overland Burma-to-Bangkok route that remains the world's major source of heroin. The most important route was the overland corridor that began as a maze of mule trails in the Shan hills of northeastern Burma and ended as a four-lane highway in downtown Bangkok. Most of Burma's and Thailand's opium followed the overland route to Bangkok and from there found its way into international markets: Hong Kong, Europe, and America. The other route was the air corridor that began among the scattered dirt airstrips of northern Laos and ended at Saigon's international airport. The opium reaching Saigon from Burma or Thailand was usually packed in northwestern Laos on muleback before being flown into South Vietnam. While very little opium, morphine, or heroin traveled from Saigon to Hong Kong, the South Vietnamese capital appeared to be the major transshipment point for Golden Triangle narcotics heading for Europe and the United States.

Since Vietnam's major source of opium was on the other side of the rugged Annamite Mountains, every South Vietnamese civilian or military group that wanted to finance its political activities by selling narcotics had to have both a connection in Laos and access to air transport. When the Binh Xuyen controlled Saigon's opium dens during the First Indochina War, the French MACG provided these services through its officers fighting with Laotian guerrillas and its air transport links between Saigon and the mountain *maquis*. Later Vietnamese politicomilitary groups used family connections, intelligence agents serving abroad, and Indochina's Corsican underworld as their Laotian connection. While almost any high-ranking South Vietnamese could establish such contacts without too much difficulty, the problem of securing reliable air transport between Laos and the Saigon area always limited narcotics smuggling to only the most powerful of the Vietnamese elite.

When Ngo Dinh Nhu, brother of and chief adviser to President Diem, decided to revive the opium traffic to finance his repression of mounting armed insurgency and political dissent, he used Vietnamese intelligence agents operating in Laos and Indochina's Corsican underworld as his contacts. From 1958 to 1960 Nhu relied mainly on small Corsican charter airlines for transport, but in 1961–1962 he also used the First Transport Group (which was then flying intelligence missions into Laos for the CIA and was under the control of Colonel Nguyen Cao Ky) to ship raw opium to Saigon. During this period and the following years, 1965–1967, when Ky was premier, most of the opium seems to have been finding its way to South Vietnam through the Vietnamese air force. By mid-1970 there was evidence that high-ranking officials in the Vietnamese navy, customs, army, port authority, national police, and National Assembly's lower house were competing with the air force for the dominant position in the traffic. To a casual observer, it must have appeared that the strong central control exercised during the Ky and Diem administrations had given way to a laissez-faire free-for-all under the government of President Nguyen Van Thieu in the late 1960s and early 1970s.

What seemed like chaotic competition among poorly organized smuggling rings actually was, on closer examination, a fairly disciplined power struggle between the leaders of Saigon's three most powerful political factions: the air force, which remained under Vice-President Ky's control; the army, navy, and lower house, which were loyal to President Thieu; and the customs, port authority, and national police, where the factions loyal to Prime Minister Tran Thien Khiem had considerable influence. To see through the confusion to the lines of authority that bound each of these groups to a higher power requires some appreciation of the structure of pre-1975 South Vietnamese political factions and the traditions of corruption.

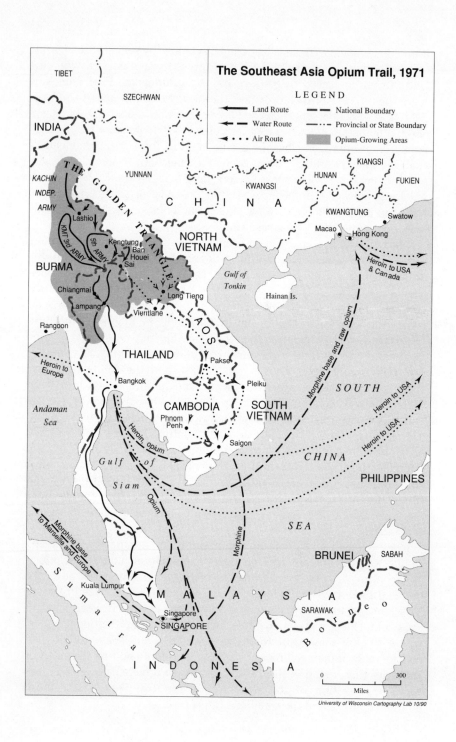

**The Southeast Asia Opium Trail, 1971**

LEGEND

Land Route — National Boundary

Water Route — Provincial or State Boundary

Air Route — Opium-Growing Areas

University of Wisconsin Cartography Lab 10/90

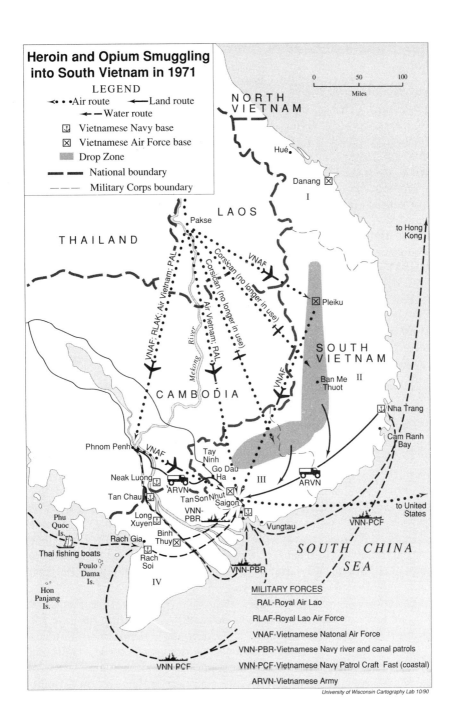

# Heroin and Opium Smuggling into South Vietnam in 1971

## LEGEND

•••• Air route   ◄— Land route
◄— — Water route
⊡ Vietnamese Navy base
⊠ Vietnamese Air Force base
▨ Drop Zone
━ ━ ━ National boundary
— — — Military Corps boundary

0    50    100
Miles

NORTH VIETNAM

Hué

Danang ⊠
I

LAOS

Pakse

THAILAND

VNAF

⊠ Pleiku

Corsican (no longer in use)

Corsican (no longer in use)

VNAF; RLAK; Air Vietnam; PAL

Air Vietnam; RAL

Mekong River

VNAF

SOUTH VIETNAM

Ban Me
Thuot
II

CAMBODIA

⊡ Nha Trang

Cam Ranh
Bay

Phnom Penh
VNAF

Tay
Ninh
Go Dau
Ha
III
ARVN

Neak Luong
ARVN ⊡

Tan Chau ⊡
Tan Son Nhut ⊠
Saigon

VNN-
PBR ⊡

Long
Xuyen ⊡

Vungtau

VNN-PCF

Binh
Thuy ⊠

Rach Gia

Phu
Quoc
Is.

Thai fishing boats

Poulo
Dama
Is.

Rach
Soi

IV

Hon
Panjang
Is.

VNN-PBR

SOUTH CHINA
SEA

to Hong
Kong

to United
States

### MILITARY FORCES

RAL-Royal Air Lao

RLAF-Royal Lao Air Force

VNAF-Vietnamese Natonal Air Force

VNN-PBR-Vietnamese Navy river and canal patrols

VNN-PCF-Vietnamese Navy Patrol Craft Fast (coastal)

ARVN-Vietnamese Army

VNN PCF

University of Wisconsin Cartography Lab 10/90

## Tradition and Corruption

As in the rest of Southeast Asia, the outward forms of Western bureaucratic efficiency were grafted onto a traditional power elite, producing a fusion of corruptions, traditional and modern. While Southeast Asian governments copied European bureaucracies in their formal trappings, the elite values of the past governed machinations over graft, patronage and power. In mainland Southeast Asia, three traditions influenced contemporary political behavior: Thailand's legacy of Hinduized god-kings; Vietnam's tradition of Chinese-style mandarin bureaucrats; and Laos's and the Shan states' heritage of fragmented, quasi-feudal kingdoms.

The Hindu worldview spread eastward from India into Siam (now Thailand), carrying its sensuous vision of a despotic god-king who squandered vast amounts of the kingdom's wealth on palaces, retinues, and personal monuments. All authority radiated from his divine, sexually potent being, and his lavish, conspicuous consumption was but further proof of his divine right to power.

After a thousand years of Chinese military occupation, Vietnam had absorbed its northern neighbor's Confucian ideal of meritocratic government: well-educated, carefully selected mandarins were given a high degree of independent administrative authority but were expected to adhere to rigid standards of ethical behavior. While the imperial court frequently violated Confucian ethics by selling offices to unqualified candidates, the emperor himself remained unaware while such men exploited the people to make a return on their investment.

Although Chinese and Indian influence spread across the lowland plains of Vietnam and Siam, the remote mountain regions of Laos and the Burmese Shan states remained less susceptible to these innovative concepts of opulent kingdoms and centralized political power. Laos and the Shan states remained a scattering of minor principalities whose princes and *sawbwas* usually controlled little more than a single highland valley. Centralized power went no further than loosely organized, feudal federations or individually powerful fiefdoms that annexed a few neighboring valleys.

The tenacious survival of these antiquated political structures is due in part to Western intervention in Southeast Asia during the last 150 years. In the mid-nineteenth century, European generals and diplomats broke down the relatively isolationist worldview of these traditional states and annexed them into their global empires. The European presence brought radical innovations—modern technology, new political ideas, and unprecedented economic oppression—which released dynamic forces of social change. While the European presence served initially as a catalyst for these changes, the colonial governments were generally conservative and allied themselves with the traditional native elite to suppress the new social forces, such as labor unions, tenants' unions, and nationalist intellectuals. When the traditional elite proved unequal to the task, the colonial powers groomed a new commercial or military class to serve their interests. In the process of serving the Europeans, both the traditional elite and the new bureaucratic class acquired values that combined the worst of two worlds. Rejecting both their own traditions of public responsibility and the Western concepts of humanism, these native leaders fused the materialism of the West with their own traditions of aristocratic prerogatives. The result was the systematic corruption that continues to trouble Southeast Asian states.

The British found the preservation of the Shan state *sawbwas* an administrative convenience and reversed the trend of gradual integration with greater Burma. Under British rule, the Shan states became autonomous regions and the authority of the reactionary *sawbwas* was reinforced.

In Laos, after denying the local princes an effective voice in the government of their own country for almost fifty years, the French returned these feudal atavisms to power when the First Indochina War made it politically expedient for them to do so.

As the gathering storm of the Vietnamese revolution forced the French to Vietnamize in the early 1950s, they created a government and an army from the only groups sympathetic to their presence—the French-educated, landowning families and the Catholic minority. When the Americans replaced the French in Indochina in 1955, they spent the next twenty years shoring up these corrupted oligarchies and keeping reform governments out of power.

In Thailand a hundred years of British councilors and twenty-five years of American advisers gave the royal government a veneer of technical sophistication, but slowed the growth of internal revolutions that might have broken with the traditional patterns of autocratic government.

At the bottom of Thailand's pyramids of corruption, dominated by police and military factions from 1947 to 1973, armies of functionaries systematically expropriated the nation's wealth and passed money up the chain of command to the top, where authoritarian leaders enjoyed an ostentatious lifestyle reminiscent of that of the god-kings. Marshal Sarit, for example, had more than a hundred mistresses, arbitrarily executed criminals at public spectacles, and died with an estate of more than $150 million.[13] Such potentates, able to control corrupt functionaries in the most remote province, were rarely betrayed during struggles with other factions. As a result, a single political faction usually was able to centralize and monopolize Thailand's narcotics traffic. In contrast, the opium trade in Laos and the Shan states reflected their feudal political tradition in which each regional warlord controlled the traffic in his territory.

Until 1975 South Vietnam's political factions were based in national political institutions and competed for control over a centralized narcotics traffic. But even the most powerful Vietnamese faction resembled a castle of cards with one mini-clique stacked gracefully, but shakily, on top of another. Balancing on top of this latticework was a high-ranking government official, usually the premier or president, who, like the old emperors, ultimately sanctioned corruption and graft but tried to remain aloof from the fray and preserve something of an honest, statesmanlike image. But behind every political leader was a power broker who was responsible for building up the coalition of factions and preventing its collapse. Using patronage and discretionary funds, the broker built a power base by recruiting small family cliques, important officeholders, and powerful military leaders. Since these ad hoc coalitions were usually unstable (betrayal preceded every Saigon coup), the broker also had to build an intelligence network to monitor his chief's supporters. Money played a key role in these affairs, and in the weeks before every coup political loyalties were sold to the highest bidder. Just before Diem's overthrow in 1963, for example, U.S. Ambassador Henry Cabot Lodge, who was promoting the coup, offered to give the plotters "funds at the last moment with which to buy off potential opposition."[14]

Since money was so crucial for maintaining power, one of the South Vietnamese broker's major responsibilities was organizing graft and corruption to finance political dealing and intelligence work. He tried to work through the leaders of existing or newly established mini-factions to generate a reliable source of income through officially sanctioned corruption. As the mini-faction sold offices lower on the bureaucratic scale, corruption seeped downward from the national level to the province, district, and village.

From the point of view of collecting money for political activities, the South Vietnamese system was not nearly as efficient as the Thai pyramidal structure. Since each layer of the Vietnamese bureaucracy skimmed off a substantial percentage of the graft (most observers felt that officials at each level kept an average of 40 percent for themselves) before passing it up to the next level, not that much steady income from routine graft reached the top. For this reason, large-scale corruption that could be managed by fewer men—such as collecting "contributions" from wealthy Chinese businessmen, selling major offices, and smuggling—were particularly important sources of political funding. It was not just coincidence that every South Vietnamese government that remained in power for more than a few months after the departure of the French was invariably implicated in the nation's narcotics traffic.

## Diem's Dynasty

Shortly after the Binh Xuyen gangsters were driven out of Saigon in May 1955, Diem, a pious Catholic, launched a determined anti-opium campaign by burning opium-smoking paraphernalia in a dramatic public ceremony. Opium dens were shut down, addicts found it difficult to buy drugs, and Saigon was no longer even a minor transit point in international narcotics traffic.[15] However, only three years later the government suddenly abandoned its moralistic crusade and took steps to revive the illicit opium traffic. The beginnings of armed insurgency in the countryside and political dissent in the cities had shown Ngo Dinh Nhu, Diem's brother and head of the secret police, that he needed more money to expand the scope of his intelligence work and political repression. Although the CIA and the foreign aid division of the State Department had provided generous funding for those activities over the previous three years, personnel problems and internal difficulties forced the U.S. embassy to deny his request for increased aid.[16]

But Nhu was determined to go ahead and decided to revive the opium traffic to provide the necessary funding. Although most of Saigon's opium dens had been shut for three years, the city's thousands of Chinese and Vietnamese addicts were willing to resume or expand their habits. Nhu used his contacts with powerful Cholon Chinese syndicate leaders to reopen the dens and set up a distribution network for smuggled opium.[17] Within months hundreds of opium dens had been reopened, and five years later one Time-Life correspondent estimated that there were 2,500 dens operating openly in Saigon's sister city, Cholon.[18]

To keep these outlets supplied, Nhu established two pipelines from the Laotian poppy fields to South Vietnam. The major pipeline was a small charter airline, Air Laos Commerciale, managed by Indochina's most flamboyant Corsican gangster, Bonaventure "Rock" Francisci. Although there were at least four small Corsican airlines smuggling between Laos and South Vietnam, only Francisci's dealt directly with Nhu. According to Lucien Conein, a former high-ranking CIA officer in Saigon, their relationship began in 1958 when Francisci made a deal with Nhu to smuggle Laotian opium into South Vietnam. After Nhu guaranteed his opium shipments safe conduct, Francisci's fleet of twin-engine Beechcrafts began making regular clandestine airdrops inside South Vietnam.[19]

Nhu supplemented these shipments by dispatching intelligence agents to Laos with orders to send back raw opium on the Vietnamese air force transports that shuttled back and forth carrying agents and supplies.[20]

While Nhu seems to have dealt with the Corsicans personally, the intelligence missions to Laos were managed by the head of his secret police apparatus, Dr. Tran Kim Tuyen. Although most accounts have portrayed Nhu as the Diem regime's arch plotter, many insiders feel that it was the ex-seminary student Tuyen who had the real capacity for intrigue. As head of the secret police, euphemistically titled Office of Social and Political Study, Tuyen commanded a vast intelligence network that included the CIA-financed special forces, the Military Security Service, and, most important, the clandestine Can Lao party.[21] Through the Can Lao party, Tuyen recruited spies and political cadres in every branch of the military and civil bureaucracy. Promotions were strictly controlled by the central government, and those who cooperated with Tuyen were rewarded with rapid advancement.[22] With profits from the opium trade and other officially sanctioned corruption, the Office of Social and Political Study was able to hire thousands of cyclo-drivers, dance hall girls ("taxi dancers"), and street vendors as part-time spies for an intelligence network that soon covered every block of Saigon-Cholon. Instead of maintaining surveillance on a suspect by having him followed, Tuyen simply passed the word to his "door-to-door" intelligence net and got back precise, reports on the subject's movements, meetings, and conversations. Some observers think that Tuyen may have had as many as 100,000 full- and part-time agents operating in South Vietnam.[23] Through this remarkable system Tuyen kept detailed dossiers on every important figure in the country, including particularly complete files on Diem, Madame Nhu, and Nhu himself, which he sent out of the country as a form of personal "life insurance."[24]

Since Tuyen was responsible for much of the Diem regime's foreign intelligence operations, he was able to disguise his narcotics dealings in Laos under the cover of ordinary intelligence work. Vietnamese undercover operations in Laos were primarily directed at North Vietnam and were related to a CIA program started in 1954. Under the direction of Colonel Edward Lansdale and his team of CIA operatives, two small groups of North Vietnamese had been recruited as agents, smuggled out of Haiphong, trained in Saigon, and then sent back to North Vietnam in 1954–1955. During this same period Civil Air Transport (later Air America) smuggled more than 8 tons of arms and equipment into Haiphong in the regular refugee shipments authorized by the Geneva accords for the eventual use of these teams.[25]

As the refugee exchanges came to an end in May 1955 and the North Vietnamese tightened their coastal defenses, CIA and Vietnamese intelligence turned to Laos as an alternative infiltration route and listening post. According to Bernard Yoh, then an intelligence adviser to Diem, Tuyen sent ten to twelve agents into Laos in 1958 after they had completed an extensive training course under the supervision of Colonel Le Quang Tung's special forces. When Yoh sent one of his own intelligence teams into Laos to work with Tuyen's agents during the Laotian crisis of 1961, he was amazed at their incompetence. Yoh could not understand why agents without radio training or knowledge of even the most basic undercover procedures would have been kept in the field for so long, until he discovered that their major responsibility was smuggling gold and opium into South Vietnam.[26] After purchasing opium and gold, Tuyen's agents had the shipments delivered to airports in southern Laos near Savannakhet or Pakse. There it was picked up and flown to Saigon by Vietnamese air force transports, which were then under the command of Nguyen Cao Ky, whose official assignment was shuttling Tuyen's espionage agents back and forth from Laos.[27]

Tuyen also used diplomatic personnel to smuggle Laotian opium into South Vietnam. In 1958 the director of Vietnam's psychological warfare department transferred one of his undercover agents to the foreign ministry and sent him to Pakse, Laos, as a consular official to direct clandestine operations against North Vietnam. Within three months Tuyen had recruited the agent for his smuggling apparatus and had him sending regular opium shipments to Saigon in his diplomatic pouch.[28]

Despite the considerable efforts Tuyen had devoted to organizing these "intelligence activities," they remained a rather meager supplement to the Corsican opium shipments until May 1961, when newly elected President John F. Kennedy authorized the implementation of an interdepartmental task force report. The report suggested:

> In North Vietnam, using the foundation established by intelligence operations, form networks of resistance, covert bases and teams for sabotage and light harassment. A capability should be created by MAAG in the South Vietnamese Army to conduct Ranger raids and similar military actions in North Vietnam as might prove necessary or appropriate. Such actions should try to avoid the outbreak of extensive resistance or insurrection which could not be supported to the extent necessary to stave off repression.
> Conduct overflights for dropping of leaflets to harass the Communists and to maintain the morale of North Vietnamese population.[29]

The CIA was assigned to carry out this mission and incorporated Aviation Investors, a fictitious parent company in Washington, D.C., to provide a cover for its operational company, Vietnam Air Transport. The agency dubbed the project Operation Haylift. Vietnam Air Transport (VIAT) hired Colonel Nguyen Cao Ky and selected members of his First Transport Group to fly CIA commandos into North Vietnam via Laos or the Gulf of Tonkin.[30]

However, Ky was dismissed from Operation Haylift less than two years after it began. One of VIAT's technical employees, S. M. Mustard, reported to a U.S. Senate subcommittee in 1968 that "Col. Ky took advantage of this situation to fly opium from Laos to Saigon."[31] Since some of the commandos hired by the CIA were Tuyen's intelligence agents, it was certainly credible that Ky was involved with the opium and gold traffic. Mustard implied that the CIA had fired Ky for his direct involvement in this traffic; Colonel Do Khac Mai, then deputy commander of the air force, said that Ky was fired for another reason. Sometime after one of its two-engine C-47s crashed off the North Vietnamese coast, VIAT brought in four-engine C-54 aircraft from Taiwan. Since Ky had been trained only in two-engine aircraft, he had to make a number of training flights to upgrade his skills; on one of these occasions he took some Cholon dance hall girls for a spin over the city. This romantic ride was in violation of Operation Haylift's strict security, and the CIA speedily replaced Ky and his transport pilots with Nationalist Chinese ground crews and pilots.[32] This change probably reduced the effectiveness of Tuyen's Laotian "intelligence activities" and forced Nhu to rely more heavily on the Corsican charter airlines for regular opium shipments.

Even though the opium traffic and other forms of corruption generated enormous amounts of money for Nhu's police state, nothing could keep the regime in power once the Americans turned against it. For several years they had been frustrated with Diem's failure to fight corruption. In March 1961 a national intelligence estimate done for President Kennedy complained of Diem:

> Many feel that he is unable to rally the people in the fight against the Communists because of his reliance on one-man rule, his toleration of corruption even to his immediate entourage, and his refusal to relax a rigid system of controls.[33]

The outgoing ambassador, Elbridge Durbrow, had made many of the same complaints, and in a cable to the secretary of state he urged that Tuyen and Nhu be sent out of the country and their secret police disbanded. He also suggested that Diem

> make a public announcement of disbandment of Can Lao party or at least its surfacing, with names and positions of all members made known publicly. Purpose of this step would be to eliminate atmosphere of fear and suspicion and reduce

public belief in favoritism and corruption, all of which the
party's semi-covert status has given rise to.[34]

In essence, Nhu had reverted to the Binh Xuyen's formula for
combating urban guerrilla warfare by using systematic corruption to
finance intelligence and counterinsurgency operations. However, the
Americans could not understand what Nhu was trying to do and kept
urging him to initiate "reforms." When Nhu flatly refused, the Americans
tried to persuade Diem to send his brother out of the country. And when
Diem agreed but then backed away from his promise, the U.S. embassy
decided to overthrow Diem.

On November 1, 1963, with the full support of the U.S. embassy, a
group of Vietnamese generals launched a coup, capturing the capital
and executing Diem and Nhu. But the coup not only toppled the Diem
regime, it destroyed Nhu's police state apparatus and its supporting
system of corruption, which, if it had failed to stop the National
Liberation Front (NLF) in the countryside, at least guaranteed a high
degree of "security" in Saigon and the surrounding area.

Shortly after the coup the chairman of the NLF, Nguyen Huu Tho, told
an Australian journalist that the dismantling of the police state had been
"gifts from heaven" for the revolutionary movement:

> The police apparatus set up over the years with great care by
> Diem is utterly shattered, especially at the base. The principal
> chiefs of security and the secret police on which mainly
> depended the protection of the regime and the repression of
> the revolutionary Communist Viet Cong movement, have been
> eliminated, purged.[35]

Within three months after the anti-Diem coup, General Nguyen Khanh
emerged as Saigon's new "strong man" and dominated South Vietnam's
political life from January 1964 until he, too, fell from grace and went
into exile twelve months later. Although a skillful coup plotter, Khanh
was incapable of using power once he got into office. Under his
leadership, Saigon politics became an endless quadrille of coups and
countercoups. Khanh failed to build any sort of intelligence structure to
replace Nhu's secret police, and during this critical period none of
Saigon's rival factions managed to centralize the opium traffic or other
forms of corruption. The political chaos was so severe that serious
pacification work ground to a halt in the countryside, and Saigon
became an open city.[36] By mid-1964 NLF-controlled territory encircled
the city, and its cadres entered Saigon almost at will.

To combat growing security problems in the capital district,
American pacification experts dreamed up the Hop Tac ("cooperation")
program. As originally conceived, the plan called for South Vietnamese

troops to sweep the areas surrounding Saigon and build a "giant oil spot" of pacified territory that would spread outward from the capital region to cover the Mekong Delta and eventually all of South Vietnam. The program was launched with a good deal of fanfare on September 12, 1964, as South Vietnamese infantry plunged into some NLF-controlled pineapple fields southwest of Saigon. Everything ran like clockwork for two days until infantry units suddenly broke off contact with the NLF and charged into Saigon to take part in one of the many unsuccessful coups that took place with distressing frequency during Khanh's twelve-month interregnum.[37]

Although presidential adviser McGeorge Bundy claimed that Hop Tac "has certainly prevented any strangling siege of Saigon,"[38] the program was an unqualified failure. On Christmas Eve 1964 the NLF blew up the U.S. officers' club in Saigon, killing two Americans and wounding fifty-eight more.[39] On March 29, 1965, NLF sappers blew up the U.S. embassy.[40] In late 1965 one U.S. correspondent, Robert Shaplen of *The New Yorker*, reported that Saigon's security was rapidly deteriorating:

> These grave economic and social conditions [the influx of refugees, etc.] have furnished the Vietcong with an opportunity to cause trouble, and squads of Communist propagandists, saboteurs, and terrorists are infiltrating the city in growing numbers; it is even said that the equivalent of a Vietcong battalion of Saigon youth has been taken out, trained, and then sent back here to lie low, with hidden arms, awaiting orders . . . The National Liberation Front radio is still calling for acts of terror ("One American killed for every city block"), citing the continued use by the Americans of tear gas and crop-destroying chemical sprays, together with the bombing of civilians, as justification for reprisals.[41]

Soon after Henry Cabot Lodge took office as ambassador to South Vietnam for the second time in August 1965, an embassy briefer told him that the Hop Tac program was a total failure. Massive sweeps around the capital's perimeter did little to improve Saigon's internal security because "the threat—which is substantial—comes from the enemy within, and the solution does not lie within the responsibility of the Hop Tac Council: it is a problem for the Saigon police and intelligence communities."[42]

In other words, modern counterinsurgency planning with its computers and game theories had failed to do the job, and it was time to go back to the proven methods of Ngo Dinh Nhu and the Binh Xuyen bandits. When the French government faced Viet Minh terrorist assaults and bombings in 1947, they allied themselves with Bay Vien, giving this river pirate a free hand to organize the city's corruption on an unprecedented scale. Confronted with similar problems in 1965–1966 and realizing the nature of their mistake with Diem and Nhu, Ambassador Lodge and the U.S. mission decided to give their full support to Premier Nguyen Cao Ky and his power broker, General Nguyen Ngoc Loan. Ky had a dubious reputation in some circles, and Diem had referred to him as "that cowboy," a term Vietnamese then reserved for only the most flamboyant of Cholon gangsters.[43]

## The New Opium Monopoly

Nguyen Cao Ky's air force career began when he returned from instrument flying school in France with his certification as a transport pilot and a French wife. As the Americans began to push the French out of air force advisory positions in 1955, the French attempted to bolster their wavering influence by promoting officers with strong pro-French loyalties to key positions. Since Lieutenant Tran Van Ho was a French citizen, he was promoted to colonel "almost overnight" and became the first ethnic Vietnamese to command the Vietnamese air force. Lieutenant Ky's French wife was adequate proof of his loyalty, and, despite his relative youth and inexperience, he was appointed commander of the First Transport Squadron. In 1956 Ky was also appointed commander of Saigon's Tan Son Nhut Air Base, and his squadron, which was based there, was doubled to a total of thirty-two C-47s and renamed the First Transport Group.[44] While shuttling back and forth across the countryside in the lumbering C-47s may have lacked the dash of fighter flying, it did have advantages. Ky's responsibility for transporting government officials and generals provided him with useful political contacts, and with thirty-two planes at his command Ky had the largest air fleet in South Vietnam. Ky lost command of the Tan Son Nhut Air Base, allegedly because of the criticism about the management of the base mess hall by his sister Madame Nguyen Thi Ly. But he remained in control of the First Transport Group until the anti-Diem coup of November 1963. Then Ky engaged in some dexterous political intrigue and, despite his lack of credentials as a coup plotter, emerged as commander of the entire Vietnamese air force only six weeks after Diem's overthrow.[45]

As air force commander, Air Vice-Marshal Ky became one of the most active of the "young Turks" who made Saigon political life so chaotic under General Khanh's brief and erratic leadership. While the air force did not have the power to initiate a coup singlehandedly as an armored or infantry division did, its ability to strafe the roads leading into Saigon and block the movement of everybody else's coup divisions gave Ky a virtual veto power. After the air force crushed the abortive September 1964 coup against General Khanh, Ky's political star began to rise. On June 19, 1965, the ten-man National Leadership Committee headed by General Nguyen Van Thieu appointed Ky to the office of premier, the highest political office in South Vietnam.[46]

Although he was enormously popular with the air force, Ky had neither an independent political base nor any claim to leadership of a genuine mass movement when he took office. A relative newcomer to politics, Ky was hardly known outside elite circles. Also, Ky seemed to lack the money, the connections, and the capacity for intrigue necessary to build up an effective ruling faction and restore Saigon's security. But he solved these problems in a traditional manner by choosing a power broker as skillful as Bay Vien or Ngo Dinh Nhu—General Nguyen Ngoc Loan.

Loan was the brightest of the young air force officers. His career had been marked by rapid advancement and assignment to such technically demanding jobs as commander of the Light Observation Group and assistant commander of the Tactical Operations Center.[47] Loan also had served as deputy commander to Ky, an old classmate and friend, in the aftermath of the anti-Diem coup. Shortly after Ky took office he appointed Loan director of the Military Security Service (MSS). Since the MSS was responsible for anticorruption investigations inside the military, Loan was in an excellent position to protect members of Ky's faction. Several months later, Loan's power increased significantly when he was also appointed director of the Central Intelligence Organization (CIO), South Vietnam's CIA, without being asked to resign from the MSS. Finally, in April 1966, Premier Ky announced that General Loan had been appointed to an additional post—director-general of the national police.[48] Only after Loan had consolidated his position and handpicked his successors did he "step down" as director of the MSS and CIO. Not even under Diem had one man controlled so many police and intelligence agencies.

In the appointment of Loan to all three posts, the interests of Ky and the Americans coincided. While Ky was using Loan to build up a political machine, the U.S. mission was happy to see a strong man take command of Saigon's police and intelligence communities to drive the NLF out of the capital. Lieutenant Colonel Lucien Conein said that Loan was given wholehearted U.S. support because

> we wanted effective security in Saigon above all else, and Loan could provide that security. Loan's activities were placed beyond reproach and the whole three-tiered US advisory structure at the district, province and national level was placed at his disposal.[49]

The liberal naiveté that had marked the Kennedy diplomats in the last few months of Diem's regime was decidedly absent. Gone were the qualms about "police state" tactics and hopes that Saigon could be secure and its politics "stabilized" without using funds from the control of the city's lucrative rackets.

With the encouragement of Ky and the tacit support of the U.S. mission, Loan revived the Binh Xuyen formula for using systematic corruption to combat urban guerrilla warfare. Rather than purging the police and intelligence bureaus, Loan forged an alliance with the specialists who had been running these agencies for the past ten to fifteen years. According to Conein, "the same professionals who organized corruption for Diem and Nhu were still in charge of police and intelligence. Loan simply passed the word among these guys and put the old system back together again."[50]

Under Loan's direction, Saigon's security improved markedly. With the "door-to-door" surveillance network perfected by Tuyen back in action, police were soon swamped with information.[51] A U.S. embassy official, Charles Sweet, who was then engaged in urban pacification work, recalled that in 1965 the NLF was actually holding daytime rallies in the sixth, seventh, and eighth districts of Cholon, and terrorist incidents were running over forty a month in district 8 alone. Loan's methods were so effective, however, that from October 1966 until January 1968 there was not a single terrorist incident in district 8.[52] That same month, correspondent Shaplen reported that Loan "had done what is generally regarded as a good job of tracking down Communist terrorists in Saigon."[53]

Putting "the old system back together again," of course, meant reviving large-scale corruption to finance the cash rewards paid to the part-time agents whenever they delivered information. Loan and the police intelligence professionals systematized the corruption, regulating how much each particular agency would collect, how much each officer would skim off for his personal use, and what percentage would be turned over to Ky's political machine. Excessive individual corruption was rooted out, and Saigon-Cholon's vice trades, protection rackets, and payoffs were strictly controlled. After several years of watching Loan's system in action, Charles Sweet felt that there were four major sources of graft in South Vietnam: (1) sale of government jobs by generals or their wives; (2) administrative corruption (graft, kickbacks, bribes, and so on); (3) military corruption (theft of goods and payroll frauds); and (4) the opium traffic. Out of the four, Sweet concluded that the opium traffic was undeniably the most important source of illicit revenue.[54]

As Premier Ky's power broker, Loan merely supervised all of the various forms of corruption at a general administrative level; he usually left the mundane problems of organization and management of individual rackets to the trusted assistants.

In early 1966 Loan appointed a rather mysterious Saigon politician named Nguyen Thanh Tung (known as "Mai Den" or "Black Mai") director of the Foreign Intelligence Bureau of the CIO. Mai Den was one of those perennial Saigon plotters who changed sides so many times in the course of twenty-five years that nobody really knew too much about them. It was generally believed that Mai Den began his career as a Viet Minh intelligence agent in the late 1940s, became a French agent in Hanoi in the 1950s, and joined Dr. Tuyen's secret police after the French withdrawal. When the Diem government collapsed, he became a close political adviser to the powerful I Corps commander, General Nguyen Chanh Thi. However, when Thi clashed with Ky during the Buddhist crisis of 1966, Mai Den began supplying Loan with information on Thi's movements and plans. After Thi's downfall in April 1966, Loan rewarded Mai Den by appointing him to the Foreign Intelligence Bureau. Although he was nominally responsible for foreign espionage operations, reportedly Mai Den's real job was to reorganize opium and gold smuggling between Laos and Saigon.[55]

Through his control over foreign intelligence and consular appointments, Mai Den would have had no difficulty placing a sufficient number of contacts in Laos. However, the Vietnamese military attaché in Vientiane, Lieutenant Colonel Khu Duc Nung,[56] and Premier Ky's sister in Pakse, Nguyen Thi Ly (who managed the Sedone Palace Hotel), were Mai Den's probable contacts.

Once opium had been purchased, repacked for shipment, and delivered to a pickup point in Laos (usually Savannakhet or Pakse), a number of methods were used to smuggle it into South Vietnam. Although no longer as important as in the past, airdrops in the Central Highlands continued. In August 1966, for example, U.S. Green Berets on operations in the hills north of Pleiku were startled when their hill tribe allies presented them with a bundle of raw opium dropped by a passing aircraft whose pilot evidently mistook the tribal guerrillas for his contact men.[57] Ky's man in the Central Highlands was II Corps commander General Vinh Loc.[58] He was posted there in 1965 and inherited the benefits of such a post. His predecessor, a notoriously corrupt general, bragged to colleagues of making $5,000 for every ton of opium dropped into the Central Highlands.

While Central Highland airdrops declined in importance and overland narcotics smuggling from Cambodia had not yet developed, large quantities of raw opium were smuggled into Saigon on regular commercial air flights from Laos. The customs service at Tan Son Nhut was rampantly corrupt, and customs director Nguyen Van Loc was an important cog in the Loan fund-raising machinery. In a November 1967 report, George Roberts, then chief of the U.S. customs advisory team in Saigon, described the extent of corruption and smuggling in South Vietnam:

> Despite four years of observation of a typically corruption ridden agency of the GVN [Government of Vietnam], the Customs Service, I still could take very few persons into a regular court of law with the solid evidence I possess and stand much of a chance of convicting them on that evidence. The institution of corruption is so much a built in part of the government processes that it is shielded by its very pervasiveness. It is so much a part of things that one can't separate "honest" actions from "dishonest" ones. Just what is corruption in Vietnam? From my personal observations, it is the following:
>
> The very high officials who condone, and engage in smuggling, not only of dutiable merchandise, but undercut the nation's economy by smuggling gold and worst of all, that unmitigated evil—opium and other narcotics;
>
> The police officials whose "check points" are synonymous with "shakedown points";
>
> The high government official who advises his lower echelons of employees of the monthly "kick in" that he requires from each of them; . . .
>
> The customs official who sells to the highest bidder the privilege of holding down for a specific time the position where the graft and loot possibilities are the greatest.[59]

It appeared that customs director Loc devoted much of his energies to organizing the gold and opium traffic between Vientiane, Laos, and Saigon. When 114 kilos of gold were intercepted at Tan Son Nhut airport coming from Vientiane, Roberts reported to U.S. customs in Washington that "there are unfortunate political overtones and implications of culpability on the part of highly placed personages."[60] Loc also used his political connections to have his niece hired as a stewardess on Royal Air Lao, which flew several times a week between Vientiane and Saigon, and used her as a courier for gold and opium shipments. When U.S. customs advisers at Tan Son Nhut ordered a search of her luggage in December 1967 as she stepped off a Royal Air Lao flight from Vientiane, they discovered 200 kilos of raw opium.[61] In his monthly report to Washington, Roberts concluded that Loc was "promoting the day-to-day system of payoffs in certain areas of Customs' activities."[62]

After Roberts filed a number of hard-hitting reports with the U.S. mission, Ambassador Ellsworth Bunker called him and members of the customs advisory team to the embassy to discuss Vietnamese "involvement in gold and narcotics smuggling."[63] The Public Administration Ad Hoc Committee on Corruption in Vietnam was formed to deal with the problem. Although Roberts admonished the committee, saying "we must stop burying our heads in the sand like ostriches" when faced with corruption and smuggling, and begged, "Above all, don't make this a classified subject and thereby bury it," the U.S. embassy decided to do just that. Embassy officials whom Roberts described as advocates of "the noble kid glove concept of hearts and minds" had decided not to interfere with smuggling or large-scale corruption because of "pressures which are too well known to require enumeration."[64]

Frustrated at the embassy's failure to take action, an unknown member of U.S. customs leaked some of Roberts's reports on corruption to a Senate subcommittee chaired by Senator Albert Gruening of Alaska. When Gruening declared in February 1968 that the Saigon government was "so corrupt and graft-ridden that it cannot begin to command the loyalty and respect of its citizens,"[65] U.S. officials in Saigon defended the Thieu-Ky regime by saying that "it had not been proved that South Vietnam's leaders are guilty of receiving 'rake-offs.' "[66] A month later Senator Gruening released evidence of Ky's 1961–1962 opium trafficking, but the U.S. embassy protected Ky from further investigations by issuing a flat denial of the senator's charges.[67]

While these sensational exposés of smuggling at Tan Son Nhut's civilian terminal grabbed the headlines, only a few hundred yards down the runway Vietnamese air force C-47 transports loaded with Laotian opium were landing unnoticed. Ky did not relinquish command of the air force until November 1967, and even then he continued to make all the important promotions and assignments through a network of loyal officers who still regarded him as the real commander. As both premier and vice-president, Air Vice-Marshal Ky refused the various official residences offered him and instead used $200,000 of government money to build a modern, air-conditioned mansion in the middle of Tan Son Nhut Air Base. The "vice-presidential palace," a pastel-colored bunker resembling a California condominium, was only a few steps away from Tan Son Nhut's runway, where helicopters sat on twenty-four-hour alert, and a minute down the road from the headquarters of his old unit, the First Transport Group. As might be expected, Ky's staunchest supporters were the men of the First Transport Group. Its commander, Colonel Luu Kim Cuong, was considered by many informed observers to be the unofficial "acting commander" of the entire air force and a principal in the opium traffic. Since command of the First Transport Group and Tan Son Nhut Air Base were consolidated in 1964, Colonel Cuong not only had aircraft to fly from southern Laos and the Central Highlands (the major opium routes) but also controlled the air base security guards and thus could prevent any search of the C-47s.[68]

Once it reached Saigon safely, opium was sold to Chinese syndicates who managed the refining and distribution. Loan's police used their efficient organization to "license" and "tax" the thousands of illicit opium dens concentrated in the fifth, sixth, and seventh wards of Cholon and scattered throughout the rest of the capital.

Although morphine base exports to Europe had been relatively small during the Diem administration, they increased during Ky's tenure as Turkey began to phase out production in 1967–1968. And according to Lucien Conein, Loan profited from this change:

> Loan organized the opium exports once more as a part of the system of corruption. He contacted the Corsicans and Chinese, telling them they could begin to export Laos's opium from Saigon if they paid a fixed price to Ky's political organization.[69]

Most of the narcotics exported from South Vietnam—whether morphine base to Europe or raw opium to other parts of Southeast Asia—were shipped from Saigon's port on oceangoing freighters. (Also, Saigon was probably a port of entry for drugs smuggled into South Vietnam from Thailand.) The director of the Saigon port authority during this period was Premier Ky's brother-in-law and close political adviser, Lieutenant Colonel Pho Quoc Chu (Ky had divorced his French wife and married a Vietnamese).[70] Under Chu's supervision, all of the trained port officers were systematically purged, and in October 1967 the chief U.S. customs adviser reported that the port authority "is now a solid coterie of GVN [Government of Vietnam] military officers."[71] However, compared with the fortunes that could be made from the theft of military equipment, commodities, and manufactured goods, opium was probably not that important.

Loan and Ky were no doubt concerned about the critical security situation in Saigon when they took office, but their real goal in building up the police apparatus was political power. Often they seemed to forget who their "enemy" was supposed to be and utilized much of their police-intelligence network to attack rival political and military factions. Aside from his summary execution of an NLF suspect in front of U.S. television cameras during the 1968 Tet offensive, General Loan was probably best known to the world for his unique method of breaking up legislative stalemates during the 1967 election campaign. A member of the Constituent Assembly who proposed a law that would have excluded Ky from the upcoming elections was murdered.[72] His widow publicly accused Loan of having ordered the assassination. When the assembly balked at approving the Thieu-Ky slate unless they complied with the election law, Loan marched into the balcony of the assembly chamber with two armed guards, and the opposition evaporated.[73] When the assembly hesitated at validating the fraudulent tactics the Thieu-Ky slate had used to gain their victory in the September elections, Loan and his gunmen stormed into the balcony, and once again the representatives relented.[74]

Under Loan's supervision, the Ky machine systematically reorganized the network of graft for the opium traffic and built up an organization many observers felt was even more comprehensive than Nhu's clandestine apparatus. Nhu had depended on the Corsican syndicates to manage most of the opium smuggling between Laos and Saigon, but their charter airlines were evicted from Laos in early 1965. This move forced the Ky apparatus to become much more directly involved in actual smuggling than Nhu's secret police had ever been. Through personal contacts in Laos, bulk quantities of refined and raw opium were shipped to airports in southern Laos, where they were picked up and smuggled into South Vietnam by the air force transport wing. The Vietnamese customs service was also controlled by the Ky machine, and substantial quantities of opium were flown directly into Saigon on regular commercial air flights from Laos. Once the opium reached the capital it was distributed to smoking dens throughout the city that were protected by General Loan's police force. Finally, through its control over the Saigon port authority, the Ky apparatus was able to derive considerable revenues by taxing Corsican morphine exports to Europe and Chinese opium and morphine shipments to Hong Kong. Despite the growing importance of morphine exports, Ky's machine was largely concerned with its own domestic opium market. The GI heroin epidemic was still five years in the future.

## The Thieu-Ky Rivalry

Politics built Premier Ky's powerful syndicate, and politics weakened it. His meteoric political rise had enabled his power broker, General Loan, to take control of the police-intelligence bureaucracy and use its burgeoning resources to increase their revenue from the lucrative rackets—which in Saigon always included the flourishing narcotics trade. However, in 1967 simmering animosity between Premier Ky and General Nguyen Van Thieu, then head of Saigon's military junta, broke into open political warfare. Outmaneuvered by his rival at every turn in the conflict, Ky's apparatus emerged from two years of internecine warfare shorn of much of its political power and its monopoly over the opium trade. The Thieu-Ky rivalry was a clash between ambitious men, competing political factions, and conflicting personalities. In both his

## 2. Air Vice-Marshal Nguyen Cao Ky's Political Power Organization, 1965-1968

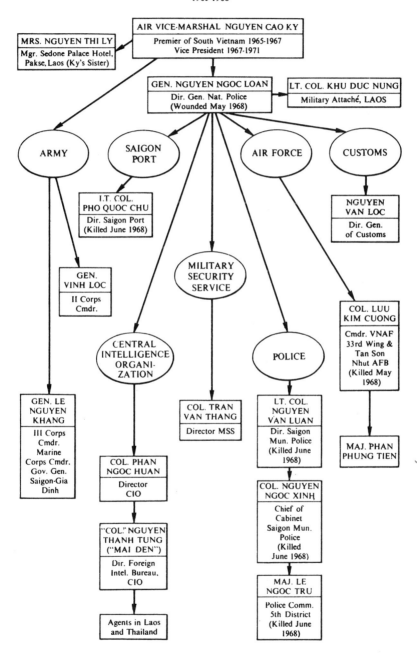

private machinations and his public appearances, Air Vice-Marshal Ky displayed all the flair of a fighter pilot. Arrayed in his midnight black jumpsuit, Ky liked to barnstorm about the countryside berating his opponents for their corruption and issuing a call for reforms. While his flamboyant behavior earned him the affection of air force officers, it often caused him serious political embarrassment, such as the time he declared his profound admiration for Adolf Hitler. In contrast, Thieu was a taciturn political operator who demonstrated the calculus of a master strategist. Although Thieu's tepid, usually dull public appearances won him little popular support, years of patient politicking inside the armed forces built him a solid political base among the army and navy officer corps.

Although Thieu and Ky managed to present a united front during the 1967 elections, their underlying enmity erupted into bitter factional warfare once their electoral victory removed the threat of civilian government. Thieu and Ky had agreed to bury their differences temporarily and run on the same ticket only after forty-eight Vietnamese generals argued behind closed doors for three full days in June 1967. On the second day of hysterical political infighting, Thieu won the presidential slot after making a scathing denunciation of police corruption in Saigon, an indirect attack on Loan and Ky, which reduced the air vice-marshal to tears and caused him to accept the number two position on the ticket.[75] But the two leaders campaigned separately, and once the election was over hostilities quickly revived.

Since the constitution gave the president enormous powers and the vice-president very little appointive or administrative authority, Ky should not have been in a position to challenge Thieu. However, Loan's extensive police-intelligence machine remained intact, and his loyalty to Ky made the vice-president a strong rival. In a report to Ambassador Bunker in May 1968, General Edward Lansdale explained the dynamics of the Thieu-Ky rivalry:

> This relationship may be summed up as follows: (1) The power to formulate and execute policies and programs which should be Thieu's as the top executive leader remains divided between Thieu and Ky, although Thieu has more power than Ky. (2) Thieu's influence as the elected political leader of the country, in terms of achieving the support of the National Assembly and the political elite, is considerably limited by Ky's influence. . . . (Suppose, for example, a U.S. President in the midst of a major war had as Vice President a leader who had been the previous President, who controlled the FBI, CIA, and DIA [Defense Intelligence Agency], who had more influence with the JCS [Joint Chiefs of Staff] than did the President, who

had as much influence in Congress as the President, who had
his own base of political support outside Congress, and who
neither trusted nor respected the President.)[76]

Lansdale went on to say that "Loan has access to substantial funds
through extra legal money-collecting systems of the police/intelligence
apparatus,"[77] which in large part formed the basis of Ky's political
strength. But, Lansdale added, "Thieu acts as though his source of money
is limited and has not used confidential funds with the flair of Ky."[78]

Since money was the key to victory in factional contests of this kind,
the Thieu-Ky rivalry became an underground battle for lucrative
administrative positions and key police-intelligence posts. Ky had used
two years of executive authority as premier to appoint loyal followers to
high office and lucrative posts, thereby building a powerful financial
apparatus. Now that President Thieu had a monopoly on appointive
authority, he tried to gain financial strength gradually by forcing Ky's
men out of office and replacing them with his own followers.

Thieu's first attack was on the customs service, where director Loc's
notorious reputation made the Ky apparatus particularly vulnerable.
The first tactic, as it often was in such factional battles, was to use the
Americans to get rid of an opponent. Only three months after the
elections, customs adviser George Roberts reported that his American
assistants were getting inside information on Loc's activities because
"this was also a period of intense inter-organizational, political infighting. Loc was vulnerable, and many of his lieutenants considered the
time right for confidential disclosure to their counterparts in this unit."[79]
Although the disclosures contained no real evidence, they forced Loc to
counterattack, and "he reacted with something resembling bravado."[80]
He requested U.S. customs advisers to come forward with information
on corruption, invited them to augment their staff at Tan Son Nhut,
where opium and gold smuggling had first aroused the controversy, and
launched a series of investigations into customs corruption. When
President Thieu's new minister of finance had taken office, he had
passed the word that Loc was on the way out. But Loc met with the
minister, pointed out all of his excellent anticorruption work, and
insisted on staying in office. But then, as Roberts reported to
Washington, Thieu's faction delivered the final blow:

> Now, to absolutely assure Loc's destruction, his enemies have
> turned to the local press, giving them the same information
> they had earlier given to this unit. The press, making liberal use
> of innuendo and implication, had presented a series of front
> page articles on corruption in Customs. They are a strong
> indictment of Director Loc.[81]

Several weeks later Loc was fired from his job,[82] and the way was open for the Thieu faction to take control over the traffic at Tan Son Nhut airport.

The Thieu and Ky factions were digging in for all-out war, and it seemed that these scandals would continue for months or even years. However, on January 31, 1968, the NLF and the North Vietnamese army launched the Tet offensive and 67,000 troops attacked 102 towns and cities across South Vietnam, including Saigon itself. The intense fighting, which continued inside the cities for several months, disrupted routine politics while the government dropped everything to drive the NLF back into the rice paddies. Not only did the Tet fighting reduce much of Saigon-Cholon to rubble, it decimated the ranks of Vice-President Ky's trusted financial cadres and crippled his political machine. In less than one month of fighting during the second wave of the Tet offensive, no less than nine of his key fund-raisers were killed or wounded.

General Loan himself was seriously wounded on May 5 while charging down a blind alley after a surrounded NLF soldier. An AK-47 bullet severed the main artery in his right leg and he was forced to resign from command of the police to undergo surgery and months of hospitalization.[83] The next day Colonel Luu Kim Cuong, commander of the air force transport wing and an important figure in Ky's network, was shot and killed while on operations on the outskirts of Saigon.[84]

While these two incidents would have been enough to seriously weaken Ky's apparatus, a mysterious incident a month later dealt a crippling blow. On the afternoon of June 2, 1968, a coterie of Ky's prominent followers were meeting, for reasons never satisfactorily explained, in a command post in Cholon. At about 6:00 P.M. a U.S. helicopter, prowling the skies above the ravaged Chinese quarter on the lookout for NLF units, attacked the building, rocketing and strafing it. Among the dead were Lieutenant Colonel Pho Quoc Chu, director of the Saigon port authority and Ky's brother-in-law; Lieutenant Colonel Dao Ba Phuoc, commander of the 5th Rangers, who were assigned to the Capital Military District; Lieutenant Colonel Nguyen Van Luan, director of the Saigon municipal police; Major Le Ngoc Tru, General Loan's right-hand man and police commissioner of the fifth district; and Major Nguyen Bao Thuy, special assistant to the mayor of Saigon. Moreover, General Loan's brother-in-law, Lieutenant Colonel Van Van Cua, the mayor of Saigon, suffered a shattered arm and resigned to undergo four months of hospitalization.[85]

These men represented the financial foundation of Ky's political machine, and once they were gone his apparatus began to crumble. As vice-president, Ky had no authority to appoint anyone to office, and all of the nine posts vacated by these casualties, with the exception of the air force transport command, were given to Thieu's men. On June 6 a loyal Thieu follower, Colonel Tran Van Hai, was appointed director-general of the national police and immediately began a rigorous purge of all of Loan's men in the lower echelons.[86] The Saigon press reported that 150 secret police had been fired and a number of these had also been arrested.[87] On June 15 Colonel Hai delivered a decisive blow to Ky's control over the police by dismissing eight out of Saigon's eleven district police commissioners.[88]

As Ky's apparatus weakened, his political fortunes went into a tailspin: loss of minor district and municipal police posts meant he could not collect protection money from ordinary businesses or from the rackets; as the "extra legal money-collecting systems of the police/intelligence apparatus" began to run dry, he could no longer counter President Thieu's legal appointive power with gifts; and once the opposition weakened, Thieu began to fire many high-ranking pro-Ky police-intelligence officials.[89]

While the quiet shift of the bureaucracy to the Thieu machine was almost imperceptible to outside observers, the desertion of Ky's supporters in the National Assembly's corrupt lower house was scandalously obvious. Shortly after the October 1967 parliamentary elections were over and the National Assembly convened for the first time since the downfall of Diem, the Thieu and Ky machines had begun competing for support in the lower house.[90] Using money provided by General Loan, Ky had purchased a large bloc of forty-two deputies, the Democratic Bloc, which included Buddhists, southern intellectuals, and a few hill tribesmen. Since Thieu lacked Ky's "confidential funds," he had allied himself with a small twenty-one-man bloc, the Independence Bloc, comprising mainly right-wing Catholics from northern and central Vietnam.[91] Both men were paying each of their deputies illegal supplemental salaries of $4,500 to $6,000 a year, in addition to bribes ranging up to $1,800 on every important ballot.[92] At a minimum it must have been costing Ky $15,000 to $20,000 a month just to keep his deputies on the payroll, not to mention outlays of more than $100,000 for the critical votes that came once or twice a year. In May 1968 General Lansdale reported to Ambassador Bunker that "Thieu's efforts . . . to create a base of support in both Houses have been made difficult by Ky's influence among some important senators . . . and Ky's influence over the Democratic Bloc in the Lower House."[93] However, throughout the summer of 1968 Ky's financial difficulties forced him to cut back the payroll, and representatives began drifting away from his bloc.

As Thieu's financial position strengthened throughout the summer, his assistant in charge of relations with the national Assembly approached a number of deputies and reportedly offered them from $1,260 to $2,540 to join a new pro-Thieu faction called the People's Progress Bloc. One deputy explained that "in the last few months, the activities of the lower house have become less and less productive because a large number of deputies have formed a bloc for personal interests instead of political credits." In September *The Washington Post* reported:

> The "Democratic Bloc," loyal to Vice President Ky, now retains 25 out of its 42 members. Thieu and Ky have been privately at odds since 1966. Thieu's ascendancy over his only potential rival has grown substantively in recent months.
> The severe blow dealt to the Ky bloc in the House has not been mentioned extensively in the local press except in the daily Xay Dung (To Construct), which is a Catholic, pro-Ky paper.[94]

These realignments in the balance of political power had an impact on the opium traffic. Despite his precipitous political decline, Air Vice-Marshal Ky retained control over the air force, particularly the transport wing. In the early 1970s the air force's transport wing was identified as one of the most active participants in South Vietnam's heroin smuggling. General Tran Thien Khiem, minister of the interior (who was to emerge as a major faction leader himself when he became prime minister in September 1969) and a nominal Thieu supporter, inherited control of Saigon's police apparatus, Tan Son Nhut customs, and the Saigon port authority. However, these noteworthy internal adjustments were soon dwarfed in importance by two dramatic developments in South Vietnam's narcotics traffic—the increase in heroin exports for the American market and the heroin epidemic among American GIs serving in South Vietnam.

## The GI Heroin Epidemic

The sudden spread of heroin addiction among GIs in 1970 was the most important development in Southeast Asia's narcotics traffic since the region attained self-sufficiency in opium production during the late 1950s. By 1968–1969 the Golden Triangle region was harvesting close to 1,000 tons of raw opium annually, exporting morphine base to European heroin laboratories, and shipping substantial quantities of narcotics to Hong Kong both for local consumption and for reexport to the United States. Although large amounts of chunky, low-grade no. 3 heroin were being produced in Bangkok and the Golden Triangle for the local market, there were no laboratories anywhere in Southeast Asia capable of producing the fine-grain, 80 to 99 percent pure, no. 4 heroin. However, in late 1969 and early 1970, Golden Triangle laboratories added the final, dangerous ether precipitation process and converted to production of no. 4 heroin. Many of the master chemists who supervised the conversion were Chinese brought in specially from Hong Kong. In a June 1971 report the CIA said that conversion from no. 3 to no. 4 heroin production in the Golden Triangle "appears to be due to the sudden increase in demand by a large and relatively affluent market in South Vietnam." By mid-April 1971 demand for no. 4 heroin in both Vietnam and the United States had increased so quickly that the wholesale price for a kilo jumped to $1,780 from $1,240 the previous September.[95]

Once large quantities of heroin became available to American GIs in Vietnam, heroin addiction spread like a plague. Previously unavailable in South Vietnam, suddenly no. 4 heroin was everywhere: fourteen-year-old girls were selling heroin at roadside stands on the main highway from Saigon to the U.S. army base at Long Binh; Saigon street peddlers stuffed plastic vials of 95 percent pure heroin into the pockets of GIs as they strolled through downtown Saigon; and "mama-sans," or Vietnamese barracks' maids, started carrying a few vials to work for sale to on-duty GIs. With this kind of aggressive sales campaign, the results were predictable: in September 1970 army medical officers questioned 3,103 soldiers of the Americal Division and discovered that 11.9 percent had tried heroin since they arrived in Vietnam and 6.6 percent were still using it on a regular basis.[96] In November a U.S. engineering battalion in the Mekong Delta reported that 14 percent of its troops were on heroin.[97] By mid-1971 U.S. army medical officers were estimating that about 10 to 15 percent, or 25,000 to 37,000, of the lower-ranking enlisted men serving in Vietnam were heroin users.[98]

As base after base was overrun by these armies of heroin pushers with their identical plastic vials, GIs and officers alike started asking themselves why this was happening. Who was behind this heroin plague? The North Vietnamese were frequently blamed, and wild rumors started floating around U.S. installations about heroin factories in Hanoi, truck convoys rumbling down the Ho Chi Minh Trail loaded with cases of plastic vials, and heroin-crazed North Vietnamese regulars making suicide charges up the slopes of Khe Sanh with syringes stuck in their arms. However, the U.S. army provost marshal laid such rumors to rest in a 1971 report, which said in part:

> The opium-growing areas of North Vietnam are concentrated in mountainous northern provinces bordering China. *Cultivation is closely controlled by the government and none of the crop is believed to be channeled illicitly into international markets.* Much of it is probably converted into morphine and used for medical purposes. [Emphasis added.][99]

Instead, the provost marshal accused high-ranking members of South Vietnam's government of being the top "zone" in a four-tiered heroin-pushing pyramid:

> Zone I, located at the top or apex of the pyramid, contains the financiers, or backers of the illicit drug traffic in all its forms. The people comprising this group may be high level, influential political figures, government leaders, or moneyed ethnic Chinese members of the criminal syndicates now flourishing in the Cholon sector of the City of Saigon. The members comprising this group are the powers behind the scenes who can manipulate, foster, protect, and promote the illicit traffic in drugs.[100]

But why were these powerful South Vietnamese officials—the very people who would lose the most if the heroin plague forced the U.S. army to pull out of South Vietnam completely—promoting and protecting the heroin traffic? The answer was $88 million. Conservatively estimated, each one of the twenty thousand or so GI addicts in Vietnam spent an average of $12 a day on four vials of heroin. Over a year this came out to $88 million, a substantial amount of money in an impoverished, war-torn country.

In probing the causes of the heroin plague, the mass media generally found fault with the U.S. army: the senior NCOs and junior officers came down too hard on strong-smelling marijuana and drove the GIs to heroin, which is odorless, compact, and much harder to detect; the GIs were being forced to fight a war they did not believe in and turned to heroin to blot out intense boredom; and, finally, the army itself was an antiquated institution from which the GIs wanted to "escape." Much of this was no doubt true, but the emphasis was misplaced. Officers and NCOs had been cracking down on marijuana for several years without the GIs turning to heroin.[101] By 1968 the emotional malaise of the Vietnam GI was already well developed; the race riot in Long Binh stockade and the My Lai massacre were only the most obvious signs of the problem. But there was no serious heroin use until the spring of 1970, when large quantities were being sold everywhere in Vietnam. And the simple fact is that there would have been no epidemic without this well-organized, comprehensive sales campaign. The roots of the problem lay not with the GI victim or the army's marijuana crackdown, but with those Vietnamese officials who organized and protected the heroin traffic.

The experience of Major General John Cushman in IV Corps, the Mekong Delta, demonstrated the extent of official involvement on the part of the Vietnamese army and the utter futility of the U.S. army's "cleanup," "crackdown" approach to dealing with the GI heroin epidemic. When Cushman took command of U.S. forces in the Delta in mid-1971 he was shocked by the seriousness of the heroin problem. U.S. army medical doctors estimated that 15 to 20 percent of the GIs in his command were regular heroin users.[102] Cushman made a desperate bid to stem the rising rate of addiction. Prepared with all the precision and secrecy of a top-priority offensive, a massive crackdown on drug use began on June 22 at 5:30 A.M.: all troops were confined to base twenty-four hours a day, guard patrols were stiffened, everyone entering the base was searched, and emergency medical clinics were opened. The price of a $3 vial of heroin shot up to $40 on the base, and 300 addicts turned themselves in for treatment. However, within six days the MPs' enthusiasm for searches began to wane, and heroin once more became available. On July 4 confinement was terminated and passes for town were reissued. Within a week the price of heroin was down to $4 and more than half of those who had turned themselves in were back on drugs.[103]

By late July Cushman realized that he could never solve the problem until the Vietnamese police and army stopped protecting the pushers. Although he wrote to the Vietnamese IV Corps commander, General Ngo Quang Truong, threatening to withdraw his "personal support" from the war effort unless Vietnamese officers stopped pushing heroin, he realized it was a futile gesture. The problem was not General Truong. Cushman explained, "Truong has a spotless reputation. I haven't heard the slightest whisper of talk that he is anything other than a man of the highest integrity. I personally admire him and I feel the same about his generals." But he could not say the same for the Vietnamese colonels and majors. While Truong himself was not involved, he was not a "free agent" and lacked the authority to stop his third-level commanders from dealing in drugs.[104] Some Vietnamese sources identified the colonels as men who were loyal to President Thieu's chief military adviser, General Dang Van Quang.[105]

The Cambodian invasion may have been another important factor in promoting the GI heroin epidemic. While this hypothesis can probably never be proved because of the clandestine, fragmented nature of the heroin traffic, it is an interesting coincidence that the invasion occurred in May 1970 and most journalistic accounts and official reports give spring 1970 or early 1970[106] as the starting date for widespread heroin addiction. (Late 1969 is the date usually given for the beginning of small-scale heroin use among GIs.[107]) The difficulties involved in smuggling between southern Laos and the Vietnamese Central High lands limited the amount of narcotics that could be brought into Vietnam; the lack of roads and rivers made air transport an absolute necessity, but the rugged mountain terrain and the relative infrequency of flights between these two unpopulated areas required excessively intricate planning.

Since the mid-1950s the Cambodian neutralist ruler Prince Sihanouk had remained hostile to the various pro-American South Vietnamese regimes. Vietnamese military transports, naval vessels, or military convoys never entered Cambodia, and most of the gold and narcotics smuggling from Laos avoided this neutralist kingdom. However, less than three months after Sihanouk's ouster in March 1970, the Vietnamese army crashed across the border and its Fifth Air Division began daily flights to Phnom Penh, the capital of Cambodia. Once Cambodia opened up, unlimited quantities of narcotics could be flown from southern Laos to Phnom Penh on any one of the hundreds of commercial, military, or clandestine flights that crowded the airways every day. From there narcotics could easily be forwarded to Saigon by boat, truck, or aircraft.[108] Since the spread of GI heroin addiction seems to have been limited only by the availability of drugs, the improved smuggling conditions that resulted from the Cambodian invasion may have played some role in promoting the GI heroin epidemic.

## South Vietnam's Heroin Market

The leap in the size and profitability of South Vietnam's narcotics trade, from both the new GI market and the increased demand on the part of international narcotics syndicates, resulted in a number of new minicliques entering the traffic.

By 1970 the traffic appeared to be divided among three major factions: (1) elements in the South Vietnamese air force, particularly the air transport wing; (2) the civil bureaucracy (police, customs, and port authority), increasingly under the control of Premier Khiem's family; and (3) the army, navy, and National Assembly's lower house, which answered to President Thieu. The enormous amounts of money involved in the drug trade produced an intense animosity among these three factions.

Involvement in the nation's narcotics traffic took a number of different forms. Usually it meant that influential Vietnamese political and military leaders worked as consultants and protectors for Chiu chau Chinese syndicates, which actually managed wholesale distribution, packaging, refining, and some of the smuggling. (Chiu chau are Chinese from the Swatow region of southern China, and Chiu chau syndicates have controlled much of Asia's illicit drug traffic since the mid-1800s and have played a role in China's organized crime similar to that of the Sicilian Mafia in Italy and the Corsican syndicates in France. See Chapter 6 for more details.) The importance of this protection, however, should not be underestimated, for without it the heroin traffic could not have continued. Also, powerful Vietnamese military and civil officials were directly involved in the smuggling of narcotics into South Vietnam. The Vietnamese military had access to aircraft, trucks, and ships that the Chinese did not, and most of the Vietnamese elite had a much easier time bringing narcotics through customs and border checkpoints than did their Chinese clients.

Of South Vietnam's three major narcotics rings, the air transport wing loyal to Air Vice-Marshal Ky was the most professional. Although Ky's apparatus lost control over the internal distribution network following his post-Tet political decline in 1968, his faction continued to manage much of the narcotics smuggling between Vietnam and Laos through the air force and its relations with Laotian traffickers. With more than ten years of experience, it had connections with the Lao elite that the other two factions could not equal. Rather than buying heroin through middlemen, Ky's apparatus dealt directly with a heroin laboratory operating in the Vientiane region. According to a U.S. police adviser stationed in Vientiane, this laboratory was one of the most active in Laos and was managed by a Chinese entrepreneur named Huu Tim-heng. Heng was the link between one of Laos's major opium merchants, General Ouane Rattikone (former commander in chief of the Laotian army), and Vietnam's air transport heroin ring.[109] From the viewpoint of the narcotics traffic, Huu's most important legitimate commercial venture was the Pepsi-Cola bottling factory on the outskirts of Vientiane. With Prime Minister Souvanna Phouma's son Panya as the official president, Huu and two other Chinese financiers began construction in 1965–1966. Although the presence of the prime minister's son at the head of the company qualified the venture for generous financial support from USAID (U.S. Agency for International Development), the plant had still not bottled a single Pepsi after five years of stop-start construction.[110] The completed factory building had a forlorn, abandoned look about it. While Pepsi's competitors were mystified at the company's lackadaisical attitude, the U.S. Bureau of Narcotics had an answer to the riddle. Bureau sources reported that Huu had been using his Pepsi operation as a cover for purchases of chemicals vital to the processing of heroin, such as ether and acetic anhydride, and for large financial transactions.[111]

Once the heroin was processed and packaged in large plastic envelopes, other experienced members of the Ky apparatus took charge of arranging shipment to South Vietnam. Mrs. Nguyen Thi Ly, Ky's elder sister, had directed much of the traffic from the Sedone Palace Hotel in Pakse when her brother was premier, but in 1967 she gave up her position as manager and moved back to Saigon. However, sources in Vientiane's Vietnamese community reported that she and her husband traveled between Saigon, Pakse, and Vientiane at least once a month after they returned to Vietnam. Mrs. Ly purchased heroin produced in Heng's clandestine laboratory and had it shipped to Pakse or Phnom Penh were it was picked up by Vietnamese air force transports.[112]

In addition, the U.S. Bureau of Narcotics believed that General Loan's former assistant Mai Den may also have been involved in this operation. After Loan was wounded in May 1968, Mai Den was forced out of his position as director of the CIO's Foreign Intelligence Bureau, and he exiled himself to Bangkok.[113] For two years this skillful operator had used his CIO agents to weave a net of drug contacts across the Golden Triangle, and the Bureau of Narcotics had reason to believe he may have used them even longer.

Normally, those air force officers responsible for directing the flow of narcotics to South Vietnam purchased the drugs and had them delivered, often by the Laotian air force, to points in Laos, particularly Pakse, or across the border in Pleiku province, South Vietnam, or in Phnom Penh, Cambodia. Most observers felt that the Cambodian capital had preempted Pleiku's importance as a drop point after the Vietnamese air force began daily sorties to Phnom Penh during the 1970 Cambodia invasion. In August 1971 *The New York Times* reported that the director of Vietnam customs "said he believed that planes of the South Vietnamese Air Force were the principal carriers" of heroin coming into South Vietnam.[114] While the director was a Thieu appointee and his remark may have been politically motivated, U.S. customs advisers, more objective observers, stated that the air force regularly unloaded large quantities of smuggled narcotics at Tan Son Nhut Air Base.[115] Here Air Vice-Marshal Ky reigned in his air-conditioned palace, surrounded by only his most loyal officers. As one U.S. air force adviser put it, "In order to get a job within shooting distance of the Vice Presidential palace a VNAF officer has to be intensely loyal to Ky."[116]

In 1973 the commander of Tan Son Nhut and the air force's transport wing, the Fifth Air Division, was Colonel Phan Phung Tien. Brother-in-law of one of Ky's close political advisers who died in the 1968 Tet offensive, Tien had served under Ky as a squadron commander in the First Transport Group from 1956 to 1960. He remained one of Ky's most loyal followers, and one U.S. air force adviser described him at the time as Ky's "revolutionary plotter" inside the air force.[117]

After the Cambodia invasion of May 1970, Fifth Air division C-47, C-119, and C-123 transports began shuttling back and forth between Phnom Penh and Tan Son Nhut with equipment and supplies for the Cambodian army, while two AC-47 gunships flew nightly missions to Phnom Penh to provide perimeter defense for the Cambodian capital.[118] All of these flights were supposed to return empty, but the director-general of Vietnam customs believed they were often filled with dutiable goods, gold, and narcotics. The director-general singled out Colonel Tien for criticism in an interview with *The New York Times* in August 1971, labeling him "the least cooperative in his efforts to narrow the channels through which heroin reached Vietnam."[119] Moreover, Vietnamese police officials reported that Tien was close to some of the powerful Corsican underworld figures who managed hotels and restaurants in Saigon.[120] This kind of evidence led many informed Vietnamese observers to conclude that Colonel Tien was a central figure in Vietnam's narcotics traffic.

## Thieu Takes Control

In the wake of Air Vice-Marshal Ky's precipitous political decline, ranking military officers responsible to President Thieu emerged as the dominant narcotics traffickers in South Vietnam. Like his predecessors, President Diem and Prime Minister Ky, President Thieu studiously avoided involving himself personally in political corruption. However, his power broker, presidential intelligence adviser General Dang Van Quang, was heavily involved in these activities. Working through high-ranking army and navy officers personally loyal to him or to President Thieu, Quang built up a formidable power base. Although Quang's international network appeared to be weaker than Ky's, Quang controlled the Vietnamese navy, which harbored an elaborate smuggling organization that imported large quantities of narcotics either by protecting Chinese maritime smugglers or by using Vietnamese naval vessels. Ky's influence among high-ranking army officers had weakened considerably, and control over the army shifted to General Quang. By 1973 the army managed most of the distribution and sale of heroin to American GIs. In addition, a bloc of pro-Thieu deputies in the lower house of the National Assembly were publicly exposed as being actively engaged in heroin smuggling, but they appeared to operate somewhat more independently of General Quang than did the army and navy.

On the July 15, 1971 edition of *NBC Nightly News*, the network's Saigon correspondent, Phil Brady, told a nationwide audience that both President Thieu and Vice-President Ky were financing their election campaigns from the narcotics traffic. Brady quoted "extremely reliable sources"[121] as saying that President Thieu's chief intelligence adviser, General Quang, was "the biggest pusher" in South Vietnam.[122] Although Thieu's press secretary issued a flat denial and accused Brady of "spreading falsehoods and slanders against leaders in the government, thereby providing help and comfort to the Communist enemy,"[123] he did not try to defend Quang, renowned as one of the most dishonest generals in South Vietnam when he was commander of IV Corps in the Mekong Delta.

In July 1969 *Time* magazine's Saigon correspondent had cabled the New York office this report on Quang's activities in IV Corps:

> While there he reportedly made millions by selling offices and taking a rake off on rice production. There was the famous incident, described in past corruption files, when Col. Nguyen Van Minh was being invested as a 21st Division commander. He had been Quang's deputy corps commander. At the ceremony the wife of the outgoing commander stood up and shouted to the assembled that Minh had paid Quang 2 million piasters [$7,300] for the position. . . . Quang was finally removed from Four Corps at the insistence of the Americans.[124]

General Quang had been transferred to Saigon in late 1966 and was made minister of planning and development, a face-saving sinecure.[125] Soon after President Thieu's election in September 1967, he was appointed special assistant for military and security affairs.[126] Quang quickly emerged as Thieu's power broker and performed the same kind of illicit fund-raising for Thieu's political machine that General Loan had done for Ky's.[127]

Thieu, however, was much less sure of Quang than Ky had been of Loan. Loan had enjoyed Ky's absolute confidence and was entrusted with almost unlimited personal power. Thieu, in contrast, took care to build up competing centers of power inside his political machine to keep General Quang from gaining too much influence. As a result, Quang never had the same control over the various pro-Thieu mini-factions as Loan had over Ky's apparatus. As control by Ky's apparatus over the Saigon rackets weakened after June 1968, various pro-Thieu factions moved in. In the political shift, Quang gained control of the special forces, the navy and the army, but one of the pro-Thieu cliques, headed by General Tran Thien Khiem, gained enough power so that it gradually emerged as an independent faction itself.[128] However, at the beginning most of the power and influence gained from Ky's downfall seemed to be securely lodged in the Thieu camp under General Quang's supervision.

There is evidence that one of the first new groups that began smuggling opium into South Vietnam was the Vietnamese special forces contingents operating in southern Laos. In August 1971 *The New York Times* reported that many of the aircraft flying narcotics into South Vietnam "are connected with secret South Vietnamese special forces operating along the Ho Chi Minh Trail network in Laos."[129] Based in Kontum province, north of Pleiku, the special forces "assault task force" had a small fleet of helicopters, transports, and light aircraft that flew into southern Laos on regular sabotage and long-range reconnaissance forays. Some special forces officers claimed that the commander of this unit was transferred to another post in mid-1971 because his extensive involvement in the narcotics traffic risked exposure.[130]

But clandestine forays were a relatively inefficient method of smuggling, and it appeared that Quang's apparatus did not become heavily involved in the narcotics trade until the Cambodian invasion of May 1970. For the first time in years the Vietnamese army operated inside Cambodia; Vietnamese troops guarded key Cambodian communication routes, the army assigned liaison officers to Phnom Penh, and intelligence officers were allowed to work inside the former neutralist kingdom. More important, the Vietnamese navy began permanent patrols along the Cambodian stretches of the Mekong and set up bases in Phnom Penh.

## Vietnamese Navy Smuggling

The Vietnamese navy used the Cambodian invasion to expand its role in the narcotics traffic, opening up a new pipeline that had previously been inaccessible. On May 9 an armada of 110 Vietnamese and 30 American river craft headed by the naval fleet commander, Captain Nguyen Thanh Chau, crossed the border into Cambodia, speeding up the Mekong in a dramatic V-shaped formation.[131] The next day the commander of Riverine Task Force 211, Captain Nguyen Van Thong, landed several hundred Vietnamese twenty miles upriver at Neak Luong, a vital ferry crossing on Route 1 linking Phnom Penh with Saigon.[132] Leaving their American advisers behind here, the Vietnamese arrived at Phnom Penh on May 11; the next day they reached Kompong Cham, seventy miles north of the Cambodian capital, thus clearing the waterway for their use.[133] Hailed as a tactical coup and a great "military humanitarian fleet" by navy publicists, the armada also had, according to sources inside the Vietnamese navy, the dubious distinction of smuggling vast quantities of opium and heroin into South Vietnam.

An associate of General Quang's, former navy commander Rear Admiral Chung Tan Cang, rose to prominence during the Cambodian invasion. Cang had been a good friend of President Thieu's since their student days at Saigon's Merchant Marine Academy (class of 1947).[134] When Cang was removed from command of the navy in 1965, after being charged with selling flood relief supplies on the black market instead of delivering them to the refugees,[135] Thieu intervened to prevent him from being prosecuted and had him appointed to a face-saving sinecure.[136]

Sources inside the Vietnamese navy said that a smuggling network that shipped heroin and opium from Cambodia back to South Vietnam was set up among high-ranking naval officers shortly after the Vietnamese navy docked at Phnom Penh. The shipments were passed

3. President Nguyen Van Thieu's Political Power Organization, 1970–1971

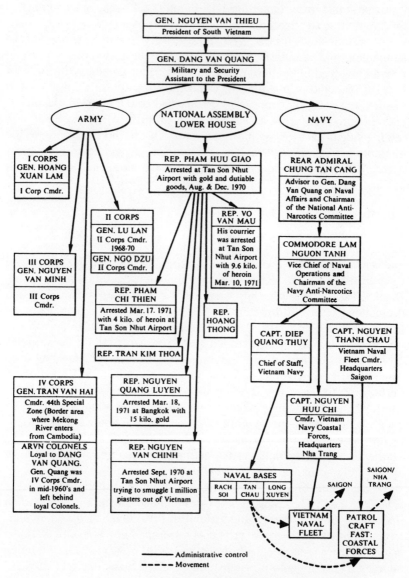

GEN. NGUYEN VAN THIEU
President of South Vietnam

GEN. DANG VAN QUANG
Military and Security
Assistant to the President

ARMY

NATIONAL ASSEMBLY
LOWER HOUSE

NAVY

I CORPS
GEN. HOANG
XUAN LAM
I Corp Cmdr.

REP. PHAM HUU GIAO
Arrested at Tan Son Nhut
Airport with gold and dutiable
goods, Aug. & Dec. 1970

REAR ADMIRAL
CHUNG TAN CANG
Advisor to Gen. Dang
Van Quang on Naval
Affairs and Chairman
of the National Anti-
Narcotics Committee

II CORPS
GEN. LU LAN
II Corps Cmdr.
1968-70
GEN. NGO DZU
II Corps Cmdr.

REP. VO
VAN MAU
His courrier
was arrested
at Tan Son
Nhut Airport
with 9.6 kilo.
of heroin
Mar. 10, 1971

COMMODORE LAM
NGUON TANH
Vice Chief of Naval
Operations and
Chairman of the
Navy Anti-Narcotics
Committee

III CORPS
GEN. NGUYEN
VAN MINH
III Corps
Cmdr.

REP. PHAM
CHI THIEN
Arrested Mar. 17. 1971
with 4 kilo. of heroin at
Tan Son Nhut Airport

REP.
HOANG
THONG

CAPT. DIEP
QUANG THUY
Chief of Staff,
Vietnam Navy

CAPT. NGUYEN
THANH CHAU
Vietnam Naval
Fleet Cmdr.
Headquarters
Saigon

REP. TRAN KIM THOA

IV CORPS
GEN. TRAN VAN HAI
Cmdr. 44th Special
Zone (Border area
where Mekong
River enters
from Cambodia)
ARVN COLONELS
Loyal to DANG
VAN QUANG.
Gen. Quang was
IV Corps Cmdr.
in mid-1960's and
left behind
loyal Colonels.

REP. NGUYEN
QUANG LUYEN
Arrested Mar. 18,
1971 at Bangkok with
15 kilo. gold

CAPT. NGUYEN
HUU CHI
Cmdr. Vietnam
Navy Coastal
Forces,
Headquarters
Nha Trang

REP. NGUYEN
VAN CHINH
Arrested Sept. 1970 at
Tan Son Nhut Airport
trying to smuggle 1 million
piasters out of Vietnam

NAVAL BASES
RACH | TAN | LONG
SOI | CHAU | XUYEN

SAIGON

SAIGON/
NHA
TRANG

VIETNAM
NAVAL
FLEET

PATROL
CRAFT
FAST:
COASTAL
FORCES

——— Administrative control
- - - - Movement

N.B.: The Vietnamese press has stated, without being
challenged, that there are more than 30 pro-government
deputies involved in narcotics and gold smuggling.

4. Vietnamese Navy Organization Established
During the Cambodia Invasion, Spring 1970

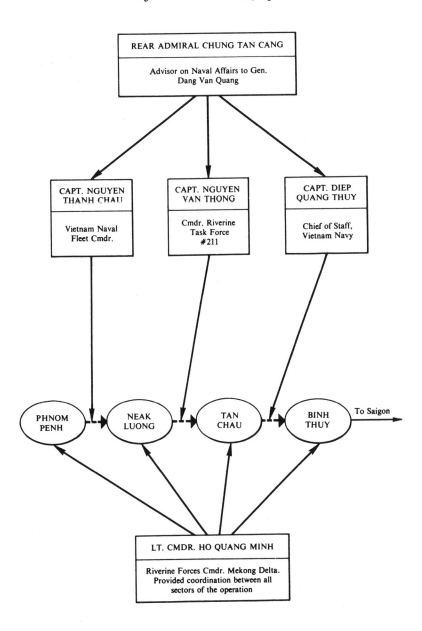

from protector to protector until they reached Saigon: the first relay was from Phnom Penh to Neak Luong; the next, from Neak Luong to Tan Chau, just inside South Vietnam; the next, from Tan Chau to Binh Thuy. From there the narcotics were shipped to Saigon on a variety of naval and civilian vessels.[137]

As the Cambodian military operation drew to a close in the middle of 1970, the navy's smuggling organization (which had been bringing limited quantities of gold, opium, and dutiable goods into Vietnam since 1968) expanded.

Commodore Lam Nguon Thanh was appointed vice-chief of naval operations in August 1970. Also a member of Thieu's class at the Merchant Marine Academy, Thanh had been abruptly removed from his post as navy chief of staff in 1966.[138] Sources inside the navy allege that high-ranking naval officials used three of the Mekong Delta naval bases under Commodore Thanh's command—Rach Soi, Long Xuyen, and Tan Chau—as drop points for narcotics smuggled into Vietnam on Thai fishing boats or Cambodian river sampans. From these three bases, the narcotics were smuggled to Saigon on naval vessels or on "swift boats" (officially known as PCFs, or Patrol Craft Fast). When, as often happened, the narcotics were shipped to Saigon on ordinary civilian sampans or fishing junks, their movements were protected by these naval units.[139]

Some of these smuggling operations within the Vietnamese navy were exposed in the summer of 1971. Shortly before this happened, the U.S. government had finally begun pressuring the South Vietnamese to crack down on the drug smuggling. According to sources inside the navy, the American demands were a cause of some concern for General Quang and Admiral Cang. Quang had Cang appointed chairman of the National Anti-Narcotics Committee and his associate, Commodore Thanh, installed as chairman of the Navy Anti-Narcotics Committee.[140]

Although these precautions should have proved adequate, events and decisions beyond General Quang's control nearly resulted in a humiliating public exposé. On July 25, 1971, Vietnamese narcotics police, assisted by Thai and American agents, broke up a major Chiu chau Chinese syndicate based in Cholon, arrested sixty drug traffickers, and made one of the largest narcotics seizures in Vietnam's history—51 kilos of heroin and 334 kilos of opium. Hailed in the press as a victory for the Thieu government's war on drugs, these raids were actually something of an embarrassment, since they exposed the navy smuggling ring.[141]

This Cholon Chiu chau syndicate was organized in mid-1970 when "Mr. Big" in Bangkok, a Chiu chau Chinese reputed to be one of the largest drug financiers in Southeast Asia, decided to start dealing in South Vietnam. He contacted a respectable Chiu chau plastics manufacturer in Cholon, Tran Minh, and the two soon came to an agreement. The Vietnamese navy was to provide protection. Sometime in mid-1970 a Thai fishing vessel arrived off the coast of Puolo Dama, a tiny Vietnamese island in the Gulf of Siam, with the first shipment. Waiting for the boat was a Vietnamese fishing boat under the command of a Chiu chau captain named Tang Hai. Hired by Tran Minh, Tang Hai was the link between the Bangkok and Cholon syndicates. After 200 kilos of opium had been transferred in mid-ocean, the Vietnamese boat headed toward its home port, Rach Gia, about fifty-five miles to the northeast. In Rach Gia, the bundles of opium were loaded onto a river sampan for the voyage to Saigon. Concealed under a layer of coconut shells, the opium appeared to be just another commercial cargo as it wound its way through the maze of canals that led to the docks of Cholon. Once the sampan docked at a wharf in Cholon's seventh district, the cargo was transferred to a microbus, driven to Tran Minh's warehouse in Cholon's sixth district, and eventually dispensed to the opium dens of Saigon-Cholon. All the traffic on these waterways was policed and protected by the Vietnamese navy. Tran Minh's business prospered and the smuggling continued.

By the third shipment Tran Minh had decided to expand into the GI market and ordered 10 kilos of Double U-O Globe brand heroin as well as the usual 200 kilos of opium. For the fourth shipment, Tran Minh was afraid the deliveries might start attracting notice and changed the transfer point to Hon Panjang, an island 115 miles southwest of Rach Gia. By mid-1971 business was going so well that the Cholon syndicate boss ordered a double shipment—400 kilos of opium and 60 kilos of heroin. The heroin alone was worth more than $720,000 retail. For the fishing captain Tang Hai and his military protectors at the Rach Soi Naval Base it turned out to be an irresistible temptation.

In early July 1971 Tang Hai kept his appointment with the Thai fishing boat and picked up the cargo near Hon Panjang Island. But instead of returning to Rach Gia, he proceeded to sail sixty miles north to Phu Quoc Island, where he buried the opium and hid the heroin in some underbrush. Then he returned to Rach Gia and told Tran Minh's contact man that the shipment had been stolen by the Vietnamese navy. Apparently this was a convincing explanation, and the contact man relayed the news to Cholon. When Tran Minh agreed to buy back half of the shipment from the navy for $25,000, Tang Hai returned to Phu Quoc Island, dug up most of the cache, and delivered half of the original shipment to the contact man in Rach Gia after burying the difference near his home. The contact man hired the usual sampan owner to smuggle the drugs to Cholon, but he was robbed, this time for real, by three Vietnamese army corporals only ten miles up the canal from Rach Gia.

The boatman returned to Rach Gia and reported his bad luck to the beleaguered contact man, who passed the word along to Cholon. Now $25,000 poorer, Tran Minh informed Bangkok that he had been robbed twice and could not pay for the shipment. The Bangkok financier, however, assumed that he was being cheated and decided to wipe out the entire Vietnamese syndicate. The Thai fishing captain was selected as the informer, and he approached Colonel Pramual Vangibandhu of the Thai Central Narcotics Bureau with a proposition: in exchange for a guarantee of complete immunity and anonymity for the Bangkok syndicate, he would name the two key men in the Saigon operation (which were, in fact, the only names the Bangkok syndicate knew).

Colonel Pramual accepted the offer and contacted U.S. narcotics agent William Wanzeck, asking him to arrange a meeting with the Vietnamese. The two men flew to Saigon, where they met with the head of the Vietnamese narcotics police, redactor Ly Ky Hoang, and U.S. narcotics agent Fred Dick. It was agreed that there should be two simultaneous raids: the Vietnamese national police would bust the Saigon syndicate while Hoang, Pramual, and Dick flew to Rach Gia to arrest Tang Hai and his cohorts.

The two raids were planned for 9:30 A.M. on July 25, less than three weeks after the drugs first arrived off Hon Panjang Island. The Saigon raid came off perfectly, but at Rach Gia, Hoang found that Tang Hai was not at home. Hoang, who was not in uniform, explained to Tang Hai's sister that the boss, Tran Minh, had sent him to negotiate for the missing drugs. After fifty minutes of skillful explanations, the sister finally agreed to take Hoang to a restaurant where her brother was "at a party drinking with some friends." The two of them clambered aboard a sputtering Lambretta taxi and disembarked about thirty minutes later in front of a restaurant in Rach Soi, a small fishing port four miles south of Rach Gia. Inside, Tang Hai was the guest of honor at a boisterous drinking party hosted by the commander of nearby Rach Soi Naval Base, Captain Hai, and attended by twenty well-armed navy officers and sailors.

Explaining that Tran Minh himself was waiting at Rach Gia, Hoang suggested that he and Tang Hai go there to discuss buying back the drugs. When the Chiu chau smuggler replied that he would rather stay at the party, Hoang elaborated on his story, explaining that the boss was willing to pay $25,000 for the remaining half of the shipment. At this the navy commander insisted that Hoang use his personal jeep and driver to bring Tran Minh to the party for negotiations.

An hour later Hoang returned in a police car, accompanied by Colonel

Pramual and Fred Dick. While the others waited outside, Hoang entered the restaurant. After suggesting that they step outside for a private word with the boss, he arrested Tang Hai, threw him into the waiting police car, and raced off for Rach Gia. Minutes later the navy officers realized that their guest had been arrested, grabbed their guns, and sped off in hot pursuit.

Even though they suspected that the navy posse was not far behind, the multinational police squad stopped en route to Rach Gia at a house belonging to Tang Hai's cousin to search for a suspected drugs cache. While Dick and Pramual took Tang Hai inside and proceeded to ransack the house, Hoang remained in the car a hundred yards down the street, radioing desperately for police assistance. Before he finally realized that the radio was out of order, navy jeeps screeched to a halt in front of the house and the officers began spreading out along the opposite side of the street with their guns drawn and aimed at the house.

Hoang was pinned down in the police car, cut off from his friends and feeling rather frightened. Suddenly he spotted a Lambretta minibus coming down the road. He cocked his gun and waited. When the minibus was just abreast of his car, Hoang jumped out, raced alongside the minibus until it was parallel with the house, and then dove through the front door. When he told the others what was happening, Dick started to break out a window with his pistol butt for a shoot-out, but Hoang, a cooler personality, stopped him.

Fortunately for these police officers, a plainclothes policeman just happened to enter the adjoining iron shop. After Hoang explained the situation, the policeman jumped on his Honda motorbike and puttered off for help. When a well-armed squad of local police arrived ten minutes later, the naval officers, realizing they were outgunned, reluctantly climbed back in their jeeps and retreated to Rach Soi.

When a search of the house turned up nothing, Hoang and the others drove Tang Hai to the Rach Gia police station for interrogation. At first the smuggler refused to talk, but after Hoang, who would not discuss his methods, finished with a few minutes of skillful interrogation, Tang Hai confessed everything—including the location of the drug cache on Phu Quoc Island. While Pramual and Dick flew Tang Hai out to the island to dig up the cache (112 kilos of opium and 3.9 kilos of heroin), Hoang himself arrested the three ARVN corporals who had actually stolen half the shipment and turned them over to the Military Security Service (MSS) for questioning. Sensing that the MSS would learn nothing, Hoang ordered the Rach Gia police commander to send a car around to his hotel when the MSS gave up. The military finished six hours of fruitless questioning at 2:00 A.M.; Hoang arrived at police headquarters an hour later and had his answers in only fifteen minutes. The next morning a police squad unearthed 32.7 kilos of heroin and 35 kilos of opium near a canal about two hours from Rach Gia. A search of Tang Hai's yard later that day uncovered an additional 7 kilos of Double U-O Globe heroin and 88 kilos of opium. Meanwhile, back in Bangkok the Thai police held a press conference on July 29, only four days after the first spectacular raids. Nervous over rumors of their involvement in the international traffic, the Thai police were eager to grab credit and repair their poor reputation. General Nitya Bhanumas, secretary general of the Thai Narcotics Board, reportedly claimed that the information that led to the seizures came from "informants *he* developed in an investigation *he* directed last month" [emphasis added].[142]

When the Vietnamese police picked up their newspapers the next morning, they were outraged.[143] Not only had the Thais claimed credit for what they felt was their work, but the investigation was still continuing and the Vietnamese police feared that the headlines might drive many of the syndicate's members into hiding. The Thai police had only given their Vietnamese counterparts the two names known to Bangkok's "Mr. Big"—Tang Hai and Tran Minh. Working from the top of the syndicate down, the Vietnamese were just beginning a roundup that eventually netted more than sixty middle- and upper-level distributors and scores of street pushers.

According to sources inside the Vietnamese navy, these raids created a near panic in the navy smuggling ring as its leaders scrambled to salvage the situation. Two of the officers involved in the Cambodia invasion command structure were transferred about the time that the smuggling ring was exposed. Captain Nguyen Van Thong was removed from his command of Riverine Task Force 211 and reassigned to a command training course only a few days before the police raids took place. The commander of the coastal patrol force, Captain Nguyen Huu Chi, was transferred to a staff college for advanced training just two weeks later.[144] Although the MSS arrested the navy officers at Rach Soi directly implicated in the affair,[145] there were reports that high-ranking military officers were doing their best to protect the navy officers and managed to make sure that their arrest received no mention in the press.[146]

## Vietnamese Army Syndicates

While the Vietnamese navy was involved in drug importing, pro-Thieu elements of the Vietnamese army managed much of the distribution and sale of heroin to GIs inside South Vietnam. Rather than risk exposure by having their own officers handle the more vulnerable aspects of the operation, high-ranking ARVN commanders generally preferred to work with Cholon's Chinese syndicates. Thus, once bulk heroin shipments were smuggled into the country—either by the military itself or by Chinese protected by the military—they were usually turned over to Cholon syndicates for packaging and shipment. From Cholon, Chinese and Vietnamese couriers fanned out across the country, delivering multi-kilo lots of heroin to military commanders from the Delta to the DMZ. In three of the four military zones, the local distribution was supervised and protected by high-ranking army officers.[147] In the Mekong Delta (IV Corps) local sales were controlled by colonels loyal to General Quang; in the south central part of the country (II Corps) heroin distribution became a subject of controversy between two feuding generals loyal to President Thieu, the former II Corps commander General Lu Lan and the present commander General Ngu Dzu;[148] and in northernmost I Corps the traffic was directed by deputies of the corps commander.[149] In June 1971 the chief U.S. police adviser filed a memorandum on Dzu's involvement in the heroin trade that described the relationship between Cholon's Chinese racketeers and Vietnamese generals:[150]

HEADQUARTERS
UNITED STATES MILITARY COMMAND, VIETNAM
APO SAN FRANCISCO 96222
Office of the Assistant Chief of Staff, CORDS
MACCORDS-PS                                            10 June 1971

MEMORANDUM FOR RECORD

SUBJECT: Alleged Trafficking in Heroin (U)

1. A confidential source has advised this Directorate that the father of General Dzu, MR 2 Commanding General, is trafficking in heroin with Mr. Chanh, an ethnic Chinese from Cholon. (Other identification not available.)

2. General Dzu's father lives in Qui Nhon. Mr. Chanh makes regular trips to Qui Nhon from Saigon usually via Air Vietnam, but sometimes by General Dzu's private aircraft. Mr. Chanh either travels to Qui Nhon alone, or with other ethnic Chinese. Upon his arrival at the Qui Nhon Airport he is met by an escort normally composed of MSS and/or QC's [military police]; Mr. Chanh is then allegedly escorted to General Dzu's father, where he turns over kilogram quantities of heroin for U.S. currency. Mr. Chanh usually spends several days in Qui Nhon, and stays at the Hoa Binh Hotel, Gia Long Street, Qui Nhon. When Chanh returns to Saigon he is allegedly also given an escort from TSN Airport.

3. The National Police in Qui Nhon, especially those police assigned to the airport, are reportedly aware of the activity between General Dzu's father and Mr. Chanh, but are afraid to either report or investigate these alleged violations fearing that they will only be made the scapegoat should they act.

4. Mr. Chanh (AKA: Red Nose) is an ethnic Chinese from Cholon about 40 years of age.

[signed] Michael G. McCann, Director
Public Safety Directorate
CORDS

After bulk shipments of heroin were delivered to cities or ARVN bases near U.S. installations it was sold to GIs through a network of civilian pushers (barracks' maids, street vendors, pimps, and street urchins) or by low-ranking ARVN officers. In Saigon and surrounding II Corps most of the heroin marketing was managed by ordinary civilian networks, but as GI addicts moved away from the capital to the isolated firebases along the Laotian border and the DMZ, the ARVN pushers became more and more predominant. "How do we get the stuff?" said one GI stationed at a desolate firebase near the DMZ, "just go over to the fence and rap with an ARVN. If he's got it you can make a purchase."[151] Even at Long Binh, the massive U.S. army installation on the outskirts of Saigon, Vietnamese officers worked as pushers. As one GI addict based at Long Binh put it, "You can always get some from an ARVN; not a Pfc., but the officers. I've gotten it from as high as Captain."[152]

## Lower House Heroin Junkets

Another avenue of the narcotics traffic that proved embarrassing to President Thieu was the smuggling operations by pro-Thieu members of the National Assembly's lower house. The ineptness of many of these politicians turned out to be more of a liability than an asset. At one point in Thieu's rivalry with Premier Khiem, the ease with which these politician smugglers could be exposed created political problems for the Thieu apparatus. While only hints of the pro-Thieu faction's massive smuggling operation leaked out of the security-conscious military, the *opéra bouffe* antics of lower house representatives rated headlines around the world. Between September 1970 and March 1971 no less than seven representatives returning from foreign study tours were caught trying to smuggle everything from gold and heroin to *Playboy* calendars and brassieres into South Vietnam.[153] Foreign observers were dismayed by the smuggling arrests, but the Vietnamese public simply regarded them as a part of the lower house's four-year history of bribery, corruption, and scandal.[154]

The outrageous behavior of its representatives on the floor of the house, where vulgar insults of every order were openly traded, cost the lower house respect among the South Vietnamese peasants. Votes on crucial issues were sold to the highest bidder, and the Saigon press kept a running tally of the going price. In addition to regular monthly stipends and special New Year's bonuses of $350,[155] pro-Thieu representatives earned up to $1,800 apiece for voting the right way on crucial government measures.[156] In fact, even staunch opposition members voted the right way to earn extra cash when defeat for their side looked inevitable.[157]

In the lower house, Thieu relied on members of the Independence Bloc to do the bargaining and make the payments, rather than negotiating personally. Consisting almost entirely of North Vietnamese Catholic refugees, this bloc had maintained a militantly anti-Communist position since it was organized in 1967. Although the bloc was nominally independent, its leader, Nguyen Quang Luyen, met with Thieu soon after it was formed and "verbally agreed" to support the president in exchange for unspecified favors.[158] The bloc had influence far beyond its numerical strength, and all its members occupied key positions as committee heads, fund-raisers, or whips. With only nineteen members, the Independence Bloc controlled six out of the lower house's sixteen committee chairmanships in 1973.[159] During the debates over the 1971 election law, for example, it was an Independence Bloc member, Pham Huu Giao, who floor-managed the passage of article 10. This controversial clause required a minimum of forty congressional signatures on every nominating petition for the upcoming presidential election and made it possible for President Thieu to eliminate Ky from the running. Early in the debates, Giao reportedly purchased a few hill tribe votes for as little as $350 apiece and most of the Cambodian minority's ballots for a mere $700 each.[160] However, in the three days of intense bargaining preceding the final balloting, the price jumped from $1,000 to $1,800 for the final handful that completed the proposal's winning tally of seventy-five votes.[161]

Loyalty to Thieu seemed to have its benefits. No opposition members were ever even implicated in a serious smuggling case. All lower house representatives implicated in the heroin and gold traffic were either present or past members of the Independence Bloc. The reason for this is simple; opposition deputies often lacked the necessary capital to finance such trips and were not guaranteed "courtesy of the port" when they returned. However, pro-government deputies who were bankrolled by an official travel grant or savings from months of voting the right way were able to take advantage of their four exit visas per year, a privilege guaranteed all deputies for foreign travel during the legislative holidays. The result was a burst of foreign junketeering on the part of pro-government deputies. In 1969–1970 representatives purchased $821,000 worth of foreign currency for their travels. One prominent pro-government representative was abroad for 119 days in 1969, 98 days in 1970, and 75 days during the first three months of 1971.[162]

Although most pro-government deputies usually returned with some form of contraband or undeclared dutiable item, they passed through customs without being checked.[163] Even if a representative was caught, customs officers merely imposed a "fine" and allowed the illegal items to pass through. For example, in August and December 1970 Vietnamese customs officers at Tan Son Nhut airport discovered gold and dutiable goods in the luggage of Representative Giao. The legislator paid a nominal fine, and the whole matter was hushed up until it was revealed during the height of the smuggling controversy several months later.[164]

The tempo of parliamentary smuggling seemed to be intensified by the eruption of the GI heroin epidemic and the liberalization of the assembly's travel laws. In December 1970 a group of pro-Thieu deputies who controlled the lower house administrative office decided to allow representatives *four* foreign trips each year instead of two.[165] When the annual January–March legislative holiday started a few weeks later, one Saigon daily reported that a record 140 out of the National Assembly's 190 members would soon be going abroad.[166]

The smuggling bonanza that followed resulted in three sensational customs seizures within ten days in March 1971 as the legislators returned to prepare for the upcoming session of the National Assembly.

The first deputy implicated was Vo Van Mau, a Catholic refugee from North Vietnam and a member of the pro-Thieu Independence Bloc. During Air Vietnam's regular Vientiane-Saigon flight on March 10, a Chinese smuggler transferred a suitcase to one of the stewardesses, Mrs. Nguyen Ngoc Qui.[167] But instead of being waved through customs at Tan Son Nhut, as Air Vietnam stewardesses usually were, Mrs. Qui was subjected to a thorough search, which turned up 9.6 kilos of Laos's leading export—Double U-O Globe heroin—and a letter addressed to Representative Vo Van Mau. Showing unusual insensitivity to Mau's high official status, officers of customs' Fraud Repression Division followed up the lead. A search of Mau's offices turned up the Chinese smuggler's identity card.[168] Although a spokesman for Premier Khiem's office later announced that this seizure was being thoroughly investigated "because it appears to implicate directly" a deputy,[169] Mau was never officially charged and quietly faded from view when he failed to stand for reelection several months later.

On March 17 another pro-Thieu representative, Pham Chi Thien, landed at Tan Son Nhut Airport on the 4:30 P.M. flight from Bangkok. Much to Representative Thien's surprise, a customs officer insisted on giving his luggage a thorough search and opened a gift-wrapped box he found in the legislator's suitcase, which turned out to contain 4 kilos of

Double U-O Globe heroin.[170] Announcing his resignation from the lower house a week later, Thien denied that he was "actually" a smuggler and claimed that he had simply agreed to carry a package to Saigon as a favor to "a soft-spoken lady I met in Vientiane."[171] He admitted to accepting money for carrying the package but denied any knowledge of its contents.[172]

While the charges against Vo Van Mau and Pham Chi Thien, both rather unimportant legislators, caused a certain dismay, the arrest of a third pro-Thieu legislator, Nguyen Quang Luyen, for gold smuggling was a major scandal. Luyen was second deputy chairman of the lower house, chairman of the Asian Parliamentary Union, and chairman of the pro-Thieu Independence Bloc from 1967 to 1970. As he was boarding a flight for Saigon at the Bangkok airport on March 18, Thai customs searched his luggage and discovered 15 kilos of pure gold, worth about $26,000 on Saigon's black market.[173] However, the Vietnamese embassy intervened and secured his immediate release after another legislator traveling with Luyen raced into downtown Bangkok to plead for assistance.[174]

Four days later one Saigon newspaper reported that Thai customs had suspected Luyen of being part of an international smuggling ring for several years but had been maintaining a discreet surveillance because of the sensitive nature of Thai-Vietnamese relations. The 15 kilos seized in Luyen's luggage were reportedly part of a larger shipment of 90 kilos of gold (worth $158,000 on the Saigon black market) being smuggled piecemeal into Saigon by this ring.[175] Reliable sources inside the lower house reported that other members of the Independence Bloc had helped finance this shipment.

By all accounts, lower house representatives had been smuggling narcotics, gold, and dutiable goods into South Vietnam for more than three years without such sensational exposés. Arrests were rare, and when they occurred the legislator almost always settled the matter quietly by paying a "fine." Why had Vietnamese customs officials suddenly become so aggressive, or, more pointedly, why was the Thieu faction suddenly subjected to the humiliating indignity of having three of its staunchest legislative supporters implicated in contraband smuggling within ten days?

The answer, as usual in South Vietnam, was political. Ironically, President Thieu's gadfly was his own handpicked prime minister, Tran Thien Khiem.

## The Khiem Apparatus

While the Independence Bloc enjoyed President Thieu's political protection, unfortunately for these three smugglers the customs service was controlled by Prime Minister Khiem's apparatus. After four years of political exile in Taiwan and the United States, Khiem had returned to Vietnam in May 1968 and was appointed minister of the interior in Thieu's administration. Khiem, probably the most aggressive of Vietnam's military leaders, proceeded to build up a power base of his own, becoming prime minister in 1969. Although Khiem had a history of betraying his allies when it suited his purposes, Thieu had been locked in an underground war with Vice-President Ky and probably appointed Khiem because he needed his talents as a political infighter.[176] First as minister of the interior and later as concurrent prime minister, Khiem appointed his relatives to lucrative offices in the civil administration and began building an increasingly independent political organization. In June 1968 he appointed his brother-in-law mayor of Saigon. He used his growing political influence to have his younger brother Tran Thien Khoi appointed chief of customs' Fraud Repression Division (the enforcement arm), another brother made director of Saigon Port, and his cousin appointed deputy governor-general of Saigon. Following his promotion to prime minister in 1969, Khiem was able to appoint one of his wife's relatives to the position of director-general of the national police.

One of the most important men in Khiem's apparatus was his brother Tran Thien Khoi. Soon after U.S. customs advisers began working at Tan Son Nhut airport in 1968, they filed detailed reports on the abysmal conditions and urged their South Vietnamese counterparts to crack down. However, as one U.S. official put it, "They were just beginning to clean it up when Khiem's brother arrived, and then it all went right out the window."[177] As chief of the Fraud Repression Division, Khoi relegated much of the dirty work to his deputy chief, and together the two men brought any effective enforcement work to a halt.[178] Khoi's partner was vividly described in a 1971 U.S. provost marshal's report:

> He has an opium habit that costs approximately 10,000 piasters a day [$35] and visits a local opium den on a predictable schedule. He was charged with serious irregularities approximately two years ago but by payoffs and political influence, managed to have the charges dropped. When he took up his present position he was known to be nearly destitute, but is now wealthy and supporting two or three wives.[179]

The report described Khoi himself as "a principal in the opium traffic" who had sabotaged efforts to set up a narcotics squad within the Fraud Repression Division.[180] Under Khoi's leadership, gold and opium smuggling at Tan Son Nhut became so blatant that in February 1971 a U.S. customs adviser reported that "after three years of these meetings

5. Prime Minister Tran Thien Khiem's Family
   Political Power Structure, 1970–1971

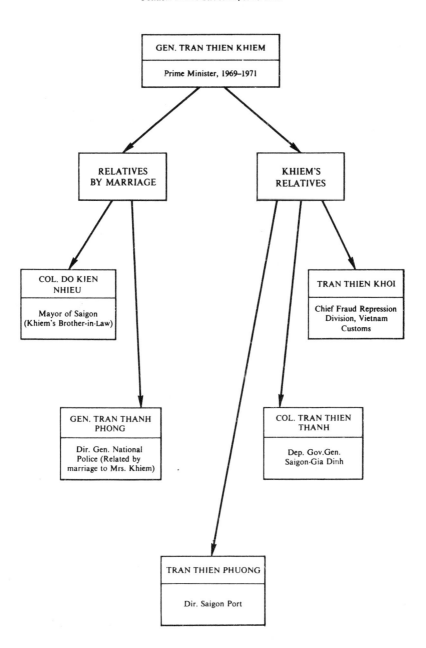

and countless directives being issued at all levels, the Customs operation at the airport has . . . reached a point to where the Customs personnel of Vietnam are little more than lackeys to the smugglers."[181] The report went on to describe the partnership between customs officials and a group of professional smugglers who seemed to run the airport:

> Actually, the Customs Officers seem extremely anxious to please these smugglers and not only escort them past the examination counters but even accompany them out to the waiting taxis. This lends an air of legitimacy to the transaction so that there could be no interference on the part of an over zealous Customs Officer or Policeman who might be new on the job and not yet know what is expected of him.[182]

The most important smuggler at Tan Son Nhut airport was a woman with impressive political connections:

> One of the biggest problems at the airport since the Advisors first arrived there and the subject of one of the first reports is Mrs. Chin, or Ba Chin or Chin Map which in Vietnamese is literally translated as "Fat Nine." This description fits her well as she is stout enough to be easily identified in any group. . . . This person heads a ring of 10 or 12 women who are present at every arrival of every aircraft from Laos and Singapore and these women are the recipients of most of the cargo that arrives on these flights as unaccompanied baggage. . . . When Mrs. Chin leaves the Customs area, she is like a mother duck with her brood as she leads the procession and is obediently followed by 8 to 10 porters who are carrying her goods to be loaded into the waiting taxis. . . .
>
> I recall an occasion . . . in July 1968 when an aircraft arrived from Laos. . . . I expressed an interest in the same type of Chinese medicine that this woman had received and already left with. One of the newer Customs officers opened up one of the packages and it was found to contain not medicine but thin strips of gold. . . . This incident was brought to the attention of the Director General but the Chief of Zone 2 . . . said that I was only guessing and that I could not accuse Mrs. Chin of any wrong doing. I bring this out to show that *this woman is protected by every level in the GVN Customs Service.* [Emphasis added.][183]

Although almost every functionary in the customs service received payoffs from the smugglers, U.S. customs advisers believed that Khoi's job was the most profitable. While most division chiefs received payoffs only from their immediate underlings, his enforcement powers enabled him to receive kickbacks from every division of the customs service.

Since even minor officials such as the chief collections officer at Tan Son Nhut cargo warehouse kicked back $22,000 a month to his superiors, Khoi's income was substantial.[184]

In early 1971 U.S. customs advisers mounted a "strenuous effort" to have the deputy chief transferred, but Khoi was adept at protecting his associate. In March American officials in Vientiane learned that Representative Pham Chi Thien would be boarding a flight for Saigon carrying 4 kilos of heroin and relayed the information to Saigon. When U.S. customs advisers asked the Fraud Repression Division to make the arrest (U.S. customs officials had no right to make arrests), Chief Khoi entrusted the seizure to his opium-smoking assistant. This official was later decorated for this "accomplishment," and U.S. customs advisers, who were still trying to get him fired, or at least transferred, had to attend a banquet in his honor.[185]

Frustrated by months of inaction by the U.S. mission and duplicity from the Vietnamese, members of the U.S. customs advisory team evidently decided to take their case to the American public. Copies of the unflattering customs advisory reports quoted earlier were leaked to the press and became the basis of an article that appeared on the front page of *The New York Times* on April 22, 1971, under the headline SAIGON AIRPORT A SMUGGLER'S PARADISE.[186]

The American response was immediate. Washington dispatched more customs advisers for duty at Tan Son Nhut, and the U.S. embassy finally demanded action from the Thieu regime. Initially, however, the Saigon government was cool to the embassy's demands for a cleanup of the Fraud Repression Division. It was not until the smuggling became a political issue between the Khiem and Thieu factions that the Vietnamese showed any interest in dealing with the problem.

## The Thieu-Khiem Struggle

When the political dividends of the Fraud Repression Division were added to Khiem's other sources of power, such as the police and the Saigon port authority, the result was the strength necessary to form an independent political faction. Prime Minister Khiem's reemergence as a political power in his own right seems to have created tensions inside the Thieu organization and produced heated political infighting.

As relations between the Thieu and Khiem factions soured, the smuggling issue became just another weapon to use against the their rivals. As one frank U.S. embassy official in Saigon put it, "Our role essentially ends up allowing one faction to use U.S. pressure to force the other faction out of business. And," he added, "the way these guys jump on each other so gleefully makes it look like they are really eager to cut themselves in on . . . an enormously lucrative traffic."[187]

When the Air Vietnam stewardess was arrested with 9.6 kilos of heroin, it was Prime Minister Khiem's office that issued an official statement confirming rumors that a pro-Thieu representative was involved.[188] Furthermore, reliable lower house sources claim that the aggressiveness shown by Khoi's Fraud Repression Division in investigating the case was politically motivated. Thieu later retaliated. According to one Saigon press report, members of Khiem's cabinet "protested . . . President Thieu's remark that the smuggling involved many high ranking officials who smuggled through the Tan Son Nhut Airport where one of the Prime Minister's brothers was in control."[189] Despite the cabinet's protest, the director-general of customs was dismissed, and in late June Tran Thien Khoi left for a short vacation in Paris. On his return several weeks later, he was transferred to a less lucrative post in the Cholon Customs House.[190] His opium-smoking assistant was likewise transferred and wound up in the Customs Library, a dumping ground for those in disgrace.[191]

Three months later the director-general of the national police, one of Mrs. Khiem's relatives, resigned under pressure. The Saigon press reported that the director-general had been involved in the heroin traffic and was being dismissed as part of the antinarcotics campaign. Providing a more credible perspective, one Saigon daily had earlier reported that President Thieu was "taking advantage of the antinarcotics smuggling drive" to force officials out of office and to replace them with his own supporters.[192] The new police director-general was Colonel Nguyen Khac Binh, a nephew of Mrs. Thieu.[193]

Despite all this political infighting over the narcotics traffic, heroin smuggling continued unabated. U.S. customs advisers have pointed out that commercial air flights were only one of several routes used to bring narcotics into South Vietnam. After airport security tightened up, smugglers simply diverted narcotics shipment to other routes, particularly military air bases and commercial shipping.[194] Throughout 1971 unlimited quantities of heroin were available near every U.S. installation in Vietnam, and there was no appreciable rise in price.

## The Mafia Comes to Asia

The flourishing heroin traffic among Vietnam-based GIs was undoubtedly the most important new market for Indochina's drug traffickers, but it was not the only one. As we have already seen, insurmountable problems in the Mediterranean basin had forced the American Mafia and Marseille's Corsican syndicates to look to Southeast Asia for new sources of heroin and morphine base. Faced with the alternative of finding a new source of morphine base or going out of business, the Corsican syndicates turned to their associates in Southeast Asia for help. "There are people who think that once the problem in Turkey is cleaned up, that's the end of the traffic," explained John Warner, chief intelligence analyst for the U.S. Bureau of Narcotics. "But the Corsicans aren't stupid. They saw the handwriting on the wall and began to shift their morphine base sources to Southeast Asia."[195]

The Corsican narcotics syndicates based in Saigon and Vientiane had been supplying European drug factories with Southeast Asian morphine base for several years, and links with Marseille were already well established. During the First Indochina War Corsican gangsters in Marseille and Saigon cooperated closely in smuggling gold, currency, and narcotics between the two ports. In 1962 Corsican gangsters in Saigon reported that Paul Louis Levet, a Bangkok-based syndicate leader, was supplying European heroin laboratories with morphine base from northern Thailand.[196] Furthermore, at least four Corsican charter airlines had played a key role in Southeast Asia's regional opium traffic from 1955 to 1965. Although they were forced out of business when the Laotian generals decided to take a larger share of the profits in 1965, most of the Corsicans had remained in Southeast Asia. They had opened up businesses or taken jobs in Vientiane and Saigon to tide themselves over until something new opened up.[197]

When General Edward G. Lansdale of the CIA returned to Saigon as a special assistant to Ambassador Henry Cabot Lodge in 1965, he quickly learned that his old enemies the Corsicans were still in town. During the fighting between the French 2$^{eme}$ Bureau and the CIA in 1955, the Corsican gangsters had been involved in several attempts on Lansdale's life. "So I wouldn't have to look behind my back every time I walked down the street," Lansdale explained in a June 1971 interview, "I decided to have a meeting with the Corsican leaders. I told them I wasn't interested in doing any criminal investigations; I wasn't in Vietnam for that. And they agreed to leave me alone. We had some kind of a truce." General Lansdale could not recall much of what transpired at that meeting. He remembered that a French-Vietnamese named Hélène took an active role in the proceedings, that the affair was amicable enough, but not much else. Lansdale later learned that the Corsicans were still heavily involved in the narcotics traffic, but since this was not his responsibility he took no action.[198]

Most of what Lansdale knew about the Corsicans came from his old friend Lieutenant Colonel Lucien Conein, the CIA agent who had helped engineer Diem's overthrow in 1963. As a former OSS liaison officer with the French Resistance during World War II, Conein had some experiences in common with many of Saigon's Corsican gangsters. During his long tours of duty in Saigon, Conein spent much of his time in Corsican-owned bars and restaurants and was close to many of

Saigon's most important underworld figures. When Conein left Vietnam several years later, the Corsicans presented him with a heavy gold medallion embossed with the Napoleonic eagle and the Corsican crest. Engraved on the back of it is *Per Tu Amicu Conein* (For your friendship, Conein). Conein proudly explained that this medallian was worn by powerful Corsican syndicate leaders around the world and served as an identification badge for secret meetings, narcotics drops, and the like.[199]

Through his friendship with the Corsicans, Conein gained a respect for them. "The Corsicans are smarter, tougher, and better organized than the Sicilians," he said. "They are absolutely ruthless and are the equal of anything we know about the Sicilians, but they hide their internal fighting better." Conein also learned that many Saigon syndicate leaders had relatives in the Marseille underworld. These family relations played an important role in the international drug traffic, Conein felt, because much of the morphine base used in Marseille's heroin laboratories came from Saigon. Corsican smugglers in Saigon purchased morphine base through Corsican contacts in Vientiane and shipped it on French merchant vessels to relatives and friends in Marseille, where it was processed into heroin.[200] "From what I know of them," said Concin, "it will be absolutely impossible to cut off the dope traffic. You can cut it down, but you can never stop it, unless you can get to the growers in the hills."[201]

This pessimism may explain why Conein and Lansdale did not pass on the information they had to the U.S. Bureau of Narcotics. It is unfortunate that General Lansdale decided to arrange "some kind of a truce" with the Corsicans during the very period when Marseille's heroin laboratories were probably beginning the changeover from Turkish to Southeast Asian morphine base. In a mid-1971 interview, Conein said that power brokers in Premier Ky's apparatus contacted the leaders of Saigon's Corsican underworld in 1965–1966 and agreed to let them start making large drug shipments to Europe in exchange for a fixed percentage of the profits. By October 1969 these shipments had become so important to Marseille's heroin laboratories that, according to Conein, there was a summit meeting of Corsican syndicate bosses from around the world at Saigon's Continental Palace Hotel. Syndicate leaders from Marseille, Bangkok, Vientiane, and Phnom Penh flew in for the meeting, when they discussed a wide range of international rackets but probably focused on reorganizing the narcotics traffic.[202] According to one well-informed U.S. diplomat in Saigon, the U.S. Embassy had a reliable Corsican informant who claimed that similar meetings were also held in 1968 and 1970 at the Continental Palace. Most significantly, American Mafia boss Santo Trafficante, Jr., visited Saigon in 1968 and was believed to have contacted Corsican syndicate leaders there. Vietnamese police officials reported that the owner of the Continental Palace was Philippe Franchini, the heir of Mathieu Franchini, the reputed organizer of currency- and opium-smuggling rackets between Saigon and Marseille during the First Indochina War. Police officials also pointed out that one of Ky's strongest supporters in the air force, Transport Division Commander Colonel Phan Phung Tien, was close to many Corsican gangsters and was implicated in the smuggling of drugs between Laos and Vietnam.

From 1965 to 1967 Lansdale's Senior Liaison Office worked closely with Premier Ky's administration, and the general himself was identified as one of the young premier's stronger supporters among U.S. mission personnel.[203] One can only wonder whether Conein's and Lansdale's willingness to grant the Corsicans a "truce" and overlook their growing involvement in the American heroin traffic might not have been motivated by political considerations, that is, their fear of embarrassing Premier Ky.

Just as most of the Corsican gangsters who were active in Saigon and Vientiane in 1973 had come to Indochina for the first time as camp followers of the French Expeditionary Corps in the late 1940s, the American Mafia followed the U.S. army to Vietnam in 1965. Like any group of investors, the Mafia was looking for new financial frontiers, and when the Vietnam war began to heat up, some of its more entrepreneurial young members were bankrolled by the organization and left for Saigon. Attracted to Vietnam by lucrative construction and service contracts, the mafiosi concentrated on ordinary graft and kickbacks at first but later branched out into narcotics smuggling as they built up their contacts in Hong Kong and Indochina.

Probably the most important of these pioneers was Frank Carmen Furci, a young mafioso from Tampa, Florida. Although any ordinary businessman would try to hide this kind of family background from his associates, Furci found that it impressed the corrupt sergeants, shady profiteers, and Corsican gangsters who were his friends and associates in Saigon. He told them all proudly, "My father is the Mafia boss of Tampa, Florida."[204] (Actually, Frank's father, Dominick Furci, was only a middle-ranking lieutenant in the powerful Florida-based family headed by Santo Trafficante, Jr., the Mafia boss of Tampa.[205]) Furci arrived in Vietnam in 1965 with good financial backing and soon became a key figure in the systematic graft and corruption that began to plague U.S. military clubs in Vietnam as hundreds of thousands of GIs poured into the war zone.[206] A lengthy U.S. Senate investigation later exposed the network of graft, bribes, and kickbacks that Furci and his fellow profiteers employed to cheat military clubs and their GI customers out of millions of dollars.

The clubs were managed by senior NCOs, usually sergeant majors, who had made the army their career and were considered dedicated, trustworthy men. While the officers were preoccupied with running a war, the sergeants were left with responsibility for managing one of the largest restaurant and nightclub chains in the world—ordering refrigerators, hiring bands, selecting liquor brands, and negotiating orders for everything from slot machines to peanuts. Accounting systems were shoddy, and the entire system was vulnerable to well-organized graft. Seven sergeants who had served together in the Twenty-fourth Infantry Division at Augsburg, Germany during the early 1960s had discovered this weakness and exploited it, stealing up to $40,000 a month from NCO clubs.[207]

In 1965 these seven sergeants started showing up in Vietnam as mess custodians and club managers at the First Infantry Division, the Americal Division, and U.S. army headquarters at Long Binh.[208] Most important of all, the group's ringleader, Sergeant William O. Wooldridge, was appointed sergeant major of the army in July 1966. As the army's highest-ranking enlisted man, he served directly under the army chief of staff at the Pentagon, where he was in an ideal position to manipulate personnel transfers and cover up the group's activities.[209]

At the apex of the system were the civilian entrepreneurs—Frank Furci and his competitor William J. Crum—who worked as agents for a host of American companies and paid the sergeants lavish kickbacks on huge Army purchase orders for kitchen equipment, snacks, and liquor.

Furci was also heavily involved in the currency black market. A U.S. Senate investigation of illegal currency manipulations in Vietnam later showed that he had exchanged $99,200 through a single unauthorized money changer at the black market rate of 300 or 400 piasters to the dollar, considerably more than the official rate of 118 piasters.[210]

Unfortunately for Furci, Crum was also aware of these illegal transactions, and he decided to use this knowledge to force Furci out of business. Furci was simply outmaneuvered by the crippled, half-blind William Crum, an old China hand who had made a profit on almost every war in Asia since 1941. Attracted by the economic potential of the growing Southeast Asia conflict, Crum came out of his retirement in Hong Kong and moved to Saigon in 1962.[211]

While the massive U.S. military buildup in 1965 had attracted other commercial agents, Crum seemed particularly resentful of Furci, whose competing line of liquor brands, slot machines, and kitchen equipment had "stolen" $2.5 million worth of his business.[212] Crum passed on information about Furci's illegal currency transactions to the Fraud Repression Division of the Vietnamese customs service through a U.S. army general whom Crum was paying $1,000 a month for protection.[213]

Vietnamese customs raided Furci's offices in July 1967, found evidence to support the accusations, and later fined him $45,000.[214] Unable to pay such a large fine, Furci left Saigon. Crum later bragged that he had "paid for" the raid that had eliminated his competitor.[215]

Furci moved to Hong Kong and in August 1967 opened a restaurant named the San Francisco Steak House with nominal capital of $100,000.[216] More important, Furci was instrumental in the formation of Maradem Ltd., a company that the Augsburg sergeants who managed NCO clubs in Vietnam used to increase illegal profits from the military clubs. Although Furci's name did not appear on any of the incorporation papers, it seems that he was the silent partner in the Mafia sense of the term.[217]

Maradem Ltd. was not a wholesale supplier or retail outlet, but a broker that used its control over NCO clubs and base mess halls to force legitimate wholesalers to pay a fixed percentage of their profits to do business.[218] Maradem's competitors were gradually "squeezed out" of business, and in its first year of operation the company did $1,210,000 worth of business with NCO clubs in Vietnam.[219]

By 1968 Frank Furci had gained three years' experience in the shadow world of Hong Kong and Indochina; he was friendly with powerful Corsican syndicate leaders in Saigon and had the opportunity to form similar relationships with Chiu chau bosses in Hong Kong.[220] Thus, it is not too surprising that the boss himself, Santo Trafficante, Jr., did Furci the honor of visiting him in Hong Kong in 1968. Accompanied by Frank's father, Dominick Furci, Trafficante was questioned by Hong Kong authorities regarding the purpose of his visit, and according to a U.S. Senate investigation, he explained that "they were traveling around the world together at the time. They stopped to visit Furci, Frank Furci in Hong Kong and to visit his restaurant."[221] After a long stopover, Trafficante proceeded to Saigon,[222] where, according to U.S. embassy sources, he met with some prominent Corsican gangsters.[223] Trafficante was not the first of Lansky's chief lieutenants to visit Hong Kong. In April 1965 John Pullman, Lansky's courier and financial expert, paid an extended visit to Hong Kong, where he reportedly investigated the narcotics and gambling rackets.[224]

Although the few Mafia watchers who were aware of Trafficante's journey to Asia were mystified by it, there is reason to believe that it was a response to the crisis in the Mediterranean drug traffic and an attempt to secure new sources of heroin for Mafia distributors inside the United States. With almost 70 percent of the world's illicit opium supply in the Golden Triangle, skilled heroin chemists in Hong Kong, and entrenched Corsican syndicates in Indochina, Southeast Asia was a logical alternative.

Soon after Trafficante's visit to Hong Kong, a Filipino courier ring started delivering Hong Kong heroin to Mafia distributors in the United States. In 1970 U.S. narcotics agents arrested many of these couriers. Subsequent interrogation revealed that the ring had successfully smuggled 1,000 kilos of pure heroin into the United States—the equivalent of 10 to 20 percent of America's annual consumption.

U.S. Bureau of Narcotics intelligence reports in the early 1970s indicated that another courier ring was bringing Hong Kong heroin into the United States through the Caribbean, Trafficante's territory. From Hong Kong heroin was usually flown to Chile on regular flights and then smuggled across the border into Paraguay in light private aircraft.[225] In the late 1960s Paraguay became the major transit point for heroin entering the United States from Latin America; both Hong Kong and Southeast Asian heroin smuggled across the Pacific into Chile and European heroin shipped across the Atlantic into Argentina were brought to Paraguay before being forwarded to the United States. Argentina and Paraguay were popular refuges for Marseille gangsters wanted in France for serious crimes. The most prominent of these was Auguste Joseph Ricort, a Marseille-born gangster who had worked with the Gestapo during World War II. Using a variety of means ranging from private aircraft to stuffed artifacts, Ricort was believed to have smuggled some $2.5 billion worth of heroin into the United States from Argentina and Paraguay from 1968 to 1973.[226] Although law enforcement officials always assumed that Ricort and his associates were being supplied from Marseille, reports of shipments from Hong Kong and Southeast Asia to Paraguay issued in 1972 raised the possibility that their sources may have been shifting to Asia.[227]

## The Politics of Complicity

In the face of the twin liabilities of the Vietnam drug problem—the heroin epidemic among GIs and the growing exports to the United States—what was the response from American diplomatic and military officials in Vietnam? On the whole, their reaction was a mix of embarrassment and apathy. Embarrassment, because they were all aware to some degree, even though they would not admit it, that elements of the Vietnamese government they had been defending were pushing heroin to American GIs. Apathy, because most of them felt that anybody who used heroin deserved what he got. Almost all U.S. officials expressed concern whenever the heroin problem was mentioned, but most did not seem to care. They were in Vietnam to beat the Communists and defend democracy; the fact that some of democracy's protégés were pushing heroin was something they did not want to think about.

In the early years of the Diem administration, American pronouncements about U.S. goals in Vietnam had an almost innocent quality. Diem was seen as a middle path between the Viet Minh's Communist dictatorship on the left and the corrupt Binh Xuyen pirates on the right. When Diem refused to fire his corrupt brother, who had revived the endemic corruption so characteristic of the Binh Xuyen, the U.S. mission helped engineer Diem's downfall in the hope that an honest, efficient government would emerge from the confusion. But as Vietnam's politics plunged into chaos and Saigon's security reached the critical level, the U.S. mission worked for the return of another "strong man."

The answer to the American dilemma was the Thieu-Ky administration. Although Thieu and Ky devoted too much of their time to fighting each other, the Americans generally were pleased with their ability to govern with a firm, if despotic, hand. Having learned that this type of authoritarian government was the most compatible with American interests, U.S. officials were unwilling to protest when the close associates of both leaders were involved in systematic corruption, including the narcotics traffic. As long as the drug trade was directed exclusively at Chinese and Vietnamese opium smokers, U.S. congressional complaints about corruption were muted. When in 1968 Senator Albert Gruening accused Air Vice-Marshal Ky of smuggling opium, the U.S. embassy in Saigon issued a firm, if inaccurate, denial, and the matter was forgotten.[228] But when South Vietnam's narcotics syndicates started cultivating the GI heroin market, the problem was not dismissed so easily. After NBC's Saigon correspondent accused President Thieu's chief adviser, General Quang, of being "the biggest pusher" of heroin to GIs in Vietnam,[229] the U.S. embassy "filed a top level report to Washington saying *it can find no evidence* to support recent charges that President Nguyen Van Thieu and Vice-President Nguyen Cao Ky were involved in or profiting from the drug trade [emphasis added]." Simultaneously, U.S. officials defended Thieu and Ky publicly by leaking the embassy report to members of the Saigon press corps in an off-the-record briefing.[230]

According to a U.S. embassy official assigned to the drug problem, the U.S. mission could "find no evidence" because it studiously avoided looking for any. It was an unwritten rule among embassy officials that nobody could mention the names of high-ranking Vietnamese during discussions of the heroin traffic. The CIA avoided gathering information on high-level involvement and even in its closed-door sessions with high embassy officials discussed only minor pushers and addicts.

The U.S. mission's handling of the accusations concerning General Ngo Dzu's involvement in the heroin trade was another case in point. Beginning in January 1971 the U.S. army's Criminal Investigation

Division (CID) began gathering detailed information on Dzu's involvement in GI heroin traffic. Although these reports were sent to the U.S. embassy through the proper channels, the U.S. mission did nothing.[231] When U.S. Representative Robert H. Steele told a congressional subcommittee in July 1971 that "U.S. military authorities have provided Ambassador Bunker with hard intelligence that one of the chief traffickers is Gen. Ngo Dzu, the commander of II Corps,"[232] the U.S. mission did its best to discredit the congressman. Rather than criticizing Dzu for pushing heroin, the senior U.S. adviser for II Corps declared publicly, "There is no information available to me that in any shape, manner or fashion would substantiate the charges Congressman Steele has made."[233] In light of the CID report quoted earlier, the U.S. mission apparently decided to protect the Thieu regime from investigation of its involvement in the heroin trade.

While the U.S. embassy did its best to shield the Thieu regime from criticism, the Nixon administration and the U.S. military command tried to defuse public concern over the GI heroin epidemic by minimizing the extent of the problem. The military offered two main arguments to justify its official optimism: (1) the definitive urinalysis test administered to every Vietnam GI just before he returned to the United States showed that no more than 5.5 percent of all army personnel in Vietnam were heroin users; (2) since only 8.0 percent of the GI addicts in Vietnam injected, or "mainlined," the great majority who smoked or snorted heroin were not seriously addicted and would have no problem kicking the habit once they returned home.[234]

Unfortunately, the army's first supposition was not true. On June 22, 1971, the U.S. military command ordered every GI leaving Vietnam to submit to a sophisticated test that could detect significant amounts of morphine in the body. Any GI who tested positive was confined to a special detoxification center and could not be allowed to return home until he had "dried out" and could pass the test. From the very first, GIs started devising ingenious ways of beating the system. Supervision of the testing centers had been lax, and many serious addicts passed by bringing a buddy's "clean" urine to the test and substituting it for their own.[235] Since the urinalysis could detect morphine in the body only if the addict had used heroin within the previous four or five days, many addicts dried themselves out voluntarily before taking the test.[236] Indeed, army nurses saw addicts who were in the midst of withdrawal pass the test.[237] Contrary to popular myth of the time, addicts could control their intake to some extent, and often alternated "sprees" with brief periods of abstinence lasting up to a week, especially the last few days before payday.[238]

Almost every American soldier in Vietnam knew the exact date of his scheduled return to the "world," and most kept a running countdown, which often included hours and minutes as the time got shorter. Every GI's DEROS (Date of Expected Return from Overseas) had a historic, even religious quality about it, and the thought of having to stay an extra week, or even a few days more was absolutely intolerable. Most GI addicts accepted the pain of voluntary withdrawal in order to pass the test and get on their scheduled flight. Those who were too weak to make it on their own volunteered for the base "amnesty" program. Many army physicians reported a disproportionately high percentage of patients with only a few weeks left in their tours.[239] When one GI was asked why he and his buddies had temporarily given up heroin, he replied, "The magic word, the absolute magic word, is DEROS."[240] The short, painful detoxification simply flushed the morphine out of the system but in no way ended the psychological craving for heroin. When these men returned home they were still, in a certain sense, "addicts".

The army's suggestion that addicts who smoked heroin in Vietnam were somehow less addicted than those who "mainlined" back in the United States was absurd. While it was true that injection was more potent than smoking, Vietnamese heroin was so pure (90 to 98 percent pure compared to 2 to 10 percent pure in the United States at the time) that smoking one vial of Vietnamese heroin was equivalent to five or six injections of the adulterated heroin available in the United States.[241] Most GI addicts in Vietnam had habits that would cost them more than $200 a day back in the United States.

The army made this claim because it was not willing to admit the impact of GI addiction in Vietnam on the worsening heroin crisis back in the United States. Despite President Nixon's promise that "all our servicemen must be accorded the right to rehabilitation," the U.S. military command in Vietnam was discharging between one thousand and two thousand GI addicts a month. These were men who were declared "of negligible value to the United States Army" after failing the urinalysis test twice. Although every GI in Vietnam had been guaranteed the right to declare himself an addict and volunteer for treatment, the army's leniency did not often extend to two-time losers. Once a commanding officer decided that a two-time loser was a hopeless case, the GI addict was flown back to the United States and discharged almost immediately.[242]

Virtually none of these addicts were given any follow-up treatment. In August 1971 the chairman of the House Subcommittee on Public Health, Representative Paul Rogers, declared that "Veterans Administration hospitals have handled only three referrals out of 12,000 servicemen on heroin. . . . in Vietnam."[243] Left to fend for themselves, many of these men returned to their home towns as confirmed addicts. A large percentage of the returning veterans were middle Americans from communities that had always been free from heroin addiction. Organized crime had never established a foothold in white middle-class communities, and most law enforcement experts considered them immune to heroin. When GI addicts started coming home to middle America, however, drug experts were concerned that they might be carriers of the heroin plague. In June 1971 one specialist said, "Each addict makes at least four more. He cannot bear his habit alone and is sure to seek recruits even if he is not himself the pusher. This is the emergency we now face."[244] Some of these fears were confirmed two years later when a White House task force surveyed Vietnam veterans and found that one-third of those who had tested positive for heroin in Saigon were continuing their addiction at home.[245]

In Vietnam heroin use was so commonplace among GIs that the traditional middle-class American antipathy toward the drug was broken. A U.S. army survey administered to 1,000 army returnees in March 1971 showed that while only 11 percent had used heroin regularly in Vietnam, 22 percent had tried it at least once.[246] Two years later the White House task force showed that 34 percent of the American soldiers in Vietnam had "commonly used" heroin.[247] For these men heroin was just another narcotic like marijuana, pep pills, or alcohol. In Vietnam soldiers handled heroin so frequently—buying it for themselves, picking up some for a buddy on duty, or selling it for profit—that the idea of pushing heroin once they got home seemed natural. "I heard from a few guys who got off it," said one twenty-two-year-old middle American at the Long Binh treatment center. "They said they were still off 'cause it was too expensive, and anyway, they were scared to use the needle. But they said they wanted me to send 'em some scag [heroin] so they could sell it and make some money. You know a jug [vial] over here only costs two dollars, but you can get a hundred dollars for it back in the world."[248] Traveling through Asia on an investigative tour, U.S. Representative John M. Murphy found "numerous examples of the slick GI who gets discharged, goes home, then comes back to set himself up in the drug traffic."[249]

According to U.S. narcotics agents, one of the more important heroin exporters in Thailand was an ex-serviceman, William Henry Jackson, who managed the Five Star Bar in Bangkok, a hangout for black GIs. Working with other ex-servicemen, Jackson recruited active-duty soldiers going home as couriers and used local GIs "to ship heroin to the United States through the army and air force postal system."[250] One U.S. agent who had arrested several of these ex-GI drug dealers said, "Most of these guys say to themselves, 'Just as soon as I get $100,000 for a gas station, home, boat, and car in California I'm going to quit.' Most of them are just regular guys." On April 5, 1971, U.S. customs officials in Fort Monmouth, New Jersey, seized 7.7 kilos of Double U-O Globe heroin in a package mailed from Bangkok, Thailand, through the U.S. military postal system.[251] It had a retail value estimated at $1.75 million. During March and April 1971 U.S. customs seized 248 pieces of mail containing narcotics in the army and air force postal systems.[252]

As the number of American troops in Vietnam rapidly dwindled, there was a natural tendency to forget the Vietnam heroin epidemic. Had not the Nixon administration met an early end with the Watergate scandal, it may have tried to claim the end of the GI heroin problem as one of the more solid accomplishments of its Vietnamization program.

Returning GI addicts came home as carriers of the disease and afflicted their communities with the heroin virus. The Golden Triangle heroin laboratories, which had been supplying American soldiers in Vietnam since late 1969, did *not* go out of business. When the number of GIs in Vietnam declined drastically in 1971, Corsican and Chinese syndicates started shipping Laotian heroin directly to the United States. In April 1971 the Laotian ambassador to France was apprehended in Paris with 60 kilos of Double U-O Globe heroin destined for the United States.[253] On November 11, 1971, a Filipino diplomat and a Bangkok Chinese merchant were arrested at the Lexington Hotel in New York City with 15.5 kilos of Double U-O Globe heroin shortly after they arrived from Vientiane.[254] For almost twenty years the U.S. Bureau of Narcotics had argued that only 5 percent of America's heroin supply came from Southeast Asia, but in November 1972 the bureau declared that an estimated 30 percent of the U.S. heroin supply was now coming from Southeast Asia.[255] Heroin was following the GIs home.

## The Fall of Saigon

The Thieu regime's corruption ultimately destroyed its capacity to govern. As U.S. troops withdrew after 1972, the regime could no longer profit from the American military presence. Nurtured by the massive corruption that had accompanied the U.S. war effort of the late 1960s, the regime now turned to its own society for the illicit incomes needed to sustain its internal political balance. "The cancer of South Vietnamese corruption," wrote war historian George Moss, "had metastasized until it suffused the entire corpus of the Saigon bureaucracy." Indicative of the changes in the patterns of corruption, the heroin networks protected by the regime compensated for their vanishing American clientele by distributing drugs to the legions of unemployed youth, prostitutes, and street dealers that were Saigon's camp follower economy. By 1974 Saigon had an estimated 150,000 heroin addicts, a new generation of drug users distinct from the aging opium smokers left by the French colonial regime.[256] The government's mounting incompetence and insensitivity came at time of major economic crisis when the society required strong leadership. In 1973–1974 the U.S. withdrawal devastated South Vietnam's fragile economy, long dependent on the American presence. As spending by American soldiers dropped from more than $500 million in 1970 to less than $100 million in 1974, some 300,000 jobs simply disappeared, a crisis that was compounded when the U.S. Congress halved American military aid in 1973.[257]

As South Vietnam spun into a crisis of corruption and economic collapse in 1974, a conservative priest, Tran Huu Thanh, launched the People's Anti-Corruption Movement with the support of Saigon's powerful Catholic Church. In a series of public manifestos, Fr. Thanh charged President Thieu with "undermining the nationalist cause for his own financial gain" and accused the regime of protecting the heroin traffic, now directed at the city's sprawling slums. Led by many of Saigon's prominent anti-Communists, Fr. Thanh's movement represented a political rebellion from within the ranks of the regime.

Alerted to Thieu's political decline, the CIA's Saigon station conducted a series of interviews with Vietnamese leaders and turned up strong evidence that corruption was crippling the regime. "The soldiers are unable to feed their families and no longer have the will to fight," said one senior source to his CIA contact. "If Thieu continues to govern with the support of corrupt and incompetent men . . . , it will be difficult for South Vietnam to win the struggle against the Communists." Instead of pressing Thieu for reforms, the CIA station chief Thomas Polgar, with support of the U.S. ambassador, suppressed the information and denied the problem.[258] After Fr. Thanh issued a new anticorruption broadside in February 1975, President Thieu, himself a Catholic, did not harass the priest and instead closed five opposition newspapers, arresting eighteen journalists.[259]

When North Vietnam launched its annual spring offensive in March 1975, ARVN, riven with corruption that corroded morale, shattered at the first contact with Hanoi's armored units and began a panicked withdrawal southward. As news of the debacle reached Saigon, support for the regime was muted. Air-Marshal Ky managed to rally just 5,000 Catholic conservatives in the city's suburbs among a population of some 4 million people. Realizing that Thieu had lost support, Polgar suggested a coup to change leaders, but CIA director William Colby refused permission.[260] Before the Americans could act, President Thieu resigned on April 25 and left for Tan Son Nhut airport under CIA protection. Just as the limousines pulled out of the palace compound, Thieu's aides loaded several mammoth suitcases. As one of the CIA escorts recalled,

"The clink of metal on metal broke through the stillness like muffled wind chimes."[261]

Five days later, North Vietnam's army broke through ARVN's last defenses and captured a city of 4 million people—including 300,000 unemployed, 150,000 heroin addicts, and 130,000 prostitutes. Within months the new regime had established the New Youth College, a residential drug center with 1,200 beds and a treatment program combining acupuncture, martial arts training, and indoctrination. "Addicts were absorbed into the culture of neo-colonialism," explained its director, Pham Nguyen Binh, in a 1981 interview, "so we have to educate them with socialist culture."[262] By 1981 the year-long program established an 80 percent cure rate among the 8,000 addicts treated at that time. Although the regime often claimed that socialism was solving the problem, Saigon retained a large addict population and drug use was still high among the city's youth gangs. The city street life of pedicab drivers, prostitutes, and black market dealers still traded in drugs, no longer no. 4 heroin but instead a low-grade processed opium that was smuggled into Saigon from Laos by corrupt, middle-ranking police, customs, and military officials.[263]

Once the gateway to the world market for Laotian heroin laboratories, Saigon had become a dead end in Southeast Asia's drug traffic. Crude opium still crossed the border from Laos to service the city's declining addict population, but the syndicates that had once moved high-grade heroin onward to markets in Europe or America had fled Vietnam with the fall of Saigon.

# 6

# Hong Kong: Asia's Heroin Laboratory

IN MANY WAYS THE BRITISH CROWN COLONY OF HONG KONG resembled Marseille. The narrow streets gave both cities an oppressive, cramped atmosphere. The waterfront areas blazed with the neon lights of bars, nightclubs, and brothels. Both had a long-standing tradition of random violence and organized crime. Marseille was the heroin laboratory for Turkish opium, and Hong Kong played a similar role for Southeast Asia. While Western journalists often wrote about the skill of Marseille's master chemists, few were aware that Hong Kong's Chiu chau chemists had a longer tradition and produced a higher grade of heroin than their Corsican counterparts. American journalists and narcotics specialists had become so accustomed to the idea of Marseille as America's heroin laboratory that few paid any attention to Hong Kong's flourishing drug trade. However, Hong Kong, along with the Golden Triangle, seemed to be the emerging heroin-producing capital of the world in the early 1970s, taking over from a Marseille beset with police crackdowns since heroin began to flood all of France in 1969, creating a severe drug problem.

Throughout the 1960s Hong Kong's heroin laboratories produced substantial quantities of pure no. 4 heroin for the American market. Since Hong Kong police were absorbed in the pursuit of petty dealers and the U.S. Bureau of Narcotics paid little attention to Asia, there were few seizures of Asian heroin and little awareness of the colony's growing role in the international traffic. It was not until American GIs serving in Vietnam began using alarming quantities of no. 4 heroin refined in the Golden Triangle that any attention was focused on the Asian heroin trade. Even then there was almost no realization that the heroin used by GIs in Vietnam was manufactured in the Golden Triangle by Hong Kong chemists who were members of international syndicates the equal of Marseille's Corsican gangs.

Like Frenchmen and Italians, the Chinese have tended to align themselves in business and voluntary groups by dialect and regional origins. In the early 1970s almost all of the gangsters belonging to Hong Kong's dominant heroin syndicates were members of the Chiu chau dialect group. Their ancestors had migrated from the region of Swatow, a city about 170 miles up the coast from the colony. However, the Chiu chau narcotics syndicates operating in Hong Kong in the 1970s did not have their origins in either Hong Kong or Swatow, but in Shanghai.

## Shanghai Syndicates

Until it was ceded to Western powers after China's humiliating defeat in the Opium War (1839–1842), Shanghai was little more than a fishing village. As Western merchants and commercial goods flooded into China in the latter half of the nineteenth century, Shanghai became China's largest and most modern city. But it was not really a Chinese city. The Chinese imperial government divided much of the city among the British, French, and Japanese, who ran their concessions as they saw fit. Westerners held all the high commercial and municipal offices and dealt with the Chinese population through a group of Chinese middlemen known as *compradores*. Since the Westerners dealt with almost no Chinese except these agents, there were soon police *compradores*, business *compradores*, and opium *compradores*.

In the so-called International Settlement, a sector administered jointly by the British and other Western powers, a group of Chiu chau became opium *compradores* soon after the Municipal Opium Monopoly was established in the 1840s.[1] Although the franchises for distribution of opium and management of the settlement's smoking dens were formally leased to Western (mainly British) merchants, the Chiu chau *compradores* actually policed the smoking dens and sold the opium. Despite their relatively low social status, the Chiu chau "prospered" from the traffic until 1918, when pressure from the new Chinese Republican government and the British Foreign Office finally forced British merchants to give up their franchises and close the dens.

Although the Chiu chau tried to maintain control over Shanghai's illicit traffic, they soon found themselves losing out to a powerful criminal syndicate named the Green Gang. A traditional "patriotic" secret society, the Green Gang had dominated Shanghai's French concession and controlled its opium traffic. When the British decided to abandon the opium trade, the Chiu chau lost their legitimate cover in the International Settlement, and the Green Gang began to challenge their well-established hegemony over the city's illicit drug traffic. As the battle between the two groups intensified, smaller gangs joined the fray, and the city's opium traffic collapsed into conflict. Realizing that an equitable division of the spoils would be more profitable for everyone involved, a young Green Gang leader named Tu Yueh-sheng, who had emerged several years earlier as the leader of one of the gang's opium syndicates, mediated between the battling gangs and convinced both sides to form a unified opium cartel. The cartel ended the bitter rivalry by dividing the traffic between the Green Gang and the Chiu chau.[2] Tu himself became known as the Opium King and used the drug business to catapult himself into the front ranks of the Shanghai underworld.

For more than thirty years Tu Yueh-sheng's cartel managed Shanghai's narcotics traffic with marked efficiency. It not only imposed order on the city's rival gangs but demonstrated an awareness of international and domestic market potential. In the early 1920s the Shanghai syndicate began promoting the sale of millions of red-colored heroin pills advertised as "anti-opium pills" and "the best medicine in the world." Thousands of Chinese opium smokers switched to heroin, and by 1923 the cartel had to import an estimated 10.25 tons of the drug annually from European and Japanese pharmaceutical companies to keep up with consumer demand. After a new Geneva convention ban on heroin marketing became law in 1928 and European pharmaceutical companies cut off their shipments to Shanghai, the city's drug dealers "began to manufacture heroin illicitly in China itself."[3] Green Gang agents purchased tons of raw opium in the market towns of distant Szechwan province and shipped it down the Yangtze River to Shanghai, where it was refined into heroin at clandestine laboratories.

Syndicate chemists had evidently mastered the new art, for in 1934 the Shanghai Municipal Council reported that heroin use had become so widespread that "it exceeds the smoking of opium itself." The council concluded that this heroin was being manufactured locally, since Shanghai police discovered one clandestine laboratory and another had blown up when a careless chemist mismanaged the volatile ether precipitation process.[4] The relative cheapness of heroin (60 percent less expensive than an equivalent dose of opium) made the "anti-opium pills" universally popular, and Shanghai heroin became the staple of addicts everywhere in China. During the late 1930s the cartel began to drop this medicinal facade, and addicts switched to straight heroin, mixed with regular tobacco and smoked in cigarettes. In addition, Shanghai became one of America's most important sources of illicit heroin in the 1930s when the American syndicates entered the drug business after their supplies of legal European heroin began to dry up.

But Tu Yueh-sheng was more than just a good businessman. Like other great criminals of the modern age such as Lucky Luciano and François Spirito, Tu was a skilled politician who understood the importance of having protectors in high office. And just as Spirito ingratiated himself with French Fascists by battling Communist street demonstrators in Marseille, so Tu served Chiang Kai-skek's Nationalist party by breaking Communist labor unions in Shanghai. Indeed, Tu's emergence as a national figure in China was intimately involved with Chiang Kai-shek's rise to power.

During the warlord era of the 1920s, Chiang Kai-shek emerged as the commander of China's new Nationalist army (Kuomintang, KMT). In 1926 Chiang led his armies on the famous Northern Campaign to establish the authority of the Nationalist government in northern and central China. As Chiang's troops approached China's industrial capital, Shanghai, in February 1927, the Communist-led labor movement rebelled against the local warlord in a show of support for the nationalists. Instead of pressing on toward Shanghai, however, Chiang halted his march while the warlord troops slaughtered the workers.[5] Although Chiang was supported by another Communist uprising when he finally entered Shanghai in late March, he was already determined to crush the Communist labor movement. Unable to rely on his own troops, many of whom were sympathetic to the workers, Chiang met with the Green Gang's leaders, including Tu, soon after he arrived in Shanghai.[6] Then, on the morning of April 12, thousands of Green Gang thugs stormed out of the French concession into Chinese sections of the city and began a reign of terror that ultimately decimated the Communist labor unions.[7]

Tu was rewarded with the rank of major general in the KMT army and soon became one of Shanghai's most respected citizens. The 1933 edition of *The China Yearbook* described Tu as the "most influential resident, French Concession" and a "well-known public welfare work-er." One Chinese historian later commented, "Perhaps for the first time in Chinese history, the underworld gained formal recognition in national politics."[8]

By 1934 Tu's control over the trade was so strong that the U.S. Treasury attaché in Shanghai, M. R. Nicholson, concluded in a formal report to his superiors in Washington that the Green Gang leader was "opium King of the nation."[9] Working through the gang's large, disciplined membership, Tu had formed an opium cartel that reached from Shanghai, where he had ten heroin laboratories, up the length of the Yangtze River to the rich opium-growing provinces of the southwest,

Szechwan and Yunnan. Through his close relations with the Nationalist regime, Tu's cartel was a major force in the Yangtze River opium trade that dominated China's drug traffic. After harvest in the southwestern highlands, the drugs were smuggled downriver on military gunboats, with at least 18,000 tons of Szechwan opium and 10,000 tons of Yunnanese passing through the major river ports every year. At the city of Hankow, halfway down the Yangtze, a garrison of 800 well-armed troops stood by to guard the opium steamers, the government's Special Tax Bureau for Hankow collected $20 million annually in opium transit fees, and two of the city's major banks were dedicated to financing the drug trade.[10]

The basis of Tu's remarkable power, in the Treasury's analysis, was his political relationships. Among the forty-eight "generations" that had joined the Green Gang since its founding in the early fifteenth century, Tu and his close ally China's President Chiang Kai-shek, were leaders of the twenty-second generation, the one currently ruling the Gang.[11] In gratitude for suppressing the Communists in Shanghai, Chiang assisted Tu in the inauguration of his ancestral temple by issuing "secret instructions to all military and civil governors . . . urging them to make appropriate gifts," just one instance that showed "Tu's influence over Chinese political life and his close relationship with General Chiang Kai-shek."[12]

Although Tu had long relied on the French concession of Shanghai as his "headquarters especially in the traffic in opium," a political miscalculation had forced him to quit the district. Several years earlier Tu had shortchanged an outgoing consul on an opium deal by $80,000. When the same official, M. Molière, was reappointed in 1932, he returned to Shanghai determined to have his revenge. After firing the concession's police chief, a Green Gang ally, Molière raised "the opium tax to an unreasonably high scale" and demanded "cash payment of a huge sum of money," forcing Tu to "flee from French Town for safety." Protected by Chiang Kai-shek, Tu took refuge in Nantao, Shanghai's Chinese city, and was continuing to dominate the opium trade.[13] Indicative of his control, the head of the government's Opium Suppression Bureau, created by Chiang in 1933, was an active member of the Green Gang who remained "loyal to his benefactor, Tu Yueh-sheng."[14]

The most disturbing sign of Tu's power was his recent political alliance with the Japanese military that was occupying much of northern China and Manchuria. Over the previous eight years, Nicholson reported, the "Japanese have been chiefly responsible for the spread of narcotics drugs . . . with the aid and protection of their military and naval forces."[15] The scale of the Japanese narcotics operation was quickly becoming the largest and best organized in China. While Japanese navy gunboats regularly carried opium down the Yangtze River, twenty-four known laboratories in northern China manufactured heroin "under the protection of Japanese authorities," and the Japanese army in northern China was "engaged actively in the traffic." Across the eighteen counties of northern China below the Great Wall, for example, a new chain of 6,900 Japanese pharmacies was selling heroin delivered by Japanese army "armed cars with armed escorts." After the Japanese army occupied Jehol province in northern China in 1930, the military government expanded opium cultivation to 130,000 acres, producing a crop of 1,660 tons worth about $30 million. Significantly, Tu had agreed "to help the Japanese in their evident scheme to monopolize . . . distribution of opium in North China and narcotics in the Yangtze Valley and Shanghai." According to their plan, the Japanese would distribute heroin produced in their northern China poppy fields across the whole of China, leaving Tu and the Chinese government "in absolute control" of the Yangtze River opium trade.[16]

The proliferation of heroin production in northern China was starting to supply a substantial, but unquantifiable, share of the U.S. domestic drug market. In 1931 the League of Nations had imposed restrictions on the manufacture of heroin in Europe, and the U.S. Treasury attaché in Shanghai was, only three years later, noticing a "sudden shift of the traffic in narcotics from Europe to the Orient." With Japanese laboratories producing "huge quantities of narcotics" and a network of Russian and Greek smugglers living in Shanghai, China would soon begin supplying America's illicit market, the world's second largest.[17] "In recent years," the attaché's report concluded, "China's opium and drug problem has become more and more a political one, both internally and externally. Its close relation with the various phases of China's . . . military and political life renders the outlook grave and seemingly hopeless."[18]

Although much of China's regular commerce was disrupted during World War II when the invading Japanese army occupied the addict-ridden coastal cities and forced Chiang Kai-shek's government into the interior, the opium trade continued unabated with Tu still the reigning "opium king." Chiang's government at Chungking in the rich opium-growing province of Szechwan gave Tu the responsibility for negotiating opium sales across the battle lines.

Writing to his superior in October 1943, a U.S. army intelligence officer reported the following about Tu's involvement in the wartime opium trade:

> Prior to 1937 Tu Yueh-sheng was one of the three bosses of
> Shanghai's underworld. He was leader in the Ching Pang (or

"Green Circle"). . . . Tu was the "opium king" and having been
friendly with Chiang Kai-shek for many years, he was never
persecuted by the Chinese authorities. When the Japs invaded
Shanghai, Tu pulled out and subsequently settled down in
Chungking. . . .

1943—In Chungking Tu became known as a great philan-
thropist and headed several relief societies. Not until Jan.
194[2] was the time ripe for Tu Yueh-sheng to go into action in
his particular line of business. Smuggling between occupied
and Free China had become so lucrative a business that the
Chungking government decided to step in and control it. It was
arranged for Tu Yueh-sheng to manage this trade with the
enemy through the firing lines, and five banks were ordered to
finance Tu's new organization to the tune of 150 million
Chinese national dollars.[19]

During the Sino-Japanese War (1937–1945), Tu and his Green Gang
became heavily involved in KMT intelligence work behind Japanese
lines, particularly in occupied Shanghai. Although Tu retreated to Hong
Kong and later to Chungking as the Japanese advanced, he retained
control over Green Gang activities in Shanghai. With Tu's cooperation,
large elements of the Gang formed the basis of Chiang Kai-shek's most
powerful secret police agency, the Statistical and Investigation Office,
under the command of the controversial General Tai Li.[20] Through its
alliance with Tai Li, the Green Gang executed espionage coups, such as
the escape of two high officials in the Japanese client regime from
Shanghai in 1940, and engaged in a bitter underground political war with
rival Chinese gangsters in the employ of the Japanese in occupied
Shanghai.[21] Among OSS officers serving in China, there were rumors
that Tai Li had "acquired great wealth through his control of the opium
trade."[22] An OSS emissary to China in 1942, Michigan professor Joseph
Hayden, described Tai Li as "the leader of the Chinese 'gestapo,' the
hatchet man of the Generalissimo [Chiang] who utilizes assassination
by poison and dagger and by subtler methods removes possible
opponents from his path and that of his chief." Despite his deep moral
revulsion, Hayden nonetheless advised the OSS command that Tai Li's
"present position and power makes it necessary for him to be used by
the United States for intelligence purposes."[23]

The agent of this pragmatic alliance with a political assassin was Navy
Captain Milton E. Miles, OSS coordinator in the Far East, and he soon
became Tai Li's ardent advocate and intimate friend. At war's end, the
two recruited Tu and his Green Gang for an elaborate scheme to save
China's premier port from destruction. Acting on intelligence that the
Japanese were planning to demolish Shanghai before the Allies could

liberate it, Miles and Tai Li decided to use Tu as "a convenient and capable tool." Some foreigners called Tu "Shanghai's Al Capone" or "sometimes insisted that this very powerful person also handled all the dives and opium dens in Shanghai," but Miles preferred to think of him as an "amiable old gentleman" who was the city's chief labor leader. After radioing Admiral Ernest King in Washington for approval, Miles worked through Tu to mobilize his "unions" and local river pirates to secure the city against Japanese sabotage. When Miles arrived at liberated Shanghai in September 1945, Tu had taken command of the city and personally escorted the OSS chief to a lavish mansion equipped with chilled champagne and "gold brocade furniture." With an ironic flair, Tu assigned his guest a limousine "with bulletproof glass and venetian blinds of quarter-inch steel with gun slits," which Miles learned had once been owned by Chicago's Al Capone.[24]

As the Chinese revolution gathered momentum in the late 1940s, Shanghai's gangsters realized it was only a matter of time until the Communist forces would occupy the city. Most of the city's gangsters had participated in the Green Gang's 1927 massacre of Communist supporters, and so almost the entire underworld migrated to Hong Kong from 1947 to 1950. This massive influx of thousands of China's toughest criminals was too much for Hong Kong police to handle, and organized crime flourished on an unprecedented scale. Both the Green Gang and Chiu chau syndicates were national organizations, and their Hong Kong branches served as welcoming committees. However, local gang leaders turned the situation to their advantage and in the case of the Green Gang, and probably the Chiu chau as well, usurped the authority of their Shanghai bosses.[25]

## The Mafia of Southeast Asia

Green Gang members had been the most powerful racketeers in Shanghai, and during their first few years in Hong Kong it seemed as though they would dominate the colony's organized crime as well. The Green Gang opened up huge dance halls, organized large-scale prostitution, and committed a series of spectacular robberies. Most important, their master chemists began producing high-grade heroin, which became increasingly popular as the colonial government's anti-opium campaign got under way. Before the Shanghai gangsters immigrated to the colony, there had been no heroin production and only a moderate level of consumption. The Green Gang's early production was aimed at exiles who had acquired the habit before coming to Hong Kong, but gradually its market expanded to include local opium smokers who switched to heroin because of the colonial government's opium suppression campaign.[26] Green Gang members were well aware of their role in introducing the technology of heroin processing into Hong Kong, and some of the society's older members claimed that all of the colony's chemists were trained by the "one-armed master chemist and his seven Green Gang disciples" who fled from Shanghai in 1949.[27]

Tu Yueh-sheng's cartel had crumbled when the underworld fled Shanghai, and the old Chiu chau–Green Gang struggle for the narcotics traffic revived soon after the two groups arrived in Hong Kong. Tu himself moved to Hong Kong in April 1949, but any possible role he might have played as a mediator ended with his death in August 1951.[28] In the ensuing struggle, the Chiu chau possessed certain advantages that contributed to their decisive victory. The Green Gang, with its predominantly northern Chinese membership, was a relative outsider in Hong Kong. But the Chiu chau syndicate had strong local connections: Chiu chau dialect speakers constituted 8 percent of the colony's population; there were a number of powerful Chiu chau street gangs;[29] and, perhaps most significant, some of the higher Chinese officials in the Hong Kong police hierarchy were Chiu chau. Rather than engaging in gun battles or street fights, the Chiu chau utilized these police connections to eliminate their rivals. Although colonial police officially ascribed the Green Gang's precipitous decline to a special police squad formed in 1950,[30] in their more candid moments police officers admitted that their success was due mainly to tips received from Chiu chau and other criminal gangs.[31] The police scored their first significant blow in 1952 when they deported reputed Green Gang leader Li Choi-fat. Although Li's arrest shocked his followers into abandoning risky robberies and concentrating on the safer vice trades, deportations and arrests continued to thin their ranks.[32] By the mid-1950s the Green Gang's narcotics import and distribution network was shattered,[33] and most of its chemists went to work for the Chiu chau syndicate.[34] Even by the early 1970s, a few independent Green Gang laboratories were still believed to be operating, but even these depended on the Chiu chau syndicate for supplies of imported morphine base and for outlets for their finished product.

The Chiu chau's victory over the Green Gang was only their first step in establishing a monopoly over the Hong Kong heroin trade. The Hong Kong syndicate then proceeded to take control of imports of Thai morphine and opium. Since most of Bangkok's commerce, including the opium traffic, was dominated by Chiu chau speakers, this was not too difficult. As Iranian, Indian, and mainland Chinese opium disappeared from the market in the mid-1950s, control over the Bangkok drug connection gave the Chiu chau an import monopoly. After defeating the Green Gang, the Chiu chau syndicate established a virtual monopoly over the manufacture and wholesale distribution phases of the colony's drug traffic. However, retail distribution, the most lucrative phase, was still managed by a collection of Cantonese family associations, secret societies, and criminal gangs. When the Chiu chau first began to edge into this sector of the business, their chances for success appeared limited: the Cantonese made up more than 80 percent of Hong Kong's population and their syndicates were much larger and more powerful. However, in the wake of three days of bloody rioting by Cantonese secret societies in October 1956, the Hong Kong police formed the Triad Society Bureau and declared it a crime for any colony resident to belong to one of these organizations. In the five years following the riots, police arrested 10,500 suspected secret society members and deported 600 more; they thus broke the powerful Cantonese organizations into impotent splinter groups.[35] Although the weakening of Cantonese secret societies removed an important barrier, the Chiu chau did not take over retail distribution until the mid-1960s, when the police began a serious effort to close smoking dens and arrest street pushers. But before the significance of the police crackdown can be fully understood, it is necessary to know something about addiction and street pushing in Hong Kong at the time.

With an estimated 100,000 narcotics addicts out of a total population of 4 million in 1970,[36] Hong Kong had the highest percentage of drug users anywhere in the world. Most of the addicts were poor wage laborers who lived in cramped tenements and sprawling slums, which many social workers considered ideal breeding grounds for addiction.[37] About 85 percent of all inmates in the colony's prisons were heroin addicts, and 47 percent of all those sentenced were narcotics offenders. Prison officials found it impossible to cut off the narcotics supply, and heroin was so common inside the prison that it was used as a form of currency.[38] The colony's addict population was increasing at an alarming rate, and the Hong Kong press noted a sharp rise in teenage addiction in 1970–1971.[39] In 1972 the U.S. Drug Enforcement Administration estimated Hong Kong's addict population at 30,000 opium smokers and 120,000 heroin users, who consumed about 35 tons of opium annually, a remarkable amount that approached the level of total U.S. opiate consumption.[40]

Although most of Hong Kong's addicts were opium smokers before World War II, twenty-five years of police opium suppression drove most addicts to heroin. By the early 1960s, 60 to 70 percent of the colony's addicts were heroin users, and most of those still smoking opium were in their fifties and sixties.[41] As the elderly addicts died off and the young turned exclusively to heroin, the percentage of addicts using heroin increased to an estimated 80 to 90 percent by 1971. But unlike the

American addict who had to shoot directly into his veins with a syringe to feel any euphoria from the diluted, 5 percent pure heroin he bought on the street, the Hong Kong addict could satisfy his craving by smoking the drug, since he could buy a much purer grade. The majority of Hong Kong addicts used a high-quality, low-cost, grayish, lumpy brand of no. 3 heroin, which was usually about 40 percent pure. The user placed several lumps of no. 3 on a piece of aluminum foil and heated it with a lighted match. As it melted and gave off smoke, he sucked in the wavering fumes through a rolled-up piece of paper ("chasing the dragon") or through a matchbox cover ("playing the mouth organ"). About 25 percent of the addict population used a higher grade of no. 3, known popularly as White Dragon Pearl. It was about 50 percent pure, and gained its characteristic chalky-white color when cut with a form of barbiturate called barbitone. The user ground the white chunks into a granular powder and smoked them in an ordinary tobacco cigarette. Since euphoria built with the short, staccato bursts of each puff, addicts called this method "shooting the ack-ack gun." The few Hong Kong addicts who used the needle usually could not afford the expensive, powdery no. 4 heroin and contented themselves with grinding down White Dragon Pearl.[42]

Before the police crackdown of the mid-1960s, addicts had the choice of smoking alone or getting high in a neighborhood "heroin den." Police were preoccupied with other matters, and pushers were dealing openly in almost every street, factory, and tenement in Hong Kong. However, as the police campaign began, small-time pushers were arrested, the more obvious dens were closed, and the entire structure was driven underground.

Previously, the government had been lax enough so that small pushers could afford to bribe the policemen on the beat. However, when the colonial government and police hierarchy took a harsher attitude toward the narcotics traffic, the street dealer became too obvious, and a small bribe was no longer worth the risk. As the petty Cantonese pushers were driven off the streets, the Chiu chau syndicates concentrated most of the colony's retail trade in seven high-volume retail distribution centers labeled "drug supermarkets" by one Hong Kong reporter. Since each of these retail centers sold from $150,000 to $300,000 a month worth of heroin,[43] the profit margin was large enough to pay the necessary bribes to Chinese and British officers in the Hong Kong police. While the police offensive in no way inhibited the growth of the narcotics traffic, it made many Chinese police sergeants millionaires. The corruption was so pervasive that in August 1969 the mere hint of an anticorruption campaign produced a wave of resignations by senior Chinese detectives and sergeants.[44] Reliable

Hong Kong sources reported that one of the Chiu chau officers who resigned invested his fortune of several million dollars in real estate, restaurants, gambling houses, and apartment buildings.

A microcosmic example of the impact of the police crackdown on the colony's narcotics traffic was the growth of the Ma Shan distribution center. Until the mid-1960s the addicts of this region on Hong Kong Island's northeast coast purchased their narcotics from neighborhood street dealers or smoked in nearby dens. When police swept the pushers off the streets and closed the dens, a Chiu chau gangster bought a small neighborhood den in the Ma Shan area from the local Cantonese secret society and made it the major "drug supermarket" for the northeast coast. Clinging to a clifflike hillside overlooking one of Hong Kong's more comfortable neighborhoods, Ma Shan was a ramshackle sprawl of squatter shacks. Although not the most convenient location, its elevation and maze of steps and ladders made it almost impossible for the police to launch a surprise raid. While ten guards patrolled the perimeter, the distribution center provided twenty-four-hour service for thousands of addicts. Although Ma Shan was a Cantonese area and all its other rackets were controlled by a local secret society, the Chiu chau reaped most of the profit from narcotics peddling and paid the Cantonese only a rather nominal rental fee. This story was repeated with minor variations throughout the entire colony: the Chiu chau had penetrated territory traditionally dominated by Cantonese gangs to establish large-scale narcotics retail operations.[45]

Although the Hong Kong press exposed their location on a number of occasions, the publicity only forced the supermarkets to move several blocks or change buildings; it did not result in any major police action.[46] The police concentrated most of their energies on shutting down smaller dens managed by entrepreneurs operating without syndicate protection. Since the police had to raid an occasional den to keep their record clean, syndicates were known to hire impoverished addicts to do a term in prison and set them up in a fake den for "discovery" by the police. The press were often invited along on these operations, and the hired addicts usually gave convincing performances complete with weeping, rage, or escape attempts.[47]

Acquisition of the retail drug traffic gave the Chiu chau a total monopoly on Hong Kong's drug traffic. Morphine base and opium were purchased from Chiu chau dealers in Bangkok, smuggled into Hong Kong, and refined into heroin by Chiu chau chemists. The wholesale distribution was managed by Chiu chau, and the "drug supermarkets" were Chiu chau–owned. Although the Chiu chau made up only 8 percent of the colony's population, Hong Kong police reported that a substantial majority of those arrested for trafficking in dangerous drugs were Chiu chau.[48] But did this mean that all of Hong Kong's drug traffic—from the heroin laboratory to the street—was controlled by a monolithic Chiu chau syndicate? Was all of Southeast Asia's narcotics traffic at the time controlled by a single Chiu chau syndicate, a veritable Chinese Mafia?

While decades of investigation by police agencies and journalists have given us a reasonably clear picture of the Sicilian Mafia and the Corsican syndicates, there is little information on the Chiu chau. Protected from scrutiny by official patrons in Thailand, Laos, Vietnam, and Hong Kong, not even the names of the prominent Chiu chau narcotics dealers were known to those outside ruling circles. However, developments in Southeast Asia's narcotics traffic in the early 1970s revealed a high degree of coordination among Chiu chau traffickers and pointed toward the existence of some kind of unified syndicate. There were indications that many of the Golden Triangle laboratories producing heroin for American GIs in Vietnam were staffed by Chiu chau chemists from Hong Kong. At Nam Keung village on the Lao side of the Mekong River, for example, the local military commander, Major Chao La, reported in September 1971 that the nearby heroin laboratory was directed by a Chiu chau chemist from Hong Kong.[49]

This was not the first time that the Chiu chau had exported Hong Kong's heroin technology to Southeast Asia. Shortly after the Thai government closed the opium dens and launched a crackdown on opium smokers in 1958, Hong Kong heroin chemists arrived in Thailand, set up laboratories in the Bangkok area, and began producing low-grade, no. 3 heroin for the local Thai market.[50] Since opium's distinctive odor made smokers vulnerable to arrest, within several years the police anti-opium campaign forced most Thai opium addicts to become heroin users. The arrival of new Chiu chau chemists from Hong Kong in 1969–1970 introduced the complex technique for producing high-grade, no. 4 heroin—a significant upgrading of the region's drug industry that later allowed it access to the U.S. market.

In July 1971 the Vietnamese police broke up a large heroin smuggling ring in Saigon and arrested more than sixty traffickers. All were Chiu chau. Although the press hailed the arrests as a major victory for the antidrug campaign, Vietnamese police had been able to make the arrests only because the Chiu chau syndicate leader in Bangkok was convinced that the Saigon operation was cheating him and decided to use the police as "enforcers."[51]

In addition, it appears that the Chiu chau played an important role in developing Southeast Asia's illicit traffic and sustaining the mass addiction fostered by old colonial opium monopolies. Through a web of international contacts, the Chiu chau provided raw materials, heroin chemists, and managerial skills necessary for the illicit traffic. Usually, they preferred to reach some sort of understanding with local governments, and in many Southeast Asian nations this relationship was so close that the Chiu chau appeared to be operating on a semiofficial basis. Like most businessmen, they would not set up operations in a country unless commercial conditions were favorable.

The success of the Singapore government's antinarcotics drive illustrates the importance of international syndicates in maintaining the region's narcotics problem. The city was the major distribution center for the Malaya Peninsula to the north and the Indonesian archipelago to the south. It was also the regional headquarters of four or five international syndicates. Unlimited drug supplies frustrated government efforts at reducing the addict population; frequent seizures of 1,000 to 2,000 kilograms (about 2 to 4 tons) by customs and police had little impact on the availability of drugs.[52] Instead of harassing opium addicts and driving them to heroin, the government decided to crack down on the syndicates. In 1962 special branch police arrested the five most powerful syndicate leaders (one of whom was Chiu chau) and had them deported after an unpublicized hearing.[53] The Chiu chau gangster went to Bangkok, where he was believed to be involved in the narcotics traffic, and the others scattered across the region. Thereafter, smugglers began avoiding Singapore, and intensified customs searches turned up only small quantities of opium.[54]

Singapore was the only Southeast Asian nation (except North Vietnam) with a declining number of addicts: in 1947 there were 25,000 registered opium smokers, and in 1970 there were only an estimated 8,000 drug addicts. Significantly, almost 7,000 of these were forty to sixty years old, a legacy of the colonial era. There were few teenage addicts and almost no heroin problem.[55] The Singapore example showed that a Southeast Asian government could reduce its local drug problem and end its role in the international traffic if it had the political will to do so.

## Heroin Free Port

Although not enough is known about Chiu chau operations in Hong Kong to detail the precise relationships between importers and "drug supermarket" operators, colonial police did know something about the syndicates' leadership and general operating methods. In 1971 police officials believed that almost all of the city's narcotics were financed and imported by only five Chiu chau gangsters.[56] The most important of these was a middle-aged Chiu chau named Ma Sik-yu, who was thought to control about 50 percent of all the morphine and opium imported into Hong Kong.[57] Ma achieved this preeminence in the narcotics traffic in only six years, and his sudden rise was something of a success story.

His family was so poor that Ma first began work as an ordinary street peddler but soon was supplementing his income by selling drugs on the side. He gradually worked his way up in the drug traffic, becoming a full-time pusher, an opium den guard, and eventually the owner of a prosperous smoking den near the Kowloon nightclub district.[58] When the police crackdown on opium dens in the mid-1960s forced him out of business, Ma was one of the Chiu chau gangsters who opened a drug supermarket. From retail distribution he moved into importing, and within several years he had become Hong Kong's most important smuggler of opium and morphine base.[59]

Although Hong Kong authorities were well aware of Ma's role in the heroin traffic, they had no way to gather sufficient evidence to convict him before a court of law. Ma maintained no direct contact with the traffic and received his share of the profits through a string of bank accounts whose trail was buried in hundreds of legitimate domestic and international money transfers. The heroin traffic was so well organized at all levels, and the Chiu chau were so disciplined and secretive, that Hong Kong authorities despaired of ever being able to convict the major traffickers; they had in fact made public admissions of their inability to halt narcotics smuggling.[60] But Hong Kong's drug industry was no longer just a local problem. The inability of the government to slow the narcotics traffic was making the colony increasingly important as a source of heroin for the American market. Hong Kong's heroin laboratories were at the end of the opium trail from Southeast Asia and the beginning of a heroin pipeline to the United States.

On September 13, 1971, a small, wooden-hulled Thai fishing trawler left Paknam, Thailand, with a cargo of 1,500 kilograms of raw opium and 260 kilograms of morphine bricks. Its destination was Hong Kong. With favorable sailing conditions, the ship would cruise along at five to ten knots an hour and arrive within a week.

This fishing boat was a member of a small but active fleet carrying narcotics between Thailand and Hong Kong. Its journey was the last leg of a voyage that began in the mountains of Burma. Almost all of Hong Kong's narcotics came from Thailand, and were smuggled into the colony on these small trawlers. This method was a relatively recent development. Until about 1968 most drug shipments had arrived on regular freighters, concealed in cargo such as refrigerators and lumber. This sort of smuggling was relatively easy for Hong Kong's Preventive Services to detect, and a number of spectacular seizures forced the smugglers to change their tactics. The new trawler method was, by contrast, virtually arrest-proof. When the trawlers left Paknam they were usually empty, but just before departure time a contact man boarded the vessel. The ship then set an easterly course, paralleling the Thai coastline until it arrived at a prearranged meeting place known only to the contact man. After coded signals were flashed from ship to shore, a high-powered speed boat darted out from the coastline, transferred the drugs, and sped away with the contact man.[61] By the time the trawler rounded Vietnam's Camau peninsula and moved into the South China Sea, it had usually been spotted by U.S. navy radar aircraft patrolling the Gulf of Siam. Within minutes after the patrol aircraft landed at its base in Uttapao, Thailand, the trawler's course, heading, and speed were radioed to the United States Navy Market Time Surveillance Patrol in Cam Ranh Bay, Vietnam. Although its primary mission was monitoring freighter traffic bound for Haiphong, North Vietnam, and coastal shipping moving toward South Vietnam, these Lockheed Electras were also responsible for spotting the "dope boats" as they chugged northward toward Hong Kong. After the dope boat had been seen for the last time by another radar patrol in the South China Sea, its course and estimated time of arrival in Hong Kong were radioed to Saigon and forwarded to British authorities.[62]

Unfortunately this precise information was of little use to Hong Kong's Preventive Services. With only six launches to patrol two hundred islands, hundreds of miles of coastline, and a local fishing fleet of 15,000 sampans and junks,[63] Preventive Services found it impossible to discourage this kind of smuggling even with detailed intelligence on the "dope boats." Once the Thai trawler reached Hong Kong it ordinarily used one of three methods for transferring its cargo to a local fishing boat: (1) it buried it on the beach of a deserted island; (2) it made a direct transfer in Chinese waters, where Hong Kong authorities could not follow; or (3) it dropped the narcotics into the shallow coastal waters in watertight steel drums. If pursued by an official launch, the trawler simply retreated to international waters and waited until the understaffed Preventive Services gave up its surveillance. Once the local fishing boat made the pickup it usually hauled the cargo into port by towing it underneath the water line in heavy steel drums. If an official launch pursued them, the crew simply cut the line and let the cargo sink to the bottom of the ocean.[64]

Since a trawler carried a cargo of 3 tons of morphine, equivalent to about "six percent of annual U.S. consumption of heroin," the U.S. Bureau of Narcotics decided that "the seizure of one trawler would be a real victory" and began to concentrate resources accordingly in early 1972. Evidently Thai smugglers somehow learned of the effort and on February 5, Hong Kong customs officers found 40 pounds of morphine base in the ventilating shaft of a cargo ship that had just arrived from

Bangkok.[65] The seizure demonstrated the dexterity of Thai smugglers in adjusting to interdiction efforts and the near impossibility of sealing Hong Kong's port against opium smuggling.

Once safely in Hong Kong, the morphine base went to one of the ten or so heroin laboratories usually operating at any time. While the largest laboratories may have had as many as seven workers and produced up to 50 pounds of heroin a day, most had only three or four employees processing about 10 pounds a day.[66] Even the most unskilled of Hong Kong's heroin chemists could manage the relatively simple chemical process required to produce an adequate grade of no. 3, and most of the morphine smuggled into the colony was used to manufacture the chunky, low-grade brands favored by local addicts.

For the United States the critical question was, of course, how much of Hong Kong's heroin industry was producing the powdery no. 4 used by American addicts, and what percentage of this output was going to the United States. It is impossible to make precise estimates of such a clandestine business, but there was every indication that Hong Kong had become a major supplier for the U.S. market. Although any chemist could go through the rather simple operations to produce no. 3, the production of the no. 4 grade required a final, dangerous step that demanded a great deal of extra skill. The chemist had to precipitate the grayish, lumpy no. 3 through a solution of ether and alcohol.[67] Unless properly handled, the ether formed a volatile gas. In 1970 one Hong Kong laboratory exploded when the chemist became a bit careless and the ventilation fan shorted out during the ether process. The chemist and several assistants escaped, leaving a badly burned co-worker lying in the smoldering rubble.[68] This final stage was not only dangerous, but it doubled the time required to complete the processing; a laboratory that could produce a batch of no. 3 in six hours required twelve to fifteen hours for the same amount of no. 4. Despite all the extra risk and time involved, the only real advantage to no. 4 was its high degree of water solubility, which made it easier to inject with a syringe. Since very few of the colony's addicts injected their heroin (and almost none of those who did could afford the more expensive no. 4), Hong Kong officials were unanimous in asserting that there was no local market for no. 4.

However, a good deal of no. 4 heroin was being produced in Hong Kong. The Government Chemist's Office reported that many of the heroin laboratories it had examined in the course of police investigations had been producing impressive quantities of no. 4. They had also been struck by the absence of any no. 4 in the confiscated street packets they tested for the police in narcotics possession cases. Their conclusion was the obvious one: large quantities of no. 4 were being produced for export.[69] Members of the narcotics police concurred with this view and added that the U.S. Bureau of Narcotics had not yet heeded their warnings on the growing importance of Hong Kong's heroin exports.[70]

Since the Hong Kong narcotics police were preoccupied with chasing pushers and addicts off the streets and the U.S. Bureau of Narcotics was understaffed in Asia, it was not until 1967 that any substantial quantities of heroin from Hong Kong were intercepted. The first breakthrough came in January of that year, when a series of coordinated police raids in Miami, New York, and Sydney, Australia, netted an entire smuggling ring operating out of Hong Kong. Its organizers were retired Australian policemen, and eleven of the fifteen arrested persons were Australians as well.[71] The ring had been operating for almost a year using standard "body packs" and a sophisticated duplicate passport system to bring $22.5 million worth of heroin into the United States.

Subsequent interrogation of the Australian suspects revealed that the ringleaders had been hired by one of Hong Kong's "big five" Chiu chau syndicate leaders to smuggle heroin into the United States. Every two weeks a group of couriers with duplicate passports flew to Hong Kong from Sydney, where they each picked up 5 to 6 kilograms of undiluted no. 4 heroin. After concealing the heroin underneath their clothing by taping the plastic-wrapped packets to their chests and stomachs, they usually caught a flight direct to London, where they disembarked. There they switched to the second passport. Once this second passport was stamped by British customs, they caught another flight to New York and passed through U.S. customs as ordinary, pot-bellied businessmen flying to New York from Australia with a brief stopover in London. Most New York authorities would be suspicious of a passport that showed a Hong Kong stopover. Those who entered the United States through Honolulu had no need for the duplicate passport, since it was common enough for Australians en route to the United States to stop off in Hong Kong.[72] Their profits were enormous; a kilogram of heroin the Australians bought from the Hong Kong Chiu chau for $1,600 was sold to American distributors for $34,000.[73]

Although these arrests drew a good deal of attention from the press, U.S. narcotics officials regarded the Australian ring as a freak phenomenon. It was not until three years later, when an even larger Hong Kong–based smuggling ring was broken up, that they began to pay serious attention to Hong Kong. In 1970 federal narcotics agents launched a coordinated series of arrests at airports across the United States that netted a group of Filipino couriers as they stepped off various transpacific flights. All were carrying body packs of no. 4 Hong Kong heroin to be delivered to Mafia contact men in the United States.

Although the Filipino ring was also working for one of Hong Kong's Chiu chau syndicate leaders, its operations were much more extensive than those of the Australian group. While the Australians usually had only three or four couriers in the air at the same time, the Filipinos "shotgunned" as many as eight couriers on a single run. During a twelve-month period in 1969–1970, the Filipinos smuggled an estimated 1,000 kilograms of Hong Kong heroin into the United States.[74] This amount alone accounted for *at least* 10 to 20 percent of all the heroin consumed in the United States in an entire year. Since Hong Kong's heroin was manufactured from Burmese and Thai opium, this syndicate added to the evidence that Southeast Asia was becoming a major source of America's heroin supply.[75]

However, the official wisdom still held that Southeast Asia accounted for only 5 percent of America's heroin. The Bureau of Narcotics was convinced that 80 percent was refined from Turkish opium and 15 percent from Mexican and had been concentrating almost all its investigative efforts in these areas.[76] But suddenly it was faced with a single Southeast Asian smuggling ring that had been supplying a substantial part of America's annual dosage. And the Filipinos were only messengers for one of five Chiu chau syndicate leaders in Hong Kong. Why couldn't the other four syndicate leaders have courier organizations just as big or even bigger?

Questions like this soon prompted a reorganization of the Bureau of Narcotics' international enforcement effort and intelligence-gathering techniques. Unprecedented quantities of heroin were flooding into the United States in the late 1960s, and top-level agents had become concerned that their old methods no longer seemed to have any effect. As one U.S. narcotics agent explained in a November 1971 interview:

> In 1961 when we . . . seized fifteen kilos there was street panic in New York City. Junkies were lined up in front of doctors' offices begging for the stuff. Even as late as 1965, when we seized fifteen or sixteen kilos, it had the same effect. Now we seize five hundred kilos in three weeks, and it has no effect whatsoever.

Yet at the same time these massive quantities of heroin were pouring into the United States, Turkey—the alleged producer of 80 percent of the opium that entered America in the form of heroin—abolished poppy cultivation in fourteen out of its twenty-one opium-producing provinces and reduced its total official output by more than 70 percent between 1967 and 1971.[77] It was evident that major changes were taking place in the international traffic, and the bureau established a special research and analysis division to deal with them. Its chief, Mr. John Warner, explained in an October 1971 interview:

> We found we knew very little about the actual pattern of drug trafficking. We were saying that 80 percent of the narcotics entering the U.S. came from Turkey and only 5 percent came from Southeast Asia. In fact, this was based on ignorance. So a year ago we created the Strategic Intelligence Office to find out what was really going on.

The bureau had not abandoned its emphasis on Turkey, but increased intelligence and enforcement work were starting to yield results in Southeast Asia and Hong Kong. Although it had not produced any arrests in 1971, investigative work seemed to indicate that the Australian and Filipino groups were only two of many courier rings the Chiu chau had been using. Intelligence showed that the Chiu chau syndicate was using a new group of couriers to smuggle large quantities of heroin into the United States through a maze of commercial air routes: Hong Kong to Okinawa, Okinawa to Buenos Aires, Buenos Aires to Paraguay, Paraguay to Panama City, and Panama City to Los Angeles. There was speculation that this new route from Hong Kong may have been contributing to the growing amounts of heroin entering the United States from Latin America.[78]

While there was room for speculation about the precise nature of the Hong Kong–Latin America link, there could no longer be any doubt about the growing importance of Southeast Asia's Chiu chau syndicates in America's heroin traffic. In 1972 U.S. customs and the Bureau of Narcotics conducted five major arrests of overseas Chinese heroin dealers, all of which revealed the emergence of a direct connection between Chiu chau syndicates in Southeast Asia and heroin distributors in the United States:

- January 1972: "U.S. Customs inspectors in Honolulu arrested three couriers who were body-carrying no. 4 heroin from Bangkok for delivery to Chinese-American buyers in San Francisco and New York." According to U.S. narcotics agents, this shipment was arranged by the "same organizations that run the trawlers" from Bangkok to Hong Kong.[79]
- April 5, 1972: A Chinese seaman was arrested in Miami, Florida, with 10 kilos of Laos's renowned Double U-O Globe brand heroin.[80]
- April 11, 1972: Seven Chinese seamen were arrested in New York with 5 kilos of Double U-O Globe brand heroin. A U.S. Bureau of Narcotics report said that "further information developed that this eleven pounds [5 kilos] was part of a 100 pound shipment which originated in Bangkok and was evidently delivered by a European diplomat assigned to Thailand. Sensitive sources have revealed that more shipments, sponsored by other groups, are on the way.[81]

• June 1972: Saigon police arrested Wan Pen Fen, a Taiwan Chinese described by the Bureau of Narcotics as "the largest heroin dealer in Vietnam and a heroin laboratory operator in Southeast Asia's Golden Triangle." According to a U.S. cabinet report, "Wan Pen Fen was reportedly in Saigon to seek channels to extend his heroin traffic to the U.S."[82]

• August 23, 1972: U.S. narcotics agents arrested four Chinese-Americans with 9 kilos of Southeast Asian heroin in New York's Chinatown.[83]

Despite the increased enforcement effort and mounting evidence of Southeast Asia's growing role in the international heroin traffic, the U.S. State Department clung to its belief in Turkey's importance. Convinced that the root of the problem still lay in the Mediterranean and unwilling to confront the political consequences of thinking otherwise, America's diplomats were reluctant to apply the same political leverage in Southeast Asia as they had in France and Turkey. It was undeniable that the State Department and the Bureau of Narcotics had made enormous strides in repressing the opium traffic in Turkey and Europe. But it was also true that the Mediterranean's loss was Southeast Asia's gain.

# 7

# The Golden Triangle

"LADIES AND GENTLEMEN," ANNOUNCED THE BRITISH DIPLO-
mat, raising his glass to offer a toast, "I give you Prince Sopsaisana, the
uplifter of Laotian youth." The toast brought a smile from the lips of the
guest of honor, cheers and applause from the luminaries of Vientiane's
diplomatic corps gathered at the send-off banquet for the Laotian
ambassador-designate to France, Prince Sopsaisana. His appointment
was the crowning achievement in a brilliant career. A member of the
royal house of Xieng Khouang, the Plain of Jars region, Prince
Sopsaisana was vice-president of the National Assembly, chairman of
the Lao Bar Association, president of the Lao Press Association,
president of the Alliance Française, and a member in good standing of
the Asian People's Anti-Communist League. After receiving his credentials from the king in a private audience at the Luang Prabang Royal
Palace on April 8, 1971, the prince was treated to an unprecedented
round of cocktail parties, dinners, and banquets.[1] For Prince Sopsaisana,
or Sopsai as his friends called him, was not just any ambassador; the
Americans considered him an outstanding example of a new generation
of honest, dynamic national leaders, and it was widely rumored in
Vientiane that Sopsai was destined for high office some day.

The send-off party at Vientiane's Wattay Airport on April 23 was one
of the gayest affairs of the season. Everybody was there: the cream of
the diplomatic corps, a bevy of Lao luminaries, and, of course,
you-know-who from the American embassy. The champagne bubbled,

the canapés were flawlessly French, and Mr. Ivan Bastouil, chargé d'affaires at the French embassy, *Lao Presse* reported, gave the nicest speech.[2] Only after the plane had left did anybody notice that Sopsai had forgotten to pay for his share of the reception.

When the prince's flight arrived at Paris's Orly Airport on the morning of April 25, there was another reception in the exclusive VIP lounge. The French ambassador to Laos, home for a brief visit, and the entire staff of the Laotian embassy had turned out.[3] There were warm embraces, kissing on both cheeks, and more effusive speeches. Curiously, Prince Sopsaisana insisted on waiting for his luggage like any ordinary tourist, and when the mountain of suitcases finally appeared after an unexplained delay, he immediately noticed that one was missing. Angrily, Sopsai insisted his suitcase be delivered at once, and the French authorities promised, apologetically, that it would be sent round to the embassy as soon as it was found. But the Mercedes was waiting, and with flags fluttering, Sopsai was whisked off to the embassy for a formal reception.

While the champagne bubbled at the Laotian embassy, French customs officials were examining one of the biggest heroin seizures in French history: the ambassador's missing suitcase contained 60 kilos of high-grade Laotian heroin worth $13.5 million on the streets of New York,[4] its probable destination. Tipped by an unidentified source in Vientiane, French officials had been waiting at the airport. Rather than create a diplomatic scandal by confronting Sopsai with the heroin in the VIP lounge, French officials impounded the suitcase until the government could decide how to deal with the matter.

Although it was finally decided to hush up the affair, the authorities were determined that Sopsaisana should not go entirely unpunished. A week after the ambassador's arrival, a French official presented himself at the embassy with the guilty suitcase in hand. Although Sopsaisana had been bombarding the airport with outraged telephone calls for several days, he must have realized that accepting the suitcase was tantamount to an admission of guilt and flatly denied that it was his. Despite his protestations of innocence, the French government refused to accept his diplomatic credentials and Sopsai festered in Paris for almost two months until he was finally recalled to Vientiane late in June.

Back in Vientiane the impact of this affair was considerably less than earthshaking. The influential American embassy chose not to pursue the matter, and within a few weeks the incident was forgotten.[5] According to reports later received by the U.S. Bureau of Narcotics, Sopsai's venture had been financed by Hmong General Vang Pao, commander of the CIA's Secret Army, and the heroin itself had been refined in a laboratory at Long Tieng, the CIA's headquarters for clandestine operations in northern Laos.[6] Perhaps these facts may explain the U.S. embassy's lack of action.

In spite of its amusing aspects, the Sopsaisana affair provided sobering evidence of Southeast Asia's rising importance in the international heroin trade. In addition to growing more than a thousand tons of raw opium annually (about 70 percent of the world's total illicit opium supply),[7] Southeast Asia's Golden Triangle had, by 1971, become a mass producer of high-grade no. 4 heroin for the American market. Its heroin laboratories rivalled those of Marseille and Hong Kong in the quantity and quality of their production.

As Turkey's opium production had declined sharply in the late 1960s and international drug syndicates had turned to Southeast Asia as an alternative source of raw materials, Southeast Asia's Golden Triangle—extending from the rugged Shan hills of northeastern Burma through the mountain ridges of northern Thailand to the Hmong highlands of northern Laos—had become the world's largest source of opium, morphine, and heroin. Its narcotics were entering the United States through Hong Kong, Latin America, and Europe. The sudden increase in Southeast Asian heroin exports to the United States was fueling a rise in heroin use among American youth. By 1972 the U.S. Bureau of Narcotics began to revise its long-standing view of the global narcotics traffic. Since the end of World War II its agents had estimated that about 80 percent of America's narcotics was supplied by a European traffic that linked the poppy fields of Turkey with the heroin laboratories of Marseille. A scientific study by the bureau's chemists in mid-1972 showed that 25.7 percent of samples tested were from Southeast Asia. Finally, in November the bureau announced that an estimated 30 percent of America's heroin supply was coming from Southeast Asia and 60 percent from Turkey.[8] While global demand was thus drawing Southeast Asian heroin out of its regional market for the first time, local political forces were transforming the Golden Triangle's opium trade to make high-volume exports possible.

In the 1960s a combination of factors—American military intervention, corrupt national governments, and international criminal syndicates—pushed Southeast Asia's opium commerce beyond self-sufficiency to export capability. Production of low-grade no. 3 heroin (3 to 6 percent pure) had started in the late 1950s when the Thai government launched an intensive opium suppression campaign that forced most of its opium habitués to switch to heroin. By the early 1960s large quantities of no. 3 heroin were being refined in Bangkok and northern Thailand, while substantial amounts of morphine base were being processed in the Golden Triangle for export to Hong Kong and Europe. However, none of the Golden Triangle's opium refineries had yet mastered the difficult technique required to produce high-grade no. 4 heroin (90 to 99 percent pure).

In late 1969 opium refineries in the Burma-Thailand-Laos tri-border region, newly staffed by master chemists from Hong Kong, began producing limited supplies of high-grade heroin for the tens of thousands of GIs serving in South Vietnam. The U.S. military command in Saigon began getting its first reports of serious heroin addiction among isolated units in early 1970. By September or October the epidemic was fully developed: seemingly unlimited quantities of heroin were available at every U.S. installation from the Mekong Delta in the south to the DMZ in the north.

When rapid U.S. troop withdrawals in 1970–1972 reduced the local market for the Golden Triangle's heroin laboratories, Chinese, Corsican, and American syndicates began sending bulk shipments of no. 4 heroin directly to the United States. As a result of these growing exports, the wholesale price for a kilo of no. 4 heroin at Golden Triangle laboratories actually increased by 44 percent—from $1,240 in September 1970 to $1,780 in April 1971—despite a 30 percent decline in the number of GIs serving in Vietnam during the same period.[9] Moreover, the rapid growth of exports to the United States spurred a dramatic leap in the price of raw opium in the Golden Triangle. One American-trained anthropologist who spent several years studying hill tribes in northern Thailand reported that "between 1968 and early 1970 . . . the price of raw opium at the producing village almost doubled from $24 to $45 a kilogram."[10] While the growing rate of addiction among remaining U.S. troops in Vietnam probably accounted for some increased demand, increased exports to the American domestic market provided the major impetus behind the price rise. Significantly, it was in April 1971 that the first bulk shipments of Laotian heroin were intercepted in Europe and the United States. On April 5 U.S. customs officials seized 7.7 kilos of Double U-O Globe heroin at Fort Monmouth, New Jersey,[11] and on April 25 French authorities seized Prince Sopsaisana's 60 kilos at Orly.

In 1970–1971 U.S. law enforcement officials became alarmed over the increased heroin supplies available to America's addict population. Massive drug seizures of unprecedented size and value did not even make the "slightest ripple" in the availability or price of heroin.[12] Knowing that Turkey's opium production was declining, U.S. narcotics experts were mystified and began asking themselves where all this heroin was coming from.[13] The answer, of course, was the Golden Triangle.

The CIA, in its 1971 analysis of narcotics traffic in the Golden Triangle, reported that the largest of the region's seven heroin factories, located just north of Ban Houei Sai, Laos, was "believed capable of processing some 100 kilos of raw opium per day,"[14] or 3.6 tons of heroin a year—an enormous output, considering that American addicts only consumed about 10.0 tons of heroin annually. Moreover, none of this production was intended for Asian addicts: high-grade no. 4 heroin was too expensive for them, and they either smoked opium or used the inexpensive no. 3 heroin. In Bangkok, for example, one gram of no. 4 heroin cost sixteen times more than one gram of no. 3.[15] The only markets for these heroin laboratories were in the affluent West: Europe, with relatively few addicts, and the United States, which had a large and growing addict population.

U.S. military and political activities had played a significant role in shaping these developments. Although opium production continued to increase in Burma and Thailand, there were no major changes in the structure of the traffic during the 1960s. Still enjoying tacit CIA support for their counterinsurgency work, Nationalist Chinese (KMT) military caravans continued to move almost all of Burma's opium exports into northern Thailand, where they were purchased by a Chinese syndicate for domestic distribution and export to Hong Kong or Malaysia. The Shan national revolutionary movement offered a brief challenge to KMT hegemony over the opium trade, but after their most powerful leader was defeated in the 1967 Opium War, the Shan threat seemed to subside.

After the 1967 Opium War, the KMT solidified its control over the Burma-Thailand opium trade. Almost none of the 700 tons of raw opium harvested annually in Burma's Shan and Kachin states reached world markets through any of Burma's ports: instead, it was packed across the rugged Shan hills by mule caravan to the tri-border junction of Burma, Thailand, and Laos. This area was the beginning of two pipelines into the illicit international markets: one crossed Laos to Saigon, and the other headed due south through central Thailand to Bangkok.[16]

Although Shan rebel bands and Burmese self-defense forces collected a heavy tax from tribal opium farmers and itinerant merchants who transported raw opium to major Shan states market towns, they controlled very few of the caravans carrying raw opium south to refineries in the tri-border area. In 1967 one CIA operative reported that 90 percent of Burma's opium harvest was carried by Nationalist Chinese army mule caravans based in northern Thailand, 7 percent by Shan armed bands, and about 3 percent by Kachin rebels.[17]

Thailand's northern hill tribes were harvesting approximately 200 tons of opium annually, according to a 1968 U.S. Bureau of Narcotics estimate.[18] The Thai government reported that KMT military units and an allied group of Chinese hill traders controlled almost all of the opium commerce in northern Thailand.

In Laos, CIA clandestine intervention produced changes in the narcotics traffic. When political infighting among the Lao elite and the escalating war forced the small Corsican charter airlines out of the opium business in 1965, the CIA's airline, Air America, began flying Hmong opium out of the hills to Long Tieng and Vientiane. CIA cross-border intelligence missions into China from Laos reaped an unexpected dividend in 1962 when the Shan rebel leader who organized the forays for the agency began financing the Shan nationalist cause by selling Burmese opium to another CIA protégé, Laotian General Phoumi Nosavan. The economic alliance between General Phoumi and the Shans opened up a new trading pattern that diverted increasingly significant quantities of Burmese opium from their normal marketplace in Bangkok. In the late 1960s U.S. air force bombing disrupted Laotian opium production by forcing the majority of the Hmong opium farmers to become refugees. However, flourishing Laotian heroin laboratories, which were the major suppliers for the GI market in Vietnam, simply increased their imports of Burmese opium through already established trading relationships.

The importance of these CIA clients in the subsequent growth of the Golden Triangle's heroin trade was revealed, inadvertently, by the agency itself when it leaked a classified report on the Southeast Asian opium traffic to *The New York Times*. The CIA analysis identified twenty-one opium refineries in the tri-border area and reported that seven were capable of producing 90 to 99 percent pure no. 4 heroin. Of these seven heroin refineries, "the most important are located in the areas around Tachilek, Burma; Ban Houei Sai and Nam Keung in Laos; and Mae Salong in Thailand."[19]

Although the CIA did not elaborate, many of these refineries were located in areas controlled by paramilitary groups closely identified with American covert operations in the Golden Triangle. Mae Salong was headquarters for the Nationalist Chinese Fifth Army, which had been continuously involved in CIA counterinsurgency and intelligence operations since 1950. According to a former CIA operative who worked in the area for several years, the heroin laboratory at Nam Keung was protected by Major Chao La, commander of Yao mercenary troops for the CIA in northwestern Laos. One of the heroin laboratories near Ban Houei Sai reportedly belonged to General Ouane Rattikone, former commander in chief of the Royal Laotian Army—the only army in the world, except for the U.S. army, that was entirely financed by the U.S. government.[20] The heroin factories near Tachilek were operated by Burmese paramilitary units and Shan rebel armies who controlled a relatively small percentage of Burma's narcotics traffic. Although few of these Shan groups had any relation to the CIA by 1971, one of the most important chapters in the history of the Shan states' opium trade involved a Shan rebel army closely allied with the agency.

Other sources revealed the existence of an important heroin laboratory operating in the Vientiane region under the protection of Ouane. Finally, the U.S. Bureau of Narcotics reported that General Vang Pao, commander of the CIA's Secret Army, was operating a heroin factory at the CIA's Long Tieng headquarters.[21] These intelligence reports indicated a clear pattern: the CIA's covert action assets had become the leading heroin dealers in Laos.

The CIA's apparent complicity in the traffic, evident in the drug dealing of its closest Laotian clients, sprang largely from the agency's alliance with the Hmong hill tribes. When the CIA began its Laos operation in the late 1950s, it inherited a French paramilitary apparatus that had used Hmong guerrillas to fight the Vietnamese Communists in the First Indochina War. After abolition of the Indochina opium monopoly in 1950, French intelligence had financed its clandestine operations through an illicit traffic that linked the Hmong poppy fields of Laos with the opium dens of Saigon. Until their defeat in 1954, French paratroopers fighting with the Hmong guerrillas had purchased the annual opium harvest and shipped it south to Saigon on regular military aircraft.

When the CIA allied itself with the same Hmong guerrillas only four years after the French withdrawal, a somewhat different logic led to a similar sort of complicity. For fifteen years, 1960–1974, the CIA maintained a secret army of 30,000 Hmong tribesmen in the mountains of northern Laos—participants in a covert war that remains the largest single operation in the agency's forty-year history. Similar to the OSS campaign with Kachin guerrillas in Japanese-occupied Burma and the OPC invasion of China by KMT irregulars, the Laos operation soon achieved a scale and tactical sophistication that made it unique. In Laos the CIA fought a new kind of war, one very different from the conventional combat in neighboring Vietnam.

Although some writers have described the Hmong as the CIA's "mercenary army,"[22] the relationship was much more complex. As a migratory hill tribe with little loyalty to any nation, the Hmong had no real interest in winning the war. Yet this small tribe absorbed extremely high casualties in heavy combat that dragged on, without promise of victory or reward, for nearly fifteen years. The CIA maintained this motivation with remarkably few field operatives. After a year of operations, in 1961 the CIA reported that it had nine operatives working in the field with 9,000 Hmong guerrillas.[23] With a ratio of only one American agent for every thousand tribal guerrillas, the CIA had to rely on its chosen Hmong commander, Major Vang Pao, to mobilize and command his people's forces. In actual combat, the role of CIA operatives was limited to planning maneuvers and providing the air power needed to sustain an advance.

Beyond the battlefield, the secret war required, through its unprecedented scale and duration, a near total integration of CIA covert action with the fabric of Hmong tribal society. For Vang Pao to be effective in mobilizing his people for war, he had to maintain the political support of Hmong villages scattered across the highlands of northern Laos. As the success of its secret war became dependent on Vang Pao, the CIA used several tactics to raise his prestige among the Hmong—most important, by giving him the resources to become a powerful patron and, second, by encouraging his alliance with more traditional tribal elite, notably the Hmong cabinet minister Touby Lyfoung. In its initial report on the Hmong army to the White House in 1961, the CIA stated that "political leadership . . . is in the hands of Touby Lyfoung, who now operates mostly out of Vientiane" and "the military leader is Lt-Col Vang Pao, who is field commander"—an effective arrangement that the CIA would work to maintain.[24] As CIA director William Colby explained, the agency promoted Vang Pao as a "new breed of tribal leadership" and simultaneously encouraged "the expression of external deference to the old leaders."[25] Accordingly, when the war intensified in the late 1960s Vang Pao acquired the vestiges of traditional legitimacy by arranging for his son and daughter to marry the children of Touby, who still had the prestige of a traditional *kaitong*.[26] These maneuvers did raise Vang Pao's prestige, but it was the material and coercive aspects of his relationship with the tribe that would remain paramount.

Living in itinerant highland villages with an austere lifestyle, the Hmong had a tribal economy based on two basic commodities—rice for subsistence and opium for cash. Since the Hmong leaders had little to gain from a French or American victory, they were free to demand air transport for their opium as partial price for tribal mercenaries. To prosecute this secret war with any efficiency, the CIA thus found that its agents, like the French paratroopers before them, had to transport the tribe's cash crop.

Although the CIA did not, like the French, profit directly from the opium trade, the strength of its secret army was nonetheless integrated with the Laotian drug trade. By flying bundles of raw opium from remote villages to refineries, the CIA allowed the Hmong to continue their cash crop income, thus reducing the agency's direct costs in maintaining tribal households. The survival of these villages was central to the success of the secret war, both as motivation for tribal guerrillas in the field and as the source of young soldiers to fill ranks depleted by high casualties. To sustain an army of 30,000 men from a tribe of only 250,000 people, the CIA relied on the Hmong villages to supply boys, often only thirteen or fourteen, to replace tribal guerrillas wounded or killed in this bloody combat. In effect, the CIA's support for the Hmong opium crop insured the economic survival of the tribal villages, thereby allowing the agency to make its annual harvest of Hmong children. More important, control over the opium crop reinforced the authority of the CIA's Hmong commander, General Vang Pao, transforming him from a minor officer into a tribal warrior who could extract adolescent recruits from villages no longer willing to accept the war's high casualties.

When fighting reached the valleys below their mountain villages, the Hmong became isolated from normal highland trade and increasingly dependent on U.S. aircraft for access to markets. As the adult male population dwindled, the villages could no longer grow sufficient rice to survive and were forced to depend on the CIA's Air America for delivery of humanitarian rice shipments. By making Vang Pao the man who approved aircraft for movement of rice into villages and opium out, the CIA gave him direct control over the two economic essentials of once autonomous Hmong households. With such power, Vang Pao could make the scattered clans and hamlets of Hmong highland society into one people, one army.

More than arms, rice, or money, it was air power that became the central factor in the CIA's relationship with Vang Pao. Long fragmented and divided by the rugged mountain terrain, the Hmong were now unified under Vang Pao through an Air America network of agile aircraft that landed rice in their villages and carried away their men to battle or their opium to market. No longer earthbound, Hmong guerrillas flew into battle backed by a cloudburst of bombs from U.S. fighters flying out of bases in nearby Thailand. In the mid-1960s Vang Pao's airborne offensives skipped along the mountaintops and established bases within fifteen miles of North Vietnam's borders. When the tides of war reversed and the Communist Pathet Lao advanced on the Plain of Jars after 1969, U.S. air power evacuated the Hmong villages to refugee camps under Vang Pao's control and devastated the enemy's territory with daily bombing. Even though the Communists had captured the countryside, Vang Pao still held the people. Air power became the medium for a political exchange that drove the secret war: Vang Pao relied on air transport to deliver his people for slaughter in the CIA's secret war, and the agency in turn did not object when his officers used Air America to transport the Hmong opium crop.

Viewed from the perspective of a CIA operative fighting in the remote and rugged terrain of northern Laos, complicity in the Hmong opium trade was driven by an ineluctable logic. Among the consequences of such a strategy, however, was the growing production of heroin supplies, first for U.S. troops in Vietnam and later for addicts in America.

## Laos: Contraband Kingdom

Laos is one of those historical oddities like Monaco, Andorra, and Liechtenstein that were somehow left behind when petty principalities were consolidated into great nations. Although both nineteenth-century empire builders and cold war summit negotiators subscribed to the fiction of Laotian nationhood out of diplomatic convenience, this impoverished little kingdom appeared to lack all of the economic and political criteria for nationhood. Not even the Wilsonian principle of ethnic determinism that Versailles peacemakers used to justify the division of the Austro-Hungarian Empire after World War I validated Laos's existence. In 1970 some 8 million Lao lived in northeast Thailand, but there were only about 1.5 million Lao in Laos. With a total population of 2 to 3 million and singularly lacking in natural resources, Laos had been plagued by fiscal problems since becoming independent in 1954. Unable to finance itself through corporate, mineral, or personal taxes, the Royal Laotian government filled its coffers and lined its pockets by legalizing or tolerating what its neighbors had chosen to outlaw, as needy principalities the world over have done. Monaco gambles, Macao facilitates the gold traffic, and the Laotian government tolerated the smuggling of gold, guns, and opium.

While the credit card revolution has displaced paper currency in America, peasants and merchants in underdeveloped countries still harbor a distrust for their nations' technicolor currency, preferring to store their savings in gold or silver. Asian governments inadvertently fostered illicit gold trafficking either by imposing a heavy revenue-producing duty on legal gold imports or by limiting the right of most citizens to purchase and hold gold freely; thus, an illicit gold traffic flourished from Pakistan to the Philippines. Purchased legally on the European market, the gold was flown to Dubai, Singapore, Vientiane, or Macao, where local governments imposed a relatively low import duty and took little interest in what happened after the tax was paid.

Laos's low duty on imported gold and its government's active participation in the smuggling trade long made it the major source of illicit gold for Thailand and South Vietnam. Although Laos was the poorest nation in Southeast Asia, Vientiane's licensed brokers imported from 32 to 72 tons of gold a year after the American buildup in Vietnam began in 1965. As thousands of free-spending GIs poured into Vietnam during the early years of the war, Saigon's black market prospered and Laos's annual gold imports shot up to 72 tons by 1967.[27] The 8.5 percent import duty provided the Royal Laotian government with more than 40 percent of its total tax revenues.[28] However, in 1968 the Tet offensive and the international gold crisis slowed consumer demand in Saigon and plunged the Laotian government into a fiscal crisis. Prime Minister Souvanna Phouma went before the National Assembly and explained that because of the downward trend in the gold market, "one of our principal sources of income will not reach our expectations this year." Faced with what the prime minister described as "an extremely complex and difficult situation," Finance Minister Sisouk na Champassak privately suggested that the government might seek an alternative source of revenue by taxing the clandestine opium trade.[29] When the establishment of a gold market in Singapore in 1969 challenged Laos's position as the major gold entrepôt in Southeast Asia and forced the finance ministry to drop the import duty from 8.5 to 5.5 percent in 1970.[30] Sisouk told a BBC reporter, "The only export we can develop here is opium, and we should increase our production and export of it."[31]

As minister of finance and acting minister of defense, Sisouk was one of the most important government officials in Laos, and his views on the opium trade were fairly representative of those of the ruling elite. Most Laotian leaders realized that their nation's only valuable export commodity was opium, and they promoted the traffic with an aggressiveness worthy of modern export executives. Needless to say, this positive attitude toward the narcotics traffic was something of an embarrassment to American advisers serving in Laos, and in deference to their patrons the Laotian elite generally did their best to maintain the fiction that opium trafficking was little more than a tribal problem.[32] As a result, coups, assassinations, and political infighting spawned by periodic struggles for control of the opium traffic often seemed quixotic to outside observers. But they suddenly gain new meaning when examined in light of the economics and logistics of the opium trade.

From the late 1950s on, the opium trade in northern Laos involved both the marketing of the locally grown produce and the transit traffic in Burmese opium. Traditionally most of Laos's domestic production was concentrated in the mountains of northeastern Laos, although it was later reduced by massive U.S. bombing and an opium eradication program in the Pathet Lao liberated zones.[33] Designated on Royal Laotian army maps as Military Region II, this area comprised the Plain of Jars and most of the Hmong highlands that extended from the northern rim of the Vientiane Plain to the border of North Vietnam. While northwestern Laos also had extensive poppy cultivation, opium production never achieved the same high level as in the northeast; soil conditions were not as favorable, the traffic was not as well organized, and tribal populations were more scattered. For example, there were between 150,000 and 200,000 Hmong living in the northeast, but only about 50,000 in the northwest. As a result, the opium trade in northwestern Laos, known as Military Region I in the 1970s, was always secondary in importance during the colonial era and the early years of the postcolonial opium traffic. However, in the mid-1960s Shan and Nationalist Chinese opium caravans began crossing the Mekong into Laos's extreme northwest with large quantities of Burmese opium. As refineries opened along the Laotian bank of the Mekong to process the Burmese opium, the center of Laos's opium trade shifted from the Plain of Jars to Ban Houei Sai in the northwest.

The mountains of northern Laos are some of the most strikingly beautiful in the world. Shrouded with mile-high clouds during the rainy season, they are reminiscent of traditional Chinese scroll paintings. Row upon row of sharp ridges wind across the landscape, punctuated by steep peaks that conjure up images of dragons' heads, towering monuments, or rearing horses. The bedrock is limestone, and centuries of wind and rain have carved a fabulous landscape from this porous, malleable material. And it is the limestone mountains that attracted the Hmong opium farmers. The delicate opium poppy, which withers and dies in strongly acidic soil, thrives in limestone soil. Tribal opium farmers were well aware of the poppy's need for alkaline soil and tended to favor mountain hollows studded with limestone outcroppings as locations for their poppy fields.

But the mountain terrain that is so ideal for poppy cultivation makes long-range travel difficult for merchant caravans. When the French tried to encourage hill tribe production during the colonial era, they concentrated most of their efforts on Hmong villages near the Plain of Jars, where communications were relatively well developed, and they abandoned much of the Laotian highlands to petty smugglers. Desperate for a way to finance their clandestine operations, French intelligence agencies expropriated the hill tribe opium trade in the last few years of the First Indochina War and used military aircraft to link the Laotian poppy fields with opium dens in Saigon. But the military aircraft that had overcome the mountain barriers for Laotian merchants were withdrawn in 1954, along with the rest of the French Expeditionary Corps, and Laos's opium trade fell upon hard times.

## Air Opium, 1955–1965

After France's military withdrawal in 1954, several hundred French war veterans, colonists, and gangsters stayed on in Laos. Some of them, mainly Corsicans, started a number of small charter airlines, which became colorfully and collectively known as Air Opium. Ostensibly founded to supply otherwise unavailable transportation for civilian businessmen and diplomats, these airlines gradually restored Laos's link to the drug markets of South Vietnam that had vanished with the departure of the French air force in 1954. At first, progress was hampered by unfavorable political conditions in South Vietnam, and the three fledgling airlines that pioneered these new routes enjoyed only limited success.[34]

Perhaps the most famous of the early French opium pilots was Gérard Labenski. His aircraft was based at Phong Savan on the Plain of Jars, where he managed the Snow Leopard Inn, a hotel that doubled as a warehouse for outgoing opium shipments.[35] Another of these aviation pioneers was René "Babal" Enjabal, a former French air force officer whose airline was popularly known as Babal Air Force.[36] The most tenacious member of the shadowy trio was Roger Zoile. His charter airline was allied with Paul Louis Levet's Bangkok-based Corsican syndicate.

In the late 1950s Levet was probably the most important Marseille underworld figure regularly supplying European heroin laboratories with morphine base from Southeast Asia. Levet had arrived in Saigon in 1953–1954 and got his start smuggling gold and piasters on the Saigon-Marseille circuit. After the gold traffic dried up in 1955, he became involved in the opium trade and moved to Bangkok, where he established the Pacific Industrial Company. According to a U.S. Bureau of Narcotics report filed in 1962, this company was used as a cover to smuggle substantial quantities of morphine base from northern Thailand to heroin laboratories in Europe. Through a network of four prominent Corsican gangsters based in Vientiane, Phnom Penh, and Saigon, Levet used Zoile's airline to move morphine base from the Golden Triangle to seaports in Thailand and Indochina.[37] There was an enormous amount of shipping between Southeast Asia and Europe, so arranging for deliveries presented no problem. Saigon was particularly convenient as a transshipment point since substantial numbers of French freighters carrying Corsican crews still sailed direct to Marseille. Even though Levet's syndicate was preoccupied with the European traffic, it also had a share of the regional opium trade.[38]

Although all these men were competent pilots and committed opium smugglers, the South Vietnamese government had adopted an intolerant attitude toward the opium traffic that seriously hampered their operations. In 1955 South Vietnam's President Diem closed most of Saigon's opium dens and announced his determination to eradicate the drug traffic. Denied secure access to Saigon, the Corsican air smugglers had to devise an elaborate set of routes, transfers, and drop zones, which complicated their work and restricted the amount of narcotics they could ship. However, only three years later Diem's chief adviser,

Ngo Dinh Nhu, reopened the dens to finance his secret police and became a silent partner in a Corsican charter airline.[39]

Named Air Laos Commerciale, the airline was managed by the most powerful member of Saigon's Corsican underworld, Bonaventure "Rock" Francisci. Tall and handsome, Francisci sported a thin black mustache and a natural charm that won friends easily. Beginning in 1958 Air Laos Commerciale made daily flights from its headquarters at Vientiane's Wattay Airport, picking up 300 to 600 kilos of raw opium from secondary Laotian airports (usually dirt runways in northern Laos) and delivering the cargo to drop points in South Vietnam, Cambodia, and the Gulf of Thailand. While these opium deliveries were destined for Southeast Asian consumers, he also supplied Corsican heroin manufacturers in Marseille. Although a relative latecomer to the field, Francisci's airline had important advantages that other Corsican airlines lacked. His rivals had to take elaborate precautions before venturing into South Vietnam, but, thanks to his relationship with Nhu, Francisci's aircraft shuttled back and forth to convenient drop zones just north of Saigon.[40]

With easy access to Saigon's market restored, opium production in northern Laos, which had declined in the years 1954–1958, quickly revived. During the opium season, Corsican charter companies made regular flights from Phong Savan or Vientiane to isolated provincial capitals and market towns scattered across northern Laos—places such as Sam Neua, Phong Saly, Muong Sing, Nam Tha, Sayaboury, and Ban Houei Sai. Each of these towns served as a center for local opium trade managed by resident Chinese shopkeepers. Every spring these Chinese merchants loaded their horses or mules with salt, thread, iron bars, silver coins, and assorted odds and ends and rode into the surrounding hills to barter with hundreds of hill tribe farmers for their bundles of raw opium.[41] Toward the end of every harvest season Corsican aircraft would land near these towns, purchase the opium, and fly it back to Phong Savan or Vientiane, where it was stored until a buyer in Saigon, Singapore, or Indonesia placed an order.[42]

Francisci also prospered, and by 1962 he had a fleet of three new twin-engine Beechcrafts making hundreds of deliveries a month. With his debonair manner he became something of a local celebrity. He gave interviews to the Vientiane press corps, speaking proudly of his air drops to surrounded troops or his services for famous diplomats. When asked about the opium business, he responded, "I only rent the planes, I don't know what missions they're used for."[43]

But unfortunately for Francisci's public image, one of his pilots was arrested in 1962 and Air Laos Commerciale's opium smuggling was given international publicity. The abortive mission was piloted by René Enjabal, the retired air force officer who had founded Babal Air Force.

In October 1962 Enjabal and his mechanic took off from Vientiane's Wattay Airport and flew south to Savannakhet where they picked up twenty-nine watertight tin crates, each packed with 20 kilos of raw opium and wrapped in a buoyant life belt. Enjabal flew south over Cambodia and dropped the 600 kilos to a small fishing boat waiting at a prearranged point in midocean. On the return flight to Vientiane, Enjabal fell asleep at the controls of his plane, drifted over Thailand, and was forced to land at a Thai air force base by two Thai T-28 fighters. When his "military charter" orders from the Laotian government failed to convince Thai authorities he was not a spy, Enjabal confessed that he had been on an opium run to the Gulf of Thailand. Relieved that it was nothing more serious, his captors allowed him to return to Vientiane after serving a nominal six-week jail sentence. While Enjabal was being interrogated by the Thai, the opium boat moved undisturbed across the Gulf of Thailand and delivered its cargo to smugglers waiting on the east coast of the Malaya Peninsula. Although Enjabal had earned a paltry $15 an hour for his trouble, Francisci may have grossed up to $20,000 for his role in this nautical adventure.[44]

While this unfortunate incident cost Francisci most of his legitimate business, it in no way hampered his opium smuggling. Even though Enjabal's downfall was the subject of a feature article in *Life* magazine, Francisci continued to operate with the same self-confidence. And with good reason. For not only was he protected by South Vietnam's most influential politician, Ngo Dinh Nhu, he was allied with the powerful Guerini syndicate of Marseille. During the period these Corsican airlines operated in Laos, the Guerini brothers were the leaders of the French underworld and heads of a criminal syndicate that stretched across the globe.[45] All of Francisci's competitors suffered mysterious accidents and sudden arrests, but he operated with absolute impunity. These political connections gave him a decisive advantage over his competitors, and he became Indochina's premier opium smuggler. Like the Guerini brothers in Marseille, Francisci despised competition and used everything from plastique explosives to the South Vietnamese police to eliminate his rivals.

Francisci's first victim had been René Enjabal. On November 19, 1959, Vietnamese police raided a remote dirt runway near Ban Me Thuot in the Central Highlands shortly after a twin-engine Beechcraft belonging to Enjabal landed carrying 293 kilos of Laotian opium. After arresting the pilot and three henchmen waiting at the airstrip, the Vietnamese impounded the aircraft.[46] With the loss of his plane, Enjabal had no alternative. Within several months he was flying for the man who in all probability was the architect of his downfall—Francisci.[47] The Vietnamese had taken no legal action against Enjabal and released the pilot,

Desclerts, after a relatively short jail term. Desclerts returned to France and reportedly continued working with Corsican syndicates to ship bulk quantities of heroin to the United States.[48]

After Enjabal's airline collapsed, Francisci's most important competitor for the lucrative South Vietnamese market was Gérard Labenski, one of Air Opium's earliest pioneers, whom many considered the best bush pilot in Laos. Francisci resented his competition and once tried to eliminate Labenski by blowing up his Cessna 195 with plastique as it sat on the runway at Phong Savan. When that failed, Francisci used his contacts with the South Vietnamese government to have his rival's entire seven-man syndicate arrested. On August 25, 1960, shortly after he landed near Xuan Loc, forty-five miles north of Saigon, with 220 kilos of raw opium, Vietnamese police descended on Labenski's entire syndicate, arrested him, and impounded his aircraft. Labenski and his chief Saigon salesman, François Mittard, were given five-year jail sentences, the others three years apiece.[49]

After languishing in a Vietnamese prison for more than two years, Labenski and Mittard were so embittered at Francisci's betrayal that they broke the Corsican rule of silence and told U.S. narcotics investigators everything they knew about his syndicate, claiming that their arrests had been engineered by Francisci to force them out of business. But Francisci was too well protected to be compromised by informers, and Air Laos Commerciale continued flying until 1965, when political upheavals in Laos forced all the Corsican airlines out of business. Mittard and Labenski were released from prison in 1964 and left Saigon almost immediately for Laos.[50]

While Enjabal and Labenski concentrated on local markets, Paul Louis Levet's Bangkok-based syndicate competed directly with Francisci for the European market. His Corsican rivals always considered Levet the "most shrewd of all the persons smuggling opium out of Laos," but he too was forced out of business by police action. On July 18, 1963, Levet received a telegram from Saigon that read:

> Everything OK. Try to have friend meet me in Saigon the 19th.
> Am in room 33 Continental Hotel.
>                         [signed] Poncho.

The wire was a prearranged signal. Levet and his assistant, Michel Libert, packed 18 kilos of Burmese opium into a brown suitcase, put it in the trunk of Levet's blue Citroen sedan, and drove out to Bangkok's Don Muang Airport. Just as they were making the transfer to a courier who was ticketed on a regular commercial flight to Saigon, Thai police closed in. The unfortunate Libert was given five years in prison, but Levet was released for "lack of evidence" and deported. Levet disappeared without a trace, while Libert, after serving his full jail term, left for Laos, where he resumed an active role in Indochina's Corsican underworld.

While Francisci was the only one of these Corsican racketeers believed to have been allied with Ngo Dinh Nhu, all of the charter airlines had to reach an accommodation with the Laotian government. All airports in Laos were classified as military terminals, and permission to take off and land required an order from the Royal Laotian army. Opium runs were usually classified as *réquisition militaire*—military charter—and as such were approved by the Laotian high command. One *Time* correspondent who examined Air Laos Commerciale's log books in November 1962 noted that a high percentage of its flights were listed as *réquisition militaire*.[51]

Despite the destructive infighting of the various Corsican airlines, they proved to be reliable opium suppliers, and the Laos-Saigon opium commerce flourished. Guaranteed reliable access to international markets, Laos's opium production climbed steadily during the ten-year period that the Corsicans controlled its opium economy; in 1953 Laos's annual harvest was estimated at 50 tons of raw opium, but in 1968 it had expanded to 100–150 tons.[52] Moreover, these syndicates, most notably Francisci's and Levet's, made regular morphine base shipments from Southeast Asia to heroin laboratories in Italy, Germany, and Marseille. Although Southeast Asian morphine still accounted for a relatively small proportion of European heroin production in the late 1950s and early 1960s, these shipments established the first links of what became a direct connection between the Golden Triangle's poppy fields and Marseille's heroin laboratories—links that would take on added importance as Turkey's opium production ebbed toward abolition in the late 1960s.

Although they were forced out of business in 1965 when Laotian General Ouane Rattikone decided to monopolize the trade, these syndicates later served as the link between Laotian heroin laboratories and American distributors when Golden Triangle laboratories began producing no. 4 heroin in the early 1970s.

## General Phoumi Nosavan: CIA Ally

According to General Ouane Rattikone, the man who issued the *réquisitions militaires* and controlled much of the opium traffic was General Phoumi Nosavan, CIA protégé and political leader of the Laotian right wing.[53] Phoumi Nosavan was just an ambitious young colonel in 1958 when an unexpected electoral victory by the leftist Pathet Lao movement brought a neutralist government to power and panicked the U.S. mission. Concerned that Laos might eventually turn

Communist, the U.S. mission decided that special measures were called for. Almost immediately the CIA financed the formation of a right-wing coalition, and several weeks later the State Department plunged the neutralist government into a fiscal crisis by cutting off all aid. Little more than three months after the elections, Prime Minister Souvanna Phouma and his neutralist government resigned. When a right-wing government took office, the new prime minister, Phoui Sananikone, declared, "We are anti-Communists."[54]

Phoumi Nosavan was one of the bright young men the CIA picked to organize the right wing. Backed by the CIA, Phoumi became a cabinet minister in February 1959 and a general several months later.[55] With his personal CIA agent always by his side, Phoumi went on to plot coups, rig elections, and help the CIA build up its Secret Army; in short, he became the major actor in the CIA's effort to keep Laos's government anti-Communist. However, in 1961 the Kennedy administration opted for a neutralist coalition rather than risk an armed confrontation with the Soviet Union over Laos, and Phoumi was ordered to merge his right-wing government into a tripartite coalition. When he refused despite personal appeals from President Kennedy and the assistant secretary of state, the State Department had his CIA contact transferred out of the country and in February 1962 cut off the $3 million a month it had been supplying his government.[56]

Desperate for funds but determined not to resign, Phoumi turned to the opium traffic as an alternative source of income for his army and government. Although he had controlled the traffic for several years and collected a payoff from both Corsican and Chinese smugglers, he was not actively involved, and his percentage represented only a small share of the total profits. Furthermore, Laotian opium merchants were still preoccupied with marketing locally grown opium, and very little Burmese opium was entering international markets through Laos. The obvious solution to Phoumi's fiscal crisis was for his government to become directly involved in the import and export of Burmese opium. This decision ultimately led to the growth of northwest Laos as one of the largest heroin-producing centers in the world.

Adhering to his nation's feudal traditions, Phoumi delegated responsibility for the task of establishing a link with the Burmese traffic to General Ouane Rattikone, commander of Military Region I and warlord of northwestern Laos. Ouane recalled that he was appointed chairman of the semiofficial Laotian Opium Administration in early 1962 and charged with the responsibility of arranging Burmese opium imports.[57] Working through a commander in the Secret Army in Ban Houei Sai, he contacted a Shan rebel leader employed by the CIA in the Golden Triangle region who arranged the first deliveries of Burmese opium

# 1. Legal Heroin and Cocaine Sales

Advertisement for cocaine and opiates typical of those appearing in popular and professional publications before the prohibition of narcotics. *Chemist and Druggist of Australasia, February 1908*

## 2. American Drug Dealers

*(Above)*
Meyer Lansky, a younger member of the so-called "Jewish Syndicate" that dominated New York's drug and alcohol rackets during prohibition, as photographed by New York City Police before World War II. *Alan A. Block Collection*

*(Right)*
Charles "Lucky" Luciano (standing, right), prewar New York Mafia leader, in exile after his deportation to Italy during the late 1940s. *Harry Anslinger Papers, Pattee Library, Pennsylvania State University*

Santo Trafficante, Jr. (center), postwar Mafia figure and alleged drug dealer, at lunch with criminal leaders in New York City in the late 1960s. *Paul de Maria, New York Daily News*

# 3. Marseille's Corsican Milieu

Barthelemy Guerini, the Marseille criminal leader who captured control of the city's waterfront from the Communist party with the support of the CIA in 1950–1951, was sentenced to twenty years for a milieu murder in 1970. *Le Provençal, Marseille*

François Spirito, prewar Corsican syndicate leader and international heroin smuggler, shown at his 1952 trial for wartime collaboration with German occupation forces. *Agence France-Presse*

# 4. War and Opium in French Indochina

A Chinese merchant trading opium with a Laotian tribeswoman at a market on the Plain of Jars, northern Laos in the early 1950s. *Touby Lyfoung collection*

French paratrooper trains Laotian guerrillas, Plain of Jars, northern Laos, 1953. *Touby Lyfoung collection*

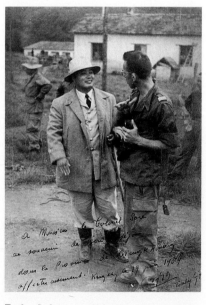

Touby Lyfoung, political leader of Hmong guerrillas fighting with the French military, confers with a French officer on the Plain of Jars in northern Laos, 1953. *Touby Lyfoung collection*

General Le Van Vien (right), leader of the Binh Xuyen bandits who controlled Saigon's opium trade, meets with Prime Minister Ngo Dinh Diem in late 1954. *Life,* © *1955*

Colonel Edward G. Lansdale, leading CIA operative in Southeast Asia, played a key role in breaking the Binh Xuyen bandits' control over Saigon during urban warfare in 1954–1955. *United Press International*

# 5. Nationalist Chinese Troops in the Golden Triangle

Nationalist Chinese soldier training at Fifth Army headquarters, Mae Salong, northern Thailand, 1967. *Weekend Telegraph, London, March 1967*

General Tuan Shi-wen, commander of the Nationalist Chinese Fifth Army, at his headquarters on the Thai-Burma border in 1967: "We have to continue to fight the evil of Communism, and to fight you must have an army, and an army must have guns, and to buy guns you must have money. In these mountains the only money is opium." *Weekend Telegraph, London, March 1967*

Nationalist Chinese officer based in northern Thailand who, like many of his comrades, married a woman from the hill tribes along the Thai-Burma border and sired sons who will be expected to join the Fifth Army. *Weekend Telegraph, London, March 1967*

# 6. CIA's Secret Army in Laos

A Yao tribeswoman near Pha Louang village in the mountains of northern Laos prepares a hillside for opium planting in 1971. *John Everingham*

Ger Su Yang, the Hmong military commander of Long Pot district in northern Laos, with his family, 1971. *John Everingham*

Hmong militia, veterans of the CIA's Secret Army, on patrol near Long Pot village, northern Laos in August 1971. *John Everingham*

Assisted by aide George Cosgrove, Edgar "Pop" Buell, organizer of the CIA's Secret Army, directs Air America cargo planes parachuting rice to dependents of Hmong soldiers in the mountains of northern Laos, 1971. *Alfred W. McCoy*

Air America helicopter lands at Long Pot village in northern Laos, 1971. *John Everingham*

Hmong women and children collect U.S. AID rice parachuted by Air America, northern Laos, 1971.
*Alfred W. McCoy*

General Ouane Rattikone (center), commander of the Royal Lao Army and Laos's leading heroin manufacturer, being decorated by King Savang Vatthana (left), on his retirement in June 1971. *Alfred W. McCoy*

The trademark for Double U-O Globe heroin brand, manufactured at Ouane Rattikone's laboratory in northwestern Laos for sale to U.S. troops serving in South Vietnam during the early 1970s. *Alfred W. McCoy*

General Vang Pao, the Hmong officer who commanded the CIA's Secret Army from 1960 to 1975, at Vientiane, Laos in July 1971. *Daniele Cavalerie*

At Nam Keung village, northern Laos in 1972, U.S. AID official Edgar "Pop" Buell lectures Major Chao La, CIA mercenary commander and heroin manufacturer, on the evils of the drug trade for the benefit of the press. *Fox Butterfield, The New York Times*

# 7. Golden Triangle Heroin Trade

Khun Sa, Burma's leading opium warlord and heroin manufacturer, in his headquarters at Mongmai in the Shan states near the Thai border, February 1989. *Piers Cavendish*

Recruits for Khun Sa's army undergo training at his camp in Mongmai, January 1989. *Piers Cavendish*

A soldier in the Shan state army, a Burmese rebel group active in the opium trade, at their camp in Man Pi, 1986. *Hseng Noung Lintner*

In the southern Shan states a Pa-O tribeswoman collects opium during the 1989 harvest at Naung Aw village, part of the territory controlled by Khun Sa. *Piers Cavendish*

# 8. Afghanistan Resistance Forces

Afghan resistance leader Gulbuddin Hekmatyar (center), chief beneficiary of CIA arms shipments, claims victory at the headquarters of the Afghan rebel alliance in Peshawar, Pakistan, the day before the Soviet withdrawal from Afghanistan began in May 1988. *Steve Galster*

Afghan guerrillas of the Harakat party celebrating a peace treaty with the Kabul Communist government at Ghor Province, central Afghanistan, August 1989. *Dr. Jochen Hippler*

several months later.[58] Ouane was proud of this historic achievement, for these were the first major opium caravans to cross the Mekong River into Laos.

When asked whether he exported the Burmese opium by dropping it in the Central Highlands of South Vietnam, Ouane responded:

> No, that is stupid and done only by small merchants and not great merchants. . . . We rented Dakotas [C-47s] from the civil aviation companies and then dropped the opium into the Gulf of Siam. The opium was wrapped in four or five layers of plastic and then attached to floats. It was dropped to small fishing boats, taken to fishing ports in South Vietnam, and then it disappeared. We are not stupid; we are serious merchants.[59]

Ouane said these early shipments were quite profitable and claimed that they provided General Phoumi with an average income of about $35,000 a month during 1962.

Despite Ouane's best efforts, a series of military and financial reverses soon forced Phoumi to merge his right-wing government into the tripartite coalition. Phoumi's government had simply ordered the National Bank to print more money when American aid was cut off in February; the foreign exchange backing for Laotian currency declined by 30 percent in six months and consumer prices in Vientiane jumped by 20 percent. Phoumi had gone on a whirlwind tour of Asia's anti-Communist nations to appeal for aid, but only South Korea had been willing to help.[60] When his rightist troops suffered a disastrous defeat at Nam Tha in northwestern Laos in May 1962, Phoumi acknowledged his failure and in June merged his government into a neutralist coalition headed by Prime Minister Souvanna Phouma.

But the price of Phoumi's compliance was high. Although he yielded some of his political power, he demanded compensatory economic concessions from the neutralist government. Bartering away several powerful ministries, Phoumi retained control over the finance ministry and won the right to monopolize much of Vientiane's thriving consumer economy. With the prime minister's tacit consent, he established a variety of lucrative monopolies over the capital's vice trades and legitimate commercial activities.[61]

One of his enterprises was an offensive but profitable gambling casino in downtown Vientiane that one journalist described as "an ugly, five-story building that stank like an Indonesian urinal." When Phoumi announced plans to erect similar monstrosities in every major Laotian city, the king categorically refused to allow one in Luang Prabang, the royal capital, and local authorities in Thakhek raised equally vehement objections. But Phoumi was not daunted by these reverses in the establishment of his financial base. Gold trafficking was even more lucrative than gambling, and the ministry of finance granted Phoumi's Bank of Laos a monopoly on the import of gold, which netted him from $300,000 to $500,000 a year.[62]

The opium trade, however, was the most profitable of all ventures. Phoumi opened a seedy opium den in Vientiane that could accommodate 150 smokers. To ward off possible criticism from his free world allies, Phoumi had a sign hung over the entrance to his palace of dreams: DETOXIFICATION CLINIC. When a French journalist asked Prime Minister Souvanna Phouma why this eyesore was allowed to remain open, he replied, "Feudalism is still with us."[63]

Although Phoumi had abandoned his plans for fiscal independence from the United States, Ouane Rattikone continued to manage the Laotian Opium Administration with considerable success. Larger Shan caravans were entering northwestern Laos every year, and from 1962 to 1964 profits on exports to South Vietnam tripled. According to the Laotian Opium Administration's ledger, which Ouane stored in an upstairs closet of his Vientiane villa, November 1963 was a typical month: 1,146 kilos of raw opium were shipped to South Vietnam, netting $97,410.[64]

But Phoumi's parsimonious management of his monopolies produced serious tensions in the right-wing camp and were a major cause of the April 1964 coup that toppled him from power. Not only did he monopolize the most lucrative portions of Vientiane's economy, but he refused to share his profits with the other right-wing generals.

The commander of the Vientiane military region, General Kouprasith Abhay, considered the capital his rightful economic preserve and was resentful of Phoumi. Ouane harbored somewhat similar feelings: more than seven years after the coup, the genial Ouane could still become angry when he recalled that Phoumi paid him a monthly salary of two hundred dollars to manage an opium administration making more than a million dollars a year.[65] Moreover, Phoumi's "understanding" with Prime Minister Souvanna Phouma had softened his hostility toward the neutralist government; and this cost him influence among the extreme right wing, which included both Kouprasith and Ouane.

Although the ostensible motivation for the right-wing coup of April 19, 1964 was to eliminate the neutralist army and make the prime minister more responsive to the right wing, the generals seem to have devoted most of their energy to breaking up Phoumi's financial empire.[66] The coup began at 4:00 A.M. as General Kouprasith's troops seized the city, captured most of the neutralist army officers, and placed the prime minister under house arrest. There was no resistance and virtually no bloodshed. While the threat of a U.S. aid cutoff convinced Kouprasith and Ouane to release the prime minister from house arrest, nothing could deter them from stripping Phoumi of his power.[67] On May 2 General Phoumi resigned his portfolio as minister of defense. That same day, the ministry of finance canceled the import license for Sogimex Company, one of Phoumi's businesses, which had enjoyed a monopoly on the import of alcoholic beverages. The Revolutionary Committee closed his gambling casino, and the ministry of finance broke the Bank of Laos's monopoly on gold imports.[68]

But in the confused manner of Laotian coups, Phoumi tried to recoup his lost power by launching a countercoup on February 2, 1965. After four separate groups of soldiers wearing three different color-coded scarves charged about Vientiane firing heavy artillery and machine guns for four or five days, Phoumi finally gave up and fled to Thailand.[69] The situation was so confusing that Ouane and Kouprasith held a press conference on February 8 to proclaim their victory and to explain that there had indeed been a coup—their coup.[70]

As the victors, Kouprasith and Ouane divided what remained of Phoumi's financial empire. While Kouprasith inherited most of the fallen general's real estate holdings, brothels, and opium dens in the Vientiane region, Ouane assumed control over the opium trade in northwestern Laos.

Ouane's accession to Phoumi's former position in the drug trade brought an end to the activities of the Corsican Air Opium charter airlines. Unwilling to tolerate any competition, Ouane refused to issue those airlines *réquisitions militaires*, thereby denying them access to Laotian airports. This ban made it impossible for the Corsican airlines to continue operating and forced them out of the opium transport business.[71] However, Ouane had seriously overestimated his air logistic capabilities, and the move produced a major crisis for Laos's opium trade.

As it turned out, Ouane probably could not have picked a worse time to force the Corsicans out of business. Laotian military air power was at a premium in 1964 and 1965: bombing operations along the Ho Chi Minh Trail were just getting under way; Laotian T-28 fighters were being used in clandestine reprisal raids against North Vietnam; and renewed fighting on the Plain of Jars required extensive air support.[72] The commander of the Laotian air force was determined to give these military operations priority and refused to allocate air transports for General Ouane's opium runs to Ban Houei Sai.

In the Hmong highlands of northeastern Laos the situation was even more critical. Capture of the Plain of Jars by Pathet Lao rebels in 1964 restricted government aircraft to temporary dirt landing strips on the surrounding mountain ridges. Heavy C-47 transports were almost useless for this kind of flying, and the Laotian air force had almost no light observation planes. Wartime conditions had increased Hmong dependence on poppy cultivation, and the lack of air transport created serious economic problems for hill tribe opium farmers. Since the CIA was using the Hmong population to combat Pathet Lao forces in the mountains of northeastern Laos, the prosperity of this tribe was central to the agency's success. By 1965 the CIA had created a Hmong army of 30,000 men that guarded radar installations vital to bombing North Vietnam, rescued downed American pilots, and battled Pathet Lao guerrillas.

Without air transport for their opium, the Hmong faced an economic crisis. There was simply no form of air transport available in northern Laos except the CIA's charter airline, Air America. Thus, according to several sources, Air America began flying opium from mountain villages north and east of the Plain of Jars to General Vang Pao's headquarters at Long Tieng.[73]

Air America was known to be flying Hmong opium as late as 1971. Hmong village leaders in the area west of the Plain of Jars, for example, claimed that their 1970 and 1971 opium harvests were bought up by Vang Pao's officers and flown to Long Tieng on Air America UH-1H helicopters. This opium was probably destined for heroin laboratories in Long Tieng or Vientiane and, ultimately, for GI addicts in Vietnam.[74]

The U.S. embassy in Vientiane adopted an attitude of benign neglect toward the opium traffic. When one American journalist wrote the embassy complaining that Laotian officials were involved in the drug trade, U.S. Ambassador G. McMurtrie Godley responded in a letter dated December 2, 1970:

> Regarding your information about opium traffic between Laos and the United States, the purchase of opium in Southeast Asia is certainly less difficult than in other parts of the world, but I believe the Royal Laotian Government takes its responsibility seriously to prohibit international opium traffic. . . . However, latest information available to me indicated that all of Southeast Asia produces only 5% of narcotics which are, unfortunately, illegally imported to Great Britain and the US. As you undoubtedly are already aware, our government is making every effort to contain this traffic and I believe the Narcotics Bureau in Washington D.C. can give you additional information if you have some other inquiries.[75]

But the latest information available to Ambassador Godley should have indicated that most of the heroin being used by American GIs in Vietnam was coming from Laotian laboratories. The exact location of Laos's flourishing laboratories was common knowledge among even the most junior U.S. bureaucrats.

To Americans living in cities and suburbs with the problem of street drugs, it may seem controversial that a U.S. government agency would condone any facet of the international drug traffic. But when viewed from the perspective of historical precedent and the demands of mountain warfare in northern Laos, Air America's involvement and the U.S. embassy's tolerance seemed almost inevitable. Rather than sending U.S. combat troops into Laos, four successive American presidents worked through the CIA to build the Hmong into the only effective army in Laos. The fundamental reason for American complicity in the Laotian opium traffic lies in these policy decisions, which can be understood only in the context of the secret war in Laos.

## Secret War in Laos

Noting the renewed guerrilla activity in South Vietnam and Laos in the late 1950s, American intelligence analysts interpreted these reports as the first signs of Communist plans for the conquest of Southeast Asia. Thus CIA operations with Hmong guerrillas in Laos began in 1959 as part of a regional intelligence-gathering program. General Edward G. Lansdale, who directed much of the Defense Department's strategic planning on Indochina during the early years of the Kennedy administration, recalled that these hill tribe operations were set up to monitor Communist infiltration:

> The main thought was to have an early warning, trip-wire sort of thing with these tribes in the mountains getting intelligence on North Vietnamese movements. This would be a part of a defensive strategy of saving the rice-producing lowlands of Thailand and Vietnam by sealing off the mountain infiltration routes from China and North Vietnam.[76]

In the minds of geopolitical strategists in the CIA's Special Operations division, potential infiltration routes stretched from the Shan hills of northeastern Burma through the rugged Laotian mountains, southward into the Central Highlands of South Vietnam. According to one CIA operative, Lieutenant Colonel Lucien Conein, agency personnel were sent to Laos in 1959 to supervise eight Green Beret teams then training Hmong guerrillas on the Plain of Jars.[77] In 1960 and 1961 the CIA recruited elements of Nationalist Chinese paramilitary units based in northern Thailand to patrol the China-Burma border area[78] and sent Green Berets into South Vietnam's Central Highlands to organize hill tribe commando units for intelligence and sabotage patrols along the Ho Chi Minh Trail.[79] Finally, in 1962 one CIA operative based in northwestern Laos began sending trained Yao and Lahu tribesmen into the heart of China's Yunnan province to monitor road traffic and tap telephones.[80]

While the U.S. military sent half a million troops to fight a conventional war in South Vietnam, this mountain warfare required only a handful of American personnel. "I always felt," said General Lansdale, "that a small group of Americans organizing the local population was the way to counter Communist wars of national liberation."[81]

American paramilitary personnel in Laos tended to serve long tours of duty, some of them for a decade or more, and were given enormous personal power. If the conventional war in South Vietnam is best analyzed in terms of the impersonal bureaucracies that produced policies and programs, the secret war in Laos is most readily understood through the men who fought it.

Three men, perhaps more than any others, left their personal imprint on the conduct of the secret war: Edgar Buell, Tony Poe, and William Young. Each in his own way illustrates a different aspect of America's conscious and unconscious complicity in the Laotian opium traffic.

William Young, one of the CIA's most effective agents, was born in the Burmese Shan states, where his grandfather had been a missionary to the hill tribes. Arriving in Burma at the turn of the century, Grandfather Young opened a Baptist mission in Kengtung and began preaching to the nearby Lahu hill tribes. Although they understood little of his Christian message, a local oracle had once prophesied the coming of a white deity, and the Lahu decided that Reverend Young was God.[82] His son Harold later inherited this presumed divinity and used it to organize Lahu intelligence-gathering forays into southern China for the CIA during the 1950s. When William was looking for a job in 1958 his father recommended him to the CIA, and he was hired as a confidential interpreter-translator. A skilled linguist who spoke five of the local languages, he probably knew more about mountain minorities than any other American in Laos, and the CIA rightly regarded him as its "tribal expert." Through his sophisticated understanding of the hill tribes, he viewed the opium problem from the perspective of a hill tribe farmer. Until a comprehensive crop substitution program was initiated, he felt nothing should be done to interfere with the opium traffic. In a September 1971 interview, Young explained his views:

> Every now and then one of the James Bond types would decide that the way to deal with the problem was to detonate or machine-gun the factories. But I always talked them out of it. As long as there is opium in Burma somebody will market it. This kind of thing would only hurt somebody and not really deal with the problem.[83]

If William Young was too sympathetic toward the hill tribes to interfere with the opium trade, Anthony Posepny, or Tony Poe, was indifferent to the problem. A marine veteran of the Pacific campaign during World War II, Poe joined the CIA's Special Operations division sometime after the war and quickly earned a reputation as one of its best clandestine warfare operatives in Asia.[84] When the CIA decided to back Tibet's religious ruler, the Dalai Lama, in 1956 in his feud with Peking, Tony Poe recruited Khamba tribesmen in northeastern India, escorted them to Camp Hale in Colorado for training, and accompanied them into Tibet on long-range sabotage missions.[85] After regional separatists declared the island of Sumatra independent of Indonesia in 1958, Tony Poe was one of the two CIA operatives sent in on the ground to lend support.[86]

His first assignment in Indochina was with anti-Sihanouk mercenaries along the Cambodian border in South Vietnam. Finally in 1963 Poe was sent to Laos as chief adviser to General Vang Pao.[87] Several years later he was transferred to northwestern Laos to supervise Secret Army operations in the tri-border area and work with Yao tribesmen. The Yao remembered "Mr. Tony" as a drinker, an authoritarian commander who bribed and threatened to get his way, and a mercurial leader who offered his soldiers 500 kip (one dollar) for an ear and 5,000 kip for a severed head when accompanied by a Pathet Lao army cap.[88] His attitude toward the opium traffic was erratic. According to a former Laos USAID official, Poe refused to allow opium on his aircraft and once threatened to throw a Lao soldier, with half a kilo of opium, out of an airborne plane. At the same time, he ignored the prospering heroin factories along the Mekong River and never stopped any of Ouane Rattikone's officers from using U.S.-supplied facilities to manage the drug traffic.

The most curious of this CIA triumvirate was Edgar "Pop" Buell, originally a farmer from Steuben County, Indiana. Buell first came to Laos in 1960 as an agricultural volunteer for International Voluntary Services (IVS), a Bible Belt edition of the Peace Corps.[89] He was assigned to the Plain of Jars, where the CIA was building up its secret Hmong army, and became involved in the agency's activities largely through circumstance and his own Christian anticommunism. As CIA influence spread through the Hmong villages ringing the Plain of Jars, Buell became a one-man supply corps, dispatching Air America planes to drop rice, meat, and other necessities the CIA had promised.[90] Buell played the naive country boy and claimed his work was humanitarian aid for Hmong refugees. However, his operations were an integral part of the CIA program.

As part of his effort to strengthen the Hmong economy and increase the tribe's effectiveness as a military force, Buell utilized his agricultural skills to improve Hmong techniques for planting and cultivating opium. "If you're gonna grow it, grow it good," Buell told the Hmong, "but don't let anybody smoke the stuff." Opium production increased but, thanks to modern drugs that Buell supplied the Hmong, local consumption for medicinal purposes declined.[91] Thus, more opium was available for the international markets.

Since there were too few U.S. operatives to assume complete responsibility for daily operations in the hills of Laos, the CIA usually selected one leader from every hill tribe as its surrogate commander. The CIA's chosen ally recruited his fellow tribesmen as mercenaries, paid their salaries with agency funds, and led them in battle. Because the CIA had only as much influence with each tribe as its surrogate commander did, it was in the agency's interest to make these men local autocrats by concentrating military and economic power in their hands. During the First Indochina War, French commandos had used the same technique to build up a force of 6,000 Hmong guerrillas on the Plain of Jars under the command of Touby Lyfoung. Recognizing the importance of opium in the Hmong economy, the French flew Hmong opium to Saigon on military transports and reinforced Touby Lyfoung's authority by making him their exclusive opium broker.

But when the CIA began organizing its Hmong army in 1960, only six years after the French disbanded theirs, it found Touby unsuitable for command. Always the politician, Touby had gotten the best of the bargain from the French and had never committed his troops to a head-on fight. As one Hmong veteran fondly remembered, "Touby always told us to fire a few shots and run." The CIA wanted a real battler who would take casualties, and in a young Hmong officer named Vang Pao they found him.

With his flair for such cost-effective combat, Vang Pao would become a hero to agency bureaucrats in Washington. "CIA had identified an officer . . . originally trained by the French, who had not only the courage but also the political acumen . . . for leadership in such a conflict . . . ," recalled retired CIA director William Colby. "His name was Vang Pao, and he had the enthusiastic admiration of the CIA officers, who knew him . . . as a man who . . . knew how to say no as well as yes to Americans."[92] Many CIA field operatives admired his ruthlessness. When agent Thomas Clines, commander of the CIA's secret base at Long Tieng, demanded an immediate interrogation of six prisoners, Vang Pao ordered them executed on the spot. Clines was impressed. "What I meant to say, general, is that I would *appreciate* it if you would *allow* us to interrogate prisoners, *please.*"[93]

Touby had once remarked of Vang Pao, "He is a pure military officer who doesn't understand that after the war there is a peace. And one must be strong to win the peace."[94] For Vang Pao, peace was a distant, childhood memory. Vang Pao saw battle for the first time in 1945 at the age of thirteen, while working as an interpreter for French commandos who had parachuted onto the Plain of Jars to organize anti-Japanese resistance.[95] Although he became a lieutenant in the newly formed Laotian army, Vang Pao spent most of the First Indochina War on the Plain of Jars with Touby Lyfoung's Hmong irregulars. In April 1954 he led 850 hill tribe commandos through the rugged mountains of Sam Neua province in a vain attempt to relieve the doomed French garrison at Dien Bien Phu.

When the First Indochina War ended in 1954, Vang Pao returned to regular duty in the Laotian army. He advanced quickly to the rank of major and was appointed commander of the Tenth Infantry Battalion, which was assigned to the mountains east of the Plain of Jars. Vang Pao had a good record as a wartime commando leader, but in his new command Vang Pao would first display the personal corruption that would later make him such an effective warlord.

In addition to his regular battalion, Vang Pao was also commander of Hmong self-defense forces in the Plain of Jars region. Volunteers had been promised regular allotments of food and money, but Vang Pao pocketed these salaries, and most went unpaid for months at a time. The rising chorus of complaints finally came to the attention of provincial army commander Colonel Kham Hou Boussarath. In early 1959 Kham Hou called Vang Pao to his headquarters in Xieng Khouang and ordered him to pay up. Several days later thirty of Vang Pao's soldiers hidden in the brush beside the road tried to assassinate Kham Hou as he was driving back from an inspection tour of the frontier areas and was approaching the village of Lat Houang. But it was twilight and most of the shots went wild. Kham Hou floored the accelerator and emerged from the gantlet unscathed.

As soon as he reached his headquarters, Kham Hou radioed a full report to Vientiane. The next morning army chief of staff Ouane Rattikone arrived in Xieng Khouang. Weeping, Vang Pao prostrated himself before Ouane and begged for forgiveness. Perhaps touched by this display of emotion or influenced by the wishes of U.S. special forces officers working with the Hmong, General Ouane decided not to punish Vang Pao. However, most of the Laotian high command seemed to feel that his career was now finished.[96]

But Vang Pao was to be rescued from obscurity by unforeseen circumstances that made his services invaluable to the Laotian right wing and the CIA.

About the same time that Vang Pao was setting up his abortive ambush, General Phoumi Nosavan was beginning his rise to power. In the April 1959 National Assembly elections, Phoumi's candidates scored victory after victory, thus establishing him as Laos's first real strong man. However, the election was blatantly rigged and aroused resentment among politically aware elements of the population. The American involvement in election fixing was obvious, and there were even reports that CIA agents had financed some of the vote buying.[97]

Angered by these American moves, an unknown army officer, Captain Kong Le, and his paratroop battalion launched a successful coup on August 8, 1960. After securing Vientiane and forcing Phoumi's supporters out of power, Kong Le turned the government over to the former neutralist prime minister Souvanna Phouma on August 16. Souvanna announced that he would end the ongoing civil war by forming a neutralist government that would include representatives from left, right, and center. The plan was on the verge of success when Phoumi suddenly broke off negotiations in early September and returned to his home in Savannakhet, where he announced the formation of the Revolutionary Committee.[98] As indication of CIA support, dozens of unmarked Air America transports began landing at Savannakhet loaded with arms, soldiers, and American advisers,[99] and Laos was plunged into a three-way civil war. The CIA-backed right wing was in Savannakhet, the neutralists were in Vientiane, and the leftist Pathet Lao was in the forests of Sam Neua province in the extreme northeast. Everything in between was virtually autonomous, and all three factions competed for territory and influence in the undeclared provinces.

While the right wingers quickly consolidated their hold over the south, the neutralists initially gained the upper hand in Xieng Khouang province, which included the Plain of Jars. This success strengthened the neutralist position considerably; with three major roads meeting on the plain, Xieng Khouang was the strategic key to northeastern Laos. The influential Hmong leader Touby Lyfoung was minister of justice for the neutralist government and seemed to be working closely with Prime Minister Souvanna Phouma.[100] The neutralist position in the northeast further improved when the newly appointed commander of Military Region II (Sam Neua and Xieng Khouang provinces), Colonel Kham Hou, declared his loyalty to the neutralist government on September 28.[101]

General Phoumi's camp was worried about its lack of support in strategic region II. After Kham Hou rebuffed their overtures, Phoumi's agents reportedly contacted Vang Pao in late September. They promised him financial support if he would lead a Hmong coup against the neutralists, thus bringing Military Region II into the rightist orbit. According to Laotian army sources, Vang Pao radioed Savannakhet on

October 1 or 2, requesting money and arms from General Phoumi. On October 5, an unmarked Air America transport from Savannakhet dropped thirty rightist paratroopers and several hundred rifles to Vang Pao's supporters on the Plain of Jars. Later that day Vang Pao called a meeting of local Hmong leaders at the village of Lat Houang. Surrounded by the paratroopers, Vang Pao told a crowd of about three hundred to four hundred Hmong that he supported General Phoumi and promised guns for all those who joined him in the fight against the neutralists.[102]

When word of the incipient Hmong revolt reached Vientiane, Prime Minister Souvanna Phouma sent his minister of justice, Hmong leader Touby Lyfoung, up to the Plain of Jars to negotiate with Vang Pao. Instead of dissuading Vang Pao, however, Touby bowed to superior force and joined him. Using his considerable talents as a negotiator, Touby met with Kham Hou and urged him not to interfere with the Hmong revolt. Unwilling to engage in unnecessary slaughter and somewhat sympathetic to the right wing, Kham Hou agreed not to fight, thus effectively conceding control of the Plain of Jars to the right wing.[103]

Confused by the murky situation, Souvanna Phouma dispatched another emissary, General Amkha, the inspector general of the neutralist army, on October 7. But the moment Amkha stepped off the plane, Vang Pao arrested him at gunpoint and had him flown aboard an unidentified transport to Savannakhet, where he remained in prison for almost three years on General Phoumi's orders. That same day Touby was "invited" to Savannakhet and left on a later flight. When Kham Hou resigned from command shortly thereafter, Phoumi rewarded Vang Pao by appointing him commander of Xieng Khouang province.[104]

In late November General Phoumi's army began its drive for Vientiane, Laos's administrative capital. Advancing up the Mekong valley, rightist forces reached the outskirts of the city on December 14 and evicted Captain Kong Le's paratroopers after three days of destructive street fighting. While Kong Le's paratroopers beat a disciplined retreat up Route 13 toward the royal capital of Luang Prabang, Phoumi was a bit lax in pursuit, convinced that Kong Le would eventually be crushed by the rightist garrisons guarding the royal capital.

About a hundred miles north of Vientiane there was a fork in the road: Route 13 continued its zigzag course northward to Luang Prabang, while Route 7 branched off eastward toward the Plain of Jars. Rather than advancing on Luang Prabang as expected, Kong Le entered the CIA-controlled Plain of Jars on December 31, 1960. While his troops captured Muong Soui and attacked the airfield at Phong Savan, Pathet Lao guerrillas launched coordinated diversionary attacks along the plain's northeastern rim. Rightist defenses crumbled, and Phoumi's troops threw away their guns and ran.[105] As mortar fire came crashing in at the end of the runway, the last Air America C-47 took off from the Plain of Jars with Edgar Buell and a contingent of U.S. military advisers.[106]

Vang Pao was one of the few commanders who did not panic at the Kong Le and Pathet Lao coordinated offensive. While Phoumi's regular army troops ran for the Mekong, Vang Pao led several thousand Hmong soldiers and refugees out of the plain on an orderly march to Padoung, a 4,000-foot mountain, twelve miles due south. Vang Pao was appointed commander of Military Region II and established his headquarters at Padoung.[107]

With General Phoumi once more in control of Vientiane and a joint Pathet Lao–neutralist force occupying the strategic Plain of Jars, the center of CIA activity shifted from Savannakhet to Padoung. In January 1961 the CIA began sending Green Berets, CIA-financed Thai police commandos, and a handful of its own agents into region II to build up an effective Hmong guerrilla army under Vang Pao. William Young was one of the CIA operatives sent to Padoung in January, and because of his linguistic skills he played a key role in the formation of the Secret Army. As he recollected ten years later, the basic CIA strategy was to keep the Pathet Lao bottled up on the plain by recruiting all of the eligible young Hmong in the surrounding mountains as commandos.

To build his army, Vang Pao's officers and the CIA operatives, including William Young, flew to scattered Hmong villages in helicopters and light Helio-courier aircraft. Offering guns, rice, and money in exchange for recruits, they leapfrogged from village to village around the western and northern perimeter of the Plain of Jars. Under their supervision, dozens of crude landing strips for Air America were hacked out of the mountain forests, thus linking these scattered villages with CIA headquarters at Padoung. Within a few months Vang Pao's influence extended from Padoung north to Phou Fa and east as far as Bouam Long.[108] However, one local Hmong leader in the Long Pot region west of the Plain of Jars said that the Hmong recruiting officers who visited his village used threats as well as inducements to win a declaration of loyalty. "Vang Pao sent us guns," he recalled. "If we did not accept his guns he would call us Pathet Lao. We had no choice. Vang Pao's officers came to the village and warned that if we did not join him he would regard us as Pathet Lao and his soldiers would attack our village."[109]

Hmong guerrilla operations on the plain itself had begun almost immediately; Hmong sappers blew up bridges and supply dumps while snipers shot at neutralist and Pathet Lao soldiers. After four months of this kind of harassment, Captain Kong Le decided to retaliate.[110] In early May 1961, Pathet Lao and neutralist troops assaulted the northern flank of Padoung mountain and began shelling the CIA base camp. After enduring an intense mortar barrage for more than two weeks, the CIA

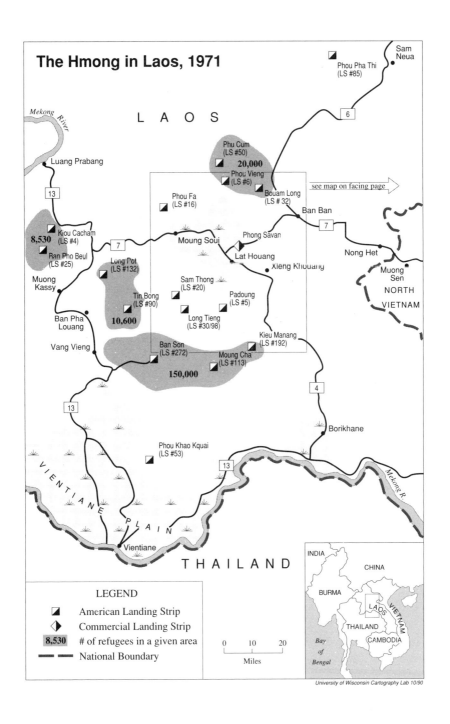

# The Hmong in Laos, 1971

L A O S

Mekong River

Sam Neua

Phou Pha Thi
(LS #85)

6

Luang Prabang

Phu Cum
(LS #50)    20,000

Phou Vieng
(LS #6)

Phou Fa
(LS #16)

Bouam Long
(LS #32)

Ban Ban

see map on facing page

13

Kiou Cacham
(LS #4)

8,530

Ran Pho Beul
(LS #25)

7

Long Pot
(LS #132)

Moung Soui

Phong Savan

Lat Houang

Xieng Khouang

7

Nong Het

Muong
Sen

NORTH
VIETNAM

Muong
Kassy

Sam Thong
(LS #20)

Tin Bong
(LS #90)

10,600

Padoung
(LS #5)

Ban Pha
Louang

Long Tieng
(LS #30/98)

Vang Vieng

Ban Son
(LS #272)

Moung Cha
(LS #113)

150,000

Kieu Manang
(LS #192)

4

Borikhane

13

Phou Khao Kquai
(LS #53)

13

Mekong R.

V I E N T I A N E   P L A I N

Vientiane

T H A I L A N D

INDIA

CHINA

BURMA

LAOS

VIETNAM

THAILAND

CAMBODIA

Bay
of
Bengal

## LEGEND

◢  American Landing Strip
◇  Commercial Landing Strip
8,530  # of refugees in a given area
▬ ▬  National Boundary

0    10    20
Miles

University of Wisconsin Cartography Lab 10/90

# The CIA's Secret Hmong Army in Retreat, 1960-1971

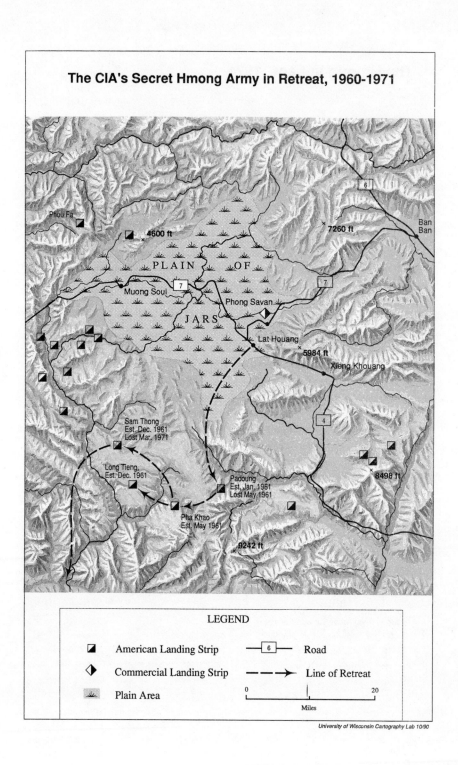

Phou Fa

4600 ft

PLAIN OF

7260 ft

Ban Ban

7

Muong Soui

Phong Savan

JARS

Lat Houang

5984 ft

Xieng Khouang

4

Sam Thong
Est. Dec. 1961
Lost Mar. 1971

8498 ft

Long Tieng,
Est. Dec. 1961

Padoung
Est. Jan. 1961
Lost May 1961

Pha Khao
Est. May 1961

9242 ft

6

## LEGEND

◢ American Landing Strip     —⊡6⊡— Road

◆ Commercial Landing Strip     ⇢ Line of Retreat

🌾 Plain Area

0           20

Miles

decided to abandon the base, and Vang Pao led his troops to a new headquarters at Pha Khao, eight miles southwest.[111] Following close behind came Edgar Buell, leading some 9,000 Hmong civilians. While Vang Pao's hardy troops made the transfer without incident, hundreds of civilians, mainly children and elderly, died in a forced march through the jungle.[112]

The only official report on Hmong operations was written by General Edward Lansdale of the CIA in July 1961 for foreign policy officials in the Kennedy administration. In it he discussed the agency's clandestine warfare potential in Indochina. "Command control of [Hmong] operations is exercised by the Chief CIA Vientiane with the advice of Chief MAAG Laos [U.S. army advisers]," reported Lansdale. Although there were only nine CIA operations officers and nine Green berets in the field, "CIA control in the [Hmong] operations has been reported as excellent." In addition, there were ninety-nine Thai police commandos working with the Hmong under CIA control. So far 9,000 Hmong had been "equipped for guerrilla operations," but Lansdale felt that at least 4,000 more of these "splendid fighting men" could be recruited. However, there was one major problem:

> As Meo [Hmong] villages are over-run by Communist forces and as men leave food-raising duties to serve as guerillas, a problem is growing over the care and feeding of non-combat Meos [Hmong]. CIA has given some rice and clothing to relieve this problem. Consideration needs to be given to organized relief, a mission of an ICA ["humanitarian" foreign aid] nature, to the handling of [Hmong] refugees and their rehabilitation.[113]

To solve this critical problem, the CIA turned to Edgar Buell, who set out on a fifty-eight-day trek around the perimeter of the plain to arrange for delivery of "refugee" supplies.[114]

In July 1962 the United States and the Soviet Union signed the Geneva Agreements on Laos and thus theoretically terminated their military operations in that chaotic kingdom. Although American Green Berets and military advisers were withdrawn by October as specified, the CIA devised a number of deceptions to continue its clandestine activities. All of the CIA operatives moved to adjacent areas of Thailand but returned almost every day by helicopter or plane to direct guerrilla operations. Civilian personnel (not covered by the Geneva Agreements) were recruited for clandestine work. In December 1962, for example, Buell trained Hmong guerrillas in demolition techniques and directed the dynamiting of six bridges and twelve mountain passes along Route 7 near Ban Ban.[115] The U.S. embassy declared that Air America flights to Hmong villages, which carried munitions as well as refugee supplies, were "humanitarian" aid and as such were exempted from the Geneva Agreements.[116]

After a relatively quiet year in 1962, the CIA went on the offensive throughout northern Laos in 1963–1964. In the northwest, William Young, assisted by IVS volunteer Joseph Flipse, led Yao commandos in an attack on Pathet Lao villages east of Ban Houei Sai. One American who took part in the offensive recalled that Pathet Lao troops had been inactive since the Geneva Agreements were signed and felt that the CIA offensive shattered the cease-fire in the northwest. In the northeast the CIA took the war to the enemy by expanding Hmong commando operations into Sam Neua province, a Pathet Lao stronghold for nearly fifteen years.[117]

Tony Poe became the new CIA man at Long Tieng, Vang Pao's headquarters since mid-1962, and organized the offensive into Sam Neua province. Rather than attacking towns and villages in the valleys where the Pathet Lao were well entrenched, the CIA concentrated on the mountain ridges populated by Hmong. Using Air America's fleet of helicopters and light aircraft, Poe led hundreds of Hmong guerrillas in a lightning advance that leaped from mountain to mountain into the heart of Sam Neua province. As soon as a village was captured and Pathet Lao cadres eliminated, the inhabitants were put to work building a crude landing strip, usually five hundred to eight hundred feet long, to receive the airplanes that followed in the offensive's wake carrying Edgar Buell's "refugee" supplies. These goods were distributed in an attempt to buy the hearts and minds of the Hmong.

Within a matter of months a fifty-mile-long strip of territory— stretching from the northeastern rim of the Plain of Jars to Phou Pha Thi mountain, only fifteen miles from the North Vietnamese border—had been added to Vang Pao's domain. More than twenty new aircraft landing strips dotted the conquered corridor, linking Hmong villages with CIA headquarters at Long Tieng. Most of these Hmong villages were perched on steep mountain ridges overlooking valleys and towns controlled by the Pathet Lao. The Air America landing strip at Hong Non, for example, was only twelve miles from the limestone caverns near Sam Neua City, where the Pathet Lao later housed their national headquarters, a munitions factory, and a cadre training school.[118]

As might be expected, the fighting on the Plain of Jars and the opening of these landing strips produced changes in northeastern Laos's opium traffic. For more than sixty years the Plain of Jars had been the hub of the opium trade in northeastern Laos. When Kong Le captured the plain in December 1960, the Corsican charter airlines abandoned Phong Savan Airport for Vientiane's Wattay Airport. The old Corsican hangout at Phong Savan, the Snow Leopard Inn, was renamed Friendship Hotel.

It became headquarters for a dozen Russian technicians sent to service the Ilyushin transports ferrying supplies from Hanoi for the neutralists and Pathet Lao.[119]

No longer able to land on the Plain of Jars, the Corsican airlines began using Air America's mountain landing strips to pick up raw opium.[120] As Vang Pao circled around the Plain of Jars and advanced into Sam Neua province, leaving a trail of landing strips behind him, the Corsicans were right behind in their Beechcrafts and Cessnas, paying Hmong farmers and Chinese traders a good price for raw opium. Since Kong Le did not interfere with commercial activity on the plain, the Chinese caravans were still able to make their annual journey into areas controlled by Vang Pao. Now, instead of delivering their opium to trading centers on the plain, most traders brought it to Air America landing strips serviced by the Corsican airlines.[121] Chinese caravans continued to use the Plain of Jars as a base until mid-1964, when the Pathet Lao drove Kong Le off the plain and forced them into retirement.

When the Laotian government in the person of Ouane Rattikone forced the Corsicans out of business in 1965, a serious economic crisis loomed in the Hmong highlands. The war had not reduced Hmong dependence on opium as a cash crop and may have actually increased production. Although thousands of Hmong recruited for commando operations were forced to leave home for months at a time, the impact of this loss on opium production was minimal. Opium farming is women's work. While men clear the fields by slashing and burning the forest, the tedious work of weeding and harvesting is traditionally the responsibility of wives and daughters. Since most poppy fields last up to five or ten years, periodic absences of the men had little impact on poppy production. Furthermore, the CIA's regular rice drops removed any incentive to grow rice and freed the people's labor for full-time poppy cultivation. To make defense of the civilian population easier, many smaller refugee villages had been evacuated and their populations concentrated in large refugee centers. Good agricultural land was at a premium in these areas, and most of the farmers devoted their labors to opium production simply because it required much less land than rice or other food crops.[122]

Hmong villages on the southern and western edges of the plain were little affected by the transportation problem caused by the end of the Corsican flights. Following the demise of the Chinese merchant caravans in mid-1964, Vang Pao's commandos dispatched Hmong military caravans from Long Tieng into these areas to buy up the opium harvest. Since there were daily flights from both Sam Thong and Long Tieng to Vientiane, it was relatively easy to get the opium to market. However, the distances and security problems involved in sending caravans into the northern perimeter of the plain and in the Sam Neua area were insuperable, and air transport became an absolute necessity. With the Corsicans gone, Air America was the only form of air transport available.[123] According to Ouane Rattikone, then commander in chief of the Laotian army, and General Thao Ma, then Laotian air force commander, Air America began flying Hmong opium to markets in Long Tieng and Vientiane.[124]

As Long Tieng swelled into a secret city of 20,000 Hmong and Vang Pao acquired the aura of a warlord, his relationship with his CIA counterpart Tony Poe, always tense, became untenable. "You don't let him run loose without a chain on him," Poe complained after the war. "You gotta control him just like any kind of animal or a baby." As their relationship deteriorated, Poe grew critical of the general's corruption, asking pointedly: "Why does he need Mercedes Benz, apartments and hotels and homes where he never had them in his life before?" Asked in a postwar television interview where the wealth came from, Poe was frank: "Oh, he was making millions 'cos he had his own source of, uh, avenue for his own, uh, heroin." In this same interview, Poe charged that Vang Pao later used a DC-3 to fly heroin across southern Laos into central Vietnam, where "the number two guy to President Thieu would receive it." Poe claimed that his opposition to Vang Pao's corruption led to his transfer from Long Tieng. Whatever the cause, in 1965 Poe was reassigned to northwestern Laos near the China border, far from Vang Pao and the main theater of covert combat.[125]

Air logistics for the opium trade were further improved in 1967 when the CIA and USAID (U.S. Agency for International Development) gave Vang Pao financial assistance in forming his own private airline, Xieng Khouang Air Transport. The company's president, Lo Kham Thy, said the airline was formed in late 1967 when two C-47s were acquired from Air America and Continental Air Services. The company's schedule was limited to shuttle flights between Long Tieng and Vientiane that carried relief supplies and an occasional handful of passengers. Financial control was shared by Vang Pao, his brother, his cousin, and his father-in-law.[126] According to one former USAID employee, USAID supported the project because officials hoped it would make Long Tieng the commercial center of the northeast and thereby reinforce Vang Pao's political position. The USAID officials involved apparently realized that any commercial activity at Long Tieng would involve opium but decided to support the project anyway.[127] Reliable Hmong sources reported that Xieng Khouang Air Transport was the airline used to carry opium and heroin between Long Tieng and Vientiane.[128]

Despite repeated dry season offensives by the Pathet Lao, the CIA's military position in the northeast remained strong, and Vang Pao's army consolidated gains it had made during the early years of the war. However, in January 1968 Pathet Lao and North Vietnamese forces mounted a general offensive that swept Vang Pao's mercenaries out of Sam Neua province. The key to the Pathet Lao victory was the capture of the CIA's eagle nest bastion, Phou Pha Thi, on March 11. The U.S. air force had built a radar guidance center on top of this 5,680-foot mountain in 1966 "to provide more accurate guidance for all-weather bombing operations" over North Vietnam.[129] Only seventeen miles from the North Vietnamese border, Pha Thi had become the eyes of the U.S. bombing campaign over Hanoi and the Red River Delta.[130] (Interestingly, President Johnson announced a partial bombing halt over North Vietnam less than three weeks after the radar installation at Pha Thi was destroyed.) Vang Pao attempted to recapture the strategic base late in 1968, but after suffering heavy losses he abandoned it to the North Vietnamese and Pathet Lao in January 1969.[131]

The loss of Sam Neua in 1968 signaled the first of the massive Hmong migrations that eventually made much of northeastern Laos a depopulated free fire zone and drastically reduced hill tribe opium production. Before the CIA-initiated Hmong guerrilla operations in 1960, Military Region II had a hill tribe population of about 250,000, most of them Hmong opium farmers evenly scattered across the rugged highlands between the Vientiane Plain and the North Vietnamese border.[132] The steady expansion of Vang Pao's influence from 1961 to 1967 caused some local concentration of population as small Hmong villages clustered together for self-defense. However, Hmong farmers were still within walking distance of their poppy fields, and opium production continued undiminished.

When Vang Pao began to lose control of Sam Neua in early 1968, the CIA decided to deny the population to the Pathet Lao by evacuating all the Hmong tribesmen under his control. By 1967 U.S. air force bombing in northeastern Laos was already heavy, and Hmong tribesmen were willing to leave their villages rather than face the daily horror of life under the bombs. Recalling Mao Tse-tung's axiom on guerrilla warfare, Edgar Buell declared, "If the people are the sea, then let's hurry the tide south."[133] Air America evacuated more than 9,000 people from Sam Neua in less than two weeks. They were flown to Buell's headquarters at Sam Thong, five miles north of Long Tieng, housed temporarily, and then flown to refugee villages in an adjacent area west of the Plain of Jars.[134]

During the next three years repeated Pathet Lao winter-spring offensives continued to drive Vang Pao's Hmong army farther and farther back, forcing tens of thousands of Hmong villagers to become refugees. As the Pathet Lao's 1970 offensive gained momentum, the

Hmong living north and west of the plain fled south, and eventually more than 100,000 were relocated in a crescent-shaped forty-mile-wide strip of territory between Long Tieng and the Vientiane Plain. When the Pathet Lao and the North Vietnamese attacked Long Tieng during the 1971 dry season, the CIA was forced to evacuate some 50,000 mercenary dependents from Long Tieng valley into the overcrowded Ban Son resettlement area south of Long Tieng. By mid-1971 USAID estimated that almost 150,000 hill tribe refugees, of which 60 percent were Hmong, had been resettled in the Ban Son area.[135]

After three years of constant retreat, Vang Pao's Hmong followers were at the end of the line. While they had once been a prosperous people living in small villages surrounded by miles of fertile, uninhabited mountains, by 1971 almost a third of all the Hmong in Laos, more than 90,000, were packed into a forty-mile-long dead end perched above the sweltering Vientiane Plain. The Hmong were used to living on mountain ridges more than 3,000 feet high where the temperate climate was conducive to poppy cultivation, the air was free of malarial mosquitoes, and the water was pure. In the refugee villages, most of which were only 2,500 feet high, many Hmong were stricken with malaria and, lacking normal immunities, became seriously ill. The low elevation and crowded conditions made opium cultivation almost impossible, and the Hmong were totally dependent on Air America's rice drops. After the North Vietnamese and Pathet Lao captured Long Tieng and advanced on Vientiane, many of the Hmong were forced down onto the Vientiane Plain, where they were susceptible to tropical diseases.

The Ban Son resettlement area served as a buffer zone, blocking any enemy advance on Vientiane. If the Pathet Lao and North Vietnamese chose to move on Vientiane they would have had no choice but to fight their way through the resettlement area. Hmong leaders, well aware of this danger, pleaded with USAID to either begin resettling the Hmong on the Vientiane Plain on a gradual, controlled basis or shift the resettlement area to the east or west, out of the probable line of an enemy advance.[136] Knowing that the Hmong fought better when their families were threatened, USAID refused to accept either alternative and seemed intent on keeping them in the area for a final, bloody stand against the North Vietnamese and Pathet Lao. Most of the Hmong had no desire to continue fighting for Vang Pao. They resented his more flamboyant excesses—personally executing his own soldiers, grafting from the military payroll, and his willingness to take heavy casualties—and regarded him as a warlord who had grown rich on their suffering.[137] Since USAID decided where the rice was dropped, the Hmong had no choice but to stand and fight.

Hmong losses by that time had already been enormous. The sudden mass migrations forced by enemy offensives frequently exceeded Air America's logistic capacity. Instead of being flown out, many Hmong had to endure long forced marches, which produced 10 percent fatalities under the best conditions and 30 percent or more if the fleeing refugees became lost in the mountain forests. Most of the mercenary dependents moved at least five times and some villages originally from Sam Neua province moved fifteen or sixteen times between 1968 and the early 1970s.[138] Vang Pao's military casualties were just as serious: with only 30,000–40,000 men under arms, his army suffered 3,272 killed and 5,426 wounded from 1967 to 1971. Hmong casualties were so heavy that Vang Pao was forced to turn to other tribes for recruits, and by April 1971 Lao Theung, the second largest hill tribe in northern Laos, constituted 40 percent of his troops.[139] Many of the remaining Hmong recruits were boys. In 1968 Edgar Buell told a *New Yorker* correspondent.

> A short time ago we rounded up three hundred fresh recruits. Thirty per cent were fourteen years old or less, and ten of them were only ten years old. Another 30 per cent were fifteen or sixteen. The remaining 40 per cent were forty-five or over. Where were the ones in between? I'll tell you—they're all dead.[140]

Despite the drop in Hmong opium production after 1968, General Vang Pao was able to continue his role in Laos's narcotics trade by opening a heroin laboratory at Long Tieng. According to reliable Laotian sources, his laboratory began operations in 1970 when a foreign Chinese master chemist arrived at Long Tieng to supervise production. The operation was so profitable that in mid-1971 Chinese merchants in Vientiane reported that Vang Pao's agents were buying opium in Vientiane and flying it to Long Tieng for processing.[141]

Although American officials in Laos vigorously denied that either Vang Pao or Air America was in any way involved, overwhelming evidence to the contrary challenged these assertions. Perhaps the best way to understand the importance of their role is to examine the dynamics of the opium trade in a single opium-growing district.

## Long Pot Village

In 1971 Long Pot district, thirty miles northwest of Long Tieng, was one of the last remaining areas in northeastern Laos where the history of the country's opium traffic could still be investigated. Located forty miles due west of the Plain of Jars, it was close enough to Long Tieng to be a part of General Vang Pao's domain but far enough away from the heavy fighting to have survived to tell its story. Viewed from Highway 13, which formed its western boundary, Long Pot district seemed a rugged, distant world. Phou Phachau mountain dominated the district, rising more than 6,200 feet into the clouds that perennially hovered about its peak during the rainy season from May to October. Steep ridges radiated outward from Phou Phachau and lesser peaks, 4,000 and 5,000 feet high, formed hollows and valleys that gouged the district's hundred square miles of territory. The landscape had once been verdant with virgin hardwood forests, but generations of slash-and-burn agriculture by hill tribe residents had left many of the ridges covered with tough, chest-high savanna grass.[142]

The district's twelve villages, seven Hmong and five Lao Theung, clung to ridges and mountain crests, where they commanded a view of the surrounding countryside. The political center of the district was the village of Long Pot, a Hmong community of forty-seven wooden, dirt-floored houses and some three hundred residents. It was not its size, but its longevity that made Long Pot village important. Founded in the latter half of the nineteenth century, it was one of the oldest Hmong villages in northeastern Laos. Its leaders had a tradition of political power, and the highest-ranking local official, District Officer Ger Su Yang, resided in Long Pot village. While most Hmong were forced to abandon their villages every ten or twenty years in search of new opium fields, Long Pot was surrounded by a surplus of fertile, limestone-laden slopes that allowed its inhabitants to remain in continuous residence for three generations. Moreover, Long Pot's high altitude was ideal for poppy cultivation; the village itself was 4,200 feet high and was surrounded by ridges ranging up to 5,400 feet. The Yunnan variety of the opium poppy found in Southeast Asia required a temperate climate; it could survive at 3,000 feet, but thrived as the altitude climbed upward to 5,000.

Despite the damage done by more than ten years of constant warfare, opium production in Long Pot village had not declined. In an August 1971 interview, the district officer of Long Pot, Ger Su Yang, said that most of the households in the village had been producing about 15 kilos of opium apiece before the fighting began and had maintained this level of production for the previous ten years. However, rice production had declined drastically.[143] During a time of war, when the Hmong of Long Pot might have been expected to concentrate their dwindling labor resources on essential food production, they had chosen instead to continue cash-crop opium farming. Guaranteed an adequate food supply by Air America's regular rice drops, the villagers were free to devote all their energies to opium production. Since Vang Pao's officers paid them a high price for their opium and assured them a reliable market, the farmers of Long Pot village tried to produce as much opium as possible.

In the past rice had always been the Hmong's most important subsistence crop and opium their traditional cash crop. However, opium and rice had conflicting crop cycles and prospered in different kinds of fields. Because the average Hmong village had a limited amount of manpower, it was capable of clearing only a few new fields every year and therefore had to opt for either opium or rice. When the opium price was high Hmong farmers concentrated their efforts on the opium crop and used their cash profits to buy rice, but if the price dropped, they gradually reduced poppy cultivation and increased subsistence rice production. With rice from Air America and good opium prices from Vang Pao's officers, the farmers of Long Pot had chosen to emphasize opium production.[144]

Every spring, as the time for cutting new fields approached, each houschold sent out a scouting party to scour the countryside for suitable field locations. Since Long Pot Hmong wanted to plant opium, they looked for highly alkaline soil near the ridgeline or in mountain hollows where the opium poppies prospered rather than midslope fields more suitable for rice. The sweeter "taste" of limestone soil can actually be recognized by a discriminating palate, and as they hiked around the nearby mountains Hmong scouts periodically chewed on a bit of soil to make sure that the prospective site was alkaline enough.[145]

Hmong farmers began clearing their new fields in March or April. Using iron-bitted axes, the men chopped away at timber stands covering the chosen site. Rather than cutting through the thick roots or immense trunks of the larger trees, they scaled the first twenty feet of the trunk, balanced themselves on a slender notched pole, and cut away only the top of the tree. A skilled woodsman could often fell three or four smaller trees with a single blow if he toppled a large tree so that it knocked down the others as it crashed to the ground. The trees were left on the ground to dry until April or early May, when the Hmong were ready for one of the most awesome spectacles in the mountains—the burn-off.[146]

After the timber had become tinderbox dry, the villagers of Long Pot formed fire brigades and gathered near the fields on the chosen day. While the younger men of the village raced down the slope igniting the timber as they came, others circled the perimeter, lighting stacked timber and brush on the edge of the field. The burn-off not only removed fallen timber from the field, but it also left a valuable layer of ash containing phosphate, calcium, and potassium scattered evenly across the field.[147]

Even though the fields were ready for planting as soon as the burn-off was completed, the poppy's annual cycle dictated that its planting be delayed until September. If the land was left unplanted, however, it lost valuable minerals through erosion and became covered with a thick crop of weeds. Dry upland rice was not harvested until November, two months after the poppies should have been planted, so the Hmong instead planted a hardy variety of mountain corn that could be harvested in August and early September. The corn kept the ground clear of weeds during the summer and provided fodder for the menagerie of hogs, mountain ponies, chickens, and cows whose wanderings turned Long Pot village into a sea of mud every rainy season.[148]

Once the corn was picked in August and early September, Hmong women began chopping and turning the soil with a heavy, triangular hoe. Just before the poppy seeds were broadcast across the surface of the ground in September, the soil had to be chopped fine and raked smooth with a bamboo broom. In November women thinned out the poppies, leaving the healthier plants standing about six inches apart. At the same time tobacco, beans, spinach, and other vegetables were planted among the poppies; they added minerals to the soil and supplemented the Hmong diet.[149]

The poppies were thinned again in late December and several weeks later the vegetables were picked, clearing the ground and allowing the poppies to make a final push. By January the bright red and white poppy flowers started to appear and the harvest began as the petals dropped away exposing an egg-shaped bulb containing the resinous opium. Since most farmers staggered their plantings to minimize demands on their time during the busy harvest season and reduce the threat of weather damage, the harvest usually continued until late February or early March.[150]

To harvest the opium, Hmong farmers tapped the poppy's resin much like a Vermont maple sugar farmer and a Malaysian rubber farmer harvest their crops. An opium farmer held the flower's egg-sized bulb with the fingers of one hand while he used a three-bladed knife to incise shallow longitudinal slits on its surface. The cuttings were made in the cool of the late afternoon. During the night the opium resin oozed out of the bulb and collected on its surface. Early the next morning, before the sun dried the moist sap, a Hmong woman scraped the surface of the bulb with a flexible rectangular blade and deposited the residue in a cup hanging around her neck. When she finished harvesting a kilo of the dark, sticky sap, she wrapped it in banana leaves and tied the bundle with string.

By the time the harvest was finished, the forty-seven households in Long Pot village had collected more than 700 kilos of raw opium.[151] Since Golden Triangle opium was usually 10 percent morphine by weight, the Long Pot harvest yielded roughly 70 kilos of pure morphine base after it was boiled, processed, and pressed into bricks. Once the morphine was chemically bonded with acetic anhydride in one of the region's many heroin laboratories, Long Pot's opium harvest became 70 kilos of high-grade no. 4 heroin.

While international criminal syndicates reaped enormous profits from the narcotics traffic, the Hmong farmers were paid relatively little for their efforts. Although opium was their sole cash crop and they devoted most of their effort to it, they received only $400 to $600 for 10 kilos of raw opium in 1971. After the opium left the village, however, the value of those 10 kilos spiraled upward. Ten kilos of raw opium yielded 1 kilo of morphine base worth $500 in the Golden Triangle. After being processed into heroin, 1 kilo of morphine base became 1 kilo of no. 4 heroin worth $2,000 to $2,500 in Bangkok. In San Francisco, Miami, or New York, the courier delivering a kilo of heroin to a wholesaler received anywhere from $18,000 to $27,000. Diluted with quinine or milk sugar, packaged in 45,000 tiny gelatin capsules and sold on the streets for $5 a shot, a kilo of heroin that began as $500 worth of opium back in Long Pot was worth $225,000.[152]

In the 1950s Long Pot's farmers had sold their opium to Chinese caravans from the Plain of Jars that passed through the area several times during every harvest season. Despite the occupation of the plain by neutralist and Pathet Lao forces in 1960 and 1961, Chinese caravans kept coming and opium growers in Long Pot district continued to deal with them.

According to Long Pot's district officer, Ger Su Yang, the Chinese merchant caravans disappeared after the 1964–1965 harvest, when heavy fighting broke out on the plain's western perimeter. But they were replaced by Hmong army caravans from Long Tieng. Commanded by lieutenants and captains in Vang Pao's army, the caravans usually consisted of half a dozen mounted Hmong soldiers and a string of shaggy mountain ponies loaded with trade goods. When the caravans arrived from Long Tieng, they usually stayed at the district officer's house in Long Pot village and used it as a headquarters while trading for opium in the area. Lao Theung and Hmong opium farmers from nearby villages, such as Gier Goot and Thong Oui, carried their opium to Long Pot and haggled over the price with the Hmong officers in the guest corner of Ger Su Yang's house.[153] While the soldiers weighed the opium on a set of balance scales and burned a small glob to test its morphine content (a good burn indicates a high morphine content), the farmer inquired about the price and examined the trade goods spread out on the nearby sleeping platform (medicines, salt, iron, silver, flashlights, cloth, thread, and so on). After a few minutes of carefully considered offers and counteroffers, a bargain was struck. At one time the Hmong would accept nothing but silver or commodities. However, during the decade of war Air America had made commodities so available that most opium farmers came to prefer Laotian government currency. (Vang Pao's Hmong subjects were unique in this regard. Hill tribesmen in Burma and Thailand still preferred trade goods or silver in the form of British India rupees, French Indochina piasters, or rectangular bars.)[154]

To buy up opium from the outlying areas, the Hmong soldiers would leave Long Pot village on short excursions, hiking along the narrow mountain trails to Hmong and Lao Theung villages four or five miles to the north and south. For example, the headman of Nam Suk, a Lao Theung village about four miles north of Long Pot, recalled that his people began selling their opium harvest to Hmong soldiers in 1967 or 1968. Several times during every harvest season, five to eight of them arrived at his village, paid for the opium in paper currency, and then left with their purchases loaded in backpacks. Previously this village had sold its opium to Lao and Chinese merchants from Vang Vieng, a market town on the northern edge of the Vientiane Plain. But the Hmong soldiers were paying 20 percent more, and Lao Theung farmers were only too happy to deal with them.[155]

Since Hmong soldiers paid almost $60 a kilo, while merchants from Vang Vieng or Luang Prabang only paid $40 or $50, Vang Pao's officers were usually able to buy up all of the available opium in the district after only a few days of trading. Once the weight of their purchases matched the endurance limits of their rugged mountain ponies, the Hmong officers packed it into giant bamboo containers, loaded it on the ponies, and headed back for Long Tieng, where the raw opium was refined into morphine base. Hmong army caravans had to return to Long Pot and repeat this procedure two or three times during every season before they had purchased the district's entire opium harvest.

However, during the 1969–1970 opium harvest the procedure changed. Ger Su Yang described this important development in a 1971 interview:

> [Hmong] officers with three or four stripes [captain or major] came from Long Tieng to buy our opium. They came in American helicopters, perhaps two or three men at one time. The helicopter leaves them here for a few days and they walk to villages over there [swinging his arm in a semicircle in the direction of Gier Goot, Long Makkhay, and Nam Pac], then come back here and radioed Long Tieng to send another helicopter for them. They take the opium back to Long Tieng.

Ger Su Yang went on to explain that the helicopter pilots were always Americans, but it was the Hmong officers who stayed behind to buy up the opium. The headman of Nam Ou, a Lao Theung village five miles north of

Long Pot, confirmed the district officer's account; he recalled that in 1969–1970 Hmong officers who had been flown into Tam Son village by helicopter hiked into his village and purchased the opium harvest. Since the thirty households in his village produced only 2 or 3 kilos of opium apiece, the Hmong soldiers continued on to Nam Suk and Long Pot.[156]

Although Long Pot's reluctant alliance with Vang Pao and the CIA at first brought prosperity to the village, by 1971 it was weakening the local economy and threatening Long Pot's very survival. The alliance began in 1961 when Hmong officers visited the village, offering money and arms if the villagers joined with Vang Pao and threatening reprisals if they remained neutral. Ger Su Yang resented Vang Pao's usurpation of Touby Lyfoung's rightful position as leader of the Hmong, but there seemed no alternative to the village declaring its support for Vang Pao.[157] During the 1960s Long Pot became one of Vang Pao's most loyal villages. Edgar Buell devoted a good deal of his personal attention to winning the area over, and USAID even built a school in the village.[158] In exchange for sending fewer than twenty soldiers to Long Tieng, most of whom were killed in action, Long Pot village received regular rice drops, money, and an excellent price for its opium.

But in 1970 the war finally came to Long Pot. With enemy troops threatening Long Tieng and his manpower pool virtually exhausted, Vang Pao ordered his villages to send every available man, including even the fifteen-year-olds. Ger Su Yang complied, and the village built a training camp for its sixty recruits on a nearby hill. Assisted by Hmong officers from Long Tieng, Ger Su Yang personally supervised the training, which consisted mainly of running up and down the hillside. After weeks of target practice and conditioning, Air America helicopters began arriving late in the year and flew the young men off to battle.

Village leaders apparently harbored strong doubts about the wisdom of sending off so many of their young men, and as early rumors of heavy casualties among the recruits filtered back, opposition to Vang Pao's war stiffened. When Long Tieng officials demanded more recruits in January 1971, the village refused. Seven months later Ger Su Yang expressed his determination not to sacrifice any more of Long Pot's youth:

> Last year I sent sixty [young men] out of this village. But this year it's finished. I can't send any more away to fight. . . . The Americans in Long Tieng said I must send all the rest of our men. But I refused. So they stopped dropping rice to us. The last rice drop was in February this year.[159]

In January Long Tieng officials warned the village that unless recruits were forthcoming Air America's rice drops would stop. Although Long

Pot was almost totally dependent on the Americans for its rice supply, opposition to Vang Pao was now so strong that the village was willing to accept the price of refusal. "Vang Pao keeps sending the Meo [Hmong] to be killed," said Ger Su Yang. "Too many Meo have been killed already, and he keeps sending more. Soon all will be killed, but Vang Pao doesn't care." But before stopping the rice shipments, Long Tieng officials made a final offer. "If we move our village to Ban Son or Tin Bong [another resettlement area] the Americans will give us rice again," explained Ger Su Yang. "But at Ban Son there are too many Meo, and there are not enough rice fields. We must stay here, this is our home."[160]

When the annual Pathet Lao–North Vietnamese offensive began in January 1971, strong Pathet Lao patrols appeared in the Long Pot region for the first time in several years and began making contact with the local population. Afraid that the Hmong and Lao Theung might go over to the Pathet Lao, the Americans ordered the area's residents to move south and proceeded to cut off rice support for those who refused to obey.[161] A far more powerful inducement was added when the U.S. bombing intensified to the east of Long Pot district and residents became afraid that it would spread to their villages. To escape from the threat of being bombed, the entire populations of Phou Miang and Muong Chim, Hmong villages five miles east of Long Pot, moved south to the Tin Bong resettlement area in early 1971. At about the same time, many of the Hmong residents of Tam Son and eight families from Long Pot also migrated to Tin Bong. Afraid that Pathet Lao patrols operating along Route 13 might draw air strikes on their villages, the Hmong of Sam Poo Kok joined the rush to Tin Bong, while three Lao Theung villages in the same general area—Nam Suk, Nam Ou and San Pakau—moved to a ridge opposite Long Pot village. Their decision to stay in Long Pot district rather than move south was largely due to the influence of Ger Su Yang. Determined to remain in the area, he used all his prestige to stem the tide of refugees and retain enough population to preserve some semblance of local autonomy. Thus, rather than moving south when faced with the dual threat of American air attacks and gradual starvation, most of the villagers abandoned their houses in January and hid in the nearby forest until March.

While U.S. officials in Laos claimed that hill tribes moved to escape slaughter at the hands of the enemy, most of the people in Long Pot district said that it was fear of indiscriminate American and Laotian bombing that drove their neighbors south to Tin Bong. These fears cannot be dismissed as ignorance on the part of "primitive" tribes; they watched the air war at work and they knew what it could do. From sunrise to sunset the mountain silence was shattered every twenty or thirty minutes by the distant roar of paired Phantom fighters en route to targets around the Plain of Jars. Throughout the night the monotonous buzz of prowling AC-47 gunships was broken only when their infrared sensors sniffed warm mammal flesh and their miniguns clattered, firing 6,000 rounds a minute. Every few days a handful of survivors fleeing the holocaust passed through Long Pot relating their stories of bombing and strafing. On August 21, 1971, twenty exhausted refugees from a Lao Theung village in the Muong Soui area reached Long Pot village. Their story was typical. In June Laotian air force T-28s had bombed their village while they fled into the forest. Every night for two months AC-47 gunships raked the ground around their trenches and shallow caves. Because of the daylight bombing and nighttime strafing, they were able to work their fields only in the predawn hours. Finally, faced with certain starvation, they fled the Pathet Lao zone and walked through the forest for eleven days before reaching Long Pot. Twice during their march the gunships found them and opened fire.[162]

When Ger Su Yang was asked which he feared most, the bombing or the Pathet Lao, his confidence disappeared and he replied in a quavering voice,

> The bombs! The bombs! Every [Hmong] village north of here [pointing to the northeast] has been bombed. Every village! Everything! There are big holes [extending his arms] in every village. Every house is destroyed. If bombs didn't hit some houses they were burned. Everything is gone. Everything from this village, all the way to Muong Soui and all of Xieng Khouang [Plain of Jars] is destroyed. In Xieng Khouang there are bomb craters like this [stretching out his arms, stabbing into the air to indicate a long line of craters] all over the plain. Every village in Xieng Khouang has been bombed, and many, many people died. From here . . . all the mountains north have small bombs in the grass. They were dropped from the airplanes.[163]

Although opium production in Long Pot village had not yet declined, by August 1971 there was concern that disruption caused by the escalating conflict might reduce the size of the harvest. Even though the village spent the 1970–1971 harvest season hiding in the forest, most families somehow managed to attain their normal output of 15 kilos. Heavy fighting at Long Tieng delayed the arrival of Air America helicopters by several months, but in May 1971 they finally began landing at Long Pot carrying Hmong army traders, who paid the expected $60 for every kilo of raw opium.[164] However, prospects for the 1971–1972 opium harvest were looking quite dismal as planting time approached in late August. There were plenty of women to plant, weed, and harvest, but a shortage of male workers and the necessity of hiding in the forest during the past winter had made it difficult for households to clear new fields. As a result, many farmers were planting their poppies in exhausted soil, and they expected to harvest only half as much opium as the year before.

However, as the war mounted in intensity through 1971 and early 1972, Long Pot district's opium harvest was drastically reduced and eventually destroyed. USAID officials reported that about 4,600 hill tribesmen had left the district in January and February 1971 and moved to the Tin Bong refugee area to the south, where there was a shortage of land.[165] Some of the villages that remained, such as the three Lao Theung villages near Long Pot village, were producing no opium at all. Even Long Pot village had lost eight of its households during the early months of 1971. Finally, on January 4, 1972, Allied fighter aircraft attacked Long Pot district. In an apparent attempt to slow the pace of a Pathet Lao offensive in the district, the fighters napalmed the district's remaining villages, destroying Long Pot village and the three nearby Lao Theung villages.[166]

The painful migration of Long Pot's villagers southward toward Vientiane was but a small part of a mass Hmong retreat away from the mountains that surrounded the Plain of Jars. By 1973 some 150,000 Hmong were crowded into a fifty-mile strip of hills at Ban Son, lying between the CIA's main base at Long Tieng and the humid Vientiane plain below. As repeated losses reduced Vang Pao's army by 10,000 troops from its peak of 40,000, the CIA imported an estimated 20,000 Thai mercenaries to replace the Hmong, now unable and unwilling to make up the losses.[167] Faced with the threat of a Pathet Lao attack on the capital Vientiane, the Royal Lao government signed a cease-fire with the Communist Pathet Lao in 1973, effectively ending the secret war. Over the next few months, Air America abandoned more than 300 landing strips and turned over a number of its transport aircraft to the Lao government. On orders from the Lao government, Air America finally gave up all of its facilities in June 1974.[168]

As Pathet Lao guerrillas began moving toward his territory in early 1975, Vang Pao led his remaining 6,000 troops in sporadic resistance that collapsed in early May when Communist troops broke through his lines guarding the main highway to Vientiane. Without U.S. air support for mobility and firepower, Vang Pao's guerrillas could no longer hold the Pathet Lao. At the insistence of his CIA case officers, Vang Pao finally agreed to flee to Thailand. On May 14, a CIA chartered aircraft landed at Long Tieng to evacuate Vang Pao and his remaining troops. Evading Communist fire from the surrounding ridges, the CIA transports made quick shuttle flights to nearby Thai air bases, maneuvering for takeoff through mobs of panicked Hmong that surged along the runway toward the aircraft.

After some 3,000 Hmong had been flown across the Mekong, Vang Pao and his CIA case officer, Jerry Daniels, a fifteen-year veteran of the secret war, flew out of Long Tieng into Thailand—and, ultimately, to Missoula, Montana, Daniels's hometown, where Vang Pao paid over a half million dollars for a cattle ranch, hog farm, and two large homes.[169] By the end of the year, more than 30,000 Hmong refugees had fled across the Mekong into Thailand,[170] the first wave of a mass exodus that would peak at 3,000 a month by 1979. "War is difficult, peace is hell," concluded General Vang Pao.[171]

## General Ouane Rattikone

General Ouane Rattikone could not have foreseen the enormous logistical problem that would be created by his ill-timed eviction of the Corsican charter airlines in 1965. While use of Air America aircraft solved the problem for Vang Pao by flying Hmong opium out of northeastern Laos, in the northwest Ouane had to rely on his own resources. Eager to establish an absolute monopoly over Laos's drug traffic, he had been confident of being able to expropriate two or three C-47s from the Laotian air force to do the job. But because of the intensification of the fighting in 1964–1965, Ouane found himself denied access to his own military aircraft. Although he still had control over enough civilian air transport to carry the local harvest and some additional Burmese imports, he could hardly hope to tap a major portion of Burma's exports unless he gained control over two or three air force C-47 transports. Ouane said that in 1964 he purchased large quantities of Burmese opium from the caravans that entered Laos through the Ban Houei Sai region in the extreme northwest, but he claimed that because of his transportation problem no large Shan or Nationalist Chinese opium caravans entered northwestern Laos in 1965.[172]

Shortly after General Phoumi Nosavan fled to Thailand in February 1965, Ouane's political ally General Kouprasith invited the commander of the Laotian air force, General Thao Ma, to Vientiane for a friendly conference. Thao Ma recalled that he did not learn the purpose of the meeting until he found himself seated at lunch with General Ouane, General Kouprasith, and General Oudone Sananikone. Kouprasith leaned forward and, with a smile, asked the diminutive air force general, "Would you like to be rich?" Thao Ma replied, "Yes. Of course." Encouraged by this positive response, Kouprasith proposed that he and Ouane pay Thao Ma 1 million kip ($2,000) a week and the air force allocate two C-47 transports for their opium-smuggling ventures. To their astonishment, Thao Ma refused; moreover, he warned Kouprasith and Ouane that if they tried to bribe any of his transport pilots he would personally intervene and put a stop to it.[173]

Very few Laotian generals would have turned down such a profitable offer, but Thao Ma was one of those rare generals who placed military considerations ahead of his political career or financial reward. As the war in South Vietnam and Laos heated up during 1964, Laotian air force T-28s became the key to clandestine air operations along the North Vietnamese border and the Ho Chi Minh Trail. Thao Ma took personal command of the squadrons bombing the Ho Chi Minh Trail and providing close air support for Secret Army operations in the northeast.[174] But his proudest accomplishment was the invention of an early version of what later became the AC-47 gunship. Aware that the Pathet Lao often attacked at night when his T-28 fighters were grounded, Thao Ma began looking for a way to provide nighttime air support for government forces and came up with the idea of arming his C-47 transports with .50 caliber machine guns. In 1964 he reduced the air force's logistic capacity by converting a number of his transports into gunships. Thus, when Kouprasith and Ouane demanded two C-47s in early 1965, Thao Ma felt there were none to spare and refused.[175]

Despite further offers and heavy political pressure, Thao Ma's intransigence continued. In 1966 Ouane was still without access to air transport and again no major Shan or Nationalist Chinese opium caravans entered northwestern Laos. Evidently the economic loss of two successive Burmese opium harvests and the prospect of continued losses convinced Ouane and Kouprasith that the Laotian air force badly needed a new commander.

In May 1966 Thao Ma was summoned to Vientiane from his headquarters in Savannakhet for a harsh dressing-down by the high command. The transport section of the air force was severed from his command and he was ordered to move his headquarters to Vientiane.[176] Fearing assassination at the hands of General Kouprasith if he moved to Vientiane, Thao Ma appealed for a six-month delay and began spending most of his time at the air base in Luang Prabang.[177] As the transfer date approached, Thao Ma sought desperately for an alternative. He begged the Americans, Captain Kong Le, and the king to intercede on his behalf, but to no avail.[178] Friend and foe alike reported that he was in a state of near panic by October, and Thao Ma himself remembered that he was functioning in a dazed stupor.[179] Thus, a coup seemed his only way out.

At 7:00 A.M. on October 22, six T-28 fighters took off from Savannakhet and headed north for Vientiane. At 8:20 A.M. the squadron reached the Laotian capital and the first bomb scored a direct hit on General Kouprasith's office at general staff headquarters. The T-28s strafed and bombed the headquarters compound extensively. Two munitions dumps at Wattay Airport on the outskirts of Vientiane were destroyed. The squadron also rocketed General Kouprasith's home at Chinaimo army camp, but all the missiles were wide of the mark and the general was unharmed.[180] More than thirty people were killed and dozens more were wounded.[181]

The squadron flew back to Savannakhet, and Vientiane waited nervously for a second round of attacks. After receiving numerous appeals from both Lao and American officials to end his revolt and go into exile, General Thao Ma and ten of his best pilots took off from Savannakhet at 1:45 A.M. October 23 and flew to Thailand, where they were granted political asylum.[182]

Although his coup was primarily an act of revenge, Thao Ma had apparently expected that his friend Kong Le, the neutralist army general, would seize Vientiane and oust the generals once Kouprasith was dead.[183] However, Kong Le was having his own problems with Kouprasith and, unknown to Thao Ma, had left for Bangkok five days before to meet with CIA officials. Shortly after the T-28s struck Vientiane, Thai officials placed Kong Le under house arrest in Bangkok and Kouprasith ordered Laotian border guards to arrest him if he tried to return. Kong Le became a political exile in Paris, and his neutralist army fell under rightist control.[184] Soon after Thao Ma flew into exile, a pliant, right-wing general was appointed air force commander.

With an ample supply of C-47 transports and helicopters now assured, General Ouane proceeded to contact Chinese and Shan opium brokers in the tri-border area and placed a particularly large order with a rising Shan warlord named Khun Sa (Chan Shee-fu).[185] As the Lahu and Wa hill tribes of northeastern Burma finished harvesting opium in the early months of 1967, Khun Sa's traders and brokers began buying up all the opium they could find. By June he had assembled one of the largest single shipments on record—16 tons of raw opium. When the caravan set out across the rugged Shan highlands for its destination near Ban Houei Sai, Laos, about two hundred miles away, its 300 pack horses and 500 armed guards marched single file in a column that extended over a mile along the narrow mountain trails.

This caravan was to spark off an armed confrontation that made headlines around the world as the 1967 Opium War. While the war struck most newspaper readers as a curiosity, in reality it was a serious struggle for control of Burma's opium exports, which at that time amounted to about 500 tons of raw opium annually—more than one-third of the world's total illicit supply. Consequently, each group's share of Burma's opium exports and its role in the Golden Triangle's heroin trade were largely determined by the war and its aftermath. All of the combatants were well aware of what was at stake and threw everything they could muster into the battle.

The confrontation started when the KMT (Nationalist Chinese army units) based in northern Thailand decided to send more than a thousand soldiers into Burma to head off Khun Sa's caravan. The KMT had been worried for some time that the rising young Shan warlord might threaten their fifteen-year domination of the opium trade, and this mammoth caravan was a serious challenge. But the Shan caravan eluded Nationalist Chinese forces, fled across the Mekong into Laos, and dug in for a fight at Ban Khwan, a lumber town twenty miles northwest of Ban Houei Sai. After several days of indecisive fighting between the Chinese and Shans, General Ouane Rattikone entered the lists. Displaying an aggressiveness rare among Laotian army commanders, Ouane bombed both sides with a squadron of T-28s and swept the field of battle with the Second Paratroop Battalion. While his friends and enemies fled in disorder, Ouane's troops scooped up the 16 tons of raw opium and delivered it to the victorious general. Almost two hundred people, mainly Shans and Chinese, died in the fighting.

As a result of Ouane's victory, the KMT lost many of its profitable prerogatives to the general. They had nevertheless crushed Khun Sa's bid for supremacy, even though they had not completely destroyed him. After the battle General Ouane emerged as one of the most important heroin manufacturers in the Golden Triangle, since his share of the Burmese opium trade increased considerably.

Although it was a relatively minor military action compared with the battles raging elsewhere in Indochina, the 1967 Opium War captured the imagination of the American press. However, all of the accounts studiously avoided any serious discussion of the Golden Triangle opium trade and emphasized the sensational. Using a cliché-studded prose usually reserved for the sports page or travel section, the media rambled on about wild animals, primitive tribes, desperadoes of every description, and the mysterious ways of the Orient. Despite its seductively exotic aspects, the 1967 Opium War remains the most revealing episode in the recent history of the Golden Triangle opium trade.

After the abolition of government opium monopolies in the 1940s and 1950s, the Golden Triangle's drug trade disappeared behind a curtain of government secrecy and it became increasingly difficult to verify official involvement or the extent of the traffic. Suddenly the curtain was snatched back, and there were 1,800 of General Ouane's best troops battling 1,400 well-armed Nationalist Chinese soldiers (supposedly evacuated to Taiwan six years before) for 16 tons of opium. But an appreciation of the subtler aspects of this sensational battle requires some background on the economic activities of the KMT units based in Thailand, the Shan rebels in Burma, and, in particular, the long history of CIA operations in the Golden Triangle.

# The CIA in Northwest Laos

CIA paramilitary operations in northwestern Laos began in 1959, but they were poorly planned and achieved far less than the ambitious Hmong program in the northeast. During the five-month battle for Nam Tha City in early 1962, a team of twelve U.S. Green Berets were active in the area as advisers to the beleaguered rightist army. What little work they did with the local hill tribes was cut short in May 1962 when the frightened garrison abandoned the city and retreated toward the Mekong River in disorder.[186]

Afraid that the Communists were about to overrun all of Nam Tha province, the CIA assigned William Young to the area in mid-1962. Young was instructed to build up a hill tribe commando force for operations in the tri-border area since regular Laotian army troops were ill-suited for military operations in the rugged mountains. Nam Tha's ethnic diversity and the scope of clandestine operations made paramilitary work in this province far more demanding than Hmong operations in the northeast.[187]

As a migration crossroads for centuries for tribes from southern China and Tibet, Nam Tha province was an area of remarkable ethnic diversity. Successive waves of Hmong and Yao tribesmen began migrating down the Red River valley into North Vietnam in the late 1700s, reaching Nam Tha in the mid-nineteenth century.[188] Nam Tha also marked the extreme southeastern frontier for advancing Tibeto-Burman tribes, mainly Akha and Lahu, who had moved south slowly through the China-Burma borderlands for centuries. Laotian officials believed that there may have been as many as thirty different ethnic minorities living in the province.

Nam Tha province itself was added to Laos in the late nineteenth century when Europe's imperial diplomats decided that the Mekong River was the most convenient dividing line between British Burma and French Indochina. Jutting awkwardly into Thailand, Burma, and China, it actually looks on maps as if it had been pasted onto Laos. There are very few Lao in Nam Tha, and most of the lowland valleys are inhabited by Lu, a Tai-speaking people who were once part of a feudal kingdom centered in southern Yunnan.

With thirty tribal dialects and languages, most of them mutually unintelligible, and virtually no Lao population, Nam Tha province had been a source of frustration for both French and American counterinsurgency specialists.

With his knowledge of local languages and his rapport with the mountain minorities, William Young was uniquely qualified to overcome these difficulties. Speaking four of the most important languages—Lu, Lao, Hmong, and Lahu—Young could deal directly with most of the tribesmen in Nam Tha. Since Young had grown up in Lahu and Shan villages in Burma, he actually enjoyed the long months of solitary work among the hill tribes, which might have strained less acculturated agents.

Rather than trying to create a tribal warlord on the Vang Pao model, Young decided to build a pan-tribal army under the command of a joint council composed of one or two leaders from every tribe. Theoretically the council was supposed to have final authority on all matters, but in reality Young controlled the money and made the decisions. However, council meetings did give various tribal leaders a sense of participation and greatly increased the efficiency of paramilitary operations. Most important, Young managed to develop his pan-tribal council and weaken the would-be Yao warlord, Chao Mai, without alienating him from the program. In fact, Chao Mai remained one of Young's strongest supporters, and his Yao tribesmen constituted the great majority of the CIA mercenary force in Nam Tha.[189]

Although his relationships with hill tribe leaders were extraordinary, William Young still used standard CIA procedures for "opening up" an area to paramilitary operations. But to organize the building of runways, select base sites, and perform all the other essential tasks connected with forging a counterguerrilla infrastructure, Young recruited a remarkable team of sixteen Shan and Lahu operatives he called the Sixteen Musketeers, whose leader was a middle-aged Shan nationalist leader, "General" U Ba Thein.[190]

With the team's assistance, Young began opening up the province in mid-1962. By late 1963 he had built up a network of some twenty dirt landing strips and a guerrilla force of 600 Yao commandos and several hundred additional troops from the other tribes. But the war in northwestern Laos had intensified and large-scale refugee relocations had begun in late 1962 when Chao Mai and several thousand of his Yao followers abandoned their villages in the mountains between Nam Tha and Muong Sing, both of which were under Pathet Lao control, and moved south to Ban Na Woua and Nam Thouei, refugee centers established by the Sixteen Musketeers.[191] The outbreak of fighting several months later gradually forced tribal mercenaries and their families, particularly the Yao, out of the Pathet Lao zone and into refugee camps.[192]

Instead of directing rice drops and refugee operations personally, Young delegated the responsibility to a pistol-packing community development worker named Joseph Flipse who, like Edgar Buell, was an IVS volunteer. While Flipse maintained a humanitarian showplace at Nam Thouei complete with a hospital, school, and supply warehouse, William Young and his tribal team opened a secret base at Nam Yu, only three miles away, which served as CIA headquarters for cross-border intelligence forays into southern China.[193] The double-dealing relationship between Nam Thouei and Nam Yu in northwestern Laos was very similar to the arrangement at Sam Thong and Long Tieng in northeastern Laos. For almost a decade reporters and visiting congressional representatives were taken to Sam Thong to see the good work Edgar Buell was doing to save the Hmong from Communist aggression but were denied access to CIA headquarters at Long Tieng.[194]

However, just as the operations were getting under way, CIA policy decisions and local opium politics combined to kill this enthusiasm and weaken the overall effectiveness of Young's hill tribe operations. A series of CIA personnel transfers in 1964 and 1965 probably did more damage than anything else. When Young became involved in a heated jurisdictional dispute with Thai intelligence officers in October 1964, the CIA pulled him out of Nam Tha and sent him to Washington for a special training course. High-ranking CIA bureaucrats in Washington and Vientiane had long been dissatisfied with the paucity of Intel-Coms (intelligence communications) and in-depth reports they were getting from Young and apparently used his squabble with the Thai as a pretext for placing a more senior agent in charge of operations in Nam Tha. After Young's first replacement, an operative named Objibway, died in a helicopter crash in the summer of 1965, Tony Poe drew the assignment.[195]

Where Young had used his skill as a negotiator and his knowledge of minority cultures to win compliance from hill tribe leaders, Poe preferred to use bribes, intimidation, and threats. The hill tribe leaders, particularly Chao Mai, were alienated by Poe's tactics and became less aggressive. Poe tried to rekindle their enthusiasm for combat by raising salaries and offering cash bonuses for Pathet Lao ears.[196] But as a former USAID official put it, "The pay was constantly going up, and the troops kept moving slower."[197]

General Ouane Rattikone's monopolization of the opium trade in Military Region I, northwestern Laos, dealt another major blow to Chao Mai's enthusiasm for the war effort. Chao Mai had inherited control over the Yao opium trade from his father, and during the early 1960s he was probably the most important opium merchant in Nam Tha province. Every year Chao Mai sold the harvest to the Chinese merchants in Muong Sing and Ban Houei Sai who acted as brokers for the Corsican charter airlines. With his share of the profits, Chao Mai financed a wide variety of social welfare projects among the Yao, from which he derived his power and prestige. However, when Ouane took over the Laotian opium trade in 1965, he forced all of his competitors, big and small, out of business. One USAID official who worked in the area remembers that all the hotels and shops in Ban Houei Sai were crowded with opium buyers from Vientiane and Luang Prabang following the 1963 and 1964 harvest seasons. But in 1965 the hotels and shops were empty and local merchants explained that "there was a big move on by Ouane to consolidate the opium business." Ouane's strategy for forcing his most important competitor out of business was rather simple; after Chao Mai had finished delivering most of the Yao opium to Ouane's broker in Ban Houei Sai, who had promised to arrange air transport to Vientiane, the Lao army officer simply refused to pay for the opium. There was absolutely nothing Chao Mai could do, and he was forced to accept the loss. Needless to say, this humiliating incident further weakened his control over the Yao, and by the time he died in April 1967 most of his followers had moved to Nam Keung where his brother Chao La was sitting out the war on the banks of the Mekong.[198]

After Chao Mai's death, Poe tried in vain to revitalize tribal commando operations by appointing Chao La commander of Yao paramilitary forces. Although Chao La accepted the position and participated in the more spectacular raids, such as the recapture of Nam Tha City in October 1967, he had little interest in the tedium of day-to-day operations that are the essence of counterguerrilla warfare. Unlike Chao Mai, who was a politician and a soldier, Chao La was a businessman whose main interests were his lumber mill, gunrunning, and the narcotics traffic. In fact, some American officials believed that Chao La worked with the CIA only to get guns (which he used to buy opium from Burmese smugglers) and political protection for his opium refineries.[199]

Although William Young was removed from command of paramilitary operations in 1964, the CIA had ordered him back to Nam Tha in August 1965 to continue supervising the Yao and Lahu intelligence teams, which were being sent deep into Yunnan province, China. Wedged between China and Burma, Nam Tha province was an ideal staging ground for cross-border intelligence patrols operating in southern China. The arbitrary boundaries between Burma, China, and Laos had little meaning for the hill tribes, who had been moving back and forth across the frontiers for centuries in search of new mountains and forests. As a result of these constant migrations, many of the hill tribes that populate the Burma-China borderlands were also found in Nam Tha province.[200] Some of the elderly Lahu and Yao living in Nam Tha were actually born in Yunnan, and many of the younger generation have relatives there. Most important, both of these tribes have a strong sense of ethnic identity, and individual tribesmen view themselves as members of larger Yao and Lahu communities that transcend national boundaries.[201] Because of the ethnic overlap between all three countries, CIA-trained Lahu and Yao agents from Nam Tha could cross the Chinese border and wander the mountains of Yunnan tapping telephone lines and monitoring road traffic without being detected.

After a year of recruiting and training agents, William Young had begun sending the first Lahu and Yao teams into China in 1963. Since the CIA and the Pentagon were quite concerned about the possibility of Chinese military intervention in Indochina, any intelligence on military activity in southern China was valued and the cross-border operations were steadily expanded. By the time Young quit the CIA in 1967, he had opened three major radio posts within Burma's Shan states, built a special training camp that was graduating thirty-five agents every two months, and sent hundreds of teams deep into Yunnan. While Young's linguistic abilities and his understanding of hill tribe culture had made him a capable paramilitary organizer, it was his family's special relationship with the Lahu that enabled him to organize the cross-border operations. The Sixteen Musketeers who recruited most of the first agents were Lahu, the majority of the tribesmen who volunteered for these dangerous missions were Lahu, and all the radio posts inside the Shan states were manned by Lahu tribesmen.[202]

This special relationship with the Lahu dated back to the turn of the century, when Young's grandfather, a Baptist missionary, converted thousands of Lahu who took him to be the God once promised by a Lahu prophet.[203] Young's father, Harold, carried the family's missionary work to the Wa states in the 1930s, but he was forced to leave Burma after World War II when the newly independent government became suspicious of his relations with minority dissidents. He moved to Chiangmai, Thailand,[204] where the second chapter in the family's special relationship with the Lahu took place.

After the establishment of the People's Republic of China in 1949, the CIA rearmed remnants of the Nationalist Chinese Army who had fled into the Shan states and launched three abortive invasions into western Yunnan in the hope that the Chinese masses would rally to their banners. The CIA needed detailed information on Chinese troop movements in Yunnan's border areas and hired Harold Young to gather this intelligence. Young in turn called on a Shan Christian in Kengtung named U Ba Thein to organize a team of Lahu Christians for intelligence work inside China. U Ba Thein, who had gained intelligence experience working for the British in World War II, sent a group of Lahu to Chiangmai, where Harold's eldest son, Gordon, trained them in radio transmission and repairs. Once their training was completed, they hiked back to the Shan states and radioed intelligence information from the Burma-China border to Chiangmai. There Gordon Young translated the information from Lahu to English and handed it over to a local CIA operative who was working undercover as the American vice-consul.[205]

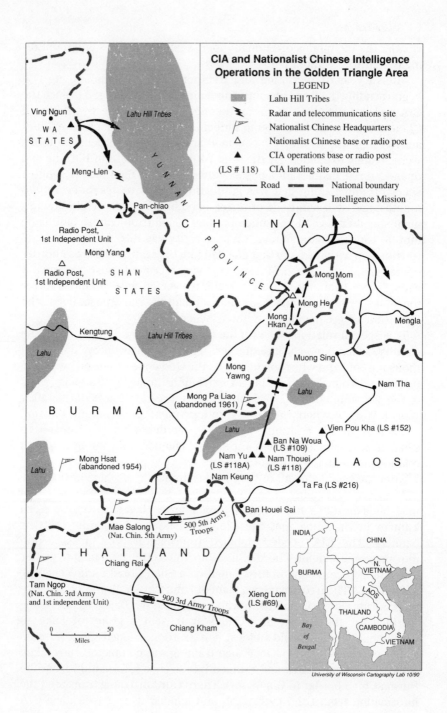

**CIA and Nationalist Chinese Intelligence Operations in the Golden Triangle Area**

LEGEND

- Lahu Hill Tribes
- Radar and telecommunications site
- Nationalist Chinese Headquarters
- △ Nationalist Chinese base or radio post
- ▲ CIA operations base or radio post
- (LS # 118) CIA landing site number
- —— Road
- ▬ ▬ ▬ National boundary
- → → → Intelligence Mission

Ving Ngun

*Lahu Hill Tribes*

WA STATES

*Y U N N A N*

Meng-Lien

Pan-chiao

△ Radio Post, 1st Independent Unit

Mong Yang

△ Radio Post, 1st Independent Unit

S H A N STATES

C H I N A

P R O V I N C E

Mong Mom

Mong He

Mong Hkan

Mengla

Kengtung

*Lahu Hill Tribes*

*Lahu*

Muong Sing

Mong Yawng

Mong Pa Liao (abandoned 1961)

*Lahu*

Nam Tha

B U R M A

*Lahu*

Vien Pou Kha (LS #152)

Ban Na Woua (LS #109)

Mong Hsat (abandoned 1954)

*Lahu*

Nam Yu (LS #118A)

Nam Thouei (LS #118)

Nam Keung

L A O S

Ta Fa (LS #216)

Ban Houei Sai

Mae Salong (Nat. Chin. 5th Army)

500 5th Army Troops

T H A I L A N D

Chiang Rai

Tam Ngop (Nat. Chin. 3rd Army and 1st independent Unit)

Xieng Lom (LS #69)

900 3rd Army Troops

Chiang Kham

0      50
Miles

INDIA

CHINA

BURMA

N. VIETNAM

LAOS

THAILAND

*Bay of Bengal*

CAMBODIA

S VIETNAM

University of Wisconsin Cartography Lab 10/90

The Lahu intelligence operations continued for almost six years, until the outbreak of the Shan national revolution in 1958 forced U Ba Thein to leave Burma. The Shan states, which had enjoyed a somewhat separate administration during British colonial days, had merged with the newly independent Union of Burma in 1947, but increasing repression by the Burmese during the 1950s fomented the independence movement. As treasurer of Kengtung state, U Ba Thein had played an important role in the early stages of the movement. But in January 1958, after Burmese intelligence had become suspicious of his activities, he fled into the hills with a sack of state pension funds from the treasury offices.

The Young family provided U Ba Thein with a hiding place in the Thai mountains for four months, until he sought refuge in Muong Sing, Laos. He remained there for three and half years, buying arms for Shan insurgents with the Kengtung pension funds and trying, without success, to organize an effective guerrilla army.[206] During the 1960s U Ba Thein's cross-border intelligence missions for the CIA became interwoven with the fabric of the Burmese opium trade, and he became involved in a series of arms-for-opium deals between General Ouane and the Shans.

Since the Pathet Lao occupied the entire Laos-China frontier in Nam Tha, CIA tribal intelligence teams had to pass through the Burmese Shan states before entering Yunnan. As a result, the CIA had to depend on Shan rebels to guide its teams up to the Chinese border, protect its forward radio posts inside the Shan states, and provide transportation between these radio posts and its forward bases in Nam Tha. Almost every aspect of these intelligence missions was somehow involved with the logistics of the Burmese opium trade.

A brief review of the cross-border operating procedures illustrates the peculiar symbiosis between opium and espionage in the Burmese Shan states. In general, the modus operandi of cross-border patrols changed very little from the time William Young initiated them in 1962 until President Nixon ordered them stopped in August 1971.[207]

After prospective agents were recruited, they were sent to secret camps not far from Nam Yu for two months of training. While the CIA planned the curriculum, Thai special forces provided most of the instructors.[208] After that initial training, the prospective agents were sent to the Thai special forces camp at Phitsanulok for four to five months of instruction in codes, radio transmission, and radio repair.[209]

Finally, the tribal agents were flown back to Nam Yu, the nerve center of cross-border espionage, and divided into five-to-fifteen-man teams. From Nam Yu the teams were flown 55 miles due north and dropped off on the Laotian bank of the Mekong River. After inflating their rubber rafts, the teams paddled across the Mekong and hiked 3 miles through the Burmese jungle until they reached the joint Nationalist Chinese–CIA base near Mong Hkan. Of the five bases the CIA maintained along the Burma-China border, Mong Hkan was by far the most exotic. It was originally established by a KMT intelligence force, the First Independent Unit, to serve as a base for its own cross-border forays into Yunnan and as a radio post for transmitting information on the availability of opium to KMT military caravans based at Mae Salong in northern Thailand. When the CIA began sending its reconnaissance patrols into Yunnan, the First Independent Unit agreed to share the base and Young opened a radio post manned by Lahu agents. According to Young, Mong Hkan was something of a "little Switzerland." Soon after the CIA arrived, British, Thai, Laotian, and even a few Indian intelligence agents began showing up to "see what they could skim off the top."[210]

From Mong Hkan, the CIA teams hiked north for several days to one of two forward bases only a few miles from the border—a joint CIA-KMT radio post at Mong He and a CIA station at Mong Mom. After crossing the lightly guarded border, the teams usually spent about three or four months inside China.

Using four-pound radios with a broadcast radius of four hundred miles, the teams transmitted their top-priority data directly to a powerful receiver at Nam Yu or to specially equipped Air America planes that flew back and forth along the Laos-China border. After these messages were translated at Nam Yu, they were forwarded to Vientiane for analysis and possible transmission to CIA headquarters in Langley, Virginia. The radio messages also served to pinpoint every team's position, all carefully recorded on a huge relief map of Yunnan province mounted in a restricted operations room at Nam Yu.[211]

During the period that William Young directed cross-border espionage, the CIA maintained two independent listening posts much deeper inside the Shan states in addition to the bases it operated jointly with the KMT. Both of these posts—one located 10 miles north of Mong Yang and the other 5 miles east of Ving Ngun—were extremely close to the Chinese border. Each was manned by twenty to thirty Lahu and Wa operatives who mounted lateral patrols along the border, went into China on reconnaissance missions, and maintained radio contact with Nam Yu.[212]

Since Mong Yang was about 80 miles from CIA headquarters at Nam Yu and Ving Ngun was more than 180 miles away, the agency found that it had to rely on U Ba Thein's guerrilla armies to protect these bases from Burmese army patrols and government self-defense forces. U Ba Thein felt that his guerrillas provided a valuable service for the CIA, pointing out that these posts were maintained with only twenty to thirty men, whereas KMT radio posts in the same areas that did not enjoy his protection needed a minimum of a hundred men.

Rather than sending Air America helicopters so far into hostile territory to keep these bases supplied, the CIA relied on Shan rebel opium caravans. Since the caravans usually returned from their frequent trips to northern Thailand and Laos with a lighter load of arms and ammunition, they were willing to pick up some extra money by carrying supplies—arms, ammunition, money, and radios—to the CIA's forward listening post, thus sparing the agency the risk of using Air America helicopters in such unknown, remote regions.[213]

## U Ba Thein: Covert Action Ally

Unlike many of the minority leaders who served the CIA in the Golden Triangle, U Ba Thein was not a simple mercenary. At the peak of his power in the mid-1960s, he was one of the most important Shan revolutionary leaders. Most of the things he did, including his work for the CIA, were designed to further the cause. While most guerrilla leaders in the Third World would hardly consider the CIA a partner in national liberation, U Ba Thein viewed the agency as his natural ideological ally. Most of the Shan rebels were anti-Communist monarchists, and the Burmese government they were fighting was Marxist and socialist. The Shan rebel leaders looked on the Burmese as aggressors who had expropriated their mineral wealth, but they remembered the British colonial administrators with fondness for having built schools and kept the Burmese at bay. Like many of his generation, U Ba Thein was educated in British schools, converted to Christianity, and learned to think of white men as his protectors. He said he was fighting for Shan independence, but he also wanted to place his independent nation under the protection of Britain or the United States. In September 1971 he spoke of his political aspirations:

> We want to be independent from the Burmese, but we are very poor and will need help. We have many minerals in the Shan states and perhaps the British or Americans will come and help develop these for us. You know, sir, we have given Bill Young twenty mineral samples to send to the U.S. to be analyzed. Then if we can get Britain or the U.S. to come in and hold hands with us we can stand independent.[214]

U Ba Thein had enjoyed organizing commando operations for British intelligence during World War II, secure in the knowledge that a great white empire was behind him. When he began building up a Shan revolutionary movement in 1958, his first thought was to seek aid from the Americans.

Soon after he fled from Burma and arrived in Muong Sing, Laos, in mid-1958, he contacted Dr. Tom Dooley, an independent American humanitarian who was operating a free clinic for the hill tribes in nearby

Nam Tha, and asked him to get aid for the Shans from the U.S. embassy or the CIA. Although Dr. Dooley was becoming an icon of America's anti-Communist crusade in Southeast Asia, he was no gunrunner. U Ba Thein eventually became associated with a fledgling rebel group called the Youth Party, but in general he accomplished very little during his first two years in Muong Sing.[215]

However, in 1961 U Ba Thein and another leader of the Youth Party, "General" Sao Gnar Kham, decided to break with the party's incompetent leader and form the Shan National Army (SNA), a loose coalition that eventually included most of the rebel bands operating in Kengtung state. While U Ba Thein was not an exceptional leader, Sao Gnar Kham was one of the few charismatic commanders the Shan rebellion produced. Before joining the rebel movement, he had been a Buddhist monk in Kengtung, where he used his personal magnetism to solicit donations for the construction of orphanages. When the Shan secessionist movement began in 1958, Gnar Kham made the mistake of openly expressing his sympathies for the dissidents and was arrested. After receiving a severe beating he fled into the hills to join the guerrillas, taking the orphanage donations with him.[216] When the Shan National Army was formed, Gnar Kham's leadership abilities made him the obvious choice for commander, and U Ba Thein became deputy commander.

During its first year, SNA operations were hampered by a lack of money and arms. In late 1961 their fortunes were at a low ebb: their absconded funds were running low, few of the independent rebel bands seemed willing to join, and they needed modern automatic weapons. At this moment in history the interests of the Shan National Army complemented those of General Ouane Rattikone, and the opium-arms traffic that later made Laos a major heroin-processing center was born. As head of General Phoumi's secret Opium Administration, Ouane was charged with the responsibility for importing large quantities of Burmese opium. Phoumi had an ample supply of surplus weapons, since the rightist army was receiving large shipments of modern arms from the CIA and its generals had inflated the troop roster to increase the payroll. For their part, Gnar Kham and U Ba Thein had contacts with rebel groups in Kengtung who were trading the local opium they collected as taxes for overpriced World War I rifles and would welcome a better bargain.

What role, if any, did William Young and the CIA play in bringing the two parties together? First, it is important to note that the Kengtung rebels and General Ouane had known of each other for a number of years. When Ouane was Pathet Lao commander in northwestern Laos during the 1940s, he was once forced to retreat into Kengtung, where he was given asylum by the *sawbwa*. The incident left Ouane with a lasting affection for the Shans, and he kept in sporadic contact over the years. William Young said that Gnar Kham pleaded with him to arrange air transportation to Vientiane so that he could meet with Ouane, but Young insisted that he had no authorization for such trips and denied the request. Young added, however, that Ouane found out about the situation independently and ordered the Secret Army commander for northwestern Laos to begin making arms available to the SNA in exchange for Burmese opium. Sometime later Ouane himself flew up to Ban Houei Sai and met with Gnar Kham to finalize the arrangements.[217] U Ba Thein generally concurred with Young's account, but added that Young knew about the arrangement, saw the arms and opium being exchanged, and never made any move to stop it. Since the Americans had denied his formal requests for military aid, U Ba Thein assumed that their benign neglect of the opium-arms trade was another form of repayment for all the services the SNA was providing the agency.[218] In fact, the security of CIA's listening posts near Mong Yang and Ving Ngun did depend on the Shans' having good automatic weapons, and the agency's logistics link with these two bases was the SNA opium caravans. Young admitted that he adopted a posture of benign neglect toward the traffic but denied any personal wrongdoing, claiming that this was the CIA policy throughout northern Laos. The CIA was afraid that pressure on local mercenary commanders to quit the traffic might damage the effectiveness of their paramilitary work.[219]

Once matters were finally settled with General Ouane and a steady stream of Shan opium and U.S. arms began moving through Ban Houei Sai, Gnar Kham and U Ba Thein launched an ambitious attempt to forge a unified guerrilla army out of Kengtung's mix of petty warlords. In late 1962 Gnar Kham and U Ba Thein left Ban Houei Sai and moved across the Mekong River into Thailand where they laid the foundation for their modern, unified army.[220]

Under Gnar Kham and U Ba Thein's supervision, the opium-arms commerce produced a marked improvement in Shan military capabilities and a dramatic shift in the balance of forces in Kengtung. In 1960–1961 most of the rebel units in Kengtung were little more than bands of outlaws hiding in the mountains. After gathering opium taxes from the few villages under their control, the local commanders led their caravans to Gnar Kham's forward caravan camp at Huei Krai, Thailand, and used the opium profits to buy U.S. automatic weapons from the Laotian army. With more weapons, the rebel groups were able to take control of additional opium-growing villages before the next year's harvest was in. More opium taxes meant more automatic weapons from U Ba Thein's headquarters near Ban Houei Sai, which in turn meant control over more villages and still more opium. The symbiotic cycle of opium and arms spiraled upward into a military whirlwind that swept the Burmese army out of the countryside into a few well-guarded cities. By 1965 the SNA's seven major local commanders had an estimated 5,000 soldiers under their command and controlled most of Kengtung's 12,000 square miles.[221]

The importance of the opium-arms dynamic in building up the SNA is illustrated by the military impact of the 1964–1965 opium harvest in Mong Yang and Kengtung districts. The two SNA commanders who controlled the mountains around Kengtung, Major Samlor and Major Tsai Noie, finished collecting the first round of their opium tax in January 1965. To protect themselves from the Burmese army and the KMT, they merged into a single caravan of ten mules carrying 650 kilos of raw opium and set off for northern Thailand with a combined force of 200 armed men. After crossing the border into Thailand, they unloaded their cargo at Gnar Kham's camp in the mountains and sold it to a merchant in the nearby town of Mae Sai for $28 a kilo, a rather low price. Then they purchased sixty rifles in Ban Houei Sai (paying $125 for an ordinary rifle and $150 for a U.S. M1 or M2) and had them smuggled across the river into Chiang Khong and delivered to Gnar Kham's camp. While the group's leader was in Chiang Khong supervising the opium-arms transfer, they visited William Young at the CIA bungalow and briefed him on the situation in their areas of the Shan states.[222] When the caravan returned to Kengtung in March, the two commanders divided the sixty rifles evenly. The thirty rifles represented an important addition to Major Samlor's arsenal of eighty rifles, four Bren automatics, and one mortar, and an equally important supplement to Major Tsai Noie's collection of fifty rifles, two Brens, and a homemade bazooka.

During the 1964–1965 harvest, the SNA commander for the Mong Yang region, Major Saeng Wan, sent two large caravans to northern Thailand, which earned more than $25,000 and brought back 120 rifles, some mortars, and several heavy machine guns. Before these two caravans returned, he had had only 280 armed men, one heavy machine gun, and four Bren automatics to protect the entire Mong Yang region, which included the nearby CIA listening post.[223]

While opium was indeed the ingredient that rushed vital arms and money into the SNA's ranks, it was also a poison that weakened its military effectiveness and finally destroyed the fragile coalition. There was enough opium in even the smallest district in Kengtung to buy arms and equipment for a rebel army and make its leader a wealthy man. As a result, rebel commanders became preoccupied with protecting territorial prerogatives and expanding their personal fiefs. Instead of sending troops into an adjoining area to launch a joint operation against the Burmese, SNA commanders kept every man on patrol inside his own territory to collect the opium tax and keep his jealous comrades at a safe distance. A British journalist who spent five months in Kengtung with the SNA in 1964–1965 reported:

> It would be far more accurate to describe the SNA as a grouping of independent warlords loosely tied into a weak federation with a president as a figurehead. This president has influence through the facilities he offers for selling opium and buying guns and because he presents a front to the outside world, but it is unlikely he will ever wield effective power unless he becomes the channel for outside aid in the forms of guns or money.[224]

The lucrative opium traffic turned into a source of internal corruption alienating commanders from their troops and prompting ranking officers to fight each other for the spoils. Shan troops frequently complained that they were left at Gnar Kham's mountain camp to feed the mules while their leaders were off in the fleshpots of Chiangmai wasting opium profits on prostitutes and gambling instead of buying arms. Often, as soon as a rebel group grew large enough to be militarily effective, the second in command killed his leader or split the force to increase his personal share of the profits.

Not surprisingly, it was this type of dispute that ultimately destroyed the Shan National Army. U Ba Thein had been concerned about Sao Gnar Kham's popularity and his control over the opium traffic for several years. Evidently there were repeated disagreements among various leaders over the opium profits. In December 1964 the charismatic commander in chief of the SNA was shot and killed at the Huei Krai caravan station. Some sources claimed that it was an opium profit dispute that led to the murder.[225]

U Ba Thein was selected commander in chief of the SNA at a meeting of the local commanders in February 1965, but he lacked the leadership abilities that Gnar Kham had used to maintain some semblance of unity within the strife-torn coalition. Afraid that he would suffer a fate similar to Gnar Kham's, U Ba Thein refused to venture out of his headquarters either to meet with subordinates or to travel through Kengtung for a firsthand look at the military situation. Local commanders began to break away from the coalition and the SNA gradually dissolved; by 1966 these leaders were marketing their own opium and U Ba Thein had become a recluse surrounded by a dwindling number of bodyguards. Six years after Gnar Kham's death, five of his seven local commanders had been captured, forced into retirement, or killed by their own men, while the remaining two had become mercenary warlords, professional opium smugglers.

But even before Gnar Kham's death, other Shan rebel armies had already begun to play a more important role in the region's opium trade. While the history of the SNA's involvement in the opium traffic is important because of its relationship with General Ouane, its caravans probably never carried more than 1 percent of the Burmese opium exported to Thailand and Laos.[226] In fact, the only Shan warlord who ran a truly professional smuggling organization capable of transporting large quantities of opium was the notorious Khun Sa. A half-Shan, half-Chinese native of Lashio district in the northern Shan states, Khun Sa became involved in opium trafficking in 1963, when the Burmese government began authorizing the formation of local self-defense forces (called Ka Kwe Ye, or KKY, in Burmese) to combat the Shan rebels. While the Burmese government gave its militia no money, rations, or uniforms and only a minimum of arms, it made up for this parsimony by giving them the right to use all government-controlled roads and towns in the Shan states for opium smuggling.

In 1963 Khun Sa was authorized to form a militia of several hundred men, and, as a young man of uncommon ambition, he quickly parlayed a number of successful opium shipments to Thailand into a well-armed militia of 800 men. After severing his ties with the Burmese army in 1964, he abandoned his bases at Lashio and Tang Yang and shifted his headquarters eastward to Ving Ngun in the Wa states (one of the most bountiful opium-growing regions in Burma), where he established an independent fiefdom. He ruled the Ving Ngun area for two years, and his ruthlessness commanded the respect of even the wild Wa, whose headhunting had forced both the British and Burmese to adopt a circumspect attitude. To increase his share of the profits, he built a crude refinery (one of the very few then operating in the Shan states) for processing raw opium into morphine bricks. In 1966 he rejoined Rangoon's militia, and, using the government's *laissez-passer* to increase his opium shipments to Thailand, he expanded his army to 2,000 men. Unlike the SNA, which could never mobilize more than 200 or 300 of its troops at any one time, Khun Sa ruled his army with an iron hand and could rely on them to do as he commanded.[227]

Despite the size and efficiency of his army, Khun Sa still controlled only a relatively small percentage of the total traffic. In fact, a CIA study prepared by William Young in 1966–1967 showed that Shan caravans carried only 7 percent of Burma's exports, the Kachin Independence Army (the dominant rebel group in Burma's Kachin state) 3 percent, and the KMT 90 percent.[228] Even though the KMT's position seemed statistically impregnable, Khun Sa's precipitous rise had aroused considerable concern among the KMT generals in northern Thailand. When his massive 16-ton opium caravan began rolling south toward Ban

Houei Sai in June 1967, the KMT realized that its fifteen-year monopoly over the Burmese opium trade was finally being challenged. The situation provoked a serious crisis of confidence in the KMT's mountain redoubts, which caused a major internal reorganization.

## The KMT in Thailand

Although by 1970 KMT armies controlled about 90 percent of Burma's opium trade, they had not maintained any major bases inside the Shan states since 1961. After 5,000 Burmese army troops and 20,000 Communist Chinese troops launched a "surprise assault" on KMT headquarters at Mong Pa Liao, Kengtung, in January 1961, most of the 10,000 KMT defenders fled across the Mekong into northwestern Laos and took refuge at Nam Tha City. Five tons of U.S. ammunition were discovered at Mong Pa Liao, and on February 16 the Burmese air force shot down an American-made Liberator bomber making supply drops to KMT holdouts inside Burma.[229] Apparently embarrassed by these incidents, the U.S. State Department offered to assist in the repatriation of KMT troops to Taiwan, and on March 14 the evacuation began. About 4,200 KMT regulars were flown from Nam Tha City to Ban Houei Sai, ferried across the Mekong, and trucked to Chiangrai, where they boarded flights for Taiwan. On April 12 the airlift came to an end, and Taiwan disclaimed any responsibility for the "few" who remained.[230]

Actually, some 2,000 to 3,000 KMT regulars had been left behind in Laos, and they were hired by the CIA to strengthen the rightist position in the area. According to William Young, these troops were placed under the nominal command of General Phoumi Nosavan and became the Bataillon Speciale 111. They remained at Nam Tha until the rightist garrison began to collapse in mid-1962, and then they moved across the Mekong River into Thailand. With the full knowledge and consent of the Thai government, the KMT established two new bases on mountains just a few miles from the Burmese border and resumed their involvement in the opium trade.[231]

Instead of hampering their commercial activities, the move to Thailand actually increased the KMT's overall importance in the Golden Triangle's opium trade. Not only did the KMT maintain their hold on Burma's opium, but they increased their share of the traffic in northern Thailand. In 1959 the Thai government had outlawed the growing and smoking of opium, and many Thai hill traders, fearful of police action, were in the process of quitting the opium trade. Most small towns and villages in the foothills of northern Thailand that had prospered as opium trading centers for the previous twelve years experienced a recession as their local opium merchants were forced out of business. While the lack of reliable data and official obfuscation make it difficult to describe this transition for the whole of northern Thailand, an Australian anthropologist has provided a portrait of the rise and fall of the Thai opium trading village Ban Wat.[232]

Situated about three miles from the base of Thailand's western mountain range, with easy access to two mountain trails leading upward into the opium-growing villages, Ban Wat was an ideal base of operations for mountain traders. Moreover, the village was only fifteen miles from Chiangmai, Thailand's northernmost rail terminus, so it was also accessible to merchants and brokers coming up from Bangkok.

Ban Wat's merchants first became involved in the opium trade in the 1920s, when four or five Hmong villages were built in the nearby mountain districts. However, the Hmong population was quite small, and their poppy cultivation was still secondary to subsistence rice production. Most of Ban Wat's traders were buying such small quantities of opium from the Hmong that they sold it directly to individual addicts in the nearby valley towns. No big brokers came to Ban Wat from Bangkok or Chiangmai, though one Ban Wat trader occasionally smuggled a bit of opium down to Bangkok on the train.[233]

After the Thai government decided to encourage poppy cultivation in 1947, however, the opium trade began to boom, and the village experienced unprecedented prosperity, becoming one of the largest opium markets in northern Thailand. The edict drew many Hmong farmers into the nearby mountains, giving Ban Wat traders access to a large supply. Much of Ban Wat's active male population became involved in the opium trade as porters, mule skinners, or independent merchants. During the harvesting and planting season the Hmong needed rice to feed themselves. The Ban Wat traders purchased rice in the Chiangmai market and sold it to the Hmong on credit. When the opium harvest began, the traders returned to the Hmong villages to collect their debts and to trade silver, salt, rice, and manufactured goods for Hmong opium.

While the abolition of legalized opium trading in 1959 did not hinder the continued expansion of Thailand's production, it was a disaster for Ban Wat. At the height of the opium boom there were twenty major opium traders operating out of Ban Wat; by 1968 there was only one. Two local merchants went broke when the police confiscated their opium, and another was ruined when his Hmong customers moved to another province without paying their debts. These examples served to chasten Ban Wat's merchant community, and many traders quit the opium trade.[234]

The vacuum was filled not by other Thai traders but by the KMT armies and an auxiliary of Yunnanese mountain traders. When the KMT and its civilian adherents were forced out of Burma in 1961, their commercial apparatus moved its headquarters into northern Thailand.[235] In 1965 a census of the most important Yunnanese villages in northern Thailand showed a total population of 6,600.[236] As the Thai traders were forced out of business after 1959, the KMT and its civilian auxiliaries were uniquely qualified to take over the opium trade. With their centralized military structure, the KMT could keep track of migrating Hmong clans and make sure that they paid their debts. With their military power, the KMT could also protect the enormous capital tied up in the merchant caravans from bandits and keep the exactions of the Thai police to a minimum.

The Yunnanese traders were the vanguard of the KMT's commercial conquest, infiltrating the mountain villages and imposing a form of debt slavery on hill tribe opium farmers. They opened permanent stores in most of the large opium-producing villages and sold such tantalizing items as flashlights, canned goods, silver ornaments, cloth, salt, and shoes. A 1962 report by the Thai Ministry of the Interior described the impact of this "commercial revolution":

> The increasing demand for merchandise deriving from outside has given a corresponding impetus to the raising of cash crops. There can be no doubt that the cultivation of poppy and the production of raw opium is by far the most profitable economic activity known to the hill peoples at present. . . . The shopkeepers and travelling merchants in the hills compete with each other to get hold of the product, readily granting credit for later sales of opium.[237]

Toward the end of the harvest season, when the Yunnanese merchants finished buying up most of the opium in their area, armed KMT caravans went from village to village collecting it. American missionaries who had seen the KMT on the march described it as a disconcerting spectacle. As soon as the caravan's approach was signaled, all the women and children fled into the forest, leaving the men to protect the village. Once the opium was loaded onto the KMT's mules, the caravan rode on and the people came back out of the forest. The Ministry of the Interior's 1962 report described the KMT-Yunnanese logistics in some detail:

> The key men of the opium traffic in the hills of Northern Thailand are the traders who come from outside the tribal societies. . . . On the basis of our observations in numerous villages of the 4 tribes we studied we have proof that the overwhelming majority of them are Haw [Yunnanese]. . . .
>
> Usually the Haw traders know each other personally, even if living in hill villages 200 km. [125 miles] and more apart. Most we encountered regard the village of Ban Yang, near Amphur

Fang, as their central place [near KMT Third Army headquar-
ters]. Quite a few of them will return to this place, after the
closing of the trading season. . . .

There seems to be a fair understanding among all the Haw in
the hills and a remarkable coherence or even silent organization.

The Haw traders keep close contacts with the armed bands
[KMT] that dwell in fortified camps along the Burmese frontier.
It is reported that they [the KMT] give armed convoy to opium
caravans along the jungle trails to the next reloading places.[238]

The fortified camps mentioned in the Ministry of the Interior's report
were the KMT Fifth Army headquarters on Mae Salong mountain, about
thirty miles northwest of Chiangrai, and the KMT Third Army
headquarters at Tam Ngop, a rugged mountain redoubt fifty miles west
of Chiangrai. Although KMT forces had always maintained a unified
command structure in Burma, they established two separate headquarters after moving to Thailand; this was symptomatic of deep internal
divisions. For reasons never fully explained, Taiwan ordered its senior
commander home in 1961 and subsequently cut back financial support
for the remaining troops. Once external discipline was removed,
personal rivalries between the generals broke the KMT into three
separate commands: General Tuan Shi-wen formed the Fifth Army with
1,800 men; General Ly Wen-huan became commander of the Third Army,
a lesser force of 1,400 men; and General Ma Ching-kuo and the 400
intelligence operatives under his command broke away to form the First
Independent Unit.[239] Since the First Independent Unit remained under
the overall supervision of President Chiang Kai-shek's son, Chiang
Ching-kuo, in Taiwan, financial support for its intelligence operations
inside China and Burma was continued.[240] As a result, its commander
General Ma could afford to remain above the bitter rivalry between
General Tuan and General Ly and came to act as mediator between the
two.[241]

After Taiwan cut off their money, Generals Tuan and Ly were forced
to rely exclusively on the opium traffic to finance their military
operations. "Necessity knows no law," General Tuan told a British
journalist in 1967. "That is why we deal with opium. We have to continue
to fight the evil of Communism, and to fight you must have an army, and
an army must have guns, and to buy guns you must have money. In these
mountains the only money is opium."[242] To minimize the possibility of
violence between their troops, the two generals apparently agreed to a
division of the opium country and used the Salween River to demarcate
their respective spheres of influence inside the Shan states; General
Tuan sent his caravans into Kengtung and the southern Wa states east of

the Salween, while General Ly confined his caravans to the west bank of the river.[243]

While the SNA's local commanders were little more than petty smugglers, Tuan and Ly had become the overlords of one of Southeast Asia's major agro-businesses. By the early 1970s their purchasing network covered most of the Shan states' 60,000 square miles, and their caravans hauled approximately 90 percent of Burma's opium exports from the Shan highlands to entrepôts in northern Thailand. To manage this vast enterprise, the KMT generals developed a private communications network inside the Shan states and imposed a semblance of order on the once chaotic hill trade. On the western bank of the Salween, Ly organized a string of seven radio posts that stretched for almost 250 miles from Third Army headquarters at Tam Ngop in northern Thailand to Lashio in the northern Shan states.[244] On the eastern bank, Tuan maintained a network of eleven radio posts supplemented by the First Independent Unit's four forward listening posts along the Burma-China border.[245] Each radio post was guarded by eighty to one hundred KMT soldiers who doubled as opium brokers and purchasing agents; as the planting season began, they canvassed the surrounding countryside, paying advances to village headmen, negotiating with Shan rebels, and buying options from local opium traders. By the time the KMT caravans began rolling north from Tam Ngop and Mae Salong in October or November, each of the radio posts had transmitted an advance report on the size and value of the harvest in its area to its respective KMT headquarters. Thus, KMT commanders were in a position to evaluate the size of the upcoming harvest in each district and plan a rough itinerary for the caravans.[246]

The enormous size of the KMT caravans made this advance planning a necessity. While most Shan rebel caravans rarely had more than fifty pack animals, the smallest KMT caravan had a hundred mules, and some had as many as six hundred.[247] The commander of a Shan rebel army active in the area west of Lashio reported that most KMT Third Army caravans that passed through this averaged about four hundred mules.[248] Since an ordinary pack animal could carry about 50 kilos of raw opium on one of these long trips, a single caravan of this size could bring back as much as 20 tons of raw opium. Despite the large number of Shan rebels and government militia patrolling the mountains, KMT caravans could afford to travel with a minimum of armed guards (usually about three hundred troops, or only one man for every one or two mules) because they carried portable field radios and could signal their scattered outposts for help if attacked. Scouts were sent out well ahead of the column to look for possible trouble. Since most of the mule drivers and guards were vigorous young tribesmen recruited from northern Thailand, KMT caravans were able to move fast enough to avoid ambush. Moreover, the KMT carried an impressive arsenal of 60 mm mortars, .50 caliber machine guns, 75 mm recoilless rifles, and semiautomatic carbines, which usually provided ample deterrence for both poorly armed Shan rebels and crack Burmese army units.

The caravans began moving south in October or November and stopped at large hill tribe villages, market towns, and KMT outposts to pick up waiting shipments of opium. Although there were KMT caravans plodding across the Shan highlands throughout most of the year, most caravans seemed to be going north from October through March (which included the harvest season) and riding south from March through August. General Ly's Third Army caravans usually went as far north as Lashio district, about 250 miles from Tam Ngop, where they picked up opium brought down from Kachin state and northern Shan districts by itinerant merchants.[249] General Tuan's Fifth Army caravans went all the way to Ving Ngun, about 170 miles north of Mae Salong, until 1969, when the Burmese Communist party began operating in the southern Wa states. After that KMT caravans began relying on itinerant merchants to bring Kokang and Wa states opium out of these Communist-controlled areas.[250]

When the KMT caravans began to head back to Thailand, they were often joined by smaller Shan rebel or merchant caravans, who traveled with them for protection. Predatory bands of Shan rebels, government militia (KKY), and Burmese army troops prowled the hills in search of vulnerable caravans. According to one Shan rebel leader, a caravan had to have an absolute minimum of 50 armed men to survive, but with 200 armed men it was completely safe unless something unusual happened. Since the smaller groups could not afford a sufficient quantity of automatic weapons to protect themselves adequately (in mid-1971 an M16 cost $250 to $300 in Chiangmai), many preferred to ride with the KMT even though they had to pay a protection fee of $9 per kilo of opium (a high fee considering that a kilo of opium retailed for $60 in Chiangmai in 1967).[251]

As a service to the Thai government, the KMT Third and Fifth armies acted as a border patrol force along the rugged northern frontier and used their authority to collect a "duty" of $4.50 on every kilo of opium entering Thailand.[252] In 1966–1967 the CIA reported that KMT forces patrolled a seventy-five-mile stretch of borderland in Chiangmai and Chiangrai provinces,[253] but in mid-1971 Shan rebel leaders claimed that KMT revenue collectors covered the entire northern border all the way from Mae Sai to Mae Hong Son. Although the rugged mountain terrain and maze of narrow horse trails would frustrate the best ordinary customs service, very few Shan caravans could enter Thailand without paying tax to the KMT. With their comprehensive radio and intelligence network, the KMT spotted most caravans soon after they began moving south and usually had a patrol waiting when one crossed into Thailand.[254]

Not having to rely on opium for funds as the Third and Fifth armies had to do, the First Independent Unit gave top priority to its military mission of cross-border espionage and regarded opium smuggling as a complementary but secondary activity. Most important from Taiwan's perspective, the First Independent Unit helped perpetuate the myth of Generalissimo Chiang Kai-shek's imminent "return to the mainland" by launching repeated sabotage raids into southern China.[255]

General Tuan's Fifth Army supported General Ma's intelligence operations, and on at least one occasion his troops participated in a full-scale raid into southern China. In exchange for such assistance, Tuan's troops were allowed to use the First Independent Unit's listening posts as opium trading centers.[256] While Tuan was taciturn about his involvement in the opium trade, he was proud of his vanguard position in the anti-Communist crusade. Describing himself as the "watchdog at the northern gate," General Tuan liked to regale his visitors with stories about his exploits battling Mao Tse-tung during the 1930s, fighting the Japanese during World War II, and raiding Yunnan province in more recent years. Although by the early 1970s the general spent most of his time in Chiangmai enjoying the personal fortune he had amassed from the opium business, he still liked to present himself as a guerrilla fighter and launched an occasional raid into China to maintain this image.[257]

Since General Ma was the only one of the three generals who enjoyed Taiwan's full support, he emerged as the senior KMT commander in the Golden Triangle. Although a number of serious disputes had poisoned relations between Tuan and Ly, Ma had remained on good terms with both. At the urging of high command on Taiwan, Ma began acting as a mediator shortly after the KMT moved to Thailand, but with little success. Taiwan was hoping to reestablish a unified command under Ma, but Tuan and Ly saw little to be gained from giving up their profitable autonomy.[258] Although the battle at Ban Khwan would heal this rift, for the moment the situation remained static.

## The Challenge of Khun Sa

General Ma had his chance as mediator in early 1967 when Generals Tuan and Ly began receiving disturbing information about Khun Sa's activities in the Shan states. The KMT's radio network was sending back reports that the Shan warlord's brokers were buying up unprecedented quantities of opium in the northern Shan and Wa states. In February,

Khun Sa had delivered a de facto declaration of war when he demanded that KMT caravans trading in the Wa states pay him the same transit tax that his caravans had to pay the KMT whenever they crossed into Thailand or Laos.[259] When Khun Sa's caravan of 300 mules assembled in June it was carrying 16 tons of raw opium worth $500,000 wholesale in Chiangmai.[260] With his share of the profits, Khun Sa could purchase at least 1,000 new carbines and expand his army from 2,000 to 3,000 men—a force almost equal in size to the combined 3,200 troops of the KMT Third and Fifth armies. If Khun Sa's caravan reached Laos, the fifteen-year dominance of the KMT would be in jeopardy. The point was not lost on the KMT, and through General Ma's mediation the two feuding generals agreed to resolve their differences and form a combined army to destroy Khun Sa.[261]

In June the main body of Khun Sa's convoy left Ving Ngun and set out on a 200-mile trek toward Ban Khwan, a small Laotian lumber town on the Mekong River that General Ouane had designated the delivery point when he placed an advance order for this large shipment with Khun Sa's broker, a Chinese merchant from Mae Sai, Thailand. The caravan was to deliver the opium to the general's refinery at Ban Khwan. As the heavily loaded mules plodded south through the monsoon downpours, the convoy was joined by smaller caravans from market towns such as Tang Yang, so that by the time it reached Kengtung its single-file column of 500 men and 300 mules stretched along the ridgelines for more than a mile.[262]

From the moment the caravan left Ving Ngun, it was kept under surveillance by the KMT's intelligence network, and the radio receivers at Mae Salong hummed with frequent reports from the mountains overlooking the convoy's line of march. After merging their crack units into a thousand-man expeditionary corps, Generals Tuan and Ly sent their forces into the Shan states with orders to intercept the convoy and destroy it.[263] Several days later the KMT expeditionary force ambushed Khun Sa's main column east of Kengtung near the Mekong River, but his rearguard counterattacked and the opium caravan escaped.[264] After crossing the Mekong into Laos on July 14 and 15, Khun Sa's troops hiked down the old caravan trail from Muong Mounge and reached Ban Khwan two days later.[265]

Shortly after they arrived, the Shan troops warned the Laotian villagers that the KMT were not far behind and that there would probably be fighting. As soon as he heard this news, the principal of Ban Khwan's elementary school raced downriver to Ton Peung, where a company of Royal Laotian Army troops had its field headquarters. The company commander radioed news of the upcoming battle to Ban Houei Sai and urged the principal to evacuate his village. During the next ten days, while Ban Khwan's twenty families moved all their worldly possessions across the Mekong into Thailand, Khun Sa's troops prepared for a confrontation.[266]

Ban Khwan was hardly a likely battlefield: the village consisted of small clearings hacked out of a dense forest, fragile stilted houses, and narrow winding lanes, which were then mired in knee-deep, monsoon-season mud. A lumber mill belonging to General Ouane sat in the only large clearing in the village, and it was here that the Shans decided to make their stand. In many ways it was an ideal defensive position: the mill was built on a long sand embankment extending a hundred feet into the Mekong and was separated from the surrounding forest by a lumberyard, which had become a moatlike sea of mud. The Shans parked their mules along the embankment, scoured the nearby towns for boats, and used cut logs lying in the lumberyard to form a great semicircular barricade in front of the mill.[267]

The KMT expeditionary force finally reached Ban Khwan on July 26 and fought a brief skirmish with the Shans in a small hamlet just outside the village. The same day the Laotian army's provincial commander flew up from Ban Houei Sai in an air force helicopter to deliver a personal message from General Ouane: he ordered them all to get out of Laos. The KMT scornfully demanded $250,000 to do so, and Khun Sa radioed his men from Burma, ordering them to stay put. After several hundred reinforcements arrived from Mae Salong, the KMT troops attacked the Shan barricades on July 29.[268] Since both sides were armed with an impressive array of .50 caliber machine guns, 60 mm mortars, and 57 mm recoilless rifles, the firefight was intense, and the noise from it could be heard for miles. However, at noon on July 30 the staccato chatter of automatic weapons was suddenly interrupted by the droning roar of six T-28 propeller fighters flying low up the Mekong River and then the thunder of the 500-pound bombs that came crashing down indiscriminately on Shans and KMT alike.

General Ouane, apparently disconcerted by the unforeseen outcome of his dealings with Khun Sa, had decided to play the part of a commander in chief defending his nation's territorial integrity. With Prime Minister Souvanna Phouma's consent, he had dispatched a squadron of T-28 fighters from Luang Prabang and air-lifted the crack Second Paratroop Battalion (Captain Kong Le's old unit) up to Ban Houei Sai. Ouane took personal command of the operation and displayed all of the tactical brilliance one would expect from a general who had just received his nation's highest state decoration, the Grand Cross of the Million Elephants and the White Parasol.[269]

Once the Second Paratroop Battalion had gone upriver to Ban Khwan and taken up a blocking position just south of the battlefield, the T-28s

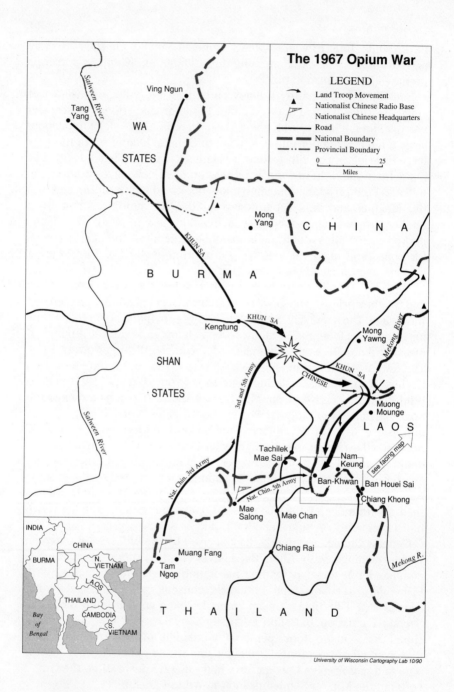

The 1967 Opium War

LEGEND

| | |
|---|---|
| ➤ | Land Troop Movement |
| ▲ | Nationalist Chinese Radio Base |
| ⚑ | Nationalist Chinese Headquarters |
| —— | Road |
| ━ ━ | National Boundary |
| —·—· | Provincial Boundary |

0                    25
Miles

Salween River

Ving Ngun

Tang
Yang

WA

STATES

KHUN SA

Mong
Yang

C  H  I  N  A

B  U  R  M  A

Kengtung          KHUN  SA

Mong
Yawng

Mekong River

SHAN

3rd and 5th Army

KHUN  SA

CHINESE

STATES

Muong
Mounge

Salween River

L  A  O  S

Nat. Chin. 3rd Army

Tachilek
Mae Sai

Nam
Keung

see facing map

Ban-Khwan          Ban Houei Sai

Nat. Chin. 5th Army

Chiang Khong

Mae
Salong          Mae Chan

Muang Fang          Chiang Rai

Tam
Ngop          Mekong R.

INDIA

CHINA

BURMA          N.
VIETNAM

LAOS

THAILAND

Bay
of
Bengal          CAMBODIA

S.
VIETNAM

T  H  A  I  L  A  N  D

University of Wisconsin Cartography Lab 10/90

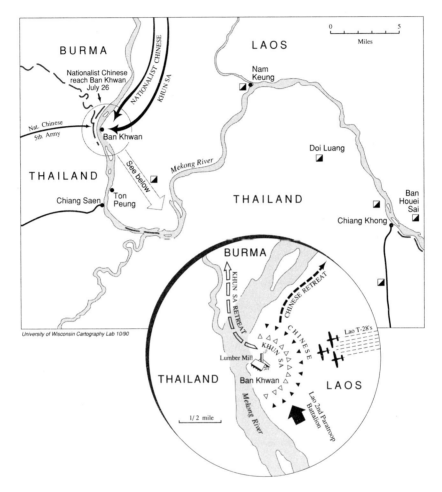

**Ban Khwan July 30: Lao Army Under General Rattikone Attacks**

LEGEND

Land troop movements — Road

Aircraft movements — National boundary

△ Khun Sa's troops ▲ Chinese troops

▨ Aircraft landing strip

began two days of bombing and strafing at the rate of four or five squadron sorties daily. To ensure against a possible retaliatory attack on Ban Houei Sai, General Ouane ordered two marine launches to patrol the upper reaches of the Mekong near Ban Khwan. Finally, two regular Laotian infantry battalions began moving down the old caravan trail from Muong Mounge to cut off the only remaining escape route.[270]

Under the pressure of the repeated bombing attacks, the four hundred surviving Shans piled into the boats tied up along the embankment and retreated across the Mekong into Burma, leaving behind eighty-two dead, fifteen mules, and most of the opium.[271] Lacking boats and unwilling to abandon their heavy equipment, the KMT troops fled north along the Mekong but got only six miles before their retreat was cut off by the two Laotian infantry battalions moving south from Muong Mounge. When the Shans and KMT had abandoned Ban Khwan, the Second Paratroop Battalion swept the battlefield, gathered up the opium, and sent it downriver to Ban Houei Sai. Reinforcements were flown up from Vientiane, and superior numbers of Laotian army troops surrounded the KMT.[272] Following two weeks of tense negotiations, the KMT finally agreed to pay General Ouane an indemnity of $7,500 for the right to return to Thailand.[273] According to Thai police reports, some 700 KMT troops crossed the Mekong into Thailand on August 19, leaving behind seventy dead, twenty-four machine guns, and a number of dead mules. Although the Thai police made a pro forma attempt at disarming the KMT, the troops clambered aboard eighteen chartered buses and drove off to Mae Salong with three hundred carbines, seventy machine guns, and two recoilless rifles.[274]

General Ouane was clearly the winner of this battle. His troops had captured most of the 16 tons of raw opium and suffered only a handful of casualties. Admittedly, his lumber mill was damaged and his opium refinery had been burned to the ground, but this loss was insignificant, since Ouane reportedly operated another five refineries between Ban Khwan and Ban Houei Sai.[275] His profits from the confiscated opium were substantial and, displaying the generosity for which he was famous, he shared the spoils with the men of the Second Paratroop Battalion. Each man reportedly received enough money to build a simple house on the outskirts of Vientiane.[276] The village of Ban Khwan itself emerged from the conflagration relatively unscathed; when the people started moving back across the Mekong River three days after the battle, they found six burned-out houses but otherwise suffered no appreciable loss.[277]

At the time it was fought, the 1967 Opium War struck even the most sober observers as a curious historical anachronism that conjured up romantic memories of China's warlords in the 1920s and bandit desperadoes of bygone eras. However, when considered in light of events in the Golden Triangle from 1968 to 1972—particularly the development of large-scale production of no. 4 heroin—the 1967 Opium War appears to have been a significant turning point in the growth of Southeast Asia's drug traffic. Each group's share of Burma's opium exports and its subsequent role in the growth of the Golden Triangle's heroin industry were largely determined by the battle and its aftermath. KMT caravans still carried the overwhelming percentage of Burma's opium exports, and Shan caravans continued to pay the KMT duty when they entered Thailand. Khun Sa, of course, was the loser; he left $500,000 worth of raw opium, thousands of dollars in arms and mules, and much of his prestige lying in the mud at Ban Khwan. Moreover, Khun Sa represented the first substantial challenge to KMT control over the Shan states opium trade—and that challenge was decisively defeated. After the destruction of Khun Sa's convoy, Shan military leaders, at least for the time being, continued to play an unimportant role in their own opium trade; Shan caravans usually had less than a hundred mules, and their opium refineries were processing only a small percentage of the opium grown in the Shan states. However, General Ouane's troops won the right to tax Burmese opium entering Laos, a prerogative formerly enjoyed by the KMT, and the Ban Houei Sai region later emerged as the major processing center for Burmese opium.

## Guardian at the Northern Gate

Although the 1967 Opium War strengthened the KMT's position inside the Shan states, it complicated the KMT's amicable relations with its host, the Thai government. Since the mid-1950s, when the Thai police commander, General Phao, became notorious as one of the major opium traffickers in Southeast Asia, the Thai government had been sensitive about concealing its involvement in the opium trade. When the KMT moved to Thailand in 1962, the government labeled them "civilian refugees" and claimed that their organized military units had been broken up.[278] The KMT reinforced this face-saving fiction by isolating themselves in their mountain redoubts and wearing civilian clothes whenever they went into nearby towns. On the whole, the Thai government was quite successful in convincing the world that the KMT Third and Fifth armies no longer existed. Only five months before the battle, for example, a full-fledged U.N. investigating team spent two months examining the drug problem in Thailand without discovering any evidence of KMT activity.[279] When the 1967 Opium War shattered this carefully constructed fiction, the Thai government claimed that it was being "invaded" by the KMT and dispatched several thousand troops to Chiangmai to defend the northern frontier.[280]

To ensure that it would not be similarly embarrassed in the future, the Thai government placed the KMT's fortified camps under the supervision of the Royal Army, and KMT generals became accountable to the high command in Bangkok for every move in and out of their headquarters. Aside from these limited gestures, however, the Thai government made no effort to weaken the KMT. In fact, the Thai military moved in the opposite direction by granting the Third and Fifth armies official status as legitimate paramilitary forces. Although the KMT had been responsible for security in the northern frontier areas for a number of years without receiving official recognition, the outbreak of the "Red Meo" revolt in Nan and Chiangrai provinces in the late 1960s brought about a gradual reversal of this nonrecognition policy.

The "Red Meo" revolt began in May 1967 when Thai officials visited the same Hmong village in Chiangrai province on three separate occasions to collect payoffs for letting the Hmong farmers clear their opium fields. The villagers paid off the first two visitors, but when the provincial police showed up to collect their rake-off the Hmong attacked them. The next day sixty police returned to the village and burned it to the ground. Although there was no further violence, this incident apparently convinced counterinsurgency strategists in Bangkok that the Hmong in Chiangrai and adjoining Nan province were about to revolt.[281] In October the Thai army and police initiated a series of heavy-handed "Communist suppression operations" that provoked a major uprising. To reduce its mounting casualties, the army began napalming selected villages and herding their inhabitants into guarded relocation centers in early 1968. The revolt spread rapidly. As the army was forced to withdraw into a series of fortified positions in June, the air force was unleashed over the insurgent areas, which had been declared free fire zones. By 1970 guerrillas were beginning to sortie out of their mountain "liberated zones," attacking lowland villages and ambushing cars along the highways.[282]

It was obvious to many Thai and American counterinsurgency planners that troops had to go in on the ground to clean up guerrilla mountain sanctuaries before the insurgency spread into the lowlands. However, as their earlier performances had shown, the Thai army was ill-suited for mountain warfare.[283] The Thai military, with American financial support, turned to the KMT for help. In the past, General Tuan had claimed credit for keeping Chiangrai province free from "communist terrorists."[284] The KMT had all the skills for mountain warfare that the Thai army lacked: they understood small unit tactics, had twenty years' experience at recruiting hill tribe paramilitary forces, and could converse with the hill tribes in their own languages or Yunnanese, which many tribesmen spoke fluently.[285] But most important of all, the KMT knew how to pit tribe against tribe. While the Thai military had tried to get Hmong to fight with little success, General Tuan recruited Akha, Lisu, and Lahu from western Chiangrai province and sent them to fight Hmong in eastern Chiangrai. In December 1969 Tuan ordered 500 of these polyglot Fifth Army troops into the mountains just north of Chiang Khong, near the Mekong, to attack the "Red Meo," and General Ly sent 900 of his Third Army troops into the mountains to the east of Chiang Kham.[286] By mid-1971 two Thai air force UH-1H helicopters were shuttling back and forth between the KMT camps and Thai army bases in eastern Chiangrai. A special photo reconnaissance lab was working round the clock, and a ranking Thai general had been placed in command. When asked what he was doing in Chiang Khong, General Krirksin replied, "I cannot tell you, these are secret operations.[287] However, the senior KMT officer at Chiang Khong, Colonel Chen Mo-sup, insisted that his forces had the "Red Meo" on the run and claimed that his troops had killed more than 150 of them.[288]

Even though the KMT had been integrated into the Thai counterinsurgency establishment, the government made no appreciable effort to reduce their involvement in the opium trade. In mid-1971 the CIA reported that Mae Salong, KMT Fifth Army headquarters, was the home of one of the "most important" heroin laboratories in the Golden Triangle, and in April 1972 NBC News reported that a laboratory was operating at Tam Ngop, the KMT Third Army headquarters.[289] In addition, Shan rebel leaders said that KMT caravans were still operating at full strength, the opium duty was being collected, and no Shan army was even close to challenging the KMT's hegemony.

## The Shan Rebellion

For Khun Sa the 1967 Opium War seemed to mark the beginning of the end. For the Shan movement as a whole, his defeat appeared to represent the last significant attempt by any rebel leader to establish himself as something more than just another petty warlord. After his troops retreated across the Mekong from Ban Khwan, Khun Sa remained in the mountains near the Thai border, reportedly waiting for another crack at the KMT.[290] However, for reasons never satisfactorily explained, the second battle never took place, and he returned to the northern Shan states in late 1967. Since Khun Sa had lost a considerable amount of money, arms, and prestige at Ban Khwan, his troops began to drift away, and by late 1968 he had considerably less than a thousand men under arms.[291] Apparently convinced that another stint as a guerrilla would revive his fortunes, Khun Sa began making contact with a number of Shan rebel leaders. When Burmese military intelligence learned that he was engaged in serious negotiations with the rebels, they had him arrested and sent off to a Rangoon jail for an indefinite period of confinement.[292] Many of his officers and men were arrested as well, but Shan rebel leaders claimed that several hundred more were still actively battling government forces in the northern Shan States.[293]

But there is a lesson to his story. The rise and apparent fall of Khun Sa and the Shan National Army show how difficult it was going to be for any Shan military leader to restore order in the strife-torn Shan states. Rather than producing an independent, unified Shan land, the Shan rebellion seemed to have unleashed political dynamics that populated the countryside with petty warlords and impoverished the people. When the rebellion began in 1958, there were only three or four rebel groups active in the entire Shan states. In mid-1971 one Shan rebel leader estimated that there were more than a hundred different armed bands in the highlands. But he cautioned that this was probably a conservative estimate and added that "it would take a computer to keep track of them all."[294] Most of these armed groups were unstable; they were constantly switching from rebel to militia (KKY) status and back again, splitting to form new armies, or entering into ineffectual alliances. Moreover, the situation became more chaotic every year as succeeding opium harvests pumped more and more weapons into the Shan states. In the early 1960s the SNA was content with semiautomatic U.S. M1 or M2 carbines, but seven years later every armed band had to have its quotient of fully automatic M16s to survive. Although the SNA had never imposed effective discipline on its local commanders, it achieved a level of unity that was not equaled by succeeding coalitions. Following its demise in 1965–1966, the military situation in the Shan States had become much more chaotic. In 1968 another faction made an attempt to draw the movement together by establishing the Shan Unity Preparatory Committee, which issued grandiose communiqués warning about communism or offering a cease-fire and then collapsed after a few acrimonious meetings in Chiangmai.[295]

Although some Shan rebel leaders spoke loftily about millions of peasants flocking to their side, a few of the franker ones admitted that people had become progressively alienated from the independence movement. Repeated taxation at gunpoint by roving Shan warlords discouraged most forms of legitimate economic activity and reduced the peasants to a state of poverty. Salt prices had become prohibitive in the hills, and goiter was a serious problem. In some of the more distant areas essential medicines like quinine had not been available for years. Vaccination programs and qualified medical treatment had all but disappeared.

Ironically, the political chaos, which damaged most other forms of agriculture and commerce, promoted a steady expansion of opium production in the Shan states. Since opium bought more guns and ammunition in Thailand than any other local product, Shan rebels and the local militia (KKY) imposed a heavy opium tax on mountain villages under their control. While mountain farmers sold all the opium they could produce to merchants who regularly visited their villages, the insurgency made it dangerous to venture into the market towns to sell other agricultural commodities. Moreover, the Burmese government controlled very few of the poppy-growing areas and was therefore in no position to discourage opium production. Other nations could be pressured into abolishing poppy cultivation, but Burma could honestly claim that it was powerless to deal with the problem. By 1972 it seemed clear that the continuing political instability in the Shan states would ensure that the Golden Triangle would be growing vast quantities of opium long after the poppy had disappeared from Turkey or Afghanistan.

The Shan states' tradition of division into thirty-four principalities ruled by autocratic *sawbwas* was only partly responsible for the lack of unity among rebel leaders in the early 1970s. Laos, for example, shared a similar tradition of petty principalities, but the Pathet Lao had managed to form a unified national liberation movement.

Indeed, there were more important reasons for the chaotic political conditions inside the Shan states. The Shan rebellion and its accompanying chaos could not have survived had not the CIA, the KMT, and the Thai government intervened. None of these groups was particularly interested in the establishment of an independent Shan nation. However, each of them had specific political or military interests that were served by providing the Shans with limited support and keeping the country in chaos. Just as the emergence of a powerful Shan leader like Khun Sa was not in the KMT's interests, so the chaotic conditions promoted by dozens of smaller rebel groups were vital to their survival. The KMT Third and Fifth armies were able to send their large, lightly guarded caravans deep into the Shan States only because the Burmese army was tied down fighting the insurgents. The KMT recognized the importance of this distraction and financed a number of small Shan rebel groups. However, the KMT tried to keep the Shan armies small by explicitly refusing to allow any Shan opium caravan larger than one hundred mules to enter Thailand, a policy adopted after the 1967 Opium War.[296] Perhaps the most notable victim of this new policy was the Shan State Army (SSA). Founded by students from Mandalay and Rangoon universities, it began operating in the mountains west of Lashio in 1958,[297] but did not start smuggling opium until five years later. After shipping 160 kilos of raw opium to Thailand in 1964, the Shan State Army increased its shipments year by year, reaching a peak of 1,600 kilos in 1967. But with the exception of 80 kilos it managed to slip by the KMT in 1969, this was its last shipment of opium to Thailand. Relations between the KMT and SSA had never been good, but the KMT embargo on SSA opium smuggling brought them to a new low. When the KMT Third Army tried to establish a radio post in SSA territory in late 1969, the two groups engaged in a series of indecisive running battles for more than three months.[298]

The CIA played an equally cynical role inside the Shan states. Although it too had no real interest in an independent Shan land, the CIA supported individual rebel armies to accomplish its intelligence-gathering missions inside China. Without the CIA's tolerance of its opium-arms traffic, the Shan National Army could never have occupied so much of Kentung state. However, the CIA refused to grant the SNA enough direct military aid to drive the Burmese out of the state and reestablish public order. During the 1950s the CIA had tried to turn the eastern Shan states into an independent strategic bastion for operations along China's southern frontier by using KMT troops to drive the Burmese army out of the area. But after the KMT were forced out of Burma in 1961, the CIA apparently decided to adopt a lower profile for its clandestine operations. While direct military support for the SNA might have produced new diplomatic embarrassments, an informal alliance and the resulting breakdown of public order in Kengtung were compatible with CIA interests. After the SNA forced the Burmese army into the cities and towns, the CIA's forward radio posts floated securely in this sea of chaos while its cross-border espionage teams passed through Burma virtually undetected.[299]

In the final analysis, the Thai government probably bore the major responsibility for the chaos. Most Thai leaders had a traditional distrust for the Burmese, who had invaded Thailand in past centuries. No Thai student graduated from elementary school without reading at least one detailed description of the atrocities committed by Burmese troops when they burned the royal Thai capital at Ayuddhya in 1769. Convinced that Burma would always pose a potential threat to its security, the Thai government granted asylum to insurgents operating along the Burma-Thailand border and supplied some of the groups with enough arms and equipment to keep operating. This low-level insurgency kept the Burmese army tied down defending its own cities, while the chaotic military situation in Burma's borderland regions gave Thailand a strategic buffer zone. Although Thai leaders had given Rangoon repeated assurances that they would not let Burmese exiles "abuse their privileges" as political refugees, they had opened a number of sanctuary areas for guerrillas near the Burmese border.[300] The Huei Krai camp north of Chiangrai had long been the major sanctuary area for Shan rebels from Kengtung state. The area surrounding KMT Third Army headquarters at Tam Ngop was the most important sanctuary for rebel armies from northeastern Burma: General Mo Heng's Shan United Revolutionary Army, Brigadier General Jimmy Yang's Kokang Revolutionary Force, General Zau Seng's Kachin Independence Army, General Jao Nhu's Shan State Army, and General Kyansone's Pa-O rebels were all crowded together on a few mountaintops under the watch of KMT General Ly. Entrances to these camps were tightly guarded by Thai police, and the guerrillas had to notify Thai authorities every time they entered or left. Even though activities at these camps were closely watched, Shan rebel leaders claimed that Thai authorities never made any attempt to interfere with their opium caravans. While foreign journalists were barred, Chiangmai opium buyers were free to come and go at will.[301]

In an effort to cope with a difficult situation, the Burmese government adopted a counterinsurgency program that legitimized some aspects of the opium trade and added to the general political instability. The Burmese army organized local militia forces (KKY), granted them the right to use government-controlled towns as opium trading centers and major highways as smuggling routes, and removed all restrictions on the refining of opium. It was their hope that the local militias' natural greed would motivate them to battle the rebels for control of the opium hills. The logic behind this policy was simple: if the local militia controlled most of the opium harvest, then the rebels would not have any money to buy arms in Thailand and would have to give up their struggle. Despite its seductive simplicity, the program had a mixed record of success. While it won a number of rebel armies to the government side, just as many local militia became rebels. On the whole, the program compounded the endemic warlordism that had become the bane of the Shan states without really reducing the level of rebel activity.

In addition, the Burmese government had sound economic reasons for tolerating the opium traffic. After seizing power from a civilian government in 1962, commander in chief of the army, General Ne Win, decreed a series of poorly executed economic reforms that crippled Burma's foreign trade and disrupted the consumer economy. After eight years of the "Burmese Way to Socialism," many of the consumer goods being sold in Burma's major cities—transistor radios, motorbikes, watches, pens, and toothpaste—were being smuggled across the border from Thailand on mule caravans. On the way down to Thailand, Shan smugglers carried opium, and on the way back they carried U.S. weapons and consumer goods. By the time a bottle of Coca-Cola reached Mandalay in northern Burma it could cost a dollar, and a

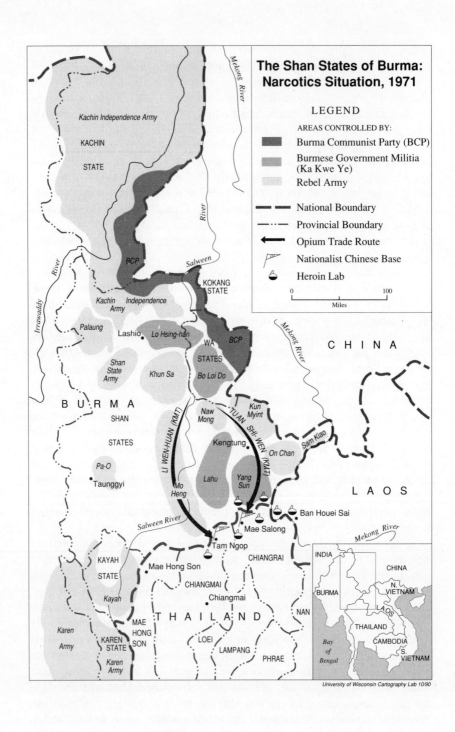

## The Shan States of Burma: Narcotics Situation, 1971

### LEGEND

AREAS CONTROLLED BY:

Burma Communist Party (BCP)

Burmese Government Militia (Ka Kwe Ye)

Rebel Army

National Boundary

Provincial Boundary

Opium Trade Route

Nationalist Chinese Base

Heroin Lab

0       100

Miles

Mekong River

Kachin Independence Army

KACHIN

STATE

River

Salween

Irrawaddy River

BCP

KOKANG STATE

Kachin Independence Army

Palaung

Lashio

Lo Hsing-han

WA STATES

BCP

CHINA

Shan State Army

Khun Sa

Bo Loi Do

B U R M A

SHAN

STATES

Pa-O

Taunggyi

Mekong River

LI WEN-HUAN (KMT)

Naw Mong

Kun Myint

TUAN SHI-WEN (KMT)

Kengtung

On Chan

Sam Kiao

Lahu

Yang Sun

L A O S

Mo Heng

Ban Houei Sai

Mekong River

Salween River

Mae Salong

Tam Ngop

CHIANGRAI

KAYAH STATE

Mae Hong Son

Kayah

CHIANGMAI

Chiangmai

NAN

T H A I L A N D

Karen Army

MAE HONG SON

KAREN STATE

LOEI

LAMPANG

PHRAE

Karen Army

INDIA

CHINA

BURMA

N. VIETNAM

LAOS

THAILAND

Bay of Bengal

CAMBODIA

S. VIETNAM

Mekong River

University of Wisconsin Cartography Lab 10/90

Japanese toothbrush went for \$3.50 in Rangoon.[302] Afraid of straining the patience of its already beleaguered consumers, the Burmese government made no real effort to close the black markets or stop the smuggling. Opium had become one of the nation's most valuable export commodities, and without it the consumer economy would have collapsed.

The opium traffic itself contributed to the chaotic conditions inside the Shan states by changing the military leaders from legitimate nationalist rebels into apolitical mercenaries. The case of Major On Chan was perhaps the most striking example. During the early 1960s he joined the Shan National Army and remained one of its more effective local commanders until the coalition split apart in 1965–1966. After deserting from the SNA, On Chan and about three hundred of his men were hired as mercenaries by the CIA and moved across the Mekong into northwestern Laos, where they fought in the Secret Army, disguised as local Lu militia. Two or three years later On Chan and his men deserted the Secret Army and moved back into the Shan states. With the ample supply of arms and ammunition he brought back to Burma, On Chan created an independent fief in eastern Kengtung, where he remained, trading in opium and fighting only to defend his autonomy.[303]

Since the Burmese army offered convenient opium trading facilities, rebel leaders frequently deserted the cause for the more comfortable life of a government militia commander. While Khun Sa was one example of this kind of Shan military leader, the case of Yang Sun was more typical. Yang Sun started his career in the opium trade as a government militia leader but switched to the rebel side in the mid-1960s and opened a base camp in the Huei Krai region of northern Thailand. Several years later he changed his allegiance once more and soon became the most powerful government militia leader in Kengtung. Although rebel leaders tried to win him back to their side, he was making so much money from the opium traffic as a militia leader that he refused their overtures.

Thanks to the good graces of the Burmese army, Yang Sun patrolled a strategic piece of geography between Kengtung and the Thai border. Caravans traveling along government-controlled roads from the opium-rich Kokang and Wa states to the north had to pass through this area on their way to opium refineries in the tri-border region to the south. Caravans belonging to both Lo Hsing-han, a powerful militia leader from Kokang, and Bo Loi Oo, the influential Wa states militia commander, were required to stop in Kengtung to have their opium weighed and taxed by Yang Sun before they could proceed down the road to their private opium refineries in Tachilek. In addition, Yang Sun's troops provided armed escorts between Kengtung and the border for private merchant caravans out of the Kokang and Wa states. For a nominal fee of $6 per kilo of opium, merchants were guaranteed safe conduct by the Burmese government and protection from bandits and rebels.[304]

Although some of the opium carried by Shan rebels and the KMT was smuggled across the border in raw form, most of the militia's opium was processed into smoking opium, morphine, or heroin at Shan militia (KKY) refineries in the Tachilek area before being shipped into nearby Thailand. Yang Sun operated a large opium refinery about six miles north of Tachilek capable of producing both no. 3 and no. 4 heroin.[305] This laboratory was only one of fourteen in the Tachilek region, which, according to a 1971 CIA report, processed a total of 30 tons of raw opium during 1970.[306] While this output represented a considerable increase from the mid-1960s when Khun Sa's morphine factory at Ving Ngun was the only known refinery, 30 tons of raw opium was still only a tiny fraction of Burma's total estimated export of 500 tons. The relative weakness of Burma's processing industry was one of the legacies of Khun Sa's defeat in the 1967 Opium War. Since KMT caravans continued to ship about 90 percent of the Shan states' opium to Thailand and Laos for processing in their own refineries, the growth of Tachilek's laboratories was hampered by a shortage of raw materials.

Until public order was restored to the Shan states, there was little chance that Burma's opium production could be eradicated or its heroin laboratories shut down. It seemed unlikely that the squabbling Shan rebels would ever be capable of driving the Burmese army out of the Shan states. It seemed even more unlikely that the profit-oriented militia commanders would be willing to divert enough effort from their flourishing opium trade to make a serious effort at driving the rebels out of the hills. Despite its claim of success, the Burmese army was even further away from victory than it had been a decade before.

If the Burmese army and the Shan military groups were out of the picture, there were only two possible contenders for immediate control over the Shan states—the Burmese Communist party and a coalition of right-wing rebels led by Burma's former prime minister U Nu. A year after he fled to Thailand in April 1969, U Nu concluded an alliance with Mon and right-wing Karen insurgents active in the Burma-Thailand frontier areas and announced the formation of a revolutionary army, the United National Liberation Front (UNLF).[307] To raise money U Nu and his assistants (among them William Young, now retired from the CIA) circled the globe, contacting wealthy financiers and offering guarantees of future oil and mineral concessions in exchange for cash donations. Burma's future was mortgaged, but by the end of 1970 U Nu had a war chest of more than $2 million.[308]

With the tacit support of the Thai government, U Nu built up his guerrilla army inside Thailand: three major bases were opened along the Thailand-Burma border at Mae Hong Son, Mae Sariang, and Mae Sot.[309] Recognizing Burma's ethnic diversity, U Nu divided the eastern part of the country into three separate military zones: the Mon and Burmese areas in the southeast, the Karen region in the east, and the Shan and Kachin states in the northeast.[310]

While the UNLF alliance gave U Nu a strong basis for operations in the Mon and Karen areas, he had almost no influence in the northeast. There were so many Shan armies that it would have been meaningless to ally with any one of them, and they were so divided among themselves that forming a coalition required special tactics.[311] Instead of allying with established rebel groups as they had done with the Mons and Karens, U Nu and his assistants assigned William Young and General Jimmy Yang the task of building an independent rebel force inside the Shan states.

A member of Kokang state's royal family, Jimmy Yang had begun organizing guerrilla resistance in 1962. Since his family had worked closely with the KMT for more than a decade, he was able to finance his infant rebellion by sending caravans loaded with Kokang opium to Thailand under the protection of General Ly's Third Army. After three years of fighting in Kokang, Jimmy and some of his men moved to northern Thailand and built a base camp in the shadow of Ly's headquarters at Tam Ngop. While his men raised chickens and smuggled opium in the mountains, Jimmy moved down to Chiangmai and became assistant manager of the most luxurious tourist hotel in northern Thailand, the Rincome Hotel.

Jimmy had known U Nu in Rangoon, and when the former prime minister first arrived in Thailand Jimmy renewed the friendship by soliciting a $10,000 contribution from General Ly.[312] U Nu returned the favor several months later by appointing Brigadier General Jimmy Yang commander of the UNLF's northern region, the Kachin and Shan states, and reportedly allocated $200,000 from the war chest to build up an effective Shan army.[313]

Rather than trying to build up the 5,000-man army he thought would be necessary to subjugate the hundred or so armed bands that roamed the hills, Jimmy decided to forge an elite strike force of about a hundred men to guarantee his security while he traveled through the strife-torn Shan states negotiating with bandits, opium armies, rebels, and government militia. In exchange for their allegiance, he planned to offer them officers' commissions and government jobs in U Nu's future government. By avoiding the opium traffic and relying on U Nu's war chest for financial support, Jimmy hoped to remain aloof from the opium squabbles and territorial disputes that had destroyed past coalitions. Once the fighting was over, Jimmy intended to return the *sawbwas* to power. They would appeal to their subjects to come out of the hills; the rebels would lay down their arms and order would be restored.[314]

To implement his plan, Jimmy recruited about a hundred young Shans and outfitted them with some of the best military equipment available on Chiangmai's black market: U.S. M2 carbines at $150 apiece, M16 rifles at $250 each, U.S. M79 grenade launchers at $500 apiece, high-grade U.S. jungle uniforms, and Communist Chinese tennis sneakers. General Ly contributed some Nationalist Chinese training manuals on jungle warfare. Confidently, Jimmy set September 1971 as his target date for jumping off into the Shan states, but almost from the beginning his program was hampered by the same problems that had destroyed similar efforts in the past. When September 1971 finally arrived, Jimmy's men were deserting, potential alliances had fallen through, and he had been forced to postpone his departure indefinitely.[315]

Jimmy Yang's men deserted because of the same type of racial and political conflicts that had promoted disunity among previous Shan armies. While almost all his troops were Shans, Jimmy's instructors, like himself and most residents of Kokang, were ethnic Chinese. Since ethnic chauvinism was the most important tenet of Shan nationalist ideology, internal discord was almost inevitable.

In April 1971 Jimmy's deputy commander, a Shan named Hsai Kiao, met with members of U Nu's revolutionary government in Bangkok and presented the Shan grievances. U Nu's assistants offered no major concessions, and several weeks later Hsai Kiao moved to Chiangrai, opening his own camp in the Huei Krai area. Shan recruits continued to desert to Hsai Kiao, and by September U Nu's northern command was a complete shambles. Jimmy was losing his men to Hsai Kiao, but Hsai Kiao, lacking any financial backing, was sending them off to work in the mines at Lampang to raise money. Hsai Kiao planned to save enough money to buy a shipment of automatic weapons in Laos, pack them into the Shan states, and trade them for opium. With the profits from the opium-arms trade, he eventually hoped to build up a large enough army to drive the Burmese out of Kengtung.[316]

While Jimmy Yang's troop training program had its problems, his attempts at forging political alliances with local warlords encountered an insuperable obstacle—William Young. After he finished a fund-raising tour in the United States, Young returned to Chiangmai and began building support for U Nu among the hill tribes of the eastern Shan states. Prior to making contact with Lahu and Wa leaders, Young spent months gathering data on every armed band in the eastern Shan states. He concluded that there were about 17,000 Lahu and Wa tribesmen armed with modern weapons. If only a fraction of these could have been mobilized, U Nu would have had the largest army in eastern Burma.[317]

Young began sending personal representatives to meet with the more important tribal leaders and arranged roundtable discussions in Chiangmai. In the mountains north of Kengtung, the Young name still commanded respect from Lahu and Wa Christians, and the enthusiastic response was to be expected.[318] However, Young's success among the animist Lahu south and west of Kengtung was unexpected. The Young family's divinity in these areas had been preempted by an innovative Lahu shaman, known as the "Man God" or "Big Shaman." In mid-1970, when William Young convened an assembly of Lahu chiefs at Chiangmai, the Man God sent one of his sons as a representative. When it was his turn to speak, the son announced that the Man God was willing to join with the other Lahu tribes in a united effort to drive the Burmese out of the Shan states.[319]

After receiving similar commitments from most of the important Lahu and Wa leaders in Burma, Young approached U Nu's war council without Jimmy's knowledge and requested $60,000 for equipment and training. The council agreed, with the proviso that the money would be channeled through Jimmy Yang. In August 1970 Young arranged a meeting between himself, Jimmy, and the tribal leaders to reach a final understanding. When Jimmy adopted a condescending attitude toward the Lahu and Wa, they conferred privately with Young, and he advised them to withhold their allegiance. Young said that all the chiefs agreed to boycott the UNLF until they were confident of full support and claimed that none of them were willing to work with Jimmy.[320]

Given these enormous problems, neither U Nu nor Jimmy Yang seemed to have a very promising future in the Shan states. In fact, Jimmy felt that the Burmese Communist party and its leader Naw Seng were the only group capable of restoring order to the Shan states. According to Jimmy, Naw Seng and the Communists had all the assets their rivals seemed to lack. First, Naw Seng was one of the best guerrilla strategists in Burma. During World War II he fought behind Japanese lines with General Wingate's British commando unit, the Chindits, and was awarded the Burma Gallantry Medal for heroism. Like many Kachin veterans, he enlisted in the First Kachin Rifles after the war and quickly rose to the rank of captain and adjutant commander.[321] The First Kachin Rifles were sent into Communist-controlled areas, and Naw Seng played such an important role in the pacification program that one British author called him "the terror of the Pyinmana Communists." However, many prominent Burmese took a dim view of Kachins attacking Burmese villages under any circumstances, and there were reports that

Naw Seng was about to be investigated by a court of inquiry. Faced with an uncertain future, Naw Seng and many of his troops mutinied in February 1949 and joined with Karen rebels fighting in eastern and central Burma.[322] After leading a series of brilliant campaigns, Naw Seng was driven into Yunnan by the Burmese army in 1949. Little was heard of him until 1969, when he became commander of a Communist hill tribe alliance called the Northeast Command and went on the offensive in the Burma-China borderlands.[323] In March 1970 the Communists captured three border towns, and by mid-1971 they controlled a 400-mile-long strip of territory paralleling the Chinese border.

While Naw Seng's tactical skills were an important asset, Jimmy Yang felt that the Communists' social policies were the key to their success. Instead of compromising with the warlords, the Communists drove them out of all the areas under their control. This policy apparently resulted in a number of violent confrontations with the Kachin Independence Army, the remnants of Khun Sa's forces, and government militia leaders such as Lo Hsing-han and Bo Loi Oo. In each case, the Communists defeated their rivals and pushed them steadily westward. Once in control of some new territory, the Communists abolished the opium tax, which had impoverished the hill tribes for the previous fifteen years, and encouraged the people to substitute other cash crops and handicrafts. In addition, the Communists distributed salt, started a public health program, and restored public order. As a result of these measures, they were able to develop a mass following, something that had eluded other army groups. However, a crop substitution program took up to five years to develop fully even under the best of circumstances, and so opium production continued. Hill traders bought opium from villagers inside the Communist zones and transported it to such market towns as Lashio and Kengtung, where it was sold to government militia, KMT buyers, and private opium armies.[324]

## Opium Warriors

In the aftermath of General Ouane's victory in the 1967 Opium War, Laos emerged as the most important processing center of raw opium in the Golden Triangle. The defeat General Ouane dealt his enemies on the Ban Khwan battlefield forced the KMT to drop its duties on Burmese opium destined for Laos. Freed from the KMT's discriminatory taxation, the Laotian army was able to impose its own import duties. Subsequently, opium refineries in the Ban Houei Sai region increased their processing of Burmese opium.

General Ouane's role in the battle had attracted a good deal of unfavorable publicity in the international press, and in 1967 and 1968 he was visited by representatives from Interpol, a multinational police force that played a major role in combating narcotics smuggling. The authorities were upset that the commander in chief of a national army was promoting the international drug traffic with such enthusiasm, such vigor. Wouldn't the general consider retiring from the opium business? General Ouane was stunned by the naiveté of their request and gave them a stern lecture about the economic realities of opium. Recalling the incident several years later, General Ouane said:

> Interpol visited me in 1967 and 1968 about the opium. I told them there would be commerce as long as the opium was grown in the hills. They should pay the tribesmen to stop growing opium. . . .
>
> I told Interpol that opium was grown in a band of mountains from Turkey to the Tonkin Gulf. Unless they stopped the opium from being grown, all their work meant nothing. I told Interpol to buy tractors so we could clear the trees off the plains. Then we would move the montagnards out of the mountains onto the plains. It's too warm there, and there would be no more opium growing. In the mountains the people work ten months a year to grow 100,000 kip [$200] worth of opium and rice. And if the weather is bad, or the insects come, or the rain is wrong they will have nothing. But on the plains the people can have irrigated rice fields, grow vegetables, and make handicrafts. On the plain in five months of work they can make 700,000 kip [$1,400] a year.
>
> I told Interpol that if they didn't do something about the people in the mountains the commerce would continue. Just as the Mekong flows downstream to Saigon, so the opium would continue to flow. But they simply wanted me to stop. And when I explained this reality to them they left my office quite discontented.[325]

Despite his apparent cockiness, General Ouane interpreted the visit as a warning and began to exercise more discretion. When the author inquired about his involvement in the opium traffic in 1971, he admitted his past complicity but claimed that he had given up his interest in the business.

Before 1967 opium caravans had followed Khun Sa's route entering Laos north of Muong Mounge, traveling down the old caravan trail, and crossing the Mekong into Thailand at Chiang Saen. To conceal Laos's growing role in the traffic, Ouane apparently discouraged caravans from crossing into Laos and ordered them to unload their cargoes on the Burmese side of the Mekong River. Residents of Chiang Saen, Thailand, reported in 1971 that the heavily armed caravans that used to ford the Mekong and ride through the center of town in broad daylight several times a year had not passed through since 1967.[326] Some Laotian air force officers described an opium-arms exchange they carried out in 1968 that illustrated the complexity of the new system: they loaded crates of weapons (M1s, M16s, M79 grenade launchers, and recoilless rifles) into an air force C-47 in Vientiane; flew to Ban Houei Sai, where they transferred the crates to a Laotian air force helicopter; and then flew the weapons to a group of Shans camped on the Burmese side of the Mekong north of Ban Khwan. The opium had already been sent downriver by boat and was later loaded aboard the C-47 and flown to Vientiane.[327]

When Golden Triangle refineries began producing no. 4 heroin in 1969–1970, access to limitless supplies of Burmese opium enabled Ban Houei Sai manufacturers to play a key role in these developments. At the time of the 1967 Opium War, morphine and no. 3 heroin were being processed at a large refinery near Ban Houei Sai and at five smaller ones strung out along the Mekong north of that city. In August 1967 one Time-Life correspondent cabled New York this description of these refineries:

> The opium refineries along the Mekong mentioned in Vanderwicken's take [earlier cable] are manned almost entirely by pharmacists imported by the syndicate from Bangkok and Hong Kong. They live moderately good lives (their security is insured by Laotian troops in some locations) and are paid far above what they would receive working in pharmacies in their home cities. Most apparently take on the job by way of building a stake and few are believed to get involved personally in the trade. Except, a course, to reduce the raw opium to morphine.[328]

At the same time another Time-Life correspondent reported that "the kingpin of the Laotian opium trade is General Ouane. . . . He is reputed to own one of Laos's two major opium refineries, near Houei Sai, and five smaller refineries scattered along the Mekong."[329]

As the demand for no. 4 heroin among GIs in South Vietnam grew, skilled Chinese chemists were brought in from Hong Kong to add the ether precipitation process and upgrade production capability. After the five smaller laboratories along the Mekong were consolidated into a single operation, Ouane's refinery at Ban Houei Tap, just north of Ban Houei Sai, became the largest, most efficient heroin laboratory in the tri-border area and its trademark, the Double U-O Globe brand, soon became infamous.[330] According to a CIA report leaked to the press in June 1971, this refinery was capable of processing a hundred kilos of raw opium per day.[331] Under the supervision of a skilled chemist, this output would yield 10 kilos of no. 4 heroin per day and exceeded the combined production of all fourteen opium refineries in Tachilek, Burma. Although belated American gestures forced the chemists to abandon the building in Ban Houei Tap in July 1971, the operation reportedly moved to a more clandestine location. The refinery operating under Major Chao La's protection north of Nam Keung was also forced to move in July, probably to a more discreet area.[332]

Moreover, Ban Houei Sai opium merchants had become the major suppliers of morphine base and raw opium for heroin laboratories in Vientiane and Long Tieng. As the massive bombing campaign and the refugee relocation program reduced the amount of Hmong opium available for heroin in northeastern Laos, Vang Pao's officers were forced to turn to northwestern Laos for supplies of Burmese opium to keep the Long Tieng laboratory running at full capacity.[333] In addition, there were reliable reports that General Ouane was supplying the raw materials for a heroin laboratory operating in the Vientiane region managed by a Sino-Vietnamese entrepreneur, Huu Tim-heng.[334]

Despite the rapid withdrawal of U.S. troops from Vietnam, Laotian prospects for continuing success in the international heroin traffic appeared to be excellent. Although most American narcotics officials hoped that the Golden Triangle's flourishing heroin laboratories would be abandoned once the GIs left Vietnam, there was every indication that Laotian drug merchants were opening direct pipelines to the United States. In 1971 two important shipments of Double U-O Globe brand heroin, which Saigon police said was manufactured in the Ban Houei Sai area, were seized in the United States:

• On April 5 a package containing 7.7 kilos of Double U-O Globe heroin was seized in Fort Monmouth, New Jersey. It had been sent through the military postal service from Bangkok, Thailand.

• On November 11 a Filipino diplomat attached to his nation's embassy in Vientiane and a Chinese merchant from Bangkok were arrested in New York City with 15.5 kilos of Double U-O Globe heroin shortly after they arrived from Laos.

While these seizures established the fact that Laotian heroin was reaching the United States, they were otherwise unexceptional cases. However, the seizure of Prince Sopsaisana's 60 kilos in Paris provided ominous evidence of connections between Laotian heroin manufacturers, Corsican gangsters in Vientiane, Corsican syndicates in France, and American heroin distributors. American narcotics officials were convinced that Corsican syndicates in France and Latin America were the most important suppliers of heroin for American distributors. But, habituated to the belief in Turkey's importance, they never investigated the links between Corsican syndicates in France and Corsican-French gangsters in Vientiane. This was a costly oversight. In fact, Vientiane's Corsican gangsters were becoming the connection between Laos's heroin laboratories and drug distributors in the United States.

When the Corsican charter airlines were forced out of business in 1965, most of the Corsican and French gangsters stayed in Vientiane waiting for something new to turn up. "Doing less well than previously," reported a Time-Life correspondent in September 1965, "are opium traders, mainly Corsicans who since the fall of grafting Phoumi have found operations more difficult. Some opium exporters have even opened bistros in Vientiane to tide them over until the good bad old days return—if they ever [do]."[335] A few of the bosses managed to stay in the drug business by serving as contact men, other Corsicans found jobs working for the Americans, and some just hung around.

After months of drinking and carousing in Vientiane's French bars, five down-and-out Corsican gangsters decided to make one last, desperate bid for the fortunes that had been snatched from their grasp. Led by a Corsican named Le Rouzic, who had reportedly owned a piece of a small charter airline, and his mechanic, Housset, the five men planned and executed the boldest crime in the history of modern Laos—the great unarmored car robbery. On the morning of March 15, 1966, two clerks from the Banque de l'Indochine loaded $420,000 cash and $260,000 in checks into an automobile and headed to Wattay Airport to put the money aboard a Royal Air Lao flight for Bangkok. As soon as the bank car stopped at the airport, a jeep pulled up alongside and three of the Corsicans jumped out. Throwing handfuls of ground pepper into the clerks' faces, they fled with the money while their victims floundered about, sneezing and rubbing their eyes.

Laotian police showed an exceptional efficiency in their handling of the case; in less than twenty-four hours they recovered almost all the money and arrested Le Rouzic, his mistress, and three of his accomplices. Acting on information supplied by Vientiane police, Thai police arrested Housset in Bangkok and found $3,940 hidden in his socks.[336] At a press conference following these arrests, the Laotian police colonel in charge of the investigation credited his astounding success to "honest citizens" and thanked the French community for "immediate cooperation."[337] Or, as one informed observer later explained, Vientiane's Corsican bosses informed on Le Rouzic and Housset to avoid a police crackdown on their involvement in the narcotics traffic.

Unlike these petty criminals, most of Vientiane's Corsican-French bosses in the early 1970s had respectable jobs and moved in the city's social circles. Roger Zoile, who owned one of the three largest Corsican charter airlines, became the president of Laos Air Charter.[338] During the

1950s and early 1960s, Zoile worked closely with the Paul Louis Levet syndicate, then smuggling morphine base from Southeast Asia to heroin laboratories in Germany, Italy, and France. Two other Air Opium pioneers still resided in Vientiane: René Enjabal, the former manager of Babal Air Force, became a pilot for one of Laos's many civil air lines, while Gérard Labenski, the former proprietor of the Snow Leopard Inn, "retired" to Laos in 1964 after serving four years in a Vietnamese prison for international narcotics smuggling. The managers of Vientiane's most popular nightclub, The Spot, had a long history of involvement in the international drug traffic: François Mittard headed one of the most powerful drug syndicates in Indochina until he was arrested for narcotics smuggling in 1960 and sentenced to five years in a Vietnamese prison; Michel Libert was Levet's right-hand man, and he served five years in a Thai prison after being arrested for drug smuggling in 1963. "My opium days are all in the past," Libert told a Thai undercover policeman in Vientiane some time after his release from prison. "Let me convince you. I'll work for you as an informer and help you make arrests to show you I'm honest." But the Thai policeman knew Libert too well to be taken in and, not wanting to become a pawn in some Corsican vendetta, refused the offer.[339] In addition, the U.S. Bureau of Narcotics identified an occasional Vientiane resident, Lars Bugatti, a former Nazi officer, as a drug trafficker with close ties to Corsican international syndicates.[340] All of these men had been linked to the clandestine Corsican narcotics networks that circled the globe. Through the efforts of these syndicates, large quantities of Laotian heroin were finding their way to France and from there to the United States.

The Prince Sopsaisana affair provided a rare glimpse into the machinations of powerful Laotian politicians and French heroin syndicates. When the king of Laos announced Prince Sopsaisana's appointment as ambassador-designate to France on April 7, 1971, he set in motion a chain of events that led to Sopsaisana's downfall and the loss of $13.5 million of top-grade Laotian heroin. Confident that his diplomatic passport would protect him from French customs, Sopsaisana apparently decided to finance his stay in Paris by smuggling this heroin into France. According to diplomatic sources in Vientiane, General Vang Pao entrusted Sopsaisana, his chief political adviser, with 60 kilos of no. 4 heroin from his laboratory at Long Tieng and a local French hotel manager on intimate terms with many of the Lao elite found a buyer in Paris.[341]

Before Sopsaisana's flight landed in Paris, however, a reliable Laotian source warned the French embassy in Vientiane that the new ambassador would be carrying heroin in his luggage. After a discreet search by airport customs officials turned up the 60 kilos, the French Foreign Ministry asked the Laotian government to withdraw its ambassador-designate. Prime Minister Souvanna Phouma, repaying his political debts, tried to keep Sopsaisana in Paris, and it took the French weeks of negotiations to secure his removal. When Sopsaisana returned to Vientiane in late June, he made a public statement claiming that his enemies had framed him by checking the heroin-filled suitcase onto the flight without his knowledge. Privately, he accused Khamphan Panya, the assistant foreign minister, of being the villain in the plot. Sopsaisana's assertion that Khamphan framed him lacks credibility, for Khamphan simply did not have $240,000 to throw away. However, until the ambitious Sopsaisana interfered, Khamphan had been assured of the ambassadorship and had spent months preparing for his new assignment. He had even ordered the staff in Paris to have the embassy refurbished and authorized a complete overhaul for the Mercedes limousine.[342]

Diplomatic sources in Vientiane reported that he was outraged by Sopsaisana's appointment. And only a few weeks after Sopsaisana returned in disgrace, the Laotian government announced that Khamphan Panya would be the new ambassador to France.[343]

If the heroin shipment had gotten through, the profits would have been enormous: the raw opium cost Vang Pao only about $30,000; Sopsaisana could sell the 60 kilos for $240,000 in Paris; Corsican smugglers could expect $1.5 million from American distributors; and street pushers in urban America would earn $13.5 million.

The important question for the United States was, of course, how many similar shipments had gotten through undetected. If someone had not informed on Sopsaisana, his luggage would have been waved through French customs, the heroin delivered as planned to a Corsican syndicate, and Sopsaisana would have joined Paris's diplomatic community. Another 60 kilos of "Marseille" heroin would have reached the United States and nobody would have been aware of its Asian origins. But the hypothetical did not happen, and suddenly here was more evidence of French gangsters in Vientiane finding ways to connect with Corsican syndicates in France. But the evidence was generally disregarded: the French government covered up the affair for diplomatic reasons, the international press generally ignored it, and the U.S. Bureau of Narcotics regarded it as a curiosity.

The U.S. Bureau of Narcotics was not entirely to blame for its ignorance about the logistics of the Laotian heroin trade. Throughout the 1950s and most of the 1960s, the bureau had concentrated its efforts in Europe and paid almost no attention to Southeast Asia. However, as thousands of GIs serving in Vietnam became addicted to Laotian heroin, the bureau tried to adjust its priorities by sending a team of agents to Laos, but its investigations were blocked by the Laotian government, the

State Department, and the CIA.[344] Although the Royal Laotian government had told the U.N. it was enforcing a "policy of absolute prohibition" of narcotics, it was in fact one of the few governments in the world with no laws against the growing, processing, and smoking of opium. Laos had become something of a free port for opium; smoking dens were found on many city blocks and the location of opium refineries was public knowledge. Laos's leading citizens controlled the opium traffic and protected it like a strategic national industry. Under these circumstances, the Laotian government could hardly have been expected to welcome the Bureau of Narcotics.

While the Laotian government's hostility toward the bureau was understandable, the reticence shown by the CIA and the U.S. embassy requires some explanation. According to U.S. narcotics agents serving in Southeast Asia, the bureau encountered a good deal of resistance from the CIA and the embassy when it first decided to open an office in Vientiane. The embassy claimed that American narcotics agents had no right to operate in Vientiane, since Laos had no drug laws of its own. The embassy said that investigative work by the bureau would represent a violation of Laotian sovereignty and refused to cooperate.[345] The U.S. embassy was well aware that prominent Laotian leaders ran the traffic and feared that pressure on them to get out of the narcotics business might somehow damage the war effort. In December 1970—as thousands of GIs in Vietnam were becoming addicted to heroin processed in laboratories protected by the Royal Laotian Army—the U.S. ambassador to Laos, G. McMurtrie Godley, told an American writer, "I believe the Royal Laotian Government takes its responsibility seriously to prohibit international opium traffic."[346]

When President Nixon issued his declaration of war on the international heroin traffic in mid-1971, the U.S. embassy in Vientiane was finally forced to take action. Instead of trying to break up drug syndicates and purge the government leaders involved, however, the embassy introduced legal reforms and urged a police crackdown on opium addicts. A new opium law, which was submitted to government ministries for consideration on June 8, went into effect on November 15. As a result of the new law, U.S. narcotics agents were allowed to open an office in early November—two full years after GIs started using Laotian heroin in Vietnam and six months after the first large seizures were made in the United States. Only a few days after their arrival, U.S. agents received a tip that a Filipino diplomat and Chinese businessman were going to smuggle heroin directly into the United States.[347] U.S. agents boarded the plane with them in Vientiane, flew halfway around the world, and arrested them with 15.5 kilos of no. 4 Laotian heroin in New York City. Even though these men were carrying a large quantity of heroin, they were still only messengers for the powerful Laotian drug merchants. But political expediency blocked any action, and the U.S. embassy made no effort to go after the men at the top.[348]

In the long run, the American antinarcotics campaign may have done more harm than good. Most of the American effort seemed to be aimed at closing Vientiane's hundreds of wide-open opium dens and harassing ordinary Laotian opium smokers. The Americans pressured the Laotian police into launching a massive crackdown on opium smoking. Since little money was being made available for detoxification centers or outpatient clinics, most of Vientiane's opium smokers were forced to become heroin users. In a September 1971 interview, General Ouane Rattikone expressed grave doubts about the wisdom of the American anti-opium campaign:

> Now they want to outlaw opium smoking. But if they outlaw opium, everyone in Vientiane will turn to heroin. Opium is not bad, but heroin is made with acid, which kills a man. In Thailand Marshal Sarit outlawed opium [1958–1959], and now everybody takes heroin in Thailand. Very bad.[349]

Although General Ouane's viewpoint may have been influenced by his own interests, he was essentially correct.

In Hong Kong, Iran, and Thailand repressive anti-opium campaigns drove the population to heroin and magnified the seriousness of the drug problem in all three nations. Vientiane's brand of no. 3 heroin seemed to be particularly high in acid content and produced some horribly debilitated zombie-addicts. One Laotian heroin pusher thought that Vientiane's brand of no. 3 could kill a healthy man in less than a year. It would have been ironic if America's antidrug campaign had driven Laos's opium smokers to a heroin death while it left the manufacturers and international traffickers untouched.

## Reflections, 1972

In the Yao village of Pa Dua, not far from the KMT headquarters at Mae Salong, in northern Thailand, there was a crude opium den in one corner of the village's general store. At almost any time during the day, three or four Yao tribesmen and KMT soldiers could be found there, flopped on the platform sucking away at their opium pipes. Occasionally as they drifted off into an opium dream one of the smokers gazed at the fading emblem of the United States Navy Seabees, a combat engineering unit, which was tacked to the wall. And the caricatured bumblebee—with a sailor's cap perched on its head and a submachine gun clutched in its gloved fists—looked down on the dreamers with the frenetic glare of an aggrieved icon. This emblem and a rotting cluster of buildings a few miles down the road were the only tangible remains of a Seabee construction team that had spent a year in this area building a road linking Mae Salong with the major provincial highway. According to local Thai officials, the Seabees' construction work was done under the auspices of USAID's Accelerated Rural Development program (ARD). Despite its neutral-sounding title, ARD was a counterinsurgency program designed to give the Thai army's heavy U.S.-style armored and infantry units access to rugged mountain areas in times of rebellion.

While this road was not much help to the Thai army, it was a boon to the KMT's involvement in the international narcotics traffic. Before the KMT caravans left for Burma, arms, mules, and supplies were shipped up this road. After they returned, opium, morphine base, and no. 4 heroin came down the road on their way to the international drug markets. The road reduced the KMT's transportation costs, increased its profit margin, and improved its competitive position in the international heroin trade. At the time the road was built, the KMT's role in the narcotics traffic was well known, but apparently USAID officials felt that the road's military advantages outweighed its positive contribution to the international drug traffic.

In many ways, this road was an example of the most innocent form of American complicity in Southeast Asia's narcotics traffic. After pouring billions of dollars into Southeast Asia for more than twenty years, the United States by 1972 had acquired considerable power in the region. And it had used this power to create new nations where none existed, handpick prime ministers, topple governments, and crush revolutions. But U.S. officials in Southeast Asia seemed to regard the opium traffic as a local problem and generally turned a blind eye to official involvement. A Laotian or South Vietnamese general who advocated neutralism was likely to find himself driven from office, but one who told the international press about his role in the opium trade did not even merit a reprimand. However, American involvement had gone far beyond coincidental complicity; embassies had covered up involvement by client governments, CIA contract airlines had carried opium, and individual CIA agents had winked at the opium traffic.

As an indirect consequence of American involvement in the Golden Triangle until 1972, opium production steadily increased, no. 4 heroin production flourished, and the area's poppy fields became linked to markets in Europe and the United States. Southeast Asia's Golden Triangle grew 70 percent of the world's illicit opium, supplied an estimated 30 percent of America's heroin, and was capable of supplying the United States with unlimited quantities of heroin for generations to come.

By early 1972 the situation had grown so critical that a special U.S.

cabinet-level task force investigating the Southeast Asian drug trade concluded: "There is no prospect of suppressing air and sea traffic in narcotics under current conditions or under any conditions that can realistically be projected." In its rather frank report, the task force explained the logic behind this conclusion:

> The most basic problem, and the one that unfortunately appears least likely of any early solution, is the corruption, collusion and indifference at some places in some governments, particularly Thailand and South Vietnam, that precludes more effective suppression of traffic by the governments on whose territory it takes place. While our Embassies have made repeated and forceful representations and stimulated some cooperation, much more clearly remains to be done. It should surely be possible to convey to the right Thai or Vietnamese officials the mood of the Congress and the Administration on the subject of drugs. It should be possible to make them see that on October 29, 1971 [date of a vote on a U.S. congressional resolution] they came perilously close to losing all military and economic aid from the United States, and that the widely accepted assumption of their corruption and their failure to perform more effectively in suppressing drug traffic played an important part in determining the mood of the Senate, even if many other factors were also involved.
>
> In any case, no real progress can be made on the problem of illicit traffic until and unless the local governments concerned make it a matter of highest priority and see in this struggle a real matter of life and death for their own countries.[350]

As this report indicates, American impact on the region's drug trade, whether covert complicity or active suppression, relied on relations with local allies. In Burma and Laos, CIA operations avoided direct involvement in combat or espionage and instead sought local clients who determined the outcome of the agency's mission. Like its clandestine operations, the agency's complicity does not, in most instances, involve actually handling opium. Instead, it is a question of the CIA's tolerance, or calculated ignorance, of drug dealing by its local allies. In many of the mountain ranges that extend westward from Laos along the southern rim of Asia, opium is the main currency of external trade and thus a major source of political power. Since CIA covert operations demand alliances with powerful warlords or tribal leaders who necessarily deal in drugs, the agency has repeatedly enmeshed its covert operations with the region's opium trade. By investing these leaders with the authority of its alliance, the CIA provides protection that a drug lord can use to expand his share of the traffic. Not only is a protected opium trader less vulnerable to arrest and prosecution, he gains, through his CIA alliance, access to international transport or commercial contacts that facilitate both the movement and the marketing of drugs.

In the opium highlands of Southeast Asia, there are certain structural givens of land, economy, and politics that have inclined the CIA toward complicity in the opium trade. In most cases, the CIA's role involved various forms of complicity, tolerance, or studied ignorance about the trade, not any direct culpability in the actual trafficking. With its vast budget, the CIA had no reason to handle heroin. Instead it was the agency's tactics of indirect intervention through local allies, some of them drug lords, that led to a similarly indirect involvement in drug trafficking. The CIA did not handle heroin, but it did provide its drug-lord allies with transport, arms, and political protection. In sum, the CIA's role in the Southeast Asian heroin trade involved indirect complicity rather than direct culpability.

Indeed, in 1972 the CIA conducted an investigation of the Laotian drug trade that corroborated these patterns of complicity. In response to my testimony on the Indochina heroin traffic before a U.S. Senate committee in June 1972, the agency's inspector general interrogated twenty operatives at its Washington headquarters and sent investigators to interview more than a hundred U.S. officials in Southeast Asia between August 24 and September 10. Not surprisingly, the inspector general concluded that there was "no evidence that . . . any senior officer of the Agency has sanctioned or supported drug trafficking as a matter of policy", thus exonerating the CIA of charges that I had not made. More important, the inspector general's final report, read carefully, confirmed the core of my argument about the agency's complicity in heroin trafficking.[351]

Reviewing the agency's relations with its Southeast Asian allies, the CIA inspector general expressed "some concern" that "local officials with whom we are in contact . . . have been or may be still involved in one way or another in the drug business. . . . What to do about these people is a particularly troublesome problem, in view of its implications for some of our operations, particularly in Laos." The inspector general found agency alliances with senior Laotian military officers particularly problematic: "The past involvement of many of these officers in drugs is well known, and the continued participation of many is suspected; yet their goodwill . . . considerably facilitates the military activities of Agency-supported irregulars."[352]

To correct the problem, the inspector general required the CIA's Vientiane station to conduct "an assessment of the possible adverse repercussions" of its relations with Laotian heroin dealers. Evidently dependent on the support of Laos's drug lords, the Vientiane station seemed reluctant to sever relations. In something akin to a public reprimand, the inspector general criticized its report as "unduly sanguine" and suggested that "the Station will need additional guidance from headquarters" in understanding the importance of current antinarcotics efforts.[353] In a frank assessment of the policies that had allowed the CIA's complicity in the drug trade, the inspector general concluded that, "The war has clearly been our overriding priority in Southeast Asia, and all other issues have taken second place in the scheme of things. It would be foolish to deny this, and we see no reason to do so."[354]

In contrast to the candor of this internal report, the CIA made repeated public statements denying any complicity in the Southeast Asian drug trade. When the U.S. Senate committee chaired by Senator Frank Church reviewed the CIA's performance in 1975, the agency convinced its members that there was "no substance" to "allegations that the Agency's air proprietaries were involved in drug trafficking."[355] By effectively denying its complicity and thus blocking reform, the CIA ensured that policies that had promoted heroin production in Burma and Laos during the 1960s would, with some variation, be repeated in Pakistan and Afghanistan during the 1980s.

# 8

# War on Drugs

SOUTHEAST ASIA HAS ACHIEVED THE DUAL DISTINCTION OF becoming the world's largest producer of raw opium and the major source of America's illicit heroin supply. In February 1990 the U.S. Drug Enforcement Administration (DEA) announced that Southeast Asia was the source of 45 percent of all the heroin consumed in the United States, up sharply from only 18 percent three years before.[1] Within weeks, the U.S. State Department released its annual review of the global drug trade with similarly sobering news. In 1989 Southeast Asia's Golden Triangle had produced an estimated 3,050 tons of raw opium, equivalent to 72 percent of the world's total illegal supply. Illicit production in Burma (now called Myanmar) jumped to 2,625 tons of raw opium, dwarfing the world's other major suppliers—Afghanistan, 585 tons; Iran, 300 tons; Pakistan, 130 tons; and Mexico, 85 tons.[2]

After twenty-five years of intensive suppression efforts by the United States, the signs of failure were clear. What American enforcement experts had long feared had finally come to pass—the globe's great opium reserve on the Shan Plateau of Burma had merged with the world's premier heroin market in the United States. In its annual review of the global traffic, the State Department noted that "Burma suspended al narcotics control programs in 1989 giving free rein to producers and traffickers."[3] Through "strengthened relationships between Thai military . . . and traffickers in Burma," Thailand had become "the major conduit for drugs exported from the region."[4] Instead of discouraging the traffic as had once been hoped, Thailand's rapid economic growth has improved its role as a transit center. The country's "excellent highway system makes it a natural conduit for drugs flowing from the Golden Triangle," and its modern banking industry allows it to "serve an important function in the financing of the Golden Triangle narcotics trade."[5]

Although Southeast Asia has remained the world's largest single source of narcotics for forty years, the United States had consistently failed to grasp the significance of the Golden Triangle opium trade. During the 1950s the head of the Federal Bureau of Narcotics (FBN) did not assign a single agent to Southeast Asia even though it was the world's largest source of narcotics by the end of the decade. The DEA, successor to the FBN, did not establish a Bangkok office until the late 1960s, some twenty years after its first foreign office opened in Rome. Although the DEA's Bangkok office has produced intelligence proving the region's importance, Washington has usually failed to react. After announcing that Southeast Asia was now producing more than 70 percent of the world's opium, the Bush administration allocated just 5 percent of its 1991 foreign suppression budget to the region. Although Southeast Asia produces three times more opium than Pakistan and Afghanistan, it receives only half the allocation for suppression efforts in those two countries. Moreover, the enforcement emphasis on cocaine at the expense of heroin has been even more extreme. Reflecting the high media visibility of crack cocaine, programs aimed at cocaine capture 86 percent of the Bush budget, leaving only 14 percent for global heroin suppression.[6]

The heroin trail that ends in New York or Los Angeles begins in the mountains of Southeast Asia's Golden Triangle, where itinerant Chinese traders still provide the link between the opium-growing villages and the heroin laboratories along the Thailand-Burma border. Descendants of merchants who once ranged as far as Mogul India, the Chinese traders who visit the mountain villages to barter city goods for raw opium are mostly Muslims who trace their origins to China's neighboring Yunnan province. Not only do the Yunnan Chinese bind the Golden Triangle together as an economic unit with their networks of debt and credit, but they also serve as managers of the heroin laboratories. Living in a remote corner of the vast Chinese empire, the greatest Yunnan merchants historically have been autonomous warlords who mobilized armed guards to accompany their trade caravans. Today the leading warlord, Khun Sa, commands an army of 3,500 men armed with M16 rifles and .50 caliber machine guns. After the 1977 harvest his mule caravans transported enough opium and heroin to supply the entire annual requirements of America's illicit drug markets.[7]

Southeast Asia's international drug traffic is controlled by the ethnic

Chiu chau Chinese syndicates. The Chiu chau have never developed the Mafia's quasi-military hierarchy and appear to organize themselves on a loose structure similar to that of Marseille's Corsican milieu. Despite their loose organization, the Chiu chau syndicates, often structured like a consortium of investors, have a proven capacity for mounting complex smuggling operations spanning several continents. Whether in Hong Kong, Malaysia, New York, or Amsterdam, these Chinese syndicates are exclusively Chiu chau. Tracing their ancestral origins to the city of Swatow on China's southern coast, the Chiu chau are described by Hong Kong police in the same manner that their French and Italian counterparts speak of Corsican and Sicilian criminals—as ruthless, clannish, loyal to their fellows, and hostile to outsiders.

The Chiu chau involvement in narcotics began in the late 1800s when a group of Swatow merchants won a government contract to sell opium in Shanghai's French concession. During the 1920s the Chiu chau syndicate opened illicit heroin laboratories in Shanghai and came to dominate a narcotics industry that served some 10 million Chinese addicts. The syndicate fled to Hong Kong when the Red Army captured Shanghai in 1949 and established new laboratories there in the 1950s, working through contacts in Bangkok's large Chiu chau community to import raw morphine base from the Golden Triangle. By 1972 five major Chiu chau syndicates dominated Hong Kong's heroin traffic, and the colony had 150,000 addicts—equivalent to 3.6 percent of the total population, the highest rate of addiction in the world. As the government opium monopolies in Thailand, Malaya, and Vietnam closed during the 1950s and narcotics were officially banned, the Chiu chau syndicates expanded their operations to cover most of Southeast Asia. By the early 1970s they were firmly in control of Southeast Asia's drug trade and were ready to penetrate the more lucrative international markets beyond the region.

## Global Heroin Trade

In explaining the global spread of mass heroin addiction over the past quarter century, media commentators have often focused on the reasons why addicts turn to heroin—structural unemployment, the youth drug culture, or the moral crisis of postindustrial societies. While all of these are factors, an exclusive emphasis on the motivations of individual addicts ignores the fundamental fact that heroin is a mass-market commodity with salesmen and distributors just like cigarettes, alcohol, or aspirin.

The rising numbers of younger users can sample drugs like heroin because they are sold at standard prices and are available at hundreds of distribution points in major cities across the globe. Without the work

of highland drug lords and urban distributors, addicts would be forced
to assuage their anguish with cannabis, synthetics, or alcohol. Simply
put, without global production and distribution systems, there can be no
mass addiction to cocaine or heroin.

In the mid-1970s Southeast Asia's Chiu chau syndicates seem to have
made a calculated decision to export to mass markets in Europe,
America, and Australia as a way to dispose of surplus production from
their Golden Triangle laboratories. In response to a series of sudden
shifts in the world heroin market, the syndicates sought export markets
first in America and then, when that market was closed to them, shifted
to Europe and Australia. After their experience with American GIs in
Vietnam, the Chiu chau became aware of the vast profits to be made in
the affluent nations, and these exports were part of an effort to win new
outlets.

The American GI heroin epidemic in Vietnam was the Chiu chau
syndicate's first experience with a non-Asian market. Realizing the
economic potential of the 500,000 American soldiers sent to Vietnam
during the late 1960s, the Chiu chau dispatched a number of skilled
Hong Kong chemists to open new no. 4 laboratories in the Burma-
Thailand-Laos tri-border area and exported thousands of kilograms of
pure no. 4 heroin to Vietnam for sale to the American troops. In early
1970 heroin pushers suddenly appeared inside every U.S. army camp
and by mid-1971 some units admitted addiction rates as high as 20
percent.

Ironically, the Chiu chau success at fostering mass addiction among
U.S. troops in Vietnam guaranteed the failure of their later attempt to
penetrate the American heroin market. In 1969 there were only three
U.S. narcotics agents stationed in Bangkok—responsible for both
answering the telephone and monitoring the flow of narcotics
throughout the whole of Southeast Asia. Convinced of the paramount
importance of the Turkey-Marseille corridor as the main source of
America's heroin supply, the U.S. Drug Enforcement Agency had paid
little attention to the increasing flow of heroin out of Southeast Asia into
the international traffic. The token DEA staff in Bangkok made few
arrests and had little expertise and less intelligence capability.

In 1970 and 1971, however, as the scandal of the GI heroin epidemic
in Vietnam immobilized combat units and broke across the front pages
of American newspapers, the DEA was forced to alter its priorities. A
special "fire brigade team" of agents was dispatched to make sure that
Asian heroin would not fill the void left by the impending abolition of
Turkish opium production. As part of President Richard Nixon's
well-publicized "war on drugs," the U.S. State Department had
pressured the Turkish government into accepting $35 million in foreign

aid in exchange for abolition of state-regulated opium cultivation for pharmaceutical companies. By the end of 1973 the 8 to 12 tons of no. 4 illicit heroin that had been manufactured from some 100 tons of raw Turkish opium in Marseille had disappeared from the market, producing a sudden shortage in the U.S. narcotics supply. During a heroin drought that continued for some twenty-four months, the New York City street price doubled and purity declined by half, strong indicators of a serious shortage. While the agreement lasted only two years and Turkey resumed state-regulated opium production in 1974, the respite was long enough to close the Turkey-Marseille pipeline, believed to be the source of 80 percent of America's heroin, and to force a major syndicate reorganization of the international drug traffic.[8]

Long-range studies prepared in 1971–1972 by the director of the DEA's Strategic Intelligence Office, John Warner, argued that Southeast Asia's Golden Triangle had the potential of replacing Turkey as the source of America's heroin supply. These reports were sent to the Nixon White House and reviewed by the Cabinet Committee on International Narcotics Control (CCINC), which decided to give Southeast Asia an increased priority. The committee's executive director, Egil Krogh, Jr., of Watergate fame, was charged with the responsibility for administering the new project and called in the selected DEA agents for pep talks before their departure for the Orient. One DEA Southeast Asian veteran can recall the young Nixon aide pulling him over to the map by his lapel, pointing to the Golden Triangle, and saying with a determined look: "Go get me opium caravans."[9] DEA increased its contingent of special agents in Southeast Asia from two in 1972[10] to thirty-one by late 1974[11] and began spending up to $12 million annually to aid local antinarcotics police.[12]

Given the impossibility of slaying what the DEA's Bangkok chief Daniel Addario called the "monster of the Golden Triangle's 1000 tons of opium," the DEA devoted its efforts to disrupting the international traffic between Thailand and the United States. Despite lack of experience in the region, by 1975 the DEA had made some advances in coping with the growing exports of Southeast Asian heroin to the United States. With a large field force of American agents, the DEA quickly developed a strong intelligence capacity in the region's major American-oriented heroin entrepôts—Hong Kong, Manila, and, most important, Bangkok. As information from informants accumulated, the DEA began intercepting shipments destined for the United States.[13]

The Nixon administration's initial supposition had been correct: by 1972 Southeast Asia's Chiu chau syndicates were in fact attempting to win a major share of the American narcotics traffic, then the only major market among the affluent nations. Reflecting on the situation several years later, DEA intelligence analysts postulated that the GI heroin epidemic in Vietnam from 1969 to 1971 may have served as a "consumer test" for the Chinese syndicates and encouraged them to make an effort to develop a mass market for Asian no. 3 and no. 4 heroin in the United States.[14] Large-scale American troop withdrawals from Vietnam in 1971–1972 left the region's Chiu chau consortium with surplus stocks of no. 4 heroin in Southeast Asia and denied them access to their best customers.

Trying in effect to follow the GI addicts home, Chiu chau syndicates initially used Chinese and Western sailors as couriers and were able to smuggle a thousand pounds of the region's heroin, much of it the Double U-O Globe brand, into New York City in 1971 and 1972.[15] A number of alternative channels were developed as well. Among the most important were a Manila-based Chiu chau group under the entrepreneur Lim Seng and a syndicate of American ex-GIs that operated from bars in Bangkok vice districts to smuggle approximately 1,000 pounds of heroin into the United States during its decade of operation.[16] Following Turkey's prohibition of poppy cultivation in 1971–1972, DEA sources estimated that Southeast Asian heroin climbed to approximately 30 percent of total U.S. consumption.[17]

Although there was every indication by 1973 that Southeast Asian heroin would enter the United States in growing quantities and would soon dominate the American narcotics trade, it failed to gain the majority share analysts had once expected. By 1975 Southeast Asian heroin had dropped from a peak of 30 to about 9 percent of the total heroin seized on the streets of American cities. Unfortunately, the sudden decrease in the amount of Southeast Asian heroin entering the United States had only a temporary impact on America's domestic drug problem. The interdiction of Southeast Asia's heroin exports, combined with the eradication of Turkey's opium crop, produced a serious narcotics drought in the United States and reduced the number of addicts from 500,000 in 1971 to 200,000 three years later.[18] As the street shortage on the East Coast raised street prices to new highs in 1973 and 1974, laboratories and poppy plantations in the Mexican tri-state area of Sinaloa, Durango, and Chihuahua undertook a quantum leap in production and increased their share of the U.S. market from 39 percent in 1972 to 90 percent by 1975.[19]

Judging from the drop of Southeast Asian heroin from 30 percent of U.S. supply in 1973 to less than 10 percent in 1975, it appears that the DEA's seizures and arrests imposed an informal but costly "customs duty" on Chiu chau heroin entering the U.S. and began to discourage further syndicate exports. Faced with the alternative of closing down their operations at a loss, the Chiu chau syndicates, according to DEA's intelligence analysts, decided to develop new markets for no. 3 heroin in Europe and Australia where there were then relatively few addicts. The Chiu chau syndicate leaders calculated, accurately enough, that there were only four regional markets with the affluence to sustain the high cost of the international heroin traffic—North America, Japan, Western Europe, and Australia. Denied access to the United States by the DEA intelligence shield and to Japan by strict customs controls and an unfavorable political situation, the Chiu chau were left with only two affluent markets—Europe and Australia. By the mid-1970s the DEA reported that "overseas Chinese traffickers, using the Netherlands as the main importation and distribution area, virtually controlled the heroin market."[20]

To supply their new European and Australian markets, Chiu chau syndicates based in Malaysia opened up no. 3 laboratories in the Thailand-Malaysia border area, supplementing ongoing no. 4 production on the Thailand-Burma border, and made Kuala Lumpur a major terminus in the international traffic.[21] Using commercial air passengers with concealed "body packs" as couriers and the large Chinese community in Amsterdam as their distribution point, the Chiu chau syndicates began making regular shipments of no. 3 heroin to Europe in early 1972. Between June 1972 and early 1975 more than sixty Chinese couriers carrying Southeast Asian heroin were arrested in Europe.[22] Total European seizures of Asian heroin increased from 22 pounds in 1972 to 195 pounds in 1974 and 1,540 pounds in 1976. Once regarded as an American problem, heroin addiction began spreading rapidly in Europe. In the Netherlands, for example, the number of heroin addicts jumped from 100 in 1970 to 10,000 in 1975.[23] Similarly in Sydney, police first observed a trickle of Southeast Asian heroin entering the city in 1968, a greatly increased flow in 1974–1975, and an unprecedented flood in 1977–1978.[24] From insignificant levels of heroin use in 1970, Western Europe had developed an addict population estimated at 190,000–330,000 by the end of the decade—a market the same size as America's.[25] Although heroin from Pakistan and Afghanistan began to compete for the European market, seizures of Southeast Asian drugs still remained four times larger than the southern Asian competition—397 kilograms to 107.[26]

The question of why Southeast Asia's Chi chau syndicates had failed to capture a major share of the American drug market was debated in U.S. drug enforcement circles.[27] Any answer to such a complex question must remain speculative, however. The DEA's explanation was largely anthropological. "The major constraint on Southeast Asian heroin reaching the United States," argued DEA administrator John R. Bartels, Jr., "seems to have been the lack of reliable connections. Traditionally, Asians have dealt primarily with other Asians."[28]

The DEA hypothesis, while no doubt true in part, ignored many of the developments in the mid-1970s that then temporarily stymied the growth of the Southeast Asia drug trade. The loose consortium of Chiu chau syndicates, as they were operating at their peak in 1972, was similar to a legitimate multinational marketing firm, with its factory and warehouse in Thailand and its newly established international outlets in Manila, Hong Kong, Saigon, and Malaysia. After the Communist takeover in Indochina, the destruction of the Manila syndicate, and the successful police campaigns in Hong Kong and Malaysia closed or crippled the firm's international outlets, management was forced to pull back to its home territory in Thailand and curtail its ambitious program for expansion into the American market.

Although the DEA had accomplished its assigned mission of reducing the heroin flow between Southeast Asia and the United States,[29] it did not devote equal effort to attacking the alliance of Chinese syndicates, Thai military officers, and Yunnanese caravan operators, which controlled the traffic—admittedly a formidable task. By simply denying Bangkok heroin exporters access to the United States without altering the structure of heroin production and the marketing within Thailand, the DEA in effect compelled the syndicates to sell heroin originally produced for American addicts in alternative markets. In short, the DEA simply diverted Southeast Asian heroin from the United States to Europe and Australia.

The net result of the American effort during the 1970s was to increase the complexity of world heroin trade by expanding the number of markets and sources, making eventual suppression even more difficult. In the mid-1960s Hong Kong and Marseille were the only major producers of heroin for the world market. A decade later, Mexico, Burma, Thailand, and Malaysia joined their ranks. In the mid-1960s the United States had the only major heroin market among the affluent nations, but a decade later major consumers included not only the United States, with still more addicts, but also Western Europe and Australia. With a larger number of markets and suppliers, the web of trafficking became far more complex and the capacity of syndicates to survive police suppression increased.

Not only did the DEA's attempt at cutting the connection between the Golden Triangle and the United States force Europe and Australia to absorb its heroin supply, it ultimately contributed to a worsening of America's own narcotics problem by adding to the number of sources and the complexity of international smuggling routes. The DEA's experience has been like that of the sorcerer's apprentice—each attempt at a solution has instead compounded the problem.

Despite the illusory aura of success in Turkey and Mexico during the

1970s, the sudden expansion of opium production in both southern and Southeast Asia during the next decade would show the failure of the DEA's interdiction effort. As Turkish supplies dwindled and Southeast Asia failed to fill U.S. demand, Mexico's production boomed and its Sierra Madre became America's major source of heroin in the mid-1970s. "It is ironic," wrote the director of DEA's Mexican office, "that the crowning success of international narcotics control efforts on the continent of Europe should be functionally related to the rise of brown heroin in North America. . . . Call it a trickle, a muddy stream, or a mighty underground river, there is nothing mysterious about it. The heroin market abhors a vacuum." In the 1950s Mexican opium cultivation had been extremely low, supplying a tiny slice of the U.S. heroin market. As poppy cultivation spread in the early 1970s, however, Mexico supplied 40 percent of U.S. heroin demand in 1972 and 89 percent in 1975.[30]

Mexico's dominance of the U.S. market with low-grade no. 3 heroin coincided with a marked decline in U.S. heroin demand during the mid-1970s and provided some hope that the brushfire approach to international trafficking might be working. In 1975 the DEA, in cooperation with the Mexican government, launched a comprehensive interdiction program that attacked highland poppy cultivation. While 25,000 Mexican troops uprooted poppy plants by hand, a fleet of eighty aircraft, most supplied through U.S. aid, sprayed the opium fields with herbicides. In early 1976 alone, 22,887 poppy fields covering 14,000 acres were destroyed. From 1975 to 1978 the eradication campaign cut the flow of Mexican heroin into the United States from 6.5 to 3 tons.[31] As U.S. enforcement efforts continued, the export of Mexican heroin continued to decline, stimulating renewed Southeast Asian exports that briefly captured about one-third of the U.S. market.

When a two-year drought cut Golden Triangle production from its usual 700 tons to only 160 tons in 1978, heroin production in southern Asia—Afghanistan and Pakistan—suddenly expanded to fill these gaps in the global narcotics supply.[32] By 1979 southern Asian heroin had captured the European market. As Dutch seizures of Southeast Asian heroin dropped from 87.6 kilograms in 1979 to 2.5 in 1980, so European seizures of southern Asian heroin jumped from 414 kilograms to 900 in the same period.[33]

At a conference called by the DEA in 1979, its agents reported that the new sources of heroin were spreading rapidly, especially in New York City, where the southern Asian heroin had captured 42 percent of the market.[34] By 1982 southern Asian heroin supplied 60 percent of the U.S. market, as Mexico's share declined to only 25 percent and Southeast Asia's remained low at 15 percent. With an estimated production of

1,600 tons, southern Asia's opium crop was three times greater than the 450 tons that the Golden Triangle had produced in its last good year, 1977–1978. In 1982 U.S. Attorney General William French Smith announced that the national addict population was approximately 450,000—in effect, back to where it had been before the drug war had started ten years before.[35]

Despite its initial success, Nixon's drug war thus produced a paradoxical strengthening of the global narcotics traffic. By the late 1970s the simplex of the Turkey–Marseille–New York heroin pipeline had been replaced by a complex of international smuggling routes that tied the disparate zones of First World consumption to Third World narcotics production. With production and consumption now dispersed about the globe, the international narcotics traffic was far more resistant to suppression than before.

With heroin consumption in Western Europe on the rise throughout the 1970s, the European authorities' awareness of the drug problem was reflected in their increased involvement in suppression efforts in Southeast Asia. Once the exclusive preserve of the American DEA, Bangkok in the late 1970s became the base for narcotics specialists from Canada, Britain, the Netherlands, France, and Australia. In 1976–1977 Norway contributed $5.4 million and Sweden $500,000 to the United Nations' antinarcotics program in the Golden Triangle.[36] In 1979 Australia for the first time posted a team of narcotics agents at its Bangkok embassy, just one indication of its growing official awareness of the threat posed by the Golden Triangle's limitless heroin supplies.

The experience of the 1970s showed the great difficulty of eliminating opium at its source or interdicting the flow of heroin into the world markets once it left the laboratories. Like opium in the nineteenth century, heroin had become a world market commodity and supplies not absorbed in one market found their way into another. Interdiction simply acted as an informal tariff barrier and encouraged syndicates to seek alternative markets in nations with less stringent international enforcement efforts.

By the early 1980s the global narcotics market had survived the natural and political reverses of the 1970s and emerged with a capacity for a decade of explosive growth. In an implicit condemnation of the suppression efforts of the 1970s, Attorney General Smith reported in 1982 that U.S. drug imports (heroin, cocaine, and marijuana) totaled $61 billion in 1980, and every significant indicator pointed to further rises.[37]

As the long drought in the Golden Triangle came to an end in 1980, farm-gate opium prices in Burma soared from $91 per kilogram in January 1979 to $399 in June 1980, boosting production from the 1979 low of 160 tons to 450–550 tons in 1981.[38] With good rain and rising prices, Burma's opium production rose steadily through the decade to 2,780 tons in 1990.[39] While heroin supplies from Mexico and southern Asia waxed and waned, Golden Triangle heroin increased its share of the New York City market from 5 percent in 1984 to 80 percent in 1989.[40]

With Thailand unwilling, the United States incapable, and Burma unable to take effective steps toward ending the opium traffic, it seemed unlikely, by the late 1980s, that anything short of major political change could reduce the Golden Triangle's vast opium harvest. During the 1970s the DEA and allied agencies had developed an impressive expertise and scored some major drug seizures in Southeast Asia. Although cautious in their predictions, international narcotics agents seemed confident of eventually reducing if not eradicating the region's illicit heroin supply. By 1980 the combination of drought and interdiction had seemingly brought the end in sight. In less than a decade, however, the Golden Triangle's production had soared,[41] and the region's future as the world's leading heroin supplier has been assured.

## Philippine Suppression

The first and most dramatic blow against the Southeast Asian heroin trade was struck at Manila in January 1973 when Lim Seng, a convicted Chiu chau heroin manufacturer, was executed by a Philippine army firing squad. Although there had been reports of a "Manila connection" by international antinarcotics agents for several years, there was still considerable surprise when Lim Seng's arrest and the seizure of his two laboratories confirmed these suspicions. Despite a mounting drug problem during five years prior to Lim Seng's arrest, the Philippines still had the smallest addict population of any nation in Southeast Asia and did not seem capable of supporting a heroin laboratory. Arrests for narcotics violations of any kind averaged only fifty to sixty annually throughout the 1950s.[42]

During the early 1960s, however, small no. 3 heroin laboratories began to open in Manila. By 1964 when Lim Seng, still a struggling restaurant proprietor, opened his first laboratory, three rival Chinese laboratories were already in operation. Financed by a leading Filipino textile magnate and an overseas Chinese insurance agency, Lim Seng hired a Chiu chau chemist from Hong Kong and began producing small quantities of no. 3 heroin for the local market. After an oversupply of no. 3 heroin forced all his competitors out of business, Lim Seng found that Manila was an inadequate market and in 1969 began manufacturing no. 4 heroin for export to the United States. He began making large purchases of morphine base from the Golden Triangle through the Hoi Se-wan–Sukree Sukreepirom partnership in Malaysia and the Lim Chiong syndicate, which operated out of the fashionable Erawan

Antique Shop in downtown Bangkok. The consortium prospered and in 1970 Lim Seng toured Southeast Asia with a portfolio of promising securities, returning with enough capital from Hoi Se-wan and Lim Chiong to take over a large mining company listed on one of the Manila stock exchanges. By 1971 Lim Seng was producing more than 100 kilograms of no. 4 heroin per month at his laboratories, which were concealed in rented mansions and protected by their owner's generosity to congressmen, customs officials, and police.[43]

Since Manila's addicts were using only 9 to 10 kilograms of heroin a month, Filipino narcotics specialists feel that Lim Seng was taking advantage of the Philippines' excellent military and civilian transportation links with the U.S. West Coast to export more than 90 percent of his annual production of 1.2 tons, an amount equivalent to 10 percent of America's annual heroin supply.[44] To meet the increased demand in the American market that developed in late 1971, Lim Seng placed a record order with the Lim Chiong syndicate in Bangkok for $1 million worth of morphine base and chartered a Royal Thai Navy gunboat to make a delivery from Bangkok to Manila. Under the guise of a goodwill tour, the Thai navy vessel docked at Manila's South Harbour, and the $1 million worth of morphine was transferred to a suite in the nearby Manila Hotel while the captain was taken out on the town by Lim Seng.[45]

Although minimal by American standards, the growing incidence of heroin addiction among the Filipino student population became a matter of grave public concern. In early 1972 the Philippine government responded by strengthening its narcotics laws and forming the Philippine Constabulary Anti-Narcotics Unit (CANU). Only weeks after its organization, CANU got its first break in the Lim Seng case on April 16 when its operatives arrested two American ex-GIs boarding a flight for Okinawa with 6 ounces of no. 4 heroin.[46] Following leads from this case, CANU agents soon identified all the members of the Lim Seng syndicate and its laboratory locations but were hesitant in applying for a search warrant for fear that corrupt court officials might warn Lim Seng of the impending raids.[47]

Finally on September 28, 1972, less than a week after President Ferdinand E. Marcos declared a state of martial law, CANU launched a series of raids that netted Lim Seng, two heroin laboratories, and more than 50 kilograms of recently processed no. 4 heroin.[48] When CANU troopers arrested him at the offices of his Forever Printing Press and discovered a concealed heroin laboratory, Lim Seng offered $150,000 if they would only arrest him and "overlook" the evidence. Rebuffed by the CANU agents, Lim Seng was evidently able to bribe a member of the military tribunal to avoid the death penalty. Soon after the court was called to order at 8:00 A.M. Lim Seng pleaded guilty, a single witness was called to give evidence, and a sentence of life imprisonment was pronounced before lunch.

Suspicious of the speed of the verdict, CANU officers posted undercover agents in Lim Seng's cell at constabulary headquarters and intercepted plans for an escape attempt.[49] After receiving a report from CANU, President Marcos announced in a television speech on January 7, 1973, that he would "sentence to death any convicted manufacturer" and ordered Lim Seng's execution a week later.[50] According to military officers who witnessed the execution, Lim Seng seemed confident until the very end that he would somehow buy his way out, and he continued to joke with the soldiers as he was marched up to the stake. Only as he was being blindfolded did the realization strike home. He was struggling against the ropes when the volley hit.[51]

The execution of Lim Seng and the breakup of his syndicate seems to have eliminated heroin trafficking in the Philippines. Within three weeks after Lim Seng's arrest there was a street panic in the Tondo slums and the price of a *papelito* containing 35 mg of heron increased from 20 cents to U.S. $2.75.[52] A 1974 survey found that heroin use had about disappeared among students, and in 1975 only 5 grams of heroin were seized in the entire country.[53] The degree of suppression was illustrated in April 1977 when a U.S. congressional committee reported that American military officers based near Manila were "more concerned with heroin imported into the Philippines from the U.S. than they are with the reverse situation."[54] Once a major center for the export of heroin to the United States, Manila was abandoned by the Chiu chau syndicates during the long years of the Marcos dictatorship.

In July 1990, four years after Marcos's downfall, a dramatic shoot-out in the streets of Manila provided compelling evidence that the Philippines is again serving as a conduit for the export of Golden Triangle heroin to the United States. The incident began when DEA special agent Philip Needham, working undercover from the U.S. embassy in Manila, met with a Filipino drug broker in a downtown hotel room to discuss the purchase of ten kilograms of heroin from dealers who turned out to be Philippine military officers. At the buy-and-bust a week later, Filipino drug agents shot the two officers in the head at close range after Needham had walked away with the heroin, sparking an explosive controversy that raged for weeks in the Manila press. In defense of its operatives, the U.S. embassy released confidential DEA reports that established an important point lost in the debate over the details of this case—senior members of the Philippine military were now principals in the trans-Pacific heroin traffic.[55]

# Hong Kong Syndicates

The Lim Seng case paled in both scope and significance to an investigation by the Royal Hong Kong police that resulted in the arrest or flight of the the colony's five major heroin brokers. Moreover, police inquiries produced a wealth of intelligence on the internal workings of the Chiu chau syndicates.

Ironically, the most important narcotics investigation in Hong Kong's history began as an ordinary homicide case in February 1974 when a Chiu chau fisherman named Leung Fat-hei was found lying stabbed to death in a road near Castle Peak in the New Territories. The homicide case was assigned to a methodical young British officer, Senior Inspector Brian Woodward, who soon learned that the dead man had been smuggling narcotics into Hong Kong harbor from Thai trawlers for the "Crippled Man," Chiu chau syndicate leader Ng Sik-ho. After a bitter disagreement several years earlier, the victim had quit Ng Sik-ho's syndicate and had recently hijacked a trawler shipment of narcotics in Hong Kong coastal waters consigned to one of Ng's close associates, Ma Sik-yu, the colony's leading narcotics dealer. In April the homicide squad arrested a Chinese hired killer who confessed that Ng Sik-ho had paid him to make sure the victim was not able to repeat the hijacking. With evidence of Ng's involvement in the murder, Inspector Woodward's team was able to use the threat of prosecution to pressure syndicate members into giving evidence about their employer's heroin operations. By September Woodward's team broadened the scope of its inquiry into a full investigation of two major import syndicates, those of Ng Sik-ho and Ng Chun-kwan.[56]

Long regarded by police as clannish, Chiu chau syndicate operatives had in years past refused information to police, and their unprecedented willingness to cooperate was the product of some major disruptions of Southeast Asia's international traffic in 1973–1975. As the DEA applied pressure on the Thai trawlers carrying opiates from Bangkok to Hong Kong, making several major seizures on the high seas, the amount of morphine base entering the colony began to dwindle. During 1973 Hong Kong syndicates were able to draw on local stockpiles, but by early 1974 reserves were low and competition between rival syndicates became intense. Arming his local junk crews with heavy machine guns, Ng Sik-ho hijacked two Thai trawlers entering Hong Kong waters in early 1974 with shipments consigned to other syndicates. His rivals retaliated, and the seizure of Ma Sik-yu's shipment by the ill-fated fisherman Leung Fat-hei was but one battle in this mounting warfare.[57] In the midst of this violence Chiu chau solidarity collapsed and embittered rivals came forward to supply the police with information. After only eight months of investigation, Hong Kong police were ready for an assault on Ng Sik-ho's operations.

On the evening of November 12, 1974, more than 140 police officers drawn from five divisions of the Hong Kong police raided Ng Sik-ho's gambling dens, offices, opium dens, and residence, arresting more than seventy suspects and seizing a cache of documents related to the syndicate's operations. The police raided Ng's home—a $500,000 mansion protected by armed guards, packs of attack dogs, automatic TV cameras, and electric fences—but the Crippled Man eluded arrest by escaping to Taiwan.[58] After Taiwan police began questioning Ng about the murder charges, he decided to return to Hong Kong, convinced that the evidence of his role in the killing was weak and unaware that Hong Kong police had already accumulated evidence of his involvement in the narcotics traffic. Shortly after his return to Hong Kong, Ng surrendered himself to police to answer questions about the homicide but instead was confronted with charges of heroin trafficking. Unprepared for these accusations, Ng Sik-ho answered police inquiries maladroitly, implicated himself in the traffic, and was formally charged with narcotics violations.

The seized documents and the eight-inch-thick dossier that police maintained on his activities for almost twenty years provide an intimate picture of Ng Sik-ho's rise from poverty to a personal fortune close to $30 million.* Born in 1932 in Swatow, the Chiu chau homeland in southern China, Ng Sik-ho migrated at the age of seventeen to Hong Kong, where his involvement with clandestine criminal brotherhoods known as Triads and street gambling soon brought him to the attention of police. It was apparently during this period that Ng was seriously wounded in a Triad war and received his nickname. During the late 1950s he began working as a street pusher in Kowloon and in 1960 was sentenced to one year in prison for possession of narcotics. After his release Ng was more successful in his narcotics dealings, and in 1967 he formed a partnership with his uncle Ng Chun-kwan to begin financing large trawler shipments of opium and morphine from Thailand. Two years later the partnership dissolved in a quarrel over the division of a morphine shipment, but by then both men had accumulated enough money to establish themselves independently as two of the three largest import syndicates in the colony.[59] During the four years prior to his arrest, Ng Sik-ho purchased $6.5 million worth of narcotics from four Chiu chau syndicates in Thailand. And from 1967 to 1974 he deposited $10 million in his four personal bank accounts; opened four new

---

* All dollar amounts are given in U.S. dollars unless otherwise indicated.

restaurants; purchased twenty-three real estate properties; and established the Hong Kong Precious Stone Company, in whose accounts he deposited an additional $13 million.[60]

The rise of this former street pusher did not go unnoticed, but police were unable and, some say, unwilling to move against him. Although Ng Sik-ho was importing substantial shipments of Thai narcotics, he never actually handled the drugs personally. Moreover, he concealed his financial dealings with the Bangkok syndicates in an impenetrable maze of codes and clandestine money transfers. Rather than risk exposure by making payment to the Bangkok syndicate by telegraphic transfer, Ng used a Hong Kong import-export firm to conceal his contacts with Bangkok. After a Thai trawler arrived with a narcotics shipment from Bangkok, Ng Sik-ho would send a courier to the offices of the Hang Choeng Yuen Company in Hong Kong's central business district with, for example, $60,000 in cash and a card that read:

SISTER-IN-LAW PAY COW BROTHER

$60,000. TEL. 744-921

After giving the courier a receipt, the company's cashier gave the message to the dispatch clerk, who translated Ng Sik-ho's private code into the company's commercial code and addressed the message to the firm's legitimate trading partners in Bangkok, the Hang Loon Company. The dispatch clerk then called a small "message center" in a low-rent apartment building in Aberdeen on the other side of Hong Kong Island. There the commercial code was again translated, this time into a transmittal code based on the reference numbers assigned to each Chinese ideogram in a standard dictionary. For a fraction of the price of a regular telegram, the message center placed a long-distance call to its correspondent in Bangkok at a prearranged time and read him, rapid-fire, Ng Sik-ho's message along with dozens of other legitimate commercial transactions for rice, teak, gems, and so on. After decoding the transmission, the Bangkok message center called the Hang Loon Company, which in turn translated the commercial code and dialed the telephone number in the message to inform "Cow Brother," Bangkok opium broker and real estate developer Sukree Sukreepirom (whose 1975 arrest is discussed later), to pick up $60,000 at its offices. Using this triple-code method, Ng Sik-ho had paid Cow Brother, his main Bangkok connection, almost $2 million for narcotics between May 13, 1970 and September 9, 1973.[61]

Not only was Ng Sik-ho circumspect in his dealings, but it was rumored that he, like most syndicate leaders, was able to "fix the police." Long the subject of speculation, reports of systematic corruption in the Hong Kong police have been confirmed since 1974–1975 by the arrests of ranking Chinese and British officers. The scandal exploded into a full-blown controversy in June 1973 when the deputy police commander for Kowloon district, Peter F. Godber, fled to England to avoid prosecution after he was asked by the police commissioner to explain how he had accumulated savings of $880,000.[62]

Although he was eventually brought back to Hong Kong and convicted on charges of corruption, the scandal of Godber's indictment and flight prompted the colonial government to establish the Independent Commission Against Corruption (ICAC) and launch a full-scale investigation. A preliminary inquiry by a Supreme Court justice reported that "narcotics has always been a tremendously lucrative source of corruption" since "it was quite possible for a police officer to make more money in one corrupt transaction . . . than he could earn honestly after twenty years of service."[63] As indictments were announced, forty-three Chinese detectives fled the colony to Taiwan, Brazil, and Canada taking an estimated total of $80 million with them.[64]

Court testimony revealed that police corruption was highly syndicated: the senior Chinese officers in each police division hired an accounting staff to make regular collections from brothels, gambling dens, and drug dealers and then divided the proceeds with the senior British officers in command of the division. The officers used the money to pay informers who assisted in the solution of violent crimes and to enjoy ostentatious lifestyles.[65]

By the time they were ready to raid Ng Sik-ho's operations, Hong Kong police were apparently sensitive to rumors of his "immunity" to arrest. "Well," commented the chief of the Police Narcotics Bureau after Ng Sik-ho was booked, "after today's events we ought to have dealt with that rumor."[66] Convicted in a precedent-setting interpretation of the colony's conspiracy laws,[67] Ng Sik-ho was sentenced to thirty years in prison in May 1975 and his one-time partner, Ng Chun-kwan, was given twenty-five years. A third major Chiu chau importer, Kong Sum-chen, fled to Taiwan, where he was arrested in November 1974, and another alleged broker, Ng Kam-cheung, was arrested in August 1975.[68]

The conviction of Ng Sik-ho and the other leading Chiu chau heroin merchants left only one of the original five Hong Kong syndicates in operation—by far the most powerful—led by the brothers Ma Sik-yu and Ma Sik-chun. The largest of the drug merchants who emerged in the mid-1960s, the Ma brothers had begun their lives as impoverished street hawkers in the lanes of Kowloon's waterfront district in the late 1940s. Accumulating wealth gradually during the 1950s as street pushers and opium den operators, the brothers emerged in the 1960s as one of Hong Kong's larger gambling and narcotics syndicates. Purchasing control over Kowloon's popular *tse-fa* lottery-style gambling racket in the early 1960s with his narcotics profits, Ma Sik-yu grossed an estimated average of $6,000 a day, or $2 million a year, from his illegal gambling operations alone. When Hong Kong police closed the colony's illegal opium dens and the Customs Preventive Services tightened search procedures on freighters arriving from Bangkok in the mid-1960s, Ma Sik-yu was one of the Chiu chau narcotics merchants instrumental in the reorganization of the traffic. To avoid interception by customs, Ma and his colleague Kong Sum-chuen imported morphine base from Bangkok in small Thai trawlers that entered the colony's waters illegally. And to minimize police detection of the malodorous opium dens, Ma and his Chiu chau confreres established laboratories for the manufacture of odorless no. 3 and no. 4 heroin. Known as "White Powder Ma" for his dominance of the heroin trade, Ma Sik-yu became the largest Hong Kong importer of Golden Triangle morphine and opium during the years 1969–1973.[69]

With the fortune they acquired from their heroin ventures, the Ma brothers established one of Hong Kong's fastest-growing business empires of the 1970s. Operating from his apartment in the Oriental Gardens on Kowloon's Prince Edward Road, the elder Ma Sik-yu managed an investment portfolio that included real estate holdings worth $2 million. The more flamboyant of the two, the younger Ma Sik-chun acquired, in addition to his own restaurants and real estate interests, a growing international media conglomerate. Beginning as a naughty-story "mosquito sheet" managed from a vest-pocket office in 1969–1970, the *Oriental Daily News*, the flagship of the Ma media fleet, rose in only eight years to become the largest Chinese-language newspaper in Hong Kong, with a daily circulation of 350,000 copies. With seemingly limitless finances, *Oriental Daily News* paid top salaries to acquire the most distinguished news staff in the colony and purchased a fleet of ten radio-equipped news cars and motorcycles, which soon gained a reputation for arriving at the scene of a crime in advance of the police. Ma Sik-chun later established Ma's Film Company to produce Cantonese and Mandarin feature films and in 1976 together with Taiwan's largest newspaper, the *United Daily*, launched a Chinese-language daily newspaper in New York City, the *World Daily*.

Seeking to shed the reputation that had tagged him White Powder Ma, Ma Sik-yu began spending thousands of dollars on charities. The Hong Kong boy scout movement became the main target of his largesse, and its grateful leaders reciprocated by showering the Ma brothers and their father with a variety of honorary titles and service awards.[70]

But perhaps most important to their ability to avoid prolonged imprisonment was the Ma brothers' alleged involvement with Taiwan intelligence operations against the People's Republic of China. Shortly after their flight from Hong Kong in 1977, the Hong Kong *Star* ran an article citing sources in the DEA to support the charge that "suspected syndicate boss Ma Sik-yu was deeply involved with a network that spied on China for Taiwan." Using their income from the heroin trade, the Ma brothers allegedly financed a "spy network" that was active in both Hong Kong and the Golden Triangle. "Much of the information," said the *Star*'s DEA source, "was actually shipped to Hong Kong with the Thai trawler trade and then dispatched to Taipei." Citing sources within the colony's Investigation Bureau, the *Star* further claimed that agents of the People's Republic of China "played a big part in giving Hong Kong Police evidence to smash the alleged syndicate, which led to the arrest of ten in Hong Kong and Ma Sik-yu in Taiwan."[71]

Following up leads gathered in the Ng Sik-ho case, Hong Kong police compiled a massive dossier on the Ma brothers' alleged narcotics syndicate and raided their homes and offices with some 300 men on August 25, 1977. Tipped off by police questioning in December 1975, Ma Sik-yu had already left the colony some time earlier and sought refuge in Taiwan once the warrant for his arrest was issued. The younger Ma Sik-chun "disappeared" for two days but later surrendered himself voluntarily at Hong Kong police headquarters in the presence of his lawyer and was released on bail. Using his freedom to expatriate his assets, Ma Sik-chun delayed court proceedings for more than a year and then fled the colony in September 1978, only one week before his trial was due to begin.[72]

Their rather lenient treatment before the Taiwan courts lends credence to the Hong Kong *Star*'s allegations of the Ma brothers' involvement in Nationalist Chinese intelligence operations. While Ma Sik-yu was detained for only 100 days in 1978 and was then released, his brother was sentenced to one year's imprisonment on charges of using forged travel documents to enter Taiwan—a sentence later reduced by the high court in May 1979 to only five months. Significantly, during these high court pleadings Ma's attorney stated that his client was a victim of "Communist persecution" and that his *Oriental Daily News* "was the staunchest anti-Communist newspaper in Hong Kong"—an indication that his publishing ventures in both New York and Hong Kong may have had motives other than financial. Although their three confederates in the narcotics syndicate were sentenced to fifteen years' imprisonment on drug charges by the Hong Kong courts, Taiwan refused to extradite the Ma brothers despite legal precedents allowing their deportation.[73]

The impact of the arrests was less than Hong Kong officials had hoped. Simply put, police operations disrupted the traffic and precipitated a major restructuring, but they did not lead to a major reduction in the level of addiction. Two months after the arrest of Ng Sik-ho, morphine prices increased 250 percent, from $8,000 to $20,000 per pound, but the traffic was soon reorganized, apparently by some smaller groups, and prices dropped to $11,500 per pound by October 1976.[74] With accommodations for only 6,000 patients and a relapse rate of more than 60 percent, Hong Kong's various treatment programs were incapable of making any inroads in an addict population estimated at 30,000 to 100,000.[75] Demand remained constant and the market adjusted to meet it.

A continuing government attack on police corruption eliminated the protection that had allowed major Chiu chau syndicates to operate a high-volume heroin industry. Although corrupt police officers protested the investigations with mass riots, the government campaign eventually overcame the opposition. Conducted in strict secrecy beyond the normal restraints of either judicial or administrative procedures, the ICAC generated great turmoil among corruption syndicates and induced five suicides and flight abroad by several European and forty-three Chinese senior police officers. The ICAC's director declared 1977 the "year that counts" and announced that he was investigating twenty-three corruption syndicates, eighteen of which were currently operating among the police. In October 1977 mounting police discontent over alleged ICAC "harassment" of active duty officers erupted in four days of mass protest rallies involving some 5,000 of the colony's 17,000 police. While representatives of the protesters were meeting with Hong Kong's police commissioner on October 28, about 100 police assaulted the ICAC's offices and injured at least five ICAC investigators. One week later a mass meeting of police threatened a strike unless its demands were met, and on November 5 the colony's governor, Sir Murray MacLehose, fearing Hong Kong to be "on the brink of anarchy," announced an amnesty for all offenses committed before January 1, 1977. Although the ICAC was not formally dissolved, observers felt that the protests slowed its investigations for some months.[76]

After the protests subsided and the most corrupt and powerful officers fled the colony, the ICAC resumed its work and maintained a slow, grinding pressure on police that blocked the reconstruction of the powerful corruption syndicates of the 1970s. In the decade following the protests, ICAC investigations of police averaged an impressive 640 a year, making its operations a model for police in England and Australia.[77] Without organized police protection, major heroin manufacturing syndicates found that repeated raids made laboratory operations in the colony's cramped quarters uneconomic.

While the breakup of Hong Kong's major syndicates did not improve the local drug problem, it did produce a dramatic change in the colony's role in the international traffic. In the early 1970s U.S. narcotics specialists were almost unanimous in asserting that Hong Kong was emerging as a major supplier of no. 4 heroin to the United States. By 1977 they were equally confident that many of the no. 4 laboratories had closed and exports to the United States had declined markedly.[78] Hong Kong authorities rightly celebrated these successes and felt they were making progress against the drug trade. Viewed from a broader perspective, these operations simply forced the Chiu chau traffickers out of the colony's narrow confines into the world market.

Reacting to police pressure in Hong Kong, the colony's syndicate operations and skilled chemists moved onward, first to Southeast Asia and later to Europe. As early as 1975 the DEA noted that "chemists who operated in Hong Kong are now working in remote inaccessible areas in northern Thailand," a trend that continued as pressures in Hong Kong mounted.[79] By 1979 seizures raised Hong Kong heroin prices to levels far beyond those elsewhere in Asia, forcing dealers to make their buys in Bangkok. In September, for example, the wholesale price for a kilogram of heroin in Hong Kong was HK$25,000 compared with only HK$3,000 in Bangkok. Although the colony could not produce heroin for export under such conditions, a good deal of refining was still required to service local demand.[80] As a crude indicator of activity, police seizures of laboratories remained constant. Rising from a low of two laboratories in 1965 to eleven in 1977, a year of intense police actions, detection remained at nine or ten per year through the 1980s.[81] As local supplies declined and prices rose correspondingly in the late 1970s, the number of addicts seeking treatment increased from 6,000 in 1975 to 16,500 in 1979. Without adequate treatment facilities, however, addiction remained steady at an estimated 40,000 to 50,000 throughout the 1980s.[82]

The loss of heroin exports in no way diminished Hong Kong's role in the global heroin traffic. As Chiu chau syndicates migrated to Europe and America during the 1980s, Hong Kong emerged as the major financial and managerial center for their global enterprise. In 1984 the U.S. State Department described the colony as "the major financial center for Southeast Asia's drug trafficking" and reported that "large numbers of heroin trafficking ventures throughout the world are financed and controlled from Hong Kong." Protected by lax banking laws that allowed unrestrained money laundering, the colony was servicing drug syndicates in Europe, America, and Southeast Asia.[83]

## Malaysia and Singapore: Radical Repression

As conditions in Hong Kong tightened up, at least four known Chiu chau chemists left the colony in 1974–1975 for the Thailand-Malaysia border area, where new no. 3 laboratories were being opened.[84] Capitalized in some cases by wealthy Singapore Chinese, four Malaysia-based Chiu chau syndicates began importing morphine base from the Golden Triangle through Haad Yai, a vice center in southern Thailand, and processing it into no. 3 heroin in the jungles of northern Malaysia. Since Malaysia had relatively few addicts, local police officials were convinced that most of the output was being exported to Europe from Kuala Lumpur's international airport.[85] Increased availability of no. 3 heroin from the local laboratories sparked a noticeable increase in Malaysian addiction during 1974, arousing suspicions of Communist involvement and grave concern among Malaysian government leaders.[86] Heroin seizures in Malaysia jumped from 3 pounds in 1972 to 130 in the first nine months of 1975.[87]

Armed with a new law passed in April 1975 that provided whipping and the death penalty for narcotics trafficking, Malaysian police began an eight-month investigation that culminated in a series of nationwide raids by 200 police. Malaysian police and their DEA counterparts felt that the new law and rigorous enforcement efforts forced the syndicates to move their laboratories and operations across the border into southern Thailand where, as one DEA agent put it, "it's a piece of cake to deal drugs."[88]

The draconian laws could not defeat the force of simple geography that inclined Malaysia toward a key role in the global heroin trade. On January 11, 1975, the arrival of Sabena flight 286 at Vienna's Schwechat Airport announced Malaysia's new importance. Among the passengers were seventeen Malaysian Chinese carrying a total of 31.6 kilograms of no. 3 heroin. Between 1972 and 1975, European seizures of Southeast Asian no. 3 jumped from 10 kilograms to 100, much of it from Malaysia.[89] Lying just to the south of Burma and Thailand, the northern states of Malaysia are home to large Chinese communities with a long tradition of Triad-dominated drug trafficking. As enforcement pressures mounted in both Hong Kong and Bangkok in the mid-1970s, the Chiu chau chemists opened heroin laboratories in the dense tropical forests of northern Malaysia to supply syndicate members then setting up their distribution networks in Western Europe. Slowed by the Golden Triangle's protracted drought from 1978 to 1980, Chiu chau laboratories revived production in the early 1980s for both export and local distribution.[90]

As heroin distribution spread in the early 1980s, Malaysian police reacted with an enforcement offensive. From 1981 to 1983 heroin seizures increased from 49 kilograms to 188 and the number of laboratories destroyed jumped from one to six, a high level by world standards. Because there were only 3,350 places in local treatment centers, these operations did little to reduce a Malaysian addict population estimated at

100,000 to 300,000, consuming about half the opium smuggled into the country.[91] Declaring the fight against narcotics to be "a national security concern," Malaysian Prime Minister Mahathir amended the Dangerous Drugs Act in 1983 to provide the death penalty for heroin possession in excess of 15 grams. By 1989 his government had hanged 68 offenders under the new law and had 179 convicted traffickers on death row. Although arrests, seizures, and executions rose steadily through the 1980s, the repression, perhaps the world's most severe, did little to change the dictates of geography. In a 1990 report, the U.S. State Department concluded, "It is unlikely that opiate supplies to and through Malaysia can be decreased. Therefore, any reduction in heroin processing . . . seems unlikely."[92]

Singapore antinarcotics laws were revised in an equally draconian manner. In December 1975 Singapore President Lee Kwan Yew signed a law that carried a mandatory death penalty for possession of more than 30 grams of narcotics. Like their Malaysian colleagues, Singapore police were empowered to use existing antisubversive laws from the emergency period to detain any suspected narcotics violator for an initial two-year period without trial, renewable indefinitely with the approval of the minister of home affairs.[93]

While Singapore's revised antinarcotics law discouraged syndicates from using its port for international narcotics smuggling, it had less success in restraining domestic drug abuse. Between 1974 and 1975 arrests for drug offenses increased more than twentyfold. Of those arrested, 88 percent were under thirty and statistics from the government's drug rehabilitation center showed that 80 percent of discharged patients returned to drugs after their release. By mid-1977 it was estimated that there were as many as 20,000 heroin addicts in Singapore, equivalent to about 0.5 to 1 percent of its 2.3 million population.[94]

Located farther down the Malay Peninsula from the Golden Triangle, Singapore did not suffer from the relentless pressure of local heroin processing and could apply repressive laws in its narrow city-state confines with much effect. Combining severe penalties with mandatory rehabilitation, Singapore police attacked the drug problem with enthusiasm, reducing the number of addicts from 13,000 in 1976 to only 9,000 in 1989.[95]

## Thailand's Transformation

At 7:00 P.M. on March 23, 1975, a middle-aged Chinese real estate developer, Sukree Sukreepirom, emerged from a high-rent apartment above the Warner Theater on Pechaburi Road in downtown Bangkok. He hesitated and then mingled briefly with the crowd leaving a late afternoon screening of *The Big Game*. Confident that he was not being watched, Sukree descended into the underground garage. Just as he reached forward to put a key into the lock of a late-model sedan, he was surrounded by a swarm of Thai police and U.S. narcotics agents. After a search turned up 25 kilograms of the famous Golden Dragon Pearl brand of no. 3 heroin, Thai police brought Sukree to headquarters for interrogation. To prevent his wife from being indicted as an accomplice, he signed a full confession.[96] Simultaneously, Thai police were raiding a hotel in a less fashionable Bangkok district where they arrested a Chinese businessman from Malaysia, Hoi Se-wan, and impounded his suitcase containing several hundred thousand dollars in Thai currency.[97]

The head of Thailand's Narcotics Suppression Center immediately called a press conference to announce the arrest of "top international drug traffickers."[98] U.S. President Gerald Ford sent the American agents letters of commendation.[99] The U.S. Drug Enforcement Administration hailed the arrests as the culmination of two years of undercover work and charged that the two Chinese had "controlled a trans-continental heroin pipeline for more than two decades."[100] These reports were not exaggerated. Confidential police files from Hong Kong, Malaysia, and the Philippines revealed that the pair were longtime partners in the overseas Chinese syndicates that dominated Southeast Asia's heroin traffic. For years Sukree and Hoi had purchased morphine in the mountains of the Golden Triangle, financed laboratories that transformed the raw morphine into heroin, and exported the granular no. 3 and powdery no. 4 to customers in Hong Kong, Manila, Amsterdam, and the United States. According to Hong Kong police, Sukree had sent more than $2 million worth of narcotics to his local Chinese syndicate contact in less than three years.[101]

Three months after the arrests, Thai police presented detailed evidence to the Department of Public Prosecutions, but the prosecutor decided not to file charges on obscure and, as it turned out, controversial procedural grounds. And on June 20, only eighty-four days after his arrest, Sukree simply walked out of prison a free man.[102]

Described in the Bangkok press as "astonished" and "outraged," ranking Thai police fired off a letter of protest to the prime minister demanding a full investigation of the Prosecutions Department.[103] As the inquiry narrowed in on the director general of public prosecutions, Aroon Israbhakdi, a Thai police general made confidential revelations to the press that the prosecutor had received $250,000 for his "sympathetic moral judgment" in the Sukree case.[104] Despite his explanation that police had used torture to extract a confession from the innocent Sukree, Aroon was found guilty of a "serious violation of discipline" and was fired from his post. As late as 1980 Thai police still had a warrant out for Sukree's arrest, as they did for the other six major drug dealers released by the prosecutor under similar circumstances.[105]

The Sukree case reveals a great deal about the complexities and characters that make up Thailand's heroin trade. In the last twenty years, Thailand has played a key role in the emergence of Southeast Asia as the world's largest producer of illicit narcotics and a major supplier of heroin for addicts in Europe and America. Despite an investment of millions of dollars in antinarcotics enforcement efforts by international agencies, Southeast Asia's heroin exports have continued to rise.

In an indication of growing dissatisfaction with Thailand's lack of progress, U.S. Representative James F. Sensenbrenner, Jr. of Wisconsin warned in February 1990 that Thailand risked becoming "stigmatized" like Columbia as a major processing center for its region's narcotics traffic. Reacting to similar reports of systematic Thai corruption, an American grand jury indicted Major General Vech Pechborom in July 1989 on charges that he allowed heroin to move through Bangkok's Don Muang Airport en route to the United States. Although Thai authorities cooperated in this case, reports of organized police corruption remain.[106]

As these complaints about Thailand's ineffective enforcement efforts indicate, Thai police have yet to achieve the high standards of professional integrity that characterize their Malaysian and Singapore counterparts. Although the cabinet-level corruption of decades past diminished during the 1980s, the trafficking syndicates simply shifted their payments downward in the police-military hierarchy to the operational level. Low pay and a long tradition of direct involvement in the narcotics trade made many Thai police willing partners in the heroin traffic. Driven from Indochina by the Communist victories in 1975 and harassed by vigorous law enforcement campaigns in Hong Kong, Manila, Singapore, and Malaysia, the Chiu chau consortium retreated into the refuge that Thailand provided. Those Thai police who made an effort to curb the traffic were hampered by narcotics laws requiring that a suspect be caught in actual physical possession of drugs. Lacking any legal equivalent to the Hong Kong conspiracy laws or Singapore's antisubversive regulations, Thai police found it impossible to charge Bangkok's fifteen or so major narcotics brokers who scrupulously insulated themselves from direct contact with the traffic.[107] DEA's regional headquarters in Bangkok maintained encyclopedic files on all of the major Thai syndicates but could do little more than send off detailed reports to its Washington headquarters. Only rarely could DEA manipulate a major dealer into handling narcotics personally, and the most important of these, Sukree, was released less than three months after his arrest.

Even with a staff of twenty agents and a narcotics assistance budget of $6 million a year, the DEA's operations were still heavily dependent on the cooperation of Thai police during the 1970s.[108] Although Thailand's addict population had grown from 71,000 opium smokers in 1959 to an estimated 300,000 to 500,000 heroin addicts in 1976,[109] five times the per capita rate in the United States for the same period, most Thai police still regarded narcotics as a "foreign problem."[110] "Thai police are so corrupt it turns my stomach," said one Bangkok-based DEA agent in a 1975 interview. "The border patrol police take payoffs for letting the opium come across the Burmese border, and the provincial police have the system to transport the narcotics themselves from northern Thailand to Bangkok. There are a few honest ones we can trust, but almost all the rest are in it for the money."[111]

Rather than grappling with the systematic corruption in the Thai police bureaucracy, the DEA encouraged the establishment of autonomous antinarcotics agencies within the Thai police. To mount any sizable antinarcotics operations, the DEA had to coordinate with Thai police and was forced, in effect, to outbid the traffickers for their services. While the syndicates could offer money, DEA rewarded its cooperative counterparts with cash bonuses for seizures, free trips to the FBI Academy in Washington, and new military hardware for their units. Adjusting to this barter arrangement was difficult for idealistic young DEA agents who were serious about antinarcotics work when they arrived in the mid-1970s. "At first I found it difficult to deal with a Thai colonel who was as corrupt as the day is long," recalled one DEA agent. "But one morning I woke up and found I could deal with it. I got as smart as they were and instead of telling the police when I was going to make a bust, I put them in the car, drove around in circles, and then slammed on the brakes in front of the house where the violator was hiding. And the Thai police knew if they didn't go in the house to make the arrest, they didn't get the new jeep or M16 rifles coming in on the boat." In late 1975, however, the DEA shifted its emphasis from seizures to strategic intelligence in northern Thailand, and its interests in Thai police operations declined. As U.S. funding and incentives decreased, Thai police returned to the narcotics syndicates for sustenance.[112]

While the DEA concentrated on interdiction and seizures, the United Nations Fund for Drug Abuse Control (UNFDAC) began a long-term crop substitution program among the opium-growing tribes of northern Thailand. While seizures may have temporarily disrupted the narcotics traffic, the only effective long-term solution, argued U.N. officials, was the substitution of other cash crops for opium in the hills of Burma and northern Thailand.[113]

Exuding an effervescent confidence, the founding U.N. program director, I. M. G. Williams, a former British colonial officer, told the press in 1975 that the program's initial five-year experimental phase had already discovered promising substitutes for opium production such as growing fruit, coffee beans, kidney beans, and flower seeds, and developing sericulture.[114] To disseminate the new commodities, the U.N. program had set up a training center in the mountains north of Chiangmai and had given instructions in new techniques such as terracing and irrigation to hill tribe opium farmers from five "key" and twenty-five "satellite" villages.[115]

Not all observers shared the optimism of the U.N. personnel, and it appeared that crop substitution began to encounter obstacles as it moved from the experimental stage to widespread implementation. While opium could be marketed profitably by footpath because of its unequaled value per kilogram, substitute crops required a costly feeder road network to reach lowland markets from the rugged highlands. The government had not yet finished paving major interprovincial highways and did not have the resources to construct such a network.[116]

Since almost one-half of the program's budget in the mid-1970s was used to maintain Thai and foreign administrators in Bangkok and much of their time was allocated to the entertainment of international dignitaries and the press, it was clear that the impact of the program was, to a certain extent, cosmetic and its rationale, from the Thai government's perspective, was to mute international criticism of the narcotics industry.[117]

Over the next ten years, the crop substitution program overcame many of these obstacles and contributed to a reduction of Thailand's poppy cultivation. But the nearby Shan Plateau remained the world's major producer with a capacity for increased production that could easily fill the void. Under the combined impact of crop substitution and ecological degradation, Thailand's production dropped from some 165 tons in 1971 to 35 tons in 1987. Simultaneously, however, Burma's harvest jumped from 500 to 1,100 tons, more than compensating for Thailand's loss.[118]

Thai police corruption and the technical failings of the U.N. crop program were not the main reasons why Bangkok continued to serve as the region's main heroin entrepôt. Simply put, the transit traffic through Thailand continued because it met the strategic and financial needs of the nation's military leaders. Instead of a conventional defense posture of regiments lining an armed frontier, the Thai military was using a traditional form of Southeast Asian statecraft to defend its northern border. Through alliances with Burma's ethnic insurgents, the Thai military fostered a situation of controlled chaos along the mountains that marked the common frontier. "We are like a 'foreign legion' for the

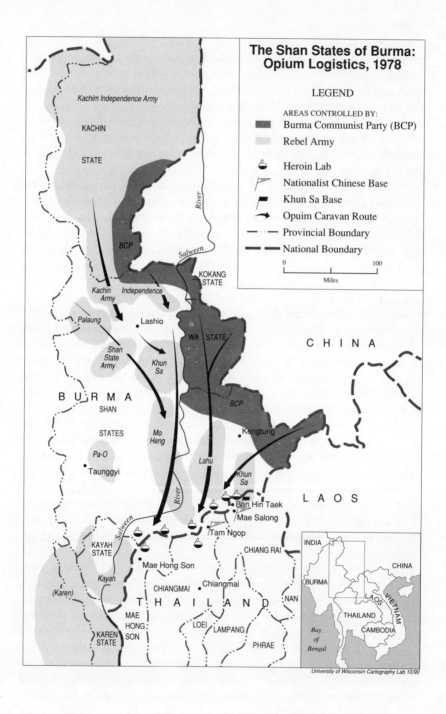

# The Shan States of Burma: Opium Logistics, 1978

## LEGEND

AREAS CONTROLLED BY:

- Burma Communist Party (BCP)
- Rebel Army

- Heroin Lab
- Nationalist Chinese Base
- Khun Sa Base
- Opuim Caravan Route
- Provincial Boundary
- National Boundary

0           100

Miles

Kachim Independence Army

KACHIN

STATE

River

Salween

BCP

KOKANG STATE

Kachin Independence Army

Palaung

Lashio

WA STATE

CHINA

BURMA

SHAN

Shan State Army

Khun Sa

BCP

STATES

Mo Heng

Kengtung

Pa-O

Taunggyi

Lahu

Khun Sa

Salween River

Ban Hin Taek

LAOS

Mae Salong

Tam Ngop

KAYAH STATE

CHIANG RAI

INDIA

CHINA

Mae Hong Son

Kayah

CHIANGMAI

Chiangmai

NAN

BURMA

LAOS

VIETNAM

THAILAND

MAE HONG SON

LOEI

LAMPANG

THAILAND

CAMBODIA

KAREN STATE

PHRAE

Bay of Bengal

University of Wisconsin Cartography Lab 10/90

Thai armed forces," remarked the Karen rebel leader General Bo Mya. "We guard the border and prevent links between the Burmese and Thai Communists."[119] For nearly forty years the Thai military provided sanctuary, arms, and an opium market for the many mini-armies it supported. Usually located in the mountains north of Chiangmai, the guerrilla camps were tightly controlled by the Thai military and housed the logistics of the Golden Triangle heroin trade—troops, mule caravans, and heroin refineries.

Following the rhythm of the annual opium harvest, guerrilla opium caravans moved south out of the Shan hills to their camps along the northern Thai border, where they sold the raw opium for cash to buy arms, ammunition, and trade goods. While the Shan opium armies blossomed and withered in their ceaseless struggle for control over the poppy fields, the Thai military stood ready to collect a regular, if informal, tax from caravans crossing its frontier. For several decades, the dominant Thai military faction expropriated a major share of the Golden Triangle's opium profits and used it for both personal consumption and clandestine political funding.

After the 1947 coup that ousted a civilian cabinet, the military ruled Thailand for a quarter century. Unchallenged by an effective civilian opposition, rival Thai military factions had relied on extensive economic activities to fund the coups and countercoups that marked their internal struggle for power. During its decade of dominion in the 1950s, the ruling clique, led by Field Marshal Phin Choonhawan and his son-in-law General Phao Siyanan, fused modern and traditional economic activities in its financial apparatus. Using the regulatory power of the state, General Phao's followers forced their way onto the boards of large companies, acquiring a significant share of the modern corporate sector. Simultaneously, his police controlled the northern borderlands and their opium trade, thereby providing an important source of extra-legal operating funds.

When Marshal Sarit Thanarat toppled the Phao-Phin faction in 1957, his army allies apparently tried to expropriate the full range of the outgoing faction's financial apparatus. Over the next fifteen years, however, Sarit and his successors proved far more skilled as opium overlords than as corporate managers. Within the faction, General Thanom Kittikhachon, later to become prime minister, proved a lackluster corporate liaison, but his longtime ally General Praphat Charusathien became an adept manager of an illicit economy that ranged from opium to arms trading.[120] From 1963 to 1973 political power was divided among Prime Minister Thanom; his minister of interior, army commander, and master of political intrigues, General Praphat; and Colonel Narong Kittikhachon, Thanom's son and Praphat's son-in-law. Following the triumvirate's forced resignation and flight into exile in October 1973, the Thai press charged that Narong had controlled a national drug trafficking network in partnership with his father-in-law, Praphat.[121] Operational control of the northern border-lands lay with Praphat's protégé General Kriangsak Chamanan, who linked the opium armies of Burma with the factional finances of the Thai military.[122]

The sudden collapse of Thailand's military dictatorship in the "democratic revolution" of October 1973 brought speculation that new civilian governments might be able to restrain military involvement in the narcotics trade. During the three years of nominal democratic rule from October 1973 to October 1976, the various civilian cabinets lacked the strength to attack what one correspondent called Thailand's "notoriously corrupt government service."[123] As left and right became locked in a protracted political confrontation, the Thai military again maneuvered for control in the midst of political instability. As right-wing vigilante groups and the border patrol police gunned down hundreds of student demonstrators in October 1976, General Praphat's military protégés launched a successful coup under General Kriangsak.[124]

Rather than installing another military government, the ruling factions chose an obscure judge, Thanin Kraiwichien, as prime minister. A moralistic conservative, Thanin soon announced that two of the prime aims of his administration would be to end official corruption and to root out the drug traffic. Unlike other Thai leaders, Thanin was evidently serious about the antinarcotics drive. His Board of Anti-Corruption Practice collected evidence against some 3,000 officials, he ordered the execution of several convicted drug smugglers under Article 21 of the new constitution, and, at a public ceremony for the diplomatic corps and the media, he personally set fire to one ton of confiscated narcotics.[125] During his year in office, Thanin's police seized 660 kilograms of heroin and 300 kilograms of morphine, substantial seizures by the standards of earlier military regimes. Most important, Thanin, drawing on legal expertise, drafted a rigorous conspiracy law with the potential of bringing indictments against the military factions that controlled the opium trade.[126]

While Prime Minister Thanin's antinarcotics efforts were rewarded with a personal letter of commendation from U.S. President Jimmy Carter, they arroused opposition from what one correspondent called "elements within the military who had profited from drug smuggling."[127] There is virtual unanimity among academic and journalistic observers that the primary source of Thanin's unpopularity with the military was his anticorruption drive, most particularly his narcotics suppression campaign.

In October 1977, after little more than a year in office, Thanin was overthrown by a military coup. Two weeks later General Kriangsak Chamanan, supreme commander of the armed forces, assumed office as prime minister, and it soon became apparent that Thanin's antinarcotics campaign was to be abandoned.[128] Given Kriangsak's personal history of involvement with the opium trade, the change in policy was not surprising. *The Washington Post* reported that Kriangsak was "long alleged to be linked to the narcotics trade." Shortly after the October 1977 coup a former Thai prime minister told the newspaper that "General Kriangsak Chamanan was a major beneficiary of the heroin/opium traffic from the Golden Triangle. . . . General Kriangsak supplied the Burmese rebels and KMT remnants in northern Thailand with arms and money in return for their opium/heroin."[129]

Prior to his appointment as deputy chief of staff of the Thai armed forces in 1973, General Kriangsak's official position for ten years had been liaison officer between the Thai supreme command and the various opium armies, particularly the Nationalist Chinese (KMT), which occupied camps along the northern border.[130] During World War II, the general acquired his knowledge of the Golden Triangle when he served as a company commander in the Thai forces that occupied the Shan states. Indeed, soon after the coup the respected business journal *Far Eastern Economic Review* described General Kriangsak as an officer best known for "his long years as the military's liaison officer with the opium-peddling Kuomintang on the Thai-Burma border."[131] In this capacity Kriangsak had arranged the burning of the KMT's "last 26 tons of opium" in 1972 for the U.S. government at a well-publicized public ceremony. He also worked to propagate the fiction that the KMT's commander General Li Wen-huan had "retired" from the opium trade and was now a jade merchant.

The transformation of General Li was accomplished at a media spectacle staged by the DEA on behalf of the CIA, which provided the funds. Parading before U.S. television cameras in March 1972, General Li's KMT troops delivered a hundred mules laden with "opium" and publicly renounced the drug trade. After the opium packs were unloaded and soaked with gasoline, the Thai military lit a bonfire that consumed the 26 tons of opium. With covert funding from the CIA, the Thai military then paid the KMT general $1,850,000 for his last opium shipment.[132] In Washington, the State Department proclaimed that "this quantity of opium if refined into heroin could have supplied one-half the U.S. market for one year." As it turned out, the opium pyre was neither the KMT's last shipment nor entirely opium at all. Four months later, Washington columnist Jack Anderson reported that only 5 tons had been opium and the balance of 21 tons was "fodder, other plant matter, chemicals."[133]

Unperturbed by the exposé, the Thai military maintained the fiction that General Li's troops had now retired from the opium trade and baptized them the "Chinese Irregular Force." The last gesture was an attempt by all parties to powder over the uncomfortable blemish of General Li's direct contact with Nationalist military intelligence on Taiwan and his longtime links to the CIA. Both Thai and American narcotics agents, however, had reliable reports that General Li was still integrally involved in Taiwan's intelligence activities on the China-Burma border. Some DEA agents had reason to suspect that KMT intelligence assisted General Li in managing the complex financial aspects of his vast opium trade.[134]

For several years following this ceremony, General Kriangsak became Li's leading public apologist and arranged interviews between the retired Chinese general and visiting reporters or congressional delegations. In 1975, for example, U.S. Representative Lester Wolff had a remarkable interview with the two men, which he described two years later in the course of taking testimony from the House Narcotics Committee's senior counsel, Joseph Nellis:

MR. WOLFF: I recall meeting General Kriangsak in the headquarters outside General Li's compound. He brought General Li to our meeting place. In my presence, he asked General Li, "Are you still in the opium business?" General Li, after translation, said no. Kriangsak took his revolver out of his belt and put it up to him and said, "If you ever get back into business, I will kill you myself."

MR. NELLIS: He [Kriangsak] hasn't done it yet.

MR. WOLFF: . . . Do we have any information at all as to General Li's complicity with the KMT?

MR. NELLIS: I am told on very good authority, and I believe, that General Li is active, if not more so than ever.[135]

Several months before his inauguration as prime minister in 1977, General Kriangsak had made a public address to Bangkok's Joint Chamber of Commerce advocating a weakening of Thanin's antinarcotics campaign. He stated that "there appears to be a conflict between our campaign against narcotics and our campaign against the Communists" and challenged the United States to seek a unilateral solution to its own narcotics problem.[136] Less than six months after General Kriangsak took office, a Bangkok correspondent reported that his administration had abandoned Thanin's campaign to eliminate the narcotics traffic.[137] Indeed, Kriangsak used his office to attack the United States for presuming to press for a crackdown on heroin: "Those who criticize Thailand for corruption among officials concerned with drug enforcement should also look into the corruption in other official circles which has made it possible for the narcotics trade to flourish in many countries."[138]

In the end, however, Kriangsak's attempt to restore military rule collapsed. Although he applied the same mix of modern and traditional economic measures that had controlled politics in the past, Thai society was undergoing an economic transformation that made authoritarian controls untenable. After Kriangsak stumbled through a succession of crises and finally resigned in 1980, the country's leading political parties formed a new coalition cabinet. Unwilling to offend the military, party leaders picked General Prem Tinsulanan, an army commander sympathetic to constitutional democracy, as the new prime minister. Unlike the other military leaders who had ruled Thailand since 1947, Prem showed no aspirations to wealth and, most important, had no prior connections to the northern borderlands or their opium trade. As Thailand's economy took off and annual growth continued at 10 percent throughout the 1980s, an unprecedented prosperity lent credibility to democracy, undercutting military pressure for a return to dictatorship.

From the moment he took power in 1980, General Prem began planning for a major military operation against the most powerful of the Shan state warlords, Khun Sa. Since the early 1970s Khun Sa's Shan United Army (SUA) had maintained a permanent headquarters for its opium caravans at the village of Ban Hin Taek, just a few miles from the main KMT base at Mae Salong. As his troops took control of nearly half the Shan state opium harvest in the late 1970s, Khun Sa began appearing in the international press as an aspiring nationalist leader, openly discussing his opium caravans as evidence of his power.[139]

While his drug trading had not concerned the Kriangsak government, Khun Sa's increasingly frank statements to the U.S. Congress and the Thai press about the traffic became an embarrassment that the prime minister, personally vulnerable on the narcotics issue, could ill afford. In a June 1977 interview with the *Bangkok World*, Khun Sa described himself as "King of the Golden Triangle" and reflected on the consequences of his business: "I know it is a social evil and understand the damage it does, not only in the West, but among my own people. But I don't feel guilty. What we are doing is justified."[140]

Apparently trying to legitimize his role as a Shan political leader, Khun Sa began granting interviews to U.S. congressional representatives and Thai media at his base inside Thailand. His media campaign culminated in an interview published on page 1 of the *Bangkok Post* on February 15, 1978, with the banner headline I CAN STOP THE DRUG FLOW. Two days later Prime Minister Kriangsak announced: "We will not allow Khun Sa to remain and operate in Thailand. Even his family will not be allowed to stay here, because they can provide him with a base for his illegal operations."[141] Despite some serious reservations among senior Thai army officers that Khun Sa's expulsion might weaken security on the northern border, his indiscretion left the Thai government little choice and in May he voluntarily moved 16 kilometers across the border into Burma. The expulsion order was not applied to the KMT's General Li, another close friend of the prime minister.[142] Within a few months, Khun Sa crossed the border into Thailand and moved back to his old headquarters at Ban Hin Taek, where he remained without opposition from Thai authorities.

In July 1980, after only four months in office, Prime Minister Prem ordered the Thai air force to bomb Khun Sa's base. Although the aircraft destroyed three chemical storage units for his heroin laboratories, Khun Sa remained defiant at Ban Hin Taek. When the Thai government next offered a reward of $21,700 for the capture of Khun Sa, dead or alive, he responded with a counteroffer of $500 rewards for information about the identity of American and Thai drug agents operating in his area.

These developments, combined with the persistent allegations against General Kriangsak, began to change the tolerant Thai attitudes that had allowed the transit traffic to flourish in decades past. During the August 1981 parliamentary elections, the Bangkok press reported that the two KMT armies had contributed $100,000 to General Kriangsak's campaign for a seat in parliament, a sum equivalent to about 15 percent of the $631,000 he spent in the campaign. The general saw nothing wrong in taking a campaign contribution from the country's leading heroin traffickers and denied any direct involvement in the drug trade. In a display of media bravado, he told reporters that if anyone had evidence that he had sold even one gram of drugs, "you can take me to the execution stand right now." Supported by these record campaign funds, General Kriangsak survived the scandal and won the seat in parliament. In the midst of the controversy, the KMT commander at Mae Salong, Lei Yu-tien, told reporters that his predecessor, the recently deceased General Tuan Shi-wen, had been Kriangsak's partner in a local "tea plantation" and in gratitude for the Thai general's kindness the KMT had built him a vacation villa in their caravan camp near the Burma border.[143]

Finally, in January 1982, the elite Thai Rangers led by General Chawalit Yongjaiyut launched a full military assault on Ban Hin Taek. Backed by aircraft and helicopter gunships, eight companies of Thai troops stormed the village and met stiff resistance. Over the next two weeks the Thai troops engaged in a protracted firefight with Khun Sa's Shan United Army that left 17 soldiers and 130 rebels dead. In mopping up, the Thai military seized 200 radio sets, 300 hand grenades and 50,000 rounds of ammunition. A survey of the site found a hundred-bed hospital, a brothel, "luxurious Chinese-style villas" with swimming pools, a vacation house for Khun Sa's "cousin in parliament" General Kriangsak, and seven heroin refineries. Despite the heavy casualties, Khun Sa's forces retreated across the border, where he quickly reestablished the heroin refineries that allowed him to control 70 percent of Burma's opium trade.[144]

Instead of letting Khun Sa slip back into Thailand as he had done in 1978, Prime Minister Prem maintained constant military pressure on the Shan United Army and began forcing other rebel groups back into Burma. In the aftermath of the assault, the press reported that the border patrol police had maintained an outpost only a mile from Khun Sa's camp for the past four years but had never disturbed the nearby heroin refineries. When several Bangkok newspapers pointed to Kriangsak as the responsible prime minister during this studied inattention to the world's largest heroin complex, General Kriangsak, now in parliament, denied any relationship with Khun Sa and threatened to sue.[145]

Despite the denial, Kriangsak's reputation had suffered and his influence in parliament waned. Three years later, in a final bid for power, Kriangsak joined two other retired generals—partners in his former ruling military triumvirate—and participated in a desperate coup with only 500 men and a tank division. With little difficulty, Prime Minister Prem crushed the uprising, as he had an earlier attempt, and then filed sedition charges against Kriangsak.[146] In 1988 Prem stepped aside in favor of Chatchai Choonhawan, Thailand's first elected prime minister since 1976, when the army seized power in a coup. Although the new prime minister is a retired army general and son of Marshal Phin Choonhawan, leader of the 1947 coup, his rise represents the triumph of business groups, not the military. After losing power in 1957, he and other military entrepreneurs used the contacts and capital acquired during a decade of power to become major businessmen. Although there was strong evidence that Kriangsak's political aspirations were financed by the opium trade, he now seemed weak compared with the new business politicians like Chatchai who could call on major Bangkok banks for their campaign funds. Opium money still flowed into Thai politics, but it now seemed far less important than the legitimate corporate contributions that surged during the long Thai economic boom of the 1980s.

These political changes were soon reflected in the operations of the Thai drug trade. Three years after Prem took office in 1980, the U.S. State Department reported that "some trafficking patterns are shifting to avoid Thai territory" and that the rebels had "moved their refineries

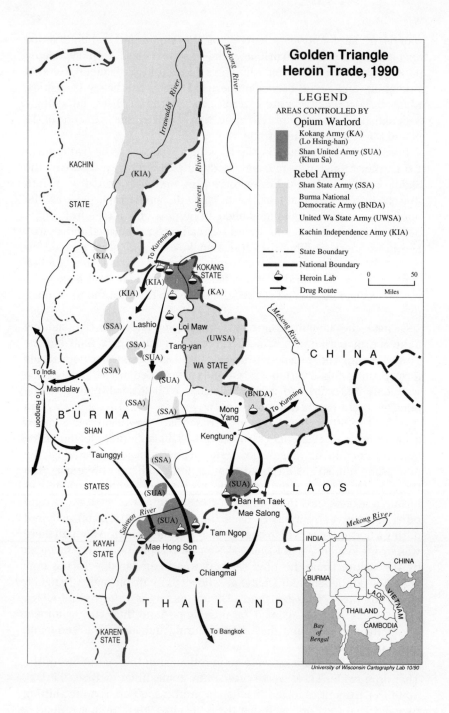

**Golden Triangle
Heroin Trade, 1990**

LEGEND

AREAS CONTROLLED BY

Opium Warlord

Kokang Army (KA)
(Lo Hsing-han)

Shan United Army (SUA)
(Khun Sa)

Rebel Army

Shan State Army (SSA)

Burma National
Democratic Army (BNDA)

United Wa State Army (UWSA)

Kachin Independence Army (KIA)

— · — · —  State Boundary

— — —  National Boundary

⚖  Heroin Lab

➜  Drug Route

0            50

Miles

KACHIN

STATE

(KIA)

(KIA)

(KIA)

To Kunming

KOKANG
STATE

(KIA)

(KIA)

(KA)

CHINA

(SSA)    Lashio

Loi Maw

(UWSA)

(SSA)    Tang-yan

(SUA)

WA STATE

To India

(SUA)

(SSA)

Mandalay

(BNDA)

(SSA)

(SSA)

Mong
Yang

To Kunming

To Rangoon

BURMA

SHAN

Kengtung

Taunggyi

(SSA)

LAOS

STATES

(SUA)

(SUA)

Ban Hin Taek

Mae Salong

(SUA)

Tam Ngop

KAYAH
STATE

(SUA)

Mae Hong Son

Chiangmai

THAILAND

KAREN
STATE

To Bangkok

Mekong River

INDIA

CHINA

BURMA

LAOS

VIETNAM

THAILAND

CAMBODIA

Bay
of
Bengal

*Irrawaddy River*

*Salween River*

*Mekong River*

*Salween River*

University of Wisconsin Cartography Lab 10/90

deeper into Burma" to avoid Thai military operations along the border. The increased pressure was reflected in Thailand's heroin seizures, which rose from 323 kilograms in 1981 to 2,400 seven years later. By 1989 the official alliance between the Thai supreme command and the opium armies seemed severed, and the transit traffic through Thailand relied more on venal middle-ranking military officials than on the cabinet-level corruption of the past. Indeed, the U.S. State Department reported that Thai military and police officials were "profiting individually from drug trafficking" with the Sino-Thai financiers who "play a leading role in narcotics trafficking within Thailand."[147]

Aside from any personal interest General Kriangsak or his military mentors may have had in the narcotics traffic, the primary rationale for aiding the opium warlords had been their role in securing the troubled Burma-Thailand frontier.[148] The transformation of Thai politics during the 1980s changed the country's relations with its troubled frontier. Instead of the traditional Southeast Asian statecraft of client warfare along the frontier, Bankok began to establish trade relations with its neighbors. As Prime Minister Chatchai put it in 1988, Thailand would change the region "from a battleground into a trading market."[149] Accordingly, in February 1990, Bangkok officially severed its ties to the opium armies and concluded an extraordinary trade agreement with Rangoon. After decades of hostility, Burma granted Thai timber corporations a chain of lumber concessions that arched from Three Pagodas Pass to Tachilek along the 500-mile frontier where the insurgents have long been active.[150] After the dismal U.S. drug suppression failure of the 1970s and the opium boom that followed in the 1980s, there was now a chance, albeit slender, that Burmese-Thai cooperation might succeed in reducing Shan state opium production during the 1990s.

## Opium and Politics in the Golden Triangle

Despite a massive international assault on the Golden Triangle's heroin trade throughout the 1970s and the severe drought of 1978–1980, the region's illicit traffic emerged from the decade more prosperous than ever. Given the limited success of the antinarcotics programs, it is hardly surprising that the critical elements of the Golden Triangle opium trade were not disturbed. Although both the Thai and Burmese governments accelerated their military operations along the border, the annual opium caravans plodded south across the Shan Plateau into Thailand with regularity. The heroin laboratories dotting the mountains of the Thailand-Burma borderlands still managed to operate without serious interference. Rather than reducing the amount of drugs flowing out of the Golden Triangle, attempts at suppression simply forced a concentration of the traffic into the hands of a warlord powerful enough to overcome these new barriers. As the KMT weakened, the Shan rebels splintered, and the Communist party of Burma collapsed, one warlord emerged as the preeminent force on the Shan Plateau—Khun Sa.

This consolidation came after decades of chronic political instability within the Shan states. Isolated on their remote plateau and denied outside support, the Shan separatist rebels, led by their traditional princely elite, turned to the opium trade to buy arms when they launched their revolt in 1959. As the caravans moved south with opium and returned north laden with guns after each annual harvest, this opium-arms cycle produced a ceaseless formation and fragmentation of new rebel fronts, armies, and coalitions. Over time, the intermingling of opium, weapons, and politics destabilized the Shan nationalist movement by splitting successive rebel alliances from within. The quick opium profits needed for weapons on the Bangkok black market required that the rebels expropriate Shan peasant opium at low prices—a simple act of exploitation that made them appear more bandit than nationalist and denied them strong popular support. The instant wealth that came when the rebel caravans crossed the Thai border often produced infighting between rival commanders, phrased in a political rhetoric that often masked a personal struggle over opium profits. Moreover, the opium encouraged fighting by allowing small guerrilla bands to grow rapidly through the opium-arms cycle—more opium paid for the purchase of more guns, which in turn allowed control of more opium territory. Thus, the opium trade that nurtured the growth of rebel armies ultimately consumed them in internecine struggles over profits and in battles with rival armies for territory. In the midst of such inherent instability, political movements like the Shan State Army fragmented and dissolved, while the pure opium warlords like Khun Sa had the strength and ruthlessness to expand.

Although these changes in the 1980s were indeed dramatic, they built on trends that were already evident in the previous decade. By the 1970s, the smaller Shan opium armies were in decline and the KMT was starting to lose ground to the warlord Khun Sa. Released from captivity in 1974, Khun Sa quickly recovered his old territory on the central Shan Plateau and seemed primed to take full control of the entire Shan opium trade. But the sudden rise of the Burmese Communist party (BCP) as lords of the prime opium country along the China-Burma border blocked Khun Sa's control. The sudden and unexpected appearance of BCP guerrilla units in the borderlands after 1970 had unleashed a complex chain of events that, by the end of the decade, produced some dramatic realignments in the region's opium politics.

Based in the Irrawaddy River delta and the Pegu Hills to the north of

Rangoon during the 1950s and 1960s, the Burmese Communist party was forced to abandon its central Burma base area in 1970 when Burma army pacification operations weakened the party's hold on the area. After a long march into southern China where its remnants were rearmed by a Peking government overtly hostile to Burma's president, General Ne Win, the BCP managed to establish new bases in mountain areas adjacent to the Chinese border in March 1970. By 1972 the BCP had consolidated its hold over the borderlands and began a recurring pattern of dual-thrust offensives—probing west across the Salween River toward central Burma and driving south into Kengtung state toward the northern Thai border. Despite a number of military reverses in their early campaigns, the BCP was reported to have mustered some 15,000 troops in the Shan states by 1975, the largest force in the area with the exception of the Burmese army's 30,000. Strengthened by its alliances with various Shan nationalist armies, the BCP advanced steadily and by 1978 controlled all territory between the Salween River and the China border, with the exception of a southern portion of Kengtung state adjacent to Thailand—success that both the Burmese and Thai governments found threatening.[151]

The rapid expansion of the BCP's strength in the Shan states between 1970 and 1978 precipitated several major shifts in the Golden Triangle's basic political alignments. Inspired by a mutual desire to restrain the BCP, the Thai and Burmese governments repaired their formerly hostile relations, epitomized by Thailand's grant of asylum to the Shan rebel armies, and began to develop an effective anti-BCP alliance along the northernmost Thailand-Burma border. The growth of the BCP's strength and the weakening of Thai support brought many of the Shan rebel armies to the point of collapse.

In this continuing history of armed battles and shifting political alliances three main protagonists were responsible for defining the Shan response to the BCP's challenge: the Shan-Chinese opium warlord Khun Sa, the Chinese warlord Lo Hsing-han, and the most political of the Shan rebel groups, the Shan State Army (SSA). The two opium warlords share common backgrounds in the Chinese trading communities of the Yunnan-Burma borderland and followed similar careers that have brought them at various times into alliance and conflict with the Burmese government, the Thai military, and the KMT. Despite their occasional espousal of the Shan nationalist ideology, the two opium warlords have remained, above all, merchants dedicated to the accumulation of opium, military power, and the enormous profit that the judicious combination of the two can yield. At the outset, the Shan nationalists thought they could control the local opium harvests as a ready weapon in their struggle for freedom. But over the next twenty years, the Golden Triangle's burgeoning opium trade gradually consumed the rebels, corrupting their movement and reducing them to simple instruments of the global heroin traffic.

Born into a Yunnanese family at Kokang state on the China border in 1934, Lo Hsing-han began his career in the 1950s as an officer for Olive Yang, a local princess then allied with the KMT. Under KMT protection, Olive soon emerged as one of the first opium warlords in the Shan states and led opium caravans guarded by a thousand troops to the Thailand border. After the military seized power at Rangoon in 1962, the Burmese army occupied Kokang state and arrested Olive, forcing her brother Jimmy Yang to flee to Thailand with the remaining troops, where he joined the KMT. By now a senior Kokang commander, Lo allied with the Burmese and became the state's new opium warlord. In exchange for supporting the Burmese army, Lo was allowed to move his opium caravans on government highways, a real competitive advantage after 1961 when the KMT were driven into Thailand.

Using his alliance with the Burmese government and his considerable skills as a merchant, Lo became one of Burma's largest opium buyers and heroin refiners.[152] In 1972 Lo gained considerable notoriety when President Richard Nixon's coordinator for international narcotics matters, Nelson Gross, anointed him "kingpin of the heroin traffic in Southeast Asia." While that title was certainly a bit of media hyperbole, Lo had in fact become the largest single opium merchant in the Shan states after his rival Khun Sa was defeated by the KMT in the 1967 Opium War. Controlling an informal empire that included more than 3,000 armed caravan guards and a complex of heroin refineries, Lo was generally considered the dominant military leader of northeastern Burma. Although he lost control of Kokang in 1968 when former comrades in Olive Yang's army crossed the border from China as the vanguard of the BCP, he retreated west to Lashio, where the Burmese allowed him to set up a new base camp. In 1971 his forces fought alongside the Burmese army in a forty-five-day battle against the BCP for control of Kunlong Bridge on the Salween River, using their superior knowledge of the terrain to ensure the army's victory. In gratitude, the Burmese army provided greater protection for Lo's opium caravans. Two years later, however, Rangoon abolished the Ka Kwe Ye (KKY), the government militia, and Lo joined a Shan nationalist coalition fighting for independence from Burma. Although Lo aspired to leadership of the Shan secessionist movement and pretended, for the benefit of the U.S. Congress, to be a Shan, at home in the city of Lashio he was very much a Yunnanese and served as a patron of the local Chinese temple.[153]

Lo's rival for the Shan states' opium harvest was the vanquished warlord of the 1967 Opium War, Khun Sa. Born to a Shan mother and a

Yunnan Chinese father at Loi Maw in the Shan states in 1933, Khun Sa was raised in a Shan aristocratic household when his mother remarried. Reflecting his mixed origins and mingled politics, he is known by two names—his Chinese birth name, Chan Shee-fu, and his Shan nom de guerre, Khun Sa, or Lord Sa.[154] At age eighteen, he joined the KMT forces then occupying the Shan states and got his training in both arms and opium in the service of this CIA-supported army. After the Burmese army drove the KMT into Thailand in 1961, Khun Sa allied with the government and used his profits to organize a KKY militia unit of some 500 men in his native Loi Maw district. Although he had become one of the region's leading opium warlords by the mid-1960s, his challenge to the KMT's dominance of the drug trade was defeated in the 1967 Opium War and his armies suffered major losses of opium, troops, and arms. Arrested in October 1969 by the Burmese army while on a visit to the city of Taunggyi, Khun Sa was placed in solitary confinement for the next five years while his army remained in control of the opium districts to the south of Lashio.[155]

The last of the three protagonists, the Shan State Army, had more ideology and less opium than either of the two warlords and was perhaps the only one of the major Shan armies with any legitimacy as a political movement. Initially founded in 1958–1959 by a number of Shan students returning from universities in Rangoon, the SSA was one of some six armed bands organized by Shan nationalists to oppose the loss of local autonomy to Rangoon and the abolition of the hereditary Shan aristocracy imposed by the central government in 1959. The other bands gradually weakened in battles with the Burmese army or were corrupted by their involvement in the opium traffic. By 1965 the SSA was the only one of the original bands that had survived but was already suffering from sharp divisions between republican and royalist factions. Funded by their opium trading, a joint venture financed by the KMT's General Li, the SSA had grown into an army of four brigades totaling some 2,700 troops armed with modern U.S. weapons purchased on the Chiangmai market.[156] As the Burmese Communist units began to advance in the early 1970s, SSA moderates began negotiations over a possible alliance and were allowed to purchase opium from villages under BCP control.[157]

By early 1973 the stage was set for a basic realignment of forces within the Shan state. While pressures for these changes had been building for several years, the immediate spark was the Burmese government's April 1973 decision to dissolve its KKY militia units. Concerned over the KKY failure to effectively stem the BCP's westward push or eliminate the Shan rebel units, the Burmese government ordered all its KKY militia units to surrender their arms. Of the twenty-three existing units, nineteen obeyed government orders and surrendered 2,086 firearms, but another four units, with some 2,000 armed men, refused. Among those who resisted was the putative "opium king" Lo Hsing-han.[158] Pressed by BCP advances on his eastern flank in Kokang state and battling with the KMT for control of the opium harvest, Lo turned to the SSA for support and opened negotiations for an alliance. Fighting the same enemies as Lo, the SSA's leaders accepted his offer of an alliance.[159]

To win a new ally in their struggle against the KMT and BCP, Lo Hsing-han and his SSA allies decided to approach the U.S. embassy in Bangkok with an offer to sell some 400 tons of Shan opium for $20 million. With the assistance of the British filmmaker Adrian Cowell, who was then in the Shan states making a documentary entitled *The Opium Warlords*, Lo Hsing-han and the leader of the SSA moderates drafted a document requesting U.S. support for the preemptive purchase of all opium controlled by rebel armies at a fixed "Thai border price." The Shans argued that preemptive purchase would result in the complete eradication of the Golden Triangle heroin trade.[160]

Before the proposals could be delivered to the U.S. embassy, where they were received with indifference, Lo was arrested in a complex series of events. The catalyst in the entire affair was the kidnapping of two Russian medical doctors from the Taunggyi hospital in the Southern Shan state by the remnants of Khun Sa's warlord army. Initially the Burmese government tried to conceal the incident, but Khun Sa's men invited a Western film crew to photograph the two doctors in their jungle prison and announced that the price of their return was the release of their leader, the imprisoned Khun Sa. Embarrassed by the publicity, the Burmese army began raiding rebel encampments throughout the Shan states in search of the doctors and in the process struck Lo Hsing-han's camp, driving him across the border into Thailand. Acting at the request of the Burmese government, the Thai police arrested Lo near Mae Hong Son on July 17, 1973 and subsequently extradited him to Rangoon where he was imprisoned.[161] Observers were surprised by the unprecedented Thai decision to arrest a major heroin dealer, but Shan rebel leaders explained it in terms of Lo's antagonism toward Bangkok's client KMT General Li and Thailand's need for a sacrificial victim to placate its American ally.[162] Instead of charging Lo with drug trafficking, Rangoon imprisoned him for "high treason" and "rebellion," an apparent slap for his dalliance with the Shan secessionists. For the next seven years, Lo remained in prison, until the general amnesty of 1980 when the Burmese government released him with funds to rebuild his opium army.[163] After Lo's capture and confinement, the SSA split several times, and the major faction joined the BCP near the border.

Less than a year after the Burmese government had eliminated one major opium warlord, it was forced to release the other. Failing to capture the two Russian doctors after months of operations, the Burmese government returned Khun Sa to his troops and they in turn released the doctors to the Thai military in June 1974.[164] And just as Lo Hsing-han had risen to a position as the preeminent Shan state warlord after Khun Sa's arrest in 1969, so Khun Sa himself now rose again to dominate the region's opium trade. According to submissions he made to the U.S. House of Representatives, Khun Sa claimed that during the 1976–1977 crop year his Shan United Army of 3,500 troops transported 70 tons of raw opium to refineries in the Thai border area—an amount sufficient to maintain the U.S. addict population for one year—in twelve caravans averaging 116 mules and 335 armed guards each.[165]

Like the preceding Chinese opium warlord, Lo Hsing-han, Khun Sa formed an alliance with the conservative SSA factions and proclaimed himself spokesman for the Shan nationalist cause. Under his leadership another approach was made to the United States, this time to the House Committee on International Relations, when Representative Lester L. Wolff visited Thailand in January 1975. At a meeting with Wolff in northern Thailand, representatives of the SSA and Khun Sa once again offered to arrange a preemptive purchase of the Shan opium crop. But the proposal was eventually rejected by the U.S. State Department during congressional hearings in April 1975 despite enthusiasm for it by Wolff and other congressional representatives.[166]

While Khun Sa prospered, the SSA continued its constant political infighting that would, within a decade, produce a virtual collapse. With its putative leader under arrest, its troops at war with the KMT, and its territory threatened by the predatory Khun Sa, the SSA faced an unpromising future. In late 1975 the majority of the SSA's remaining troops, some 700 men under Colonel Zam Mong, broke with the SSA's conservative royalist faction and joined the BCP, becoming one of several ethnic armies to rally to the Communist party during this period.[167] One of the secondary factions formed an alliance with General Mo Heng, long known as leader of the KMT's surrogate army, in a new coalition named the Tai-Land Revolutionary Council.[168]

In May 1976 the independent armies still operating in Burma's northeast joined an anti-Communist coalition, the National Democratic Front (NDF), comprising some thirteen separatist groups. The impetus for the coalition came from the Karen National Liberation Army and its commander General Bo Mya, a vocal anti-Communist closely linked to the Thai supreme command. A two-week-long conference that led to a proclamation of alliance by these disparate minority rebels was held at the Karen headquarters just inside the Thai border in Tak province, some 230 kilometers southwest of Chaingmai.[169] The formation of an anti-BCP coalition based in the Karen areas so distant from the strategic Shan states was eloquent testimony to the growing strength of the BCP along Thailand's northern frontier. While the surviving Shan armies polarized for a confrontation along ideological lines, the professional opium warlords, Khun Sa and the KMT's General Li, increased their shares of the Shan opium harvest.

After the KMT's eviction from Burma in 1961, General Li had been several steps removed from direct involvement in the Shan opium traffic. By the mid-1970s, however, now working from a more stable base inside Thailand, Li exercised an active control over the narcotics trade from his mansion in Chiangmai—purchasing opium directly from independent Chinese traders in the Shan hills, organizing his own caravans from scraps of bandit or rebel units, and outbidding the competition for the services of skilled chemists.[170] Sources in the Thai border patrol police reported that rather than use KMT regulars to protect his caravans, Li had tried to conceal his involvement by retaining the services of General Mo Heng's Shan United Revolutionary Army (SURA), whose troop strength had swelled from 1,000 to 4,200 in 1974–1975 to handle the new assignment. Despite his strong apparatus, General Li faced renewed competition from the warlord Khun Sa, the man he had defeated in the 1967 Opium War.

As an indication of Khun Sa's growing strength, the Thai military tried to counter the growing threat from the BCP by forging an alliance between the two warlords instead of relying solely on the KMT as it had in the past. Using the same statecraft they were applying to Communist threats in Cambodia and Laos, the Thai command later recruited the leading warlord armies to create a broad buffer zone along the northern border. In April 1977 the *Far Eastern Economic Review* reported that a "senior officer in the Thai armed forces" hosted a meeting between General Li and Khun Sa to "arrange a marketing agreement" for the division of the opium trade and promised arms for the fight against the BCP.[171] Under this agreement, Khun Sa was allowed to maintain an elaborate base inside Thailand at Ban Hin Taek north of Chiangmai, which served as his headquarters for the management of 40 percent of Burma's opium exports and the collection of $850,000 per year in transit taxes from other caravans.

Moreover, the Communist threat had already forced Bangkok to initiate a tentative rapprochement with Rangoon. After the Communist party of Thailand became active in the north during the early 1970s, the supreme command maneuvered to block any direct territorial link between the Thai and Burmese Communists. In 1973 the former Burma Prime Minister U Nhu, who had been granted political asylum in

Bangkok four year earlier, announced that he was resigning his leadership of a rebel coalition. In March Thailand's deputy premier visited Rangoon to discuss demarcation of frontiers,[172] and in May Burma's President Ne Win reciprocated with a visit to Bangkok. Over the coming months, Thailand showed its good faith by cutting aid to U Nhu's followers and extraditing the opium warlord Lo Hsing-han to Rangoon.[173]

Burma's government, increasingly threatened by its own Communist insurgency, moved toward an alliance with the United States and Thailand. Before the BCP became active in the northeast in 1970, the Burmese government had been satisfied that its KKY militia units were maintaining adequate control, generally tolerated the opium traffic, and showed little apparent concern over the Shan insurgency. Once these tactics failed to restrain the BCP advance, however, the Burmese government dissolved the KKY militia and began to pursue more orthodox strategy. Between 1974 and 1978 Rangoon accepted eighteen helicopters from the United States, nominally to assist in narcotics suppression, thereby more than doubling its fleet. And in 1976 the Burmese army began a series of major military operations aimed at eliminating the Shan guerrilla armies, which were drifting into the BCP orbit, and destroying their economic base—the Shan states opium trade.[174] Between April 1976 and April 1978 the Burmese army launched four major operations against insurgent heroin laboratories and opium caravans near the Thai border, in coordination with the Thai military, which netted impressive quantities of raw materials such as morphine base, acetic anhydride, and ether.

Failing, however, to eliminate either laboratories or caravans, Burmese army units began flying about the northeast in their new helicopters to burn and uproot the village poppy fields. The Burmese government and the U.S. State Department claimed a significant reduction of poppy acreage under cultivation, but these estimates must, on several grounds, be regarded as inflated. One basic problem was that the BCP controlled approximately one-third of the opium-growing region. Although the BCP was not believed to be directly involved in the traffic, it still allowed private traders to deal with opium growing villages under its control.[175]

Much of the progress in the Golden Triangle was illusory, the product of two temporary droughts—in arms and in rainfall—that cut opium production sharply from 1978 to 1980. After the American withdrawal from Vietnam in the early 1970s, the massive black market trade in U.S. infantry weapons slowed, denying Shan rebels the low-cost arms that had allowed their initial expansion. Compounding the problem, the monsoon rains failed to fall on the Shan Plateau for two seasons in

1978–1980, denying the thirsty opium poppy sufficient water for good growth. Instead of the usual 600-ton opium harvest, Burma produced only 160 tons in 1978 and 240 tons in 1979.[176]

As the rains returned and the opium armies recovered from the disruption of the drought, Thailand's Prime Minister Prem routed Khun Sa from his comfortable military cantonment in January 1982, but the warlord reacted with a series of aggressive operations that consolidated his control of the Shan states within three years.

When Khun Sa fled to a mountain range just north of the Thai border in 1982, he encountered strong opposition from an alliance of Lahu ethnic rebels and the Burmese Communist Party. Starting in July, Khun Sa showed his military mettle with a series of well-coordinated offensives that smashed the Lahu rebels under charismatic leader A Pi and drove a force of 1,500 BCP regulars out of the Doi Larng area. By late 1983 Khun Sa had secured the strategic borderlands inside Burma that contained all the major caravan routes on the east bank of the Salween River.[177] Inside this rugged hill country Khun Sa established at least ten refineries staffed by Hong Kong–trained chemists and was processing about 75 percent of the Shan opium harvest into heroin.[178] The U.S. State Department reported in 1984 that "the bulk of the Burmese opium crop is grown in areas under BCP control" but that Khun Sa "controls the major transport routes to the Thai-Burma border, where SUA . . . refineries process heroin."[179]

Now secure in his new opium zone, Khun Sa began to destroy his enemies in succession, beginning with his old rival General Li Wen-huan of the KMT. By early 1984 the continued expansion of Khun Sa's Shan United Army cut General Li's caravan routes for both jade and opium, placing pressure on his finances. With Kuhn Sa's support, the Burmese army launched attacks that destroyed a complex of nine KMT heroin refineries just north of the Thai border. Compounding Li's difficulties, a thousand Thai Rangers raided several of his heroin refineries inside the Thai border, the first time that the Thai military had attacked a KMT operation since their arrival in Thailand more than twenty years before.[180]

On March 11 Khun Sa unleashed his coup de force when a truck loaded with 7,000 sticks of dynamite detonated in the driveway of General Li's Chiangmai mansion, destroying the structure and leaving a crater twenty feet wide and six feet deep. Although General Li was away in Bangkok, the explosion damaged more than twenty houses and broke most windows within a mile, shattering the myth, so carefully constructed by the CIA ten years before, of General Li's retirement from the heroin trade.[181] In early June Bangkok announced a formal crackdown on General Li's forces, in effect a formal repudiation of the sanctuary that Bangkok had given the KMT in 1961.[182] As the KMT's heroin trading continued its collapse, Khun Sa forced an alliance with General Mo Heng's Shan United Revolutionary Army, originally created by the KMT in 1968 to serve as its main operational force inside the Shan states.[183] Although these operations did not eliminate the KMT as a force in the heroin trade, they allowed Khun Sa to expropriate a substantial share.

For the next two years Khun Sa expanded his forces without serious opposition until Thai and Burmese troops launched a loosely coordinated operation against his Doi Larng borderland bastion. Within weeks of the attack in February 1987, the Thai task force had seized thirty of Khun Sa's strategic high points along a sixteen-kilometer perimeter.[184] Simultaneously, some 300 Burmese army regulars moved into blocking positions, forcing Khun Sa to evacuate his headquarters near Mae Hong Son temporarily.[185] This pressure may have led Khun Sa to disperse his vulnerable laboratories by moving some into nearby Communist Laos. Six months after the attacks, Thai intelligence sources reported that there were now seventeen heroin refineries across the Mekong River in northwestern Laos, most of them under Khun Sa's control. Although the Thai authorities claimed that the offensive was a success, Khun Sa himself laughingly dismissed the whole operation as a "newspaper war."[186]

Khun Sa's shift toward Laos coincided with a period of Communist complicity in drug trafficking. In 1974 a major Sino-Thai trafficker named Poonsiri Chanyasak had fled to Vientiane where, with tacit Communist tolerance, he opened a heroin refinery with local drug dealer Iem Norasin, known as the chief chemist at the notorious Double U-O Globe brand heroin laboratory.[187] Under the government's informal policy of drug promotion, Laotian opium production rose from 50 tons to 1983, the last year of a non-Communist government, to 375 tons six years later.[188]

As Khun Sa's control over the drug trade expanded, his opium adversaries collapsed. In 1986 Shan State Army remnants criticized Khun Sa for running an opium army, conniving with the Burmese army, and assassinating rebel leaders. Within months, however, these Shan nationalist leaders had allied with the BCP and their independent forces had declined markedly in size.[189] Although the BCP had controlled the largest opium zone in the Shan states since 1980 and had diversified into heroin refining after 1982, its military expansion was slowed by its inability to procure arms. Initially the BCP had established its bases on the Burma-China border with Beijing's support and was rewarded with liberal arms shipments. In the late 1970s, however, the BCP leadership publicly criticized China's leader Deng Hsiao Ping. As Deng's influence rose in the coming years, China's arms shipments to the BCP correspondingly declined. With fewer arms to attract other rebel groups, the BCP sought revenues from opium trafficking and taxation of the black market trade between Burma and China. In 1987 the Burmese army occupied the BCP's main trading post on the China border, eliminating half of the BCP's annual revenues and destroying much of their influence within the Shan states. Two years later a large brigade of Wa tribal warriors, the BCP's main opium trading ally, unexpectedly attacked the main Communist headquarters, sending the BCP leadership fleeing across the border into China. Within weeks the BCP disintegrated and Wa militia took control of more than 75 percent of their former territory.[190]

With his rivals now largely destroyed, Khun Sa became the first of the Golden Triangle warlords to be worthy of his media crown as "kingpin" or "king of the opium trade." In 1986 the leading Asian business journal estimated that Khun Sa's army transported and refined about 80 percent of the Golden Triangle's opium harvest.[191] With the SSA broken, the BCP in ruins, and the KMT at its weakest point in more than thirty years, this estimate of Khun Sa's influence seems conservative. Based on intelligence reports, the U.S. State Department described Khun Sa's SUA as "the most powerful drug trafficking organization in the Golden Triangle." Translating Washington's diplomatic language into ordinary discourse, Khun Sa had become the world's largest single heroin trafficker, controlling as much as 60 percent of the world's illicit opium supply.[192]

By 1990 Khun Sa's control over the drug trade was so strong that he had become the target of a cynical diplomacy that may yet prove his downfall. Although the Bush administration's indictment of Khun Sa in February 1990[193] was meaningless as a practical exercise in law enforcement, the charges provided both Burma and Thailand with an opportunity to play politics with the drug war. Now denied its privileged status as a frontline state in the cold war against communism, Thailand is suffering a chorus of international criticism over its official tolerance of the drug trade. Under growing diplomatic pressure, Thailand may be forced to move against Khun Sa. Isolated as an international pariah after its troops slaughtered prodemocracy demonstrators in 1988, Rangoon in mid-1990 was maneuvering for a resumption of U.S. aid by hinting at its willingness to deliver Khun Sa to an American court. After the brutal military crackdown, the United States had cut all aid and Burma had abandoned its antinarcotics programs in the Shan states, forcing the DEA to quit the country. In a February 1990 visit to Washington, Burma's foreign minister failed in his attempt to lobby the State Department for a resumption of U.S. aid, but other federal agencies, notably the DEA, are keen to resume relations for the sake of the drug war.[194] If these diplomatic trends continue, Khun Sa may well find himself, like Panama's General Noriega, facing a U.S. court. Rangoon's bid for recognition, Bangkok's desire to counter charges of corruption, and Washington's need for a visible victory in the drug war may ultimately converge in a combined operation against the Shan drug lord.

As the pressures against Khun Sa mounted in 1989–1990, the Burmese government was already preparing an heir to his crown as the "king of the opium trade." When the BCP broke up in 1989, Rangoon exploited the split to revive Lo Hsing-han as the opium warlord of the northern Shan states. Only nine days after the Wa and Kokang contingents attacked the BCP's Burmese leaders and drove them into China, Lo Hsing-han was welcomed back to Kokang state by the same leaders who had driven him out in 1968. After he met with Burmese army officials in Lashio, Lo's new opium army opened some seventeen new heroin refineries in Kokang and began challenging Khun Sa's control over the northern Shan harvest. Still too weak to attack Khun Sa's hold over the Burma-Thailand border, Lo's coalition opened new overland trafficking routes across southern China to Hong Kong that supplied half the colony's heroin.[195]

Although Washington may one day announce Khun Sa's arrest and claim thereby another victory in the drug war, his trial, like General Noriega's, would make little difference to the drug trade. Even though Khun Sa may be the world's most powerful drug lord, his strength, like the poppy crop itself, is simply a product of the Golden Triangle's heroin industry. Armed by the CIA, trained by the KMT, and protected by the Burmese and Thai governments, Khun Sa has drawn his strength, even at its peak, from the complicity of powerful states and their intelligence agencies. If Khun Sa were to fall, the same forces that empowered him would soon create another opium warlord in his place.

# 9

## CIA Complicity in the Global Drug Trade

BY MAY 1980 DR. DAVID MUSTO, A YALE UNIVERSITY PSYCHIATRIST
and a White House adviser on drugs, was an angry man. In late 1977 he
had accepted President Jimmy Carter's appointment to the White House
Strategy Council on Drug Abuse with the understanding that this
statutory, policymaking body would "determine Federal strategy for
prevention of drug abuse and drug trafficking." Over the next two years,
Musto found that the CIA and other intelligence agencies denied the
council—whose members included the secretary of state and the
attorney general—access to all classified information on drugs, even
when it was necessary for framing new policy. The council's specific
inquiries took years to produce "the sketchiest information" or
"superficial responses."[1]

At one memorable briefing by CIA specialists on Colombia, Musto
came armed with current World Bank data on the role of the U.S. dollar
in the cocaine trade and began the interview with his loaded question.
To his dismay, the agency experts replied with a direct lie about the
dollar. When he confronted them with his World Bank data, the CIA men
retracted their false statements without a blush. Musto's complaints to
the White House about CIA lying produced no response.[2]

When President Carter reacted to the Soviet invasion of Afghanistan
in December 1979 by shipping arms to the mujaheddin guerrillas,
Musto's disquiet grew. "I told the council," he recalled, "that we were
going into Afghanistan to support the opium growers in their rebellion
against the Soviets. Shouldn't we try to avoid what we had done in Laos?

Shouldn't we try to pay the growers if they will eradicate their opium production? There was silence."[3] As heroin from Afghanistan and Pakistan poured into America throughout 1979, Musto noted that the number of drug-related deaths in New York City rose by 77 percent.[4]

Concerned by the mounting "heroin crisis," Musto joined another White House Drug Council member in writing an op-ed article in *The New York Times* to protest the Carter administration's failings. The two expressed their "worry about the growing of opium poppies in Afghanistan and Pakistan by rebel tribesmen" and asked: "Are we erring in befriending these tribes as we did in Laos when Air America (chartered by the Central Intelligence Agency) helped transport crude opium from certain tribal areas?" While the two drug experts could only guess at the reasons for the expanded opium production, they had no doubts about the consequence—a flood of heroin from Pakistan and Afghanistan. "On the streets, this drug is more potent, cheaper and more available than at any time in the last twenty years." Although denied official intelligence, these two medical doctors warned, quite accurately as it turned out, that "this crisis is bound to worsen."[5]

At the same time Dr. Musto was voicing his concerns about a possible flood of Afghan heroin in late 1979, field agents for the Drug Enforcement Administration (DEA) were already finding that his possibility was fast becoming their reality. Following a decade of major victories in the global drug war, the sudden surge of heroin from southern Asia—Afghanistan and Pakistan—disheartened the drug agents. As the first shipments of the new heroin began to arrive, the DEA called a special Middle East Heroin Conference at New York's Kennedy Airport in December 1979.[6]

The DEA's intelligence chief opened the gathering of his agents by introducing the "new Middle Eastern heroin threat," which seemed to be growing without restraint. Seconding the sense of crisis, the DEA's assistant intelligence administrator, Gordon Fink, spoke of the "concern and frustration that DEA is finding in dealing with the problem . . . due mainly to lack of control and intelligence at the source points, namely, Pakistan, Afghanistan and Iran."

Having arrived from the Middle East for the conference, Special Agent Ernie Staples added to the growing sense of gloom. Since the "political situations" in the region were unfavorable, he reported that the DEA's "first line of defense"—interception near the growing areas—had collapsed. In a frank admission of failure, Staples stated flatly that there were "no longer any DEA personnel working effectively in these source countries." Grown and processed without restraint, southern Asian heroin was capturing the European market. "Europe at present is being flooded with Middle Eastern heroin," said agent Staples. As supply surged, wholesale heroin prices in Europe were falling and purity had risen to a new high—a statistic confirmed by 500 recent deaths from drug overdose in West Germany.

With ample supplies of southern Asian opium and morphine, Marseille's Corsican syndicates were cooperating with Sicilian Mafia to open a new network of heroin laboratories. In February 1978 French police had seized a "working heroin laboratory" near Marseille, the first such seizure in five years, and had found 40 kilograms of morphine base supplied by the Italians. Moreover, several separate intelligence sources indicated that Lebanese smugglers were supplying opium to Sicilian heroin laboratories. Judging from a recent seizure of New York–bound heroin in Italy, it seemed that Sicilian Mafia groups based in Palermo were starting to smuggle the new heroin into the United States. "All indications," concluded Staples, "point to an increase of trafficking between Europe and the United States."

As DEA field agents from Boston to Chicago stood in succession, they added details that revealed a developing crisis. Special agents from the DEA's Newark district office identified the local "Gambino, Sollena . . . Organized Crime factions" as the dominant group distributing the new southern Asian heroin. Significantly, the faction's boss, Salvatore Sollena, who distributed the heroin through a chain of pizza parlors, was the nephew of Sicily's reigning Mafia don, Gaetano Badalamenti.

Responsible for the nation's premier heroin market, the DEA's New York agents had been the first to see the impact of the new southern Asian heroin. Black syndicates in Harlem had long operated by importing "multi-kilo lots of SEA [Southeast Asian] heroin," which were reduced "in one cutting to New York Quarters." In recent months, however, southern Asian heroin had captured 42 percent of the uptown market. In the Lower East Side, southern Asian heroin had made even more rapid progress, providing 60 percent of the supply. Most significantly, there was every sign that the New York heroin market of some 150,000 addicts was coming out of its long drought—exhibits showed a "dramatic increase in purity," hepatitis cases were up, and city police had recorded a sharp rise in heroin arrests.

Since New York City consumed 2 tons of heroin worth about $2 billion annually, changes in its market were soon felt in the rest of the country. Special Agent Bill McMullen of the DEA's Long Island office reported a rash of recent cases "involving Turkish, Spanish, and Italian principals moving Middle Eastern heroin." Philadelphia, like many district offices, noted that its heroin problem was "coming from New York." Special Agent Thomas Russo of Baltimore added that "trafficking is so easy between the two cities that the Baltimore pushers no longer keep stashes in that city." Similarly, the DEA's Washington, D.C., district office reported that a recent rise in heroin supplies from New York had produced an "increase in overdose death statistics."

Within a year, these trends, seen so clearly by both Dr. Musto and the DEA in late 1979, began to transform the nature of the U.S. drug problem. After a quarter century of rising addiction, America had enjoyed a brief respite during the mid-1970s. U.S. diplomacy in Turkey and DEA operations in Bangkok slowed Asia's drug exports, allowing America a prolonged heroin drought for the first time since World War II. The number of addicts dropped from an estimated 500,000 in 1971 to only 200,000 three years later. In New York City, the street price doubled and purity declined by half, both clear indications of short supply.[7] As Mexican heroin crossed the border to meet the demand, addiction rose briefly in 1976–1977 but then subsided when the DEA's interdiction efforts slowed the flow from Mexico. By late 1980, however, the "flood" of heroin from Pakistan and Afghanistan had captured 60 percent of the U.S. market and had brought the heroin crisis that Musto had predicted. As heroin-related injuries increased 25 percent during the year, the nation's addict population climbed back to 450,000.[8]

There were signs of worse to come. Without any restraint on production or processing, heroin exports from Pakistan and Afghanistan would continue to increase. Rising from about 100 tons in 1971, Afghanistan's opium production reached 300 tons in 1982 and then doubled to 575 tons in the next harvest.[9] Recovering from a two-year failure of the monsoon rains, Southeast Asia's Golden Triangle produced a bumper opium crop in 1981 that would, in the words of the attorney general, "provide enough heroin to glut the world market."[10] Sales of other illicit drugs were also rising. In 1980 street sales of all illicit drugs in the United States increased by 22 percent to $79 billion. While heroin imports rose by 7 percent to 4 tons, worth about $8 billion, cocaine supply jumped a remarkable 57 percent to 44 tons, worth $29 billion.[11]

During the 1980s America experienced an unprecedented drug crisis. Rising from insignificant levels, abuse of cocaine, first as pure powder and then as crack, reached pandemic proportions by the mid-1980s. Between 1982 and 1985 U.S. cocaine consumption doubled to 72 tons.[12] As supplies grew and prices dropped between 1981 and 1986, the number of Americans using cocaine rose by 38 percent to 5.8 million. When cocaine use began to taper off, the rapid spread of cut-price crack, a base form of cocaine suitable for smoking, won a growing clientele of younger users.[13]

Although eclipsed by the media glare on cocaine and crack, global heroin production and U.S. consumption rose steadily during the decade. World opium production tripled from an estimated 1,600 tons in

1982 to 4,700 in 1990.[14] The U.S. addict population stabilized at about 500,000 in the early 1980s, but there were signs of rising heroin use. Between 1983 and 1986, the number of heroin-related deaths doubled. Moreover, a new Mexican "black tar" heroin appeared in the mid-1980s with a high purity and low price that made it competitive with crack in the western United States.[15]

Of equal importance, the overall character of the U.S. illicit drug market changed in some significant ways. In general, there was every sign that the era of experimentation and casual soft-drug use was, after twenty years, coming to a close. For the first time in decades, marijuana use declined steadily in the 1980s. A survey of high school seniors showed that the percentage of current marijuana users dropped from 34 percent in 1980 to 21 percent in 1987. Indeed, the same survey showed a similar decline for most drugs—cocaine, hallucinogens, sedatives, stimulants, and tranquilizers.[16] While casual use faded, a hard core of regular cocaine and heroin users remained.

Although some local markets showed a preference for a particular drug, such as Miami for cocaine and New York for heroin, the growing tendency across the country was for regular drug users to take both. Between 1981 and 1985 deaths from "speedballs," a mixture of cocaine and heroin, rose by 754 percent.[17] In 1989–1990, moreover, a flood of Southeast Asian heroin cut the New York wholesale price of "China white" from $100,000 a kilogram to only $60,000, creating a new clientele for the drug. Crack addicts seeking an easier withdrawal were reportedly using heroin in large quantities, as were those mixing the two drugs for a more prolonged euphoria. "The heroin situation is growing on a daily basis," reported the DEA's expert Felix Jimenez in June 1990. "There's big profits, and the production of opium has doubled. . . . It is the tip of the iceberg."[18]

Although the drug pandemic of the 1980s had complex causes, the growth in global heroin supply could be traced, in large part, to two key aspects of U.S. policy: the failure of the DEA's interdiction efforts and the CIA's covert operations. By attacking heroin trafficking in separate sectors of Asia's extended opium zone in isolation, the DEA simply diverted heroin exports from America to Europe and shifted opium production from southern Asia to Southeast Asia and back again— raising both global consumption and production with each move. Moreover, the increasing opium harvests in Burma and Afghanistan, America's major suppliers, were largely the product of CIA covert operations. Just as CIA support for Nationalist Chinese (KMT) troops in the Shan states had increased Burma's opium crop in the 1950s, so the agency's aid to the mujaheddin guerrillas in the 1980s expanded opium production in Afghanistan and linked Pakistan's nearby heroin laboratories to the world market. After a decade as the sites of major CIA covert operations, Burma and Afghanistan ranked respectively as the world's largest and second largest suppliers of illicit heroin in 1989. In the decade that followed his prediction, Dr. Musto's dismal vision of America's coming drug crisis had been fulfilled.

## Southern Asian Opium

During the 1980s CIA covert operations in Afghanistan transformed southern Asia from a self-contained opium zone into a major supplier of heroin for the world market. Since the sixteenth century when recreational opium eating first developed, southern Asia had constituted a self-sufficient drug market. In the highlands spanning Iran, Afghanistan, and northwest India (now Pakistan), tribal farmers grew limited quantities of opium and sold it to merchant caravans bound for the cities of Iran to the west and India to the east. During the decade of cold war confrontation with the Soviet Union, however, CIA intervention provided the political protection and logistics linkages that joined Afghanistan's poppy fields to heroin markets in Europe and America. Although Soviet forces have withdrawn and CIA aid has now slackened, there is every indication that Afghanistan, like Burma before it, will remain a major heroin supplier for the world market long after the covert operations are over.

Unlike its effect in most of Asia, European colonialism had little impact on the tribal highlands that centered on Afghanistan. The combination of rugged terrain, a population of well-armed "martial tribes", and a deep Islamic faith that encouraged jihad, or holy war, against Western invaders made the roof of southern Asia impervious to conquest. Seeking to protect India's northwest frontier from the threat of a Russian incursion, Britain invaded Afghanistan in 1838 and 1878, suffering humiliation and heavy casualties in both attempts. After a particularly disastrous defeat in the Second Afghan War (1878–1880), Britain decided to deal with the ruling amir of Afghanistan to fix a boundary. Meeting with the amir at Kabul in 1893, Britain's emissary, Sir Mortimer Durand, drew up a boundary of mutual convenience separating Afghanistan from India.[19] As this diplomatic exercise indicates, the modern Afghan state took shape as a buffer state, with frontiers drawn to please British India, Russia, and Iran.[20] Imposing such arbitrary boundaries over sprawling tribal areas left large portions of Afghanistan's leading ethnic groups on the wrong side of the border—many of its Pushtuns in India's North-West Frontier province and a majority of its Baluch living in Iran and India.[21]

On the British side of the boundary along India's North-West Frontier, later part of Pakistan, colonial rule remained tenuous. Constantly harassed by marauding Pushtun tribes along the Afghan border, Britain dispatched forty-two military expeditions into the mountains between 1849 and 1890, nearly one every year. In 1897 the British sent 30,000 regular troops into Peshawar district to fight the redoubtable Arfidi tribe, with little effect. Unable to beat the Pushtun (or Pathan) warriors, the British adopted a punitive policy known in the officers' mess as "butcher and bolt"—that is, march into the offending village, butcher the available civilians, and bolt before the tribe's warriors could retaliate.[22] Unlike the peoples of Africa or the Americas, the Pushtun tribes did not fight with sword and spear. Supplied by merchant firearms traders from the Persian Gulf or Afghanistan, mounted tribal warriors fought effectively against British troops, first with smooth-bore muskets and later with modern European rifles.

Instead of trying to disarm the frontier tribes, an impossible task, the British adopted a policy of conciliation and control, backed by a massive military presence. Through naval patrols in the Persian Gulf, the British tried to control the arms supply by interdicting smuggling to rebellious groups.[23] By contrast, the British allowed loyal tribes to trade in arms without restraint and even recruited them for military service. The British paid tribal warriors for patrolling caravan routes through the Khyber Pass, formed them into local militia such as the Tochi Scouts or the Khyber Rifles, and, by 1915, recruited some 7,500 Pushtun into the regular Indian army. At the end of colonial rule in 1947, as the British prepared to transfer the North-West Frontier to the new nation of Pakistan, their last governor reported that over half the tribal males owned firearms—no longer just muskets, but largely high-velocity, precision rifles.[24] In effect, the British had adopted a policy of alliance or mutual conciliation with the martial Pushtun tribes that preserved their arms and autonomy, thereby bequeathing the new Pakistan state few means of controlling the tribes along its North-West Frontier.[25]

With such weak control, Britain minimized taxes to avoid provoking the tribes. Instead of encouraging opium production for revenue as they did elsewhere in India, the British saw the drug as a destabilizing factor in the North-West Frontier and worked toward its gradual abolition. Since opium production was still limited in the area, the tribes did not resist. In 1870, for example, the districts along the Afghan border cultivated only 1,130 acres of opium.[26] Through a policy of gradual interdiction, the British reduced poppy cultivation until 1901, when "it had entirely ceased." The colonial regime did not ban drug use, however, and allowed imports of Afghan opium from the nearby Jalalabad Valley where the poppy harvest was good.[27] Although the ruling amir did not restrict Afghanistan's opium production, the country's harvest was still, at century's turn, rather limited. In 1908 a

British source reported that there was opium cultivation in four Afghan districts—the Herat Valley, Kabul, Kandahar, and Jalalabad—"but not to any great extent."[28] At the end of the colonial era in 1947, the kingdom of Afghanistan and the state of Pakistan were minor opium producers with small addict populations.

The independent kingdom of Iran, by contrast, had become one of the world's major opium producers and consumers. As the global opium trade grew during the nineteenth century, Iran emerged as an important secondary supplier for the world market with an annual opium harvest of some 600 tons by century's turn.[29] Resisting diplomatic pressures to reduce production in the 1920s, Iran allowed its opium crop to peak at 1,350 tons in 1936. Its exports accounted for 40 percent of the world's medical morphine supplies and earned the country about 15 percent of its foreign exchange. Although the government banned opium smoking in 1910 and imposed prohibitive taxes in 1928, both measures found little support from a population that accepted recreational drug abuse without reservation.[30]

When the U.S. Bureau of Narcotics opened an office at Tehran in 1949, its resident agent, Garland Williams, discovered the world's most elaborate drug culture. Drawn from all regions and social classes, Iran's addict population numbered 1.3 million, or one opium user for every nine adults—a rate exceeded only by China. Williams was pessimistic about the chances of prohibition. Interviewing the head of the opium monopoly in Isfahan, Williams asked its director, Ansari, about the possibility of banning opium. "I am a thief and all my men are thieves," answered Ansari. "We have been accepting bribes for so many years that it would be impossible for us to really enforce a law like that."[31]

Nevertheless, in 1955 the Shah banned all production and consumption of opium, reducing Iran's addict population dramatically to only 350,000. Although the prohibition reduced drug use during the fourteen years that it remained in effect, it stimulated production in neighboring Turkey and Afghanistan to supply the strong illicit demand within Iran. In 1969 the Shah rescinded the ban, announcing that Iran would resume opium cultivation for sale to registered addicts. The United Nations called the Shah's decision "tragic."[32] Writing from his retirement, Harry Anslinger, former head of the U.S. Bureau of Narcotics, called the decision "highly disturbing news" and suggested that the U.N.'s Division of Narcotic Drugs "attack the proposed move as being a retrogressive step in world control."[33] The Shah responded that Iran would ban opium as soon as its neighbors did.[34]

Despite Anslinger's dire predictions about Iran's impact on the global traffic, the Shah's decision simply legitimated a portion of southern Asia's self-contained opium trade. By 1972, three years after legalization, Iran's addict population had grown by 15 percent to some 400,000, of whom 105,000 were registered opium smokers. The authorized addicts consumed the country's entire opium crop of 217 tons, while illegal smokers used 195 tons of illicit opium smuggled from Turkey, Afghanistan, and Pakistan. Still unable to produce enough opium for its own needs, Iran consumed all of Afghanistan's production, about 100 tons, and much of Pakistan's lesser crop.[35]

There was, however, a potentially disturbing new development in Iran's illicit traffic. The Shah's restrictions seem to have encouraged the growth of a local heroin industry to supply Tehran addicts who wished to avoid registration or the threat of arrest in an illegal opium den. In 1974, U.S. Ambassador Richard Helms, recently retired as head of the CIA, reported that Iran had about 30,000 heroin users supplied by illicit Tehran laboratories that refined morphine base from Turkey into a low-grade brown heroin. Despite a small seizure of Iran's brown heroin in West Germany, Helms emphasized that "there is little evidence to support the possibility that Iranian heroin produced from Turkish morphine base enters in international traffic." Quite the contrary. Helms argued that Iran's "considerable population of unregistered users . . . acts as a sponge for opiates produced elsewhere in the Middle East, thereby diverting supplies that might otherwise find their way as heroin to the United States."[36]

Over the next two years, Helms monitored Iran's drug situation closely, concluding that there were no signs of significant heroin exports. In October 1974 the U.S. embassy in Iran found the first sign of southern Asia's potential as a supplier for the world heroin market. When Tehran police intercepted 32.7 kilograms of "fairly high-grade heroin," the embassy cabled Washington that the seizure "tends to substantiate a long-held concern . . . that Iranian operators are capable of making quality heroin in commercial amounts." Moreover, the arrest provided the "first hard evidence" that Tehran's "heroin chemists have a connection with sources of opium in Afghanistan and/or Pakistan."[37]

In one of his last drug reports, in June 1975, Helms argued that, rising heroin production notwithstanding, the region's self-contained opium trade was still no threat to Western markets. On the whole, Helms found that Iran's system of legal sales to registered opium addicts "works fairly well." Growers were tightly supervised and there was little diversion to the illicit traffic. But it had been "a fiasco from the viewpoint of reducing Iran's addict population," largely because most Iranians still had a remarkably "tolerant" attitude toward opium. "In some educated, high-society circles," Helms noted, "it is smoked socially after dinner." Such tolerance made it easy for the "few influential Iranians . . . involved in the illicit opium trade" to secure protection for a traffic that supplied the country's 500,000 opium smokers and 50,000 heroin addicts. Using "every means of transport from backpacking to fast, long-range vehicles in convoys with heavily armed escorts," traffickers smuggled opium from Afghanistan and Pakistan across Iran to Tehran. Although a small group of about twenty-five men manufactured heroin in Tehran, Helms still found "no evidence" that either opium or heroin was being exported from Iran.[38]

All available evidence indicates that as late as 1975 the historic patterns of southern Asia's opium trade had not changed. The region's drug traffic was still self-contained, with the tribal areas of Pakistan and Afghanistan exporting limited opium crops to the addicts of Iran's leading cities. While Iran absorbed all the opium the region could produce, drug use in both Pakistan and Afghanistan was still uncommon. Heroin production had just started in Tehran, but heroin users were only 10 percent of all addicts and there were still no exports. Although poppy production and opium use were rising, they both seemed, to the U.S. embassy in Tehran, part of a venerable Asian drug culture beyond the ken or control of the West. Under such circumstances, Ambassador Helms's odd confidence that a region with every sign of a booming drug industry—half a million addicts, an opium harvest of 400 tons, and heroin laboratories—was still under control somehow seems justified.

Within only five years, however, southern Asia's opium trade would experience a sudden transformation. By the early 1980s Afghanistan had become the world's second largest opium grower, the Pakistan-Afghanistan border was the leading source of heroin for Europe and America, and mass heroin addiction had spread beyond Iran to Pakistan. In retrospect, this rapid change seems the result of pressures in the global drug market, local political forces, and covert operations. Although the CIA did not play the same paramount role that it had in the transformation of Burma's drug trade thirty years before, its covert warfare still served as a catalyst in the emergence of Afghanistan as a leading source of heroin for the world market.

## Covert Warfare in Afghanistan

Long something of a backwater in U.S. foreign policy, southern Asia emerged in the late 1970s as a flashpoint of cold war confrontation. As America and its allies sent in covert operatives, secret arms shipments, and military aid to meet the escalating political crisis, opium production soared and heroin poured out of the region into European and American markets. Although the causality was more complex than such simple a sketch allows, there was nonetheless a close correspondence between covert operations and the region's rising heroin exports.

The Iranian revolution of February 1979 was the first in a series of major events that changed the character of both the region's politics and its narcotics traffic. After waves of labor strikes and mass demonstrations in Tehran toppled the Shah, the apparatus of repression collapsed, breaking his controls over the country's opium traffic. His successor, Ayatollah Khomeini, leader of the new Islamic government, denounced drug dealers as "first class traitors and a danger to society." But the new religious regime, reflecting Iran's traditional tolerance for the drug, did not place opium in the same forbidden category as alcohol, thereby creating an ambiguity that allowed the traffic to flourish. Six months after the revolt, the CIA reported that drugs were being sold openly on Tehran's streets and that the Revolutionary Guards, with many addicts in their ranks, did "not interfere with the dealers."

By September CIA analysts in the U.S. embassy estimated that Iran's next poppy harvest would raise opium production from the current 200 tons to an estimated 325 tons. Since the regime banned most entertainment, "drug use has skyrocketed among the youth" and the country now had some 2 million addicts, a historic high. Agency analysts argued that Iran's opium boom had "created a new 'golden triangle' comprised of Iran, Pakistan and Afghanistan." Once the new bumper crop was harvested, Iran's opium "will join that produced in Afghanistan and Pakistan flowing over the 'silk route' of Marco Polo to Turkey and from there to Western Europe." The CIA concluded its report on Iran's opium cornucopia with a warning: "The world must brace itself for a flood of opium and heroin from Iran."[39]

As events turned out, the CIA was half right. Beginning in 1979, southern Asia sent increasing heroin exports to Europe and America. But the drugs came from the Pakistan-Afghan borderlands, not Iran. As it had for the past two centuries, Iran showed a remarkable appetite for drugs and absorbed all of its own opium harvests, now greatly expanded under the new regime. Although Iran did not produce a surplus for export, its increased harvests now met its own needs, freeing Afghanistan's opium for export to Europe. Over the next decade, the region's flood of heroin exports had far less to do with the Iranian revolution than with the CIA's own covert operations inside Afghanistan.

Initially, a peculiar twist in the global drug trade brought southern Asia's heroin to Europe in 1979. Although southern Asia's opium harvest rose steadily from 400 tons in 1971 to 1,200 tons in 1978, almost all of the increased production was consumed locally. Small quantities of Pakistan-Afghan heroin had first appeared in Europe in 1975. In the months following the region's bumper harvest of 1,200 tons in 1978, European police still seized only 49 kilograms of southern Asian heroin, only a tenth of the 451 kilograms intercepted from Southeast Asia.[40] Then the monsoon rains failed for two years in the Golden Triangle, reducing the region's opium production to a record low. As a network of heroin laboratories opened in 1979 along the Afghan-Pakistan border to service the global markets opened by the two-year drought in Southeast Asia, Pakistan's opium production soared to 800 tons, far above its 1971 harvest of some 90 tons.[41] By 1980 Pakistan-Afghan opium dominated the European market and supplied 60 percent of America's illicit demand as well.[42]

During the 1980s southern Asia's opium trade stabilized with a new pattern of production and exports. Now largely self-sufficient in opium, Iran was no longer the main market for tribal opium growers in Pakistan and Afghanistan. Pressured by the United States, an important ally, Pakistan's military regime under General Zia ul-Haq imposed an erratic suppression effort that drove the country's opium production down from its peak of 800 tons to its more normal level of 100–200 tons. As Pakistan's poppy harvest declined, Afghanistan's mujaheddin guerrillas expanded production in their zones and shipped the raw opium to the Afghan-Pakistan border refineries for processing into heroin. In January 1982 Pakistani troops attacked the heroin industry by fighting their way through armed tribesmen in the North-West Frontier province to close a single heroin refinery. After that dramatic demonstration of good intentions, General Zia's pressure on the laboratories along his border with Afghanistan remained ritualistic. Thus, by 1981–1982, Afghanistan's poppy fields were linked with laboratories in the Pakistan-Afghan borderlands to supply more than half the heroin demand in America and Europe.[43] Until Southeast Asia's opium harvest soared to some 3,000 tons in 1989, annual production in southern and Southeast Asia remained even at about 1,000 tons each, and they held roughly equal shares of First World heroin markets.[44]

During the ten years of CIA covert support for the mujaheddin resistance, U.S. government and media sources were silent about the involvement of leading Afghan guerrillas and Pakistan military in the heroin traffic. As the covert operation wound down after the Soviet withdrawal from Afghanistan in February 1989, the U.S. media began probing the scandal, gradually gathering enough data for a detailed portrait of the close relationship between the mujaheddin resistance and the region's heroin trade.

In 1978–1979 southern Asia became the focus of a major crisis in U.S. foreign policy. In February 1979 Tehran mobs toppled the Shah's dictatorship, destroying a conservative regime that had long served as America's proxy military presence in the strategic Persian Gulf, gateway for the West's oil supplies. Only eight months later, revolutionary guards seized the U.S. embassy in Tehran, taking Americans hostage. Compounding the crisis, in April 1978 Communist factions inside the Afghan army had overthrown the dictator Mohammad Daud and established a pro-Soviet regime. After months of internecine fighting between rival Communist factions, Soviet troops invaded Afghanistan in December 1979, occupying the capital Kabul and installing a more pliable Afghan Communist as president.

As Soviet troops spread across Afghanistan for a prolonged occupation, President Carter reacted with ill-concealed rage, denouncing Soviet leader Leonid Brezhnev in a television interview on December 31 and imposing a series of economic sanctions against Moscow.[45] More important, Carter used his diplomatic and covert action resources to mobilize military aid for the mujaheddin guerrillas. As chairman of the president's Special Coordination Committee on Covert Operations, national security adviser Zbigniew Brzezinski took charge and flew to the Middle East in January 1980 for meetings with Egypt's President Anwar Sadat and Pakistan's General Zia. As Sadat recalled the meeting, the White House adviser asked: " 'Please open your stores for us so that we can give the Afghanis the armaments they need to fight,' and I gave them the armaments." Simultaneously, Defense Secretary Harold Brown flew to Beijing to negotiate Chinese arms shipments, an overture that jettisoned the White House policy of evenhandedness toward the two Communist powers. Contacted for support, Saudi Arabia announced that it was giving $25 million to aid fellow Muslims fighting the Soviet invasion. Within weeks, massive arms shipments began—hand-held missiles and antitank weapons from China, Kalashnikov assault rifles from Egypt, munitions from Saudi Arabia, and a variety of U.S. weapons from the CIA.[46]

Although President Carter successfully launched the covert aid effort, his operations were limited by the coolness of his relations with General Zia, leader of the strategic frontline state of Pakistan. After seizing power in a July 1977 coup, Zia had imposed a harsh martial-law regime, toughened by his own Islamic fundamentalism, and two years later executed his chief opponent, former Prime Minister Zulfiqar Ali Bhutto—acts that provided the White House with a pretext for reducing military aid.[47] When Carter offered Pakistan $400 million in military aid to encourage its support for the Afghan resistance, Zia rejected the offer as "peanuts." Soon after President Ronald Reagan took office in 1981, the White House announced a $3 billion program of military aid to Pakistan including the latest F-16 fighters, an offer that Zia readily accepted.[48]

With Pakistan now openly committed to the mujaheddin, General Zia's military soon assumed a dominant role in supplying the Afghan resistance forces. Although the Saudis delivered their aid directly to client guerrilla units inside Afghanistan, most allied agencies, the CIA included, worked through General Zia's chosen instrument, the Inter Service Intelligence (ISI). The CIA's relationship with ISI was a complex give-and-take that makes simple caricatures inappropriate—that ISI was the agency's errand runner on the Afghan border or, conversely, that ISI manipulated the CIA into writing a blank check for General Zia's own Afghan policies. As the frontline agency in a covert guerrilla war, ISI clearly had superior intelligence and closer relations with the Afghan guerrillas. In turn, the CIA commanded a vast arsenal of funds and high-technology weapons that dwarfed ISI's meager budget. In retrospect, the CIA-ISI alliance seems a balanced relationship, with a good deal of manipulation and misrepresentation on both sides. As foreign correspondent Lawrence Lifschultz explained, "It was a proper marriage of mutual interest."[49] At the time General Zia took power in 1977, ISI had been a minor military intelligence unit with an annual budget of no more than several million dollars. With the "advice and assistance of the CIA," Zia soon built the ISI into a powerful covert operations unit and made it the strong arm of his martial-law regime.[50] In particular, Zia relied on ISI to control the troublesome Pushtun tribes in the North-West Frontier, many of whom had long been attracted to the idea of political union with the Pushtun majority inside Afghanistan.[51]

When the Soviet Union began infiltrating Afghanistan in early 1979, the CIA worked through ISI to organize the first mujaheddin resistance groups. "Throughout most of the war," explained Afghanistan expert Dr. Barnett Rubin, "the United States subcontracted to General Zia and ISI the main political decision about which Afghans to support."[52] The U.S. program to aid the Afghan guerrillas began in April 1979, eight months before the full Soviet invasion, when Brzezinski convinced the National Security Council to "be more sympathetic" to the fledgling resistance. The following month at Peshawar in Pakistan's North-West Frontier province, a CIA special envoy first met Afghan resistance leaders, all carefully selected by Pakistan's ISI.[53] Instead of arranging a meeting with a broad spectrum of resistance leaders, ISI offered the CIA's envoy an alliance with its own Afghan client, Gulbuddin Hekmatyar, leader of the small Hezbi-i Islami guerrilla group. The CIA accepted the offer and, over the next decade, gave more than half its covert aid to Hekmatyar's guerrillas. It was, as the U.S. Congress would find a decade later, a dismal decision. Unlike the later resistance leaders who commanded strong popular followings inside Afghanistan, Hekmatyar led a guerrilla force that was a creature of the Pakistan military. After the CIA built his Hezbi-i Islami into the largest Afghan guerrilla force, Hekmatyar would prove himself brutal and corrupt.[54] Not only did he command the largest guerrilla army, but Hekmatyar would use it—with the full support of ISI and the tacit tolerance of the CIA—to become Afghanistan's leading drug lord.

Among the hundreds of American correspondents who covered the Afghan resistance during the 1980s, few bothered to probe the background of Hekmatyar, the man who had become the chosen instrument for the CIA's largest covert operation. An Islamic militant and former engineering student, Hekmatyar had founded the Muslim Brotherhood and had led student demonstrations in Kabul during the late 1960s to oppose the king's secular reforms.[55] According to a later *New York Times* report, in the early 1970s "he had dispatched followers to throw vials of acid into the faces of women students who refused to wear veils."[56] Accused of murdering a leftist student in 1972, Hekmatyar fled into Pakistan's North-West Frontier where, as a member of Pushtun tribes that straddle the border, he was able to continue his political work. Living in Peshawar, Hekmaytar allied himself with Pakistan's Jamaat-i Islami (Party of Islam), a fundamentalist and quasi-fascist Muslim group with many followers inside the Pakistani officer corps.

Through these contacts with the military, Hekmatyar would become commander of a Pakistani covert operation to destabilize the new government in Kabul in 1974—five years before the Soviet invasion. When Mohammad Daud, a former prime minister, led a coup against the king and established the Republic of Afghanistan in 1973, Pakistan's Prime Minister Bhutto was rightly concerned about the security of his North-West Frontier. A direct descendant of the last Afghan ruler of the Pushtun tribes inside Pakistan, Daud was publicly committed to the unification of all Pushtun peoples under Kabul's rule.[57] To preempt any Afghan attempt to spark a Pushtun rebellion in his North-West Frontier, in 1973 Bhutto ordered his military to begin training a secret force of 5,000 Afghan rebels at clandestine camps inside Pakistan. Armed and supplied by Islamabad, Hekmatyar led these guerrillas into Afghanistan and launched a revolt in the Panjsher valley north of Kabul in July 1975. Hekmatyar's propaganda that Daud's conservative republic was a "godless communist-dominated regime" was unconvincing, and his mercenary force found itself without popular support. The Afghan army encountered little resistance when it marched into the Panjsher valley to mop up. While Kabul placed ninety-three of his captured mercenaries on trial, Hekmatyar retreated into Pakistan with most of his forces intact. Shaken by the uprising, Kabul's President Daud dropped his militant pro-Pushtun rhetoric, distanced himself from the Soviets, and began to negotiate with Iran and Pakistan. In a remarkable policy reversal, Daud made a state visit to Islamabad in 1976 and assured

Bhutto that he was at last willing to recognize the Durand line as the legal boundary between the two countries. The final agreement between the two, which would certainly have ended Hekmatyar's career as a contract revolutionary, was eclipsed by General Zia's 1977 coup that toppled Bhutto's government.[58]

A year later, a Communist coup in Kabul ousted President Daud and revived the fortunes of Hekmatyar's exile army. When John Joseph Reagan, CIA station chief in Islamabad, met the ISI's selected Afghan leaders in May 1979 and agreed to provide some arms to Hekmatyar's guerrillas, it was a momentous decision, although nobody knew it at the time. CIA covert aid would increase markedly over the next two years, but Hekmatyar remained the prime beneficiary. After the Soviet army invaded Afghanistan in December, American aid took a quantum leap—but along lines set six months earlier. Similarly, in June 1981 when President Reagan and General Zia agreed to support a full-scale war inside Afghanistan, the flood of clandestine military aid still followed the same patterns set at Peshawar by the CIA, ISI, and Hekmatyar two years earlier.

In the effect, the bargain struck at Peshawar in May 1979 and confirmed by a later executive agreement between Zia and Reagan bound the White House, and its covert action arm, to subcontract its secret war in Afghanistan to Pakistan's military. There were important advantages for both sides. With generous American aid, Pakistan opened its border to 3 million Afghan refugees and allowed the CIA to conduct its secret war without restraint. Along the border, American operatives ran training camps for the mujaheddin guerrillas and in Pakistan's capital, Islamabad, the CIA maintained one of its largest foreign stations to direct the covert war. CIA Director William Casey gained direct access to General Zia and found himself warmly received during his regular visits to Islamabad. Unique in a region where the official attitude toward America ranged from the hateful to the hostile, Zia allowed the CIA to open an electronic intelligence station facing the Soviet Union in northern Pakistan and permitted U.S. spy flights over the Indian Ocean from his air bases near the Persian Gulf. Aside from the $3 billion in U.S. aid, the Pakistan military gained control over distribution of the $2 billion in covert aid that the CIA shipped to the Afghan guerrillas during the ten-year war. For General Zia's loyalists within the military, these contracts were a source of vast wealth.[59]

At an operational level, General Zia's military loyalists controlled the delivery of the CIA's covert arms shipments when they arrived in Pakistan. Once the arms landed at the port of Karachi in the south, the Pakistan army's National Logistics Cell, acting under orders from the ISI, trucked them north to military cantonments around Peshawar and from there to the Afghan guerrilla camps in the North-West Frontier. The governor of this critical borderland province was Lieutenant-General Fazle Huq, President Zia's closest confidant and the de facto overlord of the mujaheddin guerrillas.[60] Even as the ranks of the resistance swelled after 1981, the ISI insisted on maintaining the dominance of the "pre-1978 nucleus," that is, Hekmatyar, and continued to deliver more than half of all arms to his Hezbi-i Islami guerrillas. Although Pakistan allowed formation of a few additional groups to accommodate prestigious Afghan exiles, ISI still insisted that Hekmatyar be given the bulk of CIA arms shipments. According to correspondent Lifschultz, CIA case officers were aware that ISI's distribution system "was creating a form of warlordism within the resistance command."[61]

From the outset, Hekmatyar's forces conducted themselves in a way that raised questions about the CIA's choice of clients. At the start of the covert war in 1979, other mujaheddin leaders charged that Hekmatyar's followers were using violence to take control of rival resistance groups. Although the mujaheddin's ultimate victory would require mass defections from Kabul's Communist forces, Hekmatyar's followers thought they were fighting a jihad, or holy war, and as early as 1980 were known to kill defectors. During the decade of resistance, organizations such as Asia Watch and Amnesty International received numerous reports of human rights violations by Hekmatyar's Hezbi-i Islami guerrillas.[62] Pakistan's ISI gave Hekmatyar a free hand to rule the Afghan refugee camps that sprawled around Peshawar, and he used it to run what one U.N. refugee worker called a "reign of terror."[63] During the decade-long covert war, the American press published positive reports about Hekmatyar, the leading recipient of U.S. arms shipments, ignoring his heroin dealing and human rights abuses. A year after the Soviet withdrawal in 1989 stripped the Afghan war of its national security imperatives, *The New York Times* finally reported what it called "the sinister nature of Mr. Hekmatyar" and *The Washington Post* published a page 1 exposé about his heroin syndicate.[64]

From a purely military perspective, the bankruptcy of CIA policy was exposed in the mujaheddin's abortive attack on Jalalabad in March 1989. Typical of the war's overall conduct, the attack was planned at a meeting in Islamabad attended by U.S. Ambassador Robert Oakley, senior Pakistani officials, and not a single Afghan. Since the mujaheddin had no central command to plan a major offensive, Pakistan's ISI designed the tactics and approached independent resistance forces with promises of arms and money if they would participate. Evidently, the aim of the attack was to establish a mujaheddin capital at Jalalabad, a major Afghan city near the border, in time to win recognition for the new Afghan interim government at an upcoming meeting of Islamic states in Saudi Arabia. After the Soviet withdrawal only weeks before, many U.S. observers predicted a certain defeat for government forces, the first step in an unraveling that would end with the collapse of the Communist regime in Kabul. John Glassman, chargé at the U.S. embassy in Kabul, called Afghanistan's Communist regime "a house without girders" and predicted its fall would take only a few months after Soviet troops pulled out. Around Washington, the CIA gave briefings saying that a rebel victory was assured.[65] As it turned out, the operation proved a debacle for the resistance. After weeks of lackluster fighting by the mujaheddin, the Communist garrison held Jalalabad and the guerrillas pulled back to Pakistan, defeated and humiliated. Only four months earlier, one of the fundamentalist guerrilla groups had slaughtered seventy-four defectors from the Torkham garrison, a lesson that apparently inspired an extraordinary effort by Jalalabad's Communist defenders. Indicating further discipline problems, in July the world press reported that one of Hekmatyar's commanders had slaughtered thirty members of another mujaheddin group, an atrocity that inspired the president of the Afghan interim government to denounce Hekmatyar, his own foreign minister, as a "criminal" and a "terrorist."[66]

## Hekmatyar's Heroin Trade

As the cold war confrontation wound down, the international press finally broke its decade of silence to reveal the involvement of the Afghan resistance and Pakistani military in the region's heroin trade. In May 1990, for example, *The Washington Post* published a page 1 article charging that the United States had failed to take action against Pakistan's heroin dealers "because of its desire not to offend a strategic ally, Pakistan's military establishment." The *Post* article said that U.S. officials had ignored Afghan complaints of heroin trafficking by Hekmatyar and the ISI, an allegation that at least one senior American official confirmed. Specifically, the *Post* reported that "Hekmatyar commanders close to ISI run laboratories in southwest Pakistan" and "ISI cooperates in heroin operations."[67] Although the independent Pakistani press, angered by the country's own heroin epidemic, had reported many of the details years before, the international news organizations had seemed reluctant to broach the issue as long as Afghanistan had remained a flashpoint in the cold war. While Pakistani heroin flooded Europe and America in the early 1980s, the western press had maintained a public silence on the origins of this new narcotics supply.

As the ISI's mujaheddin clients used their new CIA munitions to capture prime agricultural areas inside Afghanistan during the early 1980s, the guerrillas urged their peasant supporters to grow poppies, thereby doubling the country's opium harvest to 575 tons between 1982 and 1983.[68] Once these mujaheddin elements brought the opium across the border, they sold it to Pakistani heroin refiners who operated under the protection of General Fazle Huq, governor of the North-West Frontier province. By 1988, there were an estimated 100 to 200 heroin refineries in the province's Khyber district alone.[69] Trucks from the Pakistan army's National Logistics Cell (NLC) arriving with CIA arms from Karachi often returned loaded with heroin—protected by ISI papers from police search. "The drug is carried in NLC trucks, which come sealed from the [North-West Frontier] and are never checked by the police," reported the *Herald* of Pakistan in September 1985. "They come from Peshawar to Pirpri, Jungshahi, Jhimpir where they deliver their cargo, sacks of grain, to government godowns. Some of these sacks contain packets of heroin. . . . This has been going on now for about three and a half years."

Writing in *The Nation* three years later, Lifschultz cited numerous police sources charging that Governor Fazle Huq, General Zia's intimate, was the primary protector of the thriving heroin industry in the North-West Frontier province. Lifschultz said that General Huq "had been implicated in narcotics reports reaching Interpol" as early as 1982. Both European and Pakistani police claimed that all investigations of the province's major heroin syndicates had "been aborted at the highest level." With seventeen agents assigned to the U.S. embassy in Islamabad, the DEA compiled detailed reports identifying "forty significant narcotics syndicates in Pakistan." Despite the high quality of DEA intelligence, not a single major syndicate was investigated by Pakistani police for nearly a decade.[70] Farther south in the Koh-i-Soltan district of Pakistan's Baluchistan province, Hekmatyar himself controlled six heroin refineries that processed the large opium harvest from Afghanistan's fertile Helmand valley.[71] Describing the corruption of the Pakistani military, ISI included, the local Baluchistan governor, Mohammad Akbar Khan Bugti, a tribal nationalist often critical of Islamabad, said: "They deliver drugs under their own bayonets."[72]

The heroin boom was so large and uncontrolled that drug abuse swept Pakistan itself in the early 1980s, leaving it with one of the world's largest addict populations. In the late 1970s Pakistan did not have a significant heroin abuse problem. When the region's political upheavals of 1979 blocked the usual shipment of Afghan and Pakistani opium westward to Iran, traffickers in Pakistan's North-West Frontier perfected heroin-refining skills to reduce their mounting opium stockpiles. Operating without fear of arrest, heroin dealers began exporting their product to Europe and America, quickly capturing more than 50 percent of both markets. Unrestrained by any form of police controls, local smugglers also shipped heroin to Pakistan's own cities and towns. Addiction rose to 5,000 users in 1980, to 70,000 in 1983, and then, in the words of Pakistan's Narcotics Control Board, went "completely out of hand," exploding to more than 1.3 million addicts in less than three years.[73]

With overt official complicity and heroin exports booming beyond control, it did not take a great deal of police work to grasp the political realities of Pakistan's drug trade. During an official tour of Pakistan's own drug war in 1982, U.S. Attorney General William French Smith was surprised when one of his aides spotted heroin samples displayed in a public market near the Khyber Pass. Pakistan dealt with the problem by closing the district to foreigners.[74]

In marked contrast to the seventeen DEA agents who shuffled papers without result in the U.S. embassy at Islamabad, a single Norwegian detective broke a heroin case that led directly to General Zia's personal banker. Arrested at Oslo airport with 3.5 kilograms of heroin in December 1983, Pakistani trafficker Raza Qureshi traded details about his drug syndicate for a reduced sentence. Armed with the intelligence the Oslo detective, Oyvind Olsen, flew to Islamabad in mid-1984 and confirmed many of the leads. After Norway's public prosecutor filed formal charges against three Pakistani heroin merchants in September 1985, Pakistan's Federal Investigation Agency (FIA) ordered their arrest. When Pakistani police picked up Hamid Hasnain, vice-president of the government's Habib Bank, they searched his briefcase and found the personal banking records of President Zia. On the night of the arrest, the president's wife called senior FIA agents from Egypt to demand Hasnain's release, a request they could not grant. As Zia's intimate family friend, Hasnain had the run of the president's home and had managed his personal finances for the past five years. At the trial in June 1987, Hasnain and his coaccused screamed death threats at the prosecution witness Qureshi when he took the stand, continuing their extraordinary performance for three days until Norway threatened diplomatic protests. In the end, Hasnain was convicted and sentenced to a long prison term.

Similarly, in May 1983, a Japanese resident of Karachi posing as a boy scout was arrested in Amsterdam with 17.5 kilograms of no. 4 heroin; he named a Lahore cinema owner, Mirza Iqbal Baig, as the boss of his drug syndicate. Two years later, the British Broadcasting Corporation created a national scandal in Pakistan with the release of a television documentary, *The Scout Who Smuggled Heroin*, naming Baig as a major drug dealer.[75] After three years without an arrest in the case, Islamabad's main daily *The Muslim* quoted a Pakistani customs officer saying that Baig was "the most active dope dealer in the country." In his investigation of the case, correspondent Lifschultz found that Pakistani police were barred from arresting Baig and that American DEA agents were unwilling to press for any arrest inside Pakistan, Baig's included, with embarrassing political implications.[76] Soon after his arrest, DEA agents interviewed the Japanese smuggler in his Dutch prison cell and gained sufficient evidence to justify Baig's indictment. Concerned that Baig's trial might tug a thread that could unravel General Zia's regime, the DEA dealt with this "delicate dilemma" by trying to lure Baig abroad to a jurisdiction where the political explosion would be more easily contained. In the end, Baig was too smart to be stung and the DEA did nothing.[77]

There was evidence, moreover, of a major heroin syndicate inside the Pakistan military. In June 1986 Pakistani police arrested an army major driving from Peshawar to Karachi with 220 kilograms of heroin. Two months later, police arrested an air force lieutenant carrying an identical amount, indications of a tidy military mind organizing uniform deliveries. Before the two could be interrogated, both officers escaped from custody under what Pakistan's *Defense Journal* called "mystifying circumstances."[78] Significantly, these were only two of the sixteen military officers arrested in 1986 for heroin trafficking.[79]

The blatant official corruption continued until August 1988 when General Zia's death in an air crash brought an eventual restoration of civilian rule. Typical of the misinformation that had blocked any U.S. action against Pakistan's heroin trade, the State Department's semi-annual narcotics review in September called General Zia "a strong supporter of anti-narcotics activities in Pakistan" and speculated that his death might slow the fight against drugs.[80] Instead of fighting drugs, General Zia's regime had of course protected the country's leading heroin dealers. Soon after assuming office through open elections, Prime Minister Benazir Bhutto, by contrast, declared war on the country's drug lords by dismissing two of ISI's top military administrators and creating a new ministry to attack the drug trade. In July 1989 police arrested General Fazle Haq, the former governor of the North-West Frontier province and de facto commander of the Afghan war, who had accumulated a personal fortune estimated at several billion dollars. Unwilling to offend such a powerful man, prosecutors failed to present any evidence of his drug dealing. Instead they charged him with the murder of a popular Muslim cleric and promised further indictments against the general for destroying official records of drug cases against his brother.[81] Moreover, police arrested the general's former pilot, air force Major Farooq Hamid, on charges of heroin smuggling.[82]

Soon after Fazle Haq's arrest, Pakistan's most notorious drug dealer,

Mirza Iqbal Baig, was once the object of political controversy. In an interview with Pakistan's monthly magazine *Newsline*, President Zia's son charged that Baig had "close personal relations" with the speaker of the National Assembly, a prominent leader of Prime Minister Bhutto's ruling People's Party. Only a week later, police arrested Baig and charged him with heroin trafficking.[83] Within months, however, embarrassed government prosecutors had to release him on bail, indicating that the commitment of Benazir Bhutto's government to the drug war was already compromised.[84]

Despite Prime Minister Bhutto's good intentions, the outlook for an effective attack on Pakistan's highly developed heroin industry seemed bleak. After ten years of unchecked growth under General Zia, the country's drug trade was now too well entrenched in the country's politics and economy for simple police action. Conservative economists estimated that total annual earnings from Pakistan's heroin trade were $8–10 billion, far larger than Pakistan's government budget and equal to one-quarter of its entire gross domestic product. With so much heroin money flowing into the country, Pakistan's commentators were concerned that the country's politics would take on a Colombian cast, that is, that the drug lords would start using money and arms to influence the nation's leaders. Indeed, the first signs were not long in coming. Facing a no-confidence motion from the National Assembly in late 1989, Prime Minister Bhutto charged that "drug money was being used to destablize her government." When she claimed that heroin dealers had paid 194 million rupees for votes against her, many observers found the allegations credible.[85] Moreover, the heavily armed tribal populations of the North-West Frontier province were determined to defend their opium harvests. Police pistols would prove ineffective against tribal arsenals that now included automatic assault rifles, anti-aircraft guns, and rocket launchers. "The government cannot stop us from growing poppy," one angry tribal farmer told a foreign correspondent in 1989. "We are one force, and united, and if they come with their planes we will shoot them down."[86] In 1986, General Zia's heavy-handed attempts at poppy eradication had produced angry demonstrations in the province's Gadoon district, in which ten opium farmers were gunned down by police. In the aftermath of the massacre, almost all national and local politicians were vocal in their support for the right of tribal farmers to choose their crops—opium included. By the time Benazir Bhutto took office in December 1988, there was no consensus for opium suppression in Pakistan.[87] Even if Pakistan did eradicate all of its 130 tons of opium, Afghanistan's harvest of some 800 tons, the world's second largest, could easily expand production to supply Pakistan's network of heroin laboratories.[88]

As foreign aid declined in 1989, Afghan leaders expanded opium production to sustain their guerrilla armies. The Soviet withdrawal in February 1989 and a slackening in CIA support produced a scramble among rival mujaheddin commanders for Afghanistan's prime opium land, particularly in the fertile Helmand valley of southern Afghanistan. During most of the war, the local commander Mullah Nasim Ak-hundzada had controlled the best-irrigated lands in the northern Helmand valley, once the breadbasket of Afghanistan, and decreed that half of all peasant holdings would be planted to opium. A ruthless leader and Hekmatyar's bitter enemy, Mullah Nasim issued opium quotas to every landowner and maintained his control by killing or castrating those who defied his directives. Known as the "King of Heroin," he controlled most of the 250 tons of opium grown in Helmand province.[89] Visitors to Helmand during this period spoke "in awestruck tones of the beauty of the poppies which stretch mile after mile."[90] In early 1986 *New York Times* correspondent Arthur Bonner spent a month traveling in Helmand, where he found extensive poppy fields in every village and town. "We must grow and sell opium to fight our holy war against the Russian nonbelievers," explained Mullah Nasim's elder brother Moham-med Rasul. The mujaheddin leader's admission contradicted the assurances that the U.S. embassy in Islamabad had been giving about the Afghan drug trade. Typical of its disinformation on the subject, just two months before, the embassy had issued a formal denial that Afghan guerrillas "have been involved in narcotics activities as a matter of policy to finance their operations."[91]

While Nasim ruled the opium fields of Helmand, Hekmatyar held the complex of heroin laboratories at Koh-i-Soltan at the southern end of Helmand just across the border inside Pakistan. Beginning in 1988, Hekmatyar's local commander had challenged Mullah Nasim's rule over the Helmand opium harvest. Once the snows melted in the spring of 1989, the war revived, now focused on a bridge that linked Helmand to Pakistan's heroin refineries. In the savage fighting, both sides absorbed heavy casualties that greatly weakened the Helmand resistance forces. In the end, Nasim won the war and retained full control of the valley.[92]

In the autumn after his victory, Mullah Nasim, then deputy defense minister in the Afghan interim government, met with U.S. Ambassador to Pakistan Robert Oakley and his staff to request $2 million worth of direct aid in exchange for banning opium in the Helmand valley. With the embassy's promise to deliver the funds if he implemented the poppy ban, Nasim cut opium production and invited American officials into the Helmand valley in January and February 1990 to inspect. The U.S. officials reportedly found the poppy ban effective and noted that opium prices in the nearby Baluchistan border areas had consequently tripled. Before the U.S. embassy could honor its promise, however, in April Mullah Nasim was killed by troops loyal to Hekmatyar, reportedly angry at the sharp increase in the price of Helmand opium needed for his Baluchistan heroin refineries. Nasim's brother Mohammed Rasul succeeded to the command of their forces and was soon engaged in particularly violent clashes with Hekmatyar's troops for control of the opium routes through the Helmand valley.[93] The local war gave the U.S. embassy at Islamabad a difficult choice. It could either honor its promise of $2 million in aid or see the Helmand valley's 250 tons of opium move through Hekmatyar's heroin laboratories toward America. "We haven't been able to provide for our mujaheddin," explained Mohammed Rasul. "If the Americans don't provide assistance, the cultivation of opium will have to begin again."[94]

By early 1990 the CIA's Afghan operation had proved doubly disastrous. After ten years of covert operations at a cost of $2 billion, America was left with mujaheddin warlords whose skill as drug dealers exceeded their competence as military commanders. In 1989, as the cold war ended and the Bush administration's war on drugs began, Afghan leaders like the opium warlord Hekmatyar had become a diplomatic embarrassment for the United States. In its international edition of July 16, 1990, *Time* magazine claimed that the United States was "embarrassed by the widely bruited connections between the drug trade and elements of the insurgents, including such fundamentalist Islamic groups as Gulbuddin Hekmatyar's Hezbi-i Islami." The magazine pointed out that these drug links "are especially painful now that the U.S. is prosecuting an uncompromising war against drugs elsewhere in the world."[95] In a front-page exposé in May 1990, *The Washington Post* claimed that U.S. officials had refused for many years to investigate charges of heroin dealing by Hekmatyar and Pakistan's ISI largely "because U.S. narcotics policy in Afghanistan has been subordinated to the war against Soviet influence there."[96]

Following the policy of radical pragmatism it had used in Burma and Laos, the CIA had again allied itself with an opium warlord. Despite direct complaints from other Afghan guerrilla leaders about Hekmatyar's heroin dealing, the CIA evidently refused to do anything that might lessen his effectiveness as an instrument of its covert operations.

In mountain ranges along the southern rim of Asia—whether in Afghanistan, Burma, or Laos—opium is the main currency of external trade and thus is a key source of political power. Since agency operations involve alliances with local power brokers who serve as the CIA's commanders, the agency, perhaps unwillingly or unwittingly, has repeatedly found its covert operations enmeshed with Asia's heroin trade. By investing a local ally such as Hekmatyar or Vang Pao with the authority of its alliance, the CIA draws the ally under the mantle of its protection. So armed, a tribal leader, now less vulnerable to arrest and prosecution, can use his American alliance to expand his share of the local opium trade. Once the CIA has invested its prestige in one of these opium warlords, it cannot afford to compromise a major covert action asset with drug investigations. Respecting the national security imperatives of CIA operations, the DEA keeps its distance from agency assets, even when they are major drug lords. During the ten years of the Afghan war, some seventeen DEA agents sat in the U.S. embassy at Islamabad watching—without making a major arrest or seizure—as the flood of Afghan-Pakistan heroin captured 60 percent of the U.S. drug market. Operating along the Afghan border, CIA operatives delivered several hundred millions dollars in arms to Hekmatyar's heroin convoys and cooperated closely with his corrupt protectors in Pakistan's ISI. As David Musto demonstrated with his prescient questions at the start of this operation in 1980, CIA complicity in opium traffic had a certain predictability to it, wherever it occurred.

Over the past twenty years, the CIA has repeatedly denied any involvement in the Asian opium traffic. Although admitting that some of its allies might have dabbled in drugs, the agency insists that it has always avoided direct culpability. Regardless of whether these protests are another of the agency's plausible denials, they do not address the main issue. Indeed, critics who look for the CIA's agents to actually dirty their hands with drugs in the line of duty are missing the point. In most covert actions the CIA avoids direct involvement in combat or espionage and instead works through local clients whose success usually determines the outcome of the agency's operation. Consequently, the CIA is sensitive about allegations of drug dealing by its covert action assets. In the case of its Burma operation of the early 1950s, the CIA went to extraordinary lengths to conceal its impact on the Golden Triangle opium trade, spending nearly $2 million twenty years later to stage a bonfire in northern Thailand for the "last" opium shipment by its former covert action clients, the Nationalist Chinese irregulars. Thus, the CIA's involvement in drugs revolves around complicity in the drug dealing of covert action assets, not in most instances any direct culpability.

Instead of a direct legal culpability, CIA involvement in the Asian drug trade sprang from a more subtle political complicity. The corrosive ethos of covert operations that has led the CIA's operatives to tolerate and even protect the heroin trade is best seen in the sordid saga of the Nugan Hand Bank.

# The Nugan Hand Bank

At 4:00 A.M. on January 27, 1980, a state police officer patrolling a country road west of Sydney, Australia, noticed a late-model Mercedes sedan parked by the side of the road and stopped to examine it. Inside the constable found the body of a middle-aged male slumped forward, still holding the rifle he had apparently used to shoot himself in the head. Searching his wallet, the police found personal identification for one Frank Nugan, merchant banker of Sydney, and a calling card from one William Colby, a New York lawyer who had recently retired as director of the U.S. Central Intelligence Agency.[97]

The circumstances of Nugan's suicide and the bank's spectacular collapse only six months later have inspired hundreds of press probes, three major Australian government investigations, and a lengthy book by one of America's best investigative reporters. All have asked the same basic question: What was the relationship between the Nugan Hand Bank and the CIA? Although we have more details about the bank than about any other company with similarly ambiguous CIA connections, the question still defies a concise answer. The Nugan Hand Bank remains a great espionage mystery.

Although the large question about the bank and the agency will probably never be answered, Nugan Hand's twisted history does offer insights into the world of CIA espionage—in particular, that gray area of alumni, allies, assets, and affiliated companies that do so much of the agency's covert work. In his memoirs and public statements, William Colby has portrayed his CIA colleagues as "honorable men," patriots who simply would not, could not tolerate any involvement in drugs by either agency personnel or covert assets.[98] Whatever it may or may not have been, the Nugan Hand Bank was certainly two things: (1) an employer of many retired CIA agents and (2) heavily involved in narcotics trafficking. Unlike most of the agency's faceless espionage, the carefully documented Nugan Hand case affords a close look at the moral universe of covert operations, particularly the gray sector of CIA proprietaries and affiliates. The Nugan Hand case shows how the CIA's secret war in Laos, interwoven with the tribal opium trade, produced a covert action cadre with a tolerance for drug dealing.

The Nugan Hand Bank served several constituencies simultaneously, and its various relationships reveal a good deal about the operations of this clientele. Based in Sydney, the bank was a partnership between Australian lawyer Frank Nugan and an ex–Green Beret businessman named Michael Hand. Both worked closely with one of their senior managers, a mysterious American expatriate with impeccable intelligence contacts, Maurice Bernard Houghton. Through the three men and their separate, sometimes overlapping networks, the bank cultivated corrupt Australian politicians, Sydney crime syndicates, a fraternity of ex-CIA arms dealers, and the U.S. Central Intelligence Agency.

In less than a decade after its incorporation in Sydney in 1973, Nugan Hand Limited went through a complete cycle from modest origins to spectacular global expansion to precipitous collapse. During its eight-year life, the bank's character was shaped by its three principals. Son of a Spanish migrant fruit packer, Francis Nugan grew up in Griffith, New South Wales, in the country west of Sydney, graduated in law from Sydney University, and did some spotty postgraduate legal studies in California and Canada. Nugan would later claim that he played a major role in rewriting Canada's tax law while studying abroad, but records show that he was employed as a minor clerical assistant. His name does appear among the twenty-seven listed in the tax review's final report.[99] While his brother Ken built the family produce business, the Nugan Group Limited, into one of Australia's largest, Frank practiced law in Sydney without much success in the late 1960s.[100] Stripped of his inflated credentials, Frank Nugan was known to be an abrasive alcoholic, an incompetent manager, a mediocre lawyer, and a "pathological liar."[101]

The other founding partner, Michael Jon Hand, was born in New York in 1941, son of a senior state civil servant, and was raised in the Bronx. In 1963 he finished a year's vocational course in forestry at Syracuse University, graduating thirty-eighth among forty-nine students, and joined the U.S. Army's Special Forces, the Green Berets. After training at Fort Bragg, he was sent to Vietnam where he won the army's second highest decoration, the Distinguished Service Cross, for gallantry in fighting northwest of Saigon.[102] Sometime in 1965–1966 Hand joined the CIA for two years as a contract operative fighting with Hmong guerrillas in the mountains of northern Laos. While serving with the CIA, Hand met Theodore Shackley, the agency's Vientiane station chief in 1966–1968, and befriended a crack Air America pilot, Kermit "Buddy" King, who often flew him to remote tribal outposts.[103] The various official reports do not mention whether Hand also met Shackley's friend and deputy CIA station chief Thomas Clines, later a close associate of both Hand and his partner Bernie Houghton. Although Hand's Hmong allies grew opium and shipped it to market on Air America, it is not known whether it was here that Hand acquired the expertise in narcotics that he later applied to building the bank.

Sometime in 1967 Hand finished his CIA contract and moved to Sydney, where he met the American expatriate Bernie Houghton, who was then running the Bourbon and Beefsteak restaurant in the city's Kings Cross vice district. Through Houghton and other contacts, Hand soon became involved in selling Australian real estate to Americans serving in Southeast Asia.[104] In early 1968 the pilot Buddy King joined Hand in Australia and eventually settled with his Thai housekeeper several hours up the coast from Sydney, where their land sales were located, often flying Hand up to the property in a private aircraft for weekends.[105] As an indication of their CIA contacts, in September 1969 Hand formed Australasian and Pacific Holdings Ltd., a real estate company whose seventy-one shareholders included nineteen people then employed by the CIA's contract airlines in Indochina, Air America and Continental Air Services.[106] Sometime in the late 1960s Hand met Frank Nugan and the two are believed to have shared an apartment before they both married.[107] Crude in manner, violent in speech, and poorly educated, Hand had no banking experience and would bring little more than his cunning and covert contacts to the building of Nugan Hand Bank.

The key figure in much of the bank's history, Maurice Bernard Houghton, is a mysterious Texan who arrived in Sydney from Southeast Asia in 1967 with an impressive list of references from senior U.S. military officers. Born in Texas in 1920, Houghton finished a semester at Southern Methodist University; served in the military during World War II; and knocked about the country for twenty years in various jobs with no particular direction. In 1964 Houghton moved to Southeast Asia, where he remained for the next three years during the escalation of the Vietnam War, engaged in activities that remain unclear. Australia's Joint Task Force into the bank's affairs reported that Houghton was "part of the intelligence community" in Southeast Asia before coming to Australia.[108] *Wall Street Journal* reporter Jonathan Kwitny interviewed former U.S. intelligence officers who claimed, on the record, that Houghton was a wheeler-dealer in Southeast Asia who traded in slot machines, opium—anything.[109]

Soon after arriving in Sydney, Houghton formed a business association with a prominent Hungarian émigré, Sir Paul Strasser, owner of one of Sydney's leading property companies. With support from Strasser and his associates, Houghton opened the Bourbon and Beefsteak restaurant in October 1967, just weeks before the first American soldiers began arriving on R&R leave from Vietnam. Among Houghton's private guests at the club were the CIA's Australian station chief from 1973 to 1975, John D. Walker; the state's Premier Sir Robert Askin, a corrupt politician notorious for his contacts with criminal syndicates; and Abraham Saffron, Sydney's leading gangster and the vice lord of Kings Cross. Unlike his future partners, Houghton maintained excellent contacts with the most senior U.S. military and intelligence personnel in the Asia-Pacific region. His intelligence contacts were such that when he returned to Australia from a business trip without a visa in 1972, he rang the state director for the clandestine Australian Security Intelligence Organization (ASIO). The director, Leon Carter, vouched for Houghton, and the American received an immediate visa.[110] In dealing with his male friends, Houghton seems to have been a man of strong loyalties and antipathies. "I had a personality problem with Nugan," Houghton later told the Australian Joint Task Force. "He was harsh, abrasive, arrogant and inconsiderate."[111] By contrast, Houghton remained very close to Michael Hand, who seemed to regard the older man as a "father figure."[112] Hand would eventually tire of Frank Nugan's alcoholism and costly flamboyance, but he remained close to Bernie Houghton until the end.

In 1973 Nugan Hand Limited was born, as it would die, through a gross financial fraud. With only $80 in the company's bank account and just $5 in paid-up capital, Frank Nugan wrote his own company a personal check for $980,000 to purchase 490,000 shares of its stock. He then covered his massive overdraft by writing himself a company check for the same amount. Through this elementary accounting fraud, Nugan could claim that the company's paid-up capital was a million dollars.[113] The bank's start also coincided with the first of many allegations of drug dealing against Michael Hand. Injured in an accident, Buddy King's Thai housekeeper met a Sydney lawyer to sue for compensation. The lawyer, for reasons never explained, phoned the Australian Bureau of Narcotics to report that King, Air America's former ace pilot, was flying heroin into Australia for Michael Hand. Soon after his housekeeper's lawyer made these allegations, King fell to his death from the tenth floor of a Sydney apartment building.[114]

Over the next four years, the bank grew at a remarkable rate by providing a bridge between larger, legitimate banks and a shadow universe of organized crime, illegal money laundering, and intelligence operations. Even at its peak in 1979 with dozens of employees and a global network of offices, the bank never really made a proper profit. Most employees were not clerks or investment counselors, but salespeople who scrambled desperately to keep new deposits coming in the front door faster than the bank's officers could take them out the back—through lavish expenses, high salaries, and simple fraud. Nugan Hand was a carnival shell game, courting depositors for cash and moving money from branch to branch to conceal one fundamental fact—the bank simply had no assets behind it.

Like many corporate confidence men, Frank Nugan and Michael Hand were obsessed with creating the illusion of propriety and prosperity. Without any capital or customers, Frank Nugan's first act in opening the company was to lease expensive, well-appointed offices at 55 Macquarie

Street, a prestigious address in the heart of the Sydney business district.[115] Nugan hired a reputable money market manager who found that he could get an hour or two of credit every day from personal contacts in the business, just long enough to buy and sell. Although the trading incurred a real loss of $18,373, the total volume of transactions reached $2.4 million, giving the new company the aura of doing big business.[116] As the bank grew, so did the scale of its illusions. The bank issued glossy annual reports claiming, in 1976 for example, $22 million in "total assets," $26 million in "gross proceeds from sales of securities," and approval of its bookkeeping by reputable auditors.[117] A lavish promotional brochure described the bank as part of the Nugan Hand Group, "with assets exceeding US $20,000,000 and turnover exceeding US $1,000,000,000 per annum." Assuring potential clients "absolute security, anonymity and confidentiality," the brochure promised customers "the utmost in personal service and attentive specialist assistance." With what now seems wry irony, the bank offered, as a special service for valued customers, child welfare accounts that would "give faithful and attentive care and supervision to all aspects of the education, health, welfare and advancement in life of the children of the beneficiary."[118] All of these claims, financial and moral, were knowing lies.

While Frank Nugan concentrated on courting business clients in Sydney, other associates, Hand included, took the bank abroad. The group's first breakthrough to something approaching profit came in 1974–1975 when it opened a legal Hong Kong branch. By offering Sydney depositors a money-laundering facility for illegal transfers of Australian money to Hong Kong and reciprocally allowing Hong Kong clients a higher rate of interest for funds deposited in Sydney, the bank began to move large funds for the first time.[119]

As these global activities grew over the next six years, Nugan Hand Limited gradually divided, formally and informally, into two almost separate companies: the Sydney-based Nugan Hand Limited under Frank Nugan's control and the international branches of the Nugan Hand Bank, later registered as a Cayman Islands corporation, managed largely by Michael Hand. As Hand grew tired of Frank Nugan's incessant drinking and mounting legal problems,[120] the ex–Green Beret pulled away from his Australian partner and drew Bernie Houghton into the international side of the business. While Frank Nugan's Sydney office concentrated on tax fraud and money laundering, the Hand-Houghton partnership led the bank's international division into new fields—drug finance, arms trading, and support work for CIA covert operations.

During the bank's early days in Sydney, Michael Hand had told his junior colleagues that "it was his ambition that Nugan Hand become banker for the CIA."[121] In southern Africa during the mid-1970s, Hand, the former CIA operative, seems to have realized his ambition. At that time southern Africa was in the throes of decolonization, with guerrilla groups fighting the Portuguese in Angola and British colonials in Rhodesia. When the Portuguese regime began to crumble in Angola, rival guerrilla groups turned to their great power patrons for more arms, making Angola a cockpit of cold war confrontation. As CIA covert arms shipments began flowing into Angola in 1974–1975, first to Holden Roberto and then to UNITA, Michael Hand left Sydney in January 1975 for southern Africa, where he remained for more than a year, trading in arms and munitions.[122] During his fifteen months in Africa, Hand telexed and telephoned the bank's Sydney headquarters repeatedly, speaking with Frank Nugan and an employee, Wilhemus Hans, about shipments of pistols, helicopters, and munitions. After Nugan's death, investigators found what appeared to be phone notes in his handwriting from this period, one of which read:

> Military weapons Rhodesia
> Pay in Gold
> Recoilless Rifles
> Mortars 60/80 ml
> M79 Grenade launchers
> Quad .50 Caliber machine guns[123]

Although it has never been clearly established what, if any, arms were actually shipped from Australia, there is no doubt about the sincerity of Michael Hand's intentions. In Pretoria, South Africa, Hand incorporated a trading company, Murdoch Lewis Proprietary Ltd., to take delivery of arms shipments.[124] At one point Hand summoned his Sydney employee Wilhemus Hans to Africa and met him in Rhodesia for discussions about formation of a helicopter squadron for the white settlers.[125] Hand also made frequent phone calls to another bank employee, Frank Ward, later charged with arms dealing by Australian authorities in court proceedings that remained classified.[126]

While Hand waited in southern Africa to take delivery of arms, his close friend Bernie Houghton flew to Washington, D.C., with two Nugan Hand employees to arrange shipments. Significantly, Houghton made direct contact with CIA agent Edwin Wilson, then working for Task Force 157, a covert action arm of the Office of Naval Intelligence (ONI). With vast profits from his contract covert operations work, Wilson had purchased Mt. Airy Farms, a thousand-acre estate in northern Virginia where he often entertained his close comrades Thomas Clines and Theodore Shackley, Hand's former CIA superiors back in Laos who were now rising fast in the agency's Langley headquarters.[127] After fifteen years as a career CIA officer, Wilson had transferred to Task Force 151 in 1973 and was operating from the offices of a cover company, World Marine Inc., at 1425 K Street in Washington. It was there that Wilson would meet Houghton and the two Nugan Hand men to arrange the African arms deal.

Australia's Joint Task force investigating the bank later learned details of the meetings from Dennis Schlachter, a World Marine employee whose evidence as a protected federal witness would lead to Wilson's 1982 conviction for illegal arms sales to Libya. Sometime in 1975 or early 1976 Schlachter first learned of the Africa arms deal when two CIA agents based in Indonesia, James Hawes and Robert Moore, called on Wilson at World Marine in Washington to discuss "an African arms deal" that, in these agents' words, "had to be put together." Sometime later, Houghton arrived from Sydney and came into World Marine's offices with the two Nugan Hand men to order the arms. Schlachter recalls chauffeuring Wilson and Hawes out to the agency's headquarters in Langley while the two discussed using Nugan Hand Bank to finance the shipments. Under the "cover of Task Force 157," Wilson, in Schlachter's words, placed an order for "10 million rounds of ammunition, 3,000 weapons including machine guns, M-1s, carbines and others." With an end-user's certificate showing World Marine as the purchaser and an Australian company as the buyer, the arms left the United States from Boston for southern Africa in three separate shipments.[128]

The Australian Joint Task Force found that Ed Wilson and Bernie Houghton were also involved in an ONI operation to transfer a highly classified spy ship to the Shah of Iran. Soon after joining Task Force 157 in 1973, Wilson had earned a $500,000 fee by delivering an earlier spy ship to Iran under the cover of World Marine.[129] According to the witness Schlachter, in 1975 the U.S. navy assigned Wilson to deliver another high-technology spy ship to Iran. Schlachter recalls that Houghton "was involved" in this deal, working with "funds . . . and . . . payouts." Significantly, Australian immigration records show that Houghton flew to Iran in March 1975 in the company of a U.S. army colonel. Working through Task Force 157, Wilson purchased the ship and ordered it to sail from England around Africa to Iran. When some "mix-up" developed, Schlachter recalls that "Wilson flew to Iran to correct it." Australian immigration records show that in January 1976 Wilson flew into Sydney and stayed in Australia for three days before flying on to Iran.[130]

After fourteen months in Africa, Michael Hand returned to the bank's Sydney headquarters in March 1976 and dedicated his trade skills to a new constituency—Australia's leading international heroin smugglers.

After nearly fifty years without a serious narcotics problem, Australia showed signs of spreading addiction in the late 1970s as Sydney's criminal syndicates began organizing regular heroin shipments from Southeast Asia. In a March 1977 report, for example, Sydney's Crime Intelligence Unit monitored a series of meetings between the city's leading illegal bookmaker, George Freeman, and California crime figure Danny Stein: "Information was received that Stein was here for the purpose of organizing a network for the reception of heroin into this country from the Golden Triangle and for subsequent distribution on the local market and in the United States."[131]

Would-be Sydney heroin smugglers faced Australia's stringent currency control laws that made it difficult to export the hard cash for heroin buys in Bangkok. After two years of active money laundering through Hong Kong, Nugan Hand was becoming known in the underworld as a reliable money mover. Sometime in early 1976 George "the Duke" Countis, an American crime figure who "owned" a gaming table in an illegal Sydney casino, brought Murray Riley to the headquarters of Nugan Hand Limited. A former Sydney constable, Riley had quit the police to become a "patron" in the criminal underworld and a close associate of leading criminals like George Freeman. Just back from Africa, Hand quickly developed what the Australian police Joint Task Force called "a close business and social relationship with Riley."[132]

Starting in April 1976, only four weeks after his arrival from Africa, Hand made five cash transfers to Hong Kong for Murray Riley totalling $295,000. After each transfer, one of Riley's underlings would call at Nugan Hand's Hong Kong office to pick up the money, later using the cash to take delivery of a heroin shipment. Through this procedure, Nugan Hand handled $4.3 million in identifiable drug money for twenty-six known dealers between 1976 and 1980. Studying Hand's memorandum to his Hong Kong office about a $60,000 cash transfer for Riley's October heroin shipment, the Task Force concluded "that Hand was aware that Riley was involved in significant illegal activity."[133] As an indication of their closeness, in late 1986, acting on Riley's advice, Hand opened bank branches in Thailand, in the words of his Chiangmai branch manager, "to attract 'drug money.' "[134] Two years later, when a yacht was seized south of Sydney with 4.3 tons of high-grade cannabis and Riley was charged, Michael Hand ordered the bank's Hong Kong office to destroy all incriminating records of Riley's money transfers.[135] Reviewing this period in the bank's history, Australia's Joint Task Force concluded: "Throughout 1976 Hand was knowingly involved in drug activity with the 'Riley' group in that he permitted and even encouraged the use of Nugan Hand facilities for the movement of 'drug' money."[136]

In October 1976 Hand decided to leave the Sydney office to Frank Nugan and move to Hong Kong, where he could build the bank's international division. Over the next two years, Hand worked with some success to develop a global network of twelve branches that covered Asia, Africa, and the Americas. After months of failure, Hand's break had come in June 1986 when the Cayman Islands, a British colonial tax haven in the Caribbean, decided to charter the Nugan Hand Bank, finally giving the company the legal right to advertise itself as a "merchant bank."[137]

As the bank expanded dramatically in 1977–1978, Michael Hand recruited some of the most famous names in U.S. national security circles to join the bank as employees or associates. The key figure in making these contacts for Hand was Bernie Houghton, who had taken a more active role in the bank in 1976 after his bar business went bankrupt with debts of nearly a million dollars.[138] In early 1977 Houghton recruited an old friend, Admiral Earl Yates, retired chief strategist for the U.S. Pacific Command, to serve as president of the Nugan Hand Bank. Through the admiral's influence, a succession of such senior appointments followed:

> General Leroy J. Manor, former Pentagon counterinsurgency specialist and chief of staff of the U.S. Pacific Command, manager of the bank's Manila branch;

> General Edwin F. Black, former OSS officer and commander of U.S. forces in Thailand, president of Nugan Hand, Inc., Hawaii;

> Dr. Guy Pauker, Asia expert for the Rand Corporation, a research firm under contract to the U.S. Defense Department, bank consultant;

> Walter McDonald, retired CIA deputy director for economic research, bank executive;

> Dale Holmgren, former chairman of the CIA's Civil Air Transport, manager of the bank's Taiwan branch;

> William Colby, retired CIA director, Nugan Hand's legal counsel.[139]

The pattern of events surrounding this expansion indicates that Michael Hand may have realized his dream of becoming the "CIA's banker." Both Sydney police and *Wall Street Journal* reporter Jonathan Kwitny came away from their long investigations of Nugan Hand convinced that there may well have been some connection between the bank's sudden rise and the antecedent demise of a CIA proprietary, the Castle Bank & Trust of Nassau.[140] After retiring from the CIA, Paul Helliwell, founder of such agency "proprietaries" as SEA Supply Inc. of

Bangkok and Air America, opened a law office in Miami and formed Castle Bank offshore in nearby Nassau to cover the agency's covert money movements. In 1973 agents of the Internal Revenue Service were able to photograph the Castle Bank's customer list while a bank executive dined in a posh Key Biscayne restaurant with a woman described as an IRS "informant." Reviewing the purloined documents, IRS investigators found that the 308 Castle Bank customers on the list had moved $250 million to foreign numbered accounts. Depositors included *Playboy* publisher Hugh Hefner, *Penthouse* magazine publisher Robert Guccione, and some major organized crime figures— Morris Dalitz, Morris Kleinman, and Samuel A. Tucker. Elated by the find, investigators formed Project Haven to make "the single biggest tax-evasion strike in IRS history." Suddenly, the IRS announced that it was dropping the investigation because of "legal problems." According to a later investigation by the *Wall Street Journal,* "pressure from the Central Intelligence Agency . . . caused the Justice Department to drop what could have been the biggest tax evasion case of all time." The CIA invoked "national security" since it was using the Castle Bank "for the funding of clandestine operations against Cuba and for other covert intelligence operations directed at countries in Latin America and the Far East." By the time Helliwell died from emphysema on Christmas Eve, 1976, Castle Bank had been liquidated.[141]

Simultaneous with the closure of Castle Bank's Nassau office, Nugan Hand Bank launched its formal "banking" operations in the nearby Cayman Islands. The opening of Caribbean branches, a new area for Nugan Hand, and recruitment of retired CIA officers gave it a corporate structure similar to the collapsed Castle Bank. Indeed, a former CIA agent named Kevin Mulcahy, a key witness in the Edwin Wilson case, gave details to the *National Times* of Sydney "about the Agency's use of Nugan Hand for shifting money for various covert operations around the globe."[142]

Working through Houghton, moreover, the Nugan Hand Bank deepened its contacts with the network of ex–CIA officials surrounding Edwin Wilson. After helping Hand informally with the bank's operations for the previous five years, Houghton finally joined Nugan Hand's staff in late 1978 and opened a branch in Saudi Arabia to collect deposits from American contract employees. Under Houghton's management, the Saudi branch ran the bank's biggest—and simplest—fraud. With introductions from Beck Arabia of Dallas, a leading engineering firm with major Middle East contracts, Houghton flew into Saudi Arabia in January 1979 and rented a villa at Al-Khobar to serve as both office and residence for the bank.[143] Over the next twelve months, Houghton and his aides circulated through the U.S. construction camps along the

Persian Gulf, issuing bank receipts for cash deposits from American contract workers. Paid in cash and unable to make deposits in Saudi Arabia's backward banking system, American expatriate workers needed the deposit-taking service that Nugan Hand pretended to provide. Houghton then bought bundles of Thomas Cook traveler's checks and sent them off in commercial courier parcels to Michael Hand's new office in Singapore. Through this simple system, Houghton and Hand collected at least $5 million from their fellow Americans—all of which simply disappeared when the bank collapsed a year later.[144]

Houghton's presence in Arabia brought Nugan Hand Bank into closer contact with Wilson's network of former CIA officials, now moving its base of operations to nearby Libya. When Houghton opened his Saudi office in 1979, Wilson's network seemed a step away from unprecedented power, and Houghton apparently decided to join their rise. Within months, however, both Wilson's group and Nugan Hand were plunging precipitously toward collapse.

After decades inside the CIA, Wilson and his closest associates were finally forced out in the late 1970s, losing the mantle of CIA protection that had long masked their operations. In February 1976, Admiral Bobby Ray Inman, the new head of the Office of Naval Intelligence, ran into Ed Wilson by chance and learned to his surprise that this wheeler-dealer was one of his own operatives in Task Force 157. When Wilson's contract came up for renewal a few months later, ONI canceled it on Inman's orders, pushing the ex–CIA man into the private sector.[145] There he prospered. Between June and September 1976 Wilson supplied Libya with thousands of CIA-designed bomb timers and more than 21 tons of Composition C-4, the most powerful nonnuclear explosive in America's arsenal—thereby providing Colonel Muammar al-Qaddafi with a potent weapon for his terrorist campaign in Europe and the Middle East.[146] Over the next four years, Wilson recruited U.S. Green Berets to train Libyan commandos, delivered weapons for Qaddafi's terrorists, and even arranged assassinations for the Libyan dictator.[147] One of Wilson's employees, former CIA officer Kevin Mulcahy, became concerned by these shipments and reported them to the CIA. But Wilson's old friend Theodore Shackley, now deputy director for clandestine services, blocked any internal investigation.[148] In April 1977 *The Washington Post* published an article on Wilson's activities stating that he "may have had contact with one or more current CIA employees," and the agency's new director, Admiral Stansfield Turner, started asking questions. He soon learned about Wilson's close friendships with his former CIA colleagues Clines and Shackley, then high in the Langley hierarchy. Over the opposition of senior CIA bureaucrats, Turner transferred the two to secondary jobs.[149] A year later Thomas Clines resigned from the CIA after thirty years' service, borrowed $500,000 from Wilson to set up his own company, and soon won a $71 million contract for arms delivery to Egypt.[150] No longer heir-apparent to the post of CIA director, Theodore Shackley resigned in September 1979 and followed Clines into the consulting business.[151]

Throughout 1979 the Wilson network and the Nugan Hand Bank began to build a close commercial alliance in the netherworld of national security subcontracting. In the latter half of the year, Michael Hand renewed relations with his former CIA station chief when he met Shackley in Washington to discuss ways in which the bank could help a new company, API Distributors Inc., that the retired CIA official owned jointly with Clines and that was then trying without success to break into the Middle East oil business.[152] "Dear Ted," Hand wrote from Sydney on bank stationery on November 27, "I just checked with Dale Holmgren our Nugan Hand representative in Taipei with regards to the equipment query you gave me." Hand signed off with the suggestion that they get together with a mutual friend: "Maybe next time I am in Washington, we may be able to have the opportunity to sit down and have a bit of lunch together with Bernie Houghton." The reply was prompt and friendly. "Dear Mike," Shackley wrote on API letterhead on December 10, "I enjoyed our Washington discussion and look forward to seeing you again."[153]

Indeed, Bernie Houghton, now representing Nugan Hand in Arabia, had his own entrée to Shackley, the man who had nearly become CIA director. In 1972, Houghton had met air force Major General Richard Secord in Hawaii and seven years later the general introduced Houghton to his close friend Thomas Clines. In the mid-1960s, General Secord had been one of the triumvirate directing the CIA's secret war in Laos—CIA chief of station Ted Shackley exercised overall command, his CIA deputy Tom Clines handled the details, and air force liaison Secord supplied most of the aircraft essential to combat operations in the mountains of northern Laos.[154] As Clines and Shackley had moved into Wilson's commercial orbit after leaving Laos, General Secord seemed to follow, accepting favors large and small from the arms trader.[155] With the general's introduction, Houghton met frequently with Shackley and Clines in late 1979 to probe ways of helping API Distributors get off the ground in the Middle East oil business.[156]

All four, of course, had a mutual friend in Ed Wilson, whose growing troubles threatened their future. As a Washington grand jury started to gather incriminating evidence in early 1979 about his illegal arms sales, Wilson shifted his operations to London and Libya to avoid arrest.[157] Although he now relied on Libya as his ultimate refuge, Wilson was in deep trouble in Tripoli for his failure to deliver on an arms contract to

Colonel Qaddafi's army. Without first getting a firm delivery price, Wilson had contracted to supply 5,000 M16 automatic rifles to the Libyan army at a fixed payment. Knowing his plight, covert arms suppliers around the globe were now holding him to ransom by demanding inflated prices that Wilson could not afford to pay.[158] Since the Libyan letter of credit for $22 million specified delivery of American-made M16s, whose export to Libya were then banned under U.S. law, Wilson was finding that regular banks would not honor his Libyan letter.[159] Tom Clines and Bernie Houghton flew to Switzerland in late 1979 to confer with Wilson, who traveled up from Tripoli for the meeting. During several days of discussions, the three discussed ways of using Nugan Hand Bank to float a $22 million loan to finance the delivery.[160] According to the Australian Joint Task Force, Clines himself probably invested with the bank during this period and may have lost up to a million dollars in the coming crash.[161]

While Bernie Houghton worked closely with the Wilson network, Hand devoted his energies to launching an ambitious scheme through the CIA old boy network—the resettlement of 3,000 Hmong tribesmen from Thai refugee camps to a Caribbean island. Hand claimed some sentimental attachment to the Hmong from his service as CIA case officer with their tribal guerrillas in Laos, and in late 1979 he made several trips to the United States to promote the scheme. While seeking substantial funding from the U.N. high commissioner for refugees, Hand arranged a series of meetings with Livingston WerBell III, a former OSS officer and counterterror trainer famous in covert action circles for designing the compact Ingram submachine gun long favored by CIA operatives. In 1965–1966, WerBell had mounted an abortive coup against the Haitian dictator François "Papa Doc" Duvalier, and now Hand wanted WerBell to press the son and successor "Baby Doc" Duvalier to grant the bank a long-term lease on Jacmel Island in the bay of Port-au-Prince.[162] When that scheme collapsed, Hand, through Admiral Yates, began to explore the idea of leasing a former U.S. navy base on Turks and Caicos Islands and consulted with William Colby, the retired CIA director who had signed on as the bank's legal counsel. Interviewed by the Australian Royal Commission, Colby recalls discussing the Turks resettlement scheme with Hand. Indeed, Colby later submitted a bill to Nugan Hand for $45,684.09 for legal work on this and other matters.[163] In January 1980 Nugan Hand signed a contract with the Turks and Caicos government leasing the former U.S. navy base in exchange for a commitment to provide $1 million in future development funds.[164]

Noting that the settlement of 3,000 Hmong, almost half the population on the islands, would strain the ecology of the arid, infertile Turks and

Caicos, the Australian Joint Task Force concluded that there were "hidden motives for the project." Reviewing the evidence, Australian police investigators concluded that Michael Hand may have had a "sinister" motive in leasing a naval base complete with docks and airstrip in these islands: "The proximity . . . to a number of South American drug source countries makes them a natural transit point for illicit drug shipments destined to the North American market. The Turks and Caicos Islands are a significant transshipment point along the line of route."[165]

Before any of these deals could be worked out, Australian police found Frank Nugan's body in January 1980 and the Nugan Hand Bank began its rush to ruin. Although the collapse was sudden, the bank had been in deep trouble for more than a year. The Nugan family's produce company was being investigated for fraud, leading commercial banks were warning customers of the bank's alleged drug dealings, and the auditors were refusing to approve the books at several branches.

In retrospect, the cause of the bank's collapse seems to lie with the scandals attached to the Nugan family's fruit packing business, the Nugan Group Limited, based in the country town of Griffith, New South Wales. After an Italian criminal syndicate began producing marijuana on Griffith's irrigated farmlands in the early 1970s, persistent rumors began circulating that the Nugan family's packing plant was somehow involved. In 1977 an independent audit of the company's books turned up accounts in the names of the local drug dealers and some evidence of corporate fraud. When minority shareholders mounted a challenge to the Nugan family's management, Frank and his older brother Ken hired one of Sydney's leading crime figures, retired police detective Frederick Krahe, who filled the annual meeting with a legion of thugs and drunks, each armed with a single share of stock, to force approval of the company accounts.[166]

But the effort backfired when state Attorney-General Frank Walker ordered a full inquiry of this extraordinary episode. After the state Corporate Affairs Commission announced a formal investigation of the Nugan fruit company in October 1977, there was a run on Nugan Hand Bank offices in Sydney that took out about 30 percent of total deposits.[167] A month later, an opposition leader speaking on the floor of the state parliament accused the Nugan fruit company of marijuana dealing. In full-page advertisements in the national press, Ken Nugan denounced the attorney-general as "nothing short of despicable" and flatly denied the allegations of drug dealing—a flamboyance that fanned the media flames.[168]

While controversy over marijuana trading filled the pages of the Sydney press in late 1977, one of the bank's currency couriers was stopped and searched for drugs at Hong Kong. That news made Frank

Nugan "visibly upset."[169] Both angry and frightened, Nugan appealed to Bernie Houghton to use his U.S. contacts to fix matters in America. Advised through his contacts about local drug investigations, Nugan went to Canberra, where he demanded that the Australian Bureau of Narcotics end its inquiries of the bank's affairs. Intimidated, the bureau quietly dropped the matter.[170] To fund the legal and public relations battle for the family fruit business, Frank Nugan began stealing from the bank's accounts. Over the next two years, he would graft $1.8 million to defend the family fruit business, an amount sufficient to destabilize the bank's shaky finances.[171]

Despite Frank Nugan's extraordinary effort and expense, the state Corporate Affairs Commission issued warrants for the arrest of Ken and Frank Nugan on fraud charges in May 1978, news that made page 1 of Sydney's leading business journal, the *Financial Review*.[172] Growing ever more desperate, in October 1979, three months before his death, Nugan called a meeting of Sydney staff and ordered them to clean up the bank's business by passing the "illegitimate clients off to other banks" and refusing "illegal transactions in the future."[173] Nugan concocted a wild scheme to stop the Corporate Affairs investigation of his family fruit business. According to papers found after his death, Nugan deposited $6,000 in a numbered Swiss bank account under Attorney-General Walker's name and apparently planned to use contacts in the state's opposition party to leak the story to the press.[174] In the weeks before Nugan's death, the bad news mounted. The state attorney-general announced that the Nugan brothers would stand trial for fraud. From the Bahamas came word that auditors Price Waterhouse would not approve the books for the Nugan Hand Bank.[175] The local Sydney auditor, long the bank's loyal servant, now insisted that Nugan honor about "$4 to $5 million" of company financial paper or he would be forced to qualify his endorsement of the bank's books.[176]

As soon as police advised him of his brother's death on January 27, 1980, Ken Nugan rang Michael Hand in London, demanding: "What's going on, why has Frank committed suicide?" Told of the death of the man he had once described as his closest friend, Michael Hand said: "The little fucker, he has gone and got out of this mess and left me to clean it up."[177] After he heard of Nugan's suicide, Bernie Houghton, then in Switzerland, rang his branch office in Saudi Arabia and ordered his staff to bail out. Leaving a detachment of U.S. army troops to guard the office against angry American depositors, Houghton's staff left the country on the earliest available flight.[178] Evidently in a rush to return to Sydney, Houghton dropped by Ed Wilson's office in Geneva the day of Nugan's death and left a briefcase with bank documents for safekeeping. Several months later, one eyewitness watched while Tom Clines went through the briefcase at Wilson's office and removed one sheet of paper with his own name on it. When General Richard Secord's name was mentioned during the search, Clines said: "We've got to keep Dick's name out of this."[179]

Two days after Nugan's death, Michael Hand landed at Sydney airport and went directly to the bank's offices at 55 Macquarie Street. According to one witness, Hand told the directors when he arrived at the office that "if they did not 'cooperate' with him in the administration of the Nugan Hand Group, dissatisfied clients could cause them all to 'finish up [with] lead boots . . . concrete shoes' and they would be 'liable to find [their] wives being delivered to [them] in pieces.' " Assisted by a cooperative staff and the dutiful Admiral Earl Yates, Hand and Houghton led the directors in a systematic destruction of bank records.[180] Over the next four months, funds kept disappearing from bank branches around the world until losses reached about $25 million—a substantial sum in Australian financial circles in the late 1970s.[181] Finally, on April 17, Michael Hand announced that the bank was insolvent and asked the court to appoint liquidators.[182]

With bank records destroyed and assets stripped, Houghton and Hand fled from Australia. As Australian investigators began searching for bank records, Hand went into hiding around Sydney. On June 1 "an unnamed American" landed at Sydney airport and called for Houghton at his Bourbon and Beefsteak Restaurant. The next day Houghton and his American escort flew out of Sydney for Manila, America, and, ultimately, Acapulco. According to the Australian Joint Task Force, the "unnamed American" who assisted Houghton in his escape "has been identified as Thomas Clines."[183] Concerned about being arrested, Michael Hand was even more circumspect in his escape. With the help of one of Houghton's close friends, a former U.S. marine living in Sydney, Hand got an Australian passport under an assumed name. On May 14 James O. Spencer, an ex–Green Beret who had served in the CIA's Laos operation with Hand, landed at Sydney airport on a flight from the United States. Exactly a month later, Hand flew out of Australia with Spencer as his escort and, traveling via Fiji and Vancouver, crossed the border into America. There he disappeared.[184]

Clearly, there is more to Nugan Hand's history than mere corporate fraud. But even after a decade of intense investigation, it is difficult to be definitive about the meaning of the scandal. To enhance the plausible deniability of its operations, the CIA often works indirectly through a universe of proprietaries, alumni, assets, and affiliates. Inherent in the CIA's style of subcontracting covert operations is an ambiguity that makes precise analysis of situations like the Ed Wilson case or the Nugan Hand Bank operation almost impossible.

Even the Wilson case, after numerous trials and several convictions in U.S. courts, remains laden with ambiguities. Wilson was indicted for illegal arms sales to Libya in 1980, arrested in June 1982, tried, and sent to prison for life.[185] In 1982 Thomas Clines was indicted on charges of defrauding the U.S. government of $8 million for the shipment of military aid to Egypt by one of his companies, EATSCO. The federal prosecutor who convicted Wilson, Lawrence Barcella, had evidence that Clines was simply the front man in a criminal conspiracy. Several witnesses were ready to testify that Wilson had loaned Clines $500,000 to set up EATSCO as a company controlled by four partners—Clines; Ted Shackley, former CIA deputy director for clandestine services; Major General Richard Secord, then assistant secretary of defense responsible for military aid to Egypt; and Erich von Marbod, deputy director of the Pentagon's Defense Security Assistance Agency. Instead of pressing on with the indictment to force full revelations, another federal prosecutor allowed Clines to admit his individual guilt, pay a $10,000 fine, and return $3 million in stolen funds. Denying any involvement, General Secord resigned from the Pentagon with his pension intact.[186]

Even though none of the Nugan Hand principals has been brought to trial, there is enough evidence available for some tentative conclusions. The bank was probably not a CIA proprietary and its formation was not, like that of the Castle Bank, an agency initiative. But Hand and Houghton probably succeeded in joining Ed Wilson in that gray zone inhabited by CIA alumni, affiliates, and assets. Working with Wilson when he still belonged to ONI's Task Force 157, Hand and Houghton made some major arms shipments to southern Africa, possibly in support of the CIA's Angolan guerrilla clients, and played a role in the delivery of a spy ship to the Shah of Iran's navy.

Although there is a great deal still unknown about the activities of both Wilson and the Nugan Hand Bank, there is already enough information on the record for a moral assessment of the CIA's covert warriors. Richard Helms and William Colby, CIA directors when the agency was fighting its secret war in Laos, have insisted that the agency's faceless, nameless agents were "honorable men" morally incapable of tolerating the opium trade. "As fathers, we are . . . concerned about the lives of our children and grandchildren," CIA director Helms told the American Society of Newspaper Editors in 1971. "As an Agency, in fact, we are heavily engaged in tracing the foreign roots of the drug traffic. . . . We hope we are helping with a solution; we know we are not part of the problem."[187] The agency's anonymous operatives in Laos were, Colby insisted, moral exemplars determined to insulate their covert operations from the economic imperatives of

Laos's tribal opium trade. They would never, Colby insists, have allowed any tribal opium aboard one of the CIA's Air America aircraft.[188]

Public scrutiny of one generation of CIA commanders in this secret war now allows sufficient evidence to test the assertions of Colby and Helms about the ethics of their men. As of 1966–1967 Theodore Shackley was CIA station chief in Vientiane; Thomas Clines, deputy chief of station; General Richard Secord, U.S. air force liaison with the CIA; and Michael Hand of the U.S. Special Forces, contract CIA agent advising Hmong guerrillas in the field. After suffering a demotion for his close contact with Ed Wilson, who was then selling both classified weapons and information to a hostile foreign power, Shackley resigned from the CIA. Following plea bargaining for a lesser charge, Clines stood in an open court and admitted to defrauding the U.S. government of $8 million. General Secord testified as a defense witness for Wilson at one of his trials, denied any involvement in any wrongdoing, and resigned from the Pentagon.[189] After serving in Laos, Michael Hand founded a merchant bank whose commercial specialty was money laundering for drug dealing and tax fraud. Such men do not somehow seem extreme moralists. Instead, they appear to be pragmatists who would not have been troubled by any accommodation their secret war might have made with a local tribal opium trade.

## Contras and Cocaine

During the 1980s Latin American cocaine exports to the United States escalated, producing a pandemic of narcotics abuse. In a special report to the White House in 1982, Attorney General William French Smith stated that U.S. cocaine imports jumped to 44 tons in 1980, a 57 percent increase in just one year. Of America's total illicit drug sales of $79 billion, the attorney general estimated that cocaine now accounted for $29 billion, the largest illicit income for any single drug.[190] Even after this rapid expansion, the cocaine market continued to grow. Between 1982 and 1985 the number of cocaine users in the United States rose by 38 percent to 5.8 million, more than ten times the number of heroin addicts. In 1986 16.9 percent of American high school seniors admitted to trying cocaine at least once.[191]

Then came crack. By chemically converting cocaine powder to a granular base state suitable for smoking, American drug dealers produced a readily usable, cheap narcotic that could be sold for as little as $10 a dose. After crack became widely available in 1985–1986, its use spread to a new generation of younger users unable to afford the high price of pure cocaine or heroin. Only a year after the drug first appeared in most markets, 5.6 percent of U.S. high school seniors surveyed reported that they had used crack at least once.[192]

From the outset, the surge of exports was directed by a consortium of Colombian cocaine brokers known as the Medellín cartel. In 1980 some 75 percent of all U.S. cocaine came from Colombia, largely through networks controlled by the Medellín cartel. Unlike many such criminal names that often seem the product of police or media imagination, the Medellín cartel actually operated as a coherent group, pooling finances and making collective marketing decisions. According to a study by the U.S. Senate, the cartel began in 1980 when the Marxist revolutionary group M-19 kidnapped a member of the Ochoa family, a prominent cocaine-manufacturing clan. At a meeting in his Medellín restaurant, Jorge Ochoa convinced the major cocaine families to contribute $7 million each for the formation of a 2,000-man army equipped with the latest in automatic weapons. Over the coming months, the cartel's army fought and won a war with M-19, forcing many of its survivors into an unwilling alliance that strengthened the cartel. More important, the process of fighting a common enemy evidently tightened ties among the city's drug families, allowing a close cooperation in the years following their victory. By 1982, in the words of a congressional investigation headed by Massachusetts Senator John Kerry, the Medellín cartel had "perfected the cocaine smuggling business into a high-tech trade based on specialization, cooperation and mass production." The Escobars managed production, the Ochoas transportation, and, before its leader's arrest, the Lehders distribution.[193] By 1988 the cartel's annual income was estimated at $8 billion and *Forbes* magazine had placed two of its leaders, Jorge Ochoa and Pablo Escobar, on its list of the world's richest men.[194]

As the cartel's exports expanded in the early 1980s, there were signs that its smugglers were using CIA covert operations to protect their cocaine shipments into the United States. Indeed, the Medellín cartel's rise coincided with the start of the CIA's second largest operation of the decade, the support and supply of Contra guerrillas fighting the leftist Sandinista government in Nicaragua. All major U.S. agencies have gone on the record stating, with varying degrees of frankness, that the Medellín cartel used the Contra resistance forces to smuggle cocaine into the United States. In a July 1986 report, the State Department said that "available evidence points to involvement with drug traffickers by a limited number of persons having various kinds of affiliations with, or political sympathies for, the resistance groups."[195] In testimony before the U.S. Senate in July 1988, the DEA's assistant administrator David Westgate said that "people on both sides of the equation [in the Nicaraguan war] were drug traffickers and a couple of them were pretty significant."[196] Referring to the Contras' Southern Front commander Eden Pastora, the head of the CIA's Central American Task Force stated in May 1986: "We knew that everybody around Pastora was involved in cocaine. . . . His staff and friends . . . were drug smugglers or involved in drug smuggling."[197]

The question, then, is not whether the Contra war against the Sandinista government became involved in cocaine trafficking, but in what way and to what degree. The State Department adopted the minimalist position that a few people somehow affiliated with the Contras may have been involved with cocaine. Better-informed agencies, the DEA and CIA, reported that leading Contra commanders were major traffickers. After holding extensive hearings on the Caribbean cocaine trade, Senator Kerry's subcommittee concluded that systematic cocaine smuggling by those involved in the Contra war had become a major element in a nexus of regional corruption that allowed the drug trade to prosper. In its summary, the subcommittee concluded that "individuals associated with the Contra movement" were traffickers; cocaine smugglers had participated in "Contra supply operations"; and the U.S. State Department had made "payments to drug traffickers . . . for humanitarian assistance to the Contras, in some cases after the traffickers had been indicted . . . on drug charges."[198] At a more serious and sinister level, the subcommittee gathered evidence that John Hull, an American expatriate rancher in Costa Rica who was either a CIA asset or agent, played a leading role in the cocaine traffic across Central America.[199] Taking the Kerry subcommittee's evidence one step further, the Christic Institute, a Washington legal advocacy group, charged in a private indictment that a number of CIA agents and former agents had been principals in the Central American cocaine traffic.[200]

As in the case of the DEA's interdiction efforts, analysis of who was responsible for what aspect of the Caribbean cocaine traffic is an elusive task. In the actual drug production zones of the Andes, Afghanistan, or Burma, determining control over the drug trade is a relatively easy manner. By simply hiking through the Afghan-Pakistan borderlands, for example, a *New York Times* reporter or a DEA agent can quickly learn that Mullah Nasim rules the poppy fields of the upper Helmand valley or that Hekmatyar owns the half dozen heroin refineries at Koh-i-Soltan. The fact of territorial control makes involvement in drug dealing too obvious to conceal in these opium highlands. By the time cocaine reaches the Caribbean it is already two steps removed from its territorial source—from the Andes valleys of Bolivia or Peru to Colombia and from Medellín to the airways of the Caribbean. Deciding who controlled which aircraft in the cat's cradle of trans-Caribbean airlanes is an elusive task with uncertain results.

Despite these inherent difficulties, Senator Kerry's investigation gathered a wealth of detail that allows, for the first time, an informed assessment of the impact of covert operations on the Caribbean cocaine trade. After President Reagan took office in January 1981, the CIA, acting on White House directives, began a covert operation in support of the Contra resistance fighters based in camps along Nicaragua's border with Honduras. After the collapse of the Somoza dictatorship in 1979, the Nicaraguan National Guard had fled across the border to escape revolutionary retribution and there formed a nucleus for the Contra forces.

When the Contra camps opened along Nicaragua's borders in the early 1980s, Honduras and Costa Rica were already well-established transit points for the Medellín cartel's cocaine flights north to America. Protected by the Honduran military leaders, Colombian cocaine traffickers were, by the late 1970s, already using "Honduran airstrips for refueling and transshipment of cocaine heading north."[201] In the late 1970s the Costa Rica borderlands had been a staging area for the Sandinista revolution, and the country's police had stayed away from the area, allowing the Medellín cocaine flights to land en route to America.[202] Once the Contra war started, it was in these same areas of northern Costa Rica that the resistance developed its closest relation to the cocaine trade. In 1983 the loosely structured Contras opened the Southern Front in Costa Rica under the command of the former Sandinista guerrilla Eden Pastora, an independent, charismatic figure that both the CIA and Contra command found difficult to control. With comparatively limited U.S. military aid, the impoverished Southern Front soon turned to the cocaine trade to finance its operations. By permitting drug pilots to refuel at its camps in their flights north to America, the Southern Front financed delivery of arms and supplies.[203] Finding Pastora "disruptive and unpredictable" after his refusal to subordinate himself to the Contra command in Honduras, the CIA cut off all aid to his forces in 1984.[204]

As their troops began suffering "desperate conditions," Pastora's commanders struck a bargain with George Morales, a leading Colombian smuggler based in Miami. Already under indictment for drug smuggling, Morales sought an alliance with the Contras in the belief that their CIA contacts might help his case.[205] According to a U.S. State Department report, in late 1984 Morales supplied Pastora's Southern Front with a C-47 aircraft and money to "fly narcotics shipments from South America to sites in Costa Rica and Nicaragua for later transport to the United States."[206] Between October 1984 and February 1986 the C-47 made twenty-four flights from America to Southern Front bases along the Nicaragua–Costa Rica border with 156,000 pounds of material and returned carrying unspecified quantities of drugs.[207] The arrangement continued until early 1986 when the arrests began. In January veteran Southern Front pilot Gerardo Duran was arrested in Costa Rica for transporting cocaine to the United States.[208] At about the same time, Morales got into trouble over a cocaine flight from the Bahamas and was finally arrested in June.[209] Although the CIA's Costa Rica station chief, Thomas Castillo, told the U.S. Senate that he had reported "narcotics trafficking by Pastora's supporters and lieutenants," the smuggler Morales continued to work with the Contras for nearly two years before he was arrested for an unrelated drug flight.[210]

Apparently the Contras were not the only cocaine traffickers on the Southern Front. According to witnesses before Senator Kerry's subcommittee, an American rancher in Costa Rica named John Hull who' worked closely with the CIA was "involved in cocaine trafficking." After Congress passed the Borland Amendment cutting aid to the Contras in 1984, Hull, still nominally a private citizen, began to play a major role in the Contra supply effort.[211] When Lieutenant Colonel Oliver North of the National Security Council formed a private network to fund the Contras after the aid cutoff, he recruited General Richard Secord, recently retired from the Pentagon, to establish a covert arms supply operation. Admitting his ignorance about infantry weapons, Secord, a career air force officer, recruited the ex–agency man Thomas Clines, whom he later described as "a very close associate of mine from CIA days." The phrase "CIA days" was, of course, a reference to their service together commanding the agency's secret war in Laos during the late 1960s.

With funds from the sale of U.S. arms to Iran and gifts from private donors like the Sultan of Brunei, the Clines-Secord partnership purchased aircraft and hired veterans of past clandestine operations— "pilots, mechanics, and cargo handlers"—to ship arms south to the Contras.[212] In the words of Senator Kerry's report, John Hull became the "central figure in Contra operations when they were managed by Oliver North, from 1984 through late 1986." Scattered across Hull's sprawling ranch in northern Costa Rica, six airstrips operated beyond the control of weak local customs or police. According to testimony by Costa Rica station chief Castillo, Hull "helped the CIA with military supply" in the 1984–1986 period. Moreover, at the direction of North, Hull received a stipend of $10,000 per month from the Contra command in Honduras.[213]

In hearings on Capitol Hill, Senator Kerry's subcommittee took testimony from five witnesses who claimed direct personal knowledge of John Hull's involvement in the cocaine traffic. Among those was the Colombia drug smuggler George Morales, who passed a polygraph test to establish the credibility of his testimony.[214] A Costa Rica official, Werner Lotz, said "he heard" that drug pilots en route from Colombia to America paid Hull to stop and refuel at his airstrips. Gary Betzner, a veteran drug pilot for George Morales, testified that he was present on two occasions when John Hull actually witnessed cocaine being loaded on aircraft. In July 1984 Betzner flew into Hull's ranch in a Cessna 402-B loaded with a cargo of weapons for the Contra Southern Front. Betzner was "met at the airstrip by Hull and they watched the cargo of weapons being unloaded, and cocaine, packed in 17 duffel bags, and five or six two-foot square boxes being loaded into the now-empty Cessna." With his cargo of cocaine, Betzner flew the Cessna north and landed at a field in Lakeland, Florida, without any search. On another "guns for drugs flight" two weeks later, Betzner landed at an airstrip ten miles from Hull's ranch and again stood with Hull while they watched a half ton of cocaine being loaded for the return flight to Florida.[215]

When Hull's activities prompted investigation by the U.S. attorney for the Southern District of Florida, U.S. officials in Central America did their best to protect Hull from arrest. In March 1985 U.S. Attorney Jeffrey Feldman and two FBI agents went to Costa Rica to investigate allegations about Hull's activities. In an interview with Feldman, U.S. Ambassador Lewis Tambs and CIA station chief Castillo "gave the impression that Hull had been working for U.S. interests." A U.S. embassy security officer, Jim Nagel, told one of the FBI investigators that Hull was working for "agencies with other operational requirements and we shouldn't interfere with the work of these agencies." Since Hull was "receiving protection from some U.S. officials," Feldman gave up his attempts to interview the American expatriate. Three years later, the Justice Department had still not indicted John Hull.[216]

Other aspects of the Contra operation lent protection to the Caribbean cocaine trade. In 1986, for example, the U.S. State Department paid four contractors $806,401.20 to supply humanitarian aid to the Contra forces in Central America. All four of these companies were owned by known drug traffickers. For three years before the State Department contracted it to deliver aid to Central America, the SETCO company had been the main air transport corporation used by Honduras-based Contras to ferry supplies from America. According to a U.S. customs report, SETCO's owner was Juan Ramon Matta Ballesteros, a Honduran cocaine trafficker listed as a "class I DEA violator." Another of the four was a Costa Rican seafood company, Frigorificos de Punterennas, whose owner Luis Rodriquez was indicted on drug charges eighteen months after completing the State Department's service contract.[217]

As in Laos and Pakistan, CIA operations in the Caribbean hampered the DEA's enforcement efforts. The conflict between the DEA's drug war and the CIA's contra operation was particularly acute in Honduras, home of the critical "northern front" against Nicaragua's Sandinista government. Responding to the growing importance of the country as a transshipment point for Colombian cocaine, in 1981 the DEA opened a new office in the Honduran capital Tegucigalpa. During his two years as the DEA's chief agent in Honduras, Tomas Zepeda found that the country's ruling military officers were implicated in the transit traffic in cocaine and did everything possible to slow his operations. "It was difficult to conduct an investigation and expect the Honduran authorities to assist in arrests when it was them we were trying to investigate," Zepeda told the U.S. Senate. In June 1983 the DEA closed its Honduran office without consulting Zepeda and transferred him to Guatemala "where he continued to spend 70 percent of his time dealing with the Honduran drug problem." In his testimony before Senator Kerry's committee, Zepeda said that he would have argued, if asked, that the DEA's Honduran office should have remained open because he had "generated a substantial amount of useful intelligence."[218] Only four years later Honduras became such an important drug transshipment point that the DEA was forced to reopen its Tegucigalpa office.[219] Why, then, did the DEA close its Honduran operation in 1983 just at the point that the cocaine flow to the United States was becoming critical? As one DEA agent told a reporter who asked this question, "The Pentagon made it clear that we were in the way. They had more important business."[220]

Underlying all these allegations, official and unofficial, is one area of significant agreement: the CIA's Contra support operation coincided with a major expansion in the Caribbean cocaine trade. Even if we leave aside the question of active CIA complicity, the coincidence between cocaine trafficking and covert operations made the DEA's task of drug interdiction almost impossible. By using Contra support aircraft to carry their cocaine, the Medellín cartel's smugglers reduced the risk of seizure. For the DEA to determine which light aircraft crossing the Caribbean were CIA, cartel, or both became increasingly difficult. Simply by launching a major covert operation in a strategic drug zone, the CIA contributed, albeit indirectly, to a major expansion of America's cocaine supply.

## Search for Solutions

Reflecting public concern over the pandemic of narcotics abuse and trafficking, President Bush's "war on drugs" is becoming a major focus of U.S. foreign policy in the 1990s. To cut the flow of cocaine northward across the Caribbean, Bush invaded Panama, convened a drug summit of Latin American leaders, and made his drug war a top budgetary priority. Now that events in Eastern Europe are denying communism its sense of threat, narcotics suppression may become the main aim of U.S. foreign policy in the Third World during this decade.

Armed with a national consensus for action, President Bush and his drug administrator William Bennett have committed the country to a policy of repression far stronger than President Richard Nixon's earlier "war on drugs." In the months following Bush's declaration of "war," U.S. policy has escalated beyond drug interdiction and diplomatic pressure to military intervention. Compared with Bush's mobilization of the U.S. military, Nixon's earlier use of financial and diplomatic pressures in his war on drugs seems mild.

Now that America is fighting its second drug war, it seems time to ask some obvious questions: Can increased suppression of the international narcotics traffic slow the flow of drugs into the United States? If not, why is the policy likely to fail? Finally, what will be the consequences of such failure?

Although policy variables are too complex for prediction, historical precedents can provide the basis for assessing the probable outcome of the Bush drug war. Since the United States first prohibited narcotics use in the early 1920s, succeeding administrations have used repressive strategies that share one essential attribute—failure.

During the first decades of drug prohibition after 1920, the federal government focused on domestic drug control through specialist agencies, notably the Federal Bureau of Narcotics (FBN). Instead of eliminating drug abuse, domestic suppression changed its social character from a middle-class problem to a lower-class vice. To deal with the international supply of drugs, the United States supported, in a limited way, attempts by the League of Nations to reduce global narcotics supply through a multilateral drug diplomacy. Initially, the United States had played a pioneering role in the diplomacy by convening the first international anti-opium conference at Shanghai in 1909 and leading subsequent meetings over the next five years. After World War I, however, the United States refused to join the League of Nations and became a mere observer at the meetings of its narcotics committee.

Even without the full support of the world community, the League's drug diplomacy was remarkably successful in reducing the world's supply of opium and heroin. Between 1906 and 1934, global opium production dropped dramatically from 41,000 tons to just 7,600. Similarly, only five years after the League banned recreational heroin use in 1926, world production dropped from 9,000 to 1,000 tons. The United Nations inherited the League's antinarcotics work after World War II, and the United States resumed its leadership role in multilateral drug diplomacy.

Before World War II, U.S. narcotics agents did not operate outside America. In the late 1940s, however, the United States reduced its reliance on multilateral diplomacy and began sending its own narcotics agents to Europe and the Middle East. Using its diplomatic leverage to post FBN agents at its embassies, the United States gradually changed the character of its international drug control efforts. Operating one-on-one with the police of individual countries, U.S. drug agents were, in effect, creating a new kind of bilateral diplomacy. By placing pressure on a country such as France, Turkey, or Mexico to crack down on its local traffickers, the FBN tried to cut the drug flow to America. Instead of waiting for the U.N.'s slow, multilateral efforts to reduce the entire world's drug production, the FBN's bilateral approach targeted specific sources of America's drug supply in single countries such as Italy or Mexico. Since the 1950s American policy has invested most of its resources in these bilateral efforts to intercept shipments bound for America, thereby reducing U.S. support for the U.N.'s multilateral efforts.

In 1973 President Nixon declared his "war on drugs"—the first major U.S. attempt at bilateral suppression of narcotics production. Fighting his first battles in the Anatolian plateau, Nixon drew on the close U.S. military alliance with Turkey to force a complete eradication of legal opium production, thus cutting supplies to Marseille's heroin laboratories, then the main source of America's narcotics. The effort produced a temporary shortage in America's heroin supply and a long-term expansion of global production. Over the next decade, America's heroin dealers shifted their supplies from Turkey to Southeast Asia, then to Mexico, and then to southern Asia—remaining one step ahead of U.S. narcotics agents. Blocked from shipping their heroin to America, the Chinese syndicates of Southeast Asia shifted their exports to Europe, creating a drug market there almost as large as that in the United States. By the early 1980s it was clear that America's first war on drugs had compounded the problem. Why?

Simply put, narcotics are major global commodities resistant to any attempt at localized suppression. As long as the demand for drugs in the cities of the First World continues to grow, Third World producers will find a way to supply their markets. Ignoring these simple economic realities, the United States has, over the past seventy years, applied localized tactics to deal with a global problem. Before World War II, FBN agents tried to eradicate America's illicit narcotics supply by pursuing drug dealers inside the United States, ignoring the world market that delivered the heroin. After the war, FBN agents began operating abroad with the police of individual countries, seeking a localized interdiction of drug shipments to America from Marseille or Mexico.

Elaborating this local model of law enforcement into a global strategy, the United States has applied police methods of "buy and bust" in a way that is simply not effective against a complex global commodity trade. Confronted with local repression, say in Turkey or Mexico, the global drug market reacts by expanding production elsewhere, thereby increasing smuggling routes and making the traffic more resistant to interdiction efforts. The eradication of Turkey's opium crops in the early 1970s, for example, raised the world market price and encouraged increased production by poppy farmers in Afghanistan and Burma.

Ignoring these lessons of Nixon's Anatolian campaign, President Bush has adopted a similar bilateral strategy of local repression for his drug war in the Andes. Although both programs have tried to eradicate the drug supply at its source, Bush is employing some novel tactics, such as mobilizing the combat resources of the U.S. military. In both Anatolia and Indochina, Nixon reinforced the Drug Enforcement Administration with State Department diplomacy and CIA intelligence. But Nixon, unlike Bush, never drew on the resources of the U.S. military. Despite these formidable new weapons in his arsenal of repression, Bush's strategy remains strikingly similar to Nixon's—and is likely to fail for the same reasons.

When the blunt baton of law enforcement is brought down on a commerce as elaborate as global drug trafficking, the merchants usually react in ways not foreseen by the enforcement agencies. Dealing with global narcotics trafficking as if it were a localized vice such as pornography or prostitution, U.S. enforcement agencies are applying repression without any awareness of the complex global marketing systems involved. Instead of eradicating narcotics, suppression thus becomes another market stimulus that may actually expand drug production and distribution. Even if Bush's massive military effort wipes out the entire Andean cocaine trade, Asia's opium farmers are already producing record harvests. The heroin exporters of Pakistan and Burma stand ready to fill any void in the U.S. drug market that might appear when cocaine supplies slacken. Even under optimum circumstances, attempts at suppression can worsen the problem.

If America cannot win this war on drugs, does it have a viable alternative, short of surrender? Indeed, the public debate over drug policy in 1989–1990 gave the impression that America has only two choices—war or surrender. As the drug epidemic spread in the 1980s, bringing high crime rates and spectacular gang warfare with automatic weapons, many commentators began to question the wisdom of U.S. drug policy.

In the midst of the crisis of confidence, academics associated with the Drug Policy Foundation advocated a radical alternative to the current policy of repression—legalization. In one stroke of the president's pen, drug use, like alcohol, would become a matter of individual choice; the spread of drug-related street crime would recede; and the crack gangs would lose their markets. Legalization would not solve the problem, its advocates readily admitted, but neither will the current policy of repression. Legalization soon won some impressive converts—several U.S. congressional representatives, a New York judge, the mayor of Baltimore, and influential commentators.

Before this debate could be joined, White House advisers dismissed the idea and President Bush captured center stage with his declaration of "war." With his mobilization of military might, the president in effect closed the debate. No matter how articulate academic policy analysis might be, voices cannot compete with the dramatic images from the Latin American drug war. A talk-show drug discussion is a head and two moving hands, a weak image compared with the action news footage from the front lines of the drug war—U.S. troops shooting their way into Panama City, cocaine gangs bombing buildings in Colombia, heavily armed U.S. drug agents soaring through the Andes in combat helicopters.

Whether the battle for the Andes is won or lost, President Bush's drug war, like the capture of General Noriega, will not have any long-term impact on the U.S. domestic drug problem. As long as the demand for drugs remains, heroin can recapture the U.S. market that it held for sixty years before the advent of cocaine. The drama of the drug war has diverted the public gaze from the domestic problem, postponing the search for a new drug policy by a few months or years. Eventually, the debate will resume, and the questions asked in 1989 will have to be answered.

Is legalization the answer? The case for legalization rests on some unstated assumptions that cannot be tested with the poor information now available about drug use and users. For example, the reformers do not really explain what kind of legalization they want. Few advocates are really calling for full legalization, that is, unrestricted sale of cocaine and heroin to all buyers, including teenagers and children. Even if such a policy were proposed, it probably would not pass into law among an electorate that has recently raised the drinking age for alcohol from eighteen to twenty-one. If drugs were to be partially legalized, with restrictions on sales to persons under twenty-one, then what percentage of crack users will be denied access to legal drugs? Nobody knows. Even if we had an accurate profile of drug users in today's market, by the time legislation is enacted and implemented, the volatile drug market might have changed character radically. If we assume that half the crack users are under twenty-one, a limited legalization might well expand drug abuse among teenagers. Adult addicts could survive by buying limitless supplies of legal drugs and marking them up for resale to teenagers. Since possession and sale would no longer be illegal, police would have no control over a market mechanism that could spread narcotics abuse to levels not seen since prewar decades when China and Iran allowed legal drug sales.

If the idea of legalization were widely accepted, it could develop an unintended racial subtext, a sense of wanting to give up on the drug-infested inner cities: "Let *them* have their drugs if they want them. Just as long as *they* keep their crime and violence to themselves."

Between the extremes of war and surrender, or legalization and suppression, there is an unexplored middle ground—a policy that might be called regulation. A policy of drug regulation might be applied in four specific areas: (1) treatment and education to reduce U.S. domestic demand; (2) short-term, bilateral interdiction efforts aimed at reducing, but not eliminating, drug shipments bound for America; (3) increased cooperation with U.N. narcotics agencies to gradually reduce global drug supply; and (4) control over CIA covert operations to bar future agency alliances with powerful drug lords.

Instead of conducting interdiction with the rhetoric of war and total victory, legal controls might be used to seek a more modest, long-term improvement of the drug situation. Through a balance of international interdiction and domestic seizures, the federal government could gradually reduce the drug supply and addict population to levels where adequate treatment facilities are available for those who need or want them. Moreover, such regulation might block the periodic surges in heroin or cocaine shipments that glut the illicit market, dropping prices and forcing dealers to actively solicit new buyers. Anything that can be done to reduce U.S. demand for drugs—preventive education or curative treatment—will weaken the illicit market and make the problem more manageable. Instead of seeking a quick win in a drug war to suddenly eradicate the problem, the policy of regulation might aim at gradually reducing the number of heroin users from 500,000 to 200,000 over a period of four or five years.

Recognizing the failure of America's interdiction efforts, U.S. foreign policy might be better served by transferring resources from current bilateral U.S. programs to the U.N.'s multilateral drug agencies. The record is clear on the comparative effectiveness of both policies. Under both the League of Nations and United Nations, multilateral drug diplomacy has produced a dramatic decline in global narcotics production since the 1920s. Through the multilateral diplomacy of the League and the U.N., global opium production dropped dramatically from its high of 41,600 tons in 1906 to only 1,000 tons in 1970. By contrast, U.S. efforts at bilateral interdiction—both the DEA's foreign "buy-and-bust" operations and the presidential drug wars—have produced major increases in both production and consumption of narcotics. In the twenty years that have followed America's first war on drugs, global opium production has increased by more than 470 percent, rising from 1,000 tons in 1970 to 4,700 tons in 1990. The statistical evidence is strong: U.N. diplomacy reduced world opium supply almost 97 percent, while America's drug wars have led to a 470 percent increase in illicit production. Although slow and seemingly inefficient in reducing America's drug supply over the short term, the U.N.'s multilateral drug diplomacy has a proven record of long-term effectiveness. Narcotics are global commodities and only a world-wide approach of universal suppression can reduce supply and, ultimately, addiction. By contrast, America's bilateral efforts simply deflect production and consumption to other markets, creating a short-term illusion of success for a few years until redoubled supplies from an expanded global market sweep America, producing yet another drug epidemic of unprecedented proportions. Using the medical analogy for heroin addiction, the U.S. policy of bilateral, local drug suppression is rather like dealing with a global epidemic of smallpox or yellow fever by trying to seal the country's borders against the microbes. Instead, the United States has supported the World Health Organization in its successful worldwide campaigns to eliminate these diseases from the face of the earth. Like a communicable disease, a global commodity such as opium can be eradicated only through a cooperative, worldwide effort.

The final area of regulation is one that few in official Washington are willing to discuss—the imposition of controls over CIA covert operations to ensure that the United States does not continue to protect drug lords. Whatever the strengths or weaknesses of U.S. drug efforts might have been, they have not operated under optimum circumstances. Over the past forty years American and allied intelligence agencies have played a significant role in protecting and expanding the global drug traffic. CIA covert operations in key drug-producing areas have repeatedly restrained or blocked DEA efforts to deal with the problem.

Rather than operating as a force for repression, many government espionage agencies have acted, directly or indirectly, to structure the drug market, not destroy it. During this century, government intelligence agencies and police have often sought alliances with drug syndicates. Indeed, the list of governments whose clandestine services have had close relations with major narcotics traffickers is surprisingly long—Nationalist China, Imperial Japan, Gaullist France, French Indochina, the Kingdom of Thailand, Pakistan, and the United States. Instead of reducing or repressing drug supply, most clandestine agencies seem to regulate the traffic by protecting favored dealers and eliminating their rivals.

Adopting a pragmatic policy of accepting any effective ally in the struggle against communism, the CIA has, over the past forty years, extended the imprimatur of its protection to a number of the world's leading drug lords. Indeed, if we review the history of postwar drug traffic, we can see a repeated coincidence between CIA covert action assets and major drug dealers. During the 1950s the CIA worked with the Corsican syndicates of Marseille to restrain Communist influence on the city's docks, thereby strengthening the criminal milieu at a time when it was becoming America's leading heroin supplier. Simultaneously, the CIA installed Nationalist Chinese irregulars in northern Burma and provided them with the logistic support that they used to transform the country's Shan states into the world's largest opium producer.

During the 1960s the CIA's secret war in Laos required alliances with the Hmong tribe, the country's leading opium growers, and various national political leaders who soon became major heroin manufacturers. Although Burma's increased opium harvest of the 1950s supplied only regional markets, Laos's heroin production in the late 1960s was directed at U.S. troops fighting in South Vietnam. Constrained by local political realities, the CIA lent its air logistics to opium transport and did little to slow Laotian heroin shipments to South Vietnam. When U.S. troops withdrew from Vietnam in the early 1970s, Southeast Asian heroin followed the GIs home, capturing one-third of the U.S. drug market in the mid-1970s. After protracted complicity in the marketing of opium and heroin, the CIA emerged from Laos with an entire generation of clandestine cadres experienced in using narcotics to support covert operations.

During the 1980s the CIA's two main covert action operations became interwoven with the global narcotics trade. The agency's support for Afghan guerrillas through Pakistan coincided with the emergence of southern Asia as the major heroin supplier for the European and American markets. Although the United States maintained a substantial force of DEA agents in Islamabad during the 1980s, the unit was restrained by U.S. national security imperatives and did almost nothing to slow Pakistan's booming heroin exports to America.

Similarly, CIA support for the Nicaraguan Contras has sparked sustained allegations, yet unconfirmed, of the agency's complicity in the Caribbean cocaine trade. Significantly, many of the CIA covert warriors named in the Contra operation had substantial experience in the Laotian secret war.

Surveying CIA complicity in the narcotics trade over the past four decades produces several conclusions. First, agency alliances with Third World drug brokers have, at several key points, amplified the scale of the global drug traffic, linking new production areas to the world market. Protected by their CIA allies, these drug brokers have been allowed a de facto immunity from investigation during a critical period of vulnerability while they are forging new market linkages. Of equal importance, the apparent level of CIA complicity has increased, indicating a growing tolerance for narcotics as an informal weapon in the arsenal of covert warfare. Over the past twenty years, the CIA has moved from local transport of raw opium in the remote mountains of Laos to apparent complicity in the bulk transport of pure cocaine directly into the United States or the mass manufacture of heroin for the U.S. market. Finally, America's drug epidemics have been fueled by narcotics supplied from areas of major CIA operations, while periods of reduced heroin use coincide with the absence of CIA activity.

In effect, American drug policy has been crippled by a contradiction between DEA attempts to arrest major traffickers and CIA protection for many of the world's drug lords. This contradiction between covert operations and drug enforcement, seen most recently during Pakistan's heroin boom of the 1980s, has recurred repeatedly. The CIA's protected covert action assets have included Marseille's Corsican criminals, Nationalist Chinese opium warlords, the Thai military's opium overlord, Laotian heroin merchants, Afghan heroin manufacturers, and Pakistan's leading drug lords.

Although there are problems in many CIA divisions, complicity with the drug lords seems limited to the agency's covert operation units. In broad terms, the CIA engages in two types of clandestine work: espionage, the collection of information about present and future events; and covert action, the attempt to use extralegal means— assassination, destabilization, or secret warfare—to somehow influence the outcome of those events. In the cold war crisis of 1947, the national security act that established the CIA contained a single clause allowing the new agency to perform "other functions and duties" that the president might direct—in effect, creating the legal authority for the CIA's covert operatives to break any law in pursuit of their objectives. From this vague clause has sprung the entire CIA covert action ethos and the radical pragmatism that have encouraged repeated alliances with drug lords over the past four decades.

With the demise of the cold war in 1989–1990, it might now be possible to impose some controls over the CIA. A small reform of the national security legislation would close down the CIA's covert action apparatus, which is no longer necessary, without weakening the agency's main intelligence-gathering capabilities. Regulation of the CIA's covert operations might thus deny some future drug lord the political protection he needs to flood America with heroin or cocaine.

# Notes

## Introduction: A History of Heroin

1. *New York Times*, March 16, 1990.
2. Ibid.
3. N.S.W. Royal Commission into Drug Trafficking, *Report* (Sydney: Government Printer, October 1979), p. 267.
4. International Opium Commission, *Report of the International Opium Commission: Shanghai, China, February 1 to February 26, 1909* (Shanghai: North China Daily News, 1909), pp. 44–45.
5. Cheng U Wen, "Opium in the Straits Settlements, 1867–1910," *Journal of Southeast Asian History* 2, no. 1 (March 1961), pp. 52–75; League of Nations, Advisory Committee on the Traffic in Opium and Other Dangerous Drugs, *Annual Reports on the Traffic in Opium and Other Dangerous Drugs for the Year 1931* (Geneva: League of Nations, 1931), p. 96; Bernard M. Peyrouton, *Les Monopoles en Indochine* (Paris: Emile Larose, 1913); Virginia Thompson, *French Indochina* (New York: Macmillan, 1937), pp. 184–91.
6. United Nations, Department of Social Affairs, *Bulletin on Narcotics* 5, no. 2 (April–June 1953), pp. 3–4, 6.
7. Ibid.; David F. Musto, *The American Disease: The Origins of Narcotics Control* (New Haven: Yale University Press, 1973), pp. 6–10, 254–56.
8. Musto, *The American Disease*, pp. 6–10.
9. Ibid., p. 3.
10. E. J. Hobsbawm, *Industry and Empire: The Making of Modern English Society* (New York: Pantheon, 1968), pp. 15, 55–56, 119, 311.
11. U.S. Secretary of Commerce and Labor, Department of Commerce and Labor, *Statistical Abstract of the United States 1910* (Washington, DC: U.S. Government Printing Office, 1911), pp. 536–37, 540.
12. Musto, *The American Disease*, p. 5.
13. David T. Courtwright, *Dark Paradise: Opiate Addiction in America Before 1940* (Cambridge: Harvard University Press, 1982), pp. 9–28.
14. Terry M. Parssinen, *Secret Passions, Secret Remedies: Narcotic Drugs in British Society, 1820–1930* (Philadelphia: Institute for the Study of Human Issues, 1983), pp. 32–33.

15. Ibid., pp. 35–36; Alfred W. McCoy, *Drug Traffic: Narcotics and Organized Crime in Australia* (Sydney, NSW: Harper & Row, 1980), pp. 52–70.
16. Courtwright, *Dark Paradise*, pp. 35–42; McCoy, *Drug Traffic*, pp. 41–70.
17. Commonwealth of Australia, Parliament, *Report of the Royal Commission on Secret Drugs, Cures, and Food* (Sydney, NSW: Government Printer, 1907), paragraphs 967–1006.
18. Musto, *The American Disease*, pp. 10–14, 91–94.
19. Courtwright, *Dark Paradise*, pp. 106–7; Musto, *The American Disease*, pp. 91–150.
20. United Nations, *Bulletin on Narcotics*, p. 7.
21. See chart on following page.
22. U.S. Congress, Senate, Committee on Government Operations, *Organized Crime and Illicit Traffic in Narcotics*, 88th Cong., 1st and 2nd sess. (Washington, DC: U.S. Government Printing Office, 1964), pt. 4, p. 771.
23. Interview with Lt. Col. Lucien Conein, former CIA operative in Saigon, McLean, Virginia, June 18, 1971.
24. John C. McWilliams, *The Protectors: Harry J. Anslinger and the Federal Bureau of Narcotics, 1930–1962* (Newark, Delaware: University of Delaware Press, 1960), pp. 33–45, 48–80, 120–6.
25. Alan A. Block, "On the Origins of American Counterintelligence: Building a Clandestine Network," *Journal of Policy History* 1, no. 4 (1989), pp. 353–72.
26. James I. Matray, "Bureaucratic Cold Warrior: Harry J. Anslinger and Illicit Narcotics Traffic," *Pacific Historical Review* 50, no. 2 (May 1981), pp. 169–91.
27. Douglas Clark Kinder and William O. Walker III, "Stable Force in a Storm: Harry J. Anslinger and United States Narcotic Policy, 1930–1962," *Journal of American History* 72, no. 4 (March 1986), pp. 922–27.
28. U.S. Bureau of Narcotics and Dangerous Drugs, "Persons Known to Be or Suspected of Being Engaged in the Illicit Traffic in Narcotics," revised (Washington, DC, March 1965).
29. United Nations, Department of Social Affairs, *Bulletin on Narcotics*, p. 8; U.S. Treasury Department, Bureau of Narcotics, "History of Narcotic Addiction in the United States," in U.S. Senate, Committee on Government Operations, *Organized Crime*, pt. 3, p. 771.
30. U.S. Bureau of Narcotics and Dangerous Drugs, "The World Opium Situation" (Washington, DC: October 1970), p. 10; U.S. State Department, Bureau of International Narcotics Matters, *International Narcotics Control Strategy Report, March 1990*, pub. no. 9749 (Washington, DC: U.S. State Department, March 1990), pp. 19–20.
31. U.S. Cabinet Committee on International Narcotics Control (CCINC), *World Opium Survey 1972* (Washington, DC: CCINC, 1972), pp. 18–22, A1–A6.
32. U.S. State Department, Bureau of International Narcotics Matters, *International Narcotics Control Strategy Report, March 1990*, pp. 19–20, 239–68.
33. Ibid., pp. 19–20, 271–334.

## World Non-Medicinal Opium Production 1906–1989
### (In metric tons and % of world production)

| | 1906[a] | % | 1934[b] | % | 1970[c] | % | 1989[d] | % |
|---|---|---|---|---|---|---|---|---|
| **Southeast Asia** | | | | | | | | |
| Burma | n.d. | – | 19 | * | 500 | 47 | 2,625 | 63 |
| Thailand | n.d. | – | – | | 145 | 14 | 50 | 1 |
| Laos | 2 | * | – | | 68 | 6 | 375 | 9 |
| Total | 2 | * | 19 | * | 713 | 67 | 3,050 | 73 |
| **East Asia** | | | | | | | | |
| China | 35,364 | 85 | 6,378 | 83 | – | – | – | – |
| Japan | n.d. | – | 16 | * | – | – | – | – |
| Total | 35,364 | 85 | 6,394 | 84 | – | – | – | – |
| **Southwest Asia/Middle East** | | | | | | | | |
| Turkey | 477 | 1 | 148 | 2 | 58 | 6 | | – |
| Iran | 604 | 2 | 459 | 6 | – | – | 300 | 7 |
| India/ Pakistan | 5,177 | 12 | 344 | 5 | 139 | 13 | 130 | 3 |
| Afghani- stan | n.d. | – | 175 | 2 | 106 | 10 | 585 | 14 |
| Total | 6,258 | 15 | 1,126 | 15 | 303 | 28 | 1,015 | 24 |
| Other Total | – | – | 114 | 1 | 50 | 5 | 144 | 3 |
| **World Total** | 41,624 | | 7,653 | | 1,066 | | 4,209 | |

n.d. = Data not available.

* = Less than 1%.

[a]International Opium Commission, *Report of the International Opium Commission: Shanghai, China, February 1 to February 26, 1909* (Shanghai: North China Daily News, 1909), p. 356, "Statistics of Trade in Opium: A. Import."

[b]League of Nations, Advisory Committee on the Traffic in Opium and Other Dangerous Drugs, *Annual Reports of Governments on the Traffic in Opium and Other Dangerous Drugs for the Year 1935*, vol. 11 (Geneva: League of Nations, 1937), pp. 46–47.

[c]Figures represent the average of two U.S. government agency estimates. See U.S. Congress, Senate, Committee on Appropriations, *Foreign Assistance and Related Programs Appropriations for Fiscal Year 1972*, 92nd Cong., 2nd sess. (Washington, DC: U.S. Government Printing Office, 1971), pp. 578–84; U.S. Cabinet Committee on International Narcotics Control (CCINC), *World Opium Survey 1972* (Washington, DC: CCINC, 1972), pp. 11, A38–A39.

[d]U.S. State Department, Bureau of International Narcotics Matters, *International Narcotics Control Strategy Report, March 1990* (Washington, DC: U.S. Government Printing Office, March 1990), p. 19.

34. Alvin Moscow, *Merchants of Heroin* (New York: Dial, 1968), pp. 61–63. Southeast Asia's morphine is usually about 10 percent morphine by weight, Afghan's averages roughly 8 percent, and Pakistan's is only about 4 percent. (U.S. Cabinet Committee on International Narcotics Control, *World Opium Survey 1972* [Washington, DC: U.S. Government Printing Office, 1972], pp. A8, A36.)

35. "The Illicit Manufacture of Diacetylmorphine Hydrochloride (No. 4 Grade)," paper of a Hong Kong government chemist, n.d., pp. 1–5.

36. Max Singer (project leader), *Policy Concerning Drug Abuse in New York State* (Croton-on-Hudson: Hudson Institute, May 31, 1971).

## 1  Sicily: Home of the Mafia

1. J. M. Scott, *The White Poppy* (London: William Heinemann, 1969), pp. 167–69.

2. United Nations, Economic and Social Council, *World Trends of the Illicit Traffic During the War 1939–1945* (E/CS 7/9, November 23, 1946), pp. 10, 14.

3. William P. Morgan, *Triad Societies in Hong Kong* (Hong Kong: Government Press, 1960), pp. 76–77.

4. Charles Siragusa, *The Trail of the Poppy* (Englewood Cliffs, NJ: Prentice-Hall, 1966), pp. 180–81.

5. David Annan, "The Mafia," in Norman MacKenzie, *Secret Societies* (New York: Collier, 1967), p. 213.

6. The CIA had its origins in the wartime Office of Strategic Services (OSS), which was formed to make sure that intelligence errors like Pearl Harbor did not happen again. The OSS was disbanded on September 20, 1945, and remained buried in the State Department, the army, and the navy until January 22, 1946, when President Truman formed the Central Intelligence Group. With the passage of the National Security Act in 1947 the group became an agency, and on September 18, 1947, the CIA was born (David Wise and Thomas B. Ross, *The Invisible Government* [New York: Random House, 1964], pp. 91–94).

7. David T. Courtwright, *Dark Paradise: Opiate Addiction in America Before 1940* (Cambridge: Harvard University Press, 1982), pp. 146–47.

8. Alan A. Block, *East Side–West Side: Organizing Crime in New York, 1930–1950* (New Brunswick, NJ: Transaction Books, 1983), pp. 131–41.

9. Ibid., pp. 28–29; David Courtwright et al., *Addicts Who Survived: An Oral History of Narcotic Use in America, 1923–1965* (Knoxville: University of Tennessee Press, 1989), pp. 110, 199–203; Hank Messick, *Lansky* (New York: Putnam's, 1971), pp. 22–24.

10. Alan A. Block, "The Snowman Cometh: Coke in Progressive New York," *Criminology* 17, no. 1 (1979), pp. 75–99.

11. Albert Freid, *The Rise and Fall of the Jewish Gangster in America* (New York: Holt, Rinehart and Winston, 1980), p. 214.

12. Alan A. Block, "European Drug Traffic and Traffickers Between the Wars:

The Policy of Suppression and Its Consequences," *Journal of Social History* 23, no. 2 (1989), pp. 315–37.

13. U.S. Treasury Department, Bureau of Narcotics, *Traffic in Opium and Other Dangerous Drugs for the Year Ended December 31, 1937* (Washington, DC: U.S. Government Printing Office, 1938), pp. 20–21; U.S. Treasury Department, Bureau of Narcotics, *Traffic in Opium and Other Dangerous Drugs for the Year Ended December 31, 1939* (Washington, DC: U.S. Government Printing Office, 1940), pp. 29–30; M. R. Nicholson, Treasury Attaché, American Consulate General, Shanghai, China, "Survey of Narcotic Situation in China and the Far East," July 12, 1934, "List of Greek Narcotic Suspects Residing in Shanghai," p. 3 (Harry Anslinger Papers, Historical Collections and Labor Archives, Pennsylvania State University).

14. Block, *East Side–West Side*, pp. 168–82; Fried, *Rise and Fall*, pp. 157–74, 223–28.

15. Block, *East Side–West Side*, pp. 131–39.

16. U.S. Congress, Senate, Committee on Government Operations, *Organized Crime and Illicit Traffic in Narcotics*, 88th Cong., 1st and 2nd sess. (Washington, DC: U.S. Government Printing Office, 1964), pt. 4, p. 913.

17. Nicholas Gage, "Mafioso's Memoirs Support Valachi's Testimony About Crime Syndicate," *New York Times*, April 11, 1971.

18. Harry J. Anslinger, *The Protectors* (New York: Farrar, Straus, 1964), p. 74.

19. Courtwright, *Addicts Who Survived*, pp. 179–88.

20. Courtwright, *Dark Paradise*, pp. 107, 110–11.

21. Courtwright, *Addicts Who Survived*, pp. 186–88.

22. Block, *East Side–West Side*, pp. 141–48.

23. Anslinger, *Protectors*, p. 74.

24. Norman Lewis, *The Honored Society* (New York: Putnam's, 1964), pp. 72–73.

25. U.S. Justice Department, Federal Bureau of Investigation, "Vido Genovese, with alias Vito Genovese, Miscellaneous Information Concerning," October 7, 1944 (Alan A. Block Archive on Organized Crime, Pennsylvania State University).

26. Lewis, *Honored Society*, p. 77.

27. Michele Pantaleone, *The Mafia and Politics* (London: Chatto & Windus, 1966), p. 52.

28. William B. Herlands, Commissioner of Investigation, Executive Department, State of New York, "Report," September 17, 1954, p. 4 (Thomas E. Dewey Papers, University of Rochester).

29. Ibid., p. 31; Rodney Campbell, *The Luciano Project: The Secret Wartime Collaboration of the Mafia and the U.S. Navy* (New York: McGraw-Hill, 1977), p. 33.

30. Herlands, "Report," pp. 16–17.

31. Ibid., p. 31.

32. Ibid., pp. 34–35; Alan A. Block, "A Modern Marriage of Convenience: A Collaboration Between Organized Crime and U.S. Intelligence," in Robert J. Kelley, ed., *Organized Crime: A Global Perspective* (Totowa, NJ: Rowman & Littlefield, 1986), pp. 62–64.

33. Block, "Modern Marriage," p. 65.

34. Herlands, "Report," pp. 37–39.

35. Ibid., pp. 43–44.

36. Ibid., pp. 46–53.

37. Ibid., pp. 58–63.

38. Ibid., pp. 66–67, 93.

39. Ibid., p. 8.

40. Ibid., pp. 81–82.

41. Campbell, *Luciano Project*, pp. 169–74.

42. Max Corvo, *The O.S.S. in Italy, 1942–1945: A Personal Memoir* (New York: Praeger, 1990), pp. 64–67.

43. R. Harris Smith, *OSS: The Secret History of America's First Central Intelligence Agency* (Berkeley: University of California Press, 1972), pp. 85–87.

44. Herlands, "Report," p. 86.

45. Campbell, *Luciano Project*, pp. 174–78.

46. Herlands, "Report," pp. 86–87.

47. Ibid., p. 20; Estes Kefauver, *Crime in America*, quoted in Lewis, *Honored Society*, pp. 18–19.

48. Lt. Col. Albert N. Garland and Howard McGraw Smith, *United States Army in World War II. The Mediterranean Theater of Operations: Sicily and the Surrender of Italy* (Washington, DC: Office of the Chief of Military History, Department of the Army, U.S. Government Printing Office, 1965), p. 244.

49. Ibid., p. 238.

50. Pantaleone, *Mafia and Politics*, pp. 54–55. Michele Pantaleone was probably Italy's leading authority on the Sicilian Mafia. A native and longtime resident of Villalba, he was in a unique position to know what happened in the village between July 15 and July 21, 1943. Also, many of Villalba's residents testified in the Sicilian press that they witnessed the fighter plane incident and the arrival of the American tanks several days later (Lewis, *Honored Society*, p. 19).

51. Gay Talese, *Honor Thy Father* (New York: World Publishing, 1971), p. 201.

52. Pantaleone, *Mafia and Politics*, p. 56.

53. Ibid., pp. 56–57.

54. Harry L. Coles and Albert K. Weinberg, *United States Army in World War II. Civil Affairs: Soldiers Become Governors* (Washington, DC: Office of the Chief of Military History, Department of the Army, U.S. Government Printing Office, 1964), p. 147, cited in Gabriel Kolko, *The Politics of War* (New York: Random House, 1968), p. 57.

55. Pantaleone, *Mafia and Politics*, p. 58; Gaia Servadio, *Mafioso: A History of the Mafia from Its Origins to the Present* (New York: Dell, 1976), pp. 90–91.

56. Block, *East Side–West Side*, p. 109; Martin Gosch and Richard Hammer, *The Last Testament of Lucky Luciano* (Boston: Little, Brown, 1974, pp. 273–74.

57. Coles and Weinberg, *Civil Affairs*, p. 210.

58. Kolko, *Politics of War*, p. 48.

59. U.S. State Department, *Foreign Relations of the United States,* pt. 3, p. 1114, quoted in Kolko, *Politics of War,* p. 55.
60. Lewis, *Honored Society,* p. 102.
61. Block, *East Side–West Side,* p. 109.
62. Erwin A. Broderick, Administrative Officer, Office of the AC of S, G-2, Headquarters Peninsular Base Section, "Memorandum for Major Arnold. Subject: Genovese, Vito," October 21, 1944 (Alan A. Block Archive on Organized Crime, Pennsylvania State University).
63. Orange C. Dickey, Agent CID, Subsection No. 2, Criminal Investigation Division, Headquarters Army Air Forces, Mediterranean Theater of Operations, "Subject: Preliminary Report of Investigation," August 30, 1944 (Alan A. Block Archive on Organized Crime, Pennsylvania State University).
64. Brig. Gen. Carter W. Clarke, Deputy Chief, Military Intelligence Section, War Department, Washington, "Memorandum for the A.C. of S., G-2," June 30, 1945 (Alan A. Block Archive on Organized Crime, Pennsylvania State University).
65. Telephone conversation between Col. S. V. Constant, 2d SVC, and PMGO Duty Officer, 17:30, June 18, 1945 (Alan A. Block Archive on Organized Crime, Pennsylvania State University).
66. Clarke, "Memorandum."
67. Pantaleone, *Mafia and Politics,* p. 63.
68. Lewis, *Honored Society,* pp. 147, 173. For background information on the political relationship between the Sicilian independence movement and the Allies, see Ernest Weibel, *La Création des Régions Autonomes à Statut spécial en Italie* (Geneva: Librairie Droz, 1971), pp. 150–55, 189–96.
69. Pantaleone, *Mafia and Politics,* p. 88.
70. Ibid., p. 52.
71. Lewis, *Honored Society,* p. 18.
72. Herlands, "Report," pp. 1–3.
73. Siragusa, *Trail of the Poppy,* p. 83.
74. Ibid., pp. 83, 89.
75. U.S. Congress, Senate, Subcommittee on Improvements in the Federal Criminal Code, Committee of the Judiciary, *Illicit Narcotics Traffic,* 84th Cong. 1st sess. (Washington, DC: U.S. Government Printing Office, 1955), p. 99.
76. Official correspondence of Michael G. Picini, Federal Bureau of Narcotics, to agent Dennis Doyle, August 1963. Picini and Doyle were discussing whether to use Sami El Khoury as an informant now that he had been released from prison. The author was permitted to read the correspondence at the Bureau of Narcotics and Dangerous Drugs, Washington, DC, October 14, 1971.
77. Interview with an agent, U.S. Bureau of Narcotics and Dangerous Drugs, Washington, DC, October 26, 1971.
78. Danilo Dolci, *Report from Palermo* (New York: Viking, 1970), pp. 118–20.
79. Pantaleone, *Mafia and Politics,* p. 188.

80. Ibid., p. 192.
81. Interview with an agent, U.S. Bureau of Narcotics and Dangerous Drugs, Washington, DC, October 14, 1971.
82. Ibid.
83. Interview with an agent, U.S. Bureau of Narcotics and Dangerous Drugs, New Haven, CT, November 18, 1971.
84. Harry J. Anslinger, *The Murderers* (New York: Farrar, Straus, 1961), p. 106.
85. Messick, *Lansky*, p. 137.
86. Ibid., pp. 87–88.
87. Ibid., p. 89.
88. Ibid.
89. Ed Reid, *The Grim Reapers* (Chicago: Henry Regnery, 1969), pp. 90–92.
90. Interview with an agent, U.S. Bureau of Narcotics and Dangerous Drugs, Washington, DC, October 14, 1971.
91. William B. Herlands, Commissioner of Investigation, Executive Department, State of New York, "SE 226, Harold Meltzer et al.," June 9, 1950 (Thomas E. Dewey Papers, University of Rochester). The Bureau of Narcotics reported that in 1965 Meltzer was "active in gambling and prostitution in California and Nevada. Organized smuggler and supplier of narcotics from Mexico to the U.S. Uses business enterprises for cover of illegitimate activities. Family engaged in jewelry retail stores." See U.S. Bureau of Narcotics and Dangerous Drugs, "Persons Known to Be or Suspected of Being Engaged in the Illicit Traffic in Narcotics," revised (Washington, DC, March 1965).
92. U.S. Congress, Senate, Committee on Government Operations, *Organized Crime*, pt. 4, p. 891.
93. Ibid., p. 885.
94. *New York Times*, December 1, 1969, p. 42.
95. Messick, *Lansky*, p. 169–70.
96. United Nations, Department of Social Affairs, *Bulletin on Narcotics* 5, no. 2 (April-June 1953), p. 48.

## 2 Marseille: America's Heroin Laboratory

1. U.S. Congress, Senate, Committee on Government Operations, *Organized Crime and Illicit Traffic in Narcotics*, 88th Cong., 1st and 2nd sess. (Washington, DC: U.S. Government Printing Office, 1964), pt. 4. pp. 873–85.
2. John T. Cusack, "Turkey Lifts the Poppy Ban," *Drug Enforcement* (Fall 1974), p. 3.
3. Eugène Saccomano, *Bandits à Marseille* (Paris: Julliard, 1968), pp. 53–54.
4. U.S. Bureau of Narcotics and Dangerous Drugs, "Persons Known to Be or Suspected of Being Engaged in the Illicit Traffic in Narcotics," revised (Washington, DC, March 1965).
5. Saccomano, *Bandits*, p. 75.
6. Raymond J. Sontag, *A Broken World, 1919–1939* (New York: Harper & Row, 1971), pp. 273–75.
7. Saccomano, *Bandits*, p. 76.
8. Gabrielle Castellari, *La belle Histoire de Marseille* (Marseille: L'Ecole Technique Don Bosco, 1968), p. 120.

9. Saccomano, *Bandits,* p. 78.

10. Ibid., pp. 93–94.

11. U.S. Senate, Committee on Government Operations, *Organized Crime,* pt. 4, pp. 887–88, 960.

12. Ibid., pp. 887–88; Saccomano, *Bandits,* p. 91.

13. Maurice Choury, *La Résistance en Corse* (Paris: Editions Sociales, 1958), pp. 16–17.

14. Charles Tillon, *Les F.T.P.* (Paris: Union Générale d'Editions, 1967), pp. 167–73.

15. Gabriel Kolko, *The Politics of War* (New York: Random House, 1968), pp. 80–81.

16. Madeleine Baudoin, *Histoire des Groups francs (M.U.R.) des Bouches-du-Rhone* (Paris: Presses Universitaires de France, 1962), pp. 12–13, 163–64, 170–71.

17. Beginning in September 1941 arms drops to the Marseille Resistance was supervised by Col. Maurice J. Buckmaster of the British Special Operations Executive. The arms were dropped to a special liaison group in Marseille attached to the non-Communist Resistance. (Ibid., pp. 21–23.)

18. Ibid., pp. 51, 136–37, 158. For further details on the divisions within the Resistance movement in southern France, see B. D. Graham, *The French Socialists and Tripartism, 1944–1947* (Canberra: Australian National University, 1965), pp. 20–22; Robert Aron, *France Reborn* (New York: Scribner's, 1964), pp. 71, 163–64, 347–48; René Hostache, *Le Conseil national de la Résistance* (Paris: Presses Universitaires de France, 1958). pp. 40–44.

19. Baudoin, *Histoire,* pp. 31–32.

20. Saccomano, *Bandits,* p. 18.

21. Maurice Agulhon and Fernand Barrat, *C.R.S. à Marseille,* (Paris: Armand Colin, 1971), pp. 46–47, 75–77.

22. Harry L. Coles and Albert K. Weinberg, *United States Army in World War II. Civil Affairs: Soldiers Become Governors* (Washington, DC: Office of the Chief of Military History, Department of the Army, U.S. Government Printing Office, 1964), pp. 770–72.

23. Agulhon and Barrat, *C.R.S. à Marseille,* p. 144.

24. Tillon, *Les F.T.P.,* pp. 292–93.

25. Agulhon and Barrat, *C.R.S. à Marseille,* pp. 46–47, 75–77.

26. Castellari, *La belle Histoire,* pp. 218–19.

27. Agulhon and Barrat, *C.R.S. à Marseille,* p. 145.

28. Joyce Kolko and Gabriel Kolko, *The Limits of Power* (New York: Harper & Row, 1972), p. 157.

29. Ibid., p. 440.

30. Agulhon and Barrat, *C.R.S. à Marseille,* pp. 145–46.

31. Ibid., p. 147.

32. Ibid., p. 148.

33. Ibid., p. 171.

34. Ibid., pp. 149–150.

35. *La Marseillaise* (Marseille), November 13, 1947.
36. *La Marseillaise*, November 17 and 21, December 10, 1947.
37. Kolko and Kolko, *Limits of Power*, p. 396.
38. Ibid., p. 157.
39. Walter Lafeber, *America, Russia, and the Cold War* (New York: Wiley, 1967), p. 47.
40. Ibid., pp. 48, 56.
41. John Ranelagh, *The Agency: The Rise and Decline of the CIA* (New York: Simon & Schuster, 1986), p. 131.
42. U.S. Congress, Senate, Select Committee to Study Governmental Operations, "History of the Central Intelligence Agency," *Supplementary Detailed Staff Reports on Foreign and Military Intelligence, Book IV*, 94th Cong. 2nd sess., 1976 (Washington, DC: U.S. Government Printing Office, Senate Report No. 94-755), pp. 25–37.
43. John Loftus, *The Belarus Secret* (New York: Knopf, 1982), pp. 105–29; William Colby, *Honorable Men: My Life in the CIA* (New York: Simon & Schuster, 1978), p. 75.
44. Colby, *Honorable Men*, p. 73.
45. Ronald L. Filippelli, *American Labor and Postwar Italy, 1943–1953* (Stanford: Stanford University Press, 1989), pp. 112–13.
46. Tom Braden made these observations in November 1983. See Ranelagh, *The Agency*, pp. 247–48.
47. Peter Weiler, "The United States, International Labor, and the Cold War: The Breakup of the World Federation of Trade Unions," *Diplomatic History* 5, no. 1 (1981), p. 12.
48. Trevor Barnes, "The Secret Cold War: The C.I.A. and American Foreign Policy in Europe, 1946–1956," Part 1, *Historical Journal* 24, no. 2 (1981), pp. 411–12.
49. Filippelli, *American Labor*, pp. 112–13. Only a few months before he "provoked" the split between Communist and Socialist factions in the CGT, Socialist labor leader Léon Jouhaux came to Washington to meet with members of the Truman administration. *Le Monde* (Paris), May 12, 1967.
50. Filippelli, *American Labor*, p. 113.
51. Thomas W. Braden, "I'm Glad the C.I.A. Is 'Immoral,'" *Saturday Evening Post*, May 20, 1967, p. 14.
52. Ibid. This was not the first time that the American intelligence community had used such covert funding to create dissension within the ranks of the leftist French labor movement. During World War II, OSS's Labor Branch under the direction of Arthur Goldberg supplied funds to the "Socialist leadership" of the clandestine CGT but refused to give funds to Communist elements in the same organization. This bias created an incident that soured relations among all parties involved (R. Harris Smith, *OSS: The Secret History of America's First Central Intelligence Agency* [Berkeley: University of California Press, 1972], p. 182).
53. *Le Provençal* (Marseille), November 8–9, 14, 1947.
54. "It was on this occasion that the leaders of the *Force Ouvrière* faction

separated themselves definitively from the C.G.T., and founded, *with the aid of American labor unions,* the coalition which still bears its name [emphasis added]" (Jacques Julliard, *Le IVᵉ République* [Paris: Calmann-Lévy, 1968], p. 124).

55. Kolko and Kolko, *Limits of Power,* p. 370. This alliance between the CIA and the Socialists was apparently preceded by elaborate negotiations. While on a visit to Washington in May 1946, Socialist party leader Léon Blum told a French wire service correspondent, "Numerous American diplomats with whom I have talked are certain that Socialism can become the best rampart against Communism in Europe." It was later reported in the American press that President Truman's secretary of the treasury had urged Blum to unite the non-Communist parties and drive the Communists out of the government. *(Le Monde* [Paris], May 12, 1967).

56. *Le Provençal,* November 14, 1947.

57. *La Marseillaise,* November 19, 1947.

58. Agulhon and Barrat, *C.R.S. à Marseille,* pp. 156 73.

59. *Le Provençal,* November 14, 1947.

60. Agulhon and Barrat, *C.R.S. à Marseille,* pp. 204, 215.

61. Ibid., pp. 76, 128.

62. Ibid., p. 196.

63. Interview with Lt. Col. Lucien Conein, McLean, Virginia, June 18, 1971. (Conein worked as an OSS liaison officer with the French Resistance during World War II and later served as a CIA operative.)

64. Castellari, *La belle Histoire,* p. 221.

65. Ibid., p. 222.

66. The close relationship between Marseille's Vietnamese community and the French left also played a role in the history of the Second Indochina War. Immediately after the liberation, Marseille's left-leaning commissioner Raymond Aubrac discovered the wretched conditions at the Indochinese work camps in the city's suburbs and did everything he could to clean them up. His efforts won him the respect of Vietnamese nationalist organizations, and through them he was introduced to Ho Chi Minh, who visited France to negotiate in 1946. When the Pugwash Committee devised the deescalation proposal to end the Vietnam War in 1967, Aubrac was selected to transmit it to Ho Chi Minh in Hanoi (Agulhon and Barrat, *C.R.S. à Marseille,* p. 43).

67. *Combat* (Paris), February 4, 1950.

68. *New York Times,* February 18, 1950, p. 5.

69. *New York Times,* February 24, 1950, p. 12.

70. *Combat,* February 18–19, 1950.

71. Braden, "I'm Glad the CIA Is 'Immoral,' " p. 10.

72. Filippelli, *American Labor,* p. 181; Ronald Radosh, *American Labor and United States Foreign Policy* (New York: Random House, 1969), pp. 323–24.

73. *Time,* March 17, 1952, p. 23.

74. *New York Times,* March 14, 1950, p. 5.

75. *New York Times*, April 16, 1950, sec. 4, p. 4.
76. U.S. Drug Enforcement Administration, "The Heroin Labs of Marseille," *Drug Enforcement* (Fall 1973), pp. 11–13; Cusack, "Turkey Lifts the Poppy Ban," pp. 3–7.
77. U.S. Bureau of Narcotics and Dangerous Drugs, "Persons Known to Be."
78. *New York Times Magazine*, February 6, 1972, pp. 53–54.
79. U.S. Congress, Senate, Committee on Government Operations, *Organized Crime*, part 4, p. 888.
80. U.S. Bureau of Narcotics and Dangerous Drugs, "Persons Known to Be."
81. *France-Soir* (Paris), September 7, 1971.
82. U.S. Bureau of Narcotics and Dangerous Drugs, "Persons Known to Be."
83. *L'Express* (Paris), September 6–12, 1971, p. 18.
84. Saccomano, *Bandits à Marseille*, pp. 13–14.
85. *Le Provençal*, January 3, 1970.
86. Saccomano, *Bandits à Marseille*, p. 25.
87. *Le Provençal*, January 7, 1970.
88. *Le Provençal*, January 6–16, 1970; *La Marseillaise*, January 6–16, 1970.
89. *Le Provençal*, January 16, 1970.
90. *France-Soir*, September 7, 1971.
91. U.S. Senate, Committee on Government Operations, *Organized Crime*, pt. 4, p. 961.
92. *New York Times Magazine*, February 6, 1972, pp. 14–15.
93. U.S. Senate, Committee on Government Operations, *Organized Crime*, pt. 4, p. 956. See also Morgan F. Murphy and Robert H. Steele, *The World Heroin Problem*, 92nd Cong., 2nd sess. (Washington, DC: U.S. Government Printing Office, 1971), p. 8.
94. Phillip M. Williams and Martin Harrison, *Politics and Society in De Gaulle's Republic* (London: Longman Group, 1971), pp. 383–84.
95. *Sunday Times* (London), September 26, 1971.
96. Interview with an agent, U.S. Bureau of Narcotics and Dangerous Drugs, New Haven, CT, November 18, 1971.
97. *Sunday Times*, September 26, 1971.
98. Ibid.
99. *New York Times*, November 16, 1971, p. 1.
100. *Le Monde*, November 21–22, 23, and 27, 1971.
101. *New York Times Magazine*, February 6, 1972, pp. 53–54. During 1972 French police scored some impressive successes in their attempts to eliminate Marseille's heroin industry. In the first seven months of 1972 French police seized five heroin laboratories, more than they had been able to uncover in the previous ten years (U.S. Cabinet Committee on International Narcotics Control [CCINC], "Fact Sheet: The Cabinet Committee on International Narcotics Control—A Year of Progress in Drug Abuse Prevention," Washington, DC, September 1972, p. 2).
102. Joe Flanders, "Bad Year for French Heroin Traffickers," *Drug Enforcement* (February–March 1974), p. 29.
103. Lucien Aimé-Blanc, "France," *Drug Enforcement* (Winter 1975–1976), p. 38.

104. Joe Flanders "The Key to Success: Franco-American Cooperation," *Drug Enforcement* (Fall 1973), p. 15.

105. Aimé-Blanc, "France," pp. 37–38.

106. U.S. Drug Enforcement Administration, "Summary of Middle East Heroin Conference," John F. Kennedy Airport, December 6–7, 1979, pp. 14–17 (Alan A. Block Archive on Organized Crime, Pennsylvania State University).

107. John Bacon, "Is the French Connection Really Dead?" *Drug Enforcement* (Summer 1981), pp. 19–21.

108. Anton Blok, *The Mafia of a Sicilian Village, 1860–1960: A Study of Violent Peasant Entrepreneurs* (New York: Harper & Row, 1975), pp. 215–22.

109. Gaia Servadio, *Mafioso: A History of the Mafia from Its Origins to the Present* (New York: Dell, 1976), pp. 176–79.

110. Michele Pantaleone, *The Mafia and Politics* (London: Chatto & Windus, 1969), pp. 167–79.

111. Norman Lewis, *The Honored Society* (New York: Putnam's, 1964), pp. 297–307; U.S. Senate, Committee on Government Operations, *Organized Crime*, pt. 4, pp. 893–94.

112. *Life*, June 18, 1971, pp. 35–36.

113. Claire Sterling, *Octopus: The Long Reach of the International Sicilian Mafia* (New York: Norton, 1990), pp. 102–4.

114. Alan A. Block, "Thinking About Violence and Change in the Sicilian Mafia," *Violence, Aggression and Terrorism* 1, no. 1 (1987), pp. 67–70.

115. E. Meade Feild, Newark, NJ, Strike Force, "Report of Investigation: Michael Piancone et al.," U.S. Treasury Department, Bureau of Customs, November 16, 1973, pp. 1–3 (Alan A. Block Archive on Organized Crime, Pennsylvania State University).

116. Anthony Mangiaracina, Special Agent, Drug Enforcement Administration, "Report of Investigation: Report Re. Salvatore Sollena," July 27, 1981, pp. 1–11 (Alan A. Block Archive on Organized Crime, Pennsylvania State University).

117. Murphy and Steele, *World Heroin Problem*, pp. 12, 16.

118. Ibid.

119. Cusak, "Turkey Lifts the Poppy Ban," pp. 2–7.

120. Interview with John Warner, U.S. Bureau of Narcotics and Dangerous Drugs, Washington, DC, October 14, 1971.

121. Ed Reid, *The Grim Reapers* (Chicago: Henry Regnery, 1969), p. 16.

122. Hank Messick, *Lansky* (New York: Putnam's, 1971), p. 175.

123. Reid, *Grim Reapers*, p. 97.

124. U.S. Senate, Committee on Government Operations, *Organized Crime*, pt. 4, p. 928.

125. U.S. Bureau of Narcotics and Dangerous Drugs, "Persons Known to Be."

126. U.S. Senate, Committee on Government Operations, *Organized Crime*, pt. 2, pp. 524–25; interview with an agent, U.S. Bureau of Narcotics and Dangerous Drugs, New Haven, CT, November 18, 1971.

127. U.S. Senate, Committee on Government Operations, *Organized Crime*, pt. 2, pp. 527, 539. (In 1954 Santo Trafficante, Jr., was arrested by the Saint Petersburg police when he tried to bribe a police officer into destroying evidence of his involvement in the *bolita* lottery.)

128. U.S. Bureau of Narcotics and Dangerous Drugs, Washington, DC, press release, June 27, 1970.

129. Interview with an agent, U.S. Bureau of Narcotics and Dangerous Drugs, Washington, DC, October 14, 1971.

130. U.S. Congress, Senate, Permanent Subcommittee on Investigations, *Fraud and Corruption in Management of Military Club Systems*, 91st Cong., 1st sess. (Washington, DC: U.S. Government Printing Office, 1969), p. 279; Reid, *Grim Reapers*, p. 296.

## 3  Opium for the Natives

1. International Opium Commission, *Report of the International Opium Commission: Shanghai China, February 1 to February 26, 1909* Shanghai: North China Daily News, 1909), vol. 2, p. 44.

2. David Edward Owen, *British Opium Policy in China and India* (New Haven: Yale University Press, 1934), pp. 5–6.

3. Ibid., p. 2.

4. Ibid., p. 6.

5. Jonathan Spence, "Opium Smoking in Ch'ing China" (Honolulu: Conference on Local Control and Protest During the Ch'ing Period, 1971), pp. 5–8.

6. Om Prakash, *The Dutch East India Company and the Economy of Bengal, 1630–1720* (Delhi: Oxford University Press, 1988), pp. 145–57.

7. J. F. Richards, "The Indian Empire and Peasant Production of Opium in the Nineteenth Century," *Modern Asian Studies* 15, no. 1 (1981), pp. 59–62.

8. International Opium Commission, *Report*, vol. 2, pp. 44–66, 356, U.S. Department of Commerce, Bureau of Foreign and Domestic Commerce, *Statistical Abstract of the United States 1915* (Washington, DC: U.S. Government Printing Office, 1916), p. 713.

9. Owen, *British Opium Policy*, pp. 18–27.

10. Ibid., pp. 31–44.

11. Sir John Strachey, *India: Its Administration and Progress* (London: Macmillan, 1903), pp. 133–42.

12. Richards, "The Indian Empire," pp. 66–76.

13. Michael Greenberg, *British Trade and the Opening of China 1800–42* (Cambridge: Cambridge University Press, 1951), pp. 109–10.

14. Owen, *British Opium Policy*, p. vii; Richards, "The Indian Empire," p. 66.

15. Tan Chung, "The Britain-China-India Trade Triangle, 1771–1840," in Sabyasachi Bhattacharya, ed., *Essays in Modern Indian Economic History* (New Delhi: Munshiram Manoharlal Publishers, 1987), pp. 114–30; Richards, "The Indian Empire," pp. 67–69.

16. Charles C. Stelle, "American Trade in Opium to China in the Nineteenth Century," *Pacific Historical Review* 9 (December 1940), pp. 427–42.

17. Greenberg, *British Trade*, pp. 124–31, 221.

18. Charles C. Stelle, "American Trade in Opium to China, 1821–39," *Pacific Historical Review* 10 (March 1941), pp. 57–74.
19. Ibid., pp. 127, 221.
20. Owen, *British Opium Policy*, pp. 104–8; Richards, "Indian Empire," p. 65.
21. Basil Lubbock, *The Opium Clippers* (Glasgow: Brown, Son & Ferguson, 1933), pp. 14, 62–79.
22. Ibid., pp. 92–93, 382–83; Basil Lubbock, *The China Clippers* (Glasgow: James Brown & Son, 1914), pp. 22–23.
23. Lubbock, *Opium Clippers*, pp. 382–83.
24. Greenberg, *British Trade*, pp. 221; Owen, *British Opium Policy*, pp. 113–45.
25. Rev. A. S. Thelwall, M.A., *The Iniquities of the Opium Trade with China: Being a Development of the Main Causes Which Exclude the Merchants of Great Britain from the Advantages of an Unrestricted Commercial Intercourse with that Vast Empire* (London: William H. Allen, 1839), p. 13.
26. Ibid., p. 177.
27. Ibid., pp. 52–54.
28. Ibid., pp. 65–82.
29. John K. Fairbank, Edwin O. Reischauer, and Albert M. Craig, *East Asia: The Modern Transformation* (Boston: Houghton Mifflin, 1965), p. 131. The Chinese opium trade and the Opium War attracted considerable comment by contemporary observers and was the subject of a number of monographs a century later. See Chang Hsin-pao, *Commissioner Lin and the Opium War* (Cambridge: Harvard University Press, 1964); John K. Fairbank, *Trade and Diplomacy on the China Coast: The Opening of the Treaty Ports, 1842–1854* (Cambridge: Harvard University Press, 1953); P. C. Kuo, *A Critical Study of the First Anglo-Chinese War* (Shanghai: Commercial Press, 1935); Teng Ssu-yu, *Chang Hsi and the Treaty of Nanking* (Chicago: University of Chicago Press, 1944); Arthur Waley, *The Opium War Through Chinese Eyes* (New York: Macmillan, 1958).
30. Owen, *British Opium Policy*, pp. 146–89.
31. Joshua Rowntree, *The Imperial Drug Trade* (London: Methuen, 1905), p. 286.
32. Lubbock, *Opium Clippers*, pp. 280–85.
33. Edouard Stackpole, *Captain Prescott and the Opium Smugglers* (Mystic, CT: Marine Historical Association, July 1954), pp. 34–43; Owen, *British Opium Policy*, pp. 183–93; Lubbock, *Opium Clippers*, pp. 382–84.
34. Stackpole, *Captain Prescott*, p. 35.
35. Arthur H. Clark, *The Clipper Ship Era: An Epitome of Famous American and British Clipper Ships, Their Owners, Builders, Commanders, and Crews 1853–1869* (New York: Putnam's, 1910), pp. 57–72.
36. W. C. Costin, *Great Britain and China* (Oxford: Oxford University Press, 1937), pp. 206–86.
37. Owen, *British Opium Policy*, 221–29.
38. International Opium Commission, *Report*, vol. 2, pp. 44–66; U.S. Department of Commerce, *Statistical Abstract 1915*, p. 713.

39. Rowntree, *Imperial Drug Trade*, pp. 286–87.

40. Shlomo Avineri, *Karl Marx on Colonialism and Modernization* (Garden City, NY: Doubleday, 1969), p. 361.

41. Spence, "Opium Smoking," p. 16. Opium was so important to Szechwan's economy that a local opium suppression campaign in 1901–1911 alienated much of the province's population from the imperial government and created support for the 1911 revolution. (S. A. M. Adshead, "The Opium Trade in Szechwan 1881 to 1911," *Journal of Southeast Asian History* 7, no. 2 [September 1966], 98–99).

42. Owen, *British Opium Policy*, pp. 266–67.

43. International Opium Commission, *Report*, vol. 2, pp. 56–57.

44. Owen, *British Opium Policy*, pp. 266–67.

45. *L'Asie française* (Hanoi), July 1901, pp. 163–65.

46. Bernard-Marcel Peyrouton, *Les Monopoles en Indochine* (Paris: Emile Larose, 1913), p. 146; G. Ayme, *Monographie de Vᵉ Territoire militaire* (Hanoi: Imprimerie d'Extrême-Orient, 1930), pp. 117–22; League of Nations, Commission of Inquiry into the Control of Opium Smoking in the Far East, *Report to the Council*, vol. 1 (Geneva: League of Nations, 1930), p. 86.

47. Rhoads Murphey, "Traditionalism and Colonialism: Changing Urban Roles in Asia," *Journal of Asian Studies* 29, no. 1 (November 1969), pp. 68–69.

48. League of Nations, Advisory Committee on the Traffic in Opium and Other Dangerous Drugs, *Annual Reports of Governments on the Traffic in Opium and Other Dangerous Drugs for the Year 1935*, vol. 11 (Geneva: Series of League of Nations Publications, 1937), pp. 72–75.

49. G. William Skinner, *Chinese Society in Thailand: An Analytical History* (Ithaca: Cornell University Press, 1957), pp. 29–30.

50. Victor Purcell, *The Chinese in Southeast Asia* (London: Oxford University Press, 1951), pp. 28, 215; Skinner, *Chinese Society*, pp. 29–30, 87.

51. League of Nations, Advisory Committee on the Traffic in Opium and Other Dangerous Drugs, *Summary of Annual Reports*, vol. 11 (Geneva: Series of League of Nations Publications, 1930), "Part III: Prepared Opium Statistics."

52. Ibid., pp. 16–18; League of Nations, *Annual Reports for 1935*, p. 23.

53. James R. Rush, *Opium to Java* (Ithaca: Cornell University Press, 1990), pp. 234–37.

54. John G. Butcher, "The Demise of the Revenue Farm System in the Federated Malay States," *Modern Asian Studies* 17, no. 3 (1983), pp. 410–11.

55. The Philippines became an exception soon after the Spanish were replaced by the American colonial government in 1898. The Spanish opium franchise had been established in 1843 and had earned the colonial government about $600,000 in silver per year. It was abolished by the American colonial government shortly after the U.S. army occupied the island (Arnold H. Taylor, *American Diplomacy and the Narcotics Traffic, 1900–1939: A Study in International Humanitarian Reform* [Durham: Duke University Press, 1969], pp. 31–32, 43).

56. Alleyne Ireland, *Colonial Administration in the Far East: The Province of Burma* (Boston: Houghton Mifflin, 1907), pp. 848–49.

57. Carl A. Trocki, *Prince of Pirates: The Temenggongs and the Development of Johor and Singapore* (Singapore: Singapore University Press, 1979), pp. 85–117, 203–15.

58. Carl A. Trocki, "The Rise of Singapore's Great Opium Syndicate, 1840–86," *Journal of Southeast Asian Studies* 18, no. 1 (1987), pp. 58–80.

59. Butcher, "Demise of the Revenue Farm System," pp. 394–97.

60. Prakash, *Dutch East India Company,* pp. 145–57.

61. International Opium Commission, *Report,* vol. 2, "Statistics of the Trade in Opium: A. Import"; Rush, *Opium to Java,* pp. 126–27.

62. James R. Rush, "Opium in Java: A Sinister Friend," *Journal of Asian Studies* 44, no. 3 (1985), pp. 550–53.

63. International Opium Commission, *Report,* vol. 2, p. 315.

64. League of Nations, *Annual Reports for 1935,* pp. 72–75.

65. Rush, *Opium to Java,* pp. 65–82.

66. James R. Rush, "Social Control and Influence in Nineteenth Century Indonesia: Opium Farms and the Chinese of Java," *Indonesia* 35 (1983), pp. 56–64.

67. Robert Cribb, "Opium and the Indonesian Revolution," *Modern Asian Studies* 22, no. 4 (1988), pp. 701–22.

68. International Opium Commission, *Report,* vol. 2, pp. 359–65.

69. For a discussion of the opium franchise operations in the Philippines, see Edgar Wickberg, *The Chinese in Philippine Life* (New Haven: Yale University Press, 1965), pp. 114–19. For statistics on the percentage of revenues derived from opium sales, see League of Nations, Advisory Committee on the Traffic in Opium and Other Dangerous Drugs, *Annual Reports,* 1921–1937. Revenue from opium in the British Malayan Straits Settlements was even higher. In 1880 it accounted for 56.7 percent of all government revenues, in 1890 it dropped slightly to 52.2 percent, and in 1904 it climbed back up to 59 percent (Cheng U Wen, "Opium in the Straits Settlements, 1867–1910," *Journal of Southeast Asian History* 2, no. 1 [March 1961], pp. 52, 75).

70. International Opium Commission, *Report,* vol. 2, p. 329.

71. Andrew D. W. Forbes, "The 'Cin-Ho' (Yunnanese Chinese) Caravan Trade with North Thailand During the Late Nineteenth and Early Twentieth Centuries," *Journal of Asian History* 21, no. 1 (1987), pp. 1–47.

72. Ibid., pp. 27–28.

73. Geoffrey C. Gunn, "Shamans and Rebels: The Batchai (Meo) Rebellion of Northern Laos and North-West Vietnam (1918–1921)," *Journal of the Siam Society* 74 (1986), pp. 110–11; Dr. Thaung, "Panthay Interlude in Yunnan: A Study in Vicissitudes Through the Burmese Kaleidoscope," *Burmese Research Society Fiftieth Anniversary Publication,* no. 1 (1961), pp. 479–81.

74. John Anderson, M.D., *Mandalay to Momien: A Narrative of the Two Expeditions to Western China of 1868 and 1879 Under Colonel Edward B. Sladen and Colonel Horace Browne* (London: Macmillan, 1876), pp. 333–45.

75. Andrew D. W. Forbes, "The Yunnanese ('Ho') Muslims of North Thailand," in Andrew D. W. Forbes, *The Muslims of Thailand*, vol. 1: *Historical and Cultural Studies* (Gaya, Bihar, India: Centre for South East Asian Studies, 1988), pp. 91–95.

76. Terry B. Grandstaff, "The Hmong, Opium and the Haw: Speculations on the Origin of Their Association," *Journal of the Siam Society* 71, no. 2 (1979), pp. 76–79.

77. Moshe Yegar, "The Panthay (Chinese Muslims) of Burma and Yunnan," *Journal of Southeast Asian Studies* 7, no. 1 (1966), pp. 80–82; Forbes, "Yunnanese," p. 93.

78. Grandstaff, "Hmong," pp. 77–78.

79. Eugène Picanon, *Le Laos français* (Paris: Augustin Challamel, 1901), pp. 284–85.

80. League of Nations, *Summary of Annual Reports* (1930), pp. 29–30.

81. League of Nations, *Annual Reports for 1935*, p. 9.

82. International Opium Commission, *Report*, vol. 2, pp. 124, 357.

83. League of Nations, *Annual Reports for 1935*, pp. 46–47.

84. Ibid., pp. 9, 46–47.

85. League of Nations, Advisory Committee on the Traffic in Opium and Other Dangerous Drugs, *Application of Part II of the Opium Convention with Special Reference to the European Possessions and Countries in the Far East*, vols. 11–12 (Geneva: League of Nations, 1923), "Raw Opium Statistics"; League of Nations, *Summary of Annual Reports* (1930), "Raw Opium Statistics."

86. League of Nations, Advisory Committee on the Traffic in Opium and Other Dangerous Drugs, *Minutes of the Twelfth Session*, January 17–February 2, 1929 (Geneva: League of Nations, 1969), p. 209.

87. Ibid., p. 205; League of Nations, Advisory Committee on the Traffic in Opium and Other Dangerous Drugs, *Summary of Annual Reports in the Traffic in Opium and Other Dangerous Drugs for the Years 1929 and 1930* (Geneva: League of Nations, March 22, 1932), p. 317.

88. Paul Doumer, *Situation de l'Indochine, 1897–1901* (Hanoi: F. H. Schneider, 1902), pp. 157, 162.

89. Owen, *British Opium Policy*, pp. 261–63.

90. Rev. A. E. Moule, *The Use of Opium and Its Bearing on the Spread of Christianity in China* (Shanghai: Celestial Empire Office, 1877), pp. 13–15.

91. Owen, *British Opium Policy*, pp. 263–65; Rowntree, *Imperial Drug Trade*, pp. 228–29.

92. Wie T. Dunn, *The Opium Traffic in Its International Aspects* (New York: Columbia University, 1920), pp. 118–30; 281–354.

93. International Opium Commission, *Report*, vol. 2, pp. 21–26.

94. David Musto, *The American Disease: Origins of Narcotic Control* (New Haven: Yale University Press, 1973), pp. 25–28.

95. International Opium Commission, *Report*, vol. 2, pp. 22–26.

96. Musto, *American Disease*, pp. 28–37; Peter D. Lowes, *The Genesis of International Narcotics Control* (Geneva: Librairie Droz, 1966), pp. 102–11.

97. International Opium Commission, *Report*, vol. 2, pp. 79–84.

98. Musto, *American Disease*, pp. 49–63; Taylor, *American Diplomacy and the Narcotics Traffic*, pp. 120, 129–31.

99. Vladimir Kusevic, "Drug Abuse Control and International Treaties," *Journal of Drug Issues* 7, no. 1, pp. 34–53; Bertil A. Renborg, *International Drug Control: A Study of International Administration by and Through the League of Nations* (Washington, DC: Carnegie Endowment for International Peace, 1944), pp. 20–26.

100. International Opium Commission, *Report*, vol. 2, pp. 355–65; League of Nations, *Annual Reports for 1935*, pp. 46–47.

101. League of Nations, *Application of Part II*, p. 4; League of Nations, *Annual Reports for 1935*, pp. 70–71.

102. League of Nations, *Annual Reports for 1935*, pp. 72–75.

103. Hong Lysa, *Thailand in the Nineteenth Century: Evolution of the Economy and Society* (Singapore: Institute of Southeast Asian Studies, 1984), p. 128.

104. International Opium Commission, *Report*, vol. 2, pp. 330, 364.

105. Ibid., p. 346.

106. Virginia Thompson, *Thailand: The New Siam* (New York: Macmillan, 1941), pp. 728–30.

107. League of Nations, *Summary of Annual Reports* (1930), "Raw Opium Statistics," pp. 42–43.

108. Purcell, *Chinese in Southeast Asia*, pp. 105–6. The Thai government also did its best to restrict local opium production. A British official traveling in northern Thailand in the 1920s came across a party of Thai police leading a group of captured Hmong opium smugglers into Chiangrai. He reported that opium cultivation was prohibited, but "the small scattered tribes living among the remote mountains still pursue their time-honored habits, and although it is, as a rule, dangerous and profitless work for the gendarmes to attack the tribes in their own fastness, still captures are occasionally made . . . when the poppy is brought down for sale" (Reginald le May, *An Asian Arcady* [Cambridge: W. Heffer & Sons, 1926], p. 229).

109. Skinner, *Chinese Society*, pp. 118–19.

110. Ibid., pp. 120–21; Hong, *Thailand in the Nineteenth Century*, p. 128; Constance M. Wilson, "State and Society in the Reign of Mongkut, 1851–1868: Thailand on the Eve of Modernization," Ph.D. thesis, Cornell University, 1970, Table Q.2, "Estimate of Revenue Received from Tax Farms," pp. 995–1000.

111. International Opium Commission, *Report*, vol. 1, p. 331.

112. League of Nations, *Traffic in Opium*, Appendix 2, June 1, 1922; League of Nations, *First Opium Conference*, November 3, 1924–February 11, 1925, p. 134.

113. League of Nations, Advisory Committee on the Traffic in Opium and Other Dangerous Drugs, *Application of Part II of the Opium Convention with Special Reference to the European Possessions and the Countries of the Far East*, (Geneva: League of Nations, 1923), p. 12.

114. League of Nations, Advisory Committee on the Traffic in Opium and Other Dangerous Drugs, *Annual Reports for the Year 1931* (Geneva: League of Nations, 1931), p. 96.

115. League of Nations, Commission of Inquiry into the Control of Opium Smoking in the Far East, *Report to the Council*, vol. 1 (Geneva: League of Nations, 1930), pp. 78–79.

116. Thompson, *Thailand*, p. 734.

117. Benjamin A. Batson, "The Fall of the Phibun Government, 1944," *Journal of the Siam Society* 62, part 2 (July 1974), pp. 91–94; Nigel J. Brailey, *Thailand and the Fall of Singapore: A Frustrated Asian Revolution* (Boulder: Westview, 1986), p. 77.

118. Kenneth P. Landon, *The Chinese in Thailand* (New York: Russell & Russell, 1941), pp. 92–93.

119. Ibid., pp. 93–94.

120. League of Nations, *Annual Reports for 1935*, p. 9; Thompson, *Thailand*, p. 733.

121. Landon, *Chinese in Thailand,*p. 93.

122. League of Nations, *Annual Reports for 1935*, pp. 46–47.

123. Thompson, *Thailand*, pp. 734–36.

124. Landon, *Chinese in Thailand*, p. 93.

125. Thompson, *Thailand*, p. 737.

126. League of Nations, *Application of Part II*, "Raw Opium Statistics."

127. Landon, *Chinese in Thailand*, pp. 94–95; Thompson, *Thailand*, p. 737.

128. W. R. Geddes, "Opium and the Miao: A Study in Ecological Adjustment," *Oceania* 41, no. 1 (September 1970), pp. 1–2; Peter Kandre, "Autonomy and Integration of Social Systems: The Iu Mien ('Yao' or 'Man') Mountain Population and Their Neighbors," in Peter Kundstadter, ed., *Southeast Asian Tribes, Minorities, and Nations*, vol. 2 (Princeton: Princeton University Press, 1967), p. 585.

129. Paul T. Cohen, "Hill Trading in the Mountain Ranges of Northern Thailand" (1968), pp. 1–3. One anthropologist who traveled in northern Thailand during the 1930s reported that although the Akha were devoting full attention to the opium crop and were engaged in regular opium commerce, Hmong production was quite sporadic (Hugo Adolf Bernatzik, *Akha and Meo* [New Haven: Human Relations Area Files Press, 1970], pp. 522–23).

130. Brailey, *Thailand and the Fall of Singapore*, pp. 73–78, 89–102.

131. E. Bruce Reynolds, "The Fox in the Cabbage Patch: Thailand and Japan's Southern Advance," paper prepared for presentation at the annual meeting of Asian Studies on the Pacific Coast, Honolulu, July 1, 1989, pp. 2–20.

132. John Costello, *The Pacific War 1941–1945* (New York: Rawson Wade, 1981), pp. 236–44.

133. Thak Chaloemtiarana, ed., *Thai Politics: Extracts and Documents, 1932–1957* (Bangkok: Social Science Association of Thailand, 1978), pp. 692–96.

134. This can be inferred from data on Thai wartime imports. The opium

imported in 1943 was valued at 9.7 million baht (the Thai currency). Countries exporting goods into Thailand in excess of this amount were Malaya, China, Japan, Penang, Singapore, and Burma. However, only exports from Burma in 1943 show a peculiar jump in value of 10 million baht. In 1942, Burma's exports into Thailand were valued at 500,000 baht. In 1943, the value rose to 11 million before resuming a more stable level of 1 million in 1944 and 900,000 in 1945. The uncharacteristic single-year rise of 10 million baht in the value of exports from Burma in 1943 is most likely accounted for by Shan state opium imported by the Thai opium monopoly. Furthermore, unlike exports from other Japanese-held territories, no Burmese exports were received in Thai ports in 1943, indicating that what Thailand did import from Burma came overland as would be expected with Shan state opium (Thailand Department of His Majesty's Customs, *Annual Statement of the Foreign Trade and Navigation* [Bangkok, 1946], pp. 53, 81–91).

135. Thak Chaloemtiarana, *Thai Politics*, pp. 568–70.
136. Ibid.
137. Brailey, *Thailand and the Fall of Singapore*, pp. 100–101.
138. Nicol Smith and Blake Clark, *Into Siam, Underground Kingdom* (Indianapolis: Bobbs-Merrill, 1946), pp. 142–46.
139. General Phao, as personal aide to Prime Minister Phibun Songkhram, was no doubt assigned to serve as a liaison between Bangkok and Shan state military groups during the war. When Phibun fell from power in 1944, Phao was placed on inactive duty. In 1947, he joined his father-in-law, General Phin, to launch a coup that brought down the civilian government. Phao reached his peak of power in the mid-1950s as director-general of the Thai police and deputy minister of the ministries of finance and interior, but his police repression and his involvement in illicit opium trading eventually compromised his position. In the aftermath of the 1957 coup, he was exiled to Switzerland, where he died a few years later.

With the expulsion of Phao from the country, members of the Sarit faction, many of them veterans of the Shan state campaign, quickly moved in to take over the opium trade. Sarit had commanded the 33rd Infantry Battalion, which proved a key unit in the seizure of Mong Hsat and later in the Northern Army's drive to the Chinese border and the occupation of Chieng Lo. By 1945, Sarit was a colonel and military commander of Lampang province, one of the major transit points in the illicit opium trade. As commander of the 1st Regiment, Sarit played an important role in the 1947 military coup. In the 1950s, he rose through the ranks, replacing Phin as commander in chief of the army in 1954 and becoming a field marshal in 1956. A year later, he engineered a coup, driving Phibun and Phao from the country. Before he died in the early 1960s, Sarit outlawed opium use and distribution, but allowed his protégés to take control of the illicit drug trade.

Reputedly the last "strongman" of the Thai military, General Krit Siwara had served as company commander under Sarit in the Shan states and was a member of both the 1947 and 1957 coup groups. Although he was never linked to the opium trade, Krit's rise through the military was made possible through his association with Praphat Charusathien, a military dictator who dominated heroin trafficking through Thailand in the 1960s. Weeks before the student demonstrations brought Praphat down in 1973, Krit became commander of the Thai army. Krit died only two days after being appointed defense minister under a civilian government in 1976.

Another Shan state veteran with confirmed links to the drug-running armies of the Kuomintang (KMT) and Khun Sa is General Kriangsak. In 1941, Kriangsak was a lieutenant and commander of the 1st Company, 27th Infantry Battalion. In 1943, he became captain and was awarded a medal for his part in securing a Thai victory in the Shan states. After serving in the Korean War, Kriangsak was sent to the United States for military training. In 1959, he became chief of the SEATO Affairs Division. As perhaps the most significant of Praphat's protégés throughout the 1960s, Kriangsak was involved at the operational level of the drug trade while serving as the Thai military command's liaison to the KMT. After staging a coup that toppled the civilian government in 1976 and more firmly establishing his power in yet another coup in 1977, Kriangsak became prime minister, supreme commander of the Thai armed forces, and minister of the interior. After a series of political challenges by his political opponents, Kriangsak resigned as prime minister in 1980. The following year Kriangsak formed his own political party and was elected to the Thai parliament. In 1985, he joined with one of the Thai Young Turks in an unsuccessful coup and was subsequently charged with sedition. He has recently been pardoned by Prime Minister Chatchai Choonhawan. See David K. Wyatt, *Thailand: A Short History* (New Haven: Yale University Press, 1984), p. 273. See also "List of Members of the Coups of 1932–1957"; Phin Choonhawan, "Events in the Life of Field Marshal Phin Chunnahawan"; Khana Ratthamontri, "The History and Works of Field Marshal Sarit Thanarat," in Thak Chaloemtiarana, *Thai Politics*, pp. 556–61, 568–71, 692–703; *Who's Who in Thailand 1987* (Bangkok: Advance Publishing, 1987).

140. U.S. Congress, Senate, Committee of the Judiciary, *The AMERASIA Papers: A Clue to the Catastrophe of China*, 91st Cong., 1st sess., January 1970 (Washington, DC: U.S. Government Printing Office, 1970), pp. 272–73.

141. For example, in 1947 the Thai government imported 9,264,000 baht worth of opium, compared with 10,135,000 baht worth of alcoholic beverages (*Far Eastern Economic Review* [November 23, 1950], p. 625).

142. *The Burmese Opium Manual* (Rangoon: Government Printing, 1911), pp. 21–45, 65.

143. League of Nations, Advisory Committee on the Traffic in Opium and Other Dangerous Drugs, *Annual Reports on the Traffic in Opium and Other Dangerous Drugs for the Year 1939* (Geneva: League of Nations, 1939), p. 42.

144. League of Nations, *Report to the Council*, vol. 1, p. 51.

145. E. R. Leach, *Political Systems of Highland Burma* (Boston: Beacon Press, 1968), pp. 36–37.

146. Ibid., pp. 56–59.
147. Sao Saimong Mangrai, *The Shan States and the British Annexation* (Ithaca: Cornell University, Southeast Asia Program, Data Paper no. 57, August 1965), p. 150.
148. Ibid., pp. 215, xxxiii–xxxvii.
149. "Report of the Administration of the Northern Shan States for the Year Ended the 30th June 1923," in *Report on the Administration of the Shan and Karenni States* (Rangoon: Government Printing, 1924), p. 125.
150. League of Nations, *Annual Reports for 1939*, p. 42.
151. *Report by the Government of the Union of Burma for the Calendar Year 1950 of the Traffic in Opium and Other Dangerous Drugs* (Rangoon: Government Printing, 1951), p. 1.
152. *New York Times*, November 9, 1968, p. 8.
153. Alexander Barton Woodside, *Vietnam and the Chinese Model* (Cambridge: Harvard University Press, 1971), pp. 278–79.
154. Ibid., p. 269.
155. Le Thanh Khoi, *Le Viet-Nam: Histoire et Civilisation* (Paris: Les Editions de Minuit, 1955), p. 369.
156. C. Geoffray, *Réglementation des Régies indochinoises*, Tome Iⁱᵉʳ (*Opium, Alcools, Sel*) (Haiphong: Imprimerie Commerciale du "Colon français," Edition 1938), pp. 30–32.
157. Exposition coloniale internationale, Paris, 1931, Indochine française, Section d'Administration générale Direction des Finances, *Histoire budgétaire de l'Indochine* (Hanoi: Imprimerie d'Extrême-Orient, 1930), p. 7.
158. Ibid., p. 8.
159. Jacques Dumarest, "Les Monopoles de l'Opium et du Sel en Indochine" (Ph.D. thesis, Université de Lyon, 1938), p. 34.
160. Doumer, *Situation de l'Indochine*, p. 158.
161. Ibid., p. 163.
162. Virginia Thompson, *French Indochina* (New York: Octagon, 1968), pp. 76–77.
163. *L'Asie française*, pp. 163–65.
164. Naval Intelligence Division, *Indochina*, Handbook Series (Cambridge, England, December 1943), p. 361.
165. In an essay written in the 1920s Ho Chi Minh attacked the governor-general of Indochina for ordering an expansion of the opium franchise (Ho Chi Minh, *Selected Works* [Hanoi: Foreign Languages Publishing House, 1961], vol. 2, pp. 30–31). For an example of later nationalist antiopium propaganda see Harold R. Isaacs, *No Peace for Asia* (Cambridge: MIT Press, 1967), pp. 143–44.
166. A. Viollis, *Indochine S.O.S.*, quoted in Association Culturelle pour le Salut du Viet-Nam, *Témoinages et Documents français relatifs à la Colonisation française au Viet-Nam* (Hanoi, 1945).
167. Dumarest, *Les Monopoles de l'Opium*, pp. 96–98.
168. Nguyen Cong Hoan, *The Dead End* (originally published in 1938), quoted in

Ngo Vinh Long, *Before The Revolution: The Vietnamese Peasants Under the French* (Cambridge: MIT Press, 1973), pp. 183–84.

169. Picanon, *Le Laos français*, pp. 284–85; interview with Yang Than Dao, Paris, March 17, 1971 (Yang Than Dao was doing graduate research on the Hmong at the University of Paris); Charles Archaimbault, "Les Annales de l'ancien Royaume de S'ieng Khwang," *Bulletin de l'Ecole française d'Extrême-Orient*, 1967, pp. 595–96.

170. Henri Roux, "Les Meo ou Miao Tseu," in *France-Asie*, nos. 92–93 (January–February, 1954), p. 404. The most detailed report of this uprising was written by a French missionary to the Laotian hill tribes. See F. M. Savina, "Rapport Politique sur la Revolte des Meos au Tonkin et au Laos, 1918–1920" (Xieng Khouang, unpublished manuscript, April 17, 1920).

171. André Boutin, "Monographie de la Province des Houa-Phans," *Bulletin des Amis du Laos*, no. 1 (September 1937), p. 73; Ayme, *Monographie du V^e Territoire militaire*, pp. 117–22.

172. Circular no. 875-SAE, July 22, 1942, from Resident Superior of Tonkin, Desalle, to the residents of Laokay, Sonla, and Yenbay and to the commanders of the military regions of Cao Bang, Ha Giang, and Lai Chau, quoted in Association culturelle pour le Salut du Viet-Nam, *Témoinages et Documents français* (Hanoi, 1945), p. 115.

173. Ibid., p. 116.

174. Herold J. Wiens, *China's March toward the Tropics* (Hamden, CT: Shoe String Press, 1954), pp. 202, 207.

175. Ibid., p. 222.

176. Frank M. Lebar, Gerald C. Hickey, and John K. Musgrave, *Ethnic Groups of Mainland Southeast Asia* (New Haven: Human Relations Area Files Press, 1964), p. 69.

177. Wiens, *China's March*, p. 90.

178. F. M. Savina, *Histoire des Miao* (Hong Kong: Imprimerie de la Societé des Missions-Etrangères de Paris, 1930), pp. 163–64.

179. Lebar, Hickey, and Musgrave, *Ethnic Groups*, p. 73.

180. The information on these clans is based on interviews with Hmong clan leaders who were living in Vientiane in the early 1970s. Information on the Lynhiavu family was supplied by Nhia Heu Lynhiavu, Nhia Xao Lynhiavu, and Lyteck Lynhiavu. Touby Lyfoung himself provided most of the information on the Lyfoung branch of the clan. Since almost all of the prominent Lo clansmen were living in the Pathet Lao liberated zones, it was impossible to interview them directly. However, Touby Lyfoung's mother was a Lo clanswoman, and he was a nephew of Lo Faydang, currently vice-chairman of the Pathet Lao. Nhia Xao Lynhiavu's father, Va Ku, was a close political adviser to *kaitong* Lo Bliayao for a number of years and absorbed a good deal of information, which he passed on to his son.

181. Interview with Nhia Heu Lynhiavu and Nhia Xao Lynhiavu, Vientiane, Laos, September 4, 1971.

182. Ibid.

183. Ibid.

184. Interview with Touby Lyfoung, Vientiane, Laos, August 31, 1971.

185. Interview with Lyteck Lynhiavu, Vientiane, Laos, August 28, 1971; interview with Touby Lyfoung, Vientiane, Laos, September 1, 1971; interview with Nhia Heu Lynhiavu and Nhia Xao Lynhiavu, Vientiane, Laos, September 4, 1971.

186. Interview with Touby Lyfoung, Vientiane, Laos, September 1, 1971.

187. Ibid.

188. Interview with Touby Lyfoung, Vientiane, Laos, September 4, 1971.

189. Interview with Nhia Heu Lynhiavu and Nhia Xao Lynhiavu, Vientiane, Laos, September 4, 1971.

190. Charles Rochet, *Pays Lao* (Paris: Jean Vigneau, 1949), p. 106. In 1953 a French spokesman estimated Laos's annual opium production at 50 tons (*New York Times*, May 8, 1953, p. 4).

191. Michel Caply, *Guérilla au Laos* (Paris: Presses de la Cité, 1966), pp. 58–82.

192. Interview with Touby Lyfoung, Vientiane, Laos, September 1, 1971.

193. Interview with Nhia Heu Lynhiavu and Nhia Xao Lynhiavu, Vientiane, Laos, September 4, 1971. A former Viet Minh officer who was in Muong Sen when Faydang arrived from his village was quite certain that Faydang had no prior contact with the Viet Minh (interview with Lo Kham Thy, Vientiane, Laos, September 2, 1971). At the time Thy was manager of Xieng Khouang Air Transport, which flew between Long Tieng and Vientiane.

194. Joseph John Westermeyer, "The Use of Alcohol and Opium Among Two Ethnic Groups in Laos" (M.A. thesis, University of Minnesota, 1968), p. 98.

195. Wilfred Burchett, *Mekong Upstream* (Hanoi: Red River Publishing House, 1957), p. 267.

196. Jean Jerusalemy, "Monographie sur le Pays Tai," mimeographed (n.d.), p. 20.

197. Interview with Jean Jerusalemy, Paris, France, April 2, 1971. (Jerusalemy was an adviser to the Tai Federation from 1950 to 1954.)

198. Jerusalemy, "Monographie," p. 50.

199. Interview with Jean Jerusalemy, Paris, France, April 2, 1971.

200. Jerusalemy, "Monographie," p. 29. One American scholar places the figure for marketable Tai country opium at 8–9 tons annually, or about 20 percent of all the opium in North Vietnam (John R. McAlister, "Mountain Minorities and the Viet Minh: A Key to the Indochina War," in Kunstadter, *Southeast Asian Tribes*, vol. 2, p. 822).

201. Association culturelle pour le Salut du Viet-Nam, *Témoinages et Documents français*, p. 115.

202. U.S. Bureau of Narcotics and Dangerous Drugs, "The World Opium Situation" (Washington, DC: U.S. Government Printing Office, October 1970), p. 13.

203. Ibid.

204. Ibid., pp. 22, 27.

205. C. P. Spencer and V. Navaratnam, *Drug Abuse in East Asia* (Kuala Lumpur: Oxford University Press, 1981), pp. 50–51, 154–55.

206. U.S. Drug Enforcement Administration, Office of Intelligence, International

Intelligence Division, "People's Republic of China and Narcotic Drugs," *Drug Enforcement* (Fall 1974), pp. 35–36.

207. Harry J. Anslinger, *The Murderers* (New York: Farrar, Straus and Cudahy, 1961), p. 230.

208. U.S. Drug Enforcement Administration, "People's Republic of China," pp. 35–36.

209. U.S. Bureau of Narcotics and Dangerous Drugs, "World Opium Situation," p. 22.

210. United Nations, Economic and Social Council, Commission on Narcotic Drugs, *Illicit Traffic* (E/CN.7/L.115), May 4, 1955, p. 4.

211. Garland H. Williams, District Supervisor, Bureau of Narcotics, letter to Harry Anslinger, February 1, 1949, p. 3 (Historical Collections and Labor Archives, Pennsylvania State University).

212. Ibid.

213. Garland H. Williams, District Supervisor, Bureau of Narcotics, "Opium Addiction in Iran," memo to Mr. H. J. Anslinger, Commissioner of Narcotics, February 1, 1949, pp. 1–12 (Historical Collections and Labor Archives, Pennsylvania State University).

214. U.S. Bureau of Narcotics and Dangerous Drugs, "World Opium Situation," p. 23.

215. Directorate of Intelligence, Central Intelligence Agency, "Intelligence Memorandum: International Narcotics Series No. 13, Narcotics in Iran," June 12, 1972, p. 3.

216. U.S. Bureau of Narcotics and Dangerous Drugs, "World Opium Situation," pp. 27–28.

## 4  Cold War Opium Boom

1. U.S. State Department, Public Affairs, "An Historical Overview" (Washington, DC: State Department, January 1982), p. 2.

2. U.S. Bureau of Narcotics and Dangerous Drugs, "The World Opium Situation," (Washington, DC, October 1970), p. 29.

3. *Weekend Telegraph* (London), March 10, 1967, p. 25.

4. Gen. Vo Nguyen Giap, *Peoples' War, Peoples' Army* (Hanoi: Foreign Languages Publishing House, 1961), p. 79.

5. Lt. Col. Grimaldi, Inspecteur des Forces supplétives, Inspection des Forces Supplétives du Sud Vietnam, *Notions de Case sur les Forces supplétives du Sud Vietnam* (S.P.50.295, May 15, 1954), p. 7.

6. Interview with Col. Roger Trinquier, Paris, March 25, 1971.

7. Ibid.

8. United Nations, Economic and Social Council, Commission on Narcotic Drugs, *Summary of the Fourth Meeting* (E/C.S.7/25), November 29, 1946, p. 4.

9. United Nations, Economic and Social Council, Commission on Narcotic Drugs, *Abolition of Opium Smoking* (E/CN.7/244), November 17, 1952, p. 34.

10. Ibid., p. 36. In 1952 French customs purchased absolutely no opium in

Indochina (United Nations, *Abolition of Opium Smoking,* add. 2, "Laos Report for the Year 1952," March 12, 1953, p. 4).

11. Ibid., p. 18.
12. Interview with Col. Roger Trinquier, Paris, March 25, 1971. A number of high-ranking South Vietnamese officials also confirmed the existence of Operation X, including Col. Tran Dinh Lan, former director of military intelligence for the chief of staff of the Vietnamese army (interview, Paris, March 18, 1971), and Nghiem Van Tri, former minister of defense (interview, Paris, March 30, 1971). One former CIA agent reports that it was General Salan who first organized Operation X in the late 1940s (interview with Lt. Col. Lucien Conein, McLean, Virginia, June 18, 1971).
13. Interview with Gen. Mai Huu Xuan, Saigon, Vietnam, July 19, 1971.
14. Interview with Gen. Maurice Belleux, Paris, March 23, 1971.
15. Interview with Touby Lyfoung, Vientiane, Laos, September 1, 1971.
16. Interview with Gen. Maurice Belleux, Paris, March 23, 1971.
17. Bernard B. Fall, "Portrait of the 'Centurion,' " in Roger Trinquier, *Modern Warfare* (New York: Praeger, 1964), p. xiii.
18. Interview with Col. Roger Trinquier, Paris, March 23, 1971. (Colonel Trinquier read from a training manual he prepared for MACG officers during the First Indochina War. All of the following material on his four-stage method is based on this manual.)
19. Trinquier, *Modern Warfare,* p. 105.
20. For Trinquier's account of his role in the Katanga revolt, see Colonel Roger Trinquier, Jacques Duchemin, and Jacques Le Bailley, *Notre Guerre au Katanga* (Paris: Editions de la Pensée Moderne, 1963); Fall, "Portrait of the 'Centurion,' " p. xv.
21. Trinquier, *Modern Warfare,* p. 109.
22. Ibid., p. 111.
23. Interview with Touby Lyfoung, Vientiane, Laos, September 1, 1971.
24. Interview with Col. Roger Trinquier, Paris, March 25, 1971.
25. Donald Lancaster, *The Emancipation of French Indochina* (New York: Oxford University Press, 1961), p. 257.
26. Bernard B. Fall, *Anatomy of a Crisis* (Garden City, NY: Doubleday, 1969), pp. 49–52.
27. Interview with Gen. Albert Sore, Biarritz, France, April 7, 1971.
28. Interview with Gen. Edward G. Lansdale, Alexandria, Virginia, June 17, 1971.
29. Bernard B. Fall, *Hell in a Very Small Place* (Philadelphia: Lippincott, 1967), pp. 33–37.
30. Interview with Col. Then, Versailles, France, April 2, 1971.
31. Bernard B. Fall, *Hell in a Very Small Place,* pp. 318–20.
32. Interview with Col. Roger Trinquier, Paris, March 25, 1971. Jules Roy said that on May 4 the Dien Bien Phu defenders learned that "Colonel Trinquier, thanks to a fund in the form of bars of silver, had just recruited fifteen hundred Meos [Hmong] and was beginning to come upcountry with them from the Plain of Jarres toward Muong Son, about sixty miles south of

Dienbienphu as the crow flies" (Jules Roy, *The Battle of Dienbienphu* [New York: Harper & Row, 1965], p. 261).

33. Fall, *Hell in a Very Small Place*, p. 442.
34. Interview with Jean Jerusalemy, Paris, April 2, 1971.
35. John T. McAlister, "Mountain Minorities and the Viet Minh," in Peter Kunstadter, ed., *Southeast Asian Tribes, Minorities, and Nations* (Princeton: Princeton University Press, 1967), vol. 2 pp. 812, 825–26.
36. Jean Jerusalemy, "Monographie sur le Pays Tai," mimeographed (n.d.), p. 18.
37. McAlister, "Mountain Minorities," pp. 813–14.
38. Jerusalemy, "Monographie," p. 79.
39. Interview with Jean Jerusalemy, Paris, April 2, 1971.
40. Jerusalemy, "Monographie," pp. 29–30.
41. Interview with Jean Jerusalemy, Paris, April 2, 1971. For background on opium and the Hmong in the Tai highlands, see McAlister, "Mountain Minorities," pp. 817–20.
42. McAlister, "Mountain Minorities," pp. 823–24.
43. Ibid., p. 825.
44. Jerusalemy, "Monographie," p. 29.
45. Interview with Jean Jerusalemy, Paris, April 2, 1971.
46. McAlister, "Mountain Minorities," p. 830.
47. Giap, *Peoples' War*, p. 183.
48. Fall, *Hell in a Very Small Place*, pp. 320–21.
49. Philippe Devillers and Jean Lacouture, *End of a War* (New York: Praeger, 1969), pp. 151–52.
50. Interview with Col. Roger Trinquier, Paris, March 25, 1971.
51. Interview with Gen. Maurice Belleux, Paris, March 23, 1971.
52. Conversation with Commandant Désiré, Paris, March 31, 1971.
53. Interview with Touby Lyfoung, Vientiane, Laos, September 1, 1971. After reading the first edition of this book, Col. Roger Trinquier sent the following letter to Harper & Row, Publishers. It contains additional noteworthy details on MACG's involvement in the opium trade, as well as presenting Col. Trinquier's explanation.

Paris
November 24, 1972

Gentlemen:

Thank you for having sent me a copy of your book, *The Politics of Heroin in Southeast Asia*, which I found particularly interesting on the whole and relatively precise if I judge by the parts that I know and certain of which concern me. This did not offer any difficulties to your authors since for that part I gave them in full confidence the information that I possessed.

I did this all the more voluntarily since I always strictly controlled the use of the X funds, as I did others, in order that they never be turned away from their destination: the upkeep of the Meo [Hmong] maquis in Laos.

This is the reason why I could expose in all good conscience facts which it would have been easy for me to keep quiet if I had had something for which to reproach myself or my officers.

However, in the second paragraph of page 107, you write, "There was an ironic footnote to this last MACG. . . . What irony. What irony."

This paragraph leads one to believe that I or my officers were able to use for ourselves the 5 million piasters, the balance of the MACG funds when it was dissolved. This is therefore a very serious accusation which it is my duty to rectify. Here are therefore the exact facts.

When Touby had collected the opium from his Meo with the aid of the officers of MACG Laos, he asked me to assure its transport by air to its recipient in Saigon. Then he came to collect the funds and gave me the agreed price for the transport, 5,000 piasters per kilo which were deposited in the account of the MACG X funds.

All the officers of the Meo maquis in Laos knew about the sums I had deposited for the upkeep of their maquis. I sent funds back to these officers according to their needs when they presented the requisite vouchers. The control was therefore absolute.

I left command of MACG on September 1, 1954. Not having been able to settle my accounts between the end of hostilities and the end of my command, I asked to stay in Saigon for the time necessary to do this. In fact this was a large job since the MACG was spread out over all of Indochina, from Dong Van in the north to the Ca Mau peninsula in the south.

The accounts were settled about December 15, 1954. There remained in the account of MACG, the regional representatives having sent me their accounts, a sum slightly above 5 million piasters.

I then went to the chief of cabinet for General Elie, High Commissioner and Commander in Chief for Indochina, General Noiret, in order to present my accounts to him—a large chest of documents—and the remainder of the funds. I insisted particularly that the accounts be verified before my departure and that a release be given me. The general answered that the accounts of the special services did not have to be verified and that he did not have the intention of doing so. In spite of my insistence, he refused. But I informed him that I would take the accounts back to France with me and that I would hold them at the disposition of any verifying organization wishing to examine them. They never have been. But I kept them and they still could be verified today.

Concerning the 5 million piasters, General Noiret seemed concerned for a moment about their fate and then said to me:

"We will give them to the casualties of Orleansville." Orleansville was a city in Algeria which had just been destroyed by an earthquake. General Noiret only came to Indochina for short, infrequent inspections of the airborne troops. On the other hand, he had spent a long part of his career in North Africa and, obviously, if I judge by this decision, Algeria interested him more at the time than Indochina.

I parted from the General, took away my accounts and left the funds. Since then I have never heard of them.

I was, however, disappointed. These funds would have been very useful to compensate the men in our services who had dedicated themselves to France and who we were going to abandon.

But I had left my command; their fate no longer depended on me, but on my successor, an artillery captain newly arrived from France who did not know any of our problems.

Here are therefore the exact facts which are still easy to verify today since General Noiret as well as General Elie are still alive. . . .

Yours sincerely,
(signed) R. Trinquier

54. Interview with Lt. Col. Lucien Conein, McLean, Virginia, June 18, 1971. One anonymous American officer interviewed by an Australian journalist attributed the American refusal to the myopia of Lt. Gen. Samuel T. Williams: "The French officer handling the intelligence organization embracing all the montagnard tribes in the High Plateau and the Annamite Chain offered to turn it all over to Williams. He was not interested" (Denis Warner, *The Last Confucian* [London: Angus & Robertson, 1964], pp. 129–30).

55. Interview with Col. Roger Trinquier, Paris, March 25, 1971.

56. Interview with Gen. Maurice Belleux, Paris, March 23, 1971. This is Gen. Belleux's version of the incident; a French author has a simpler account:

For opium it was exactly the same. The MACG aircraft made millions of piasters transporting the merchandise, and each level took its cut of this traffic, often in good faith. Until the day when, at a base, an ingenuous officer noticed the transfer of mysterious trunks from one DC-3 to another, which was none other than that of the commander in chief. Shocked, he reported it to his superiors. Then, by chance, the Vietnamese Police (who were hardly a model of virtue) made a raid on a Saigon warehouse where there were stockpiles of hundreds of kilos of opium.

This was the beginning of a shadowy and sordid affair in which everybody attacked and defended himself over the extent to which he was hostile or favorable to the conduct of the "dirty war." (Claude Paillat, *Dossier secret de l'Indochine* [Paris: Les Presses de la Cité, 1964], p. 340)

57. Ibid.

58. In 1929, for example, out of 71.7 tons of opium sold by the Indochina Opium Régie, 38.0 tons were consumed in Cochin China (Exposition coloniale internationale, Paris, 1931, Indochine française, Section générale, *Administration des Douanes et Régies en Indochine* [Hanoi: Imprimerie d'Extrême-Orient, 1930], pp. 61–62).

59. Chef de Bataillon A. M. Savani, "Notes sur les Binh Xuyen" (mimeographed, December 1945), pp. 4–5. In making this analogy it is the intention of the author to point out that the Binh Xuyen can be considered representative of the historical phenomenon of "social banditry." For a discussion of social banditry, see Eric J. Hobsbawm, *Primitive Rebels* (New York: Norton, 1959), pp. 13–29, and *Bandits* (New York: Delacorte, 1969). Hobsbawm's argument that the social bandit's diffuse internal structure

and lack of ideology generally make him incapable of playing a major role in a social revolution is borne out by the Binh Xuyen's experience. However, one interesting aspect of the Binh Xuyen's history is not touched on by Hobsbawm—the transformation of a social bandit from an active revolutionary force into a counterrevolutionary force with strong "Mafia" characteristics. The decline of the armed wing of the Philippine Communist party, the Hukbalahap, from an effective guerrilla force to a local "Mafia" living off the bars and bordellos near the U.S. air force base at Clark Field, is a similar case of the phenomenon. (See Eduardo Lachica, *The Huks, Philippine Agrarian Society in Revolt* [New York: Praeger, 1971], pp. 139–43).

60. Ngo Vinh Long, *Before the Revolution: The Vietnamese Peasants Under the French* (Cambridge: MIT Press, 1973); pp. 113–14.

61. Savani, "Notes sur les Binh Xuyen," pp. 22–25.

62. Ibid., pp. 6–8.

63. Interview with Lai Van Sang, Paris, March 22, 1971. (Lai Van Sang was Binh Xuyen military counselor and head of the national police, 1954–1955.)

64. Huynh Kim Khanh, "Background of the Vietnamese August Revolution," *Journal of Asia Studies* 25, no. 4 (August 1971), pp. 771–72.

65. Savani, "Notes sur les Binh Xuyen," pp. 13–14.

66. Ibid., p. 16.

67. Bernard B. Fall, *The Two Vietnams* (New York: Praeger, 1967), pp. 64–65.

68. Ellen J. Hammer, *The Struggle for Indochina, 1940–1955* (Stanford: Stanford University Press, 1967), pp. 113–19; Jean Julien Fonde, *Traitez à tout Prix* (Paris: Robert Laffront, 1971), pp. 18–22. For an account of the diplomatic negotiations and military preparations surrounding the French return to Indochina after World War II, see Marcel Vigneras, *United States Army in World War II: Rearming the French* (Washington, DC: Office of the Chief of Military History, Department of the Army, 1957), pp. 391–99. For the official British version of General Gracey's actions in Saigon, see Maj. Gen. S. Woodburn Kirby, *The War Against Japan,* vol. 5: *The Surrender of Japan* (London: Her Majesty's Stationery Office, 1969), pp. 297–306.

69. Savani, "Notes sur les Binh Xuyen," p. 17.

70. The Avant-Garde Youth Movement had been started by Governor-General Decoux to channel the enthusiasms of Vietnamese youth in a pro-French direction, and by 1945 it was one of the most powerful political groups in Saigon, with a cell in each city ward. By this time its tone was strongly anticolonialist, and its director, Dr. Pham Ngoc Thach, was a secret member of the Viet Minh (Philippe Devillers, *Histoire de Vietnam de 1940 à 1952* [Paris: Editions du Seuil, 1952], pp. 140–41).

71. Interview with Lai Van Sang, Paris, March 22, 1971.

72. Hammer, *Struggle for Indochina,* p. 120.

73. Savani, "Notes sur les Binh Xuyen," p. 44.

74. Interview with Lai Van Sang, Paris, March 22, 1971.

75. Interview with Gen. Maurice Belleux, Paris, March 23, 1971.

76. Savani, "Notes sur les Binh Xuyen," p. 35–36.
77. Ibid., pp. 70–71.
78. Antoine Savani, "Notes sur le Phat Giao Hoa Hao" (mimeographed, n.d.), pp. 30–33.
79. Savani, "Notes sur les Binh Xuyen," pp. 103–4.
80. Ibid., pp. 110–11.
81. Lucien Bodard, *The Quicksand War: Prelude to Vietnam* (Boston: Little, Brown, 1967), p. 114; Fonde, *Traitez à tout Prix*, p. 32.
82. Savani, "Notes sur les Binh Xuyen," p. 118–19.
83. Ibid., pp. 121–22.
84. Interview with Lai Huu Tai, Paris, March 28, 1971.
85. Interview with President Nguyen Van Tam, Paris, March 1971.
86. Lancaster, *Emancipation of French Indochina*, p. 164.
87. Interview with Lai Van Sang, Paris, March 22, 1971; Lucien Bodard, *L'Humiliation* (Paris: Gallimard, 1965), p. 120.
88. F.T.S.V. 2eme Bureau, "Les Binh Xuyen" (carbon typescript, 1953–1954), p. 17.
89. Bodard, *Quicksand War*, p. 110.
90. F.T.S.V. 2eme Bureau, "Les Binh Xuyen," p. 18.
91. Lancaster, *Emancipation of French Indochina*, p. 379.
92. In reference to the Binh Xuyen's involvement in opium trade, the 2eme Bureau commented, "Naturally all of the clandestine traffics, the most interesting by definition, are not forgotten and cover a wide range including arms, opium, and contraband of all forms as well as other unsavory activities" (F.T.S.V. 2eme Bureau, "Les Binh Xuyen," p. 16).
93. Edward G. Lansdale, "Subject: The Cao Dai," to Ambassador Ellsworth Bunker and members, U.S. Mission Council (May 1968), p. 17.
94. Warner, *Last Confucian*, p. 17.
95. The French had few illusions about Bay Vien as a 1954 report noted: "The thundering success of this former resident of Puolo Condore [Con Son Prison Island] should not be surprising if one considers that he has preserved intact from his tumultuous past certain methods which are closer to those of the celebrated bands of the heroic epoch of Chicago than to ordinary commercial transactions" (F.T.S.V. 2eme Bureau, "Les Binh Xuyen," p. 15). However, in contrast to this frankness in classified documents, 2eme Bureau officials avoided any mention of the Binh Xuyen's criminal character and described it in public statements simply as an "extreme nationalist" force. (See, for example, A. M. Savani, *Visages et Images du Sud Viet-Nam* [Saigon: Imprimerie Française d'Outre-Mer, 1955], pp. 100–105.).
96. F.T.S.V. 2eme Bureau, "Les Binh Xuyen," p. 17.
97. Ibid., p. 15.
98. Lansdale, "Subject: The Cao Dai," p. 17.
99. Lancaster, *Emancipation of French Indochina*, pp. 187–88.
100. Mike Gravel, ed., *The Pentagon Papers*, 5 vols. (Boston: Beacon Press, 1971), vol. 1, pp. 180–81.

101. Ibid., p. 182. Although U.S. support for Diem remained an open question on the diplomatic level, the CIA gave him its unqualified support from the very beginning of his tenure as prime minister. According to a State Department official, "the Central Intelligence Agency was given the mission of helping Diem" in June 1954 and Col. Lansdale was sent to Saigon to carry out this mission (Chester L. Cooper, *The Lost Crusade* [New York: Dodd, Mead, 1970], p. 129).

102. Pierre Brocheux, "L'Economie et la Société dans L'Ouest de la Cochinchine pendant la Periode coloniale (1890–1940)" (Ph.D. thesis, University of Paris, 1969), p. 298.

103. Eugène Saccomano, *Bandits à Marseille* (Paris: Julliard, 1968), p. 44.

104. In 1958 a U.S. narcotics agent told a Senate subcommittee, "When French Indochina existed, there were quantities of opium that were shipped to the labs . . . around Marseille, France, to the Corsican underworld there, and then transshipped to the United States" (U.S. Congress, Senate, Select Committee on Improper Activities in the Labor Management Field, *Hearings,* 85th Cong., 2nd sess. (Washington, DC: U.S. Government Printing Office, 1959), p. 1225.

105. Bodard, *L'Humiliation,* pp. 80–81.

106. Bodard, *Quicksand War,* pp. 121, 124.

107. Interview with Gen. Edward G. Lansdale, Alexandria, Virginia, June 17, 1971.

108. Fall, *Two Vietnams,* Praeger, pp. 245–46; New York Times, *The Pentagon Papers* (New York: Quadrangle, 1971), p. 60.

109. Lansdale, "Subject: The Cao Dai," p. 14.

110. Ibid., p. 2.

111. Ibid., p. 11.

112. Grimaldi, *Notions de Case,* p. 24.

113. Fall, *Two Vietnams,* pp. 245–46.

114. Lansdale, "Subject: The Cao Dai," pp. 15–16.

115. Interview with Gen. Edward G. Lansdale, Alexandria, Virginia, June 17, 1971; Edward G. Lansdale, *In the Midst of Wars* (New York: Harper & Row, 1972), pp. 221–24.

116. Lansdale, *In the Midst of Wars,* pp. 245–47; Gravel, *Pentagon Papers,* vol. 1, p. 230.

117. New York Times, *Pentagon Papers,* p. 21.

118. Interview with Gen. Mai Huu Xuan, Saigon, Vietnam, July 19, 1971.

119. Lansdale, *In the Midst of Wars,* p. 270.

120. Gravel, *Pentagon Papers,* vol. 1, p. 231.

121. Ibid., p. 233.

122. New York Times, *Pentagon Papers,* p. 22.

123. Interview with Lt. Col. Lucien Conein, McLean, Virginia, June 18, 1971.

124. Lansdale, "Subject: The Cao Dai," p. 17.

125. Lansdale, *In the Midst of Wars,* pp. 316–17.

126. Ibid., p. 318.

127. Gravel, *Pentagon Papers,* vol. 1, pp. 238–39.

128. *New York Times*, March 28, 1955, p. 26.
129. Savani, "Notes sur les Binh Xuyen," p. 198.
130. See Chapter 5.
131. *New York Times*, September 17, 1963, p. 45.
132. Interview with William Young, Chiangmai, Thailand, September 8, 1971; *New York Times*, August 11, 1971, p. 1.
133. Archimedes L. A. Patti, *Why Vietnam: Prelude to America's Albatross* (Berkeley: University of California Press, 1980), pp. 216–17.
134. Ibid., pp. 34, 265, 354–55, 487.
135. John T. McAlister, *Vietnam: The Origins of the Revolution* (New York: Knopf, 1969), pp. 235, 242.
136. Lancaster, *Emancipation of French Idonchina*, p. 150.
137. Bodard, *Quicksand War*, p. 12. For a detailed analysis of Yunnan politics during this period, see A. Doak Barnett, *China on the Eve of Communist Takeover* (New York: Praeger, 1963), 282–95.
138. *New York Times*, July 28, 1951, p. 3; Bodard, *Quicksand War*, pp. 162–63.
139. Lancaster, *Emancipation of French Indochina*, p. 203.
140. Union of Burma, Ministry of Information, *Kuomintang Aggression Against Burma* (Rangoon: Government Printing, 1953), p. 8.
141. The Chargé in China (Strong) to Secretary of State, August 11, 1950, in *Foreign Relations of the United States 1950*, vol. 6: *East Asia and the Pacific* (Washington, DC: U.S. Government Printing Office, 1976), pp. 249–50.
142. New York Times, *Pentagon Papers*, p. 10.
143. Joint Chiefs of Staff, "Memorandum for the Secretary of Defense," April 10, 1950, in Gravel, *Pentagon Papers*, vol. 1, p. 366.
144. Ibid.
145. David Wise and Thomas B. Ross, *The Invisible Government* (New York: Random House, 1964), pp. 130–31; Thomas Powers, *The Man Who Kept the Secrets: Richard Helms and the CIA* (New York: Knopf, 1979), pp. 81–82.
146. U.S. Congress, Senate, Select Committee to Study Governmental Operations, "History of the Central Intelligence Agency," *Supplementary Detailed Staff Reports on Foreign and Military Intelligence*, Book 6, 94th Cong., 2nd sess., 1976 (Washington, DC: U.S. Government Printing Office, Senate Report No. 94-755), pp. 30–32.
147. William Colby, *Honorable Men: My Life in the CIA* (New York: Simon & Schuster, 1978), p. 96.
148. John Ranelagh, *The Agency: The Rise and Decline of the CIA* (New York: Simon & Schuster, 1986), pp. 134–35.
149. Colby, *Honorable Men*, pp. 23–56.
150. Ibid., pp. 147–48.
151. *Wall Street Journal*, April 18, 1980.
152. Claire Lee Chennault, *Way of a Fighter: The Memoirs of Claire Lee Chennault* (New York: Putnam's, 1949), pp. xx–xxi.
153. William M. Leary, *Perilous Missions: Civil Air Transport and CIA Covert*

*Operations in Asia* (Montgomery: University of Alabama Press, 1984), pp. 67–83; *Wall Street Journal*, April 18, 1980.

154. Leary, *Perilous Missions*, pp. 100–112, 208.

155. Ibid., pp. 84–93, 128–31.

156. For an explanation of the concept of "plausible denial," see U.S. Congress, Senate, Select Committee to Study Governmental Operations, *Alleged Assassination Plots Involving Foreign Leaders* (New York: Norton, 1976), pp. 11–12.

157. *Wall Street Journal*, April 18, 1980.

158. Y. C. Hsueh, "The Minutes of a Conference with General Li Mi in Taipei on March 2, 1953, and Prepared by Waichaiaopu, Marked Secret," Wellington Koo, Oral History, Butler Library, Columbia University. *The New York Times* biography of Lt. Gen. Graves B. Erskine states that he was commander of the First Marine Division in Korea when the war there broke out but "was detached from command to head a survey mission to Indochina on France's problems in dealing with local insurgents" (*New York Times*, May 23, 1973).

159. Leary, *Perilous Missions*, pp. 131–32.

160. Catherine Lamour, *Enquête sur une Armée secrète* (Paris: Editions de Seuil, 1975), pp. 41–43.

161. After 1960, William Bird, through his construction firm Bird & Son, began constructing CIA landing strips in Laos and acquired a fleet of fifty aircraft to fulfill a CIA contract for air transport in Laos. In 1965, Bird sold his airline for about one million dollars to Continental Air Services, headed by Robert Rousselot, the CAT pilot who had flown the first arms for the KMT to Chiangmai in February 1951 (Peter Dale Scott, *The War Conspiracy: The Secret Road to the Second Indochina War* [Indianapolis: Bobbs-Merrill, 1972], pp. 207–8; Leary, *Perilous Missions*, pp. 129–31).

162. Memorandum, Special Assistant for Mutual Security Affairs (Merchant), *Foreign Relations of the United States 1951*, Vol. 6: *Asia and the Pacific*, part 1 (Washington, DC: U.S. Government Printing Office, 1977), pp. 316–17.

163. Leary, *Perilous Missions*, pp. 129–32.

164. Hsueh, "Minutes of a Conference."

165. For a useful compilation of secondary sources and a simple chronicle of the KMT operation, see Robert H. Taylor, *Foreign and Domestic Consequences of the KMT Intervention in Burma* (Ithaca: Southeast Asia Program, Cornell University, Data Paper No. 93, 1973); Union of Burma, *Kuomintang Aggression*, p. 15.

166. Union of Burma, *Kuomintang Aggression*, p. 35.

167. Ibid., pp. 13–15.

168. Joseph and Stewart Alsop, *Nippon Times*, March 23, 1953, quoted in Union of Burma, *Kuomintang Aggression*, pp. 13–14, 120.

169. The Ambassador in Burma (Key) to the Secretary of State [Top Secret Priority], Rangoon, August 29, 1951, *Foreign Relations of the United States 1951*, pp. 290–91.

170. Ambassador in Burma, *Foreign Relations of the United States 1951*, pp. 288–89.

171. Union of Burma, *Kuomintang Aggression*, p. 16.

172. Ibid., p. 13; Peter Dale Scott, "Air America: Flying the U.S. into Laos," in Nina S. Adams and Alfred W. McCoy, eds., *Laos: War and Revolution* (New York: Harper & Row, 1970), pp. 306–7; *New York Times*, February 22, 1952.

173. Wise and Ross, *Invisible Government*, p. 131.

174. Union of Burma, *Kuomintang Aggression*, pp. 40–41.

175. Interview with Rev. Paul Lewis, Chiangmai, Thailand, September 7, 1971.

176. Union of Burma, *Kuomintang Aggression*, p. 15. Smuggling across the Chinese border became increasingly difficult after the defeat of the Nationalist government. After interviewing Chinese Muslim exiles in Rangoon in June and July 1962, an Israeli scholar reported, "The frontier, which had never been clearly marked or demarcated, was closed and strictly guarded after 1950 when the Government of Communist China established its authority in these regions. Until then the Panthays [Chinese Muslims] had been able to move freely and easily between Yunnan and Burma" (Moshe Yegar, "The Panthay (Chinese Muslims) of Burma and Yunnan," *Journal of Southeast Asian History* 7, no. 1 [March 1966], 82).

177. Union of Burma, *Kuomintang Aggression*, p. 14.

178. Leary, *Perilous Missions*, pp. 131–32.

179. William R. Corson, *The Armies of Ignorance: The Rise of the American Intelligence Empire* (New York: Dial, 1977), pp. 320–21.

180. Hsueh, "Minutes of a Conference." The precise nature of Gen. Frank Merrill's assignment in Southeast Asia was evidently concealed. After retirement from the U.S. army in 1948, Merrill became New Hampshire state highway commissioner but was recalled by the army in December 1951 for an active-duty assignment that did not appear on the regular army roster. By May 1952, Merrill was back in New Hampshire planning the state's new tollway system. His activities during his last Asian tour are omitted from all biographies. See *New York Times*, August 2, 1950; December 15, 1951; and December 13, 1955; and *The Cyclopedia of American Biography* (New York: James T. White, 1963), vol. 46, p. 134.

181. Union of Burma, *Kuomintang Aggression*, p. 16.

182. Interview with Rev. Paul Lewis, Chiangmai, Thailand, September 7, 1971.

183. Union of Burma, *Kuomintang Aggression*, p. 12.

184. Ibid., p. 15.

185. *New York Times*, March 9, 1952, p. 8.

186. Wise and Ross, *Invisible Government*, pp. 132–33.

187. Hugh Tinker, *The Union of Burma* (London: Oxford University Press, 1957), p. 53.

188. Wise and Ross, *Invisible Government*, pp. 132–33.

189. Anthony Cave Brown, *The Last Hero: Wild Bill Donovan* (New York: Times Books, 1982), pp. 822–24.

190. Interview with William vanden Heuvel, New York City, June 21, 1971.

(William vanden Heuvel was executive assistant to Ambassador Donovan and had noted this incident in his personal journal.)

191. Tinker, *Union of Burma*, pp. 53–54.

192. Interview with Rev. Paul Lewis, Chiangmai, Thailand, September 7, 1971. (At the time of this interview, Rev. Lewis was acting as a mail link for many of these separated Lahu families and received two or three letters a week from Taiwan.)

193. Leary, *Perilous Missions*, pp. 196–97.

194. *The Nation* (Rangoon), March 19, 1954, p. 1.

195. Ibid., March 21, 1954, p. 1.

196. *New York Times*, May 31, 1954, p. 2.

197. Tinker, *Union of Burma*, p. 55.

198. Interview with Col. Chen Mo Su, Chiang Khong, Thailand, September 10, 1971. (Colonel Chen was KMT commander at Chiang Khong.)

199. Elaine T. Lewis, "The Hill Peoples of Kengtung State," *Practical Anthropology* 4, no. 6 (November–December 1957), p. 226.

200. *New York Times*, May 19, 1959, p. 6.

201. *Time*, February 10, 1961, p. 22.

202. Interview with Colonel Chen Mo Su, Chiang Khong, Thailand, September 10, 1971.

203. *The Guardian* (Rangoon), January 30, 1961, p. 1.

204. Wise and Ross, *Invisible Government*, p. 134.

205. *New York Times*, February 23, 1961.

206. Ibid., February 18, 1961; March 3, 1961.

207. Seymour Topping, *Journey Between Two Chinas* (New York: Harper & Row, 1972), pp. 130–31.

208. *New York Times*, April 6, 1961.

209. Ibid., April 12, 1961.

210. Interview with William Young, Chiangmai, Thailand, September 8, 1971.

211. Topping, *Journey Between Two Chinas*, pp. 129–30.

212. Memorandum of conversation, Deputy Assistant Secretary of State for Far Eastern Affairs (Merchant), Subject: KMT Troops in Burma, Washington, August 10, 1951 [Top Secret], *Foreign Relations of the United States 1951*, pp. 287–88.

213. Ibid., p. 131; Leary, *Perilous Missions*, p. 131.

214. Ranelagh, *Agency*, pp. 220–21.

215. Powers, *Man Who Kept the Secrets*, pp. 47–51.

216. U.S. Senate, "History of the Central Intelligence Agency," pp. 37–38.

217. Ranelagh, *Agency*, p. 221.

218. Corson, *Armies of Ignorance*, pp. 320–22.

219. *New York Times*, March 9, 1952, p. 8.

220. Anon Puntharikapha, "The 'Manhattan' Incident," in Thak Chaloemtiarana, ed., *Thai Politics: Extracts and Documents, 1932–1957* (Bangkok: Social Science Association of Thailand, 1978), pp. 594–603.

221. Fred W. Riggs, *Thailand: The Modernization of a Bureaucratic Polity* (Honolulu: East-West Center Press, 1966), pp. 242–45.

222. Thongchai Winnichakul, *Siam Mapped: The Geobody of Thailand* (Honolulu: University of Hawaii Press, forthcoming).

223. Phin Choonhawan, "Events in the Life of Field Marshal Phin Chunnahawan," in Thak Chaloemtiarana, *Thai Politics*, pp. 579–81.

224. Riggs, *Thailand*, p. 236.

225. Nigel J. Brailey, *Thailand and the Fall of Singapore: A Frustrated Asian Revolution* (Boulder: Westview, 1986), pp. 130–31.

226. Phin Choonhawan, "Events in the Life," pp. 568–92.

227. Khana Ratthamontri, "The History and Works of Field Marshal Sarit Thanarat," in Thak Chaloemtiarana, *Thai Politics*, pp. 681–715.

228. Thak Chaloemtiarana, "On Coups d'Etat," in Thak Chaloemtiarana, *Thai Politics*, pp. 564–67.

229. Anon Puntharikapha, "The 'Manhattan' Incident," pp. 595–99.

230. Frank C. Darling, *Thailand and the United States* (Washington, DC: Public Affairs Press, 1965), pp. 88–89; Anon Puntharikapha, "The 'Manhattan' Incident," pp. 594–99; Brailey, *Thailand and the Fall of Singapore*, p. 156.

231. *New York Times*, July 23, 1951.

232. Phin Choonhawan, "Events in the Life," pp. 568–92; Darling, *Thailand and the United States*, p. 117.

233. United Nations, *Summary of the Fourth Meeting*, p. 4.

234. United Nations, Economic and Social Council, Commission on Narcotic Drugs, *Agenda of the Ninth Meeting* (E/C.S.7/27), December 3, 1946, pp. 6–9.

235. *Far Eastern Economic Review*, November 23, 1950, p. 625.

236. Paul T. Cohen, "Hill Trading in the Mountain Ranges of Northern Thailand" (1968), p. 4.

237. Darrell Berrigan, "They Smuggle Dope by the Ton," *Saturday Evening Post*, May 5, 1956, p. 157.

238. *New York Daily News*, February 13, 1955.

239. *New York Times*, November 7, 1948, p. 30.

240. Berrigan, "They Smuggle Dope," pp. 157–58.

241. Warner, *Last Confucian*, p. 284.

242. Thomas Lobe, *The United States National Security Policy and Aid to the Thailand Police* (Denver: Graduate School of International Studies, University of Denver, 1977), pp. 27–28.

243. *New York Times*, September 20, 1957, p. 7.

244. Riggs, *Thailand*, p. 239.

245. Darling, *Thailand and the United States*, pp. 115–22.

246. *New York Times*, November 6, 1957, p. 34.

247. Warner, *Last Confucian*, p. 282.

248. William J. Donovan, "Our Stake in Thailand," *Fortune* (July 1955), pp. 94–95.

249. Darling, *Thailand and the United States*, p. 106.

250. G. William Skinner, *Chinese Society in Thailand: An Analytical History* (Ithaca: Cornell University Press, 1957), p. 325.

251. Ibid., p. 326.

252. U.S. National Security Council, "Statement of Policy by the National Security Council on United States Objectives and Courses of Action with Respect to Southeast Asia," in Gravel, *Pentagon Papers*, vol. 1, p. 438.

253. Skinner, *Chinese Society*, pp. 328, 330, 335, 340–43.

254. Wendell Blanchard, *Thailand, Its People, Its Society, Its Culture* (New Haven: Human Relations Area Files Press, 1958), p. 198.

255. For examples of such incidents, see *Bangkok Post*, March 11, 1955; July 14, 1955.

256. For some of Phao's public statements, see *Bangkok Post*, February 10, 1950; February 20, 1950.

257. Ibid., December 3, 1953; December 4, 1953.

258. Ibid., July 14, 1955.

259. Berrigan, "They Smuggle Dope," pp. 42, 156.

260. *Bangkok Post*, July 15, 1955.

261. Ibid., July 29, 1955.

262. Berrigan, "They Smuggle Dope," p. 156.

263. *New York Times*, August 25, 1955, p. 3.

264. Ibid., September 4, 1955, p. 5.

265. Prasert Rujirawong, "Kanluk Supfin" (Abolishing Opium Smoking), in Khana Ratthamontri, *Prawat lae phonngan khong jomphon Sarit Thanarat, phim nai ngan phraratchathan pleong sop phon jomphon Sarit Thanarat* (The Life and Works of Field Marshal Sarit Thanarat, Published on the Occasion of the Cremation of Field Marshal Sarit Thanarat) (Bangkok: Prime Minister's Office, 1964), pp. 32–33.

266. The percentage is inferred from data provided in Skinner, *Chinese Society*, pp. 364–65.

267. *Bangkok Post*, September 21, 1955.

268. Skinner, *Chinese Society*, p. 343.

269. Warner, *Last Confucian*, p. 286.

270. Blanchard, *Thailand, Its People*, p. 199.

271. *New York Times*, September 20, 1957, p. 7.

272. Interview with William Young, Chiangmai, Thailand, September 14, 1971.

273. *Bangkok World*, November 17, 1957.

274. *Bangkok Post*, February 10, 1958.

275. Warner, *Last Confucian*, pp. 289–91.

276. Interview with a retired CIA operative, Chiangmai, Thailand, August 1971. This operative was a Thai language specialist and was involved in monitoring CIA audio intercepts from Field Marshal Sarit's home and offices as a part of his agency duties.

277. The text of this decree is found in Prasert Rujirawong, "Kanluk Supfin," pp. 34–35.

278. Field Marshal Sarit is quoted in Prasert Rujirawong, "Kanluk Supfin," pp. 35–36.

279. *Far Eastern Economic Review* (November 5, 1973).

280. *Far Eastern Economic Review* (April 28, 1978).

281. W. W. Rostow, *The Stages of Economic Growth* (New York: Cambridge University Press, 1968), pp. 6–9; Hla Myint, *The Economics of the Developing Countries* (New York: Praeger, 1964), pp. 14–16.

282. League of Nations, Advisory Committee on the Traffic in Opium and Other Dangerous Drugs, *Annual Reports on the Traffic in Opium and Other Dangerous Drugs for the Year 1939* (Geneva: League of Nations, 1939), p. 42.

283. *New York Times*, September 17, 1963, p. 45.

284. League of Nations, Advisory Committee on the Traffic in Opium and Other Dangerous Drugs, *Minutes of the First Session* (Geneva: League of Nations, May 24–June 7, 1923), p. 187. Anthropological research has shown that there was no substantial increase in Thai opium production until 1947 (Cohen, "Hill Trading," pp. 1–2).

285. In 1967 a U.N. survey team estimated Thailand's opium production at 145 tons. Since most of the expansion in production had taken place during the 1950s, an estimate of more than 100 tons for the early 1960s is believed to be a conservative one (*Report of the United Nations Survey Team on the Economic and Social Needs of the Opium Producing Areas in Thailand* [Bangkok: Government House Printing Office, 1967], p. 59).

286. U.S. Bureau of Narcotics and Dangerous Drugs, "World Opium Situation," p. 29.

## 5  South Vietnam's Heroin Trade

1. Mike Gravel, ed., *The Pentagon Papers*, 5 vols. (Boston: Beacon Press, 1971), vol. 1, pp. 221–22.

2. Robert Scheer, "Hang Down Your Head Tom Dooley," in *A Muckraker's Guide* (San Francisco: Ramparts Magazine, 1969), p. 18.

3. Gravel, *Pentagon Papers*, vol. 2, p. 22.

4. Ibid., vol. 1, p. 240.

5. Philippe Devillers and Jean Lacouture, *End of a War* (New York: Praeger, 1969), p. 377.

6. Thomas A. Dooley, M.D., *Deliver Us from Evil* (New York: Farrar, Straus and Cudahy, 1956), pp. 41, 60.

7. Ibid., p. 71.

8. Ibid., p. 159. For a description of American moralism in this period see Chester L. Cooper, *The Lost Crusade* (New York: Dodd, Mead, 1970), pp. 12–14.

9. Edward G. Lansdale, *In the Midst of Wars* (New York: Harper & Row, 1972), p. ix.

10. David Halberstam, *The Making of a Quagmire* (New York: Random House, 1964), p. 42.

11. Lt. Col. Lucien Conein was one of Lansdale's chief assistants during the 1955 battles that put Diem in power, and he was the CIA liaison man with the coup plotters who overthrew Diem in November 1963. Interestingly, Diem's two key supporters in the 1955 fighting—Gen. Mai Huu Xuan and Gen. Duong Van Minh—were two of the leaders of the 1963 coup group.

12. Interview with Col. Roger Trinquier, Paris, March 25, 1971.

13. Fred. W. Riggs, *Thailand: The Modernization of a Bureaucratic Polity* (Honolulu: East-West Center Press, 1966), p. 245.

14. New York Times, *The Pentagon Papers* (New York: Quadrangle, 1971), p. 235.

15. Interview with Bernard Yoh, Washington, DC, June 15, 1971. (Bernard Yoh was an adviser to President Ngo Dinh Diem during the 1950s.)

16. Interview with Lt. Col. Lucien Conein, McLean, Virginia, June 18, 1971.

17. Gen. Mai Huu Xuan claimed that most of Nhu's dealings with the Chinese syndicates and business community were conducted through a Chinese businessman named Ma Tuyen (interview with Gen. Mai Huu Xuan, Saigon, Vietnam, July 19, 1971). Following the November 1963 coup, Diem and Nhu hid in Ma Tuyen's house in Cholon just prior to their murder (*New York Times*, November 4, 1971, p. 8).

18. Stanley Karnow, Time-Life Editorial Reference Files (unpublished manuscript, April 1963).

19. Interview with Lt. Col. Lucien Conein, McLean, Virginia, June 18, 1971.

20. Ibid. Ironically, Nhu reportedly spent the latter months of his life as a heroin addict. According to correspondent Robert Shaplen's account, Diem's secretary of state said, "We knew that Nhu was smoking opium in the last year and maybe taking heroin, too, and this helped create his moods of extremism" (Robert Shaplen, *The Lost Revolution: The U.S. in Vietnam, 1946–1966* [New York: Harper & Row, 1966], p. 189).

21. The Can Lao was a clandestine organization formed by Ngo Dinh Nhu shortly after Diem took office. Party members were recruited from every branch of the military and civil bureaucracy but were usually conservative Catholics. The party functioned as a government within the government, and through it Nhu was able to exercise direct control over every aspect of the government. Its membership list was kept secret to enable party cadres to spy more effectively on their co-workers.

22. Interview with an exiled Vietnamese army colonel, Paris, March 25, 1971.

23. Interview with an exiled Can Lao party official, Paris, April 1, 1971.

24. Denis Warner, *The Last Confucian* (London: Angus & Robertson, 1964), p. 224; for one U.S. official's opinion of Dr. Tuyen, see Cooper, *Lost Crusade*, p. 205. Ironically, Tuyen later became one of the earliest plotters of the coup that ultimately overthrew the Diem regime in November 1963. After a series of quarrels with Madame Nhu that cost him Nhu's friendship, Tuyen began to elaborate plans for a coup, which were postponed in September 1963 when Nhu sent him to Cairo as consul. Immediately after the coup, Tuyen returned to Saigon but was imprisoned by the military regime (Shaplen, *Lost Revolution*, pp. 197–98, 211).

   For a description of the Diem regime's intelligence operations, see Frances FitzGerald, *Fire in the Lake* (Boston: Atlantic Monthly Press, 1972), pp. 97–98.

25. New York Times, *Pentagon Papers*, p. 19.

26. Interview with Bernard Yoh, Washington, DC, June 15, 1971.

27. Interview with an exiled Can Lao party official, Paris, April 1, 1971.

28. Ibid.; interview with Tran Van Dinh, Washington, DC, April 30, 1971.

29. Interdepartmental Task Force, "A Program of Action for South Vietnam," in New York Times, *Pentagon Papers*, p. 129.

30. A number of sources confirmed that Ky was hired to fly these missions: interview with Col. Phan Phung Tien, Tan Son Nhut Air Base, South Vietnam, July 29, 1971 (Colonel Tien was commander of the Fifth Air Division, the air transport division); interview with Lt. Col. Lucien Conein, McLean, Virginia, June 18, 1971; interview with Bernard Yoh, Washington, DC, June 15, 1971.

31. S. M. Mustard, letter to Senator Ernest Greuning, March 9, 1968; *New York Times*, April 19, 1968, p. 11.

32. Interview with Col. Do Khac Mai, Paris, March 29, 1971. (Col. Do Khac Mai was commander of the Vietnamese air force in 1963.)

33. New York Times, *Pentagon Papers*, p. 91.

34. Cablegram from Elbridge Durbrow, United States Ambassador to South Vietnam, to Secretary of State Christian A. Herter, September 16, 1960, in ibid., p. 122.

35. Marguerite Higgins, *Our Vietnam Nightmare* (New York: Harper & Row, 1965), p. 241.

36. Interview with Lt. Col Lucien Conein, McLean, Virginia, June 18, 1971; Cooper, *Lost Crusade*, p. 247.

37. Gravel, *Pentagon Papers*, vol. 2, pp. 522–23.

38. Ibid., p. 524.

39. New York Times, *Pentagon Papers*, p. 347.

40. Ibid., p. 410.

41. Robert Shaplen, *The Road from War* (New York: Harper & Row, 1970), pp. 22–23.

42. Gravel, *Pentagon Papers*, vol. 2, pp. 525–26.

43. Interview with an exiled Can Lao party official, Paris, April 1, 1971.

44. Interview with Nguyen Xuan Vinh, Ann Arbor, MI, June 22, 1971. (Nguyen Xuan Vinh was commander of the Vietnamese air force from 1958 until 1962.)

45. Interview with Col. Do Khac Mai, Paris, March 29, 1971. According to Colonel Mai, Mrs. Ly had raised prices and was grafting from the base food budget. Air force officers complained to the high command, and Ky was removed from command of Tan Son Nhut after an investigation by a ranking army general.

46. George McTurnan Kahin and John W. Lewis, *The United States in Vietnam* (New York: Dial, 1967), p. 241.

47. Interview with Nguyen Xuan Vinh, Ann Arbor, MI, June 22, 1971.

48. *New York Times*, April 22, 1966, p. 22.

49. Interview with Lt. Col. Lucien Conein, McLean, Virginia, June 18, 1971.

50. Ibid.

51. Ibid.

52. Interview with Charles Sweet, Washington, DC, May 1971. (Charles Sweet

was an adviser to Air Vice-Marshal Ky when Ky was minister of sports and youth in 1965. Sweet later served as an assistant to Gen. Edward G. Lansdale in the senior liaison office attached to the U.S. embassy in Saigon.)

53. Shaplen, *Road from War,* p. 185.

54. Interview with Charles Sweet, Washington, DC, May 1971.

55. Interview with a Vietnamese intelligence official, Saigon, Vietnam, July 1971.

56. Interview with Tran Van Dinh, Washington, DC, February 16, 1971. (Tran Van Dinh was a South Vietnamese ambassador to the United States.)

57. *Vietnam Guardian* (Saigon), August 18, 1966.

58. Interview with a Vietnamese intelligence official, Saigon, Vietnam, July 1971; Shaplen, *Road from War,* pp. 36–37, 53.

59. George Roberts, Report to Robert R. Johnson, Public Administration Ad Hoc Committee on Corruption in Vietnam, November 29, 1967.

60. Roberts, Report, October 5, 1967.

61. *Los Angeles Times,* February 29, 1968.

62. Roberts, Report, December 6, 1967.

63. Ibid.

64. Roberts, Report, November 29, 1967.

65. U.S. Congress, Senate, *Congressional Record* 114, no. 16 (February 5, 1968).

66. *Christian Science Monitor,* March 9, 1968.

67. *New York Times,* April 19, 1968, p. 11.

68. Interview with a Vietnamese intelligence official, Saigon, Vietnam, July 1971.

69. Interview with Lt. Col. Lucien Conein, McLean, Virginia, June 18, 1971.

70. "Nationalist Politics in Viet-Nam," Report of the Senior Liaison Office, U.S. Embassy, Saigon, Vietnam, May 1967, p. 11. (Those who prepared this report were Edward G. Lansdale, David E. Hudson, Calvin E. Mehlert, and Charles F. Sweet.)

71. Roberts, Report, October 5, 1967.

72. Kahin and Lewis, *United States in Vietnam,* pp. 347–48.

73. Keesing's Research Report, *South Vietnam: A Political History, 1954–1970* (New York: Scribner's, 1970), pp. 124–25.

74. Kahin and Lewis, *United States in Vietnam,* p. 358.

75. Shaplen, *Road from War,* pp. 156–57.

76. "Nationalist Politics in Viet-Nam," p. 9.

77. Ibid., pp. 11, 15.

78. Ibid., p. 10.

79. Roberts, Report, December 6, 1967.

80. Ibid.

81. Ibid.

82. Roberts, Report, January 19, 1968.

83. Interview with Col. Tran Van Phan, Saigon, Vietnam, July 23, 1971. (Colonel Phan was information officer for the national police.)

84. Interview with Col. Phan Phung Tien, Tan Son Nhut Air Base, Vietnam, July 29, 1971.

85. Interview with Col. Tran Van Phan, Saigon, Vietnam, July 23, 1971. (Colonel Phan was then assistant to the director-general of the national police for personnel training. He suffered a serious leg wound in the accident and was hospitalized for three months.)

86. Keesing's Research Report, *South Vietnam*, p. 138.

87. Richard Critchfield, *The Long Charade* (New York: Harcourt, Brace and World, 1968), p. 387.

88. Keesing's Research Report, *South Vietnam*, p. 138.

89. Interview with a senior MACCORDS official, Saigon, Vietnam, July, 1971.

90. Most of the visible corruption in the National Assembly seems to have been the work of lower house members. As in many European parliaments, the Senate had less nominal authority and its members were generally more reserved.

91. "Nationalist Politics in Viet-Nam," pp. 19–20.

92. Interview with a lower house representative, Saigon, Vietnam, July 1971.

93. "Nationalist Politics in Viet-Nam," p. 18.

94. *Washington Post*, September 8, 1968.

95. *New York Times*, June 6, 1971, p. 2.

96. Capt. Gary C. Lulenski (MC), Capt. Larry E. Alessi (MC), and Sp4c Charles E. Burdick, "Drug Abuse in the 23rd Infantry Division (Americal)," September 1970, p. 9.

97. Major Richard H. Anderson (MC) and Sp4c Wade Hawley, "Subject: Analysis of 482 Questionnaires on Illicit Drug Use in an Engineering Battalion in Vietnam," November 11, 1970, p. 6.

98. *New York Times*, May 16, 1971, p. 1.

99. "The Drug Abuse Problem in Vietnam," Report of the Office of the Provost Marshal, U.S. Military Assistance Command Vietnam (Saigon, 1971), p. 4.

100. Ibid., p. 6.

101. For an analysis of the impact of the army's marijuana suppression campaign, see Norman E. Zinberg, "GIs and OJs in Vietnam," *New York Times Magazine*, December 5, 1971, p. 120. Dr. Zinberg said that the crackdown on marijuana began in 1968. Since large numbers of GIs did not start using heroin until spring 1970, it is obvious that the crackdown on marijuana was only a contributing factor in the switch to heroin.

102. Interview with Captain Higginbotham, Can Tho, Vietnam, July 23, 1971. (Captain Higginbotham was a medical doctor working in the IV Corps amnesty program.)

103. *Washington Post*, July 13, 1971.

104. Interview with Maj. Gen. John H. Cushman, Can Tho, Vietnam, July 23, 1971.

105. *New York Times*, May 18, 1971, p. 10.

106. "Drug Abuse Problem in Vietnam," p. 3.

107. Interview with U.S. Rep. Robert H. Steele, Washington, DC, June 16, 1971.

108. *Milford Citizen* (Connecticut), June 29, 1971. (The paper carried a UPI dispatch from Phnom Penh that said, "Since its inclusion in the Indochina War 15 months ago Cambodia has become a small but growing 'way station' for hard drugs bound for American Servicemen in Vietnam.")

109. Interview with an agent, Washington, DC, October 21, 1971. (Huu Tim-heng's involvement in the heroin traffic was confirmed by the U.S. Bureau of Narcotics and Dangerous Drugs, October 21, 1971).

110. Telephone interview with Richard J. Hynes, USAID/Laos, Vientiane, Laos, September 7, 1971.

111. Interview with an agent, U.S. Bureau of Narcotics and Dangerous Drugs, Washington, DC, October 21, 1971.

112. Interview with Vietnamese residents of Vientiane, Laos, August 1971; interview with a Vietnamese intelligence official, Saigon, Vietnam, September 1971; interview with Estelle Holt, London, March 1971 (Estelle Holt is a former foreign correspondent in Laos); interview with an agent, U.S. Bureau of Narcotics and Dangerous Drugs, New Haven, CT, May 3, 1972.

113. Interview with an agent, U.S. Bureau of Narcotics and Dangerous Drugs, Saigon, Vietnam, July 27, 1971.

114. *New York Times*, August 30, 1971, p. 1.

115. Interview with a U.S. customs adviser, Saigon, Vietnam, July 16, 1971.

116. Interview with the U.S. air force adviser to the Fifth Air Division, Tan Son Nhut Air Base, Vietnam, July 1971.

117. Ibid.

118. On June 29, 1971, United Press International reported, "Vietnamese air force C 119 flying boxcars or C 123 providers, which fly military cargo to Cambodia, return to Saigon empty, except for the drug shipments, sources claim" (*Milford Citizen*, June 29, 1971).

119. *New York Times*, August 30, 1971, p. 1.

120. Interview with the U.S. air force adviser to the Fifth Air Division, Tan Son Nhut Air Base, Vietnam, July 1971; interview with a Vietnamese intelligence official, Saigon, Vietnam, July 1971.

121. *Washington Post*, July 21, 1971.

122. Ibid., July 17, 1971.

123. Ibid., July 18, 1971.

124. "Corruption in Vietnam," memo from Bill Marmon, Saigon, to Time World, New York, July 23, 1969.

125. Shaplen, *Road From War*, pp. 88, 125. According to the official Defense Department study of the Vietnam War, Gen. Quang was considered one of the "most corrupt generals" in South Vietnam in 1965–1966. His removal from command by IV Corps in late 1966 was the result of American pressure on the Ky regime to do something about the corruption problem (Gravel, *Pentagon Papers*, vol. 2, pp. 384, 391).

   According to one of the most acute American observers of South Vietnamese politics, "a brisk trade in rice and opium" were the chief forms of corruption engaged in by Gen. Quang when he was IV Corps commander in 1965–1966 (FitzGerald, *Fire in the Lake* p. 311.)

126. "National Politics in Viet-Nam," p. 12.

127. Interview with a senior MACCORDS official, Saigon, Vietnam, July 1971. As of late 1972, Gen. Quang continued to play a key role in President Thieu's apparatus despite accusations about the general's involvement in the

heroin traffic. Following the peace negotiations in Paris, the *New York Times* reported "that on Oct. 7 President Thieu set up a 50-member Central Study Committee headed by his close aide, Lt. Gen. Dang Van Quang, to draw up detailed plans on what Government ministries should do in the event of a ceasefire" (*New York Times*, October 23, 1972, p. 1).

128. Ibid.

129. *New York Times*, August 8, 1971, p. 1.

130. Interview with a Vietnamese intelligence official, Saigon, Vietnam, July 1971.

131. *New York Times*, May 11, 1970, p. 1.

132. *Washington Post*, May 11, 1970.

133. *New York Times*, May 12, 1970, p. 1; *Washington Post*, May 13, 1970.

134. Interview with Vietnamese naval officers, Saigon, Vietnam, July 1971.

135. The floods were some of the worst in central Vietnam's history. The typhoon rains killed 5,000 people and left thousands homeless (Don Luce and John Sommer, *Vietnam: The Unheard Voices* [Ithaca: Cornell University Press, 1969], pp. 243–44). Adm. Cang's grafting outraged the residents of central Vietnam, and the I Corps commander, Gen. Nguyen Chanh Thi, initiated an official investigation of the affair. It was largely due to Gen. Thi's persistent demands for punishment that Rear Adm. Cang was removed from command (interview with Gen. Nguyen Chanh Thi, Washington, DC, October 21, 1971).

136. Vietnamese navy records show that Rear Adm. Chung Tan Cang held the following positions after he was removed from command in 1965: (1) 1966, special assistant to the joint generals staff; (2) December 1, 1966–August 14, 1969, commander of the Military Academy; (3) August 14, 1969–July 1, 1970, detached to the Ministry of Defense; (4) July 1, 1970–July 1, 1971, detached as a research assistant.

137. Interview with Vietnamese naval officers, Saigon, Vietnam, July 1971.

138. Vietnamese naval records show that Commo. Lam Nguon Thanh reached the position of deputy commander in chief of the navy before being sent to the U.S. Naval War College in Newport, RI, in 1966. From 1966 until August 1970 he served successively as assistant to the chief, political warfare directorate and commandant, Political Warfare College in Dalat.

139. Interview with Vietnamese naval officers, Saigon, Vietnam, July 1971.

140. Ibid. President Thieu's choice of key officials to carry out this "antinarcotics" campaign in mid-1971 was a source of some irony for high-level American officials in Saigon. On May 4, 1971, President Thieu "designated a team of five experienced intelligence and police officials, headed by Lieutenant General Dang Van Quang, to develop and carry out an effective program of action" against drug traffic in South Vietnam. On June 17 Prime Minister Khiem "appoints Rear Admiral Cang as his Special Assistant for anti-narcotics effort . . . to prepare a three-month campaign from July 1 through September 30, similar to three-month campaigns conducted in field of pacification." The irony lay in the fact that these officers, particulary Lt. Gen. Quang, were then believed to be the "biggest pushers" in South Vietnam (Department of State,

Briefing Paper, "Significant Events and Activities in Vietnamese Efforts to Suppress Drug Traffic" [Washington, DC, 1972], pp. 4, 7; interview with a senior MACCORDS official, Saigon, Vietnam, July 1971).

141. All of the following information is based on extensive interviews with Redactor Ly Ky Hoang, chief of the Narcotics Bureau of the national police (interviews with Ly Ky Hoang, Saigon, Vietnam, August 5 and 12 and September 11, 1971). Agents of the U.S. Bureau of Narcotics and Dangerous Drugs who participated in the raids were unwilling or unable to be interviewed. The Thai official involved, Col. Pramual Vanigbandhu, was out of the country when the author was in Bangkok.

142. *Pacific Stars and Stripes*, July 30, 1971. This reputation for corruption was apparently well deserved. Indeed, Col. Pramual himself, the Thai police official in charge of these raids, engaged in corruption. On January 16, 1973 the *Miami Herald* printed a photograph of a luxurious Bangkok villa, complete with manicured gardens and swimming pool, with the following caption:

> This luxurious home in Bangkok is the residence of Col. Pramual Wanigbhand, a top narcotics suppression official in the government of Thailand. The colonel's salary is about $250 a month. The house is reported to be worth more than $100,000 and the colonel's private bank account stands at $500,000. The *Herald* obtained the photograph privately from Bangkok.

In January 1973 Col. Pramual was arrested by the Thai police for "narcotics trafficking as well as dereliction of duty, falsifying official documents, and using his position to earn money." According to the *New York Times* report, "the Colonel was suspected of accepting bribes from traffickers operating through Thailand from Asia's opium-producing area." The colonel learned he was under suspicion while in the United States attending an international conference of narcotics officers in October 1972. He disappeared until January when he surrendered to Thai police in Bangkok (*New York Times*, February 3, 1973, p. 6).

143. Competition between the Vietnamese and Thai police created complications in the investigation and arrests. Redactor Hoang was openly resentful of the Thai police for the commanding attitude they displayed at the various planning meetings. Hoang told the authors "the whole story" because "the Thais are claiming all the credit" (interview with Ly Ky Hoang, Saigon, Vietnam, August 12, 1971).

144. Vietnamese navy records show that Capt. Nguyen Huu Chi was transferred from command of Task Force 213/DP to an unspecified post on August 9, 1971.

145. Interview with Ly Ky Hoang, Saigon, Vietnam, September 11, 1971.

146. Interview with a senior MACCORDS official, Saigon, South Vietnam, August 1971.

147. Corps commanders had been a key feature of the Vietnamese corruption system since the early 1960s. In a report prepared for Ambassador Ellsworth Bunker in May 1968, Gen. Edward G. Lansdale of the CIA described how the corps commanders tended to become corrupt warlords:

... the civil apparatus and Armed Forces in most of the country have operated more on the basis of a system of the patronage revolving around each corps commander under which . . . each has appointed and replaced virtually all province and district chiefs and to a considerable degree division and regimental commanders in the Corps Tactical Zone. As a result, these officers are more responsive to the corps commander than to the central government . . . and not infrequently the corps commander's policies differ from those of Saigon. Certain facets of this system have also led to considerable corruption within the government" ("Nationalist Politics in Viet-Nam," p. 6).

148. The competition between Gen. Dzu and Gen. Lu Lan sparked a major controversy in South Vietnam during the summer of 1971. In a widely publicized speech in early 1971, Gen. Dzu claimed that he could not clean up the II Corps drug traffic because he had inherited the problem from his predecessor, Gen. Lu Lan. After U.S. Representative Robert Steele accused Ngo Dzu of being one of the chief drug traffickers in South Vietnam, Gen. Lu Lan, who had since been promoted to inspector general of ARVN, announced that he was undertaking a full investigation of the charges. Gen. Dzu counterattacked, accusing Lu Lan of being the man responsible for Steele's allegations (Auchincloss, Johnson, and Lynch, *Newsweek* dispatch [Saigon Bureau], July 9, 1971; *New York Times*, July 8, 1971, p. 1; July 10, 1971, p. 2).

In his report to Ambassador Bunker cited in note 147, Gen. Lansdale reported that "General Lu Lan is personally loyal to Thieu" and implied that Gen. Lu Lan was fast becoming a corrupt warlord. ("Nationalist Politics in Viet-Nam," p. 6).

149. Interview with a high-ranking police-intelligence official, Saigon, Vietnam, July 1971.

150. The U.S. army's Criminal Investigation Division (CID) also filed three reports on Gen. Ngo Dzu's involvement in the drug traffic.

1. Dated January 6, 1971. Source reported to CID that Gen. Dzu and his father were involved in narcotics trafficking. This source said that Gen. Dzu was cooperating with a number of other individuals, including the ARVN provost marshal in Qui Nhon, certain South Vietnamese navy officers, and an officer in a South Korean division.

2. Dated May 12, 1971. Source reported that Gen. Ngo Dzu's father, Ngo Khoung, was trafficking in heroin with an ethnic Chinese. According to this source, Gen. Dzu's father was working with a former special assistant to President Thieu.

3. Dated July 10, 1971. Source alleged that Gen. Dzu controlled a sizable heroin ring through a number of associates, including his mistress, Mrs. Tran Thi Khanh.

151. *Dispatch News Service International* (weekly Asian release), August 16, 1971.

152. Interview with U.S. army enlisted men, Operation Crossroads Rehabilitation Center, Long Binh, Vietnam, July 1971.

153. *Dien Tin*, (Saigon), March 23, 1971.

154. D. Gareth Porter, "Saigon National Assembly Racked by Corruption and Smuggling," *Dispatch News Service International*, April 19, 1971.

155. *Dien Tin*, May 1–2, 1971.

156. *Cong Luan* (Saigon), May 19, 1971.

157. Porter, "Saigon National Assembly."

158. *Hoa Binh* (Saigon), March 29, 1971.

159. The bloc committee chairman and their committees, as of June 12, 1971, were as follows:

> Rep. Tran Quy Phong, Communications and Public Works
> Rep. Nguyen Dinh Ly, Economics
> Rep. Pham Huu Giao, Foreign Affairs
> Rep. Hoang Thong, Interior
> Rep. Le Van Dien, Information and Open Arms
> Rep. Truong Dinh Tu, Public Health

Also, a former Independence Bloc member, Rep. Tran Kim Thoa, was chairman of the Labor, Social Welfare, and Veterans Committee.

160. Interview with a lower house representative, Saigon, Vietnam, July 1971; *Tin Sang* (Saigon), May 19, 1971.

161. *Cong Luan*, May 19, 1971; *Chinh Luan* (Saigon), May 19, 1971.

162. *Tin Sang* (Saigon), April 18, 1971.

163. Porter, "Saigon National Assembly."

164. *Cong Luan*, May 17, 1970.

165. Porter, "Saigon National Assembly."

166. *Dien Tin*, January 31, 1971.

167. "Drug Abuse Problem in Vietnam," p. 13.

168. Interview with a Vietnamese customs official, Saigon, Vietnam, July 22, 1971.

169. Announcement from the residence of the prime minister, Republic of Vietnam, March 19, 1971.

170. "Drug Abuse Problem in Vietnam," p. 13.

171. *Saigon Post*, March 25, 1971.

172. *Vietnam Guardian* (Saigon), March 25, 1971.

173. Ibid., March 24, 1971.

174. *Bao Den* (Saigon), March 24, 1971.

175. *Dien Tin* (Saigon), March 22, 1971.

176. Gen. Khiem had a history of successful coup plotting. During the November 11, 1960, coup against President Diem, he advanced on Saigon from the Delta, telling both sides that he was coming to help them. When it was apparent that the coup group was weakening, he ordered his troops to attack the rebels, delivered the decisive blow, and took credit for saving the Diem regime. Three years later he allied with Gen. Duong Van Minh to topple President Diem, but only three months after that he played a key role in the coup that overthrew Gen. Minh's government. Although he occupied a number of important positions in succeeding governments, he was one of the architects of a coup against the new regime in February 1965. This last coup is perhaps

General Khiem's most remarkable achievement; he organized it from the Vietnamese embassy in Washington, DC, nine thousand miles from Saigon (Kahin and Lewis, *United States in Vietnam*, p. 173).

177. *New York Times*, May 18, 1971, p. 10.
178. Interview with a U.S. customs adviser, Saigon, Vietnam, July 16, 1971.
179. "Drug Abuse Problem in Vietnam," p. 10.
180. Ibid., p. 10.
181. "Excerpts from Report of Customs Advisor Joseph R. Kvoriak; Date: February 8, 1971," United States Government Memorandum, to James E. Townsend, Chief of Party/Customs, from Joseph R. Kvoriak, Customs Adviser, on the subject "Lack of Controls and Enforcement, Tan Son Nhut," February 25, 1971, p. 1.
182. Ibid., p. 2.
183. Ibid., pp. 4–5.
184. "Drug Abuse Problem in Vietnam," p. 7.
185. *New York Times*, August 30, 1971, p. 1.
186. *New York Times*, April 22, 1971, p. 1.
187. Interview with a U.S. embassy official, Saigon, Vietnam, July 1971.
188. Announcement from the residence of the prime minister, Republic of Vietnam, March 19, 1971.
189. *Lap Truong* (Saigon), May 29, 1971.
190. Interview with a Vietnamese customs official, Saigon, Vietnam, July 1971.
191. *New York Times*, August 8, 1971, p. 1.
192. *Lap Truong*, May 31, 1971. D. Gareth Porter provided additional details on the workings of Prime Minister Khiem's political entourage.

> Prime Minister Khiem has quietly established a family empire in the years since 1968, when he first emerged as Vietnam's second most powerful man. His relatives now control many of the most sensitive government positions dealing with smuggling.
>
> Two relatives of Khiem still hold key posts guarding access to Saigon by land and by sea. Colonel Tran Thien Thanh, a first cousin, who in 1964 had been in charge of the ill-fated Saigon municipal bus company when it was disintegrating under the weight of massive corruption, was named in 1968 to the position of deputy commander of the Capital Military District and assistant to the military government of Saigon-Gia Dinh. . . .
>
> In this post he has the authority over all transportation in and out of the capital. It is Thanh who signs all authorizations for travel on the roads during curfew hours and in other special circumstances.
>
> Lieutenant Colonel Tran Thien Phuong, the second brother of Khiem placed in a key post in 1968, was named director of the port of Saigon. Possibilities for enrichment in such a position are enormous, according to political observers in Saigon, through collusion with smugglers. Former Premier Nguyen Cao Ky had named his brother-in-law to the post.
>
> General Tran Thanh Phong, a relative of Khiem's wife, was

minister of Rural Development from 1968 to early 1971, when he became head of the National Police. He was replaced in September 1971, and Saigon newspapers reported that he had been accused of involvement in drug trafficking and had been removed under American pressure.

Colonel Do Kien Nhieu, Khiem's brother-in-law, was named mayor of Saigon-Cholon in 1968 and still remains in city hall. The Minister of Defense had protested his nomination on the grounds he had a past record of flagrant corruption. Mayor Nhieu was among 27 government officials on a list of those known to be involved in significant corruption, compiled by the Ky government in 1966 at the request of the U.S. mission.

With his grip on the administrative apparatus in Saigon-Cholon, Colonel Nhieu exercises extensive power over the enormous commerce, both legitimate and illegal, that is centered in the capital.

Do Kien Nhieu's brother, Do Kien Nuoi, has been chief of the Fraud Repression section of the National Police since 1968. (D. Gareth Porter, "Premier Khiem's Family Mafia," *Indochina Chronicle*, no. 18 [August 1, 1972], pp. 23–24)

193. Interview with a Vietnamese intelligence officer, Saigon, Vietnam, July 1971. (Some other sources reported that Colonel Binh was a member of Khiem's army faction during the early 1960s. These sources felt that Colonel Binh may have been a member of the Khiem faction until the 1970s, even though he was Mrs. Thieu's nephew.)

194. *New York Times*, August 8, 1971, p. 1; interview with a U.S. customs adviser, Saigon, Vietnam, July 1971.

195. Interview with John Warner, Washington, DC, October 14, 1971; other U.S. officials, including Representative James H. Scheuer, the comptroller general of the United States, and the assistant secretary of state for East Asia and Pacific Affairs observed this shift to Southeast Asia (U.S. Congress, House, Committee on Foreign Affairs, *International Aspects of the Narcotics Problem*, 92nd Cong., 1st sess., 1971 [Washington, DC: U.S. Government Printing Office, 1971], pp. 61, 119, 149). In mid-1972 the U.S. Bureau of Narcotics supplied the following supplemental testimony in response to questioning concerning "shifts in this geographical pattern of heroin trafficking" by Sen. William Spong of the U.S. Senate Foreign Relations Committee: "Immediate shifts for which there is already some indication involve greater exploitation of Southeast Asia and Mexican sources." Moreover, in September 1972 the former deputy director of BNDD issued the following statement to the press:

Increasingly the American heroin market is being supplied from the Golden Triangle region of Laos, Burma, and Thailand. Southeast Asia clearly has the potential to replace Turkey as the major supplier of heroin to the illicit market places of this country. We are at present in the midst of a dramatic changeover. Although the seizures of heroin from Southeast Asia are smaller than those from Europe, the incidence of seizures are growing at an alarming rate. (Statement of John Finlator, Former Deputy Director, Bureau of Narcotics and Dangerous Drugs, Justice Department, September 18, 1972)

196. Interview with police Col. Smith Boonlikit, Bangkok, Thailand, September 17, 1971.
197. Cabled dispatch from Shaw, Vientiane (Hong Kong Bureau), to Time Inc., received September 16–17, 1965.
198. Interview with Gen. Edward G. Lansdale, Alexandria, Virginia, June 17, 1971.
199. Interview with Lt. Col. Lucien Conein, McLean, Virginia, June 18, 1971.
200. As of the early 1970s, French commercial shipping companies still maintained regular schedules between Saigon and France. In August 1971, for example, there were four scheduled departures from Saigon to either Le Havre or Marseille.
201. Interview with Lt. Col. Lucien Conein, McLean, Virginia, June 18, 1971.
202. Ibid.
203. In September 1965 Gen. Lansdale's Senior Liaison Office began advising the Vietnamese Central Rural Construction Council, headed by Premier Ky, on pacification and social reform. (Kahin and Lewis, *United States in Vietnam*, p. 242.)
204. Interview with Norma Sullivan, Singapore, September 24, 1971. (Norma Sullivan was a special assistant to William Crum and had worked in Saigon business circles since the early 1960s.)
205. Ed Reid, *The Grim Reapers* (Chicago: Henry Regnery, 1969), Appendix III, Chart 8.
206. U.S. Congress, Senate, Permanent Subcommittee on Investigations, *Fraud and Corruption in Management of Military Club Systems—Illegal Currency Manipulations Affecting South Vietnam*, 91st Cong., 2nd sess., 1970; 92nd Cong., 1st sess., 1971 (Washington, DC: U.S. Government Printing Office, 1971), pt. 4, p. 1017.
207. Ibid., pp. 28, 34.
208. Ibid., p. 68.
209. Ibid., p. 43.
210. Ibid., pt. 3, p. 637.
211. Ibid., pp. 12–13.
212. Ibid., p. 73.
213. Ibid., pt. 5, p. 1045.
214. Ibid., pt. 2, pp. 478–79.
215. Ibid., pt. 5, pp. 1046–47.
216. Fine Foreign Foods Ltd., described as the "restaurant proprietor" of the San Francisco Steak House (Ground Floor, 67 Peking Road, Kowloon), registered with the Inland Revenue Department, Hong Kong, on August 1, 1967.
217. U.S. Senate, Permanent Subcommittee on Investigations, *Fraud and Corruption Report*, pp. 75–77.
218. Ibid., p. 85.
219. Ibid., p. 86.

220. According to corporate records filed with the Hong Kong government, Frank Carmen Furci resigned from his position as director of Fine Foreign Foods Ltd. on March 18, 1970. He transferred 1,667 shares to James Edward Galagan, his partner for the previous few years, and 1,666 shares to Setsui Morten on March 25, 1970. Since the corporate report filed in 1969 showed that Frank Carmen Furci owned 3,333 shares, it is presumed that these events marked the end of his connection with the company and its restaurant.

221. U.S. Senate, Permanent Subcommittee on Investigations, *Fraud and Corruption*, pt. 2, p. 279. This testimony before the committee was given by Senate investigator Carmine Bellino, "conceded to be the best investigative accountant in the country" (Victor S. Navasky, *Kennedy Justice* [New York: Atheneum, 1971], p. 53).

222. Reid, *Grim Reapers*, p. 296.

223. Interview with a U.S. embassy official, Saigon, Vietnam, July 1971.

224. Hank Messick, *Lansky* (New York: Putnam's, 1971), p. 241.

225. Interview with an agent, U.S. Bureau of Narcotics and Dangerous Drugs, Washington, DC, November 18, 1971.

226. *New York Times*, January 9, 1972, p. 25; in September 1972 Ricord was extradited to the United States and in December was found guilty by a New York Federal District Court. Subsequent investigations by U.S. narcotics agents turned up more evidence of the same pattern, and in November more Corsican heroin dealers residing in Latin America were arrested (*New York Times*, November 18, 1972, p. 1; December 2, 1972, p. 1; December 8, 1972, p. 90; December 16, 1972, p. 1).

227. *Evening Star* (Washington, DC), January 6, 1972; U.S. Congress, Senate, Committee on Appropriations, *Foreign Assistance and Related Programs Appropriations for Fiscal Year 1972*, 92nd Cong., 1st sess., 1971 (Washington, DC: U.S. Government Printing Office, 1972), p. 614. This and other evidence contradict Secretary of State William Rogers's assertion that the narcotics problem in Southeast Asia was being dealt with effectively (Secretary of State William Rogers, Testimony Before the Foreign Operations Subcommittee of the Senate Appropriations Subcommittee, uncorrected transcript, May 15, 1972).

228. *New York Times*, April 19, 1968, p. 11.

229. *Washington Post*, July 17, 1971.

230. *Saigon Post*, July 25, 1971.

231. The army CID filed reports detailing Gen. Ngo Dzu's involvement in the heroin traffic on January 6, May 12, and July 10, 1971. These reports and other information gathered by the U.S. Bureau of Narcotics and Dangerous Drugs convinced several of its ranking agents that Gen. Dzu was involved.

232. *New York Times*, July 8, 1971, p. 1.

233. Ibid., July 10, 1971, p. 2. Whether by design or by accident, the U.S. embassy failed to forward these reports on Gen. Ngo Dzu's involvement in the heroin traffic to the State Department in Washington. Testifying in July 1971, the assistant secretary of state for East Asia and Pacific Affairs,

Marshall Green, said that he had "no information" on Gen. Ngo Dzu's involvement in the traffic (U.S. House Committee on Foreign Affairs, *International Aspects of the Narcotics Problem*, p. 157).

234. *New York Times*, December 19, 1971, p. 1.
235. *Washington Post*, August 3, 1971.
236. *Pacific Stars and Stripes*, August 7, 1971.
237. *New York Times*, June 24, 1971, p. 4.
238. Interview with Maj. Richard A. Ratner, Long Binh Rehabilitation Center, Vietnam, July 22, 1971.
239. Interview with Sp4c James Baltz, Long Binh Rehabilitation Center, Vietnam, July 22, 1971.
240. *Pacific Stars and Stripes*, July 19, 1971.
241. *New York Times*, May 19, 1971, p. 6.
242. Ibid., December 19, 1971, p. 1.
243. *Washington Post*, August 3, 1971.
244. *New York Times*, June 16, 1971, p. 21.
245. U.S. Executive Office of the President, Special Action Office for Drug Abuse Prevention, *The Vietnam Drug User Returns: Final Report* (Washington, DC: U.S. Government Printing Office, 1974), p. 57.
246. *Washington Post*, August 20, 1971.
247. U.S. Executive Office, *Vietnam Drug User Returns*, p. 57.
248. Interview with a U.S. serviceman, Long Binh Rehabilitation Center, South Vietnam, July 22, 1971.
249. *Washington Post*, August 19, 1971.
250. Morgan F. Murphy and Robert H. Steele, *The World Heroin Problem*, Report of Special Study Mission, 92nd Cong., 1st sess. (Washington, DC: U.S. Government Printing Office, 1971), p. 20.
251. Telephone interview with Jerome Hollander, Los Angeles, California, June 25, 1971. (Jerome Hollander was the public information officer, U.S. Customs Regional Commission.)
252. Murphy and Steele, *World Heroin Problem*, p. 20.
253. *New York Times*, August 11, 1971, p. 1.
254. Ibid., November 12, 1971, p. 93.
255. *Christian Science Monitor*, November 16, 1972.
256. Alfred W. McCoy, "A Tale of Three Cities: Hanoi, Saigon, and Phnom Penh, *Geo* (Sydney) 5, no. 2 (1983), p. 34.
257. George Donelson Moss, *Vietnam: An American Ordeal* (Englewood Cliffs, NJ: Prentice Hall, 1990), pp. 358–59.
258. Frank Snepp, *Decent Interval: The American Debacle in Vietnam and the Fall of Saigon* (London: Allen Lane, 1980), pp. 96–100.
259. Ibid., pp. 125–26. The Anti-Corruption Movement's first manifesto accused President Nguyen Van Thieu of five specific kinds of corruption and cited this book's first edition as documentation for the charge that the Saigon regime was involved in heroin trafficking ("Phong Trao Nhan Dan Chong Tham Nhung De Cuu Nuoc Va Kien Tao Hao Binh," [Hue, mimeograph, September 8, 1974]).

260. Stanley Karnow, *Vietnam: A History* (New York: Viking/Penguin, 1983), pp. 667–68.

261. Ibid., p. 343.

262. Interview with Pham Nguyen Binh, Ho Chi Minh City, September 4, 1981.

263. Interviews with bar employees, taxi drivers, cyclo drivers, and taxi dancers, Ho Chi Minh City, September 3–6, 1981. These conclusions about the role of middle-grade corruption in sustaining the traffic were confirmed in an interview with a member of the Politburo, Lao Dong Workers party, Hanoi, Vietnam, September 8, 1981.

## 6 Hong Kong: Asia's Heroin Laboratory

1. Y. C. Wang, "Tu Yueh-sheng (1888–1951): A Tentative Political Biography," *Journal of Asian Studies* 26, no. 3 (May 1967), p. 435.

2. Ibid., p. 436; Howard L. Boorman, ed., *Biographical Dictionary of Republican China* (New York: Columbia University Press, 1970), vol. 3, pp. 328–30.

3. United Nations, Department of Social Affairs, *Bulletin on Narcotics* 5, no. 2 (April–June 1953), 49.

4. Ibid., p. 52.

5. Harold R. Isaacs, *The Tragedy of the Chinese Revolution* (Stanford: Stanford University Press, 1951), p. 135.

6. Ibid., pp. 142–45.

7. Ibid., pp. 174–80; Wang, "Tu Yueh-sheng," pp. 437–38.

8. Wang, "Tu Yueh-sheng," pp. 438–39. According to one history of wartime China, Tu used these "welfare" activities to good advantage: "As a member of the Opium Suppression Bureau, for example, Tu expanded his control over the narcotics distribution network of Shanghai, which flourished as never before" (John Hunter Boyle, *China and Japan at War, 1937–1945* [Stanford: Stanford University Press, 1972], p. 278).

9. M. R. Nicholson, U.S. Treasury Attaché, Shanghai, "Survey of Narcotic Situation in China and the Far East," To: Commissioner of Customs, Washington, DC, July 12, 1934, Annex 2, p. 7 (Harry Anslinger Papers, Historical Collections and Labor Archives, Pennsylvania State University).

10. Ibid., Annex 6, pp. 2–7.

11. Ibid., Survey, pp. 16–17.

12. Ibid., Annex 3, pp. 3–4.

13. Ibid., Annex 3, pp. 4–6.

14. Ibid., Annex 3, pp. 6–7.

15. Ibid., Survey, p. 7.

16. Ibid., Survey, pp. 7–15.

17. Ibid., Survey, pp. 18–26.

18. Ibid., Survey, p. 7.

19. U.S. Congress, Senate, Committee on the Judiciary, *The AMERASIA Papers: A Clue to the Catastrophe of China*, 91st Cong., 1st sess., 1970 (Washington, DC: U.S. Government Printing Office, 1970), pp. 272–73. (In the original document the date given for the beginning of Tu Yueh-sheng's opium dealings in Chungking was 1944. However, since the report was submitted in

October 1943, this must be a misprint. The author believes that 1942 was the likely date.)

20. U.S. Senate, Committee on the Judiciary, *AMERASIA Papers*, pp. 239, 265.

21. John Hunter Boyle, *China and Japan at War, 1937–1945* (Stanford: Stanford University Press, 1972), p. 278.

22. R. Harris Smith, *OSS: The Secret History of America's First Intelligence Agency* (Berkeley: University of California Press, 1972), p. 245.

23. Letter from J. R. Hayden, To: General William J. Donovan, Subject: A Certain Agreement, May 13, 1943 (J. R. Hayden Papers, Michigan Historical Collections, Ann Arbor, MI).

24. Milton E. Miles, *A Different Kind of War* (New York: Doubleday, 1967), pp. 508–9, 526–27, 532–33.

25. W. P. Morgan, *Triad Societies in Hong Kong* (Hong Kong: Government Press, 1960), pp. 76–77.

26. Ibid., pp. 77–78.

27. Interview with a retired Green Gang member, Hong Kong, July 13, 1971.

28. Wang, "Tu Yueh-sheng," p. 453.

29. Interview with George Dunning, Hong Kong, July 6, 1971. (George Dunning was superintendent of police, Narcotics Bureau, Royal Hong Kong Police.)

30. Morgan, *Triad Societies*, p. 78.

31. Interview with a retired Royal Hong Kong police officer, London, March 2, 1971.

32. Morgan, *Triad Societies*, p. 78.

33. Interview with George Dunning, Hong Kong, July 6, 1971.

34. Interview with a retired Green Gang member, Hong Kong, July 13, 1971. In August 1972 the U.S. cabinet published the following summary account of the recent history of the Hong Kong drug trade:

> Before the 1950s the drug of choice in Hong Kong was opium. Opium dens were operated chiefly by vice syndicates in Hong Kong's large Ch'ao-chou [Chiu chau] community. Ch'ao-chou is a coastal region of China, on the Fukien-Kwangtung border, from which millions of people have migrated in the past century to nearly every country in Southeast Asia. They are notorious throughout the area for their activities in vice and smuggling rings. Because of these proclivities and their clannishness they are sometimes called the Mafia of Southeast Asia.
>
> Heroin was introduced to Hong Kong by refugees who fled Shanghai in 1949 and 1950. As consumption gradually shifted from opium to heroin, the Ch'ao-chou organizations began to take over and today are again in firm control of Hong Kong's narcotics trade. (U.S. Cabinet Committee on International Narcotics Control [CCINC], *World Opium Survey 1972* [Washington, DC: CCINC, 1972], p. A41.)

35. Interview with Brian Webster, Hong Kong, July 9, 1971. (Brian Webster was superintendent of police, Triad Society Bureau and Juvenile Liaison Office.)

36. *Hong Kong Standard*, October 17, 1970.

37. *South China Morning Post* (Hong Kong), May 25, 1971.

38. Interview with T. G. P. Garner, Hong Kong, July 7, 1971. (T. G. P. Garner was deputy commissioner of prisons.)
39. *Hong Kong Standard,* January 20, 1971.
40. U.S. CCINC, *World Opium Survey 1972,* p. A41.
41. Albert G. Hess, *Chasing the Dragon* (New York: Free Press, 1965), p. 42.
42. Interview with T. G. P. Garner, Hong Kong, July 7, 1971; interview with James Chien, Hong Kong, July 8, 1971. (James Chien was director of the Society for the Aid and Rehabilitation of Drug Addicts.)
43. *Hong Kong Standard,* December 1, 1970.
44. *South China Morning Post,* August 28, 1969.
45. Interview with a Ma Shan customer, Hong Kong, July 1971; interview with a Chiu chau secret society member, Hong Kong, July 1971.
46. Interview with a government narcotics expert, Hong Kong, July 8, 1971.
47. Interview with a retired Royal Hong Kong police officer, London, March 2, 1971.
48. Interview with George Dunning, Hong Kong, July 6, 1971.
49. Interview with Maj. Chao La, Ban Nam Keung, Laos, September 12, 1971.
50. Interview with police Col. Smith Boonlikit, Bangkok, Thailand, September 17, 1971. (Col. Smith Boonlikit was employed in the Foreign Bureau of the Central Narcotics Bureau, Thailand.)
51. Interview with Redactor Ly Ky Hoang, Saigon, Vietnam, August 12, 1971. (Ly Ky Hoang was chief of the Narcotics Bureau of the National Police, Vietnam.)
52. See, for example, *New York Times,* June 3, 1955, p. 9.
53. *Malay Mail* (Singapore), April 2, 1965.
54. Interview with Liao Long-sing, Singapore, September 24, 1971. (Liao Long-sing was deputy director of the Central Narcotics Intelligence Bureau, Singapore.)
55. T. A. Mugan, "Drugs Addiction," mimeographed (Singapore, 1970). (T. A. Mugan was senior superintendent of customs, Harbour Division, Singapore.) See also *New York Times,* May 5, 1970, p. 10.
56. Interview with George Dunning, Hong Kong, July 6, 1971.
57. Police records show that he was a Kowloon resident who was known to the police for his involvement in gambling and narcotics. He had never been arrested and had no provable Triad connections (interview with Brian Webster, Hong Kong, July 10, 1971). Privately, one narcotics officer labeled him as Hong Kong's major drug importer and provided much of the following information (interview with a Narcotics Bureau police officer, Hong Kong, July 13, 1971).
58. Interview with a Chiu chau secret society member, Hong Kong, July 1971.
59. Interview with a Narcotics Bureau police officer, Hong Kong, July 13, 1971.
60. *Hong Kong Standard,* January 25, 1971.
61. Interview with an agent, U.S. Bureau of Narcotics and Dangerous Drugs, Bangkok, Thailand, September 16, 1971.
62. Interview with flight crew, Market Time Surveillance Patrol, Cam Ranh Bay, Vietnam, August 2, 1971. In January 1972 an interagency task force with members from the State Department, CIA, and BNDD was dispatched to

Southeast Asia to investigate the international drug traffic. A month later the committee filed a report containing suggestions for disrupting the trawler smuggling.

63. Interview with Graham Crookdake, Hong Kong, July 5, 1971. (Graham Crookdake was assistant chief preventive officer, Royal Hong Kong Preventive Services.)

64. John Hughes, *The Junk Merchants* (Boston: Christian Science Publishing Company, 1970), p. 31. (This description assumed that the Market Time intelligence data were actually finding their way through the maze of British and American bureaucracies to the Preventive Services. Sources in South Vietnam assured the author that this information was in fact being used by Hong Kong authorities.)

65. Frederick W. Flott, Chairman, Task Force on Air and Sea Smuggling, Cabinet Committee on International Narcotics Control, "Report of the Cabinet Committee on International Narcotics Control Task Force on Air and Sea Smuggling," February 21, 1972.

66. Interview with George Dunning, Hong Kong, July 6, 1971.

67. "The Illicit Manufacture of Diacetylmorphine Hydrochloride," photocopy (Hong Kong, n.d.), p. 1.

68. Interview with a Hong Kong government chemist, Hong Kong, July 9, 1971.

69. Ibid.

70. Interview with a Narcotics Bureau police officer, Hong Kong, July 13, 1971.

71. *The Age* (Melbourne, Australia), January 16, 1971.

72. Interview with a Narcotics Bureau police officer, Hong Kong, July 13, 1971.

73. *New York Times*, January 14, 1967, p. 13.

74. Interview with an agent of the U.S. Bureau of Narcotics and Dangerous Drugs, Washington, DC, October 14, 1971. This incident was only the beginning of known Filipino involvement in the Southeast Asian heroin traffic. In October 1972 the Philippine government seized a heroin laboratory operating in the greater Manila area and arrested seven alleged drug manufacturers and dealers. On January 15, 1973, a firing squad executed a fifty-two-year-old Chinese printer named Ling Seng (alternately, Lim Seng) who had been convicted of manufacturing and selling millions of dollars worth of heroin over a ten-year period (*New York Times*, October 5, 1972, p. 19; January 15, 1973, p. 3).

75. In March 1970 the director of the Bureau of Narcotics and Dangerous Drugs estimated that the United States consumed a total of 2.5–3.0 tons of heroin a year (*New York Times*, March 6, 1970, p. 44), but later estimates were revised upward: to 3.0–3.5 tons annually in 1964–1966 and about 10 tons in 1971 (interview with John Warner, Washington, DC, October 14, 1971).

76. *New York Times*, April 3, 1970, p. 3.

77. Morgan F. Murphy and Robert H. Steele, *The World Heroin Problem*, Report of Special Study Mission, 92nd Cong., 1st sess. (Washington, DC: U.S. Government Printing Office, 1971), p. 12.

78. Interview with an agent, U.S. Bureau of Narcotics and Dangerous Drugs, New Haven, CT, November 18, 1971.

79. U.S. CCINC, *World Opium Survey 1972*, p. 29.

80. *Daily News* (New York), June 27, 1972.

81. *New York Times*, July 28, 1972, p. 3.

82. U.S. Cabinet Committee on International Narcotics Control, "Fact Sheet: The Cabinet Committee on International Narcotics Control—A Year of Progress in Drug Abuse Prevention" (Washington, DC, September 1972), p. 1.

83. *New York Times*, August 24, 1972, p. 1.

## 7 The Golden Triangle

1. *Lao Presse* (Vientiane: Ministry of Information, #1448/71), April 8, 1971.

2. Ibid. (#1459/71), April 24, 1971.

3. Ibid. (#1460/71), April 26, 1971.

4. *New York Times*, August 11, 1971, p. 1.

5. Interview with diplomatic officials, Vientiane, Laos, August and September 1971.

6. Interview with an agent, U.S. Bureau of Narcotics and Dangerous Drugs, New Haven, CT, November 18, 1971.

7. *Report of the United Nations Survey Team on the Economic and Social Needs of the Opium-Producing Areas in Thailand* (Bangkok: Government Printing, 1967), pp. 59, 64, 68; *New York Times*, September 17, 1963, p. 45; June 6, 1971, p. 2.

8. *New York Times*, April 3, 1970, p. 3; the director of the U.S. Bureau of Narcotics, John E. Ingersoll, testified that the 80 percent figure was "handed down from very obscure beginnings" and admitted that he had not been able to verify the figure (U.S. Congress, Senate, Committee on Appropriations, *Foreign Assistance and Related Programs Appropriations for Fiscal Year 1972*, 92nd Cong., 1st sess. [Washington, DC: U.S. Government Printing Office, 1971], p. 610). See also U.S. Bureau of Narcotics and Dangerous Drugs, Strategic Intelligence Office, "Special Report: China and Drugs" (Report no. 112, 1972), p. 6; *Christian Science Monitor*, November 16, 1972.

9. *New York Times*, June 6, 1971, p. 2.

10. Alain Y. Dessaint, "The Poppies Are Beautiful This Year," *Natural History*, February 1972, p. 31. A cabinet-level report published in mid-1972 contained the following details on the impact of the GI heroin epidemic on the Southeast Asian drug trade:

> Up to 1970, Southeast Asian farmers apparently received around $17 per kilogram for their opium, most of which was used for production of smoking opium and no. 3 heroin. The Hong Kong wholesale price for white heroin—for which there was little demand at that time—averaged around $2,000. The sharp increase in demand for heroin, engendered by growing use of the drug by U.S. troops in Vietnam in 1970, led to an increase in prices paid to farmers for opium to $20 per kilogram and by mid-1971 to a doubling of the Hong Kong wholesale price to $4,000. Furthermore, new operators entered the heroin production business at this time.

By early 1972, the collapse of the U.S. serviceman market had led to a drop in prices paid to farmers and a decline in the Hong Kong wholesale heroin price to around $3,500. (U.S. Cabinet Committee on International Narcotics Control [CCINC], *World Opium Survey 1972* [Washington, DC: CCINC, 1972], pp. 36–37.)

11. Morgan F. Murphy and Robert H. Steele, *The World Heroin Problem*, Report of Special Study Mission, 92nd Cong., 1st sess. (Washington, DC: U.S. Government Printing Office, 1971), p. 20.

12. *Milford Citizen* (Connecticut), September 28, 1971.

13. Interview with an agent, U.S. Bureau of Narcotics and Dangerous Drugs, Washington, DC, October 21, 1971.

14. *New York Times*, June 6, 1971, p. 2.

15. Interview with police Col. Smith Boonlikit, Bangkok, Thailand, September 17, 1971. In mid-1971 the going price for a gram of no. 4 heroin in Bangkok was about $2 (40 baht), compared with about 12¢ (2.5 baht) for no. 3 heroin.

16. About 65 tons of opium were smuggled into the major cities in upper and central Burma for local consumption, but almost none got beyond these cities into the international markets (interview with William Young, Chiangmai, Thailand, September 8, 1971). (William Young worked for the CIA from 1958 until 1967.)

17. Ibid.

18. U.S. Bureau of Narcotics and Dangerous Drugs, "The World Opium Situation," mimeographed (Washington, DC, October 1970), p. 10.

19. *New York Times*, June 6, 1971, p. 2.

20. *Evening Star* (Washington, DC), June 19, 1972.

21. Interview with Elliot K. Chan, Vientiane, Laos, August 15, 1971. (Elliot K. Chan was a USAID police adviser to the Royal Laotian government.) Interview with an agent, U.S. Bureau of Narcotics and Dangerous Drugs, New Haven, CT, November 18, 1971.

22. Catherine Lamour and Michel R. Lamberti, *The International Connection: Opium from Growers to Pushers* (New York: Pantheon, 1974), p. 117.

23. Mike Gravel, ed., *The Pentagon Papers*, 5 vols. (Boston: Beacon Press, 1971), vol. 2, pp. 646–47.

24. Ibid., p. 646.

25. William Colby, *Honorable Men: My Life in the CIA* (New York: Simon & Schuster, 1978), p. 197.

26. Alfred W. McCoy, "The Politics of the Poppy in Indochina: A Comparative Study of Patron-Client Relations Under French and American Administrations," in Luiz R. S. Simmons and Abdul S. Said, eds., *Drugs Politics and Diplomacy: the International Connection* (Beverly Hills: Sage, 1974), pp. 122–29.

27. Interview with Edward Fillingham, Vientiane, Laos, September 5, 1971. (Edward Fillingham was the director of the Foreign Exchange Operations Fund.)

28. Louis Krarr, "Report from Laos," *Fortune*, September 1, 1968, p. 52.

29. Ibid., p. 54.

30. Far Eastern Economic Review, *1971 Yearbook* (Hong Kong), p. 216; *Straits*

*Times* (Singapore), August 22, 1969; *Eastern Sun* (Singapore), February 24, 1971.

31. British Broadcasting Corporation interview with Sisouk na Champassak, Vientiane, Laos, 1970. (The quotation is filed at BBC Lime Grove Studios, London.)

32. For example, Sisouk himself made this statement before the U.N. Commission on Narcotic Drugs in 1957:
    The Royal Government is determined, as it always has been:
    1. to prohibit the production or consumption of opium derivatives throughout the national territory under its control;
    2. to take vigorous measures to combat illicit traffic;
    3. to ensure effective and complete enforcement of the prohibition of the consumption of opium.
    (United Nations, Economic and Social Council, Commission on Narcotic Drugs, *Illicit Traffic*, 12th sess., agenda item no. 4 [E/CN.7/L.169], May 28, 1957; [295/MPL/ONU], May 29, 1957)

33. *Washington Post,* July 8, 1971.

34. Interview with police Col. Smith Boonlikit, Bangkok, Thailand, September 21, 1971. (Col. Boonlikit allowed the author to read and copy reports from U.S. customs, U.S. Bureau of Narcotics, and Interpol relating to Corsican syndicates in Southeast Asia. Practically all of the following information is based on these reports unless otherwise noted.)

35. Interview with Touby Lyfoung, Vientiane, Laos, September 4, 1971; *Time,* February 29, 1960, p. 35.

36. Paule Bernard, *Lotus, Opium et Kimonos* (Paris: Robert Laffont, 1959), p. 90; telephone interview with an agent, Bureau of Narcotics and Dangerous Drugs, Washington, DC, December 20, 1971.

37. Paul Louis Levet's syndicate consisted of six men, including himself:
    1. Jacques Texier.
    2. Jean "Jeannot" Giansily, who reportedly arrived in Indochina from France in 1954–1955 and first worked for Bonaventure Francisci. Later hired by Levet.
    3. Barthélemy "Mémé" Rutilly, Levet's contact man in Saigon.
    4. Charles Orsini, an elderly Corsican resident of Phnom Penh who served as the contact man in Cambodia.
    5. Tran Hung Dao, an alias for a Vietnamese member of the syndicate.

38. In late 1959 or early 1960, for example, a small Beaver aircraft chartered from Roger Zoile picked up 300 kilos of opium at Muong Sing, in northwestern Laos, for Levet's "account." The aircraft landed at a small strip on the western edge of Tonle Sap lake in Cambodia, where the opium was repacked in orange crates and trucked to the Cambodian seaport of Kompot. From there half was shipped to Hong Kong and the other half to Singapore.

39. Interview with Lt. Col. Lucien Conein, McLean, Virginia, June 18, 1971.

40. Interview with Gen. Ouane Rattikone, Vientiane, Laos, September 1, 1971.

41. Joel Halpern, "The Role of Chinese in Lao Society," *Journal of the Siam Society* 49, pt. 1 (July 1961), pp. 31–34.

42. Joel M. Halpern, *Economy and Society of Laos* (New Haven: Southeast Asian Studies, Yale University, 1964), pp. 117–18.

43. Stanley Karnow, "The Opium Must Go Through," *Life*, August 30, 1963, pp. 11–12; Hong Kong Dispatch #4222, from Jerry Rose to Time Inc. (November 9, 1962).

44. Ibid.

45. *L'Express*, no. 1052 (September 6–12, 1971), p. 18. (This article identified Jean-Baptiste Andréani, a Guerini partisan during the vendetta discussed in Chapter 2, as an associate of Antoine Guerini and Bonaventure Francisci.)

46. U.S. Bureau of Narcotics and Dangerous Drugs has the following information on this incident:
    1. Owners of the aircraft: René Enjabal and Lucien Don Carlini.
    2. Vientiane opium dealers: Roger Lasen, Maurice Lecore, Ao Thien Hing (Chinese resident of Laos), and Thao Shu Luang Prasot (Chinese resident of Laos).
    3. Waiting for the opium on the ground in Ban Me Thuot were Charles Merelle (French), Padovani (French Corsican), and Phan Dao Thuan (Vietnamese).
    4. Opium was destined for two Chinese distributors in Cholon: Ky Van Chan and Ky Mu.
    5. Also believed to be involved as financiers: Roger Zoile and François Mittard.
    (Telephone interview with an agent, U.S. Bureau of Narcotics and Dangerous Drugs, Washington, DC, December 20, 1971)

47. Karnow, "Opium Must Go Through," p. 12.

48. Telephone interview with an agent, U.S. Bureau of Narcotics and Dangerous Drugs, Washington, DC, December 20, 1971.

49. Also arrested were Mme. Isabela Mittard, Roger Boisviller, Roger Paul Jean, Etienne Kassubeck, and Jean Roger Barbarel. Barbarel escaped from prison to 1960 and by 1972 had not been apprehended.

50. According to Vietnamese Passport Control, François Mittard visited Laos briefly from December 28 to 30, 1964, and left Saigon for Laos on January 31, 1965. As of 1972 he had not returned to Vietnam (interview with Ton That Binh, Vietnamese Passport Control, Saigon, Vietnam, September 10, 1971).

51. Hong Kong Dispatch #222, from Jerry Rose (November 9, 1962).

52. *New York Times*, May 8, 1953, p. 4; U.S. Bureau of Narcotics and Dangerous Drugs, "World Opium Situation," p. 10.

53. Interview with Gen. Ouane Rattikone, Vientiane, Laos, September 1, 1971.

54. Len E. Ackland, "No Place for Neutralism: The Eisenhower Administration and Laos," in Nina S. Adams and Alfred W. McCoy, eds., *Laos: War and Revolution* (New York: Harper & Row, 1970), p. 149.

55. Arthur J. Dommen, *Conflict in Laos* (New York: Praeger, 1971), p. 116; Roger Hilsman, *To Move a Nation* (Garden City, NY: Doubleday, 1967), pp. 114–15.

56. David Wise and Thomas B. Ross, *The Invisible Government* (New York: Random House, 1964), p. 153.

57. Interview with Gen. Ouane Rattikone, Vientiane, Laos, September 1, 1971.

58. Interview with William Young, Chiangmai, Thailand, September 14, 1971.
59. Interview with Gen. Ouane Rattikone, Vientiane, Laos, September 1, 1971.
60. Dommen, *Conflict in Laos*, p. 219.
61. *Le Monde* (Paris), May 24–25, 1964.
62. *Far Eastern Economic Review*, May 28, 1964, p. 421.
63. *Le Monde*, May 24–25, 1964.
64. General Ouane gave the author the following statistics:

*Contrôle du Opium au Laos*

| Month | Report no. | Amount exported | Profits | Dollar equivalent |
|---|---|---|---|---|
| November 1963 | Report 1/A | 1,146 kgs. | 1,948,200 baht | $97,410 |
| December 1963 | Report 2/V | 1,128 kgs. | 1,917,000 baht | $95,880 |
| January 1964 | Report 2/V | 1,125 kgs. | 1,912,500 baht | $95,625 |

(Interview with Gen. Ouane Rattikone, Vientiane, Laos, September 1, 1971)
65. Ibid.
66. General Kouprasith told one reporter that "some of the things he [Phoumi] has done with the economy of the nation are wrong, including the introduction of gambling and the monopolies. Some of the things he has done have helped to support and strengthen the Communists in their attack on us" (Dommen, *Conflict in Laos*, p. 265); *Lao Presse* (Vientiane: Ministry of Information #3764), April 20, 1964.
67. D. Gareth Porter, "After Geneva: Subverting Laotian Neutrality," in Adams and McCoy, *Laos: War and Revolution*, p. 204.
68. *Far Eastern Economic Review*, May 28, 1964, p. 421.
69. Dommen, *Conflict in Laos*, pp. 286–87.
70. *Lao Presse* (Vientiane: Ministry of Information #3998), February 8, 1965.
71. Cabled dispatch from Shaw, Vientiane (Hong Kong Bureau), to Time Inc., received September 16–17, 1965.
72. The New York Times, *The Pentagon Papers* (New York: Quandrangle, 1971), pp. 313–14.
73. Interview with Gen. Ouane Rattikone, Vientiane, Laos, September 1, 1971; interview with Gen. Thao Ma, Bangkok, Thailand, September 17, 1971; Don A. Schanche, *Mister Pop* (New York: David McKay, 1970), pp. 240–45.
74. The author visited Long Pot village in the region west of the Plain of Jars in August 1971 and interviewed local officials, opium farmers, and soldiers who confirmed Air America's role in the local opium trade.
75. James Hamilton-Paterson, *The Greedy War* (New York: David McKay, 1971), pp. 275–76.
76. Interview with Gen. Edward G. Lansdale, Alexandria, Virginia, June 17, 1971.
77. Interview with Lt. Col. Lucien Conein, McLean, Virginia, June 18, 1971.
78. Interview with Gen. Edward G. Lansdale, Alexandria, Virginia, June 17, 1971.

79. Peter Kunstadter, "Vietnam: Introduction," in Peter Kunstadter, ed., *Southeast Asian Tribes, Minorities, and Nations* (Princeton: Princeton University Press, 1967), vol. 2, pp. 681–82; Howard Shochurek, "Americans in Action in Vietnam," *National Geographic* 127, no. 1 (January 1965), pp. 38–64.

80. Interview with William Young, Chiangmai, Thailand, September 8, 1971.

81. Interview with Gen. Edward G. Lansdale, Alexandria, Virginia, June 17, 1971.

82. Genevieve Sowards and Erville Sowards, *Burma Baptist Chronicle* (Rangoon: Board of Publications, Burma Baptist Convention, 1963), pp. 411–14.

83. Interview with William Young, Chiangmai, Thailand, September 8, 1971.

84. *Boston Globe*, September 3, 1970.

85. The CIA's Tibetan operations began in August 1959, when twenty Khamba tribesmen from southern Tibet arrived in Camp Hale, Colorado, for special training. These men, and others like them, served as cadres in the CIA's guerrilla army, which devoted most of its resources to mining the two major roads between Tibet and China. Through these operations the CIA hoped to slow the flow of Chinese men and matériel moving into Tibet and thereby strengthen the political position of the exiled Dalai Lama. When the operations were curtailed in May 1960, there were an estimated 42,000 Khamba guerrillas fighting for the CIA inside Tibet (L. Fletcher Prouty, *Empire Gazette* [Denver, CO], February 6, 1972).

86. Thomas Powers, *The Man Who Kept the Secrets: Richard Helms and the CIA* (New York: Knopf, 1979), pp. 90, 326.

87. Interview with Don A. Schanche, Larchmont, New York, February 12, 1971.

88. Interview with Maj. Chao La, Ban Nam Keung, Laos, September 12, 1971. (Maj. Chao La was commander of Yao mercenary troops in Nam Tha province for the CIA.)

89. Schanche, *Mister Pop*, p. 5.

90. John Lewallen, "The Reluctant Counterinsurgents: International Voluntary Services in Laos," in Adams and McCoy, *Laos: War and Revolution*, pp. 361–62. For an official USAID admission of the military character of these "humanitarian" refugee operations, see U.S. Congress, Senate, Committee of the Judiciary, *Refugee and Civilian War Casualty Problems in Indochina*, 91st Cong., 2nd sess. (Washington, DC: U.S. Government Printing Office, 1970), pp. 22–24.

91. Schanche, *Mister Pop*, pp. 241–42.

92. Colby, *Honorable Men*, p. 197.

93. Christopher Robbins, *The Ravens: The Men Who Flew in America's Secret War in Laos* (New York: Crown, 1987), p. 125.

94. Interview with Touby Lyfoung, Vientiane, Laos, September 1, 1971.

95. Dommen, *Conflict in Laos*, pp. 294–95.

96. Interview with a Royal Laotian army officer, Vientiane, Laos, August 1971. (This interview is the basis for the foregoing description of Vang Pao's early career.)

97. Dommen, *Conflict in Laos,* pp. 133–34.

98. *Lao Presse* (Vientiane: Ministry of Information #2,700), September 12, 1960.

99. Dommen, *Conflict in Laos,* p. 154.

100. *Lao Presse* (Vientiane: Ministry of Information #2,692), September 1, 1960.

101. Ibid. (#2,716), September 29, 1960.

102. Interview with a Royal Laotian army officer, Vientiane, Laos, August 1971.

103. Interview with Touby Lyfoung, Vientiane, Laos, September 1, 1971.

104. Dommen, *Conflict in Laos,* pp. 161, 296; interview with Touby Lyfoung, Vientiane, Laos, September 1, 1971.

105. Hugh Toye, *Laos: Buffer State or Battleground* (New York: Oxford University Press, 1968), p. 161.

106. Schanche, *Mister Pop,* pp. 75–76.

107. Dommen, *Conflict in Laos,* pp. 179, 207.

108. Interview with William Young, Chiangmai, Thailand, September 8, 1971.

109. Interview with Ger Su Yang, Long Pot village, Laos, August 19, 1971.

110. Interview with Capt. Kong Le, Paris, March 22, 1971.

111. Dommen, *Conflict in Laos,* p. 207.

112. Schanche, *Mister Pop,* pp. 97–100.

113. Brig. Gen. Edward G. Lansdale, "Resources for Unconventional Warfare, S.E. Asia," in New York Times, *Pentagon Papers,* pp. 138–40.

114. Schanche, *Mister Pop,* pp. 103, 115–16.

115. Ibid., pp. 162–63.

116. U.S. Congress, Senate, Committee on Foreign Relations, Subcommittee on United States Security Agreements and Commitments Abroad, *United States Security Agreements and Commitments Abroad, Kingdom of Laos,* 91st Cong., 1st sess. (Washington, DC: U.S. Government Printing Office, 1970), pt. 2, p. 473.

117. Interview with William Young, Chiangmai, Thailand, September 8, 1971; interview with a former USAID official in Nam Tha province, Laos, June 1971.

118. Interview with William Young, Chiangmai, Thailand, September 8, 1971; Schanche, *Mister Pop,* pp. 171–73.

119. Dommen, *Conflict in Laos,* p. 183.

120. *New York Times,* April 25, 1963, p. 7.

121. Interview with Capt. Kong Le, Paris, March 22, 1971.

122. An Australian anthropologist working in northern Thailand has shown that the high price of opium enabled the Hmong in one village to support themselves on only one-third of the land it would have required to produce an adequate amount of rice for the village's subsistence (Douglas Miles, "Shifting Cultivation—Threats and Prospects," in *Tribesmen and Peasants in North Thailand,* Proceedings of the First Symposium of the Tribal Research Center [Chiangmai, Thailand: Tribal Research Center, 1967], p. 96).

123. Schanche, *Mister Pop,* pp. 240–45.

124. Interview with Gen. Ouane Rattikone, Vientiane, Laos, September 1, 1971; interview with Gen. Thao Ma, Bangkok, Thailand, September 17, 1971.

125. "Guns, Drugs and the CIA," reported by Judy Woodruff, produced by Andrew and Leslie Cockburn, *Frontline*, Documentary Consortium, WGBH, Boston, 1988; Robbins, *Ravens*, pp. 124–25.

126. Interview with Lo Kham Thy, Vientiane, Laos, September 2, 1971.

127. Interview with a former USAID official, Washington, DC, June 1971.

128. Interview with high-ranking Hmong officials, Vientiane, Laos, September 1971.

129. U.S. Senate, Committee on Foreign Relations, *United States Security Agreements*, pt. 2, p. 465.

130. Ibid., pp. 470, 490.

131. Dommen, *Conflict in Laos*, pp. 297, 299.

132. A Hmong social scientist of Paris working for his doctorate at the University of Paris estimated that there were 80,000 Hmong in Xieng Khouang province and 55,000 in Sam Neua province before the mass migrations began (interview with Yang Than Dao, Paris, March 17, 1971). One USAID refugee official at Ban Son estimated that there were a total of about 250,000 hill tribesmen living in the mountains of these two provinces (interview with George Cosgrove, Ban Son, Laos, August 30, 1971).

133. Schanche, *Mister Pop*, pp. 294–95; U.S. Senate Committee of the Judiciary, *Refugee and Civilian War Casualty Problems*, pp. 24–28.

134. Interview with George Cosgrove, Ban Son, Laos, August 30, 1971.

135. Ibid.; U.S. Congress, Senate, Committee of the Judiciary, *War-Related Civilian Problems in Indochina, Part II: Laos and Cambodia*, 92nd Cong., 1st sess. (Washington, DC: U.S. Government Printing Office, 1971), p. 48.

136. Interview with Lyteck Lynhiavu, Vientiane, Laos, August 28, 1971. (Lyteck Lynhiavu was a member of one of the most prestigious Hmong clans in Laos and director of administration in the Ministry of the Interior.)

137. Ibid.; interviews with Hmong villagers, Long Pot village, Laos, August 1971. The Royal Laotian government conducted an investigation of Vang Pao's regular infantry battalions in September 1970 and found that all of them were far below their reported payroll strength of 550 men: the Twenty-first Battalion had 293 men, the Twenty-fourth Battalion had 73, the Twenty-sixth Battalion had 224, and the Twenty-seventh Battalion had 113. According to Laotian army sources, Vang Pao was pocketing the difference.

138. Interview with George Cosgrove, Ban Son, Laos, August 30, 1971. (George Cosgrove was a USAID refugee officer for Military Region II.)

139. James G. Lowenstein and Richard M. Moose, U.S. Congress, Senate, Committee on Foreign Relations, Subcommittee on United States Security Agreements and Commitments Abroad, *Laos: April 1971*, 91st Cong., 1st sess. (Washington, DC: U.S. Government Printing Office, 1971), p. 16.

140. Robert Shaplen, *Time Out of Hand* (New York: Harper & Row, 1970), p. 352.

141. Interview with Chinese merchants, Vientiane, Laos, August 1971. It is very difficult to measure the exact impact that the U.S. bombing campaign and refugee movements had on Laotian opium production. However, the U.S. Bureau of Narcotics made an attempt. In 1968 the Bureau estimated Laos's production at 100–150 tons. In mid-1971 it estimated Laos's total production at 35 tons (U.S. Bureau of Narcotics and Dangerous Drugs, "World Opium Situation," p. 10; U.S. Senate, Committee on Appropriations, *Foreign Assistance and Related Programs Appropriations for 1972,* p. 583).

142. The author visited Long Pot District from August 18 to August 23, 1971. Most of the following information is based on these six days in Long Pot unless otherwise noted.

143. Interview with Ger Su Yang, Long Pot village, Laos, August 19, 1971.

144. For a detailed examination of the problem of "choice" in a Hmong village in Thailand, see W. R. Geddes, "Opium and the Miao: A Study in Ecological Adjustment," *Oceania* 41, no. 1 (September 1970).

145. One Thai government study reported that "tasting" is an important part of opium cultivation: "In each village, one or a few men are able to determine the suitability of the terrain for poppy by tasting the soil; apparently a highly respected qualification. When the ph [soil acidity index], after several years of continual use, begins to decrease, these men can 'taste' when the soil becomes unsuitable for further poppy cultivation" (F. R. Moormann, K. R. M. Anthony, and Samarn Panichapong, "No. 20: Note on the Soils and Land Use in the Hills of Tak Province," in *Soil Survey Reports of the Land Development Department* [Bangkok: Kingdom of Thailand, Ministry of National Development, March 1964], p. 5).

146. F. B. G. Keen, *The Meo of North-West Thailand* (Wellington, New Zealand: Government Printer, 1966), p. 32.

147. For a description of the burn-off in other hill tribe villages, see Paul J. Zinke, Sanga Savuhasri, and Peter Kunstadter, "Soil Fertility Aspects of the Lua Forest Fallow System of Shifting Cultivation," Seminar on Shifting Cultivation and Economic Development in Northern Thailand, Chiangmai, Thailand, January 18–24, 1970, pp. 9–10.

148. Geddes, "Opium and the Miao," pp. 8–9.

149. Keen, *The Meo of North-West Thailand,* p. 35.

150. Ibid., p. 36; Dessaint, "The Poppies Are Beautiful," p. 36.

151. In comparison, Geddes found that the Hmong village of seventy-one houses he surveyed in northern Thailand produced a minimum of 1,775 kilos, or more than 1 3/4 tons of raw opium. This is an average of 25 kilos per household, compared with an estimated 15 kilos for Long Pot village (Geddes, "Opium and the Miao," p. 7).

152. Interview with an agent, U.S. Bureau of Narcotics and Dangerous Drugs, Southeast Asia, August 1971.

153. Interview with Ger Su Yang, Long Pot village, Laos, August 19, 1971.

154. *A Report on Tribal Peoples of Chiangrai Province North of the Mae Kok River,* Bennington-Cornell Anthropological Survey of the Hill Tribes in

Thailand (Bangkok: Siam Society, 1964), pp. 28–29; Delmos Jones, "Cultural Variation Among Six Lahu Villages, Northern Thailand," (Ph.D. thesis, Cornell University, 1967), pp. 40–41, 136.

155. Interview with the headman of Nam Suk village, refugee village, Long Pot District, Laos, August 21, 1971.

156. Interview with the headman of Nam Ou village, refugee village, Long Pot District, Laos, August 21, 1971.

157. Many Hmong clan leaders regarded Vang Pao as something of a usurper. According to a number of influential Hmong, Vang Pao was aware of his low social stature and tried to compensate for it by marrying his relatives into Touby's family. In 1967 Vang Pao's daughter May Keu married Touby's son Touxa Lyfoung. In 1969 Vang Pao's son François Vangchao married Touby's daughter May Kao Lyfoung. Finally, in 1970 Vang Pao's nephew Vang Geu married Touby's niece May Choua Lyfoung. Vang Pao was threatened by military setbacks and mounting opposition from the Lynhiavu clan and so felt compelled to arrange this last marriage to shore up his declining political fortunes.

158. Interview with Edgar Buell, Ban Son, Laos, August 31, 1971.

159. Interview with Ger Su Yang, Long Pot village, Laos, August 22, 1971.

160. Ibid.

161. When I left Long Pot district on August 23, a number of village headmen explained that their people would begin dying from starvation in several months and urged me to somehow force the Americans into making a rice drop. Upon return to Vientiane, I explained the situation to the local press corps and an article appeared several days later in the *Washington Post* (August 31, 1971) and on the Associated Press wires. As might be expected, many American officials denied that the rice had been cut off.

Edgar Buell was incensed and told me, "When you're saying that no f——— rice gets into that village you're not saying that Charlie Mann [USAID director] won't send it in. And sending or not sending soldiers don't make any difference. Hell, hippies, yippies, and every other thing won't go. Now if they won't send soldiers we don't take 'em out of college or put 'em in jail; we give 'em rice. . . .

"You shouldn't have snuck into that village and then talked to Charlie Mann. You should have come here right off and talked to Pop Buell and got the real story. You've caused a lot of trouble for people here. Hell, I'd kill anybody who'd say old Pop Buell would let somebody starve" (interview with Edgar Buell, Ban Son, Laos, August 30, 1971).

On September 2 Norman Barnes, director of United States Information Service, and Charles Mann, director of USAID/Laos, flew to Long Pot village to make a report on the situation for USAID/Washington. Barnes later contradicted Buell's assertion that the rice drops had not been cut off and admitted that there had been no deliveries since early March. Barnes denied that there were any ulterior motives and explained that the presence of Pathet Lao troops in the immediate area from early March until August 20 made it impossible for aircraft to operate in Long Pot district. But Barnes was now happy to report that deliveries had been restored and a rice drop had been made on August 30 (interview with Norman Barnes, Vientiane, Laos, September 3, 1971).

However, I saw an Air America UH-1H helicopter land at Long Pot on the afternoon of August 19 and was told by villagers at the time that Air America's helicopters had been flying in and out of the village since the rice drops stopped. Moreover, villagers reported that Pathet Lao forces had left the area several months earlier.

162. Interview with the assistant headman of Ban Nam Muong Nakam, Long Pot village, Laos, August 21, 1971.

163. Interview with Ger Su Yang, Long Pot village, Laos, August 19, 1971. In late 1971 one American reporter flew over the Plain of Jars and described what he saw:

> A recent flight around the Plain of Jars revealed what less than three years of intensive American bombing can do to a rural area, even after its civilian population has been evacuated. In large areas, the primary tropical color—bright green—has been replaced by an abstract pattern of black, and bright metallic colors. Much of the remaining foliage is stunted, dulled by defoliants.
>
> Today, black is the dominant color of the northern and eastern reaches of the Plain. Napalm is dropped regularly to burn off the grass and undergrowth that covers the Plain and fills its many narrow ravines. The fires seem to burn constantly, creating rectangles of black. During the flight plumes of smoke could be seen rising from bombed areas. . . .
>
> From an enlarged negative of a photograph covering one small, formerly grass-covered hill about 100 feet high, I spotted several hundred distinct craters before losing count. In many places it is difficult to distinguish individual craters; the area has been bombed so repeatedly that the land resembles the pocked, churned desert in storm hit areas of the North African desert. (T. D. Allman, "Plain Facts," *Far Eastern Economic Review,* January 8, 1972, p. 16)

For a description of life under the bombs in northern Laos, see Fred Branfman, ed., *Voices from the Plain of Jars* (New York: Harper & Row, 1972).

164. Interview with Ger Su Yang, Long Pot village, Laos, August 19, 1971.

165. Interview with George Cosgrove, Ban Son, Laos, August 30, 1971.

166. The bombing seriously disrupted opium production even in villages that managed to survive the attacks and remain in their original location. In August 1971 the author visited the Yao village of Pha Louang, in the mountains eighty miles north of Vientiane. Residents reported that their village had been bombed in August 1964 by a squadron of T-28s bearing Royal Laotian air force markings. When the planes first appeared over the village, people hid in their houses. But as the bombs began hitting the houses they tried to flee into the forest. The aircraft strafed the village, shooting the people as they tried to climb up the steep ridges that

surrounded the village. All the houses were destroyed, most of the livestock was killed, and twelve people (about 20 percent of the inhabitants) were killed. There were five Pathet Lao soldiers hiding in a cave about a mile away and villagers felt they might have been the cause of the attack. Once the planes left, the Pathet Lao emerged from the cave unharmed and marched off. Villagers reported that the mid-1971 opium harvest would equal the harvests before the bombing attack. However, intervening harvests had been much smaller because of the material and human losses they suffered.

Four months after our visit, Long Pot itself was no longer producing opium. In late 1971 Royal Laotian Army troops turned the village into a forward combat base in preparation for the upcoming dry season offensive by Pathet Lao forces. When the offensive got under way in December, Pathet Lao forces attacked the area and reportedly "overran" Long Pot on January 10, 1972. (*South Vietnam in Struggle* [Hanoi, DRVN], January 17, 1972, p. 7).

But this disruption was not the end of Ger Su Yang's troubles. Around the time of the first publication of this book, the CIA pressured Ger Su Yang into retracting his statements about Air America's involvement in the Long Pot opium trade. In September 1971, following the publicity about the CIA's rice cutoff in Long Pot district, officers in the CIA's Secret Army had visited Long Pot village to advise Ger Su Yang that he would be arrested and taken away if any more news came out of Long Pot. The ultimatum was delivered in such a way as to convince Ger Su Yang that he would never come back alive if that happened.

Similarly, Ger Su Yang was more than apprehensive when a CIA helicopter arrived in his village sometime in July 1972 and CIA mercenaries ordered him aboard the aircraft for a flight to CIA headquarters in northern Laos, Ban Son. Coincidentally, my photographer, John Everingham, arrived in the Long Pot area the very day that Ger Su Yang returned from his ordeal, and so we have a remarkably complete report of what actually passed between the CIA and this Hmong district officer.

According to Everingham's account, Ger Su Yang reported that he was interrogated for more than an hour by a "short, fat," rather irate American in a building near the runway at a CIA base. Ger Su Yang later recounted to Everingham the following details of the interrogation.

> The American [CIA agent] asked if I had a photo of you [Everingham], if I knew how to contact you in Vientiane. It was easy to see the American was angry that you had come to Long Pot to talk to me.
>
> I was afraid. I didn't know what was best to say to him. So I said I knew nothing about everything he asked me.
>
> He also asked if it's true the American helicopters carried away our opium. Again I didn't know what was best to say. So I said I didn't know if it was true or not.

How frightened and intimidated Ger Su Yang had been is revealed by his last question to Everingham: "Do you think they will send a helicopter to arrest me or send Vang Pao's soldiers [CIA mercenaries] to shoot me?" (Alfred W. McCoy, "A Correspondence with the CIA", *New York Review of Books* 19, no. 4 [September 21, 1972], p. 34).

167. Lamour and Lamberti, *International Connection*, pp. 124–26.

168. Christopher Robbins, *Air America* (New York: Putnam's, 1979), pp. 220–25.

169. Ibid., pp. 332–38. For the details of Vang Pao's move to Montana, see Charles E. Hood, "Vang Pao Guerrilla General," *The Sunday Missoulian* (Missoula, Montana), November 21, 1976.

170. Grant Evans, *The Yellow Rainmakers* (London: Verso, 1983), pp. 26–28.

171. Robbins, *Ravens*, p. 332.

172. Interview with Gen. Ouane Rattikone, Vientiane, Laos, September 1, 1971.

173. Interview with Gen. Thao Ma, Bangkok, Thailand, September 17, 1971.

174. New York Times, *Pentagon Papers*, pp. 313–14, 362.

175. Interview with Gen. Thao Ma, Bangkok, Thailand, September 17, 1971.

176. *New York Times*, October 22, 1966, p. 2.

177. Gen. Thao Ma had good reason to fear Kouprasith. Following the February 1965 coup, Gen. Phoumi's right-hand man Gen. Siho fled to Thailand. After consulting with a monk in Ubon, Thailand, who told him that it would be good luck to go home, Siho returned to Laos. Kouprasith had him arrested and imprisoned at Phou Khao Kquai, where he was shot while "attempting to escape" (Dommen, *Conflict in Laos*, p. 287). According to a former USAID official, Loring Waggoner, Kouprasith's right-hand man Gen. Thonglith Chokbengboung told him at a funeral for one of Thonglith's relatives several years after the incident that "Siho was dirty and corrupt" and that he was "glad" that he had a hand in eliminating him (interview with Loring Waggoner, Las Cruces, New Mexico, June 23, 1971).

178. Interview with Capt. Kong Le, Paris, March 22, 1971.

179. Ibid.; interview with Gen. Ouane Rattikone, Vientiane, Laos, August 21, 1971; interview with Gen. Thao Ma, Bangkok, Thailand, September 17, 1971.

180. *Lao Presse* (Vientiane: Ministry of Information #232/66), October 22, 1966.

181. Dommen, *Conflict in Laos*, p. 290.

182. Interview with Gen. Thao Ma, Bangkok, Thailand, September 17, 1971; *New York Times*, October 22, 1966, p. 1; October 24, 1966, p. 4.

183. Dommen, *Conflict in Laos*, p. 291.

184. Interview with Capt. Kong Le, Paris, March 22, 1971.

185. Interview with Jimmy Yang, Chiangmai, Thailand, August 12, 1971.

186. Dommen, *Conflict in Laos*, pp. 217–18.

187. Interview with William Young, Chiangmai, Thailand, September 8, 1971.

188. Interview with Maj. Chao La, Nam Keung, Laos, September 12, 1971; Peter Kandre, "Autonomy and Integration of Social Systems: The Iu Mien ('Yao' or 'Man') Mountain Population and Their Neighbors," in Kunstadter, *Southeast Asian Tribes*, vol. 2, p. 585.

189. Interview with a former USAID official in Nam Tha Province, Laos, June 1971.

190. Interview with William Young, Chiangmai, Thailand, September 8, 1971.

191. Interview with a former USAID official in Nam Tha Province, Laos, June 1971.

192. J. Thomas Ward, "U.S. Aid to Hill Tribe Refugees in Laos," in Kunstadter, *Southeast Asian Tribes*, vol. 1, p. 297.

193. Interview with William Young, Chiangmai, Thailand, September 8, 1971.

194. Fred Branfman, "Presidential War in Laos, 1964–1970," in Adams and McCoy, *Laos: War and Revolution*, p. 270.

195. Interview with William Young, Chiangmai, Thailand, September 8, 1971.

196. Interview with Maj. Chao La, Nam Keung, Laos, September 12, 1971.

197. Interview with a former USAID official in Nam Tha Province, Laos, June 1971.

198. Ibid.

199. Interview with a former USAID official from Nam Tha province, Laos, New York, June 1971; interview with William Young, Chiangmai, Thailand, September 8, 1971.

About the time of this book's first publication, the CIA stated publicly that "last year CIA identified a refinery operated by Chao La and had it confiscated. The production equipment was dismantled and forwarded to the Bureau of Narcotics and Dangerous Drugs (BNDD) in Washington, D.C." (Alfred W. McCoy, "A Correspondence with the CIA," *New York Review of Books* 19, no. 4 [September 21, 1972], p. 31).

Despite the CIA's implications in that statement that the drug trade in Nam Keung was cleaned up, a *New York Times* correspondent on a USAID public relations tour of northwestern Laos several months later reported: "Shortly after the delegation of officials arrived in Nam Keung, a pack train of 20 mules, like those that carry most of the opium in this area, moved silently and swiftly through the village. The visitors [which included Edgar Buell] were too polite to inquire about the carefully wrapped cargo carried by the mules." The correspondent also reported that a contingent of KMT troops was camped in the forest near Nam Keung and a KMT officer lived in Chao La's home in the village (*New York Times*, October 16, 1972, p. 12).

200. In the early 1950s for example, anthropologists estimated that there were 139,000 Lahu in China's Yunnan Province, 66,000 in northeastern Burma, and 2,000 in Nam Tha. In 1970 there were 16,000 Yao in Nam Tha and probably more than 100,000 in Yunnan, most of whom dwelled in the border regions (Frank M. Lebar, Gerald C. Hickey, and John K. Musgrave, *Ethnic Groups of Mainland Southeast Asia* [New Haven: Human Relations Area Files Press, 1964], pp. 31, 82; interview with Maj. Chao La, Nam Keung, Laos, September 12, 1971; Peter Kunstadter, "China: Introduction, " in Kunstadter, *Southeast Asian Tribes*, vol. 1, p. 154).

201. Kandre, "Autonomy and Integration of Social Systems," p. 607.

202. Interview with William Young, Chiangmai, Thailand, September 14, 1971.

203. Sowards and Sowards, *Burma Baptist Chronicle*, p. 409. For one of Rev. William Young's reports of his mission work among the Lahu, see Lizbeth B. Hughes, *The Evangel in Burma* (Rangoon: American Baptist Mission Press, 1926), pp. 124–29.

204. Interview with William Young, Chiangmai, Thailand, September 14, 1971.

205. Ibid. For a flattering biography of Gordon Young see Cherrie French, "The Adventures of Gordon Young," *Sawaddi* 6, no. 3 (January–February 1968), pp. 14–27.

206. Interview with U Ba Thein, Chiang Khong District, Thailand, September 11, 1971.

207. *Washington Post*, August 6, 1971.

208. One of the first camps used for training was located in a river valley about twelve miles due north of Nam Keung, but this was closed in 1965 when Chao La and a group of Chinese opium smugglers opened an opium refinery nearby. Young was afraid that the constant movement of mule caravans and boats in and out of the area would compromise the base's security; eventually it was moved across the Mekong River into Thailand and rebuilt in an uninhabited mountain valley, known only by its code name, "Tango Pad" (interview with William Young, Chiangmai, Thailand, September 8, 1971).

209. Interview with a former USAID official in Nam Tha province, New York, June 1971.

210. Interview with William Young, Chiangmai, Thailand, September 14, 1971; interview with U Ba Thein, Chiang Khong district, Thailand, September 11, 1971.

211. *Boston Globe*, September 3, 1970; interview with a former USAID official in Nam Tha province, Laos, New York, June 1971. In general, the security on these cross-border operations was terrible, and many hill tribesmen in the Golden Triangle region knew about them. In mid-1971 the authors met several Yao tribesmen in northern Thailand who knew the names of the five or six Yao who had been on the forays and could recite their itinerary with remarkable accuracy. Both the Chinese and Burmese governments knew about the operations, since they had captured a number of teams. In retrospect, it seems that the American public were the only interested party ignorant of their existence.

212. Interview with William Young, Chiangmai, Thailand, September 14, 1971; interview with U Ba Thein, Chiang Khong district, Thailand, September 11, 1971.

213. Interview with U Ba Thien, Chiang Khong district, Thailand, September 11, 1971. There were a number of reports that Air America helicopters had been forced to land in Burma because of mechanical failure. According to one report by Dispatch News Service International correspondent Michael Morrow, an Air America helicopter was forced to make an emergency landing in May 1971 in the eastern Shan states. The helicopter had been chartered from Air America and was reportedly carrying a CIA operative (Dispatch News Service International, November 8, 1971).

214. Interview with U Ba Thein, Chiang Khong district, Thailand, September 11, 1971.

215. Ibid.; for an account of Dr. Dooley's adventures in Nam Tha province, see Thomas A. Dooley, M.D. *The Night They Burned the Mountain* (New York: Farrar, Straus & Cudahy, 1960).

216. Interview with Rev. Paul Lewis, Chiangmai, Thailand, September 7, 1971; interview with William Young, Chiangmai, Thailand, September 8, 1971.

217. Interview with William Young, Chiangmai, Thailand, September 14, 1971.

218. Interview with U Ba Thien, Chiang Khong district, Thailand, September 11, 1971.

219. Interview with William Young, Chiangmai, Thailand, September 14, 1971.

220. Interview with U Ba Thein, Chiang Khong district, Thailand, September 11, 1971.

221. Adrian Cowell, "Report on a Five Month Journey in the State of Kengtung with the Shan National Army," typescript (1965).

222. Ibid.; *Far Eastern Economic Review*, July 24, 1971, p. 40; interview with Adrian Cowell, London, March 9, 1971.

223. Cowell, "Report on a Five Month Journey"; *Far Eastern Economic Review*, July 24, 1971, p. 40.

224. Cowell, "Report on a Five Month Journey."

225. Interview with Jimmy Yang, Chiangmai, Thailand, September 14, 1971. (This story was confirmed by several former members of the SNA, leaders of other Shan armies, and residents of the Huei Krai area.)

226. Out of the 700 tons of raw opium produced in northeastern Burma, approximately 500 tons were exported to Laos and Thailand. A maximum of 15 percent of the opium harvest was consumed by hill tribe addicts before it left the village (Gordon Young, *The Hill Tribes of Northern Thailand* [Bangkok: The Siam Society, Monograph no. 1, 1962], p. 90). In addition, an estimated 65 tons were smuggled into Burma's major cities for local consumption (interview with William Young, Chiangmai, Thailand, September 8, 1971).

227. Interview with Jimmy Yang, Chiangmai, Thailand, August 12, 1971.

228. Interview with William Young, Chiangmai, Thailand, September 8, 1971.

229. *New York Times*, February 17, 1961, p. 4; February 18, 1961, p. 1.

230. Dommen, *Conflict in Laos*, p. 193; according to President Kennedy's assistant secretary of state for Far Eastern affairs, Roger Hilsman, Kennedy pressured Taiwan to withdraw the KMT forces from Burma to improve relations with mainland China. However, Taiwan insisted that the evacuation be voluntary and so "a few bands of irregulars continued to roam the wilds" (Hilsman, *To Move a Nation*, pp. 304–5).

231. Interview with William Young, Chiangmai, Thailand, September 8, 1971.

232. Paul T. Cohen, "Hill Trading in the Mountain Ranges of Northern Thailand" (1968).

233. Ibid., pp. 2–3.

234. Ibid., pp. 11–14.

235. Young, *Hill Tribes of Northern Thailand*, p. 83.

236. F. W. Mote, "The Rural 'Haw' (Yunnanese Chinese) of Northern Thailand," in Kunstadter, *Southeast Asian Tribes*, p. 489.
237. Ministry of the Interior, Department of Public Welfare, "Report on the Socio-Economic Survey of the Hill Tribes in Northern Thailand," mimeographed (Bangkok, September 1962), p. 23.
238. Ibid., p. 37.
239. Interview with Col. Chen Mo-su, Chiang Khong district, Thailand, September 10, 1971; *New York Times*, August 11, 1971, p. 1.
240. Interview with Col. Chen Mo-su, Chiang Khong district, Thailand, September 10, 1971.
241. Interview with William Young, Chiangmai, Thailand, September 8, 1971.
242. *Weekend Telegraph* (London), March 10, 1967, p. 25.
243. Interview with Jimmy Yang, Chiangmai, Thailand, August 12, 1971; interview with Jao Nhu, Chiangmai, Thailand, September 8, 1971; interview with U Ba Thein, Chiang Khong district, Thailand, September 11, 1971.
244. *New York Times*, August 11, 1971, p. 1; interview with Jao Nhu, Chiangmai, Thailand, September 8, 1971.
245. *New York Times*, August 11, 1971, p. 1; interview with U Ba Thein, Chiang Khong district, Thailand, September 11, 1971.
246. Interview with Jao Nhu, Chiangmai, Thailand, September 8, 1971.
247. Interview with Jimmy Yang, Chiangmai, Thailand, August 12, 1971.
248. Interview with Jao Nhu, Chiangmai, Thailand, August 12, 1971.
249. Ibid.; *New York Times*, June 6, 1971, p. 2.
250. *New York Times*, June 6, 1971, p. 2; interview with Jimmy Yang, Chiangmai, Thailand, August 12, 1971.
251. Interview with William Young, Chiangmai, Thailand, September 8, 1971.
252. Ibid.
253. *New York Times*, August 11, 1971, p. 1.
254. Interview with Jimmy Yang, Chiangmai, Thailand, August 12, 1971.
255. In May 1965, for example, the *New York Times* reported that General Ma was operating in a mountainous area of western Yunnan about twenty miles across the border from Ving Ngun and said that unmarked aircraft were making regular supply drops to his troops (*New York Times*, May 18, 1965, p. 1).
256. Interview with U Ba Thein, Chiang Khong district, Thailand, September 11, 1971.
257. *Weekend Telegraph* (London), March 10, 1967, pp. 27–28. In September 1966 400 of Gen. Tuan's best troops left their barren wooden barracks on top of Mae Salong mountain, saluted the twenty-foot-high portrait of Generalissimo Chiang Kai-shek that decorated the parade ground, and marched off into the jungle. After plunging across the Burma-China border into western Yunnan province, Gen. Tuan's troops fell back across the border, leaving 80 casualties behind (*New York Times*, September 9, 1966, p. 3; *Weekend Telegraph*, March 10, 1967, p. 27).
258. Interview with William Young, Chiangmai, Thailand, September 8, 1971.

259. "Opium War—Take Three," dispatch from McCulloch, Hong Kong, filing from Saigon, to Time World, New York, August 22, 1967, p. 10.

260. Jeffrey Race, "China and the War in Northern Thailand," typescript (1971), p. 26.

261. Interview with William Young, Chiangmai, Thailand, September 8, 1971.

262. Interview with Jimmy Yang, Chiangmai, Thailand, August 12, 1971; "Opium War Add," dispatch from McCulloch, Hong Kong, filing from Saigon, to Time World, New York, August 23, 1967, p. 2.

263. "Opium War—Take Two," dispatch from Vanderwicken, Hong Kong, filing from Saigon, to Time World, New York, August 22, 1967, p. 4.

264. New York Times, August 11, 1971, p. 1.

265. Race, "China and the War in Northern Thailand," p. 27; interview with Lawrence Peet, Chiangrai, Thailand, August 9, 1971. (Lawrence Peet was a missionary working in Lahu villages near the caravan trail at the time of the Opium War.)

266. Interview with the principal of Ban Khwan public school, Ban Khwan, Laos, August 9, 1971.

267. Ibid.; interview with Gen. Ouane Rattikone, Vientiane, Laos, September 1, 1971.

268. Race, "China and the War in Northern Thailand," p. 27.

269. Interview with Gen. Ouane Rattikone, Vientiane, Laos, September 1, 1971.

270. Ibid.

271. "Opium War—Take Two," p. 5.

272. Interview with Gen. Ouane Rattikone, Vientiane, Laos, September 1, 1971.

273. New York Times, August 11, 1971, p. 1.

274. Race, "China and the War in Northern Thailand," p. 28.

275. "Opium War—Take Two," pp. 4, 6; Evening Star, (Washington, DC), June 19, 1972.

276. New York Times, August 11, 1971, p. 1.

277. Interview with the principal of Ban Khwan Public School, Ban Khwan, Laos, August 9, 1971.

278. Race, "China and the War in Northern Thailand," p. 28; Mote, "The Rural 'Haw,'" pp. 488, 492–93.

279. Report of the United Nations Survey Team on the Economic and Social Needs of the Opium-Producing Areas in Thailand, p. 64.

280. Race, "China and the War in Northern Thailand," pp. 21–23.

281. Ibid.

282. Ibid., pp. 29–31. The insurgency in northern Thailand was regarded as the "most serious" military problem facing Thai government in the early 1970s (U.S. Congress, Senate, Committee on Foreign Relations, Thailand, Laos, and Cambodia: January 1972, 92nd Cong., 2nd sess. [Washington, DC: U.S. Government Printing Office, 1972], p. 14).

283. Alfred W. McCoy, "Subcontracting Counterinsurgency: Academics in Thailand, 1954–1970," Bulletin of Concerned Asian Scholars (December 1970), pp. 64–67.

284. Weekend Telegraph, p. 27.

285. According to a 1961 report by Gordon Young, 50 percent of the Hmong, 20 percent of the Lahu, 75 percent of the Lisu, and 25 percent of the Akha tribesmen in northern Thailand had some fluency in Yunnanese. In contrast, only 5 percent of the Hmong, 10 percent of the Lahu, 50 percent of the Lisu, and 25 percent of the Akha spoke Thai or Laotian (Young, *Hill Tribes of Northern Thailand,* p. 92).
286. Interview with Col. Chen Mo-su, Chiang Khong district, Thailand, September 10, 1971.
287. Interview with General Krirksin, Chiang Khong district, Thailand, September 10, 1971.
288. Interview with Col. Chen Mo-su, Chiang Khong district, Thailand, September 10, 1971.
289. *New York Times,* June 6, 1971, p. 2; *NBC Chronolog,* April 28, 1972.
290. "Opium War—Take Three," pp. 1–2.
291. Interview with Jimmy Yang, Chiangmai, Thailand, August 12, 1971.
292. Interview with Hsai Klao, Chiangrai, Thailand, September 13, 1971.
293. Interview with Jao Nhu, Chiangmai, Thailand, September 8, 1971.
294. Interview with Jimmy Yang, Chiangmai, Thailand, August 12, 1971.
295. The Shan Unity Preparatory Committee was a coalition of the right-wing Shan rebel groups formed mainly to provide effective joint action against the Burmese Communist party. This quotation from one of their communiqués conveys the group's conservative character and its anti-Communist first principles: "In the areas bordering Communist China in the Kachin and Northern Shan States particularly, armed bands trained and armed by the Communist Chinese composed mostly of China born Kachins and Shans are now very active. . . . The Shan Unity Preparatory Committee (SUPC) believes unity within the Union of Burma is definitely attainable and there is no reason why unity based on anti-communism, a belief in Parliamentary democracy and free economy, and last but not least, a unity based on the principles of Federalism cannot be achieved." (Shan Unity Preparatory Committee, "Communiqué No. 5," mimeographed [Shan State, March 14, 1968], pp. 1–2).
296. Interview with Jimmy Yang, Chiangmai, Thailand, August 12, 1971.
297. Communiqué from the Central Executive Committee, Shan State Progress party, September 1971, pp. 1–2.
298. The Shan State Army admitted to having transported the following quantities of raw opium from the northern Shan states to northern Thailand: 160 kilos in 1964, 290 kilos in 1965, 960 kilos in 1966, 1,600 kilos in 1967, nothing in 1968, and 80 kilos in 1969 (interview with Jao Nhu, Chiangmai, Thailand, September 8, 1971).
299. Interview with William Young, Chiangmai, Thailand, September 8, 1971.
300. *Far Eastern Economic Review, 1968 Yearbook* (Hong Kong), p. 123; *Far Eastern Economic Review, 1971 Yearbook* (Hong Kong), p. 108.
301. In September 1971, for example, the author was invited to visit a Shan rebel camp near Huei Krai. However, on the morning of the visit (September 13) the author received the following note:

Sorry to inform you that your trip with us to Mae Sai is not approved by the Thai authorities. Because it is near the Burmese border and it might be possible for the Burmese to know it.

It is better to stay within the regulations since the host, the Thais, is giving us a warm and friendly reception.

[signed] Hsai Kiao

302. *Far Eastern Economic Review*, May 1, 1971, pp. 47–49; April 17, 1971, pp. 19–20.

303. Interview with William Young, Chiangmai, Thailand, September 8, 1971; interview with Jao Nhu, Chiangmai, Thailand, September 8, 1971.

304. Interview with Hsai Kiao, Chiangrai, Thailand, September 21, 1971; interview with Jimmy Yang, Chiangmai, Thailand, September 14, 1971. The foregoing description of the Shan states' opium trade focused mainly on the traffic in the eastern Shan states (Kengtung, Wa, and Kokang) since this was the most important opium-growing area in northeastern Burma. However, it should be noted that guerrillas in the southern Shan states were also actively involved in the trade. The Palaung National Force, Gen. Mo Heng's Shan United Revolutionary Army, the Mong Ngai KKY, and the Pa-O rebels (divided between Chairman Hla Mong's Shan National Liberation Organization and Gen. Kyansone's Pa-O National Freedom League) were the major indigenous participants in the southern Shan states' opium trade. On the divisions within the Pa-O rebels, see The Pa-O National Freedom League, General Kyansone (Chan Son), "The Opinion of the Pa-O National Freedom League Concerning the Shan National Liberation Organization" (Chiangmai, January 1970).

Perhaps to blunt criticism of Thai and Laotian complicity in the Golden Triangle opium trade, U.S. officials exaggerated the importance of Lo Hsing-han. In June 1972 the senior adviser to the secretary of state and coordindator for international narcotics matters, Nelson Gross, testified before a congressional committee in response to earlier testimony by the author:

> Mr. McCoy somehow missed the name of the kingpin of the heroin traffic in Southeast Asia. The man is Lo Hsing Han of Burma. His control of the area opium runs the gamut from opium poppy fields, along the smuggling routes, to his heroin refineries. Lo has a virtual monopoly on heroin refining in the section. Many of the refineries driven out of Laos and Thailand have come under Lo's control in Burma. (U.S. Congress, *Congressional Record*, 92nd Cong., 2nd sess., 118, no. 106, June 28, 1972, p. H6274)

305. Interview with Hsai Kiao, Chiangrai, Thailand, September 12, 1971.

306. *New York Times*, June 6, 1971, p. 2.

307. *Far Eastern Economic Review*, December 12, 1970, p. 22; April 17, 1971, p. 20.

308. *Newsweek*, March 22, 1971, p. 42; interview with William Young, Chiangmai, Thailand, September 8, 1971.

309. *New York Times*, January 3, 1971, p. 9; January 31, 1971, p. 3.

310. Interview with William Young, Chiangmai, Thailand, September 8, 1971.

311. It was not possible for U Nu to ally with the Kachin Independence Army (KIA), which controlled much of Kachin State. Its leaders were Baptist Christians who resented U Nu's establishment of Buddhism as a state religion. The head of the KIA was a Baptist Christian named Zau Seng. He founded the Kachin Independence Army with his brothers in 1957 and with the exception of brief negotiations with Ne Win in 1963, continued to fight the Burmese government. When he was in Thailand trading in opium and buying arms, his brothers, Zau Dan and Zau Tu, directed military operations in Kachin State. Unlike the Shans, Zau Seng was the undisputed leader of the conservative Kachins, and his troops controlled most of the Kachin state. Relations between Zau Seng and the Kachin Communist leader, Naw Seng, were reportedly quite hostile.

  The Kachin Independence Army was also distinguished by the fact that it was associated with an American Baptist Mission couple from Louisianna, Robert and Betty Morse. As of late 1972, Betty Morse had retired to Baton Rouge, but her husband Robert was still in the hills with the Kachin guerrillas.

312. Interview with Jimmy Yang, Chiangmai, Thailand, September 14, 1971.
313. Interview with William Young, Chiangmai, Thailand, September 8, 1971.
314. Interview with Jimmy Yang, Chiangmai, Thailand, September 14, 1971.
315. Interview with William Young, Chiangmai, Thailand, September 14, 1971.
316. Interview with Hsai Kiao, Chiangrai, Thailand, September 13, 1971; interview with Brig. Gen. Tommy Clift, Bangkok, Thailand, September 21, 1971.
317. Interview with William Young, Chiangmai, Thailand, September 8, 1971.
318. Interview with Hsai Kiao, Chiangrai, Thailand, September 13, 1971.
319. It appeared that the Young family was revered mainly by the Black Lahu of northern Kengtung state and western Yunnan. The original prophecy of the White God was made by a Black Lahu, and the Youngs had a remarkable conversion rate among them. In contrast, the Red Lahu generally remained animist and regarded Bu-jong Luang, the "Man God," or "divine deliverer," as their living deity. The "Man God" had his headquarters west of Mong Hsat and was influential among the Red Lahu of southern Kengtung state. The terms "red" and "black" derive from the different-colored clothing worn by different Lahu subgroups. On the other hand, the term "Red Meo" was a political term used to designate Communist Hmong insurgents. Many Red Lahu tribesmen in the 1970s feared that their ethnolinguistic designation would be misinterpreted as a political label. Red Lahu tribesmen in northern Thailand usually claimed to be Black Lahu when questioned by anthropologists. Thus, when Bu-jong Luang's son spoke, he said that the Red Lahu were not Communists as many people thought and would willingly join their fellow Lahu in the struggle against Ne Win (interview with William Young, Chiangmai, Thailand, September 8, 1971).
320. Ibid.
321. Tinker, *Union of Burma,* pp. 38, 395.

322. Ibid., pp. 40–41.

323. *Pacific Research and World Empire Telegram* 2, no. 3 (March–April 1971), p. 6.

324. The Burmese Communist party's (BCP) reasons for abolishing the opium trade were very pragmatic:

    1. Since the BCP was a political enemy of the Burmese government, the KMT, and the Shan rebels, it would be impossible for it to send an opium caravan into Thailand even if it had wanted to.

    2. Continuing the exploitative opium tax would have alienated the people.

    3. Since Shan rebels and government militia were interested only in occupying opium-producing territories, opium eradication weakened their desire to retake lost territory (interview with Jimmy Yang, Chiangmai, Thailand, August 12, 1971).

325. Interview with Gen. Ouane Rattikone, Vientiane, Laos, September 1, 1971.

326. Interview with residents of Chiang Saen, Thailand, August 1971.

327. Interview with officers in the Royal Laotian air force, Vientiane, Laos, July–August 1971.

328. "Opium War Add," p. 2.

329. "Opium War—Take 2," p. 6.

330. According to a U.S. narcotics analyst, Gen. Ouane's control over the opium traffic in the Ban Houei Sai region was further improved in 1968 when Col. Khampay, a loyal Ouane follower, was appointed regional commander. Col. Khampay reportedly devoted most of his military resources to protecting the Ban Houei Tap refinery and moving supplies back and forth between Ban Houei Sai and the refinery (interview with an agent, U.S. Bureau of Narcotics and Dangerous Drugs, New Haven, CT, May 3, 1972); *Evening Star* (Washington, DC), June 19, 1972.

331. *New York Times*, June 6, 1971, p. 2.

332. Interview with William Young, Chiangmai, Thailand, September 8, 1971. According to a U.S. cabinet report, these laboratories in the tri-border area were in Bangkok before 1969, "but during 1969 and 1970 most or all moved upcountry for security reasons." The same report goes on to say: that "A consortium of Chinese merchants in Vientiane handles the processing and distribution of most smoking heroin and opium to urban markets in Laos and Vietnam. They also produced much of the no. 4 heroin supplied to U.S. servicemen in Vietnam in 1970 and 1971." This consortium apparently shifted these Laotian laboratories across the Burmese side of the border in mid-1971 (U.S. CCINC, *World Opium Survey 1972*, pp. 27, 29).

333. The attack on Long Tieng in early 1972 inevitably created problems for narcotics dealings among Vang Pao's troops. It was entirely possible that they were no longer in the heroin business.

334. Interview with Elliot K. Chan, Vientiane, Laos, August 15, 1971.

335. Cabled dispatch from Shaw, Vientiane (Hong Kong Bureau), to Time Inc., received September 16–17, 1965.

336. *Lao Presse* (Vientiane: Ministry of Information #56/66), March 16, 1966.

337. *Lao Presse* (Vientiane: Ministry of Information #58/66), March 18, 1966.

338. Direction du Protocole, Ministre des Affaires Etrangères, "Liste des Personnalités Lao," mimeographed (Royaume du Laos n.d.), p. 155.

339. Interview with a Thai police official, Bangkok, Thailand, September 1971.

340. Interview with an agent, U.S. Bureau of Narcotics and Dangerous Drugs, New Haven, CT, May 3, 1972.

341. Interview with Western diplomatic official, Vientiane, Laos, August 1971; interview with Third World diplomatic official, Vientiane, Laos, August 1971 (this account of the incident was corroborated by reports received by the U.S. Bureau of Narcotics and Dangerous Drugs [interview with an agent, U.S. Bureau of Narcotics and Dangerous Drugs, New Haven, CT, November 18, 1971]); interview with a Laotian political observer, Vientiane, Laos, August 1971.

342. Interview with a Laotian political observer, Vientiane, Laos, August 1971.

343. *Lao Presse* (Vientiane: Ministry of Information #1566/71), September 6, 1971.

344. Interview with an agent, U.S. Bureau of Narcotics and Dangerous Drugs, Southeast Asia, September 1971.

345. Ibid.

346. Hamilton-Paterson, *Greedy War*, p. 194.

347. *Far Eastern Economic Review*, December 4, 1971, pp. 40–41.

348. In its July 19, 1971, issue, *Newsweek* magazine hinted that the United States had used its "other means of persuasion" to force Gen. Ouane Rattikone into retirement. This suggestion was based only on the imagination of *Newsweek*'s New York editorial staff. According to the Vientiane press corps, *Newsweek* cabled its Vientiane correspondent for confirmation of this story and he replied that Ouane's retirement had been planned for more than a year (which, in fact, it had been). Reliable diplomatic sources in Vientiane found *Newsweek*'s suggestion absurd and Gen. Ouane himself flatly denied that there had been any pressure on him to retire (*Newsweek*, July 19, 1971, pp. 23–24).

349. Interview with Gen. Ouane Rattikone, Vientiane, Laos, September 1, 1971.

350. State Department, "Report of the Cabinet Committee on International Narcotics Control Task Force on Air and Sea Smuggling," Washington, DC, February 21, 1972, pp. 1, 5.

351. U.S. Senate, Select Committee to Study Governmental Operations with Respect to Intelligence Activities, *Foreign and Military Intelligence, Book I: Final Report*, 94th Cong., 2nd sess. (Washington, DC: U.S. Government Printing Office, 1976, Report No. 94-755), pp. 228.

352. Ibid., pp. 228, 232.

353. Ibid., p. 233.

354. Ibid., p. 229.

355. Ibid., p. 205.

## 8 War on Drugs

1. *New York Times*, February 11, 1990.

2. U.S. State Department, Bureau of International Narcotics Matters, *Interna-*

*tional Narcotics Control Strategy Report, March 1990,* pub. no. 9749 (Washington, DC: State Department, March 1990), p. 20.

3. Ibid., p. 13.

4. Ibid., pp. 33, 324.

5. Ibid., p. 325.

6. Ibid., p. 43.

7. U.S. Congress, House, Select Committee on Narcotics Abuse and Control, *Southeast Asian Narcotics,* 95th Cong., 1st sess. (Washington DC: U.S. Government Printing Office, 1978), p. 249.

8. John T. Cusack, "Turkey Lifts the Poppy Ban," *Drug Enforcement* (Fall 1974), pp. 3–7.

9. Confidential interview with DEA special agent, Southeast Asia, December 1975.

10. U.S. Congress, House, Committee on Foreign Affairs, *The U.S. Heroin Problem and Southeast Asia: The Asian Connection,* 93rd Cong., 1st sess. (Washington DC: U.S. Government Printing Office, 1973), pp. 6–7.

11. U.S. Congress, House, Committee on International Relations, *The Narcotics Situation in Southeast Asia: The Asian Connection,* 94th Cong., 1st sess. (Washington, DC: U.S. Government Printing Office, 1975), p. 40; interview with Daniel J. Addario, Bangkok, December 15, 1975.

12. U.S. House Committee on International Relations, *Narcotics Situation,* p. 38.

13. Lester L. Wolff et al., "The Narcotics Situation in Southeast Asia," *Drug Enforcement* (Summer 1975), pp. 28–33.

14. Confidential interview with DEA special agent, Southeast Asia, December 1975.

15. *Drug Enforcement* (Winter 1975), cited in U.S. House Committee on International Relations, *Narcotics Situation,* p. 49.

16. *Asia Week,* May 20, 1977.

17. U.S. Congress, House, Committee on International Relations, *Proposal to Control Opium from the Golden Triangle and Terminate the Shan Opium Trade,* 94th Cong., 1st sess. (Washington, DC: U.S. Government Printing Office, 1975), p. 91.

18. Cusack, "Turkey Lifts the Poppy Ban," pp. 3–7.

19. U.S. Congress, House, Committee on International Relations, *The Shifting Pattern of Narcotics Trafficking: Latin America,* 94th Cong., 2nd sess. (Washington, DC: U.S. Government Printing Office, 1976), pp. 7–13; U.S. Drug Enforcement Administration, "Heroin Source Identification for U.S. Heroin Market" (Washington, DC, unpublished documents, 1972, 1973, 1974, 1975); U.S. Cabinet Committee on International Narcotics Control (CCINC), *World Opium Survey 1972* (Washington DC: CCINC, 1972), pp. 10–13. These statistics on relative percentage of Southeast Asian heroin entering the United States are based on an interpretation of published statistics after discussions with DEA agents. The DEA's Signature program of determining origin of samples from various U.S. cities through chemical analysis gives a similar downward trend. In 1973 Southeast Asian heroin

accounted for 16 percent of U.S. samples, down to 12 percent in 1974, down to 10 percent in 1975, and down to 8 percent in 1976. See U.S. House Select Committee on Narcotics Abuse and Control, *Southeast Asian Narcotics*, pp. 151–52.

20. Laura M. Wicinski, "Europe Awash with Heroin," *Drug Enforcement* (Summer 1981), pp. 14–15.

21. Confidential interview with DEA special agent, Southeast Asia, December 1975.

22. U.S. House Committee on International Relations, *Narcotics Situation*, pp. 50–51; U.S. House Select Committee on Narcotics Abuse and Control, *Southeast Asian Narcotics*, pp. 154–55.

23. Confidential interview with DEA agent, Singapore, December 1975.

24. Interview with officer, New South Wales police, Sydney, Australia, October 1978.

25. Wicinski, "Europe Awash with Heroin," pp. 14–15.

26. U.S. Drug Enforcement Administration, Office of Intelligence, "Heroin Seized in Europe During 1978," *Drug Enforcement* (February 1979), pp. 20–21.

27. U.S. House Committee on International Relations, *Proposal to Control Opium*, p. 101.

28. Ibid., p. 94; confidential interview with DEA special agent, Singapore, December 1975.

29. Confidential interview with DEA agent, Bangkok, December 1975.

30. Irvin C. Swank, "North American Heroin," *Drug Enforcement* (February 1977), pp. 3–12.

31. Ibid., pp. 3–9; U.S. General Accounting Office, *Report to the Congress, Drug Control: U.S.–Mexico Opium and Marijuana Aerial Eradication Program* (Washington, DC: U.S. Government Printing Office, January 1988), pp. 2–16.

32. U.S. Congress, Senate, Committee on Appropriations, *Foreign Assistance and Related Program Appropriations for Fiscal Year 1972*, 92nd Cong., 1st sess. (Washington, DC: U.S. Government Printing Office, 1971), pp. 578–84; Richard M. Gibson, "Hilltribes of the Golden Triangle," *Drug Enforcement* (February 1979), pp. 27–36; Thomas H. Becker, "Footnote on the Golden Triangle," *Drug Enforcement* (Summer 1981), pp. 25–26.

33. Malthea Falco, "Asian Narcotics: The Impact on Europe," *Drug Enforcement* (February 1979), pp. 2–7; John P. Lyle, "Southwest Asian Heroin: Pakistan, Afghanistan, and Iran," *Drug Enforcement* (Summer 1981), pp. 2–6.

34. U.S. Drug Enforcement Administration, "Summary of Middle East Heroin Conference, December 6–7, 1979, John F. Kennedy International Airport," pp. 1–16 (Alan A. Block Archive on Organized Crime, Pennsylvania State University).

35. William French Smith, "Drug Traffic Today: Challenge and Response," *Drug Enforcement* (Summer 1982), pp. 2–5; Lyle, "Southwest Asian Heroin," pp. 2–6. For different figures that give a similar market

breakdown, see U.S. State Department, Bureau of International Narcotics Matters, *International Narcotics Control Strategy Report* (Washington, DC: U.S. Government Printing Office, February 1984), p. 4.

36. U.S. House Select Committee on Narcotics Abuse and Control, *Southeast Asian Narcotics*, pp. 67, 77, 95.

37. French, "Drug Traffic Today," pp. 2–5.

38. Thomas H. Becker, Asian Heroin Section, Office of Intelligence, Drug Enforcement Administration, "Footnote on the Golden Triangle," *Drug Enforcement* (Summer 1981), pp. 25–26.

39. U.S. State Department, Bureau of International Narcotics Matters, *International Narcotics Control Strategy Report* (1990), pp. 271–79.

40. *New York Times*, February 11, 1990.

41. U.S. State Department, Bureau of International Narcotics Matters, *International Narcotics Control Strategy Report* (1990), p. 20.

42. Ricardo M. Zarco, "Drugs in School 1974: A Five Philippine City Study," *Two Research Monographs on Drug Abuse in the Philippines* (Manila: Government Printing Office, 1975), pp. 81–82.

43. Confidential interview with Philippine constabulary, Manila, Philippines, November 1975.

44. Interview with Romeo J. Sanga, Dangerous Drugs Board, Manila, Philippines, November 27, 1975.

45. Confidential interview with Philippine constabulary, Manila, Philippines, November 1975.

46. Constabulary Anti-Narcotics Unit, *Third Anniversary* (Quezon City: Philippine Constabulary, 1975).

47. Confidential interview with Philippine constabulary, Manila, Philippines, November 1975.

48. Constabulary Anti-Narcotics Unit, *First Anniversary* (Quezon City: Philippine Constabulary, 1973).

49. Confidential interview with Philippine constabulary, Manila, Philippines, November 1975.

50. A. P. Sta Ana, *The Golden Triangle Revisited* (Manila: Philippines Daily Express, 1975).

51. Confidential interview with Philippine constabulary, Manila, Philippines, November 1975.

52. Ricardo M. Zarco, *Street Corner Drug Use in Metropolitan Manila: A Comparison of Two Socio-Economic Categories of Illicit Social Drug Users* (Manila: Narcotics Foundation of the Philippines, 1972), p. 34.

53. Ricardo M. Zarco, "Drugs in School," pp. 11–12; Dangerous Drugs Board, *Annual Report 1974* (Manila, 1975), p. 18; Dangerous Drugs Board, "Seizures and Apprehensions: Aggregate Total for the Period January–September 30, 1975" (Manila, unpublished document).

54. U.S. Congress, House, Select Committee on Narcotics Abuse and Control, *Opium Production, Narcotics Financing, and Trafficking in Southeast Asia*, 95th Cong., 1st sess. (Washington, DC: U.S. Government Printing Office, 1977), pp. 4, 11.

55. *The Manila Chronicle,* August 3, 1990; *Philippine Daily Globe,* August 5, 1990; *Philippine Daily Inquirer,* August 8, 1990.
56. Interview with Senior Inspector Brian Woodward, Hong Kong, December 3–4, 1975.
57. *South China Morning Post* (Hong Kong), November 17, 1974.
58. *South China Morning Post,* November 13, 1974.
59. Interview with David Hodson, Narcotics Bureau, Royal Hong Kong Police, December 2, 1975.
60. Interview with Senior Inspector Brian Woodward, Hong Kong, December 3–4, 1975.
61. Ibid.
62. *First Report of the Commission of Inquiry Under Sir Alistair Blair-Kerr* (Hong Kong: Government Printer, 1973), pp. 3–9.
63. *Second Report of the Commission of Inquiry Under Sir Alistair Blair-Kerr* (Hong Kong: Government Printer, 1973), p. 25.
64. Interview with Martin Bishop, ICAC, Hong Kong, December 3, 1975; *Annual Report by the Commissioner of the Independent Commission Against Corruption* (Hong Kong: Government Printer, 1974), Appendix 10; *Hong Kong Star,* December 1, 1975; U.S. House Select Committee on Narcotics Abuse and Control, *Opium Production,* pp. 17–18.
65. *South China Morning Post,* November 4–8, 1975; *Far Eastern Economic Review,* January 17, 1976.
66. *South China Morning Post,* November 13, 1974.
67. R. J. Faulkner and R. A. Field, *Vanquishing the Dragon: The Law of Drugs in Hong Kong* (Hong Kong: Center for Asian Studies, University of Hong Kong, 1975), pp. 65–72.
68. Interview with John Johnston, Narcotics Bureau, Royal Hong Kong Police, December 4, 1975.
69. Confidential interviews with Hong Kong police, December 1975; correspondence with senior Hong Kong police narcotics officer, November 1976.
70. *Far Eastern Economic Review,* September 9, 1977.
71. *Hong Kong Star,* September 17, 1977.
72. *Hong Kong Standard,* August 26, 1977; *Far Eastern Economic Review,* September 9, 1977.
73. *Hong Kong Star,* January 10, 1979; *Hong Kong Standard,* May 16, 1979.
74. U.S. House Select Committee on Narcotics Abuse and Control, *Opium Production,* pp. 21–22.
75. *Report on the Action Committee Against Narcotics for 1973–1974* (Hong Kong: Government Printer, 1974), p. 11; "Analysis Report on the Central Registry for Drug Addicts, April 1972–March 1974" (Hong Kong, unpublished document), pp. 2, 13; *The Problem of Dangerous Drugs in Hong Kong* (Hong Kong: Government Printer, 1974), pp. 1–4; Discharged Prisoner's Aid Society, *Three Years Experience (1967–1970) with Treatment of Ex-Prisoner Female Narcotic Addicts* (Hong Kong: Government Printer, 1970), pp. 1–12; Society for the Aid and Rehabilitation of Drug Addicts, *Annual Report 1973–1974* (Hong Kong: SARDA, 1974), pp. 38–41.

76. *Far Eastern Economic Review,* November 11, 1977, November 18, 1977, January 27, 1978, March 24, 1978.
77. *Far Eastern Economic Review,* December 8, 1988.
78. Confidential interview with narcotics agent, Hong Kong, December 1975; U.S. Drug Enforcement Administration, "Heroin Source Identification"; *Far Eastern Economic Review,* December 26, 1975.
79. Wolff, "Narcotics Situation in Southeast Asia," p. 31.
80. *Far Eastern Economic Review,* September 14, 1979, p. 41.
81. U.S. State Department, Bureau of International Narcotics Matters, *International Narcotics Control Strategy Report* (1990), pp. 290–291.
82. U.S. State Department, Bureau of International Narcotics Matters, *International Narcotics Control Strategy Report* (1984), pp. 105–6; U.S. State Department, Bureau of International Narcotics Matters, *International Narcotics Control Strategy Report* (1990), p. 288.
83. U.S. State Department, Bureau of International Narcotics Matters, *International Narcotics Control Strategy Report* (1984), p. 103.
84. Interview with John Johnston, Narcotics Bureau, Royal Hong Kong Police, December 4, 1975.
85. Confidential interview with Royal Malaysian Police, Kuala Lumpur, December 1975.
86. *Philippines Daily Express,* November 25, 1975.
87. Abdul Rahman bin H. J. Ismail, "The Prevention of Drug Abuse in Malaysia: Intelligence, Enforcement, and Control" (Genting Highlands: National Workshop on the Prevention of Drug Abuse, 1975), pp. 8–9; *Far Eastern Economic Review,* April 30, 1976.
88. Confidential interview with DEA special agent, Kuala Lumpur, December 1975.
89. Michael A. Antonelli, "Asian Heroin on the Rise in Europe," *Drug Enforcement* (Summer 1975), pp. 34–35.
90. Wicinski, "Europe Awash with Heroin," pp. 14–15.
91. U.S. State Department, Bureau of International Narcotics Matters, *International Narcotics Control Strategy Report* (1984), pp. 115–19.
92. U.S. State Department, Bureau of International Narcotics Matters, *International Narcotics Control Strategy Report* (1990), pp. 309–12.
93. Confidential interview with DEA special agent, Singapore, December 1975.
94. *Far Eastern Economic Review,* April 30, 1976; *Asia Week,* May 20, 1977.
95. U.S. State Department, Bureau of International Narcotics Matters, *International Narcotics Control Strategy Report* (1990), pp. 320–21.
96. *Bangkok Post,* July 16, 1975.
97. *Bangkok Post,* March 24, 1975.
98. *Bangkok Post,* March 25, 1975.
99. Interview with Daniel J. Addario, Bangkok, Thailand, December 15, 1975.
100. *Drug Enforcement* (Summer 1975), p. 36.
101. Confidential interviews with Philippine constabulary, Royal Hong Kong Police, DEA Southeast Asia, Royal Malaysia Police, November–December 1975.

102. *Bangkok Post,* June 21, 1975.

103. *Bangkok Post,* July 10, 1975.

104. *Bangkok Post,* June 25, 1975; confidential interviews with *Bangkok Post* staff reporter, and an officer, Narcotics Suppression Center, Bangkok, Thailand, December 1975.

105. *Bangkok Post,* July 17, 1975; December 5, 1975; interview with police Maj. Gen. Pow Sarasin, Bangkok, Thailand, December 15, 1975.

106. *New York Times,* February 11, 1990.

107. Interview with Col. Chawalit Yodmani, Narcotics Suppression Center, Bangkok, Thailand, December 11, 1975.

108. U.S. House Committee on International Relations, *Narcotics Situation,* pp. 38–40.

109. Interview with Col. Chawalit Yodmani, Narcotics Suppression Center, Bangkok, Thailand, December 11, 1975.

110. Confidential interview with Royal Thai Police, Chiangmai, Thailand, December 1975.

111. Confidential interview with DEA special agent, Bangkok, Thailand, December 1975.

112. Confidential interviews with DEA special agents, Southeast Asia, December 1975.

113. Interview with Daniel J. Addario, Bangkok, Thailand, December 15, 1975; Interview with Col. Chawalit Yodmani, Narcotics Suppression Center, Bangkok, Thailand, December 11, 1975.

114. Interview with I. M. G. Williams, Bangkok, Thailand, December 12, 1975.

115. United Nations Fund for Drug Abuse Control, "Crop Replacement and Community Development Project: Progress Report, September 1972–June 1973" (Bangkok, unpublished document, 1973), pp. 1–17.

116. Confidential interview with DEA special agent, Southeast Asia, December 1975.

117. United Nations Fund for Drug Abuse Control, UN/Thai Program for Drug Abuse Control in Thailand, "Progress Report No. 5" (Geneva: UNFDAC, September 1975, NAR/THA.5); "Progress Report No. 6" (Geneva: UNFDAC, June 1976, NAR/THA.6); W. R. Geddes, "Hmong Opium and Attempts to Replace It," Seminar: The Asian Opium Trade, Center for Asian Studies, University of Syndey, October 20, 1978; George K. Tanham, *Trial in Thailand* (New York: Crane, Russak, 1974), pp. 7–8, 57–62, 98–99; Interview with I. M. G. Williams, Bangkok, Thailand, December 12, 1975.

118. U.S. CCINC, *World Opium Survey 1972,* p. A-38; U.S. State Department, Bureau of International Narcotics Matters, *International Narcotics Control Strategy Report* (1990), p. 20.

119. *Far Eastern Economic Review,* May 21, 1976.

120. *Far Eastern Economic Review,* April 28, 1978.

121. *Far Eastern Economic Review,* November 5, 1973.

122. *Far Eastern Economic Review,* October 7, 1977.

123. *Far Eastern Economic Review,* June 10, 1974, October 24, 1975.

124. Thomas Lobe, *United States National Security Policy and Aid to the*

*Thailand Police* (Denver: Monograph Series in World Affairs, University of Denver, 1977), pp. 117–123.

125. Frank C. Darling, "Thailand in 1977: The Search for Stability and Progress," *Asian Survey* 18, no. 2 (February 1978), pp. 158–59; Kamol Somvichian, " 'The Oyster and the Shell': Thai Bureaucrats in Politics," *Asian Survey* 18, no. 8 (August 1978), pp. 834–87.

126. *Far Eastern Economic Review*, April 15, 1977.

127. *Christian Science Monitor*, October 25, 1977.

128. *Bangkok Post*, July 17, 1977; October 27, 1978; *Bangkok World*, October 26, 1977.

129. *Washington Post*, February 6, 1978.

130. *Far Eastern Economic Review*, April 28, 1978.

131. *Far Eastern Economic Review*, October 7, 1977.

132. The conclusion that the CIA was responsible for this rather curious public ceremony was revealed inadvertently by John Doyle, DEA deputy chief of operations for the Far East, in July 1977 testimony before the U.S. Congress. In answering a question about responsibility for the decision to purchase the KMT's 26 tons, Doyle denied that the Bureau of Narcotics and Dangerous Drugs had made the decision and implicated the CIA: "But the only thing I am aware of is there was a decision made certainly above the then BNDD to do this. We in some small fashion as an *overt* agency were involved as an agent in transferring the certain moneys that were involved" [emphasis added]. Doyle's use of the word *overt* is significant since the CIA is generally referred to in administrative parlance as the reverse—a "covert" agency. (See U.S. House Select Committee on Narcotics Abuse and Control, *Southeast Asian Narcotics*, pp. 178–79.) The CIA was then being criticized for its complicity in the Southeast Asian narcotics traffic and was sensitive about its long-standing relationship with the KMT 3rd and 5th armies. It is likely that the ceremony was designed as a way to remove the CIA from further criticism on the subject of its relations with the KMT rather than as a serious attempt at retiring the KMT from the narcotics traffic.

133. Jack Anderson, "Thai Opium Bonfire Mostly Fodder," *Washington Post*, July 31, 1972, p. B-11.

134. Confidential interviews with Royal Thai Police, DEA special agent, Thailand, December 1975; U.S. House Committee on International Relations, *Narcotics Situation*, pp. 15–16, 31–32.

135. U.S. House Select Committee on Narcotics Abuse, *Southeast Asian Narcotics*, p. 145.

136. *Bangkok Post*, April 20, 1977.

137. *Christian Science Monitor*, April 5, 1978.

138. *Bangkok Post*, April 10, 1977.

139. *Far Eastern Economic Review*, April 28, 1978.

140. *Bangkok World*, June 16, 1977.

141. *Bangkok Post*, February 15, 1978; February 17, 1978.

142. *Far Eastern Economic Review*, April 25, 1978, June 2, 1978.

143. *Asiaweek* (Hong Kong), September 4, 1981; *Far Eastern Economic Review*, July 24, 1981.

144. *Asiaweek*, February 19, 1982; *Far Eastern Economic Review*, February 19, 1982; June 18, 1982.

145. *Far Eastern Economic Review*, February 19, 1982.

146. *Far Eastern Economic Review*, September 19, 1985; September 26, 1985.

147. U.S. State Department, Bureau of International Narcotics Matters, *International Narcotics Control Strategy Report* (1984), pp. 122–29; U.S. State Department, Bureau of International Narcotics Matters, *International Narcotics Control Strategy Report* (1990), pp. 324–34.

148. *Far Eastern Economic Review*, May 21, 1976; *Bangkok Post*, February 13, 1977.

149. *Far Eastern Economic Review*, August 25, 1988.

150. *Far Eastern Economic Review*, February 22, 1990.

151. *Far Eastern Economic Review*, January 14, 1974; April 15, 1974; May 23, 1975; October 3, 1975; January 6, 1978.

152. Chao Tzang Yawnghwe, *The Shan of Burma: Memoirs of a Shan Exile* (Singapore: Institute of Southeast Asian Studies, 1987), p. 204; *Far Eastern Economic Review*, August 6, 1987.

153. *Far Eastern Economic Review*, August 6, 1973; June 29, 1990; U.S. *Congressional Record*, 92nd Cong. 2nd sess., June 28, 1972, 118, no. 106, p. H6274; Bertil Lintner, *Land of Jade: A Journey Through Insurgent Burma* (Edinburgh: Kiscadale White Lotus, 1990), pp. 224–26.

154. Chao Tzang Yawnghwe, *Shan of Burma*, p. 189.

155. *Bangkok World*, June 16, 1977; *Bangkok Post*, February 17, 1978; *Far Eastern Economic Review*, April 28, 1978.

156. Shan State Army, "An Outline of the Political History of the Shan State from World War II to the Present," in U.S. House Committee on International Relations, *Proposal to Control Opium*, pp. 253–66.

157. Greg Huddleston, "The Politics of Pre-Emptive Purchase: Opium, Shan Liberation, and the United States," typescript (Sydney University, June 1978). Huddleston was a University of Sydney student who spent two months interviewing leading Shan rebels in Thailand and Burma in January and February 1978.

158. *Far Eastern Economic Review*, July 9, 1973.

159. *Far Eastern Economic Review*, August 6, 1973; Huddleston, "Politics of Pre-Emptive Purchase," pp. 3–4.

160. U.S. House Committee on International Relations, *Proposal to Control Opium*, pp. 16–17.

161. *Far Eastern Economic Review*, July 9, 1973; August 6, 1973.

162. Huddleston, "Politics of Pre-Emptive Purchase," p. 6.

163. Chao Tzang Yawnghwe, *Shan of Burma*, p. 204–5; *Far Eastern Economic Review*, June 1, 1989; June 28, 1990.

164. *Bangkok Post*, June 21, 1974.

165. U.S. House Select Committee on Narcotics Abuse and Control, *Opium Production*, pp. 55–58.

166. U.S. House Committee on International Relations, *Narcotics Situation,* pp. 9–14; U.S. House Committee on International Relations, *Proposal to Control Opium,* pp. 42–54.

167. *The Burma Committee* (Montreal) 4, no. 3 (Summer 1978), p. 4; Huddleston, "Politics of Pre-Emptive Purchase," pp. 12–13; *Bangkok Post,* February 13, 1977.

168. *Far Eastern Economic Review,* July 29, 1983.

169. *Far Eastern Economic Review,* May 21, 1976.

170. Confidential interview with DEA special agent, Thailand, December 1975.

171. *Far Eastern Economic Review,* April 15, 1977.

172. *Far Eastern Economic Review,* April 2, 1973.

173. *Far Eastern Economic Review,* April 16, 1973; October 18, 1974.

174. U.S. House Committee on International Relations, *Proposal to Control Opium,* p. 59; U.S. House Select Committee on Narcotics Abuse and Control, *Southeast Asian Narcotics,* pp. 2–3.

175. *The Guardian* (Rangoon), April 24, 1978; U.S. House Select Committee on Narcotics Abuse and Control, *Southeast Asian Narcotics,* pp. 9–33, 243–46; U.S. House Committee on International Relations, *Proposal to Control Opium,* p. 25.

176. Becker, "Footnotes on the Golden Triangle," p. 25.

177. *Far Eastern Economic Review,* May 10, 1984; *Asiaweek,* January 13, 1984.

178. *Far Eastern Economic Review,* January 20, 1983; August 13, 1987.

179. U.S. State Department, Bureau of International Narcotics Matters, *International Narcotics Control Strategy Report* (1984), p. 96.

180. *Far Eastern Economic Review,* May 10, 1984.

181. *Far Eastern Economic Review,* May 3, 1984; August 13, 1987.

182. *Far Eastern Economic Review,* September 6, 1984.

183. *Far Eastern Economic Review,* February 20, 1986; Chao Tzang Yawnghwe, *Shan of Burma,* p. 209.

184. *Far Eastern Economic Review,* April 16, 1987.

185. *Far Eastern Economic Review,* March 26, 1987.

186. *Far Eastern Economic Review,* May 22, 1986; August 13, 1987; June 28, 1990.

187. *Far Eastern Economic Review,* September 5, 1980; January 30, 1981.

188. U.S. State Department, Bureau of International Narcotics Matters, *International Narcotics Control Strategy Report* (1984), p. 112; U.S. State Department, Bureau of International Narcotics Matters, *International Narcotics Control Strategy Report* (1990), p. 300.

189. *Far Eastern Economic Review,* January 1, 1987.

190. *Far Eastern Economic Review,* June 1, 1989; June 22, 1989. A recent history of the Burmese Communist Party (BCP) explains its opium trading as a response to economic pressures from its patron, the Chinese Communist Party. During the 1970s the BCP's border zone contained some 80 percent of Burma's poppy lands but the party discouraged opium in order to increase food crops. When China reduced its aid in 1980, the BCP, like the KMT in the 1950s, took control of the local opium traffic to survive in these

rugged highlands. Officially, the BCP limited its involvement to collection of a 20 percent tax from opium farmers. In reality, the party dominated the drug trade in its zone by (1) collecting a 10 percent tax on local opium sales and a 5 percent tax on any exports from its zones; (2) transporting opium to Thai-Burma border refineries operated by Khun Sa and the KMT; (3) taxing Chinese syndicate heroin refineries operating in its zones; and (4) failing to discipline any BCP local commanders active in the traffic. In 1985 the BCP announced a death penalty for cadre involved in heroin trading, a decision prompted by the party's embarrassment at the scale of its drug dealing and China's objections to the transit of heroin across its territory to Hong Kong. The attempted suppression produced "severe frictions" between the party's aging leadership and local BCP commanders who were now opium warlords, thereby contributing to the BCP's collapse in 1989 (Bertil Lintner, *The Rise and Fall of the Communist Party of Burma (BCP)* [Ithaca: Southeast Asia Program, Cornell University, 1990], pp. 39–46).

191. *Far Eastern Economic Review,* February 20, 1986.

192. U.S. State Department, Bureau of International Narcotics Matters, *International Narcotics Control Strategy Report* (1990), p. 271.

193. *New York Times,* March 16, 1990.

194. *Far Eastern Economic Review,* June 28, 1990.

195. Ibid.; U.S. State Department, Bureau of International Narcotics Matters, *International Narcotics Control Strategy Report* (1990), p. 286.

# 9  CIA Complicity in the Global Drug Trade

1. *New York Times,* May 22, 1980.

2. Interview with Dr. David Musto, Madison, WI, May 12, 1990.

3. Ibid.

4. *New York Times,* May 22, 1990.

5. Ibid.

6. U.S. Drug Enforcement Administration, "Summary of Middle East Heroin Conference, December 6–7, 1979, John F. Kennedy International Airport," pp. 1–16 (Alan A. Block Archive on Organized Crime, Pennsylvania State University).

7. John T. Cusack, "Turkey Lifts the Poppy Ban," *Drug Enforcement* (Fall 1974), pp. 3–7.

8. William French Smith, "Drug Traffic Today: Challenge and Response," *Drug Enforcement* (Summer 1982), pp. 2–3.

9. U.S. Cabinet Committee on International Narcotics Control (CCINC), *World Opium Survey 1972* (Washington, DC: CCINC, 1972), p. A-7; U.S. State Department, Bureau of International Narcotics Matters, *International Narcotics Control Strategy Report* (Washington, DC: U.S. Government Printing Office, February 1984), p. 4.

10. Smith, "Drug Traffic Today," p. 3.

11. Ibid., pp. 2–5.

12. U.S. Comptroller General, *Controlling Drug Abuse: A Status Report* (Washington, DC: Comptroller General, March 1, 1988), p. 7.

13. Ibid., pp. 7–8.
14. U.S. State Department, Bureau of International Narcotics Matters, *International Narcotics Control Strategy Report* (1984), p. 4; U.S. State Department, Bureau of International Narcotics Matters, *International Narcotics Control Strategy Report, March 1990*, pub. no. 9749 (Washington, DC: U.S. Government Printing Office, March 1990), pp. 19–20.
15. U.S. Comptroller General, *Controlling Drug Abuse*, pp. 11–13.
16. Ibid., p. 6.
17. Ibid., p. 13.
18. *Daily News* (New York), June 25, 1990.
19. *Imperial Gazetteer of India: Provincial Series, North-West Frontier Province* (Calcutta: Superintendent of Government Printing, 1908), p. 25.
20. Barnett R. Rubin, "The Fragmentation of Afghanistan," *Foreign Affairs* 68, no. 5 (1989), pp. 150–68.
21. Thomas T. Hammond, *Red Flag over Afghanistan* (Boulder: Westview, 1984), pp. 4–6.
22. C. Colin Davies, *The Problem of the North-West Frontier, 1890–1908* (London: Curzon Press, 1932), pp. 26–28.
23. Arnold Keppel, *Gun-Running and the Indian North-West Frontier* (London: John Murray, 1911), pp. 141–49.
24. R. O. Christensen, "Tribesmen, Government, and Political Economy on the North-West Frontier," in Clive Dewey, ed., *Arrested Development in India: The Historical Dimension* (New Delhi: Manohar Publications, 1988), pp. 179–82.
25. Davies, *Problem of the North-West Frontier*, pp. 24–26.
26. *Report on the Administration of the Punjab and its Dependencies for the Year 1870–71* (Lahore: Government Civil Secretariat Press, 1871), p. cxxxiii.
27. *Imperial Gazetteer of India*, pp. 65–66.
28. *Imperial Gazetteer of India: Afghanistan and Nepal* (Calcutta: Superintendent of Government Printing, 1908), p. 30.
29. U.S. Central Intelligence Agency, Directorate of Intelligence, "Intelligence Memorandum: Narcotics in Iran," International Narcotics Series no. 13 (Washington, DC: Central Intelligence Agency, June 12, 1972), pp. 1–2.
30. U.S. CCINC, *World Opium Survey 1972*, p. A-11.
31. Garland H. Williams, "Opium Addiction in Iran," report to H. J. Anslinger, Commissioner of Narcotics, February 1, 1949, pp. 1–12 (Historical Collections and Labor Archives, Pennsylvania State University).
32. U.S. Central Intelligence Agency, "Intelligence Memorandum: Narcotics in Iran," pp. 2–3.
33. Harry J. Anslinger, letter to William J. Stibravy, Director, Office of International Economic and Social Affairs, United Nations, October 28, 1968 (Historical Collections and Labor Archives, Pennsylvania State University).

34. U.S. CCINC, *World Opium Survey 1972*, p. A-12.

35. U.S. Central Intelligence Agency, "Intelligence Memorandum: Narcotics in Iran," pp. 2–10.

36. Richard Helms, From: Amembassy Tehran; To: Department of State; Subject: Revised Narcotics Action Plan; Date: March 4, 1974; airgram, Department of State.

37. Richard Helms, From: Amembassy Tehran; To: SecState WashDC; R: 260919Z Nov 74; telegram, Department of State.

38. Richard Helms, From: Amembassy Tehran; TO: SecState Wash DC 2222; SUBJ: Narcotics Matters Related to Iran; R: 261315Z Jun 75; Department of State.

39. U.S. Central Intelligence Agency, memorandum, "Subject: Iran—An Opium Cornucopia," September 27, 1979.

40. Malthea Falco, "Asian Narcotics: The Impact on Europe," *Drug Enforcement* (February 1979), pp. 2–3; U.S. CCINC, *World Opium Survey 1972*, pp. A-7, A-14, A-17.

41. U.S. State Department, Bureau of International Narcotics Matters, *International Narcotics Control Strategy Report* (1984), pp. 4, 7–8.

42. Smith, "Drug Traffic Today," p. 2–3.

43. U.S. State Department, Bureau of International Narcotics Matters, *International Narcotics Control Strategy Report* (1984) pp. 4, 7–8.

44. U.S. State Department, Bureau of International Narcotics Matters, *International Narcotics Control Strategy Report* (1990), pp. 19–20.

45. Hammond, *Red Flag over Afghanistan*, pp. 98–99, 118–21.

46. Ibid., pp. 158–59.

47. Tariq Ali, *Can Pakistan Survive?* (New York: Penguin, 1983), pp. 133–40.

48. Hammond, *Red Flag over Afghanistan*, pp. 218–21.

49. Lawrence Lifschultz, "Dangerous Liaison: The CIA-ISI Connection," *Newsline* (Karachi), November 1989, p. 52.

50. Barnett R. Rubin, testimony before the House Foreign Affairs Committee, Subcommittee on Europe and the Middle East and Subcommittee on Asia and the Pacific, "Answers to Questions for Private Witnesses," March 7, 1990, p. 3–4.

51. Tariq Ali, *Can Pakistan Survive?*, pp. 164–68.

52. Barnett R. Rubin, "The Fragmentation of Afghanistan," p. 154.

53. Lifschultz, "Dangerous Liaison," pp. 49–54. Rubin, testimony before the House Subcommittee on Europe and the Middle East, p. 5.

54. Lifschultz, "Dangerous Liaison," pp. 49–54.

55. Steven Galster, "Biography: Hekmatyar, Gulbuddin," National Security Archives, Washington, DC, March 14, 1990; Tariq Ali, *Can Pakistan Survive?*, pp. 139–42.

56. John F. Burns, "Afghans: Now They Blame America," *New York Times Magazine*, February 4, 1990, p. 37.

57. Hammond, *Red Flag over Afghanistan*, p. 38.

58. Lifschultz, "Dangerous Liaison," pp. 51–52.

59. Ibid., pp. 52–53.

60. Lawrence Lifschultz, "Inside the Kingdom of Heroin," *The Nation* (New York), November 14, 1988, pp. 492–93.
61. Lifschultz, "Dangerous Liaison," pp. 52–53.
62. Ibid., pp. 53–54.
63. Rubin, testimony before the House Subcommittee on Europe and the Middle East, p. 29.
64. Burns, "Afghans," p. 37; *Washington Post*, May 13, 1990.
65. Ibid., pp. 27–28.
66. Rubin, "Fragmentation of Afghanistan," pp. 156–60.
67. *Washington Post*, May 13, 1990.
68. U.S. State Department, Bureau of International Narcotics Matters, *International Narcotics Control Strategy Report* (1984), p. 4.
69. Kathy Evans, "The Tribal Trail," *Newsline* (Karachi), December 1989, p. 26.
70. Lifschultz, "Inside the Kingdom of Heroin," pp. 495–96.
71. Rubin, testimony before the House Subcommittee on Europe and the Middle East, pp. 18–19; *Washington Post*, May 13, 1990.
72. *Washington Post*, May 13, 1990.
73. Pakistan Narcotics Control Board, *National Survey on Drug Abuse in Pakistan* (Islamabad: Narcotics Control Board, 1986), pp. iii, ix, 23, 308; Zahid Hussain, "Narcopower: Pakistan's Parallel Government?," *Newsline* (Karachi), December 1989, p. 17.
74. Richard Reeves, *Passage to Peshawar* (New York: Simon & Schuster, 1984), p. 159.
75. Hussain, "Narcopower," p. 14-b.
76. Lifschultz, "Inside the Kingdom of Heroin," pp. 492–95.
77. Lawrence Lifschultz, "Turning a Blind Eye?," *Newsline* (Karachi), December 1989, p. 32.
78. Ibid., p. 495.
79. Hussain, "Narcopower," p. 14-b.
80. *New York Times*, September 7, 1988.
81. *Far Eastern Economic Review*, August 10, 1989.
82. Hussain, "Narcopower," p. 14-b.
83. Lifschultz, "Turning a Blind Eye?," p. 32.
84. Hussain, "Narcopower," pp. 14-a, 14-b.
85. Ibid., pp. 14-a, 17.
86. Evans, "Tribal Trail," p. 24.
87. Rahimullah Yusufzai, "Poppy Polls," *Newsline* (Karachi), December 1989, p. 29.
88. U.S. State Department, Bureau of International Narcotics Matters, *International Narcotics Control Strategy Report* (1990), p. 239.
89. Rubin, testimony before the House Subcommittee on Europe and the Middle East, pp. 18–19.
90. Evans, "Tribal Trail," p. 30.
91. *New York Times*, June 18, 1986.
92. Rubin, testimony before the House Subcommittee on Europe and the Middle East, pp. 20, 35.

93. *Washington Post*, May 13, 1990.

94. *Time* (Australian edition), July 16, 1990, pp. 28–29.

95. Ibid.

96. *Washington Post*, May 13, 1990.

97. Jonathan Kwitny, *The Crimes of Patriots* (New York: Simon & Schuster, 1987), pp. 19–22; Commonwealth of Australia, Royal Commission of Inquiry into the Activities of the Nugan Hand Group, *Final Report, Volume 1* (Canberra: Australian Government Publishing Services, 1985), pp. 131–32, 525–26.

98. W. E. Colby, Executive Director, Central Intelligence Agency, Letter, *Harper's*, October 1972, pp. 116–18.

99. Kwitny, *Crimes of Patriots*, pp. 79–80.

100. *Sydney Morning Herald*, May 2, 1980; *National Times* (Sydney), August 17, 1980.

101. Australia Royal Commission, *Final Report, Volume 1*, pp. 50–52, 514–15.

102. Commonwealth of Australia–New South Wales, Joint Task Force on Drug Trafficking, *Report, Volume 2: Nugan Hand*, part 1 (Canberra: Australian Government Printer, June 1982), p. 289.

103. Commonwealth of Australia–New South Wales, Joint Task Force on Drug Trafficking, *Report, Volume 4: Nugan Hand*, part 2 (Canberra: Australian Government Printer, March 1983), pp. 675–77, 689–91.

104. Australia Royal Commission, *Final Report, Volume I*, pp. 64–65.

105. Australia–New South Wales Joint Task Force, *Report, Volume 4: Nugan Hand*, p. 676; Kwitny, *Crimes of Patriots*, p. 88.

106. Australasian and Pacific Holdings Limited, "Prospectus," September 15, 1969; List of Shareholders, May 18, 1970, N.S.W. Corporate Affairs Commission (Sydney).

107. Australia Royal Commission, *Final Report, Volume 1*, p. 403.

108. Australia–New South Wales Joint Task Force, *Report, Volume 4: Nugan Hand*, p. 670.

109. Kwitny, *Crimes of Patriots*, p. 59.

110. Australia–New South Wales Joint Task Force, *Report, Volume 2: Nugan Hand*, pp. 404–5.

111. Australia–New South Wales Joint Task Force, *Report, Volume 2: Nugan Hand*, p. 409.

112. Ibid., p. 441.

113. Australia Royal Commission, *Final Report, Volume 1*, pp. 409–11.

114. Australia–New South Wales Joint Task Force, *Report, Volume 4: Nugan Hand*, pp. 691–92; Kwitny, *Crimes of Patriots*, pp. 88–89.

115. Australia Royal Commission, *Final Report, Volume 1*, p. 407.

116. Ibid., pp. 408–9.

117. Nugan Hand Limited, Investment Bankers, Sydney, Australia, Annual Report, January 31, 1977.

118. Nugan Hand Bank, brochure, n.d.

119. Australia Royal Commission, *Final Report, Volume 1*, pp. 434–41; Kwitny, *Crimes of Patriots*, pp. 165–75.

120. Australia Royal Commission, *Final Report, Volume 1*, pp. 83–84.

121. Ibid., p. 98.

122. Kwitny, *Crimes of Patriots*, pp. 95–113.

123. N.S.W. Corporate Affairs Commission, *Seventh Interim Report of the Corporate Affairs Commission into the Affairs of Nugan Hand Limited and Other Companies*, vol. 2 (Sydney: Government Printer, New South Wales, 1983), pp. 649–52.

124. Kwitny, *Crimes of Patriots*, p. 113.

125. N.S.W. Corporate Affairs Commission, *Seventh Interim Report*, vol. 2, pp. 657–58.

126. Kwitny, *Crimes of Patriots*, p. 113.

127. Peter Maas, *Manhunt* (New York: Random House, 1986), pp. 50–53.

128. Kwitny, *Crimes of Patriots*, pp. 114–17; Australia–New South Wales Joint Task Force, *Report, Volume 4: Nugan Hand*, pp. 697–99.

129. Maas, *Manhunt*, p. 49.

130. Australia–New South Wales Joint Task Force, *Report, Volume 4: Nugan Hand*, pp. 704–6.

131. New South Wales Police, Crime Intelligence Unit, "Report to the Superintendent," March 1977, pp. 1–9.

132. Australia–New South Wales Joint Task Force, *Report, Volume 2: Nugan Hand*, p. 330.

133. Ibid., pp. 304–34, 484–86.

134. Ibid., p. 319–20.

135. Ibid., pp. 331–32.

136. Ibid., p. 442.

137. Australia Royal Commission, *Final Report, Volume 1*, pp. 72–73, 452–53.

138. N.S.W. Corporate Affairs Commission, *Seventh Interim Report*, vol. 2, pp. 530–31.

139. *Wall Street Journal*, August 24, 1982; *National Times* (Sydney), June 6, 1982.

140. Kwitny, *Crimes of Patriots*, pp. 161–64.

141. *Wall Street Journal*, April 18, 1980.

142. *National Times*, February 21, 1982.

143. N.S.W. Corporate Affairs Commission, *Seventh Interim Report*, vol. 2, pp. 535–37.

144. Ibid., pp. 536–53; Kwitny, *Crimes of Patriots*, pp. 261–71.

145. Kwitny, *Crimes of Patriots*, pp. 100–101.

146. Maas, *Manhunt*, pp. 61–63, 94–96.

147. Ibid., pp. 89–93, 122–23, 162–64.

148. Kwitny, *Crimes of Patriots*, 101–3.

149. Maas, *Manhunt*, pp. 6–9.

150. Ibid., pp. 108–9, 137–41.

151. Kwitny, *Crimes of Patriots*, pp. 291–92.

152. Australia–New South Wales Joint Task Force, *Report, Volume 4: Nugan Hand*, pp. 735–36.

153. N.S.W. Corporate Affairs Commission, *Seventh Interim Report,* vol. 2, pp. 558–59.

154. Australia–New South Wales Joint Task Force, *Report, Volume 4: Nugan Hand,* pp. 675–77, 736–37.

155. Maas, *Manhunt,* pp. 278–80.

156. Australia–New South Wales Joint Task Force, *Report, Volume 4: Nugan Hand,* pp. 736–37.

157. Maas, *Manhunt,* pp. 108–23.

158. Ibid., pp. 142–43.

159. Kwitny, *Crimes of Patriots,* pp. 312–13.

160. Australia–New South Wales Joint Task Force, *Report, Volume 4: Nugan Hand,* pp. 734–40.

161. Ibid., pp. 745–56; Kwitny, *Crimes of Patriots,* pp. 317–18.

162. Australia–New South Wales Joint Task Force, *Report, Volume 4: Nugan Hand,* pp. 679–82, 767–71.

163. Kwitny, *Crimes of Patriots,* pp. 71–72; Australia Royal Commission, *Final Report, Volume 1,* pp. 131–32.

164. Australia–New South Wales Joint Task Force, *Report, Volume 4: Nugan Hand,* p. 771.

165. Ibid., pp. 771–74.

166. *Sydney Morning Herald,* October 28, 1977; *The Bulletin* (Sydney), May 11, 1977.

167. Australia Royal Commission, *Final Report, Volume 1,* p. 478.

168. *The Australian* (Sydney), November 12/13, 1977.

169. Australia Royal Commission, *Final Report, Volume 1,* p. 191.

170. Ibid., p. 491.

171. Ibid., pp. 478–88.

172. *Australian Financial Review* (Sydney), May 29, 1978.

173. Australia Royal Commission, *Final Report, Volume 1,* pp. 50–51.

174. Kwitny, *Crimes of Patriots,* pp. 258–59.

175. *Wall Street Journal,* August 26, 1982.

176. Australia Royal Commission, *Final Report, Volume 1,* p. 520.

177. Ibid., p. 531.

178. Ibid., p. 533; Australia–New South Wales Joint Task Force, *Report, Volume 2: Nugan Hand,* pp. 411–15.

179. Australia–New South Wales Joint Task Force, *Report, Volume 4: Nugan Hand,* pp. 744–45.

180. Ibid., pp. 86–89, 91–92.

181. Interview with John Willis, special investigator, N.S.W. Corporate Affairs Commission, Sydney, July 16, 1990.

182. Australia Royal Commission, *Final Report, Volume 1,* pp. 557–58.

183. Australia–New South Wales Joint Task Force, *Report, Volume 4: Nugan Hand,* pp. 747–48.

184. Ibid., pp. 778–79; *Report, Volume 2: Nugan Hand,* pp. 467–73.

185. Maas, *Manhunt,* pp. 281–89.

186. Ibid., pp. 138–39, 278–80.
187. Richard Helms, quoted in W. E. Colby, letter, *Harper's*, October 1972, p. 118.
188. William Colby, *Honorable Men: My Life in the CIA* (New York: Simon & Schuster, 1978), pp. 196–98.
189. Maas, *Manhunt*, pp. 278–79.
190. Smith, "Drug Traffic Today," pp. 2–5.
191. U.S. Comptroller General, *Controlling Drug Abuse*, pp. 7–9, 11.
192. Ibid., pp. 7–8.
193. U.S. Congress, Senate, Committee on Foreign Relations, Subcommittee on Terrorism, Narcotics, and International Operations, *Drugs, Law Enforcement, and Foreign Policy*, 100th Cong., 2nd sess. (Washington, DC: U.S. Government Printing Office, December 1988), report, pp. 26–29.
194. *Forbes*, July 25, 1988, p. 64.
195. U.S. Senate Committee on Foreign Relations, *Drugs, Law Enforcement, and Foreign Policy*, report, p. 37.
196. Ibid., p. 39.
197. Ibid., p. 38.
198. Ibid., p. 36.
199. Ibid., pp. 53–58.
200. Christic Institute, *Inside the Shadow Government* (Washington, DC: Christic Institute, June 1988), pp. 100–14.
201. U.S. Senate Committee on Foreign Relations, *Drugs, Law Enforcement, and Foreign Policy*, report, pp. 73–75.
202. Ibid., pp. 39–40.
203. Ibid., p. 41.
204. Ibid., p. 49.
205. Ibid., p. 50.
206. Ibid., p. 49.
207. Ibid., p. 51.
208. Ibid., p. 49.
209. Ibid., p. 53.
210. Ibid., p. 53.
211. Ibid., pp. 53–54.
212. Kwitny, *Crimes of Patriots*, pp. 310–12.
213. U.S. Senate Committee on Foreign Relations, *Drugs, Law Enforcement, and Foreign Policy*, report, pp. 53–54.
214. Ibid., pp. 53–54.
215. Ibid., pp. 54–55.
216. Ibid., pp. 55–56.
217. Ibid., pp. 42–49.
218. Ibid., p. 75.
219. *The Washington Post*, December 7, 1987.
220. Mort Rosenblum, "Hidden Agendas," *Vanity Fair*, March 1990, p. 120.

# Bibliography

## Articles and Theses

Ackland, Len, "No Place for Neutralism: The Eisenhower Administration and Laos," in Nina S. Adams and Alfred W. McCoy, eds., *Laos: War and Revolution* (New York: Harper & Row, 1970).

Adshead, S. A. M., "The Opium Trade in Szechwan, 1881–1911," *Journal of Southeast Asian History* 7, no. 2 (September 1966).

Aimé-Blanc, Lucien, Chief, Marseille Narcotics Office, Service Régional de Police Judiciaire, "France," *Drug Enforcement* (Winter 1975–76).

Anderson, Major Richard, and Wade Hawley, "Subject: Analysis of 482 Questionnaires on Illicit Drug Use in an Engineering Battalion in Vietnam" (November 11, 1970).

Annan, David, "The Mafia," in Norman MacKenzie, *Secret Societies* (New York: Collier, 1967).

Anon Puntharikapha, "The 'Manhattan' Incident," in Thak Chaloemtiarana, ed., *Thai Politics: Extracts and Documents, 1932–1957* (Bangkok: Social Science Association of Thailand, 1978).

Antonelli, Michael A., "Asian Heroin on the Rise in Europe," *Drug Enforcement* (Summer 1975).

Archaimbault, Charles, "Les Annales de l'ancien Royaume de S'ieng Khwang," *Bulletin de l'Ecole française d'Extrême-Orient* (1967).

Bacon, John, "Is the French Connection Really Dead?" *Drug Enforcement* (Summer 1981).

Barnes, Trevor, "The Secret Cold War: The C.I.A. and American Foreign Policy in Europe, 1946–1956," part 1, *Historical Journal* 24, no. 2 (1981).

Batson, Benjamin A., "The Fall of the Phibun Government, 1944," *Journal of the Siam Society* 62, part 2 (July 1974).

Bayley, David H., "The Effects of Corruption in a Developing Nation," *Western Political Science Quarterly* 19, no. 4 (December 1966).

Becker, Thomas H., Asian Heroin Section, Office of Intelligence, Drug Enforcement Administration, "Footnote on the Golden Triangle," *Drug Enforcement* (Summer 1981).

Berrigan, Darrell, "They Smuggle Dope by the Ton," *Saturday Evening Post*, May 5, 1956.

Block, Alan A., "European Drug Traffic and Traffickers Between the

Wars: The Policy of Suppression and Its Consequences," *Journal of Social History* 23, no. 2 (1989).

Block, Alan A., "A Modern Marriage of Convenience: A Collaboration Between Organized Crime and U.S. Intelligence," in Robert J. Kelly, ed., *Organized Crime: A Global Perspective* (Totowa, NJ: Rowman & Littlefield, 1986).

Block, Alan A., "On the Origins of American Counterintelligence: Building a Clandestine Network," *Journal of Policy History* 1, no. 4 (1989).

Block, Alan A., "The Snowman Cometh: Coke in Progressive New York," *Criminology* 17, no. 1 (1979).

Block, Alan A., "Thinking About Violence and Change in the Sicilian Mafia," *Violence, Aggression, and Terrorism* 1, no. 1 (1987).

Boutin, André, "Monographie de la Province des Houa-Phans," *Bulletin des Amis du Laos*, no. 1 (September 1937).

Braden, Thomas, "I'm Glad the C.I.A. Is 'Immoral,'" *Saturday Evening Post*, May 20, 1967.

Braibanti, Ralph, "Reflections on Bureaucratic Corruption," *Public Administration* 40 (London), (Winter 1962).

Branfman, Fred, "Presidential War in Laos, 1964–1970," in Nina S. Adams and Alfred W. McCoy, eds., *Laos: War and Revolution* (New York: Harper & Row, 1970).

British Broadcasting Corporation (BBC), interview with Sisouk na Champassak, Vientiane, Laos, 1970.

Brocheaux, Pierre, "L'Economie et la Société dans l'Quest de la Cochinchine pendant la Periode coloniale (1890–1940)," (Ph.D. thesis, University of Paris, 1969).

Burns, John F., "Afghans: Now They Blame America," *New York Times Magazine*, February 4, 1990.

Butcher, John G., "The Demise of the Revenue Farm System in the Federated Malay States," *Modern Asian Studies* 17, no. 3 (1983).

Cheng U Wen, "Opium in the Straits Settlements, 1867–1910," *Journal of Southeast Asian History* 2, no. 1 (March 1961).

Christensen, R. O., "Tribesmen, Government, and Political Economy on the North-West Frontier," in Clive Dewey, ed., *Arrested Development in India: The Historical Dimension* (New Delhi: Manohar Publications, 1988).

Cohen, Paul T., "Hill Trading in the Mountain Ranges of Northern Thailand," typescript (1968).

Colby, W. E., Executive Director, Central Intelligence Agency, Letter, *Harper's* (October 1972).

Cowell, Adrian, "Report on a Five Month Journey in the State of Kengtung with the Shan National Army," typescript (1965).

Cribb, Robert, "Opium and the Indonesian Revolution," *Modern Asian Studies* 22, no. 4 (1988).

Cusack, John T., Director, International Operations Division, Office of Enforcement, Drug Enforcement Administration, "Turkey Lifts the Poppy Ban," *Drug Enforcement* (Fall 1974).

Darling, Frank C., "Thailand in 1977: Search for Stability and Progress," *Asian Survey* 18, no. 2 (February 1978).

Dessaint, Alain Y., "The Poppies Are Beautiful This Year," *Natural History* (February 1972).

Donovan, William J., "Our Stake in Thailand," *Fortune* (July 1955).

Dorsey, John T., Jr., "Stresses and

Strains in a Developing Administrative System," in Wesley R. Fishel, ed., *Problems of Freedom: South Vietnam Since Independence* (Glencoe, IL: Free Press, 1961).

"The Drug Abuse Problem," Report of the Office of the Provost Marshal, U.S. Military Assistance Command Vietnam (Saigon, 1971).

Dumarest, Jacques, "Les Monopoles de l'Opium et du Sel en Indochine" (Ph.D. thesis, Université de Lyon, 1938).

Evans, Kathy, "The Tribal Trail," *Newsline* (Karachi) (December 1989).

Everingham, John, "Let Them Eat Bombs," *Washington Monthly* (September 1972).

Falco, Malthea, Senior Adviser to the Secretary of State, Director for International Narcotics Control Matters, State Department, "Asian Narcotics: The Impact on Europe," *Drug Enforcement* (February 1979).

Fall, Bernard B., "Portrait of the 'Centurion,'" in Roger Trinquier, *Modern Warfare* (New York: Praeger, 1964).

Fishel, Wesley R., "Problems of Democratic Growth in Free Vietnam," in Wesley R. Fishel, ed., *Problems of Freedom: South Vietnam Since Independence* (Glencoe, IL: Free Press, 1961).

Flanders, Joe, U.S. Drug Enforcement Administration Paris, "Bad Year for French Heroin Traffickers," *Drug Enforcement* (February–March 1974).

Flanders, Joe, U.S. Drug Enforcement Administration Paris, "The Key to Success: Franco-American Cooperation," *Drug Enforcement* (Fall 1973).

Forbes, Andrew D. W., "The 'Cin-Ho' (Yunnanese Chinese) Caravan Trade with North Thailand During the Late Nineteenth and Early Twentieth Centuries," *Journal of Asian History* 21, no. 1 (1987).

Forbes, Andrew D. W., "The Yunnanese ('Ho') Muslims of North Thailand," in Andrew D. W. Forbes, ed., *The Muslims of Thailand*, vol. 1: *Historical and Cultural Studies* (Gaya, Bihar, India: Centre for South East Asian Studies, 1988).

French, Cherrie, "The Adventures of Gordon Young," *Sawaddi* 6, no. 3 (January–February 1968).

Geddes, W. R., "Hmong Opium and Attempts to Replace It," Seminar: The Asian Opium Trade, Center for Asian Studies, University of Sydney, October 20, 1978.

Geddes, W. R., "Opium and the Miao: A Study in Ecological Adjustment," *Oceania* 41, no. 1 (September 1970).

Gibson, Richard M., Special Assistant, Office of International Narcotics Control Matters, State Department, "Hilltribes of the Golden Triangle," *Drug Enforcement* (February 1979).

Grandstaff, Terry B., "The Hmong, Opium, and the Haw: Speculations on the Origin of Their Association," *Journal of the Siam Society* 71, no. 2 (1979).

Gunn, Geoffrey C., "Shamans and Rebels: The Batchai (Meo) Rebellion of Northern Laos and North-West Vietnam (1918–1921), *Journal of the Siam Society* 74 (1986).

"Guns, Drugs and the CIA," reported by Judy Woodruff, produced by Andrew and Leslie Cockburn, *Frontline*, Documentary Consortium, WGBH, Boston, 1988.

Halpern, Joel, "The Role of the Chinese in Lao Society," *Journal of the Siam Society* 49, part 1 (July 1961).

Hood, Charles E. "Vang Pao Guerrilla General," *The Sunday Missoulian* (Missoula, Montana), November 21, 1976.

Huddleston, Greg, "The Politics of Pre-Emptive Purchase: Opium, Shan Liberation, and the United States," typescript (Sydney University, June 1978).

Hussain, Zahid, "Narcopower: Pakistan's Parallel Government?," *Newsline* (Karachi), December 1989.

"The Illicit Manufacture of Diacetylmorphine Hydrochloride (No. 4 Grade)," paper of a Hong Kong government chemist, typescript (n.d.).

Ismail, Abdul Rahman bin H. J., "The Prevention of Drug Abuse in Malaysia: Intelligence, Enforcement, and Control" (Genting Highlands: National Workshop on the Prevention of Drug Abuse, 1975).

Jerusalemy, Jean, "Monographie sur le Pays Tai," typescript (n.d.).

Jones, Delmos, "Cultural Variation Among Six Lahu Villages, Northern Thailand" (Ph.D. thesis, Cornell University, 1967).

Jumper, Roy, "Mandarin Bureaucracy and Politics in South Vietnam," *Pacific Affairs* 30, no. 1 (March 1957).

Kandre, Peter, "Autonomy and Integration of Social Systems: The Iu Mien ('Yao' or 'Man') Mountain Population and Their Neighbors," in Peter Kunstadter, ed., *Southeast Asian Tribes, Minorities, and Nations* (Princeton: Princeton University Press, 1967).

Karnow, Stanley, "The Opium Must Go Through," *Life*, August 30, 1963.

Khana Ratthamontri, "The History and Works of Field Marshal Sarit Thanarat," in Thak Chaloemtiarana, ed., *Thai Politics: Extracts and Documents, 1932–1957* (Bangkok: Social Science Association of Thailand, 1978).

Kim Khanh, Huynh, "Background of the Vietnamese August Revolution," *Journal of Asia Studies* 25, no. 4 (August 1971).

Kinder, Douglas Clark, and William O. Walker, III, "Stable Force in a Storm: Harry J. Anslinger and United States Narcotic Policy, 1930–1962," *Journal of American History* 72, no. 4 (March 1986).

Kraar, Louis, "Report from Laos," *Fortune*, September 1, 1968.

Kramol Somvichian, "The Oyster and the Shell: Thai Bureaucrats in Politics," *Asian Survey* 18, no. 8 (August 1978).

Kunstadter, Peter, "China: Introduction," in Peter Kunstadter, ed., *Southeast Asian Tribes, Minorities, and Nations* (Princeton: Princeton University Press, 1967).

Kunstadter, Peter, "Vietnam: Introduction," in Peter Kunstadter, ed., *Southeast Asian Tribes, Minorities, and Nations* (Princeton: Princeton University Press, 1967).

Kusevic, Vladimir, "Drug Abuse Control and International Treaties," *Journal of Drug Issues* 7, no. 1 (Winter 1977).

Leff, Nathaniel H., "Economic Development Through Bureaucratic Corruption," *American Behavioral Scientist* 8, no. 3 (November 1964).

Lehman, F. K., "Ethnic Categories in Burma and the Theory of Social Systems," in Peter Kunstadter, ed.,

*Southeast Asian Tribes, Minorities, and Nations* (Princeton: Princeton University Press, 1967).

Lewallen, John, "The Reluctant Counterinsurgents: The International Voluntary Services in Laos," in Nina S. Adams and Alfred W. McCoy, eds., *Laos: War and Revolution* (New York: Harper & Row, 1970).

Lewis, Elaine T., "The Hill Peoples of Kengtung State," *Practical Anthropology* 4, no. 6 (November–December 1957).

Lifschultz, Lawrence, "Dangerous Liaison: The CIA-ISI Connection," *Newsline* (Karachi) (November 1989).

Lifschultz, Lawrence, "Inside the Kingdom of Heroin," *The Nation* (New York), November 14, 1988.

Lifschultz, Lawrence, "Turning a Blind Eye?," *Newsline* (Karachi) (December 1989).

Lulenski, Capt. Gary C., Larry E. Alessi, and Charles E. Burdick, "Drug Abuse in the 23rd Infantry Division (Americal)," typescript, (September 1970).

Lyle, John P., Bureau of International Narcotics Matters, State Department, "Southwest Asian Heroin: Pakistan, Afghanistan, and Iran," *Drug Enforcement* (Summer 1981).

McAlister, John T., "Mountain Minorities and the Viet Minh: A Key to the Indochina War," in Peter Kunstadter, ed., *Southeast Asian Tribes, Minorities, and Nations* (Princeton: Princeton University Press, 1967).

McCoy, Alfred W., "A Correspondence with the CIA," *New York Review of Books*, September 21, 1972.

McCoy, Alfred W., "The Politics of the Poppy in Indochina: A Comparative Study of Patron-Client Relations Under French and American Administrations," in Luiz R. S. Simmons and Abdul S. Said, eds., *Drugs, Politics, and Diplomacy: The International Connection* (Beverly Hills: Sage, 1974).

McCoy, Alfred W., "Subcontracting Counterinsurgency: Academics in Thailand, 1954–1970," *Bulletin of Concerned Asian Scholars* (December 1970).

McCoy, Alfred W., "A Tale of Three Cities: Hanoi, Saigon, and Phnom Penh," *Geo* (Sydney) 5, no. 2 (1983).

McWilliams, John C., *The Protectors: Harry J. Anslinger and the Federal Bureau of Narcotics, 1930–1962* (Newark, Delaware: University of Delaware Press, 1960).

Matray, James I., "Bureaucratic Cold Warrior: Harry J. Anslinger and Illicit Narcotics Traffic," *Pacific Historical Review* 50, no. 2 (May 1981).

Miles, Douglas, "Shifting Cultivation: Threats and Prospects," in *Tribesmen and Peasants in North Thailand*, Proceedings of the First Symposium of the Tribal Research Center (Chiangmai, Thailand: Tribal Research Center, 1967).

Moormann, F. R., K.R.M. Anthony, and Samarn Panichapong, "No. 20: Note on the Soils and Land Use in the Hills of Tak Province," in *Soil Survey Reports of the Land Development Department* (Bangkok: Kingdom of Thailand, Ministry of National Development, March 1964).

Mote, F. W., "The Rural 'Haw' (Yunnanese Chinese) of Northern Thailand," in Peter Kunstadter, ed.,

*Southeast Asian Tribes, Minorities, and Nations* (Princeton: Princeton University Press, 1967).

Murphey, Rhoads, "Traditionalism and Colonialism: Changing Urban Roles in Asia," *Journal of Asian Studies* 29, no. 1 (November 1969).

O'Kearney, John, "Thai Becomes Opium Center for SE Asia," *Daily News* (New York), February 13, 1955.

Phin Choonhawan, "Events in the Life of Field Marshal Phin Chunnahawan," in Thak Chaloemtiarana, ed., *Thai Politics: Extracts and Documents, 1932–1957* (Bangkok: Social Science Association of Thailand, 1978).

Porter, D. Gareth, "After Geneva: Subverting Laotian Neutrality," in Nina S. Adams and Alfred W. McCoy, eds., *Laos: War and Revolution* (New York: Harper & Row, 1970).

Porter, D. Gareth, "National Assembly Racked by Corruption and Smuggling," *Dispatch News Service International*, April 19, 1971.

Porter, D. Gareth, "Premier Khiem's Family Mafia," *Indochina Chronicle*, no. 18 (August 1, 1972).

Prasert Rujirawong, "Kanluk Supfin" (Abolishing Opium Smoking), in Khana Ratthamontri, *Prawat lae phonngan khong jomphon Sarit Thanarat, phim nai ngan phraratchathan pleong sop phon jomphon Sarit Thanarat* (The Life and Works of Field Marshal Sarit Thanarat, Published on the Occasion of the Cremation of Field Marshal Sarit Thanarat) (Bangkok: Prime Minister's Office, 1964).

Race, Jeffrey, "China and the War in Northern Thailand," typescript (1971).

Reynolds, E. Bruce, "The Fox in the Cabbage Patch: Thailand and Japan's Southern Advance," paper prepared for presentation at the annual meeting of Asian Studies on the Pacific Coast, Honolulu, July 1, 1989.

Richards, J. F., "The Indian Empire and Peasant Production of Opium in the Nineteenth Century," *Modern Asian Studies* 15, no. 1 (1981).

Rosenblum, Mort, "Hidden Agendas," *Vanity Fair*, March 1990.

Roux, Henri, "Les Meo ou Miao Tseu," *France-Asie*, nos. 92–93 (January–February 1954).

Rubin, Barnett R., "The Fragmentation of Afghanistan," *Foreign Affairs* 68, no. 5 (1989).

Rush, James R., "Opium in Java: A Sinister Friend," *Journal of Asian Studies* 44, no. 3 (1985).

Rush, James R., "Social Control and Influence in Nineteenth Century Indonesia: Opium Farms and the Chinese of Java," *Indonesia* 35 (1983).

Savini, A. M., Chef de Bataillon, "Notes sur les Binh Xuyen," typescript (December 1945).

Savini, Antoine, "Notes sur le Phat Giao Hoa Hao," typescript (n.d.).

Savini, F. M., "Rapport Politique sur la Revolte des Meos au Tonkin et au Laos, 1918–1920," typescript (Xieng Khoung, April 17, 1920).

Scheer, Robert, "Hang Down Your Head Tom Dooley," in *A Muckraker's Guide* (San Francisco: Ramparts Magazine, 1969).

Scott, James C., "Patron-Client Politics and Political Change in Southeast Asia," *American Political Science Review* 66, no. 1 (March 1972).

Scott, Peter Dale, "Air America: Flying the U.S. into Laos," in Nina S.

Adams and Alfred W. McCoy, eds., *Laos: War and Revolution* (New York: Harper & Row, 1970).

Shan State Army, "An Outline of the Political History of the Shan State from World War II to the Present," in U.S. Congress, House, Committee on International Relations, *Proposal to Control Opium from the Golden Triangle and Terminate the Shan Opium Trade*, 94th Cong., 1st sess. (Washington DC: U.S. Government Printing Office, 1975).

Shan State Progress Party, Central Executive Committee, "Communiqué," September 1971.

Shan Unity Preparatory Committee, "Communiqué No. 5," (Shan State, March 14, 1968).

Shochurek, Howard, "Americans in Action," *National Geographic* (January 1965).

Silverstein, Josef, "Politics in the Shan State: The Question of Secession from the Union of Burma," *Journal of Asian Studies* 18, no. 1 (November 1958).

Smith, William French, U.S. Attorney General, "Drug Traffic Today: Challenge and Response," *Drug Enforcement* (Summer 1982).

Spence, Jonathan, "Opium Smoking in Ch'ing China," Honolulu: Conference on Local Control and Protest During the Ching Period, 1971.

Stelle, Charles C., "American Trade in Opium to China in the Nineteenth Century," *Pacific Historical Review* 9 (December 1940).

Stelle, Charles C., "American Trade in Opium to China, 1821–39," *Pacific Historical Review* 10 (March 1941).

Swank, Irvin C., Director, Special Action Office for Mexico, Drug Enforcement Administration, "North American Heroin," *Drug Enforcement* (February 1977).

Tan Chung, "The Britain-China-India Trade Triangle, 1771–1840," in Sabyasachi Bhattacharya, ed., *Essays in Modern Indian Economic History* (New Delhi: Munshiram Manoharlal Publishers, 1987).

Thak Chaloemtiarana, "On Coups d'Etat," in Thak Chaloemtiarana, ed., *Thai Politics: Extracts and Documents, 1932–1957* (Bangkok: Social Science Association of Thailand, 1978).

Thaung, Dr., "Panthay Interlude in Yunnan: A Study in Vicissitudes Through the Burmese Kaleidoscope," *Burmese Research Society Fiftieth Anniversary Publication*, no. 1 (1961).

Tilman, Robert O., "Emergence of Black-Market Bureaucracy: Administration, Development, and Corruption in New States," *Public Administration Review* 28, no. 5 (September–October 1968).

Trocki, Carl A., "The Rise of Singapore's Great Opium Syndicate, 1840–86," *Journal of Southeast Asian Studies* 18, no. 1 (1987).

U.S. Drug Enforcement Administration, "The Heroin Labs of Marseille," *Drug Enforcement* (Fall 1973).

U.S. Drug Enforcement Administration, Office of Intelligence, "Heroin Seized in Europe During 1978," *Drug Enforcement* (February 1979).

U.S. Drug Enforcement Administration, Office of Intelligence, International Intelligence Division, "People's Republic of China and Narcotic Drugs," *Drug Enforcement* (Fall 1974).

Wang, Y. C., "Tu Yueh-sheng (1888–1951): A Tentative Political Biography," *Journal of Asian Studies* 26, no. 3 (May 1967).

Ward, J. Thomas, "U.S. Aid to Hill Tribe Refugees in Laos," in Peter Kunstadter, ed., *Southeast Asian Tribes, Minorities, and Nations* (Princeton: Princeton University Press, 1967).

Weiler, Peter, "The United States, International Labor, and the Cold War: The Breakup of the World Federation of Trade Unions," *Diplomatic History* 5, no. 1 (1981).

Wertheim, W. F., "Sociological Aspects of Corruption in Southeast Asia," in W. F. Wertheim, ed., *East-West Parallels* (Chicago: Quadrangle, 1964).

Westermeyer, Joseph John, "The Use of Alcohol and Opium Among Two Ethnic Groups in Laos" (M.A. thesis, University of Minnesota, 1968).

Wicinski, Laura, M., Europe/Middle East Heroin Section, Office of Intelligence, Drug Enforcement Administration, "Europe Awash with Heroin," *Drug Enforcement* (Summer 1981).

Wilson, Constance M., "State and Society in the Reign of Mongkut, 1851–1868: Thailand on the Eve of Modernization" (Ph.D. thesis, Cornell University, 1970).

Wolff, Lester L., et al., Special Study Mission to Southeast Asia, U.S. House Committee on Foreign Affairs, "The Narcotics Situation in Southeast Asia," *Drug Enforcement* (Summer 1975).

Yegar, Moshe, "The Panthay (Chinese Muslims) of Burma and Yunnan," *Journal of Southeast Asian Studies* 7, no. 1 (March 1966).

Yusufzai, Rahimullah, "Poppy Polls," *Newsline* (Karachi) (December 1989).

Zinberg, Norman E., "GIs and OJs in Vietnam," *New York Times Magazine,* December 5, 1971.

Zinke, Paul J., Sanga Savuhasri, and Peter Kunstadter, "Soil Fertility Aspects of the Lua Forest Fallow System of Shifting Cultivation," Seminar on Shifting Cultivation and Economic Development in Northern Thailand, Chiangmai, Thailand, January 18–24, 1970.

## Books

Agulhon, Maurice, and Fernand, Barrat, *C.R.S. Marseille* (Paris: Armand Colin, 1971).

Ali, Tariq, *Can Pakistan Survive?* (New York: Penguin, 1983)

Anderson, John, M.D., *Mandalay to Momien: A Narrative of the Two Expeditions to Western China of 1868 and 1879 Under Colonel Edward B. Sladen and Colonel Horace Browne* (London: Macmillan, 1876).

Anslinger, Harry J., *The Murderers* (New York: Farrar, Straus & Cudahy, 1961)

Anslinger, Harry J., *The Protectors* (New York: Farrar, Straus, 1964).

Aron, Robert, *France Reborn* (New York: Scribner's, 1964).

Association Culturelle pour le Salut du Viet-Nam, *Témoinages et Documents français relatifs à la Colonisation française au Viet-Nam* (Hanoi, 1945).

Avineri, Shlomo, *Karl Marx on Colonialism and Modernization* (Garden City, NY: Doubleday, 1969).

Ayme, G., *Monographie de Vᵉ Territoire militaire* (Hanoi: Imprimerie d'Extrême-Orient, 1930).

Barnett, A. Doak, *China on the Eve of Communist Takeover* (New York: Praeger, 1963).

Baudoin, Madeleine, *Histoire des Groups francs (M.U.R.) des Bouches-du-Rhone* (Paris: Presses Universitaires de France, 1962).

Bennington-Cornell Anthropological Survey of the Hill Tribes in Thailand, *A Report on Tribal Peoples of Chiangrai Province North of the Mae Kok River* (Bangkok: Siam Society, 1964).

Bernard, Paule, *Lotus, Opium, et Kimonos* (Paris: Robert Laffont, 1959).

Bernatzik, Hugo Adolph, *Akha and Meo* (New Haven: Human Relations Area Files Press, 1970).

Blanchard, Wendell, *Thailand, Its People, Its Society, Its Culture* (New Haven: Human Relations Area Files Press, 1958).

Block, Alan A., *East Side–West Side: Organizing Crime in New York, 1930–1950* (New Brunswick, NJ: Transaction Books, 1983).

Blok, Anton, *The Mafia of a Sicilian Village, 1860–1960: A Study of Violent Peasant Entrepreneurs* (New York: Harper & Row, 1975).

Boddard, Lucien, *L'Humiliation* (Paris: Gallimard, 1965).

Boddard, Lucien, *The Quicksand War: Prelude to Vietnam* (Boston: Little, Brown, 1967).

Boorman, Howard L., ed., *Biographical Dictionary of Republican China* (New York: Columbia University Press, 1970).

Boyle, John Hunter, *China and Japan at War, 1937–1945* (Stanford: Stanford University Press, 1972).

Brailey, Nigel J., *Thailand and the Fall of Singapore: A Frustrated Asian Revolution* (Boulder: Westview, 1986).

Branfman, Fred, ed., *Voices from the Plain of Jars* (New York: Harper & Row, 1972).

Brown, Anthony Cave, *The Last Hero: Wild Bill Donovan* (New York: Times Books, 1982).

Burchett, Wilfred, *Mekong Upstream* (Hanoi: Red River Publishing House, 1957).

Buttinger, Joseph, *Vietnam: A Dragon Embattled* (New York: Praeger, 1967).

Campbell, Rodney, *The Luciano Project: The Secret Wartime Collaboration of the Mafia and the U.S. Navy* (New York: McGraw-Hill, 1977).

Caply, Michel, *Guérilla au Laos* (Paris: Presses de la Cité, 1966).

Castellari, Gabrielle, *La Belle Histoire de Marseille* (Marseille: L'Ecole Technique Don Bosco, 1968).

Chao Tzang Yawnghwe, *The Shan of Burma: Memoirs of a Shan Exile* (Singapore: Institute of Southeast Asian Studies, 1987).

Chennault, Claire Lee, *Way of a Fighter: The Memoirs of Claire Lee Chennault* (New York: Putnam's, 1949).

Choury, Maurice, *La Résistance en Corse* (Paris: Editions Sociales, 1958).

Christic Institute, *Inside the Shadow Government* (Washington, DC: Christic Institute, June 1988).

Clark, Arthur H., *The Clipper Ship Era: An Epitome of Famous American and British Clipper Ships, Their Owners, Builders, Commanders, and Crews, 1853–1869* (New York: Putnam's, 1910).

Colby, William, *Honorable Men: My*

*Life in the CIA* (New York: Simon & Schuster, 1978).

Coles, Harry L., and Albert K. Weinberg, *United States Army in World War II. Civil Affairs: Soldiers Become Governors* (Washington, DC: Office of the Chief of Military History, Department of the Army, U.S. Government Printing Office, 1964).

Cooper, Chester L., *The Lost Crusade* (New York: Dodd, Mead, 1970).

Corson, William R., *The Armies of Ignorance: The Rise of the American Intelligence Empire* (New York: Dial, 1977).

Corvo, Max, *The O.S.S. in Italy, 1942–1945: A Personal Memoir* (New York: Praeger, 1990).

Costello, John, *The Pacific War, 1941–1945* (New York: Rawson Wade, 1981).

Costin, W. C., *Great Britain and China* (Oxford: Oxford University Press, 1937).

Courtwright, David T., *Dark Paradise: Opiate Addiction in America Before 1940* (Cambridge: Harvard University Press, 1982).

Courtwright, David, et al., *Addicts Who Survived: An Oral History of Narcotic Use in America, 1923–1965* (Knoxville: University of Tennessee Press, 1989).

Critchfield, Richard, *The Long Charade* (New York: Harcourt, Brace and World, 1968).

*The Cyclopedia of American Biography* (New York: James T. White, 1963), vol. 46.

Darling, Frank C., *Thailand and the United States* (Washington, DC: Public Affairs Press, 1965).

Davies, C. Colin, *The Problem of the North-West Frontier, 1890–1908* (London: Curzon Press, 1932).

De Quincey, Thomas, *Confessions of an English Opium-Eater and Other Writings* (New York: Signet, 1966).

Devillers, Philippe, *Histoire de Vietnam de 1940 à 1952* (Paris: Editions du Seuil, 1952).

Devillers, Philippe, and Jean Lacouture, *End of a War* (New York: Praeger, 1969).

Dolci, Danilo, *Report from Palermo* (New York: Viking, 1970).

Dommen, Arthur J., *Conflict in Laos* (New York: Praeger, 1971).

Dooley, Thomas, M.D., *Deliver Us from Evil* (New York: Farrar, Straus and Cudahy, 1956).

Doumer, Paul, *Situation de l'Indochine, 1897–1901*, Hanoi: F. H. Schneider, 1902).

Duncanson, Dennis J., *Government and Revolution in South Vietnam* (London: Oxford University Press, 1968).

Dunn, Wie T., *The Opium Traffic in Its International Aspects* (New York: Columbia University, 1920).

Evans, Grant, *The Yellow Rainmakers* (London: Verso, 1983).

Fairbank, John K., *Trade and Diplomacy on the China Coast: The Opening of the Treaty Ports, 1842–1854* (Cambridge: Harvard University Press, 1953).

Fairbank, John K., Edwin O. Reishauer, and Albert M. Craig, *East Asia: The Modern Transformation* (Boston: Houghton Mifflin, 1965).

Fall, Bernard B., *Anatomy of a Crisis* (Garden City, NY: Doubleday, 1969).

Fall, Bernard B., *Hell in a Very Small Place* (Philadelphia: Lippincott, 1967).

Fall, Bernard B., *The Two Vietnams* (New York: Praeger, 1967).

Far Eastern Economic Review, *1968 Yearbook* (Hong Kong).

Far Eastern Economic Review, *1971 Yearbook* (Hong Kong).

Faulkner, R. J., and R. A. Field, *Vanquishing the Dragon: The Law of Drugs in Hong Kong* (Hong Kong: Center for Asian Studies, University of Hong Kong, 1975).

Filippelli, Ronald L., *American Labor and Postwar Italy, 1943–1953* (Stanford: Stanford University Press, 1989).

FitzGerald, Frances, *Fire in the Lake* (Boston: Atlantic Monthly Press, 1972).

Freid, Albert, *The Rise and Fall of the Jewish Gangster in America* (New York: Holt, Rinehart and Winston, 1980).

Fronde, Jean Julien, *Traitez à tout Prix* (Paris: Robert Laffront, 1971).

Garland, Lt. Col. Albert, and Howard McGraw, *United States Army in World War II. The Mediterranean Theater of Operations: Sicily and the Surrender of Italy* (Washington, DC: Office of the Chief of Military History, Department of the Army, U.S. Government Printing Office, 1965).

Geoffray, C., *Réglementation des Régies indochinois*, tome 1ier: *Opium, Alcools, Sel* (Haiphong: Imprimerie Commerciale du "Colon français" Edition, 1938).

Giap, Gen. Vo Nguyen, *Peoples' War, Peoples' Army* (Hanoi: Foreign Languages Publishing House, 1961).

Gosch, Martin, and Richard Hammer, *The Last Testament of Lucky Luciano* (Boston: Little, Brown, 1974).

Graham, B. D., *The French Socialists and Tripartism, 1944–1947* (Canberra: Australian National University, 1965).

Gravel, Mike, ed., *The Pentagon Papers: The Defense Department History of United States Decisionmaking on Vietnam*, 5 vols. (Boston: Beacon Press, 1971).

Greenberg, Michael, *British Trade and the Opening of China, 1800–42* (Cambridge: Cambridge University Press, 1951).

Grimaldi, Lt. Col., Inspecteur des Forces supplétive, Inspection des Forces supplétives du Sud Vietnam, *Notions de Case sur les Forces supplétives du Sud Vietnam* (S.P.50.295, May 15, 1954).

Halberstam, David, *The Making of a Quagmire* (New York: Random House, 1964).

Halpern, Joel, *Economy and Society of Laos* (New Haven: Southeast Asian Studies, Yale University, 1964).

Hamilton-Paterson, James, *The Greedy War* (New York: David McKay, 1971).

Hammer, Ellen J., *The Struggle for Indochina, 1940–1955* (Stanford: Stanford University Press, 1967).

Hammond, Thomas T., *Red Flag over Afghanistan* (Boulder: Westview, 1984).

Hess, Albert G., *Chasing the Dragon* (New York: Free Press, 1965).

Higgins, Marguerite, *Our Vietnam Nightmare* (New York: Harper & Row, 1965).

Hilsman, Roger, *To Move a Nation* (Garden City, NY: Doubleday, 1967).

Hla Myint, *The Economics of the Developing Countries* (New York: Praeger, 1964).

Hobsbawm, Eric J., *Bandits* (New York: Delacorte, 1969).

Hobsbawm, Eric J., *Industry and*

*Empire: The Making of Modern English Society* (New York: Pantheon, 1968).

Hobsbawm, Eric J., *Primitive Rebels* (New York: Norton, 1959).

Ho Chi Minh, *Selected Works* (Hanoi: Foreign Languages Publishing House, 1961).

Hong, Lysa, *Thailand in the Nineteenth Century: Evolution of the Economy and Society* (Singapore: Institute of Southeast Asian Studies, 1984).

Hostache, René, *Le Conseil national de la Résistance* (Paris: Presses Universitaires de France, 1958).

Hsin-pao, Chang, *Commissioner Lin and the Opium War* (Cambridge: Harvard University Press, 1964).

Hughes, John, *The Junk Merchants* (Boston: Christian Science Publishing Company, 1971).

Hughes, Lizbeth B., *The Evangel in Burma* (Rangoon: American Baptist Mission Press, 1926).

Ireland, Alleyne, *Colonial Administration in the Far East: The Province of Burma* (Boston: Houghton Mifflin, 1907).

Isaacs, Harold R., *No Peace for Asia* (Cambridge: MIT Press, 1967).

Isaacs, Harold R., *The Tragedy of the Chinese Revolution* (Stanford: Stanford University Press, 1951).

Julliard, Jacques, *Le IVᵉ République* (Paris: Calmann-Levy, 1968).

Kahin, George McTurnan, and John W. Lewis, *The United States in Vietnam* (New York: Dial, 1967).

Karnow, Stanley, *Vietnam: A History* (New York: Viking/Penguin, 1983).

Keen, F. B. G., *The Meo of North-West Thailand* (Wellington, New Zealand: Government Printer, 1966).

Keesing's Research Report, *South Vietnam: A Political History,* *1954–1970* (New York: Scribner's 1970).

Keppel, Arnold, *Gun-Running and the Indian North-West Frontier* (London: John Murray, 1911).

Kirby, Maj. Gen. S. Woodburn, *The War against Japan,* vol. 5: *The Surrender of Japan* (London: Her Majesty's Stationery Office, 1969).

Kolko, Gabriel, *The Politics of War* (New York: Random House, 1968).

Kolko, Joyce, and Gabriel Kolko, *The Limits of Power* (New York: Harper & Row, 1972).

Kwitny, Jonathan, *The Crimes of Patriots* (New York: Simon & Schuster, 1987).

Lachica, Eduardo, *The Huks: Philippine Agrarian Society in Revolt* (New York: Praeger, 1971).

Lafeber, Walter, *America, Russia, and the Cold War* (New York: Wiley, 1967).

Lamour, Catherine, *Enquête sur une Armée secrète* (Paris: Editions de Seuil, 1975).

Lamour, Catherine, and Michel R. Lamberti, *The International Connection: Opium from Growers to Pushers* (New York: Pantheon, 1974).

Lancaster, Donald, *The Emancipation of French Indochina* (New York: Oxford University Press, 1961).

Landon, Kenneth P., *The Chinese in Thailand* (New York: Russell & Russell, 1941).

Lansdale, Edward G., *In the Midst of Wars* (New York: Harper & Row, 1972).

Leach, E. R., *Political Systems of Highland Burma* (Boston: Beacon Press, 1968).

Leary, William M., *Perilous Missions: Civil Air Transport and CIA Covert Operations in Asia*

(Montgomery: University of Alabama Press, 1984).

Lebar, Frank M., Gerald C. Hickey, and John K., Musgrave, *Ethnic Groups of Mainland Southeast Asia* (New Haven: Human Relations Area Files Press, 1964).

Le May, Reginald, *An Asian Arcady* (Cambridge: W. Heffer & Sons, 1926).

Le Thanh Khoi, *Le Viet-Nam: Histoire et Civilisation* (Paris: Les Editions de Minuit, 1955).

Lewis, Norman, *The Honored Society* (New York: Putnam's, 1964).

Lintner, Bertil, *Land of Jade: A Journey Through Insurgent Burma* (Edinburgh: Kiscadale White Lotus, 1990).

Lintner, Bertil, *The Rise and Fall of the Communist Party of Burma (CPB)* (Ithaca: Southeast Asia Program, Cornell University, 1990).

Lobe, Thomas, *United States National Security Policy and Aid to the Thailand Police* (Denver: Monograph Series in World Affairs, University of Denver, 1977).

Loftus, John, *The Belarus Secret* (New York: Knopf, 1982).

Lowenstein, James G., and Richard M. Moose, U.S. Congress, Senate, Committee on Foreign Relations, Subcommittee on United States Security Agreements and Commitments Abroad, *Laos: April 1971*, 91st Cong., 1st sess. (Washington, DC: U.S. Government Printing Office, 1971).

Lowes, Peter D., *The Genesis of International Narcotics Control* (Geneva: Librairie Droz, 1966).

Lubbock, Basil, *The China Clippers* (Glasgow: James Brown & Son, 1914).

Lubbock, Basil, *The Opium Clippers* (Glasgow: Brown, Son & Ferguson, 1933).

Luce, Don, and John, Sommer, *Vietnam: The Unheard Voices* (Ithaca: Cornell University Press, 1969).

Maas, Peter, *Manhunt* (New York: Random House, 1986).

McAlister, John T., *Vietnam: The Origins of the Revolution* (New York: Knopf, 1969).

McCoy, Alfred W., *Drug Traffic: Narcotics and Organized Crime in Australia* (Sydney: Harper & Row, 1980).

McWilliams, John C., *The Protectors: Harry J. Anslinger and the Federal Bureau of Narcotics, 1930–1962* (Newark, Delaware: University of Delaware Press, 1990).

Messick, Hank, *Lansky* (New York: Putnam's, 1971).

Miles, Milton E., USN, *A Different Kind of War* (New York: Doubleday, 1967).

Mintz, Sidney W., *Sweetness and Power: The Place of Sugar in Modern History* (New York: Viking, 1985).

Morgan, William P., *Triad Societies in Hong Kong* (Hong Kong: Government Press, 1960).

Moscow, Alvin, *Merchants of Heroin* (New York: Dial, 1968).

Moss, George Donelson, *Vietnam: An American Ordeal* (Englewood Cliffs, NJ: Prentice Hall, 1990).

Moule, Rev. A. E., Church Missionary Society, *The Use of Opium and Its Bearing on the Spread of Christianity in China* (Shanghai: Celestial Empire Office, 1877).

Murphy, Morgan F., and Robert H. Steele, *The World Heroin Problem*, Report of Special Study Mission, U.S. Congress, 92nd Cong., 2nd sess. (Washington, DC: U.S. Government Printing Office, 1971).

Musto, David F., *The American Disease: The Origins of Narcotics Control* (New Haven: Yale University Press, 1973).

Naval Intelligence Division, *Indochina* (Cambridge, England: Handbook Series, 1943).

Navasky, Victor S., *Kennedy Justice* (New York: Atheneum, 1971).

New York Times, *The Pentagon Papers* (New York: Quandrangle, 1971).

Nghiem Dang, *Viet-Nam: Politics and Public Administration* (Honolulu: East-West Center, 1966).

Ngo Vinh Long, *Before the Revolution: The Vietnamese Peasants Under the French* (Cambridge: MIT Press, 1973).

Owen, David Edward, *British Opium Policy in China and India* (New Haven: Yale University Press, 1934).

Paillat, Claude, *Dossier secret de l'Indochine* (Paris: Les Presses de la Cité, 1964).

Pantaleone, Michele, *The Mafia and Politics* (London: Chatto & Windus, 1966).

Parssinen, Terry M., *Secret Passions, Secret Remedies: Narcotic Drugs in British Society, 1820–1930* (Philadelphia: Institute for the Study of Human Issues, 1983).

Patti, Archimedes L. A., *Why Vietnam: Prelude to America's Albatross* (Berkeley: University of California Press, 1980).

Peyrouton, Bernard-Marcel, *Les Monopoles en Indochine* (Paris: Emile Larose, 1913).

Picanon, Eugene, *Le Laos français* (Paris: Augustin Challamel, 1901).

Powers, Thomas, *The Man Who Kept the Secrets: Richard Helms and the CIA* (New York: Knopf, 1979).

Prakash, Om, *The Dutch East India Company and the Economy of Bengal, 1630–1720* (Delhi: Oxford University Press, 1988).

Purcell, Victor, *The Chinese in Southeast Asia* (London: Oxford University Press, 1951).

Radosh, Ronald, *American Labor and United States Foreign Policy* (New York: Random House, 1969).

Ranelagh, John, *The Agency: The Rise and Decline of the CIA* (New York: Simon & Schuster, 1986).

Reeves, Richard, *Passage to Peshawar* (New York: Simon & Schuster, 1984).

Reid, Ed, *The Grim Reapers* (Chicago: Henry Regnery, 1969).

Renborg, Bertil A., *International Drug Control: A Study of International Administration by and Through the League of Nations* (Washington, DC: Carnegie Endowment for International Peace, 1944).

Riggs, Fred W., *Thailand: The Modernization of a Bureaucratic Polity* (Honolulu: East-West Center Press, 1966).

Robbins, Christopher, *Air America* (New York: G. P. Putnam's Sons, 1979).

Robbins, Christopher, *The Ravens: The Men Who Flew in America's Secret War in Laos* (New York: Crown, 1987).

Rochet, Charles, *Pays Lao* (Paris: Jean Vigneau, 1949).

Rostow, W. W., *The Stages of Economic Growth* (New York: Cambridge University Press, 1968).

Rowntree, Joshua, *The Imperial Drug Trade* (London: Methuen, 1905).

Roy, Jules, *The Battle of Dienbienphu* (New York: Harper & Row, 1965).

Rush, James R., *Opium to Java*

(Ithaca: Cornell University Press, 1990).

Saccomano, Eugène, *Bandits à Marseille* (Paris: Julliard, 1968).

Sao Saimong Mangrai, *The Shan States and the British Annexation* (Ithaca: Southeast Asia Program, Cornell University, data paper no. 57, August 1965).

Savini, A. M., *Visages et Images du Sud Viet-Nam* (Saigon: Imprimerie Française d'Outre-Mer, 1955).

Savini, F. M., *Histoire des Miao* (Hong Kong: Imprimerie de la Société des Missions-Étrangères de Paris, 1930).

Schanche, Don A., *Mister Pop* (New York: David McKay, 1971).

Scigliano, Robert, *South Vietnam: Nation Under Stress* (Boston: Houghton Mifflin, 1963).

Scott, J. M., *The White Poppy* (London: William Heinemann, 1969).

Scott, Peter Dale, *The War Conspiracy: The Secret Road to the Second Indochina War* (Indianapolis: Bobbs-Merrill, 1972).

Servaidio, Gaia, *Mafioso: A History of the Mafia from Its Origins to the Present* (New York: Dell, 1976).

Shaplen, Robert, *The Lost Revolution: The U.S. in Vietnam, 1946–1966* (New York: Harper & Row, 1966).

Shaplen, Robert, *The Road from War* (New York: Harper & Row, 1970).

Shaplen, Robert, *Time Out of Hand* (New York: Harper & Row, 1970).

Singer, Max, project leader, *Policy Concerning Drug Abuse in New York State* (Croton-on-Hudson: Hudson Institute, May 31, 1970).

Siragusa, Charles, *The Trail of the Poppy* (Englewood Cliffs, NJ: Prentice-Hall, 1966).

Skinner, G. William, *Chinese Society in Thailand: An Analytical History* (Ithaca: Cornell University Press, 1957).

Smith, Nicol, and Blake Clark, *Into Siam, Underground Kingdom* (Indianapolis: Bobbs-Merrill, 1946).

Smith, R. Harris, *OSS: The Secret History of America's First Central Intelligence Agency* (Berkeley: University of California Press, 1972).

Snepp, Frank, *Decent Interval: The American Debacle in Vietnam and the Fall of Saigon* (London: Allen Lane, 1980).

Society for the Aid and Rehabilitation of Drug Addicts, *Annual Report 1973–1974* (Hong Kong: SARDA, 1974).

Sontag, Raymond J., *A Broken World, 1919–1939* (New York: Harper & Row, 1971).

Sowards, Genevieve, and Erville Sowards, *Burma Baptist Chronicle* (Rangoon: Board of Publications, Burma Baptist Convention, 1963).

Spencer, C. P., and V. Navaratnam, *Drug Abuse in East Asia* (Kuala Lumpur: Oxford University Press, 1981).

Sta Ana, A. P., *The Golden Triangle Revisited* (Manila: Philippines Daily Express, 1975).

Stackpole, Edouard, *Captain Prescott and the Opium Smugglers* (Mystic, CT: Marine Historical Association, no. 26, July 1954).

Sterling, Claire, *Octopus: The Long Reach of the International Sicilian Mafia* (New York: Norton, 1990).

Strachey, Sir John, *India: Its Administration and Progress* (London: Macmillan, 1903).

Talese, Gay, *Honor Thy Father* (New York: World, 1971).

Tanham, George K., *Trial in Thai-*

*land* (New York: Crane, Russak, 1974).

Taylor, Arnold H., *American Diplomacy and the Narcotics Traffic, 1900–1939: A Study in International Humanitarian Reform* (Durham: Duke University Press, 1969).

Taylor, Robert H., *Foreign and Domestic Consequences of the KMT Intervention in Burma* (Ithaca: Southeast Asia Program, Cornell University, data paper no. 93, 1973).

Teng Ssu-yu, *Chang Hsi and the Treaty of Nanking* (Chicago: University of Chicago Press, 1944).

Thak Chaloemtiarana, ed., *Thai Politics: Extracts and Documents, 1932–1957* (Bangkok: Social Science Association of Thailand, 1978).

Thelwall, Rev. A. S., *The Iniquities of the Opium Trade with China: Being a Development of the Main Causes Which Exclude the Merchants of Great Britain from the Advantages of an Unrestricted Commercial Intercourse with That Vast Empire* (London: William H. Allen, 1839).

Thompson, Virginia, *French Indochina* (New York: Macmillan, 1937).

Thompson, Virginia, *Thailand: The New Siam* (New York: Macmillan, 1941).

Thongchai, Winnichakui, *Siam Mapped: The Geobody of Thailand* (Honolulu: University of Hawaii Press, forthcoming).

Tillon, Charles, *Les F.T.P.* (Paris: Union Générale d'Editions, 1967).

Tinker, Hugh, *The Union of Burma* (London: Oxford University Press, 1957).

Topping, Seymour, *Journey Between Two Chinas* (New York: Harper & Row, 1972).

Toye, Hugh, *Laos: Buffer State or Battleground* (New York: Oxford University Press, 1968).

Trinquier, Roger, Jacques Duchemin, and Jacques Le Bailley, *Notre Guerre au Katanga* (Paris: Editions de la Pensée moderne, 1963).

Trocki, Carl A., *Prince of Pirates: The Temenggongs and the Development of Johor and Singapore* (Singapore: Singapore University Press, 1979).

Vigneras, Marcel, *United States Army in World War II: Rearming the French* (Washington, DC: Office of the Chief of Military History, Department of the Army, 1957).

Waley, Arthur, *The Opium War Through Chinese Eyes* (New York: Macmillan, 1958).

Warner, Denis, *The Last Confucian* (London: Angus & Robertson, 1964).

Weibel, Ernest, *La Création des Régions autonomes à Status spécial en Italie* (Geneva: Librairie Droz, 1971).

*Who's Who in Thailand 1987* (Bangkok: Advance Publishing, 1987).

Wickberg, Edgar, *The Chinese in Philippine Life* (New Haven: Yale University Press, 1965).

Wiens, Herold J., *China's March toward the Tropics* (Hamden, CT: Shoe String Press, 1954).

Williams, Phillip M., and Martin Harrison, *Politics and Society in De Gaulle's Republic* (London: Longmans Group, 1971).

Wise, David, and Thomas B. Ross, *The Invisible Government* (New York: Random House, 1964).

Woodside, Alexander Barton, *Vietnam and the Chinese Model* (Cambridge: Harvard University Press, 1971).

Wyatt, David K., *Thailand: A Short History* (New Haven: Yale University Press, 1984).

Young, Gordon, *The Hill Tribes of Northern Thailand* (Bangkok: Siam Society, monograph no. 1, 1962).

Zarco, Ricardo M., *Street Corner Drug Use in Metropolitan Manila: A Comparison of Two Socio-Economic Categories of Illicit Social Drug Users* (Manila: Narcotics Foundation of the Philippines, 1972).

Zarco, Ricardo M., *Two Research Monographs on Drug Abuse in the Philippines* (Manila: Government Printing Office, 1975).

## Government Publications

### Australia

Australasian and Pacific Holdings, Limited, "Prospectus," September 15, 1969; List of Shareholders, May 18, 1970, N.S.W. Corporate Affairs Commission (Sydney).

Commonwealth of Australia, Parliament, *Report of the Royal Commission on Secret Drugs, Cures, and Food* (Sydney: N.S.W. Government Printer, 1907).

Commonwealth of Australia–New South Wales, Joint Task Force on Drug Trafficking, *Report, Volume 2: Nugan Hand*, part 1 (Canberra: Australian Government Printer, June 1982).

Commonwealth of Australia–New South Wales, Joint Task Force, *Report, Volume 4: Nugan Hand*, part 2 (Canberra: Australian Government Printer, March 1983).

Commonwealth of Australia, Royal Commission of Inquiry into the Activities of the Nugan Hand Group, *Final Report, Volume 1* (Canberra: Australian Government Publishing Services, 1985).

N.S.W. Corporate Affairs Commission, *Seventh Interim Report of the Corporate Affairs Commission into the Affairs of Nugan Hand Limited and Other Compa-*nies, vol. 2 (Sydney: Government Printer, New South Wales, 1983).

N.S.W. Royal Commission into Drug Trafficking, *Report* (Sydney: Government Printer, October 1979).

### Burma (Myanmar)

*The Burmese Opium Manual* (Rangoon: Government Printing, 1911).

*Report by the Government of the Union of Burma for the Calendar Year 1950 of the Traffic in Opium and Other Dangerous Drugs* (Rangoon: Government Printing and Stationery, 1951).

"Report of the Administration of the Northern Shan States for the Year Ended the 30th of June 1923," in *Report on the Administration of the Shan and Karenni States* (Rangoon: Government Printing, 1924).

Union of Burma, Ministry of Information, *Kuomintang Aggression Against Burma* (Rangoon: Government Printing, 1953).

### Hong Kong

"Analysis Report on the Central Registry for Drug Addicts, April 1972–March 1974," unpublished document (Hong Kong).

*Annual Report by the Commis-*

sioner of the Independent Commission Against Corruption (Hong Kong: Government Printer, 1974).

Discharged Prisoner's Aid Society, *Three Years Experience (1967–1970) with Treatment of Ex-Prisoner Female Narcotic Addicts* (Hong Kong: Government Printer, 1970).

*First Report of the Commission of Inquiry Under Sir Alistair Blair-Kerr* (Hong Kong: Government Printer, 1973).

*The Problem of Dangerous Drugs in Hong Kong* (Hong Kong: Government Printer, 1974).

*Report of the Action Committee Against Narcotics for 1973–74* (Hong Kong: Government Printer, 1974).

*Second Report of the Commission of Inquiry Under Sir Alistair Blair-Kerr* (Hong Kong: Government Printer, 1973).

## India

*Imperial Gazetteer of India: Afghanistan and Nepal* (Calcutta: Superintendent of Government Printing, 1908)

*Imperial Gazetteer of India: Provincial Series, North-West Frontier Province* (Calcutta: Superintendent of Government Printing, 1908).

*Report on the Administration of the Punjab and Its Dependencies for the Year 1870–71* (Lahore: Government Civil Secretariat Press, 1871).

## Laos

Direction du Protocole, Ministre des Affaires Etrangères, "Liste des Personnalités Lao," mimeographed (Royaume du Laos, n.d ).

## Pakistan

Pakistan Narcotics Control Board, *National Survey on Drug Abuse in Pakistan* (Islamabad: Narcotics Control Board, 1986).

## Philippines

Constabulary Anti-Narcotics Unit, *First Anniversary* (Quezon City: Philippine Constabulary, 1973).

Constabulary Anti-Narcotics Unit, *Third Anniversary* (Quezon City: Philippine Constabulary, 1975).

Dangerous Drugs Board, *Annual Report 1974* (Manila, 1975).

Dangerous Drugs Board, "Seizures and Apprehensions: Aggregate Total for the Period January–30 September 1975," unpublished documents (Manila).

## Thailand

Department of His Majesty's Customs, *Annual Statement of the Foreign Trade and Navigation* (Bangkok, 1946).

Ministry of Interior, Department of Public Welfare, "Report on the Socio-Economic Survey of the Hill Tribes in Northern Thailand," typescript (Bangkok, September 1962).

*Report of the United Nations Survey Team on the Economic and Social Needs of the Opium Producing Areas in Thailand* (Bangkok: Government Printing Office, 1967).

## United States

U.S. Bureau of Narcotics and Dangerous Drugs, "Persons Known to Be or Suspected of Being Engaged in the Illicit Traffic in Narcotics," revised (Washington, DC, March 1965).

U.S. Bureau of Narcotics and Dangerous Drugs, "The World Opium Situation," (Washington, DC, October 1970).

U.S. Cabinet Committee on International Narcotics Control (CCINC), "Fact Sheet: The Cabinet Committee on International Narcotics Control—A Year of Progress in Drug Abuse Prevention" (Washington, DC, September 1972).

U.S. Cabinet Committee on International Narcotics Control (CCINC), *World Opium Survey 1972* (Washington, DC: CCINC, 1972).

U.S. Comptroller General, *Controlling Drug Abuse: A Status Report* (Washington, DC: Comptroller General, March 1, 1988).

U.S. Congress, *Congressional Record*, 92nd Cong., 2nd sess., 118, no. 106, June 28, 1972.

U.S. Congress, House, Committee on Foreign Affairs, *The U.S. Heroin Problem and Southeast Asia: The Asian Connection*, 93rd Cong., 1st sess. (Washington, DC: U.S. Government Printing Office, 1973).

U.S. Congress, House, Committee on Foreign Relations, *International Aspects of the Narcotics Problem*, 92nd Cong., 1st sess., 1971 (Washington, DC: U.S. Government Printing Office, 1971).

U.S. Congress, House, Committee on International Relations, *The Narcotics Situation in Southeast Asia: The Asian Connection*, 94th Cong., 1st sess. (Washington, DC: U.S. Government Printing Office, 1975).

U.S. Congress, House, Committee on International Relations, *Proposal to Control Opium from the Golden Triangle and Terminate the Shan Opium Trade*, 94th Cong., 1st sess. (Washington, DC: U.S. Government Printing Office, 1975).

U.S. Congress, House, Committee on International Relations, *The Shifting Pattern of Narcotics Trafficking: Latin America*, 94th Cong., 2nd sess. (Washington, DC: U.S. Government Printing Office, 1976).

U.S. Congress, House, Select Committee on Narcotics Abuse and Control, *Opium Production, Narcotics Financing, and Trafficking in Southeast Asia*, 95th Cong., 1st sess. (Washington, DC: U.S. Government Printing Office, 1977).

U.S. Congress, House, Select Committee on Narcotics Abuse and Control, *Southeast Asian Narcotics*, 95th Cong., 1st sess. (Washington, DC: U.S. Government Printing Office, 1978).

U.S. Congress, Senate, Committee of the Judiciary, *Refugee and Civilian War Casualty Problems in Indochina*, 91st Cong., 2nd sess. (Washington, DC: U.S. Government Printing Office, 1970).

U.S. Congress, Senate, Committee of the Judiciary, *War-Related Civilian Problems in Indochina, Part II: Laos and Cambodia*, 92nd Cong., 1st sess. (Washington, DC: U.S. Government Printing Office, 1971).

U.S. Congress, Senate, Committee on Foreign Relations, *Thailand, Laos, and Cambodia: January 1972*, 92nd Cong., 2nd sess. (Washington, DC: U.S. Government Printing Office, 1972).

U.S. Congress, Senate, Committee on Foreign Relations, Subcommittee on United States Security Agreements and Commitments Abroad, *United States Security Agreements and Commitments Abroad, Kingdom of Laos*, 91st Cong., 1st sess. (Washington, DC:

U.S. Government Printing Office, 1970).

U.S. Congress, Senate, Committee on Foreign Relations, Subcommittee on Terrorism, Narcotics, and International Operations, *Drugs, Law Enforcement, and Foreign Policy*, 100th Cong., 2nd sess. (Washington, DC: U.S. Government Printing Office, December 1988).

U.S. Congress, Senate, Committee on Government Operations, *Organized Crime and Illicit Traffic in Narcotics*, 88th Cong., 1st and 2nd sess. (Washington, DC: U.S. Printing Office, 1964).

U.S. Congress, Senate, *Congressional Record* 114, no. 16, February 5, 1968.

U.S. Congress, Senate, Permanent Subcommittee on Investigations, *Fraud and Corruption in Management of Military Club Systems*, 91st Cong., 1st sess. (Washington, DC: U.S. Government Printing Office, 1969).

U.S. Congress, Senate, Permanent Subcommittee on Investigations, *Fraud and Corruption in Management of Military Club Systems: Illegal Currency Manipulations Affecting South Vietnam*, 91st Cong., 2nd sess. 92nd Cong., 1st sess. (Washington, DC: U.S. Government Printing Office, 1971).

U.S. Congress, Senate, Select Committee on Improper Activities in the Labor Management Field, *Hearings*, 85th Cong., 2nd sess. (Washington, DC: U.S. Government Printing Office, 1959).

U.S. Senate, Select Committee to Study Governmental Operations with Respect to Intelligence Activities, *Foreign and Military Intelligence, Book I: Final Report*, 94th Cong., 2nd sess. (Washington, DC: U.S. Government Printing Office, Senate Report No. 94-755, 1976).

U.S. Congress, Senate, Select Committee to Study Governmental Operations with Respect to Intelligence Activities, "History of the Central Intelligence Agency," *Supplementary Detailed Staff Reports on Foreign and Military Intelligence*, Book 4, 94th Cong., 2nd sess. (Washington, DC: U.S. Government Printing Office, Senate Report No. 94-755, 1976).

U.S. Congress, Senate, Subcommittee on Improvements in the Federal Criminal Code, Committee of the Judiciary, *Illicit Narcotics Traffic*, 84th Cong., 1st sess. (Washington, DC: U.S. Government Printing Office, 1955).

U.S. Department of Commerce, Bureau of Foreign and Domestic Commerce, *Statistical Abstract of the United States 1915* (Washington, DC: U.S. Government Printing Office, 1916).

U.S. Executive Office of the President, Special Action Office for Drug Abuse Prevention, *The Vietnam Drug User Returns: Final Report* (Washington, DC: U.S. Government Printing Office, 1974).

U.S. General Accounting Office, *Report to the Congress, Drug Control: U.S.–Mexico Opium And Marijuana Aerial Eradication Program* (Washington, DC: U.S. Government Printing Office, January 1988).

U.S. Secretary of Commerce and Labor, Department of Commerce and Labor, *Statistical Abstract of the United States* (Washington,

DC: U.S. Government Printing Office, 1911).

U.S. State Department, Bureau of International Narcotics Matters, *International Narcotics Control Strategy Report* (Washington, DC: U.S. Government Printing Office, February 1984).

U.S. State Department, Bureau of International Narcotics Matters, *International Narcotics Control Strategy Report, March 1990*, pub. no. 9749 (Washington, DC: State Department, March 1990).

U.S. Treasury Department, Bureau of Narcotics, "History of Narcotic Addiction in the United States," in U.S. Senate Committee on Government Operations, *Organized Crime and Illicit Traffic in Narcotics*, 88th Cong., 1st and 2nd sess. (Washington, DC: U.S. Government Printing Office, 1964).

U.S. Treasury Department, Bureau of Narcotics, *Traffic in Opium and Other Dangerous Drugs for the Year Ended December 31, 1937* (Washington, DC: U.S. Government Printing Office, 1938).

U.S. Treasury Department, Bureau of Narcotics, *Traffic in Opium and Other Dangerous Drugs for the Year Ended December 31, 1939* (Washington, DC: U.S. Government Printing Office, 1940).

U.S. Treasury Department, Bureau of Narcotics, *Traffic in Opium and Other Dangerous Drugs for the Year Ended December 31, 1965* (Washington, DC: U.S. Government Printing Office, 1966).

### Vietnam

"Announcement," from the residence of the prime minister, Republic of Vietnam, March 19, 1971.

Exposition coloniale internationale, Paris, 1931, Indochine française, Section d'Administration générale, Direction des Finances, *Histoire bugetaire de l'Indochine* (Hanoi: Imprimerie d'Extrême-Orient, 1930).

Exposition coloniale internationale, Paris, 1931, Indochine française, Section générale, *Administration des Douanes et Régies en Indochine* (Hanoi: Imprimerie d'Extrême-Orient, 1930).

### International Bodies

International Opium Commission, *Report of the International Opium Commission Shanghai, China, February 1 to February 26, 1909*, 2 vols. (Shanghai: North China Daily News, 1909).

League of Nations, Advisory Commission of Enquiry into the Control of Opium Smoking in the Far East, *Report to the Council*, vol. 1 (Geneva: League of Nations, 1931).

League of Nations, Advisory Committee on the Traffic in Opium and Other Dangerous Drugs, *Annual Reports of Governments on the Traffic in Opium and Other Dangerous Drugs for the Year 1935*, vol. 11, (Geneva: Series of League of Nations Publications, 1937).

League of Nations, Advisory Committee on the Traffic in Opium and Other Dangerous Drugs, *Annual Reports on the Traffic in Opium and Other Dangerous Drugs for the Year 1931* (Geneva: League of Nations, 1931).

League of Nations, Advisory Committee on the Traffic in Opium and Other Dangerous Drugs, *Annual Reports on the Traffic in Opium and Other Dangerous Drugs for the Year 1939* (Geneva: League of Nations, 1939).

League of Nations, Advisory Committee on the Traffic in Opium and Other Dangerous Drugs, *Application of Part II of the Opium Convention with Special Reference to the European Possessions and Countries in the Far East*, vols. 11–12 (Geneva: League of Nations, 1923).

League of Nations, Advisory Committee on the Traffic in Opium and Other Dangerous Drugs, *Minutes of the First Session* (Geneva: League of Nations, May 24–June 7, 1923).

League of Nations, Advisory Committee on the Traffic in Opium and Other Dangerous Drugs, *Minutes of the Twelfth Session* (Geneva: League of Nations, February 2, 1929).

League of Nations, Advisory Committee on the Traffic in Opium and Other Dangerous Drugs, *Summary of Annual Reports*, vol. 11 (Geneva: Series of League of Nations Publications, 1930).

League of Nations, Advisory Committee on the Traffic in Opium and Other Dangerous Drugs, *Summary of Annual Reports in the Traffic in Opium and Other Dangerous Drugs for the Years 1929 and 1930* (Geneva: League of Nations, March 22, 1932).

League of Nations, Commission of Inquiry into the Control of Opium Smoking in the Far East, *Report to the Council*, vol. 1 (Geneva: League of Nations, 1930).

United Nations, Department of Social Affairs, *Bulletin on Narcotics* 5, no. 2 (April–June 1953).

United Nations, Economic and Social Council, *World Trends of the Illicit Traffic During the War, 1939–1945* (E/CS 7/9), November 23, 1946.

United Nations, Economic and Social Council, Commission on Narcotic Drugs, *Abolition of Opium Smoking* (E/CN.7/244), November 17, 1952.

United Nations, Economic and Social Council, Commission on Narcotic Drugs, *Agenda of the Ninth Meeting* (E/C.S.7/27), December 3, 1946.

United Nations, Economic and Social Council, Commission on Narcotic Drugs, *Illicit Traffic* (E/CN.7/L.115), May 4, 1955.

United Nations, Economic and Social Council, Commission on Narcotic Drugs, *Illicit Traffic*, 12th sess., agenda item no. 4 (E/CN.7/L.169), May 28, 1957; (295/MPL/ONU), May 29, 1957.

United Nations, Economic and Social Council, Commission on Narcotic Drugs, "Laos Report for the Year 1952," in *Abolition of Opium Smoking* (E/CN.7/244), November 17, 1952.

United Nations, Economic and Social Council, Commission on Narcotic Drugs, *Summary of the Fourth Meeting* (E/C.S.7/25), November 29, 1946.

United Nations Fund for Drug Abuse Control, "Crop Replacement and Community Development Project: Progress Report September 1972–June 1973," (Bangkok, 1973).

United Nations Fund for Drug Abuse Control, UN/Thai Program for Drug Abuse Control in Thailand, "Progress Report No. 5" (Geneva:

UNFDAC, September 1975, NAR/
THA. 5); "Progress Report No. 6"

(Geneva: UNFDAC, June 1976,
NAR/THA. 6).

## Interviews

Daniel J. Addario, Bangkok, December 15, 1975.

Gen. Maurice Belleux, Paris, March 23, 1971.

Martin Bishop, ICAC, Hong Kong, December 3, 1975.

Edgar Buell, Ban Son, Laos, August 30–31, 1971.

Elliot K. Chan, Vientiane, Laos, August 15, 1971.

Maj. Chao La, Ban Nam Keung, Laos, September 12, 1971.

Col. Chawalit Yodmani, Narcotics Suppression Center, Bangkok, December 11, 1975.

Col. Chen Mo Su, Chiang Khong, Thailand, September 10, 1971.

James Chien, Hong Kong, July 8, 1971.

Brig. Gen. Tommy Clift, Bangkok, Thailand, September 21, 1971.

Col. Co Khac Mai, Paris, March 29, 1971.

Lt. Col. Lucien Conein, McLean, Virginia, June 18, 1971.

George Cosgrove, Ban Son, Laos, August 30, 1971.

Adrian Cowell, London, England, March 9, 1971.

Graham Crookdae, Hong Kong, July 5, 1971.

Maj. Gen. John H. Cushman, Can Tho, Vietnam, July 23, 1971.

George Dunning, Hong Kong, July 6, 1971.

Edward Fillingham, Vientiane, Laos, September 5, 1971.

G. P. Garner, Hong Kong, July 7, 1971.

Ger Su Yang, Long Pot village, Laos, August 19, 1971.

Capt. Higginbotham, Can Tho, Vietnam, July 23, 1971.

David Hodson, Narcotics Bureau, Royal Hong Kong Police, December 2, 1975.

Jerome Hollander, Los Angeles, California, June 25, 1971.

Estelle Holt, London, England, March 1971.

Hsai Kiao, Chiangmai, Thailand, September 12–13, 21, 1971.

Richard J. Hynes, USAID/Laos, Vientiane, Laos, September 7, 1971.

Jao Nhu, Chiangmai, Thailand, September 8, 1971.

Jean Jerusalemy, Paris, April 2, 1971.

John Johnston, Narcotics Bureau, Royal Hong Kong Police, December 4, 1975.

Capt. Kong Le, Paris, March 22, 1971.

Gen. Krirksin, Chiang Khong District, Thailand, September 10, 1971.

Lai Huu Tai, Paris, March 28, 1971.

Lai Van Sang, Paris, March 22, 1971.

Gen. Edward G. Lansdale, Alexandria, Virginia, June 17, 1971.

Rev. Paul Lewis, Chiangmai, Thailand, September 7, 1971.

Liao Long-sing, Singapore, September 24, 1971.

Lo Kham Thy, Vientiane, Laos, September 2, 1971.

Redactor Ly Ky Hoang, Saigon, Vietnam, August 5, 12, September 11, 1971.

Lyteck Lynhiavu, Vientiane, Laos, August 28, 1971.

Gen. Mai Huu Xuan, Saigon, South Vietnam, July 19, 1971.

Dr. David Musto, Madison, WI, May 12, 1990.

Nghiem Van Tri, Paris, March 30, 1971.

Gen. Nguyen Chanh Thi, Washington, DC, October 21, 1971.

Nguyen Van Tam, Paris, March 1971.

Nguyen Xuan Vinh, Ann Arbor, MI, June 22, 1971.

Nhia Heu Lynhiavu and Nhia Xao Lynhiavu, Vientiane, Laos, September 4, 1971.

Gen. Ouane Rattikone, Vientiane, Laos, September 1, 1971.

Lawrence Peet, Chiangrai, Thailand, August 9, 1971.

Pham Nguyen Binh, Ho Chi Minh City, September 4, 1981.

Col. Phan Phung Tien, Tan Son Nhut Air Base, South Vietnam, July 29, 1971.

Police Maj. Gen. Pow Sarasin, Bangkok, December 15, 1975.

Maj. Richard A. Ratner, Long Binh Rehabilitation Center, Vietnam, July 22, 1971.

Romeo J. Sanga, Dangerous Drugs Board, Manila, November 27, 1975.

Don A. Schanche, Larchmont, NY, February 12, 1971.

Police Col. Smith Boonlikit, Bangkok, Thailand, September 17, 1971.

Gen. Albert Sore, Biarritz, France, April 7, 1971.

U.S. Representative Robert H. Steele, Washington, DC, June 16, 1971.

Norma Sullivan, Singapore, September 24, 1971.

Charles Sweet, Washington, DC, May 1971.

Thao Ma, Bangkok, Thailand, September 17, 1971.

Col. Then, Versailles, France, April 2, 1971.

Ton That Binh, Saigon, Vietnam, September 10, 1971.

Touby Lyfoung, Vientiane, Laos, August 31–September 1, 4, 1971.

Col. Tran Dinh Lan, Paris, March 18, 1971.

Tran Van Dinh, Washington, DC, April 30, 1971.

Col. Tran Van Phan, Tan Son Nhut Air Base, Vietnam, July 29, 1971.

Col. Roger Trinquier, Paris, March 25, 1971.

U Ba Thien, Chiang Khong District, Thailand, September 11, 1971.

William vanden Heuvel, New York City, June 21, 1971.

Loring Waggoner, Las Cruces, New Mexico, June 23, 1971.

John Warner, U.S. Bureau of Narcotics and Dangerous Drugs, Washington, DC, October 14, 1971.

Brian Webster, Hong Kong, July 9, 1971.

I. M. G. Williams, Bangkok, December 12, 1975.

John Willis, Special Investigator, N.S.W. Corporate Affairs Commission, Sydney, July 16, 1990.

Senior Inspector Brian Woodward, Hong Kong, December 3–4, 1975.

Yang Than Dao, Paris, March 17, 1971.

Jimmy Yang, Chiangmai, Thailand, August 12, 14, 1971.

Bernard Yoh, Washington, DC, June 15, 1971.

William Young, Chiangmai, Thailand, September 8, 14, 1971.

# Index

Alfred W. McCoy is professor of Southeast Asian history at the University of Wisconsin-Madison. Educated at Columbia and Yale, he has spent the past twenty years writing about Southeast Asian history and politics. His writing on Philippine political history has won the country's National Book Award and Catholic Press Award. He is the author of *Drug Traffic: Narcotics and Organized Crime in Australia* and editor of *Southeast Asia under Japanese Occupation.*